WEB DESIGN HANDBOOK

DESIGN SUR INTERNET | WEBDESIGN | WEBDESIGN

D1531636

FEB 17 2010

© 2009 **booQs** publishers bvba
Godefriduskaai 22
2000 Antwerp
Belgium
Tel: + 32 3 226 66 73
Fax: + 32 3 226 53 65
www.booqs.be
info@booqs.be

ISBN: 978-94-60650-04-8
WD: D/2009/11978/005
(Q005)

Editor & texts: Paz Diman
Art direction: Mireia Casanovas
Layout: Esperanza Escudero
Translation: Cillero & de Motta Traducción

Editorial project:

maomao publications
Via Laietana, 32, 4.º, of. 104
08003 Barcelona, Spain
Tel.: +34 932 688 088
Fax: +34 933 174 208
maomao@maomaopublications.com
www.maomaopublications.com

Printed in China

All rights reserved. No part of this book may be used or reproduced in any manner whatsoever without written permission except in the case of brief quotations embodied in critical articles and reviews.

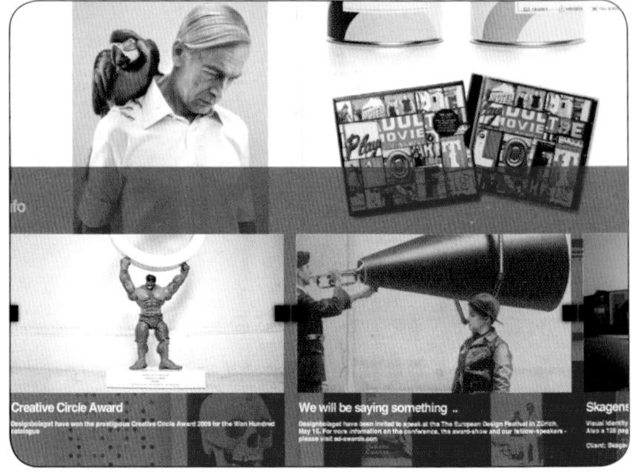

Baldwinsville Public Library
33 East Genesee Street
Baldwinsville, NY 13027-2575

WEB DESIGN HANDBOOK

DESIGN SUR INTERNET | WEBDESIGN | WEBDESIGN

CONTENTS

Less than twenty years ago, the Internet was a kind of Pandora's Box that the first users first found the courage to open, though with great caution. The most popular search engine then was Yahoo, and even the most innocent of searches threw up thousands of XXX hits. The most abundant sites were those of Geocities, where texts occupied a vertical space over predetermined background textures, only lightly sprinkled with links that were either underlined or marked in bold.

Back then, the great 'network of networks' was something that mankind was beginning to explore. And, despite the jaw-dropping amazement of a person in the former Yugoslavia being able to communicate in real time with someone in the southernmost country of South America, the Internet was still a primitive imitation of printed material.

The Internet is the form of technology gaining the most rapid acceptance to date. Every day, every minute, every second, it just gets better. Internet is also inextricably linked to enhancing new software, and it never fails to surprise us with a level of interactivity that draws us in, taking us to unpredictable, imaginary worlds.

Within this cutting-edge context, this book is an essential source of inspiration for all those who want to become real virtual whiz kids.

Web Design is a collection of websites from all latitudes of the planet, containing hundreds of extraordinary examples that demonstrate the many opportunities new technologies bring us.

In addition to basic graphic design elements applied to web design (such as the use of color, fonts, the layout of elements on the page), the examples in this book also encompass the possibilities of animation —previously elements were always static— and, in particular, interactivity, which leads us to question the frontiers of time and space.

Web Design also has a chapter on blogs, not just because these intimate diaries are unique in that each new post is automatically published, but because more and more companies are using them to project an up-to-date image. Blogs are an important channel for communicating with potential clients and have features enabling companies to generate the dialog needed to stimulate creativity.

Portfolios, advertising campaigns, online stores and personal universes... These are the first steps along a journey with infinite possibilities. Is there anyone on the planet who wouldn't want to peep into the future and see what awaits us there?

Il y a à peine vingt ans, Internet ressemblait à une boîte de Pandore dont les premiers utilisateurs se décidaient à retirer le couvercle avec précaution. Le moteur de recherche le plus utilisé était Yahoo, et presque tous les résultats de la plus innocente des recherches aboutissaient à des milliers de pages XXX. La plupart des sites étaient hébergés par Geocities, on déroulait leurs textes verticalement sur des fonds aux textures prédéfinies, à peine émaillés de quelques liens soulignés ou en gras pour qu'on les repère bien.

L'humanité commençait juste à explorer le grand « réseau des réseaux », la possibilité de communiquer en temps réel avec un habitant de l'ex-Yougoslavie depuis le pays le plus reculé de l'Amérique du Sud provoquait l'étonnement, mais ce n'était encore que l'imitation primitive d'une page imprimée.

Aujourd'hui, Internet est la technologie qui a été le plus rapidement acceptée. Chaque jour, chaque minute, chaque seconde, Internet dépasse ses propres possibilités grâce à sa connexion permanente aux nouveaux logiciels puissants, et nous surprend avec un niveau d'interactivité qui nous capture et nous transporte dans des mondes imaginaires imprévisibles.

Dans le cadre d'un contexte incroyablement actuel, ce livre est une source d'inspiration indispensable pour tous ceux qui sont désireux de devenir de véritables prestidigitateurs du monde virtuel. Web Design est une collection de sites Internet issus des quatre coins de la planète qui présente des centaines d'exemples exceptionnels illustrant les multiples possibilités des nouvelles technologies.

Outre le fait qu'il tient compte des éléments basiques du design graphique appliqués au design web (comme l'utilisation de la couleur, la typographie et la disposition des éléments sur la page), ce livre présente également des travaux qui reflètent des possibilités d'animation des éléments, autrefois inévitablement statiques, et met l'accent sur l'interactivité qui nous fait interpeler le cadre délimité du temps et de l'espace.

D'autre part, Web Design comprend un chapitre spécial consacré aux blogs, non seulement pour l'aspect particulier de ces journaux intimes dont chaque mise à jour est automatiquement accessible à tous, mais aussi parce que les entreprises les utilisent de plus en plus pour être à la pointe de la modernité. Les blogs constituent une voie de communication essentielle avec des clients potentiels, et leur fonctionnalité leur permet de maintenir le dialogue indispensable au développement de la créativité.

Portfolios, campagnes publicitaires, boutiques online et de nombreux espaces personnels. Ces exemples sont les premiers pas vers un avenir aux possibilités infinies. Y'a-t-il vraiment quelqu'un qui n'aimerait pas savoir de quoi l'avenir sera fait ?

Es ist noch keine zwanzig Jahre her, dass Internet eine Art Pandoras Büchse war, das die ersten Anwender mit großer Vorsicht öffneten. Die meistverwendete Suchmaschine war Yahoo und fast alle Ergebnisse unschuldiger Suchen enthielten mehrere tausend Pornoseiten. Die am häufigsten vorkommenden Homepages waren von Geocities, deren Texte sich vertikal über vorbestimmte Hintergründe ausdehnten und einige wenige Links enthielten, die durch Unterstreichen oder Fettschrift hervorgehoben waren.

Damals begann die Menschheit, das „Netz der Netze" zu erforschen. Trotz der Verwunderung darüber, dass man in Istzeit mit jemandem aus dem ehemaligen Jugoslawien Kontakt aufnehmen konnte, während man sich im südlichsten Land Südamerikas aufhielt, war das Netz immer noch eine primitive Nachbildung gedruckter Seiten.

Heutzutage ist Internet die am schnellsten akzeptierte Technologie. Abhängig von der Leistung neuer Software übertrifft es sich jeden Tag, jede Minute und jede Sekunde selbst und überrascht mit der Interaktion, die uns einfängt und in unvorhersehbare Phantasiewelten versetzt.

In diesem Rahmen absoluter Aktualität ist dieses Buch eine unverzichtbare Quelle der Anregung für alle, die echte Zauberkünstler des virtuellen Lebens werden wollen. Web Design ist eine Homepage-

Sammlung aus allen Breitengraden des Planeten und stellt mehrere hundert außergewöhnliche Beispiele für die zahlreichen Möglichkeiten dieser neuen Technologie vor.

Zusätzlich zu den grundlegenden Elementen aus dem Grafikdesign (wie Farbeinsatz, Typographie und Anordnung der Elemente auf der Seite), die auf das Webdesign übertragen werden, zeigen die in diesem Buch enthaltenen Arbeiten die Animationsmöglichkeit vorher unweigerlich statischer Elemente, und vor allem die Interaktion – die dazu führt, dass wir festgesetzte Zeit- und Raumgrenzen mit Fragen angehen.

Web Design enthält außerdem ein Extrakapitel über Blogs – und zwar nicht nur aufgrund der Besonderheit dieser privaten Tagebücher, die mit jeder Aktualisierung automatisch öffentlich werden – sondern weil immer mehr Unternehmen sie verwenden, um aktuell zu bleiben. Die Blogs stellen einen wichtigen Kommunikationskanal zu möglichen Kunden dar. Aufgrund ihrer Funktionalität kann der notwendige Dialog zur Förderung der Kreativität geführt werden.

Portfolios, Werbekampagnen, Online-Geschäfte und mehrere persönliche Welten. Diese Beispiele sind die ersten Schritte in eine Zukunft unbegrenzter Möglichkeiten. Gibt es tatsächlich jemanden, der nicht auskundschaften will, was schon bald auf uns zukommt?

Minder dan twintig jaar geleden was Internet een soort doos van Pandora die de eerste gebruikers heel voorzichtig open maakten. De meest gebruikte zoekmachine was Yahoo en bijna alle resultaten van de meest onschuldige zoekopdrachten leverden duizenden pornosites op. De meest voorkomende websites waren die van Geocities, waarvan de teksten zich verticaal uitstrekten over een achtergrond van vooraf vastgelegde texturen met een enkele link die opviel omdat deze was onderstreept of vetgedrukt.

Toen was het grote «netwerk der netwerken» iets dat de mensheid nog aan het onderzoeken was en dat nog een primitieve nabootsing van de gedrukte pagina was, ondanks de verwondering die werd veroorzaakt door de mogelijkheid om in real time vanuit het zuidelijkste land van Zuid-Amerika met iemand in het oude Joegoslavië te communiceren.

Vandaag de dag is Internet de snelst geaccepteerde technologie. Internet, dat voor altijd verbonden is met het vermogen van de nieuwe software, overtreft zichzelf elke dag, elke minuut, elke seconde en verbaast ons met een interactiviteitsniveau dat ons overvalt en ons naar onvoorspelbare denkbeeldige werelden voert.

Binnen deze razend actuele context, is dit boek een onontbeerlijke bron van inspiratie voor iedereen die een ware goochelaar van het virtuele leven wil zijn. Web Design is een verzameling websites uit alle windstreken van de wereld en toont honderden uitzonderlijke voorbeelden die de talloze mogelijkheden van de nieuwe technologieën aantonen.

Er wordt niet alleen rekening gehouden met basiselementen voor het grafisch ontwerp dat wordt omgezet in webdesign (zoals het gebruik van kleur, lettertypes en de opstelling van de elementen op de pagina), maar de ontwerpen die in dit boek zijn opgenomen zijn eveneens een weerspiegeling van de mogelijkheden van het animeren van - voorheen onvermijdelijk statische - elementen en, met name, van de interactiviteit, die ervoor zorgt dat de grenzen van de tijd en de ruimte worden verlegd.

Anderzijds bevat Web Design een hoofdstuk dat speciaal is gewijd aan blogs, niet alleen vanwege het bijzondere karakter van deze dagboeken die bij elke update automatisch openbaar worden gemaakt, maar ook omdat er steeds meer bedrijven zijn die ze gebruiken om actueel te blijven. Blogs vertegenwoordigen een fundamenteel communicatiekanaal voor potentiële klanten en dankzij de functionaliteit ervan kan een dialoog gevoerd worden die nodig is om de creativiteit te bevorderen.

Portfolio's, reclamecampagnes, online winkels en diverse persoonlijke werelden. Deze voorbeelden zijn de eerste stappen naar een toekomst met oneindig veel mogelijkheden. Is er iemand die eraan kan weerstaan een kijkje te nemen in de toekomst?

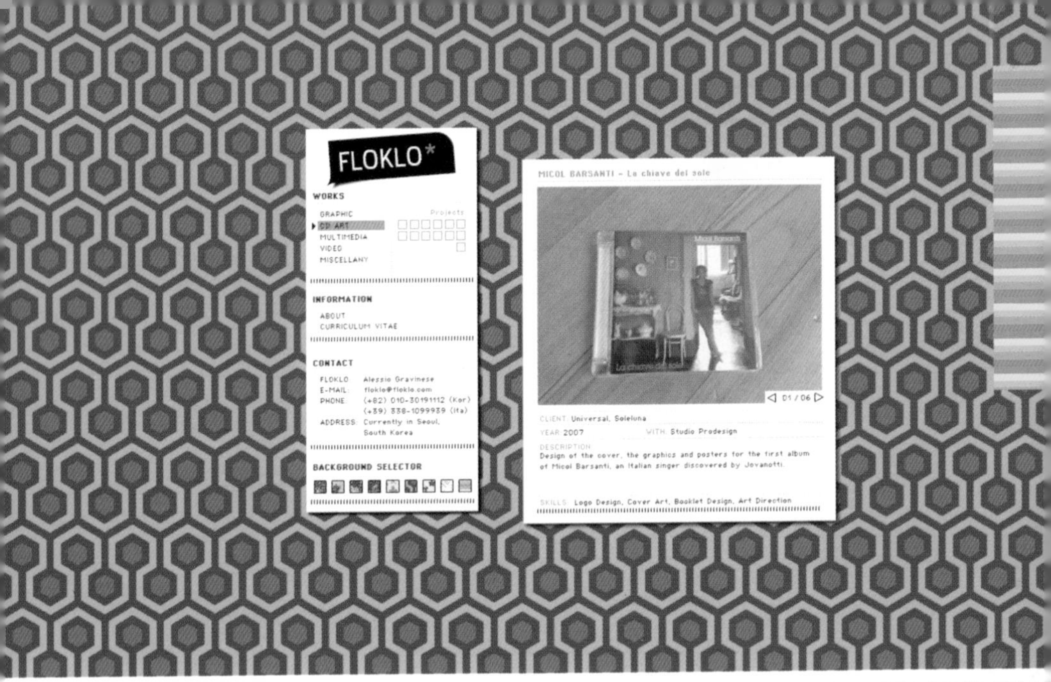

FLOKLO*

WORKS

GRAPHIC
CD ART
MULTIMEDIA
VIDEO
MISCELLANY

Projects

INFORMATION

ABOUT
CURRICULUM VITAE

CONTACT

FLOKLO: Alessio Gravinese
E-MAIL: floklo@floklo.com
PHONE: (+82) 010-30191112 (Kor)
(+39) 338-1099939 (Ita)
ADDRESS: Currently in Seoul,
South Korea

BACKGROUND SELECTOR

MICOL BARSANTI – La chiave del sole
01 / 06
CLIENT: Universal, Soleluna
YEAR: 2007
WITH: Studio Prodesign
DESCRIPTION:
Design of the cover, the graphics and posters for the first album of Micol Barsanti, an Italian singer discovered by Jovanotti.
SKILLS: Logo Design, Cover Art, Booklet Design, Art Direction

...ds, commissioned Hello Monday to
...een strategy is not about creating
...blue ocean view to 17,000 people.
...water canals, and recreational

Back to top

WEBSITES 01/10

SITES INTERNET

WEBSEITEN

WEBSITES

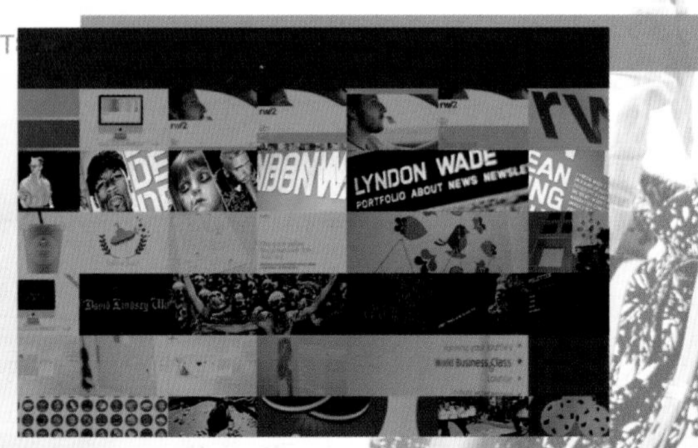

To make a website memorable, one of its strong points should be that it provides a unique user experience. The information should also be easy to understand and the contents accessed as naturally and logically as possible. But, what can be done to stop visitors from being turned off and going elsewhere while the intro is loading?
The following pages show examples of how the first impression created by color and the use of different web applications are the key to holding attention. Full screen viewing recommended!

Si l'on veut qu'un site marque les esprits, l'une de ses principales caractéristiques doit être d'offrir à l'utilisateur une expérience unique. Mais un site doit également veiller à la facilité de compréhension de l'information et à l'accès aux différents éléments qui doit pouvoir se faire le plus naturellement possible. Comment empêcher l'utilisateur de fuir pendant le chargement de l' « intro » ?
Les pages suivantes illustrent comment la première impression de la couleur et l'utilisation des différentes applications internet sont la clé pour y parvenir. À voir en plein écran !

Um sich an eine Homepage erinnern zu können, muss sie als Haupteigenschaft für den Anwender eine einzigartige Erfahrung darstellen. Dazu kommen die Verständlichkeit der Informationen und der einfache Zugriff auf die einzelnen Elemente. Wie erreicht man dies, ohne dass jemand schon beim Laden des Intros die Seite wechselt?
Auf den folgenden Seiten sind Beispiele für die Schlüsselfunktionen des ersten Farbeindrucks und Einsatzes unterschiedlicher Webanwendungen dargestellt. Es wird empfohlen, den gesamten Bildschirm zur Anzeige zu nutzen!

Om een website te kunnen onthouden is het heel belangrijk dat de site de gebruiker een unieke ervaring biedt. En toch moet de informatie eveneens gemakkelijk te begrijpen zijn en dient men zo eenvoudig mogelijk toegang te kunnen krijgen tot de verschillende onderdelen. Hoe zorgen we ervoor dat niemand op de vlucht slaat terwijl de «homepage» wordt geladen?
De volgende pagina's tonen voorbeelden die laten zien dat de eerste indruk van de kleur en het gebruik van verschillende webtoepassingen de sleutel tot succes kunnen zijn. Liefst te bekijken op volledig scherm!

310k // www.310k.nl

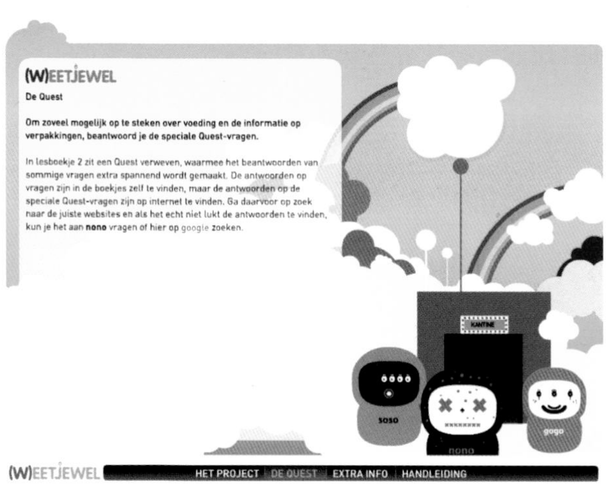
(W)EETJEWEL
De Quest
Om zoveel mogelijk op te steken over voeding en de informatie op verpakkingen, beantwoord je de speciale Quest-vragen.
In lesboekje 2 zit een Quest verweven, waarmee het beantwoorden van sommige vragen extra spannend wordt gemaakt. De antwoorden op vragen zijn in de boekjes zelf te vinden, maar de antwoorden op de speciale Quest-vragen zijn op internet te vinden. Ga daarvoor op zoek naar de juiste websites en als het echt niet lukt de antwoorden te vinden, kun je het aan nono vragen of hier op google zoeken.
KANTINE
soso
nono
gogo
(W)EETJEWEL
HET PROJECT | DE QUEST | EXTRA INFO | HANDLEIDING

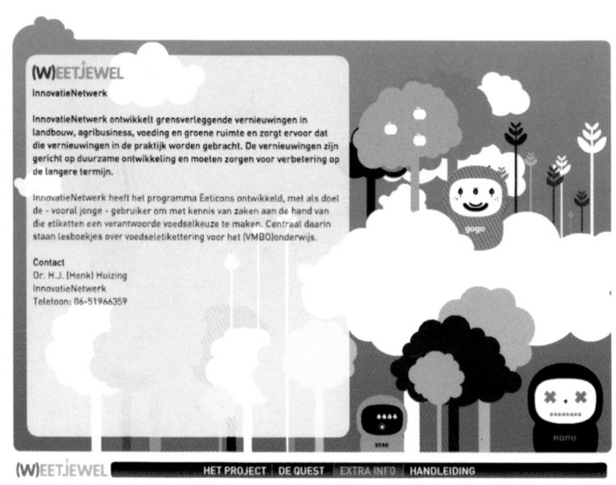
(W)EETJEWEL
InnovatieNetwerk
InnovatieNetwerk ontwikkelt grensverleggende vernieuwingen in landbouw, agribusiness, voeding en groene ruimte en zorgt ervoor dat die vernieuwingen in de praktijk worden gebracht. De vernieuwingen zijn gericht op duurzame ontwikkeling en moeten zorgen voor verbetering op de langere termijn.
InnovatieNetwerk heeft het programma Eeticons ontwikkeld, met als doel de - vooral jonge - gebruiker om met kennis van zaken aan de hand van die etiketten een verantwoorde voedselkeuze te maken. Centraal daarin staan lesboekjes over voedseletikettering voor het (VMBO)onderwijs.
Contact
Dr. H.J. (Henk) Huizing
InnovatieNetwerk
Telefoon: 06-51966359
gogo
soso
nono
(W)EETJEWEL
HET PROJECT | DE QUEST | EXTRA INFO | HANDLEIDING

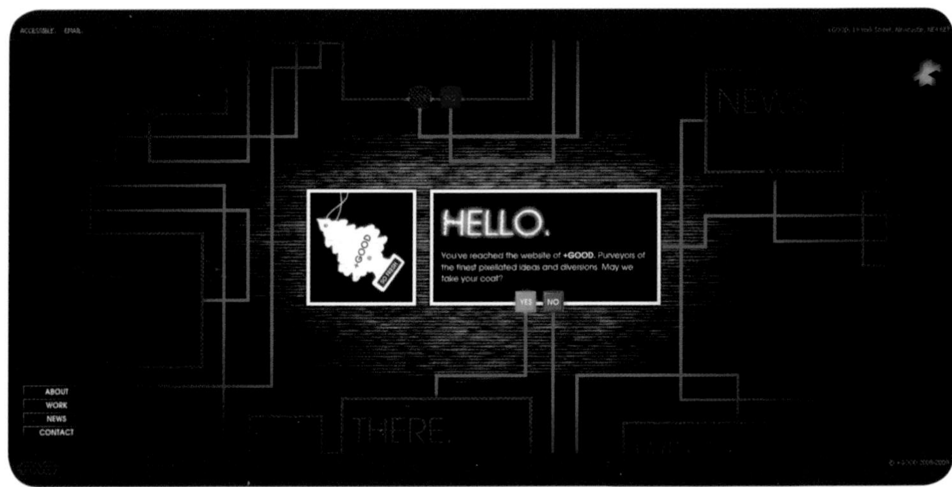

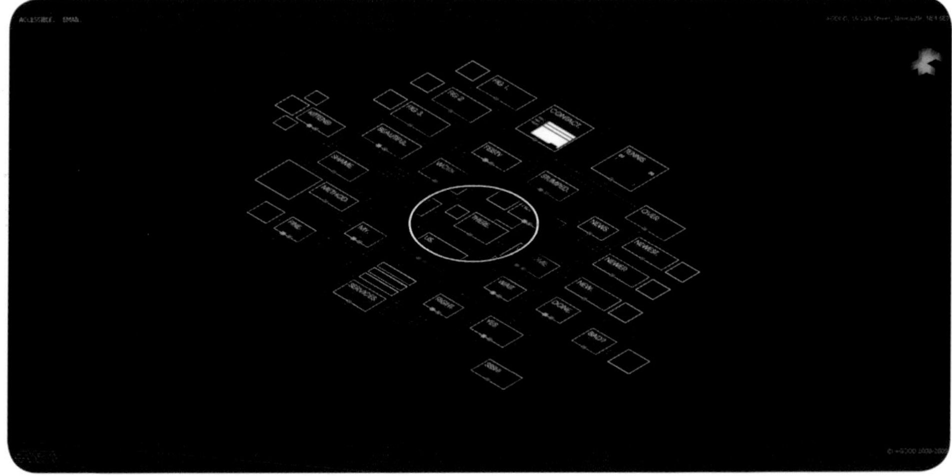

James Lattimore // www.plusgood.co.uk

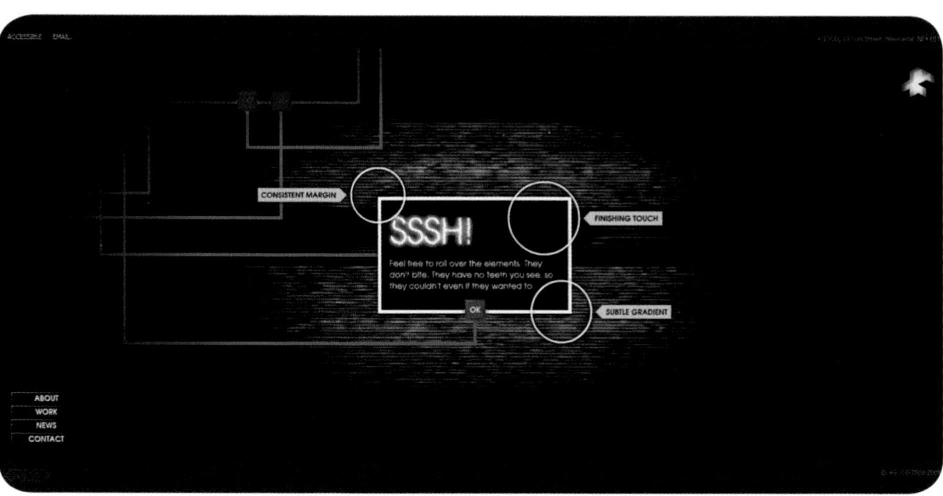
ACCESSIBLE EMAIL
CONSISTENT MARGIN
SSSH!
Feel free to roll over the elements. They don't bite. They have no teeth you see, so they couldn't even if they wanted to.
OK
FINISHING TOUCH
SUBTLE GRADIENT
ABOUT
WORK
NEWS
CONTACT

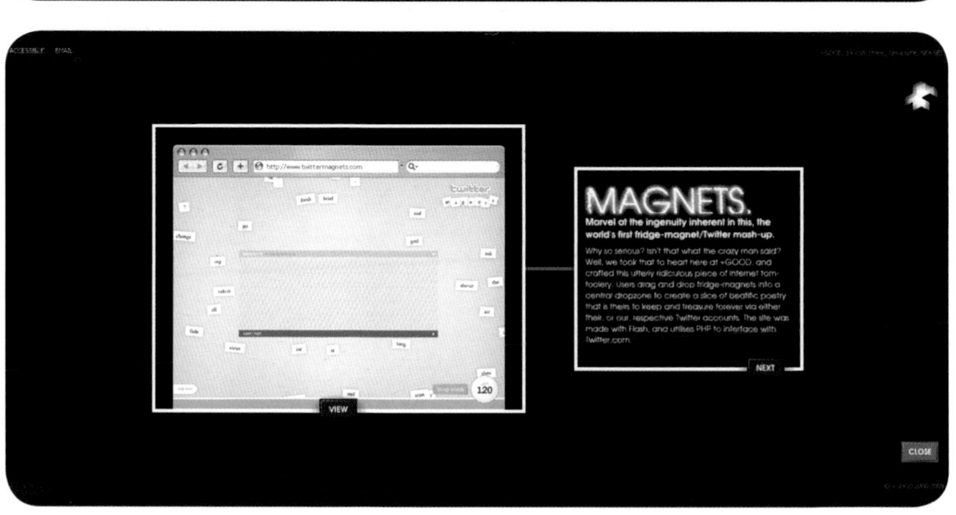
ACCESSIBLE EMAIL
http://www.twittermagnets.com
twitter
120
VIEW
MAGNETS.
Marvel at the ingenuity inherent in this, the world's first fridge-magnet/Twitter mash-up.
Why so serious? Isn't that what the crazy man said? Well, we took that to heart here at +GOOD, and crafted this utterly ridiculous piece of internet tom-foolery. Users drag and drop fridge-magnets into a central dropzone to create a slice of beatific poetry that is theirs to keep and treasure forever via either their, or our, respective Twitter accounts. The site was made with Flash, and utilises PHP to interface with Twitter.com.
NEXT
CLOSE

WE DON'T SEE THINGS AS THEY ARE. WE SEE THEM AS WE ARE. ANAIS NIN

ANDREAS ENNEMOSER
JAN WISCHERMANN
GORAN POZNANOVIC

KREATIVSTUDIO
DIEGUTGESTALTEN
DEUTSCHE VERSION ENGLISH VERSION

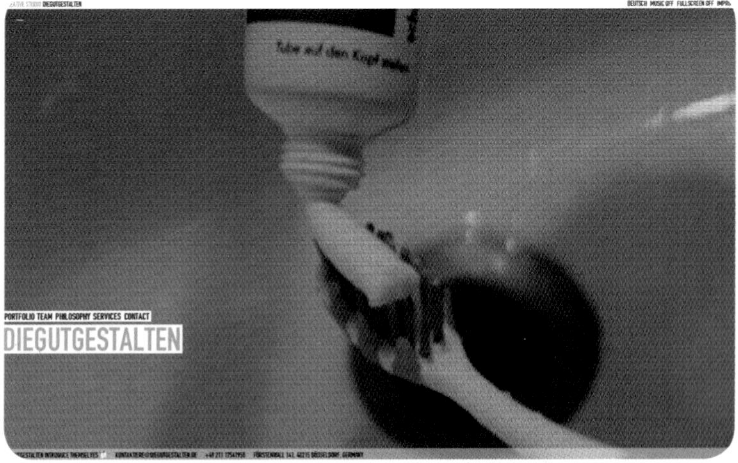

Andreas Ennemoser
Jan Wischermann
Goran Poznanovic/
DIEGUTGESTALTEN // www.diegutgestalten.de

DEUTSCH MUSIC OFF FULLSCREEN OFF
PORTFOLIO BACK
PRINT
ONE
TWO
THREE
FOUR
FIVE
SIX
SEVEN DOGS HAVE FLEAS
EIGHT
NINE
TEN FREE FALL
ONLINE
ELEVEN
TWELVE
DIGITAL ART
THIRTEEN
FOURTEEN
FIFTEEN
PROJECT INFORMATION
Freier Fall
ADDITIONAL PORTFOLIO PDF 15MB

DEUTSCH MUSIC OFF FULLSCREEN OFF
PORTFOLIO BACK
PRINT
ONE
TWO THEMA21
THREE
FOUR
FIVE
SIX
SEVEN
EIGHT
NINE
TEN
ONLINE
ELEVEN
TWELVE
DIGITAL ART
THIRTEEN
FOURTEEN
FIFTEEN
PROJECT INFORMATION
ADDITIONAL PORTFOLIO PDF 15MB

26000 Vodka // www.26000vodka.com

PRESS DISTRIBUTORS CONTACT

29.64 MILLION

A / meals prepared by the average Australian in 26000 years

B / grams of skin shed by the human body over 26000 years

C / people saved by surf life guards in the United States in 26000 years

D / phone calls will be made by the average person in 26000 years

Resn // www.resn.co.nz

PRESS DISTRIBUTORS CONTACT

Infusions

PRESS DISTRIBUTORS CONTACT

Slippery When Wet

45ml **26000 Vodka Lychee**
5ml Elder Flower Syrup
60ml Pineapple Juice
Shake & Strain
Martini Glass
Pineapple Wedge

Island Dancer

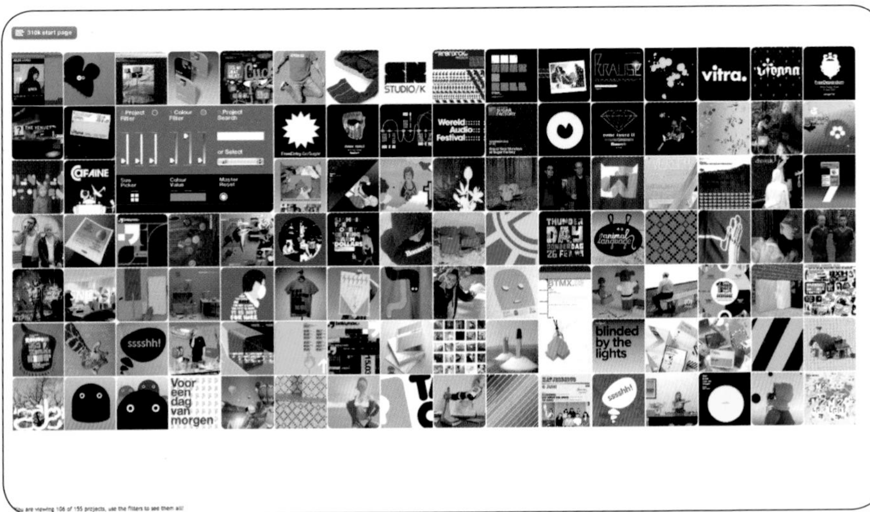

310k // www.310k.nl
Use media // Usemedia.com
Mikoon webservices // Mikoon.nl

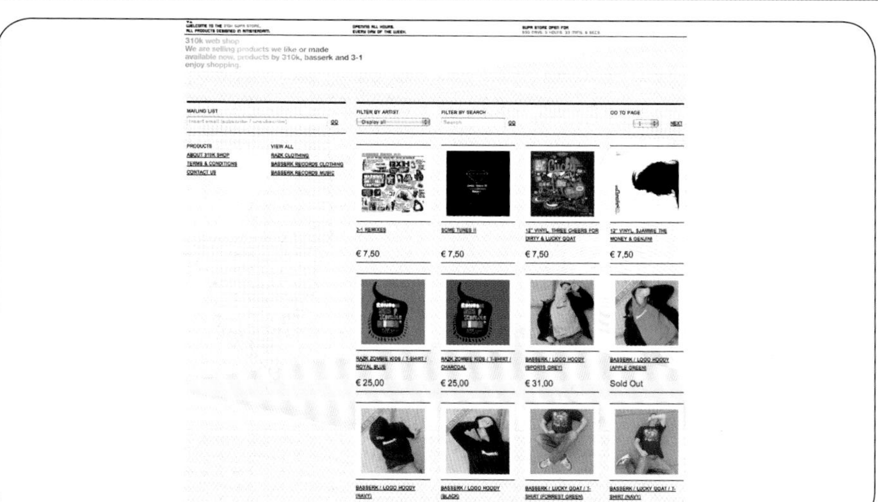
OPENING ALL HOURS.
EVERY DAY OF THE WEEK.
310k web shop
We are selling products we like or made
available now. products by 310k, basserk and 3-1
enjoy shopping.
MAILING LIST
GO
FILTER BY ARTIST
Display all
FILTER BY SEARCH
Search
GO
GO TO PAGE
NEXT
PRODUCTS
ABOUT 310K SHOP
TERMS & CONDITIONS
CONTACT US
VIEW ALL
RAZK CLOTHING
BASSERK RECORDS CLOTHING
BASSERK RECORDS MUSIC
3-1 REMIXES
€ 7,50
SOME TUNES II
€ 7,50
12" VINYL, THREE CHEERS FOR DIRTY & LUCKY GOAT
€ 7,50
€ 7,50
€ 25,00
€ 25,00
€ 31,00
Sold Out
Sold Out
Sold Out
€ 20,00
€ 20,00

310k start page
Basserk
home - news
catalog
artists
dj's
parties
about
reviews - feedback
downloads
links
contact
news:
02-06-09
The last Kiss off before summer, hot line up!!!
read more>>>>
01-06-09
Matjesdisco summer parties
read more>>>>
New distribution partner: Painted dog records
read more>>>>
Fat Sauce, the new release by Petr Passive
read more>>>>
13 Horrible remixes. The new CD by 3-1 is out now!!!
read more>>>>
Tanzkonsol, a new artist with a new release.
read more>>>>
Petr Passive a new artist on Basserk
310k / Basserk webshop
Check this site for all the Basserk releases on cd and vinyl.
Also available: T-shirts and other Basserk gear
buy tracks at Beatport
buy mp3's at the iTunes store
go to basserk myspace
go to Toolbox for vinyl
buy vinyl at rec-order
listen on LastFM
mailinglist
your details please

Kinetic // www.kinetic.com.sg

BACK
WHAT WE DO
THE UBIQUITOUS NEED FOR BRANDS, BIG OR SMALL, TO BE ESTABLISHED THEMSELVES IN THE EVER CHANGING WORLD LENDS THE NEED FOR A RESOURCEFUL, CREATIVE AND RELIABLE PARTNER. ONE THAT WILL GO THE DISTANCE, BEYOND THE TRADITIONAL MEANS OF MASS COMMUNICATION, TO
WHO ARE WE?
WHY ARE WE HERE?
WHAT IS OUR PURPOSE?
SOUND ON

PROFILE
E-MAIL
WEB SITE
industrie
BACK
PROFILE
EVOLVED FROM THE NEED TO PACE UP TO THE DEMANDS OF A RAPIDLY CHANGING DIGITAL WORLD, INDUSTRIE IS POSITIONED TO MEET NEW CHALLENGES WITH ITS ABILITY TO INTEGRATE OFF-LINE AND ON-LINE MARKETING AND PUBLICITY EFFORTS. HOUSING BEST-OF-BREED
+ AGENCY PROFILE
+ LAWRENCE YEAP, MANAGING DIRECTOR
SOUND ON

designedmemory // www.designedmemory.com

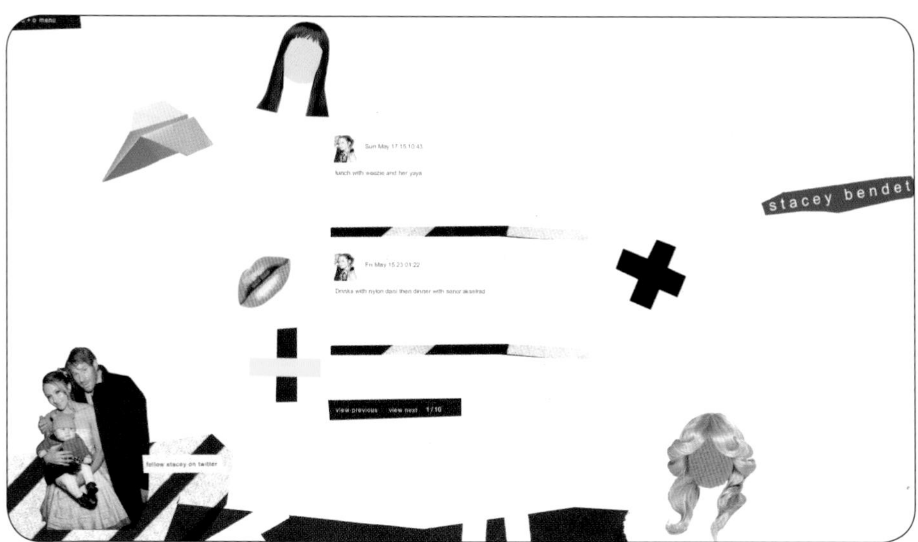

stacey bendet
lunch with weezie and her yaya
view previous
view next
1/10
follow stacey on twitter

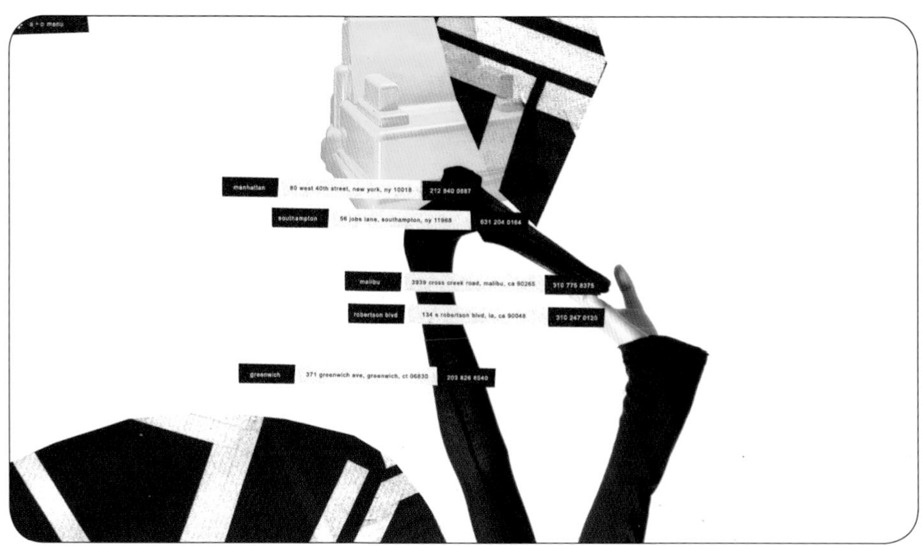

manhattan
80 west 40th street, new york, ny 10018
212 840 0887
southampton
56 jobs lane, southampton, ny 11968
631 204 0164
malibu
3939 cross creek road, malibu, ca 90265
310 775 8375
robertson blvd
134 s robertson blvd, la, ca 90048
310 247 0120
greenwich
371 greenwich ave, greenwich, ct 06830
203 826 6540

Coloring Book Studio // www.coloringbookstudio.com

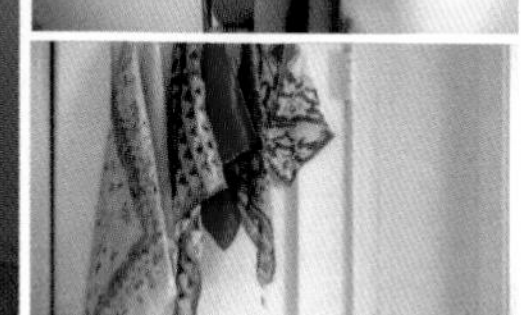

Bra, belt and long leggings

Limited edition belts made from found fabric

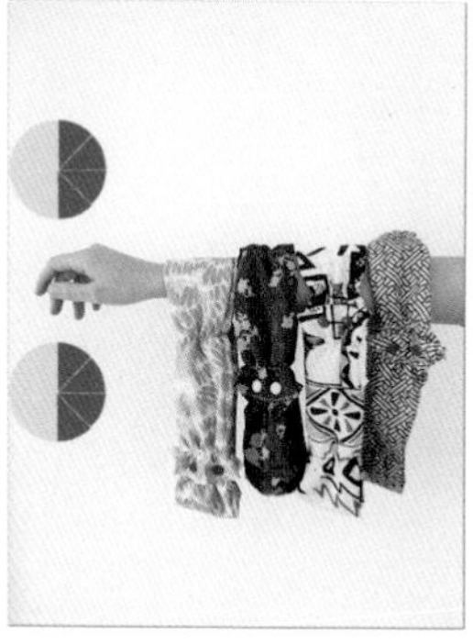

Watch Videos
Buy on iTunes
Buy on CD or Vinyl
Buy at Insound

SHOWS

6/03 Monkeytown
w/ Infernal Devices & Purple Crush
58 N. 3rd St., Brooklyn, New York 11211

4/25 Bokenstock Music Festival
1 Castle Point On Hudson, Hoboken, New Jersey

5/02 Vassar College w/ Francis & The Lights, Bear Hands, Holy Ghost!, !!!
124 Raymond Ave, Poughkeepsie, New York

5/08 Europa w/ Buke and Gass
98 Meserole Ave (corner of Manhattan Ave) Brooklyn, NY

TUMBLELOG

HEYYY BOSTON

We're playing at the Middle East tonight with Harry & the Potters and Previously on Lost

It'll be fun fun fun!

WE ARE A HAPPY FAMILY (photo by marjorie becker)

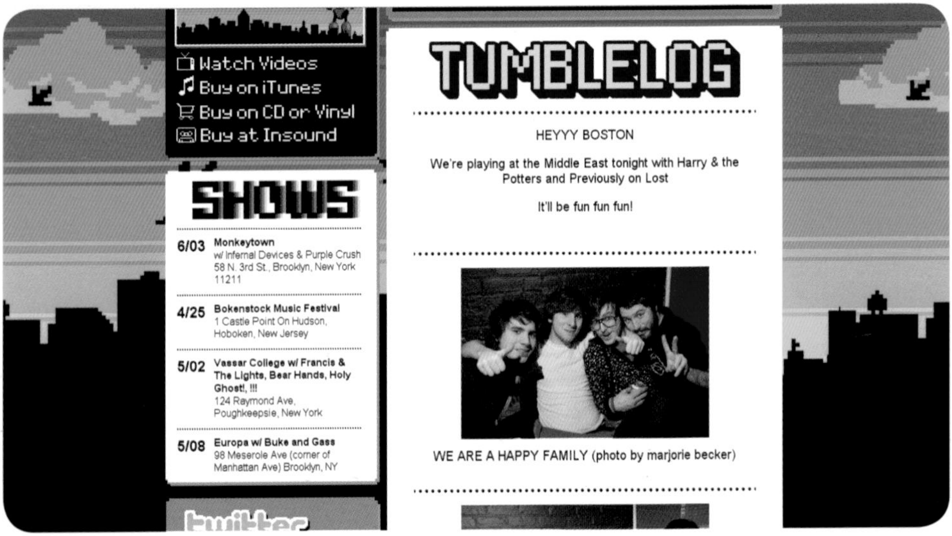

Adam Conover
David Mauro // www.anamanaguchi.com

> fullscreen
> embed

ANAMANAGUCHI
dawn metropolis

BUY THE ALBUM / about the band / the normative music co

SITE BY: LOLZ

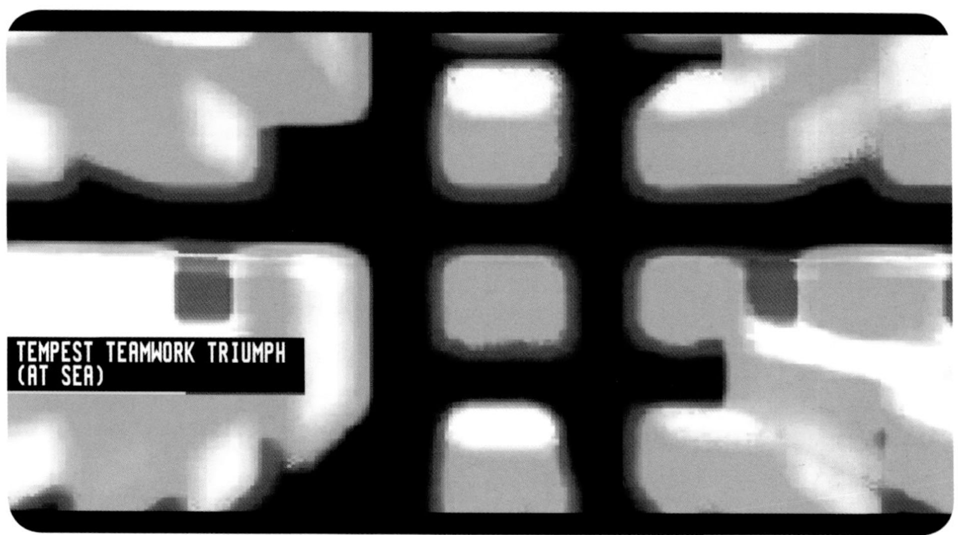

Outside Line & Arla Foods // www.outsideline.co.uk

Table of Contents
Welcome to the recipes of Anchor Real Dairy Cream. Here you will find some delicious creations that can be made and enjoyed by all of the family.
Please select which recipes you would like to see from the tabs sticking out of the recipe book. While reading the recipes you can jump to and from the sections in the book by clicking the tabs or you can just page through the book by clicking on the page curls on the top left and bottom right of the pages.
Featured Recipe
Divine Eton Mess
User Rating:
Serves: 4
Prep Time: 10 mins
Cook Time: 0
Difficulty: Easy
Impress the guests or treat the family with this quick, simple...
View this Recipe
Light Real Dairy Cream
View Recipe!
Real Dairy Cream
View Recipe!
Extra Thick Real Dairy Cream
View Recipe!
Chocolate Flavour Mousse
View Recipe!
LITTLE SQUIRT
SQUIRTY ART
SQUIRTY FUN
RECIPES
SQUIRTY RANGE
EVENTS
WIN!

Eraser
Fruits are good!!!
CHOCOLATE
Print Art
Clear
Save Art
LITTLE SQUIRT
SQUIRTY ART
SQUIRTY FUN
RECIPES
SQUIRTY RANGE
EVENTS
WIN!

Version Industries // versionindustries.com

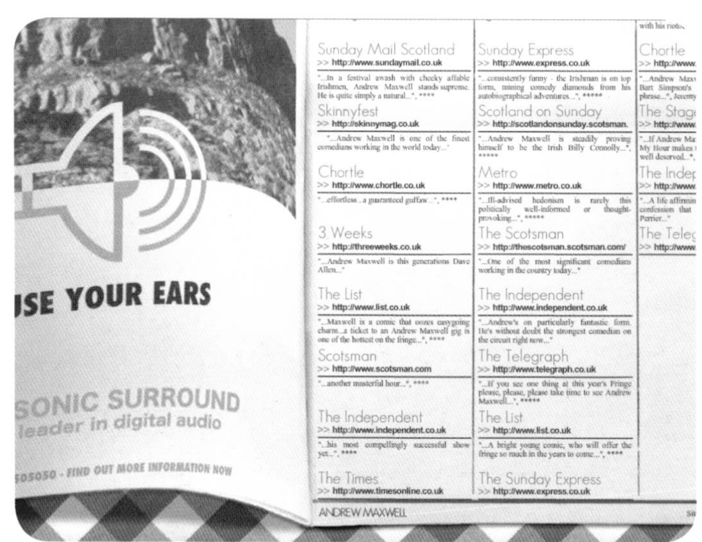

Sunday Mail Scotland
>> http://www.sundaymail.co.uk
"...In a festival awash with cheeky affable Irishmen, Andrew Maxwell stands supreme. He is quite simply a natural...", ****

Skinnyfest
>> http://skinnymag.co.uk
"...Andrew Maxwell is one of the finest comedians working in the world today..."

Chortle
>> http://www.chortle.co.uk
"...effortless...a guaranteed guffaw...", ****

3 Weeks
>> http://threeweeks.co.uk
"...Andrew Maxwell is this generations Dave Allen..."

The List
>> http://www.list.co.uk
"...Maxwell is a comic that oozes easygoing charm...a ticket to an Andrew Maxwell gig is one of the hottest on the fringe...", ****

Scotsman
>> http://www.scotsman.com
"...another masterful hour...", ****

The Independent
>> http://www.independent.co.uk
"...his most compellingly successful show yet...", ****

The Times
>> http://www.timesonline.co.uk

Sunday Express
>> http://www.express.co.uk
"...consistently funny - the Irishman is on top form, mining comedy diamonds from his autobiographical adventures...", *****

Scotland on Sunday
>> http://scotlandonsunday.scotsman.
"...Andrew Maxwell is steadily proving himself to be the Irish Billy Connolly...", *****

Metro
>> http://www.metro.co.uk
"...Ill-advised hedonism is rarely this politically well-informed or thought-provoking...", *****

The Scotsman
>> http://thescotsman.scotsman.com/
"...One of the most significant comedians working in the country today..."

The Independent
>> http://www.independent.co.uk
"...Andrew's on particularly fantastic form. He's without doubt the strongest comedian on the circuit right now..."

The Telegraph
>> http://www.telegraph.co.uk
"...If you see one thing at this year's Fringe please, please, please take time to see Andrew Maxwell...", *****

The List
>> http://www.list.co.uk
"...A bright young comic, who will offer the fringe so much in the years to come...", ****

The Sunday Express
>> http://www.express.co.uk

Chortle
The Stage
The Indep
The Teleg

ANDREW MAXWELL

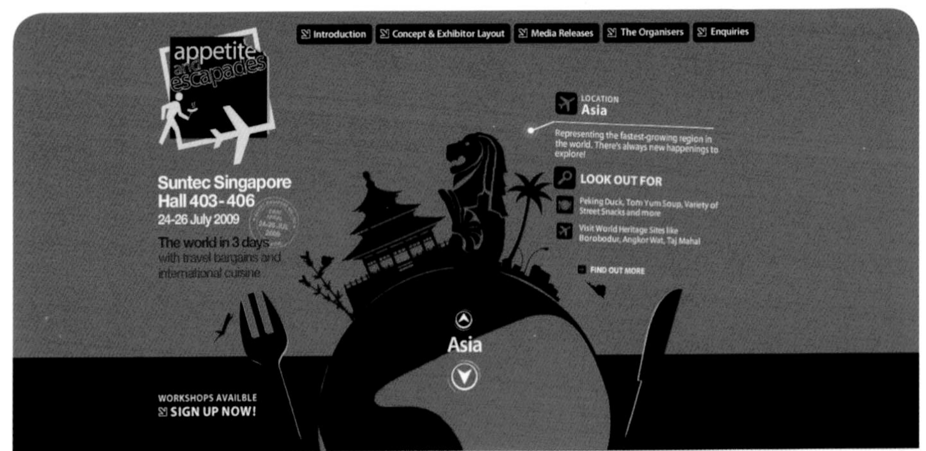

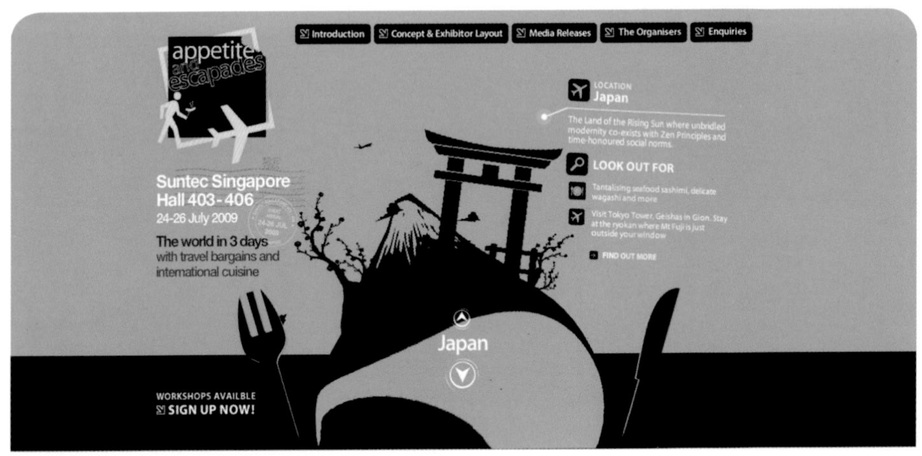

Kilo Studio // www.kilostudio.net

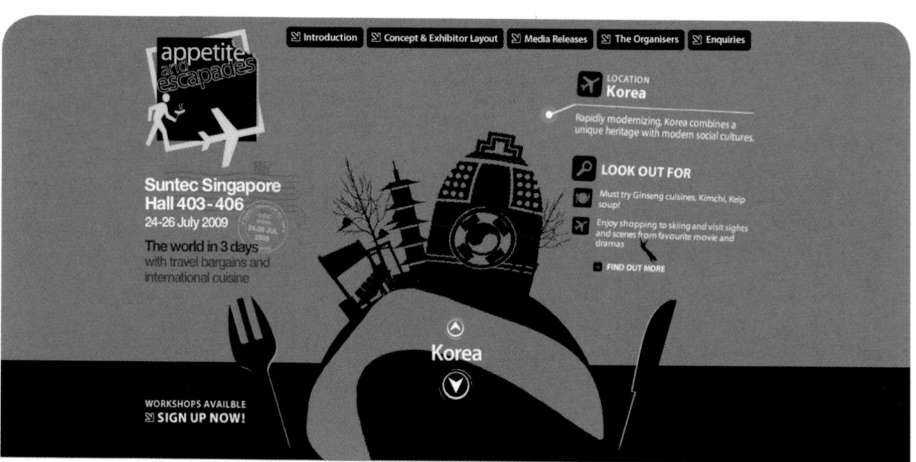
Introduction
Concept & Exhibitor Layout
Media Releases
The Organisers
Enquiries
appetite and escapades
LOCATION
Korea
Rapidly modernizing, Korea combines a unique heritage with modern social cultures.
LOOK OUT FOR
Must try Ginseng cuisines, Kimchi, Kelp soup!
Enjoy shopping to skiing and visit sights and scenes from favourite movie and dramas
FIND OUT MORE
Suntec Singapore
Hall 403-406
24-26 July 2009
The world in 3 days
with travel bargains and international cuisine
Korea
WORKSHOPS AVAILBLE
SIGN UP NOW!

Organiser:
sphere

Introduction
Concept & Exhibitor Layout
Media Releases
The Organisers
Enquiries
appetite and escapades
LOCATION
USA / Europe
Be part of the enticing region that is thriving with city life and steeped in history!
LOOK OUT FOR
Breweries, Italian cuisine etc
Visit the Louvre, Rocky Mountains, Colosseum, Athens etc
FIND OUT MORE
Suntec Singapore
Hall 403-406
24-26 July 2009
The world in 3 days
with travel bargains and international cuisine
USA/Europe
WORKSHOPS AVAILBLE
SIGN UP NOW!

Organiser:
sphere

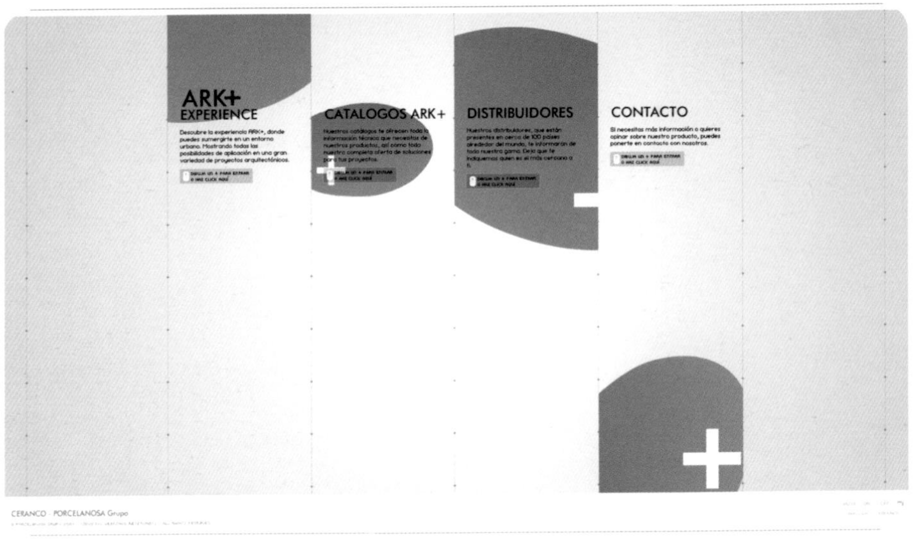

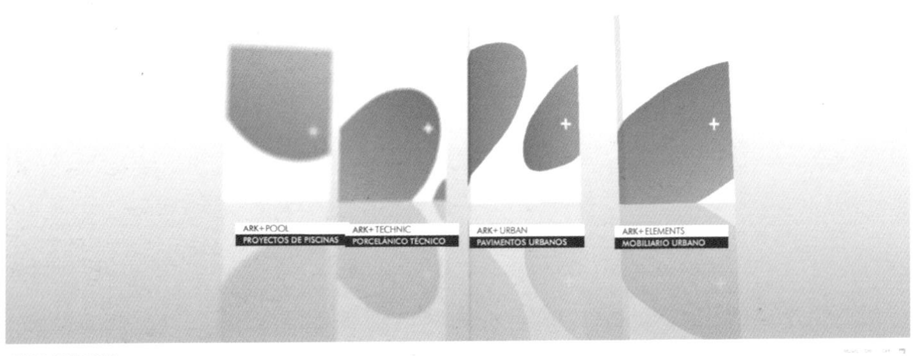

Pixelinglife // www.pixelinglife.com

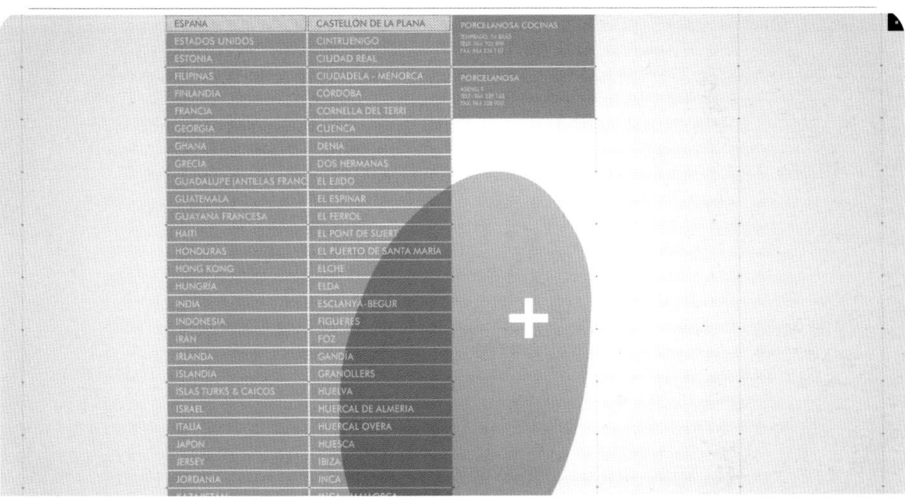
ESPAÑA
ESTADOS UNIDOS
ESTONIA
FILIPINAS
FINLANDIA
FRANCIA
GEORGIA
GHANA
GRECIA
GUADALUPE (ANTILLAS FRANC
GUATEMALA
GUAYANA FRANCESA
HAITÍ
HONDURAS
HONG KONG
HUNGRÍA
INDIA
INDONESIA
IRÁN
IRLANDA
ISLANDIA
ISLAS TURKS & CAICOS
ISRAEL
ITALIA
JAPÓN
JERSEY
JORDANIA
CASTELLÓN DE LA PLANA
CINTRUÉNIGO
CIUDAD REAL
CIUDADELA - MENORCA
CÓRDOBA
CORNELLÀ DEL TERRI
CUENCA
DENIA
DOS HERMANAS
EL EJIDO
EL ESPINAR
EL FERROL
EL PONT DE SUERT
EL PUERTO DE SANTA MARÍA
ELCHE
ELDA
ESCLANYÀ-BEGUR
FIGUERES
FOZ
GANDIA
GRANOLLERS
HUELVA
HUERCAL DE ALMERÍA
HUERCAL OVERA
HUESCA
IBIZA
INCA
PORCELANOSA COCINAS
PORCELANOSA
CERANCO - PORCELANOSA Grupo

PASEO MARÍTIMO
AL ENTORNO
PASEO MARÍTIMO
CERANCO - PORCELANOSA Grupo

Vergani & Gasco // www.verganiegasco.it

ART&FORM
made in italy
01.MENU'
[SALONE INTERNAZIONALE DEL MOBILE 07]
POKER&TOGETHER
REA01&REA02
LORD&MILORD
LE PIEGHEVOLI

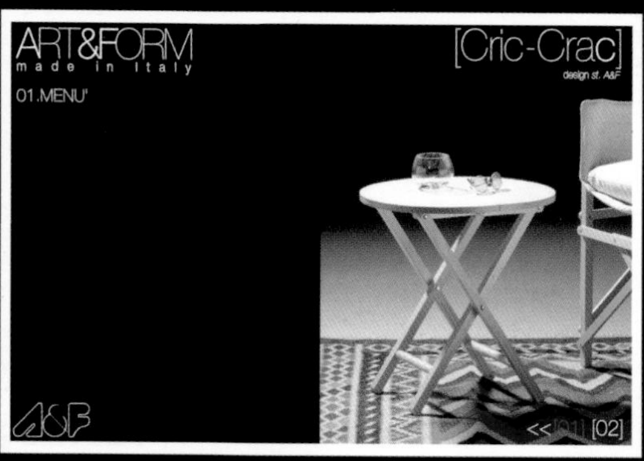
ART&FORM
made in italy
01.MENU'
[Cric-Crac]
design st. A&F
<< [01] [02]

Arte Antiqua // www.arteantiqua.it

Vergani & Gasco // www.verganiegasco.it

MENU

MENU

Asylum Films // www.asylumfilms.co.uk

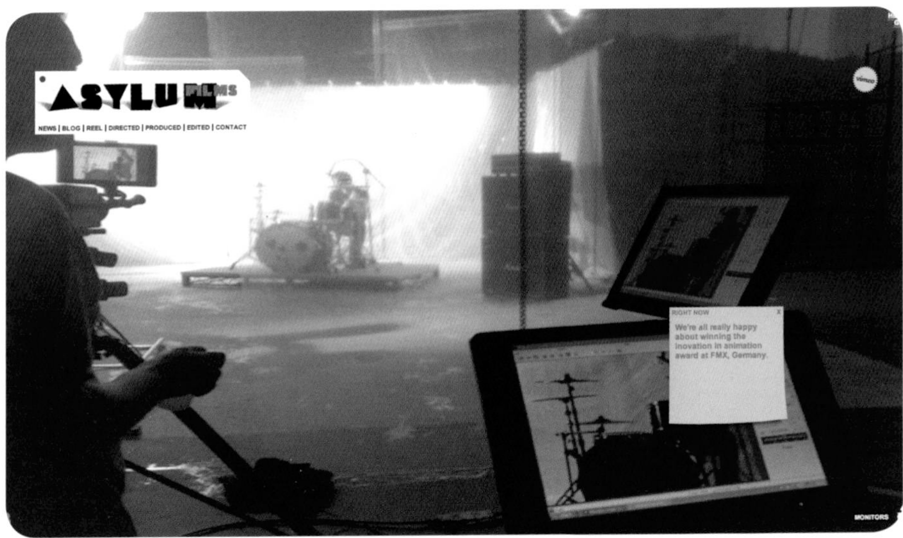

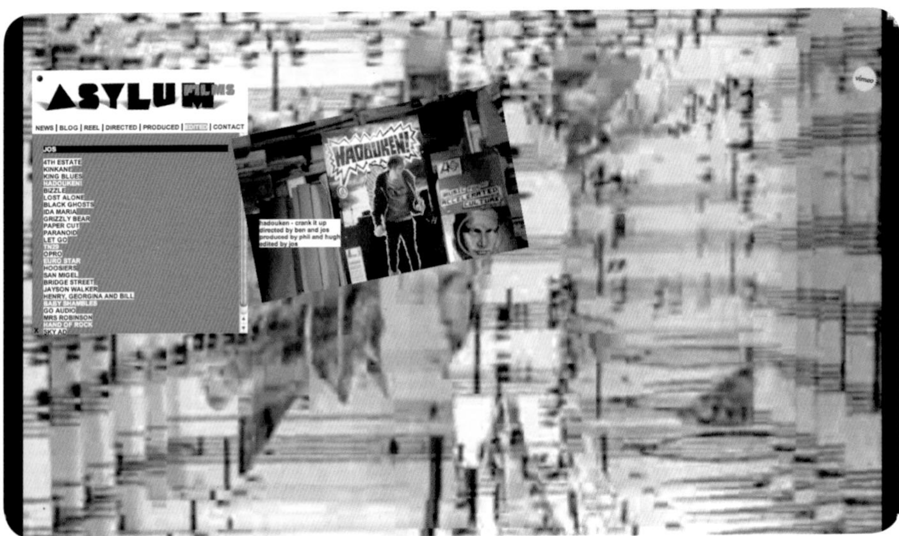

Version Industries // versionindustries.com

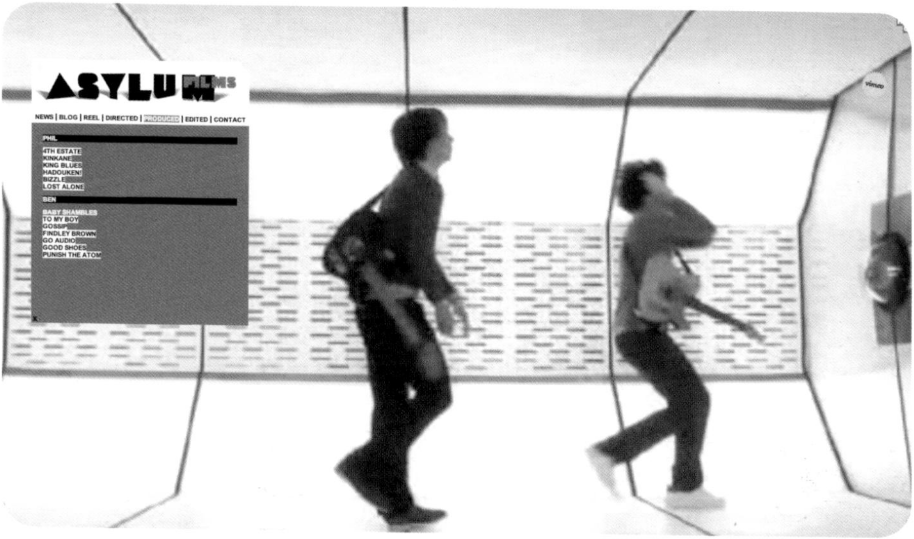

ASYLUM FILMS

NEWS | BLOG | REEL | DIRECTED | PRODUCED | EDITED | CONTACT

PHIL

4TH ESTATE
KINKANE
KING BLUES
HADOUKEN!
BIZZLE
LOST ALONE

BEN

BABY SHAMBLES
TO MY BOY
GOSSIP
FINDLEY BROWN
GO AUDIO
GOOD SHOES
PUNISH THE ATOM

X

vimeo

designedmemory // www.designedmemory.com

loading
go home.
ARS downloads
*press quotes
*press one sheet
*band biography

Thu May 21
Hello Friends!
Download Still Night, Still Light from thinkindie.com and receive The Teenagers remix of Shadows as a bonus. And if you buy Still Night, Still Light from one of the following fine independent record stores, you'll also get a copy of Reverse Migration, a collection of our favorite remixes from The Bird of Music. While supplies last!
Boo Boo Records San Luis Obispo, CA
Cactus Music Houston, TX
CD Central Lexington, KY
CD Connection Jacksonville Beach, FL
go home.

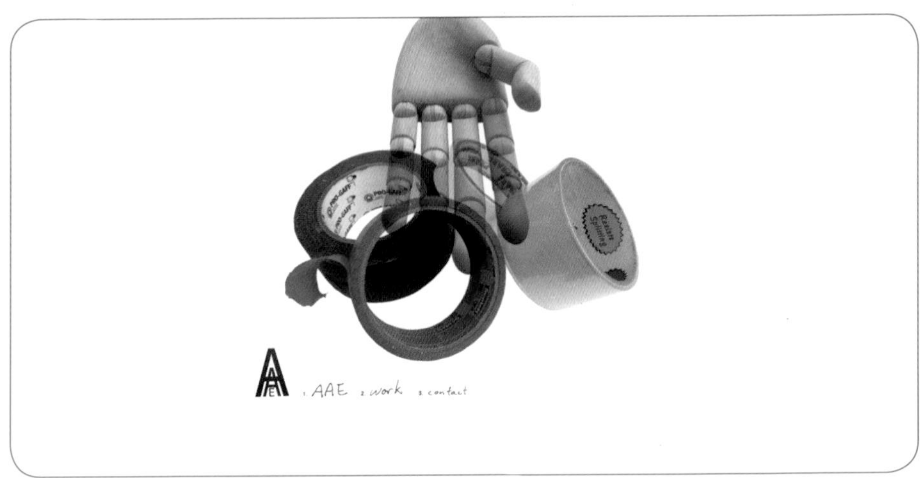

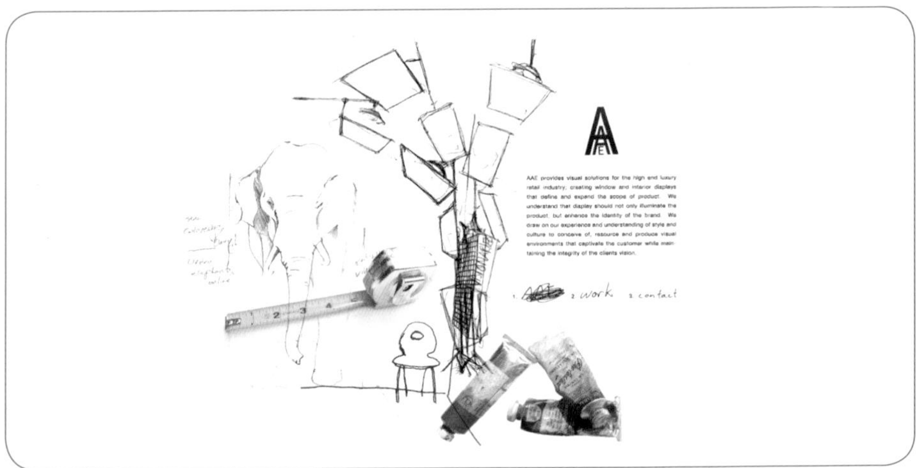

designedmemory // www.designedmemory.com

1. AAE 2. work 3. contact
DVF
HERMÈS PARIS
MISSONI
BARNEYS NEWYORK
HELMUT LANG
VALENTINO
ROSA CHÁ
BURBERRY
curve
JILLSTUART
steven alan

1. AAE 2. work 3. contact
ROSA CHÁ
a. move back b. move forward
ROSA CHÁ

Bagua Jody // www.baguajody.nl

310k // www.310k.nl

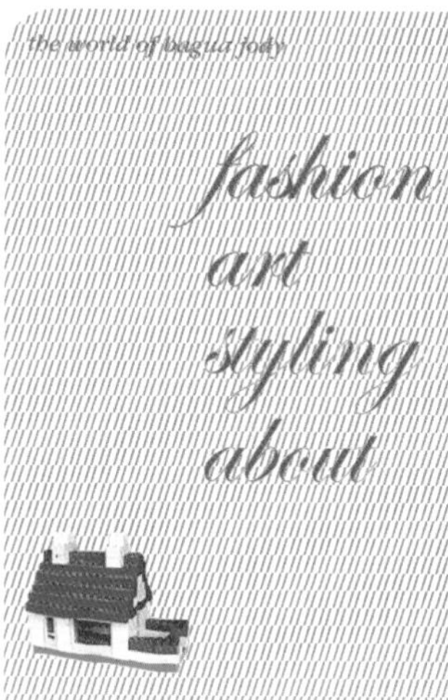
the world of bagua jody
fashion
art
styling
about
cream of the crop
eclectique c'est chic
paris oh my

eclectique c'est chic
< back next >
Editorial Colurfull magazine, fall
Photography: feriattumo
Model: Jessica @ Tony Jones Management

the world of bagua jody
fashion
art
styling
about
nudes
illustrations
me blood
fashion drawings
< back next >
Different styles with humor.

...da Swinging London Mary Quant foi uma grande percursora do estilo quando criou ... Criou sua célebre butique chamada Bazaar, uma loja ... a mistura de estilos e novos acessórios, que ... época se identificavam, pois estavam cansad... ...lo de suas mães. Elas queriam uma roupa cont... ...ir ao trabalho e também para ...

...tinha como protagonista a lendária rua ... a Carnaby Street, na zona londrina de Soho. Lá ...dade e fama os desenhos de John Stephen, Michael ...ark. Outros estilistas animados pelos preços incrível... ...de aluguéis, abriram suas próprias butiques, que atraíam com letreiros e vitrines chamativas, onde ninguém poderia resistir.

O "Swinging London" também marcou o desenho gráfico da ... O desenho pop, as cores e a inspiração psicodélica invadiram ... revistas, fotografias e capas dos discos dos grupos musicais ... de Beatles a Rolling Stones, passando por Pink Floyd e Jimi... Hendrix. Entre os mais destacados da época estão os cartazes-retratos dos Beatles, feitos pelo famoso fotógrafo Richard Avedon, nos quais a estética psicodélica e hippie se misturaram com a iconogra... ...adicional utilizada para as bandas. O " Swinging London" te... ...o início dos anos 70. Sua estética fervilhante, contudo, de... ...que continuam a contaminar a arte e a moda dos nos dias ... hoje.

de uma grande diversidade de sapatarias.

A lendária rua reúne mais de 30 flagships de grandes marcas do mundo todo e não pode passar desapercebida. Por uma estreita entrada pela Oxford Street ou pelo acesso principal via Regent Street, a charmosa Carnaby Street têm de tudo! É um grande ponto turístico de Londres com uma variedade grande de lojas de marcas internacionais muito popular entre a juventude consumidora londrina, sempre tomada por turistas de todas as partes do mundo, atraídos por sua fama. É um lugar qu... ...rece visita obrigatória para quem gosta de moda.

Como che...

Não importa a maneira co... até a Carnaby Street, o qu... em Oxford Circus

Pegue o metrô até Oxford Circu... e Central todas essas linhas ... Desça da estação pela saíd... instruções a seguir a pé.

A partir de Piccadilly ... Street, em direcção a O... Street ao seu lado direi... Street está agora a ape...

De Oxford Circus: ... Marlborough Stree... ough Str. e ande p... principal 'para C... adiante à sua di...

Outra alternativa é pegar um ... ista para levá-lo a Carnaby Street. Todos ... Londres sabem onde fica a Carnaby Street.

INVERNO 2009
Noite e Diversão
Lugares para dançar até cansar
Música
Rock´n Roll
Entre o novo e o antigo, o bom rock de verdade é aquele que vem do coração
O primeiro sucesso de rock n' roll verdadeiramente britânico foi a música "Move It" de Cliff Richard. A partir daí vários grupos de rock começaram a se formar para tocar em clubes e bailes locais. A chegada da Guerra do Vietnã provocou o rock a tomar partido contra ela. Começaram a ficar conhecidas as contestações políticas de Bob Dylan.
O rock inglês ganhou notoriedade mundial com o surgimento dos Beatles. Em 1962 os garotos de Liverpool estouraram nas paradas com o single "Love Me Do". A partir daí o
ref. 17496
ref. 19190

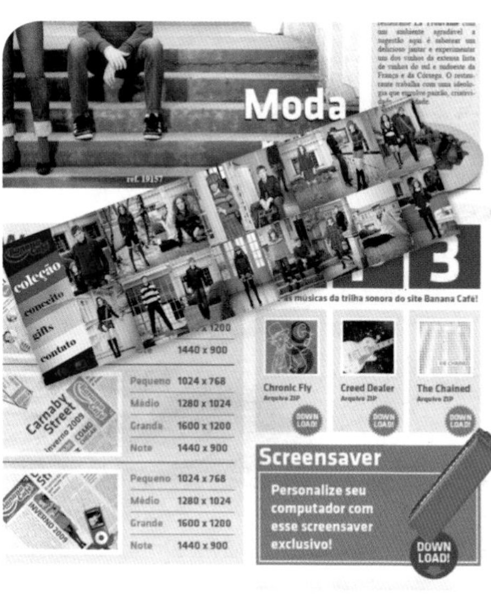

Conceito

Carnaby Street

Carnaby Street já foi palco de grandes acontecimentos na cena urbana de Londres e arrastava multidões de modernos atrás das últimas novidades dos mundos da música e da moda nos anos 60 e 70. A Atmosfera cosmopolita londrina e o lifestyle dos jovens ingleses são grande fonte de inspiração para a coleção Banana Café.

Um passeio pelas ruas e becos do Soho ou pelo Piccadilly Circus, visitando o Trocadero; circular pela feirinha de Portobello Road em busca da "mais nova" peça vintage para incrementar a produção, são programas indispensáveis nessa "viagem". E como ninguém é de ferro, no final do dia, um "esquenta" num autêntico pub e terminar a noite curtindo um show ao vivo da "banda do momento" ou mesmo dançando e arrasando nas pistas dos famosos clubes londrinos.

O figurino das bandas Libertines, Razor Lights e Amy Winehouse; cenários das baladas como Ministry of Sound, Cherry Jam e Neibourhood; além da eterna musa Kate Moss são fontes de inspiração para a coleção da Banana Café.

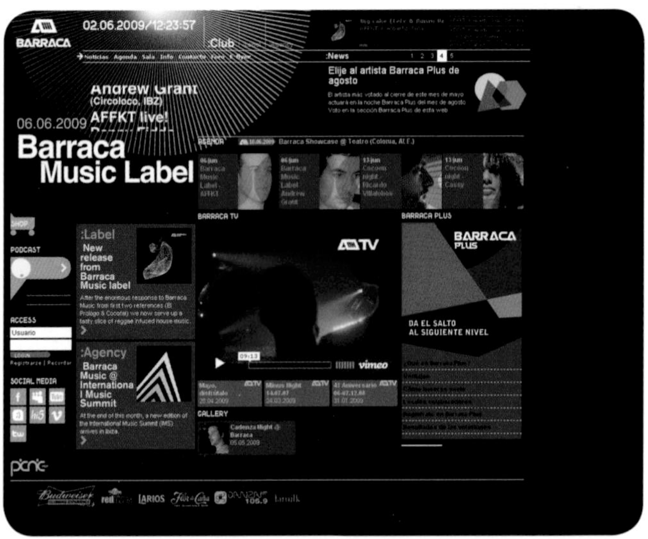

Inklude // www.inklude.com

Círculo Rojo // www.circulorojo.es

BARRACA
02.06.2009/12:50:58
:Agency :Club :Label
Noticias Agenda Artistas Contacto Foro
Artistas
Andrew Grant
SHOP
PODCAST
ACCESS
Usuario
SOCIAL MEDIA
Danny Fiddo
Barraca Music Agency, ESP
BOOKING
Chart Mayo 2009
1- REBOOT "PAR DIZER" (CDR)
2- SPENCER PARKER "THE BEGINNING (AFFKT & FIDDO RMX)" (BUZZIN FLY)
3- RADIOSLAVE "ORCHESTRATING MANOUVRES IN THE DARK" (CDR)
4- AME "ENSOR" (INNERVISIONS)
5- GUISEPPE CENNAMO "CANADIAN SALSA (DANNY FIDDO & J.M ABOGA RMX)" (MONIQUE MUSIQUE)
6- JOHN TALABOT "SUNSHINE(AFFKT RMX)" (CDR)
7- FELIPE VENEGAS & ALLENDES "NUNCA CAMINARAS SOLO" (CDR)
8- ALEX CELLER "LA PALMA" (AREA REMOTE)
9- SASCHA DIVE "JED CLAYTON (SAMUEL DAVIS DARK BEAT MIX)" (DEEP VIBES)
10- DAMIAN SCHWARZ "IN THE MOOD" (MUPA)
Danny Fiddo's time in the Spanish electronic music scene is steeped in history and tradition.
His years as resident of iconic Barraca club in Valencia coupled with over 15 years of playing experience prove that his personal style and touch remain as important and relevant as ever.
Having played mainly throughout Spain and Europe, Danny has played alongside with artists such as Ricardo Villalobos, Richie Hawtin, Sven Vath, Carl Craig, Luciano, Tania Vulcano and many big names. All of whom have had added their touches of influence to his playing style and production ideas. Now sharing the studio with production partner AFFKT, Danny is quickly establishing his own name in electronic music.
His first full release alongside AFFKT on the 'Barraca Music' label entitled 'Points' on El Prologo EP has been widely acclaimed being loved and played by Richie Hawtin, Ricardo Villalobos, Luciano, Marco Carola, 2000 And One, Radio Slave, Loco Dice and many other big names in the DJ world. Not a bad achievement for someone's very first release in music.
He is well respected as one of the most consistent and personable DJ's in Spain and capped off a stellar 2008 schedule in both performance and production, with a year that included shows at Rex Club (Paris), Tresor (Berlin), Amnesia (Ibiza) Cocoon Disco Invaders 2008 (alongside Ricardo Villalobos and Dandy Jack), Russia's largest club, Arma 17 (Moscow) and most recently this year at Weekend (Berlin). The very near future will bring to light more solo work, on the 'Barraca Music' and '3rd Floor Records' (La Safa) labels alongside remix work for Radio Slave and Martinez.
Danny's time is now...
AGENDA
BOOKING

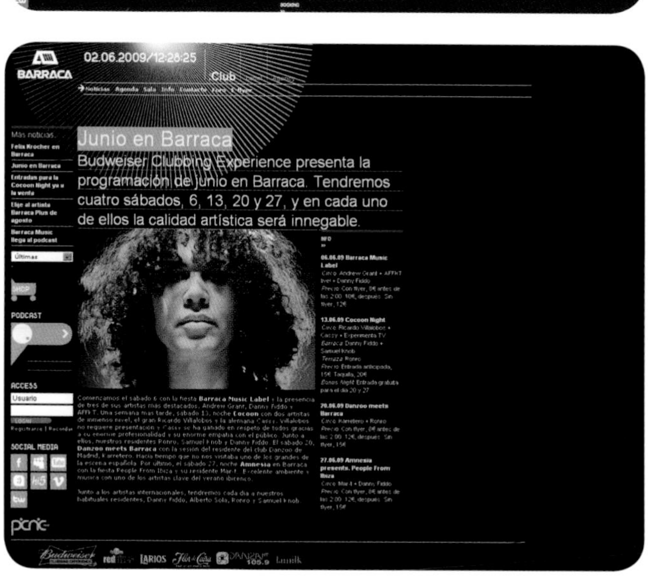
BARRACA
02.06.2009/12:28:25
Club
Noticias Agenda Sala Info Contacto Foro E-flyer
Mas noticias.
Felix Krocher en Barraca
Junio en Barraca
Entradas para la Cocoon Night ya a la venta
Elije al artista Barraca Plus de agosto
Barraca Music llega al podcast
Últimas
SHOP
PODCAST
ACCESS
Usuario
SOCIAL MEDIA
Junio en Barraca
Budweiser Clubbing Experience presenta la programación de junio en Barraca. Tendremos cuatro sábados, 6, 13, 20 y 27, y en cada uno de ellos la calidad artística será innegable.
Comenzamos el sabado 6 con la fiesta Barraca Music Label y la presencia de tres de sus artistas mas destacados, Andrew Grant, Danny Fiddo y AFFKT. Una semana mas tarde, sábado 13, noche Cocoon con dos artistas de inmenso nivel, el gran Ricardo Villalobos y la alemana Cassy. Villalobos no requiere presentacion y Cassy se ha ganado en respeto de todos gracias a su enorme profesionalidad y su enorme empatia con el público. Junto a ellos, nuestros residentes Ronro, Samuel Knob y Danny Fiddo. El sabado 20, Danzoo meets Barraca con la sesión del residente del club Danzoo de Madrid, Karretero. Hacia tiempo que no nos visitaba uno de los grandes de la escena española. Por ultimo, el sábado 27, noche Amnesia en Barraca con la fiesta People From Ibiza y su residente Mar-T. Excelente ambiente y musica con uno de los artistas clave del verano ibicenco.
Junto a los artistas internacionales, tendremos cada dia a nuestros habituales residentes, Danny Fiddo, Alberto Sola, Ronro y Samuel Knob.
06.06.09 Barraca Music Label
13.06.09 Cocoon Night
20.06.09 Danzoo meets Barraca
27.06.09 Amnesia presents. People From Ibiza
picnic
Budweiser
LARIOS
Flor de Caña

Jordan Stone/ sofake // www.sofake.com

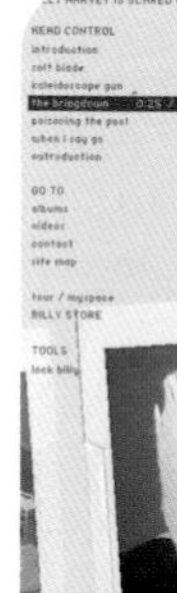

LY HARVEY IS SCARED OF FIRE
HEAD CONTROL
introduction
colt blade
kaleidoscope gun
the bringdown 0:25 / 3:59
poisoning the pool
when i say go
outroduction
GO TO
albums
videos
contact
site map
tour / myspace
BILLY STORE
TOOLS

we forgot to call Jordan.

I wonder if anyone has seen the site
now that its on the internet?

Web site Launch Party 11/6 2004

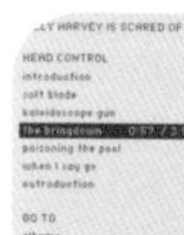

LY HARVEY IS SCARED OF FIRE
HEAD CONTROL
introduction
colt blade
kaleidoscope gun
poisoning the pool
when i say go
outroduction
GO TO
albums
videos
contact
site map
tour / myspace
BILLY STORE
TOOLS
lock billy

The bluebird of happiness
Spires of castles and cathedrals far
above the Feeble

999-9091

The ground that aches for the sky and it
has never seen him fly, but does hear him
sing high up there with his wing
tucked underneath his coat

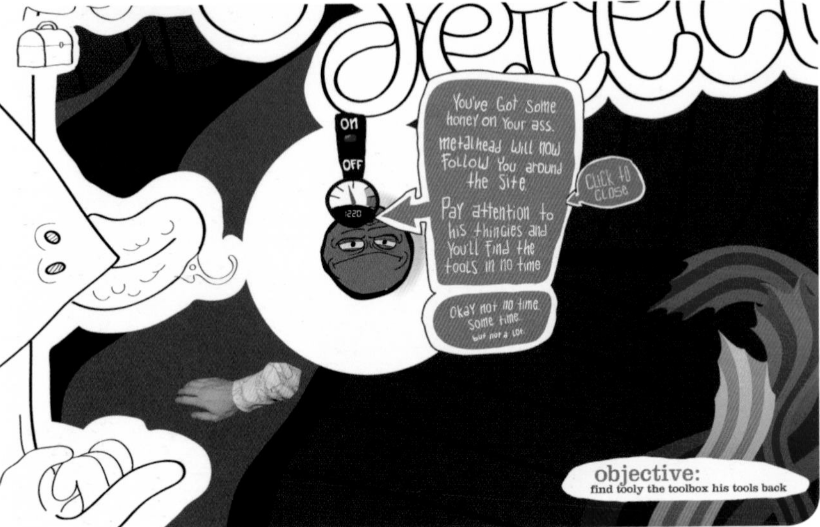

Coen Grift // www.bio-bak.nl

objective:
find tooly the toolbox his tools back

bio-bak
contact
take me home
Insert
here

BIRDMAN INC. // www.birdman.ne.jp

BIRDMAN
NEWS
PORTFOLIO
INFORMATION
CONCEPT
MEMBERS
AWARDS
CONTACT
ACCESSMAP
CREDITS
© BIRDMAN ALL RIGHTS RESERVED
SOUND

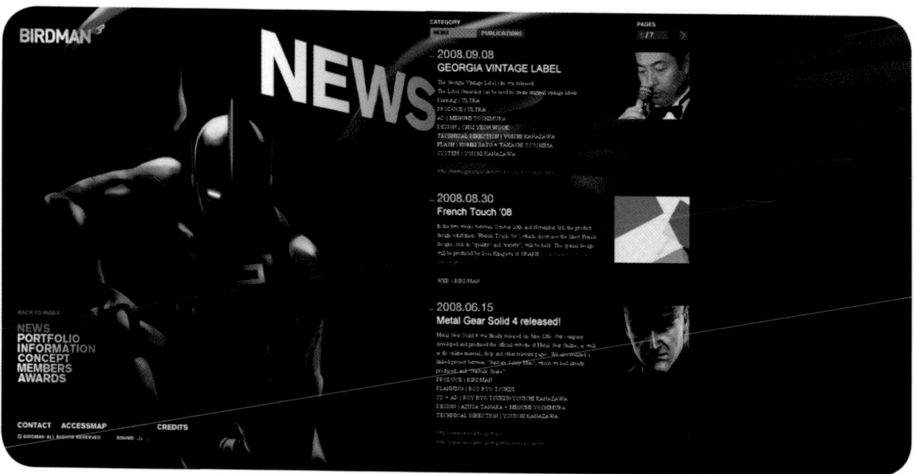
BIRDMAN
NEWS
CATEGORY
NEWS
PUBLICATIONS
PAGES
2008.09.08
GEORGIA VINTAGE LABEL
2008.08.30
French Touch '08
2008.06.15
Metal Gear Solid 4 released!
BACK TO INDEX
NEWS
PORTFOLIO
INFORMATION
CONCEPT
MEMBERS
AWARDS
CONTACT
ACCESSMAP
CREDITS
© BIRDMAN ALL RIGHTS RESERVED
SOUND

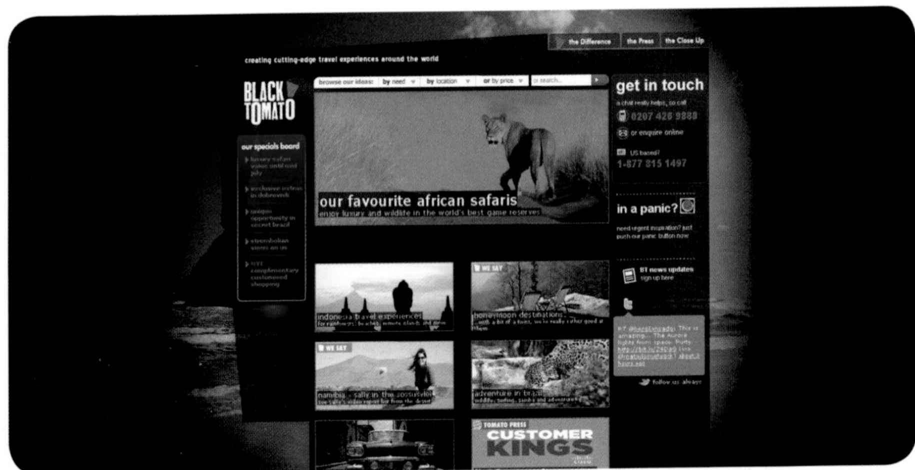

We Are Swede // www.weareswede.com

creating cutting-edge travel experiences around the world
the Difference
the Press
the Close Up
BLACK TOMATO
browse our ideas:
by need
by location
or by price
or search...
get in touch
a chat really helps, so call
0207 426 9888
or enquire online
US based?
1-877 815 1497
our specials board
luxury safari value until mid july
buy NOW for a four night safari including luxury stopover
in a panic?
need urgent inspiration? just push our panic button now
Travel before 9th July 2009 to save £500 per person. A week in South Africa from £2169 per person including flights, transfers, luxury accomodation, all meals and game drives.
THE FACTS
Price: from £2169 pp full board including flights
Location: south africa
Flight Time: 11 hrs
When to go: until 9th July
Ideal length: 7 nights, including two overnight flights
BT news updates
sign up here
Enjoy four nights prime (we mean really amazing) game watching in the Manyeleti Reserve concession at very special rates, including a luxury stopover at stylish Tintswalo Waterfalls in Johannesburg en route. Staying at the lush, exclusive Tintswalo Safari lodge, nestled between three of the countries' best game reserves, you'll wake up to see an ancient sycamore tree grove overlooking a waterhole surrounded by large herds of elephant and other big game. This is african wilderness at it's best. The big game watching is top notch and so is your accommodation. An indulgent bush spa treatment and private dinner in the wine cellar are included too. Snap it up while while you still can.
follow us always
Contact us to see leopards for less
have a look at...
Interested in South Africa? Have a look here for more information.
Interested? Why not get in touch by filling in the form below or calling us on 0207 426 9888
name

Image 2 of 3
getting under the skin of Cuba at a road side juice bar
Close X

Boeven Maskers // www.boevenmaskers.nl

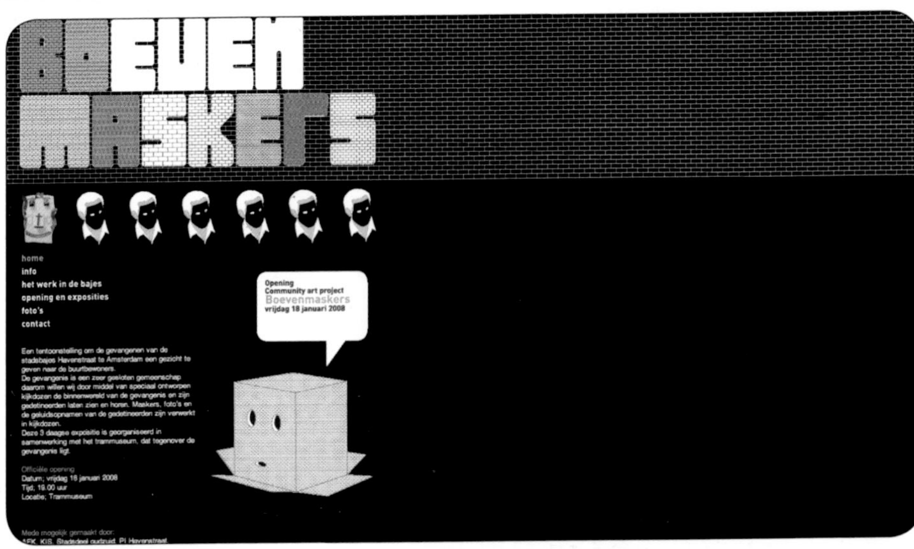

310k // www.310k.nl

Mikoon webservices // www.mikoon.nl

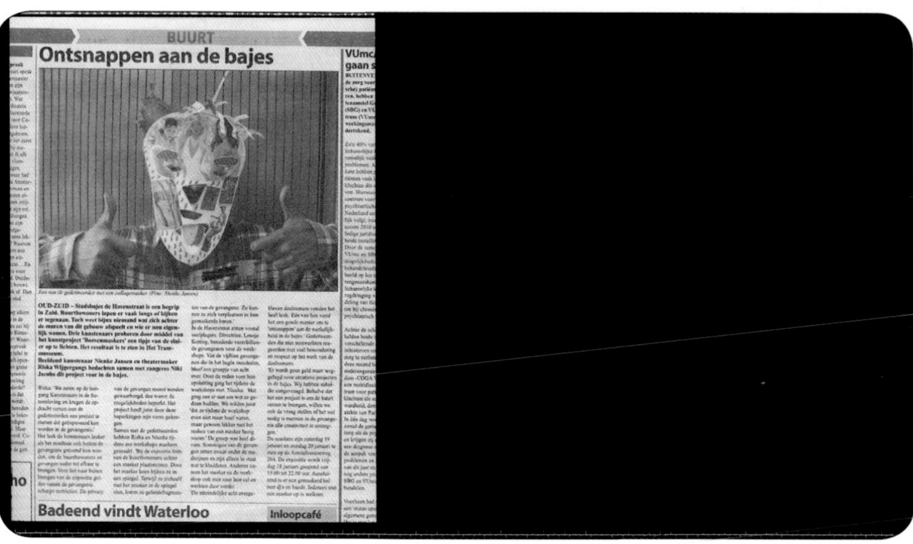

BUURT

Ontsnappen aan de bajes

Een van de gedetineerden met een collagemasker. (Foto: Nienke Jansen)

OUD-ZUID – Stadsbajes de Havenstraat is een begrip in Zuid. Buurtbewoners lopen er vaak langs of kijken er tegenaan. Toch weet bijna niemand wat zich achter de muren van dit gebouw afspeelt en wie er nou eigenlijk wonen. Drie kunstenaars proberen door middel van het kunstproject 'Boevenmaskers' een tipje van de sluier op te lichten. Het resultaat is te zien in Het Trammuseum.
Beeldend kunstenaar Nienke Jansen en theatermaker Riska Wijgergangs bedachten samen met zangeres Niki Jacobs dit project voor in de bajes.

Riska: 'We zaten op de leergang Kunstenaars in de Samenleving en kregen de opdracht samen met de gedetineerden een project te starten dat geïnspireerd kon worden in de gevangenis.'
Het leek de kunstenaars leuker als het resultaat ook buiten de gevangenis getoond kon worden, om de buurtbewoners en gevangen nader tot elkaar te brengen. Voor het naar buiten brengen van de expositie golden vanuit de gevangenis scherpe restricties. De privacy van de gevangen moest worden gewaarborgd, dus waren de mogelijkheden beperkt. Het project heeft juist door deze beperkingen zijn vorm gekregen.
Samen met de gedetineerden hebben Riska en Nienke tijdens zes workshops maskers gemaakt. 'Bij de expositie kunnen de buurtbewoners achter een masker plaatsnemen. Door het masker kijken ze in een spiegel. Terwijl ze zichzelf met het masker in de spiegel zien, horen ze geluidsfragmenten van de gevangene. Zo kunnen ze zich verplaatsen in hun gemaskerde buren.'
In de Havenstraat zitten vooral veelplegers. Directrice, Louise Koning, benaderde verschillende gevangenen voor de workshops. Van de vijftien gevangenen die in het begin meededen, bleef een groepje van acht over. Over de reden voor hun opsluiting ging het tijdens de workshops niet. Nienke: 'Het ging ons er niet om wat ze gedaan hadden. We wilden juist dat ze tijdens de workshop even niet meer boef waren, maar gewoon lekker met het maken van een masker bezig waren.' De groep was heel divers. Sommigen van de gevangenen zitten zwaar onder de medicijnen en zijn alleen in staat wat te kladderen. Anderen namen het masker na de workshop ook mee naar hun cel en werkten daar verder.
De uiteindelijke acht overgebleven deelnemers vonden het heel leuk. Eén van hen vond het een goede manier om te 'ontsnappen' aan de werkelijkheid in de bajes.' Gedetineerden die niet meewerkten reageerden met veel bewondering en respect op het werk van de deelnemers.
'Er wordt geen geld meer weggelegd voor creatieve projecten in de bajes. Wij hebben subsidie aangevraagd. Behalve dat het een project is om de buurt samen te brengen, willen we ook de vraag stellen of het wel nodig is mensen in de gevangenis alle creativiteit te ontnemen.'
De maskers zijn zaterdag 19 januari en zondag 20 januari te zien op de Amstelveenseweg 264. De expositie wordt vrijdag 18 januari geopend van 19.00 tot 22.00 uur. Aansluitend is er een gemaskerd bal met dj's en bands. Iedereen met een masker op is welkom.

Badeend vindt Waterloo

Inloopcafé

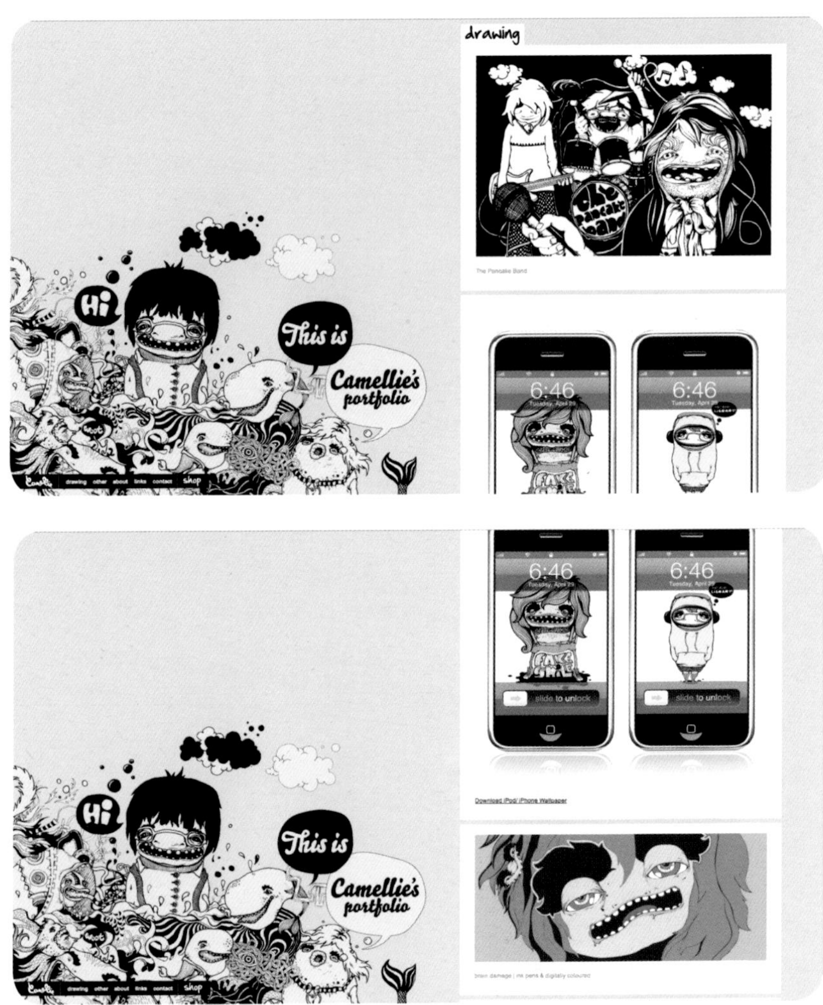

Daniel Aga // www.danielaga.com

Hi
This is
Camellie's portfolio
drawing other about links contact shop
shop
Pack of 4 badges · 25mm (free shipping)
-- Select size --
buy now

Hi
This is
Camellie's portfolio
drawing other about links contact shop

raindownonme

unit9 // www.unit9.com
CHI & Partners London // www.chiandpartners.com

home
sing a song
judge a song
people's chart
judge a song
Carphone Warehouse

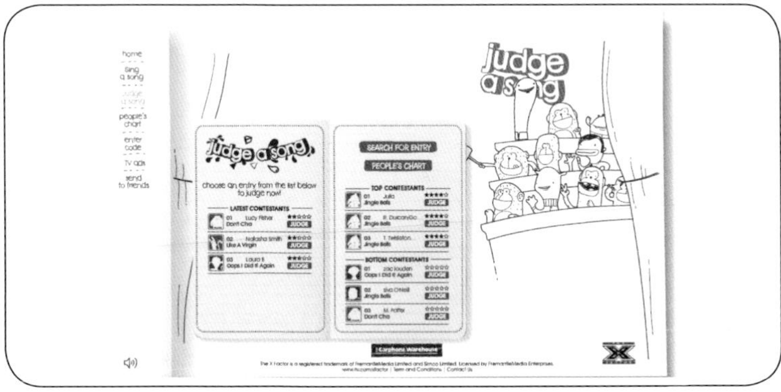
home
sing a song
judge a song
people's chart
enter code
TV ads
send to friends
judge a song
judge a song
choose an entry from the list below to judge now!
LATEST CONTESTANTS
SEARCH FOR ENTRY
PEOPLE'S CHART
TOP CONTESTANTS
BOTTOM CONTESTANTS
Carphone Warehouse

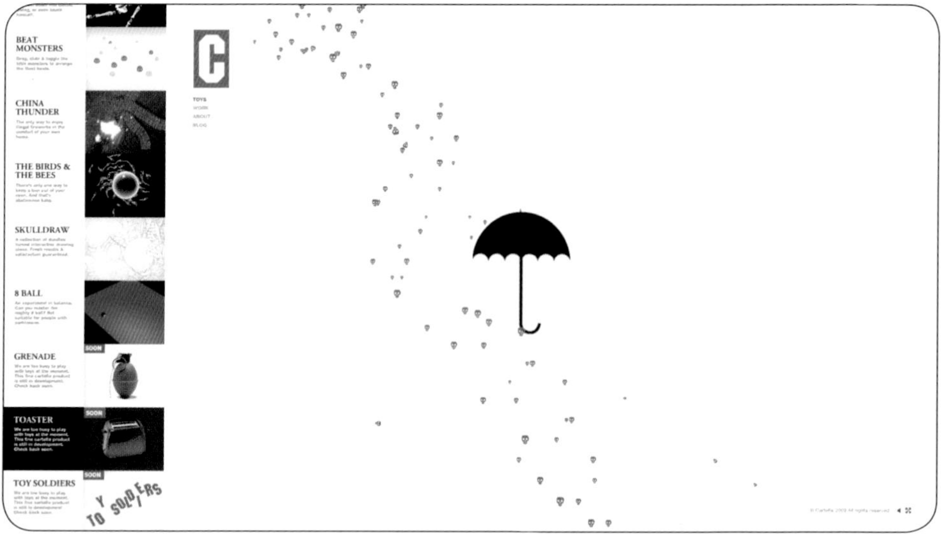

BEAT MONSTERS

CHINA THUNDER

THE BIRDS & THE BEES

SKULLDRAW

8 BALL

GRENADE

TOASTER

TOY SOLDIERS

TOYS

WORK

ABOUT

BLOG

Cartelle, Interactive Studio // www.cartelle.nl

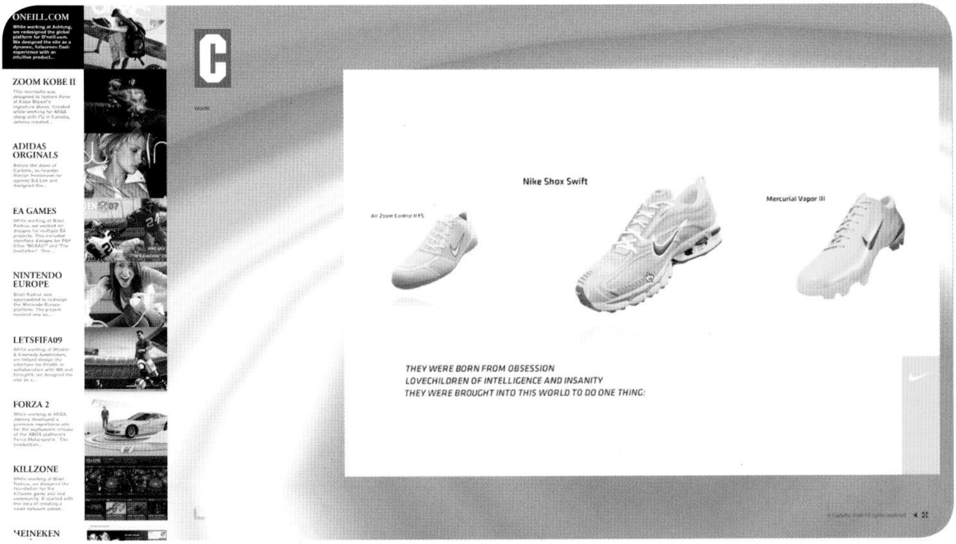

ONEILL.COM

While working at Achtung, we redesigned the global platform for O'neill.com. We designed the site as a dynamic, fullscreen flash experience with an intuitive product...

ZOOM KOBE II

ADIDAS ORGINALS

EA GAMES

NINTENDO EUROPE

LETSFIFA09

FORZA 2

KILLZONE

HEINEKEN

WORK

Nike Shox Swift

Air Zoom Control II FS

Mercurial Vapor III

THEY WERE BORN FROM OBSESSION
LOVECHILDREN OF INTELLIGENCE AND INSANITY
THEY WERE BROUGHT INTO THIS WORLD TO DO ONE THING:

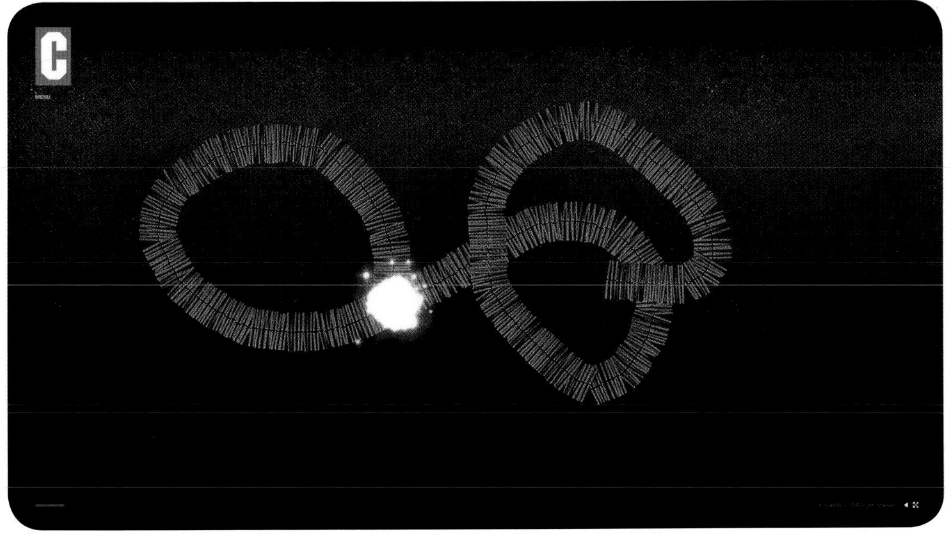

Cavalera // www.grafikonstruct.com.br/works/cavalera/inverno05/home/home.html

Camila Chaves
Danilo Figueiredo
Rodrigo Teco
Cauê Teixeira // www.grafikonstruct.com.br

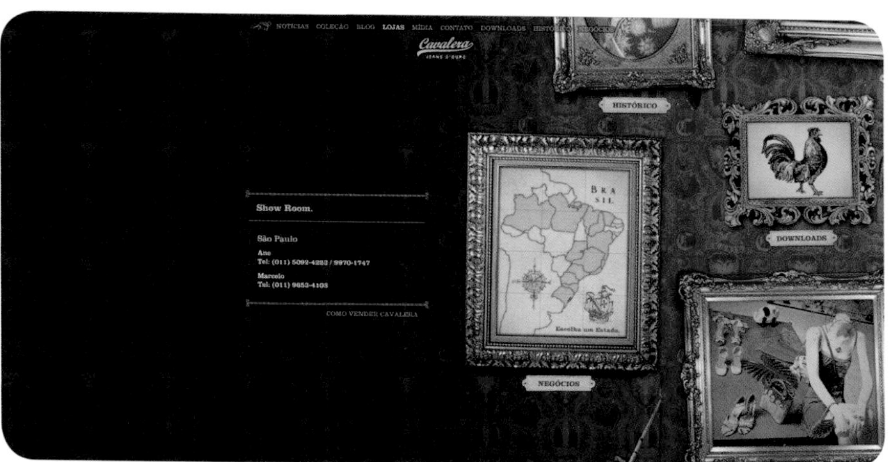
NOTÍCIAS COLEÇÃO BLOG LOJAS MÍDIA CONTATO DOWNLOADS
Cavalera
Show Room.
São Paulo
Ane
Tel: (011) 5092-4223 / 9970-1747
Marcelo
Tel: (011) 9653-4103
COMO VENDER CAVALERA
BRA
SIL
Escolha um Estado.
HISTÓRICO
DOWNLOADS
NEGÓCIOS

COLEÇÃO
HISTÓRICO
CONTATO
DOWNLOADS
MÍDIA
Cavalera
NOVIDADES NA TELA
NOTÍCIAS

Pixelinglife // www.pixelinglife.com

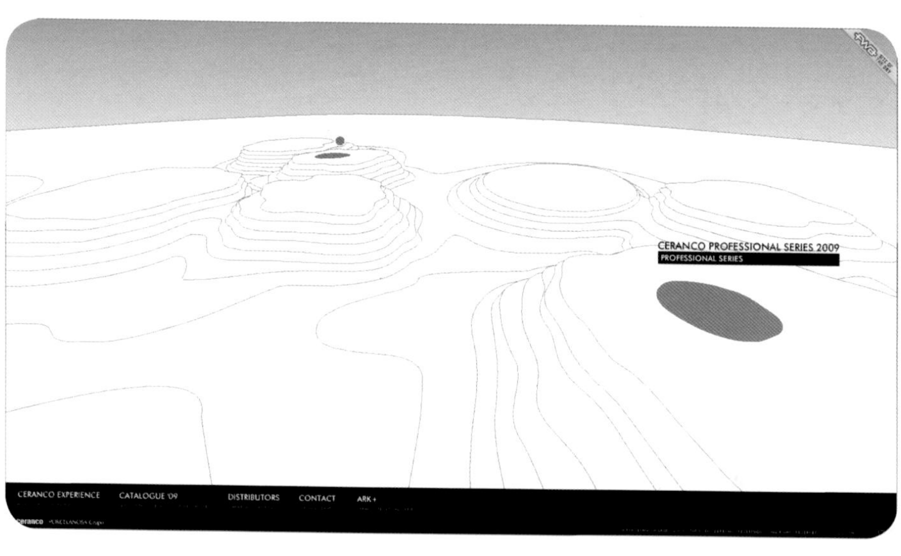
CERANCO PROFESSIONAL SERIES 2009
PROFESSIONAL SERIES
CERANCO EXPERIENCE
CATALOGUE '09
DISTRIBUTORS
CONTACT
ARK+
ceranco

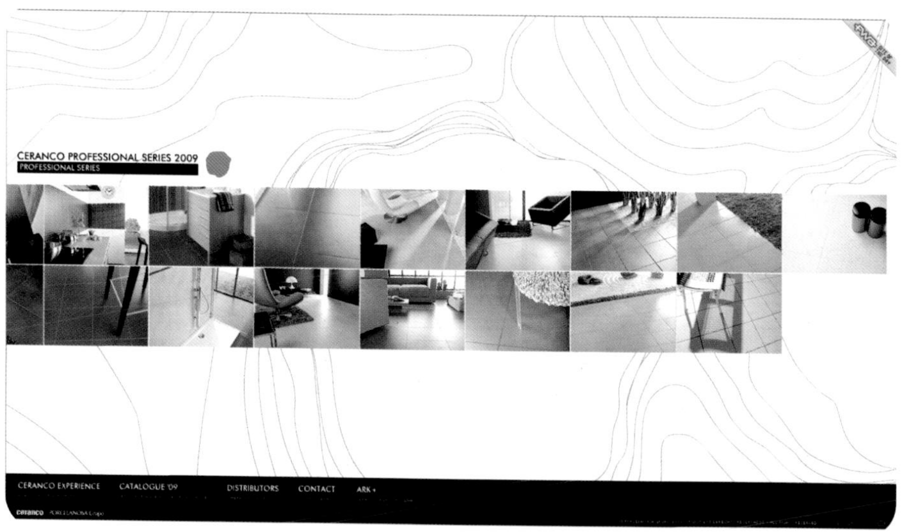
CERANCO PROFESSIONAL SERIES 2009
PROFESSIONAL SERIES
CERANCO EXPERIENCE
CATALOGUE '09
DISTRIBUTORS
CONTACT
ARK+
ceranco

unit9 // www.unit9.com
Goodby Silverstein & Partners San Francisco // www.goodbysilverstein.com

Welcome to
COMCAST TOWN
Bank
Click to login
Guest Book
Bunny
Extras

Welcome to
COMCAST TOWN
Bank
Click to login
Watch the commercials
Pick a commercial to watch from the menu on the right. You can also download the lyrics.
One
Lyrics
Two
Lyrics
Three
Lyrics
Four
Lyrics
Five
Lyrics
Get started
Extras

Kinetic // www.kinetic.com.sg

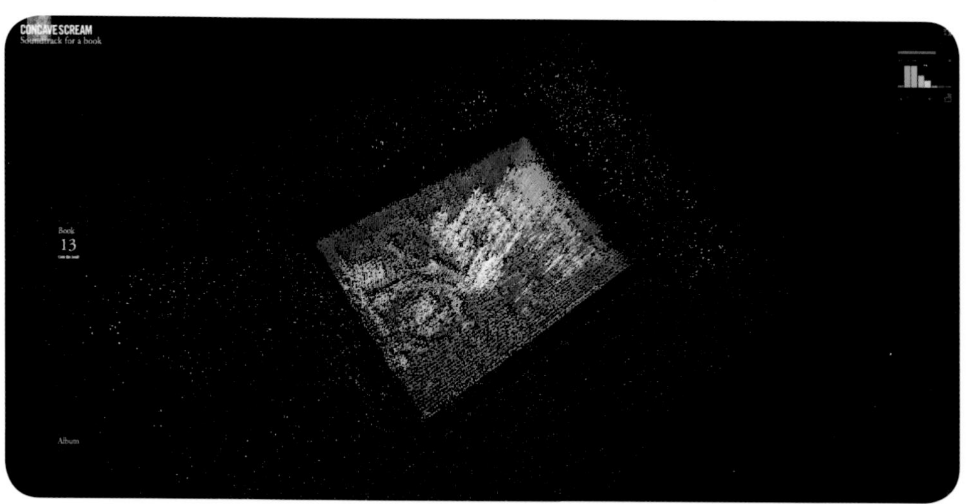
CONCAVE SCREAM
Soundtrack for a book
Book
13
Album

CONCAVE SCREAM

Converse Century // century.onclick.es

OnClick Studio // www.onclick.es

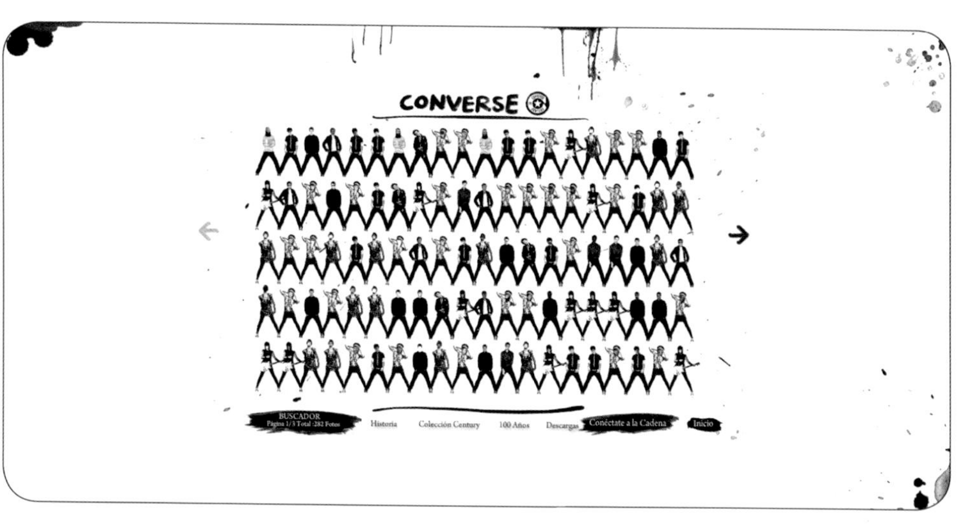
CONVERSE
BUSCADOR
Página 1/3 Total :282 Fotos
Historia
Colección Century
100 Años
Descargas
Conéctate a la Cadena
Inicio

CONVERSE
CENTURY
WELCOME
TO THE
CONVERSE
CENTURY
CONVERSE
Conéctate a la Cadena
Ver la Cadena
Inicio
Historia
Colección Century
100 Años
Descargas

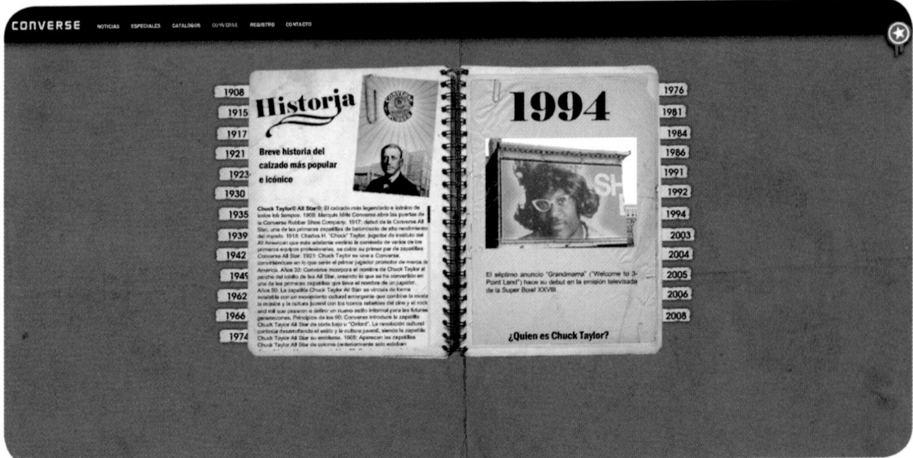

OnClick Studio // www.onclick.es

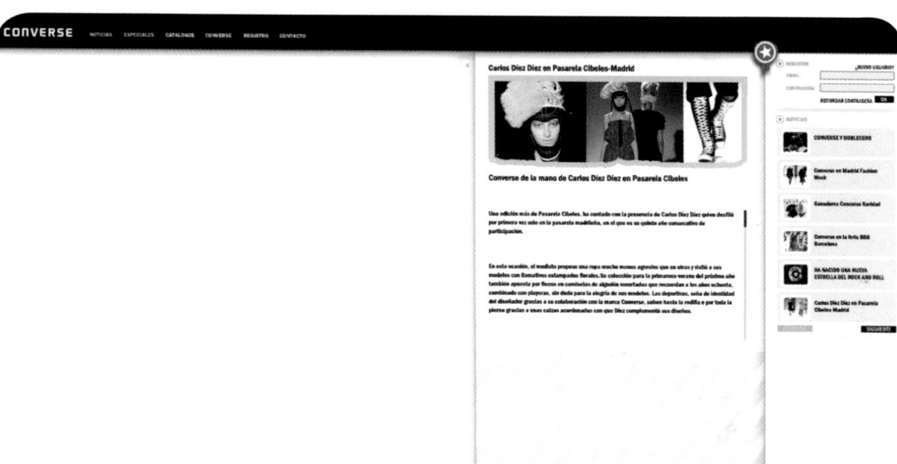
CONVERSE
NOTICIAS
ESPECIALES
CATALOGOS
CONVERSE
REGISTRO
CONTACTO
Carlos Díez Díez en Pasarela Cibeles-Madrid
Converse de la mano de Carlos Díez Díez en Pasarela Cibeles
¿NUEVO USUARIO?
EMAIL
CONTRASEÑA
RECORDAR CONTRASEÑA
CONVERSE Y DOBLECERO
Converse en Madrid Fashion Week
Ganadores Concurso Karidad
Converse en la feria BBB Barcelona
HA NACIDO UNA NUEVA ESTRELLA DEL ROCK AND ROLL
Carlos Díez Díez en Pasarela Cibeles-Madrid
SIGUIENTE

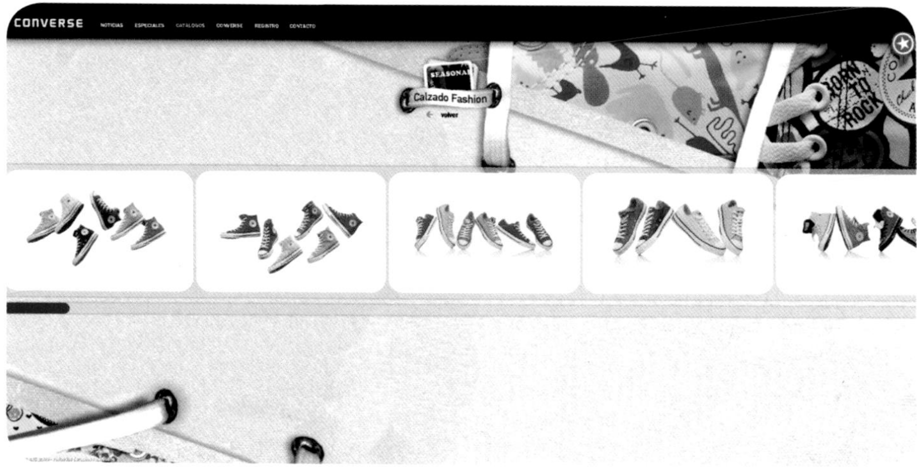
CONVERSE
NOTICIAS
ESPECIALES
CATALOGOS
CONVERSE
REGISTRO
CONTACTO
SEASONAL
Calzado Fashion
volver
BORN TO ROCK

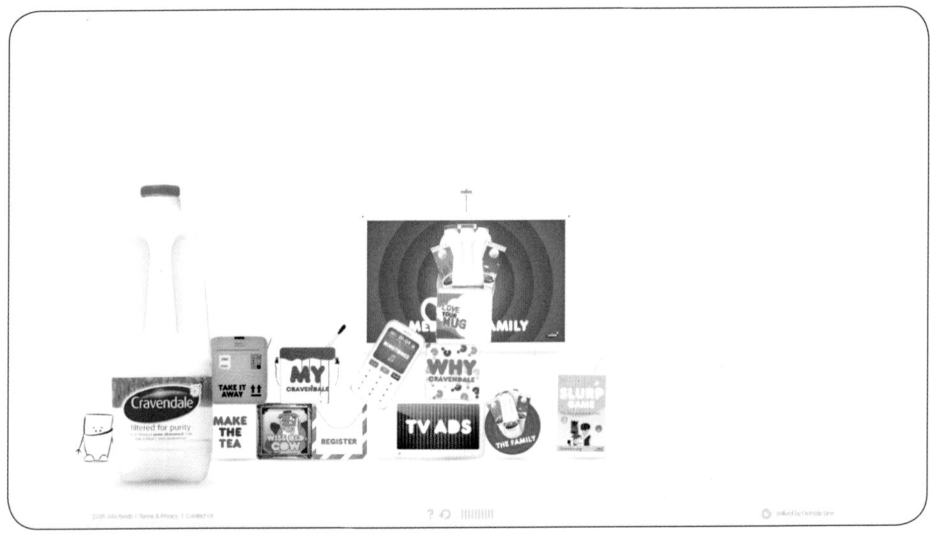

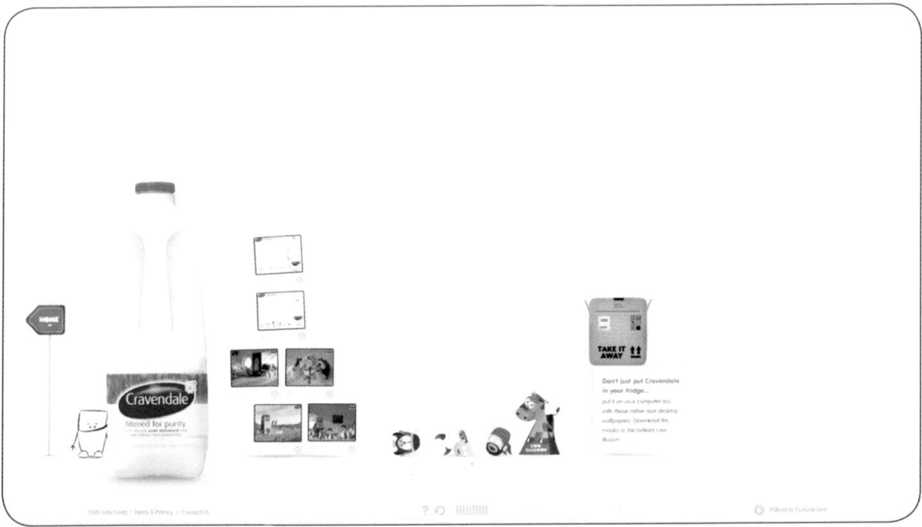

Outside Line & Arla Foods // www.outsideline.co.uk

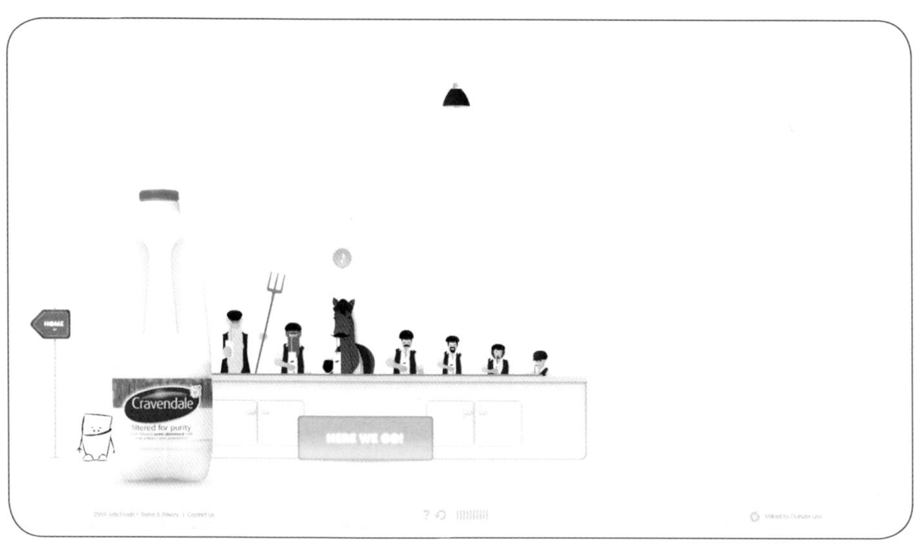

HOME
Cravendale
filtered for purity
HERE WE GO!

HOME
Cravendale
filtered for purity
SLURP GAME
PAUSE
PROJECTOR
TV ADS
BAD BULL
The thirsty rampaging bull arrives on the scene.

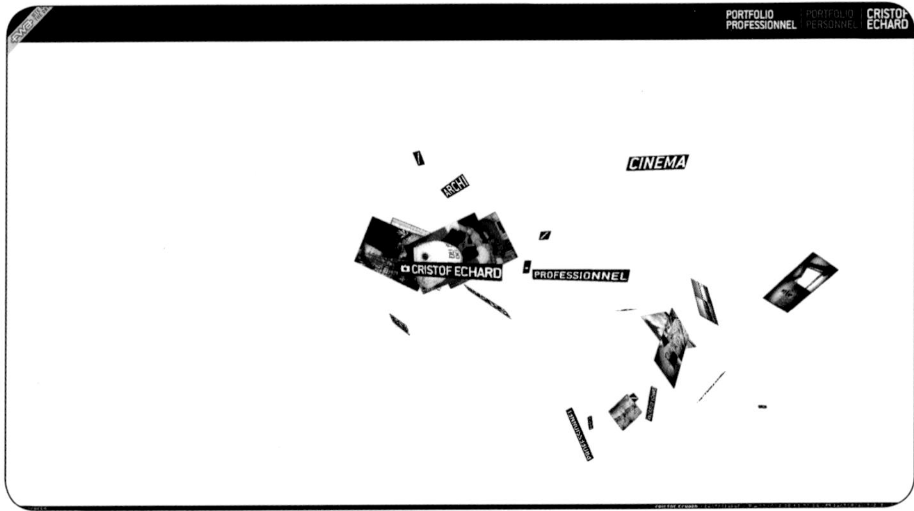

Jocker / CREAKTIF ! // www.creaktif.com/jocker/
noMatter // www.nomatter.eu

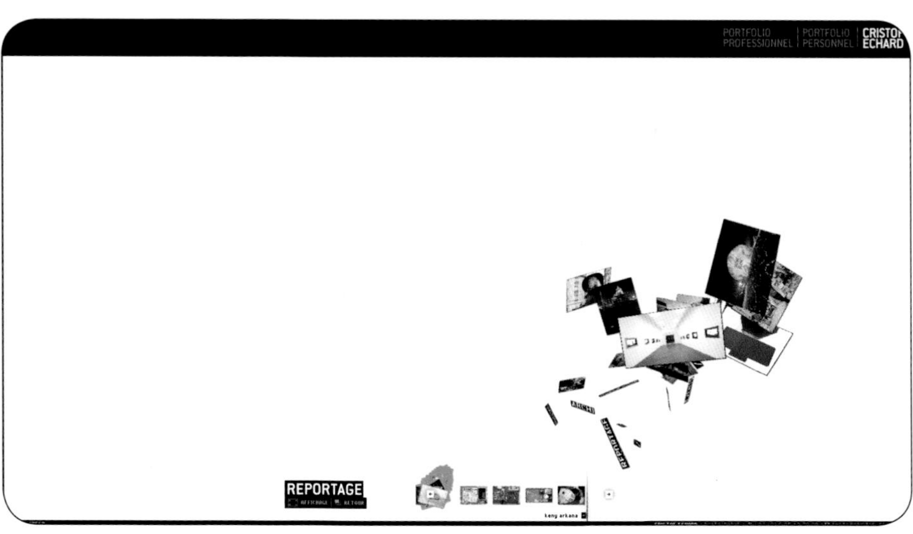
PORTFOLIO PROFESSIONNEL
PORTFOLIO PERSONNEL
REPORTAGE
keny arkana

Super
DIPTIC

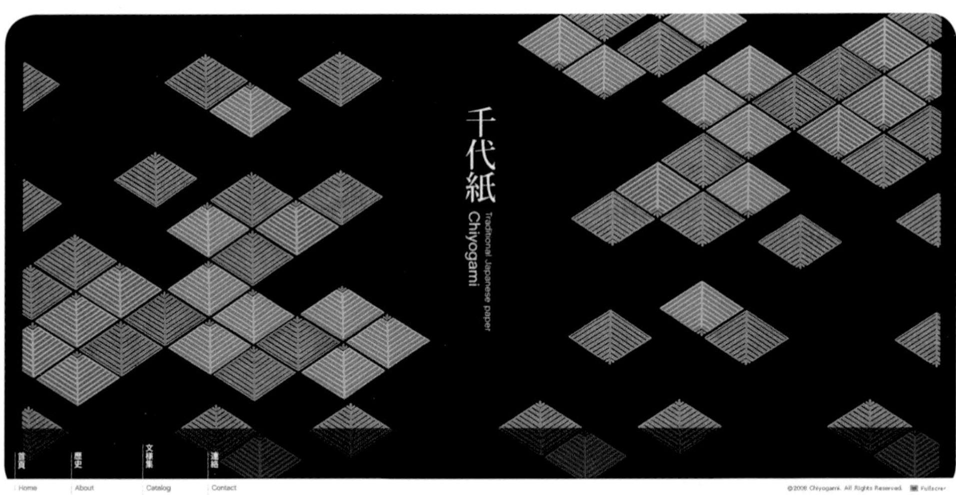

Chris Wang // www.chris-wang.com

Asanoha
目錄 01.Plant
02.Animal
03.Pattern
04.Geometry
首頁
歷史
文様集
連絡
Home
About
Catalog
Contact
©2008 Chiyogami. All Rights Reserved.

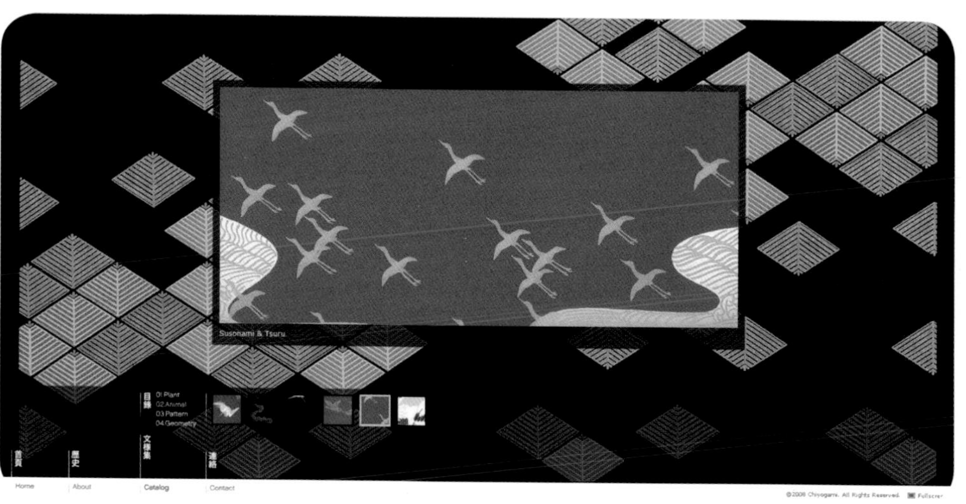
Susonami & Tsuru
目錄 01.Plant
02.Animal
03.Pattern
04.Geometry
首頁
歷史
文様集
連絡
Home
About
Catalog
Contact
©2008 Chiyogami. All Rights Reserved.

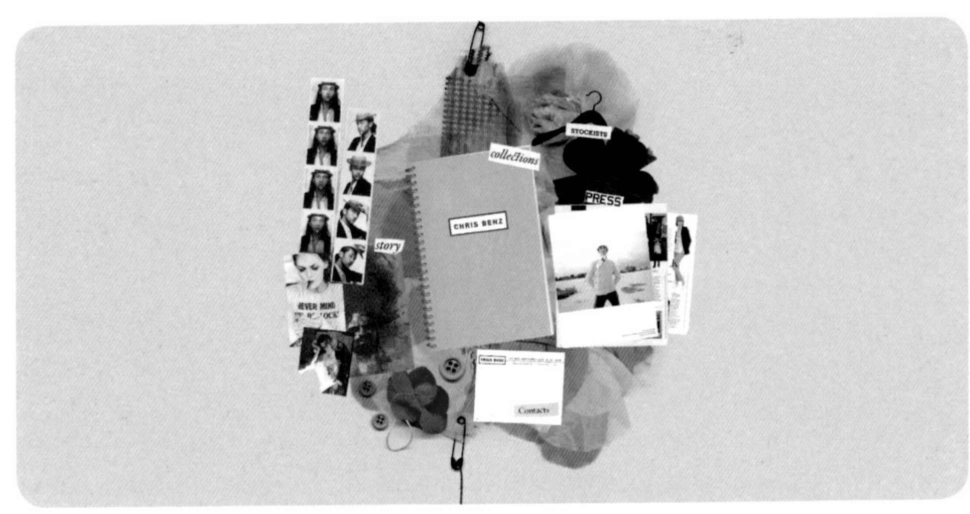

designedmemory // www.designedmemory.com

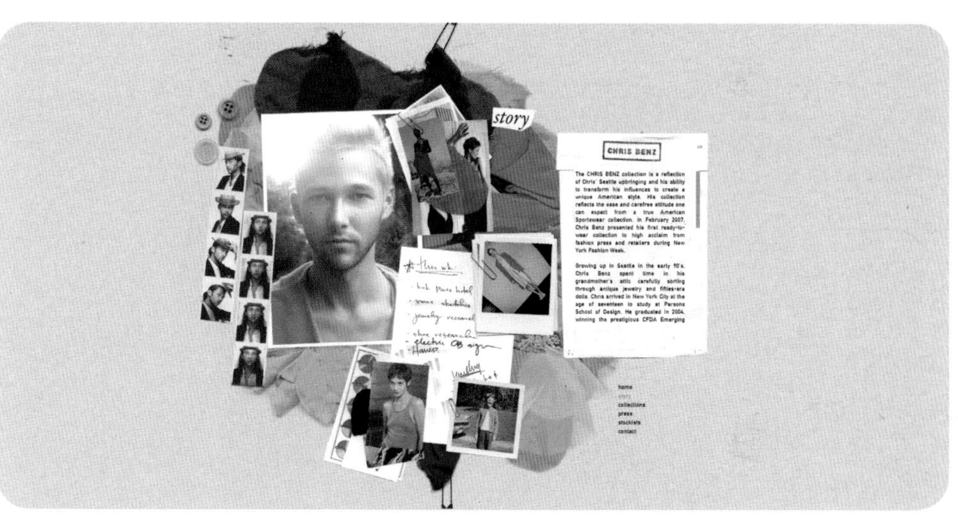
story
CHRIS BENZ
The CHRIS BENZ collection is a reflection of Chris' Seattle upbringing and his ability to transform his influences to create a unique American style. His collection reflects the ease and carefree attitude one can expect from a true American Sportswear collection. In February 2007, Chris Benz presented his first ready-to-wear collection to high acclaim from fashion press and retailers during New York Fashion Week.
Growing up in Seattle in the early 90's, Chris Benz spent time in his grandmother's attic carefully sorting through antique jewelry and fifties-era dolls. Chris arrived in New York City at the age of seventeen to study at Parsons School of Design. He graduated in 2004, winning the prestigious CFDA Emerging
home
story
collections
press
stockists
contact

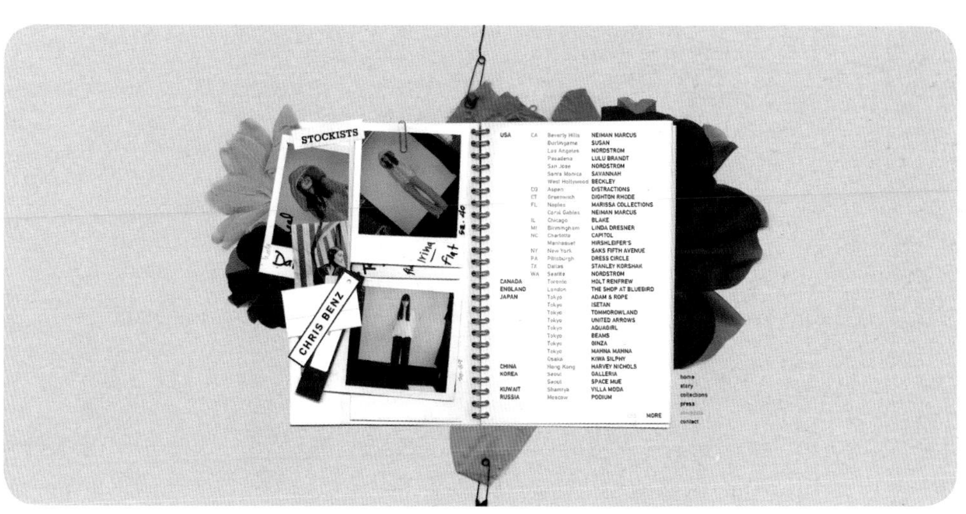
STOCKISTS
CHRIS BENZ
USA CA Beverly Hills NEIMAN MARCUS
Burlingame SUSAN
Los Angeles NORDSTROM
Pasadena LULU BRANDT
San Jose NORDSTROM
Santa Monica SAVANNAH
West Hollywood BECKLEY
CO Aspen DISTRACTIONS
CT Greenwich DIGHTON RHODE
FL Naples MARISSA COLLECTIONS
Coral Gables NEIMAN MARCUS
IL Chicago BLAKE
MI Birmingham LINDA DRESNER
NC Charlotte CAPITOL
Manhasset HIRSHLEIFER'S
NY New York SAKS FIFTH AVENUE
PA Pittsburgh DRESS CIRCLE
TX Dallas STANLEY KORSHAK
WA Seattle NORDSTROM
CANADA Toronto HOLT RENFREW
ENGLAND London THE SHOP AT BLUEBIRD
JAPAN Tokyo ADAM & ROPE
Tokyo ISETAN
Tokyo TOMMOROWLAND
Tokyo UNITED ARROWS
Tokyo AQUAGIRL
Tokyo BEAMS
Tokyo GINZA
Tokyo MAHNA MAHNA
Osaka KIWA SILPHY
CHINA Hong Kong HARVEY NICHOLS
KOREA Seoul GALLERIA
Seoul SPACE MUE
KUWAIT Shamiya VILLA MODA
RUSSIA Moscow PODIUM
MORE
home
story
collections
press
stockists
contact

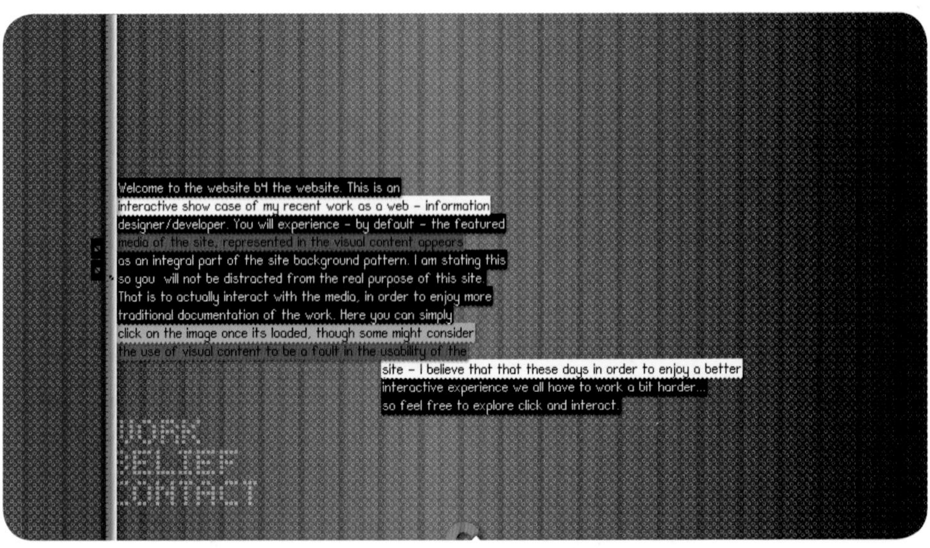

Welcome to the website b4 the website. This is an
interactive show case of my recent work as a web - information
designer/developer. You will experience - by default - the featured
media of the site, represented in the visual content appears
as an integral part of the site background pattern. I am stating this
so you will not be distracted from the real purpose of this site.
That is to actually interact with the media, in order to enjoy more
traditional documentation of the work. Here you can simply
click on the image once its loaded, though some might consider
the use of visual content to be a fault in the usability of the
site - I believe that that these days in order to enjoy a better
interactive experience we all have to work a bit harder...
so feel free to explore click and interact.
WORK
BELIEF
CONTACT

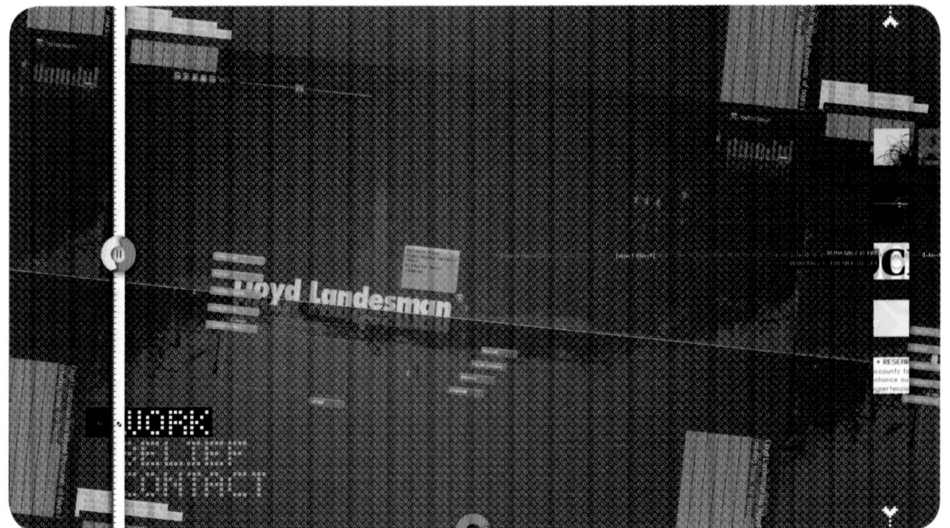

Alon Zouaretz // www.dawebsiteb4dawebsite.com

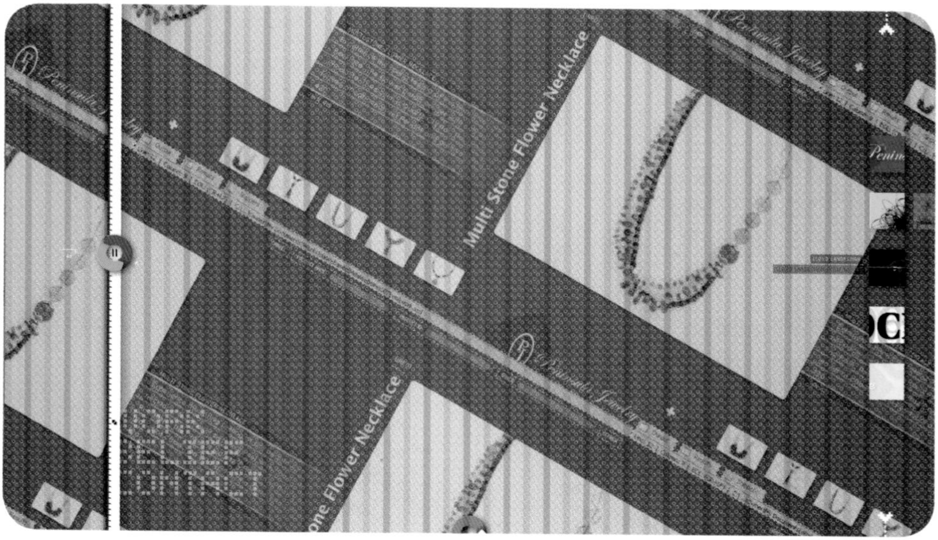

Multi Stone Flower Necklace
Multi Stone Flower Necklace
CONTACT

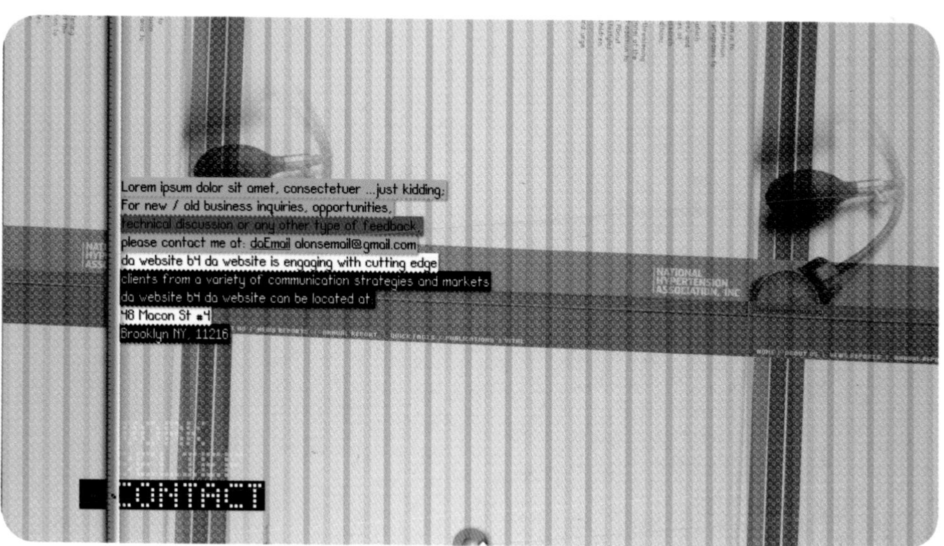
Lorem ipsum dolor sit amet, consectetuer ...just kidding;
For new / old business inquiries, opportunities,
technical discussion or any other type of feedback,
please contact me at: daEmail alonsemail@gmail.com
da website b4 da website is engaging with cutting edge
clients from a variety of communication strategies and markets
da website b4 da website can be located at:
48 Macon St #4
Brooklyn NY, 11216
NATIONAL
HYPERTENSION
ASSOCIATION, INC.
CONTACT

David Mikula // www.davidmikula.com

Listen
ADD TO CART
BIRD
PEACH TREES
TROLLEY FRIEND
NEW MATH
SUDAFED PE
NASAL DECONGESTANT
Sami's Holiday
The story of a Sami, his reindeer and his holiday surprise
CLOSE

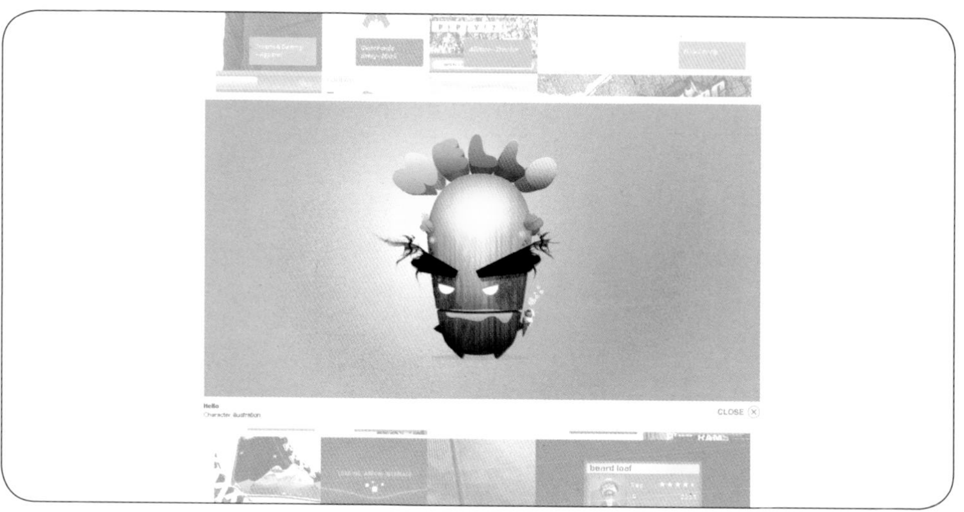
Hello
Character illustration
CLOSE
beard loaf

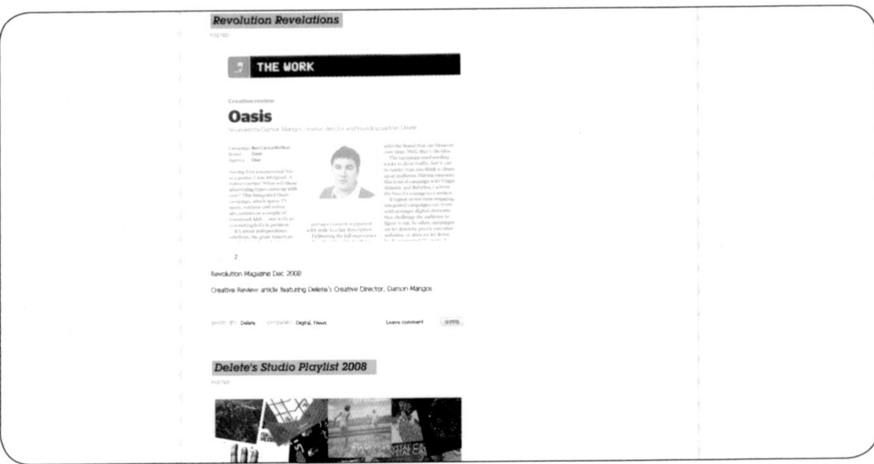

Matt Barron
David Bonas
Tom Dougherty
Thomas Garrod
Damon Mangos
Tom Peck/ Delete // www.deletelondon.com

THE BLIGHTY CHALLENGE
UKTV
Jan 2009
uktv.co.uk/blighty/homepage/aid/7116
VISIT SITE
What's the ideal amount of time to dunk a biscuit?
The Great British Tea Dunk
YOUR TIME
HOLD TO DUNK
DUNK
BLIGHTY
Overview
What's the optimal dunk time for a biscuit? What spicy food makes a bulldog blush? – Working on UKTV's new channel, Blighty, we discovered some fascinating facts about the eccentricities of our great nation.
Delete were asked to create an engaging, humorous quiz to support the launch of UKTV's new channel, which would drive

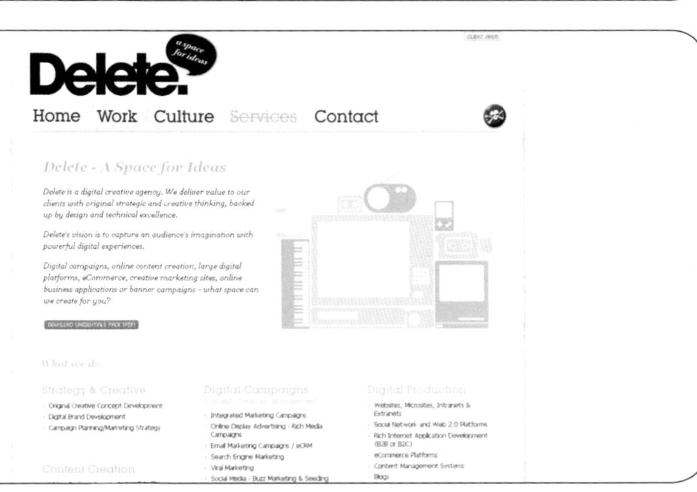
Delete.
a space for ideas
Home
Work
Culture
Services
Contact
Delete - A Space for Ideas
Delete is a digital creative agency. We deliver value to our clients with original strategic and creative thinking, backed up by design and technical excellence.
Delete's vision is to capture an audience's imagination with powerful digital experiences.
Digital campaigns, online content creation, large digital platforms, eCommerce, creative marketing sites, online business applications or banner campaigns - what space can we create for you?
What we do
Strategy & Creative
- Original Creative Concept Development
- Digital Brand Development
- Campaign Planning/Marketing Strategy
Content Creation
Digital Campaigns
- Integrated Marketing Campaigns
- Online Display Advertising - Rich Media Campaigns
- Email Marketing Campaigns / eCRM
- Search Engine Marketing
- Viral Marketing
- Social Media - Buzz Marketing & Seeding
Digital Production
- Websites, Microsites, Intranets & Extranets
- Social Network and Web 2.0 Platforms
- Rich Internet Application Development (B2B or B2C)
- eCommerce Platforms
- Content Management Systems
- Blogs

Pelle Martin/ I AM PELLE // iampelle.com

The Sandmen

AD / Graphic design.
Album, posters, ads etc.

Photos from the bands scrap-books, previous albums etc.

dolphinsonline // www.dolphinsonline.gr

dolphins // communication design // www.dolphinsonline.gr

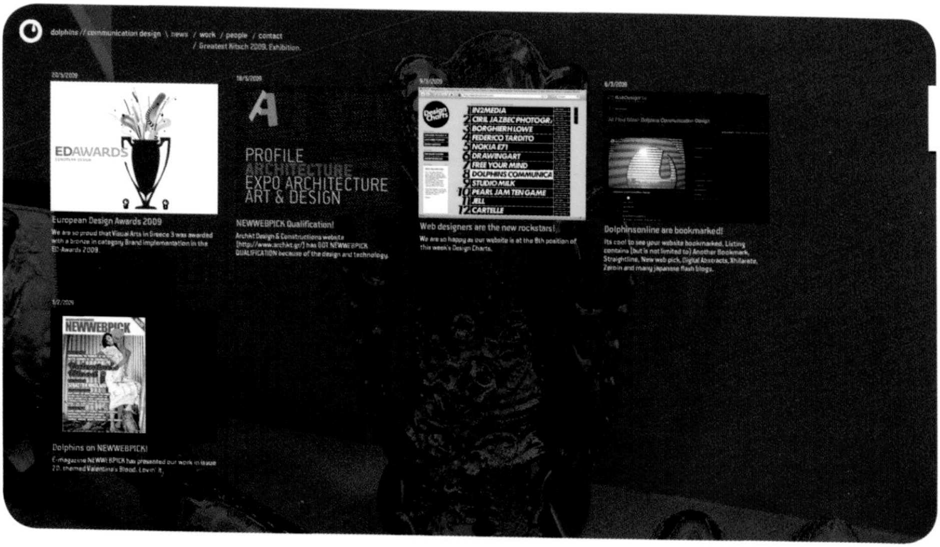

dolphins // communication design \ news / work / people / contact
/ Greatest Kitsch 2009. Exhibition.

European Design Awards 2009

We are so proud that Visual Arts in Greece 3 was awarded with a bronze in category Brand implementation in the ED-Awards 2009.

NEWWEBPICK Qualification!

Archkt Design & Constructions website [http://www.archkt.gr/] has GOT NEWWEBPICK QUALIFICATION because of the design and technology.

Web designers are the new rockstars!

We are so happy as our website is at the 8th position of this week's Design Charts.

Dolphinsonline are bookmarked!

Its cool to see your website bookmarked. Listing contains [but is not limited to] Another Bookmark, Straightline, New web pick, Digital Abstracts, Xhilarate, Zeroin and many japanese flash blogs.

Dolphins on NEWWEBPICK!

E-magazine NEWWEBPICK has presented our work in issue 20, themed Valentine's Blood. Lovin' it.

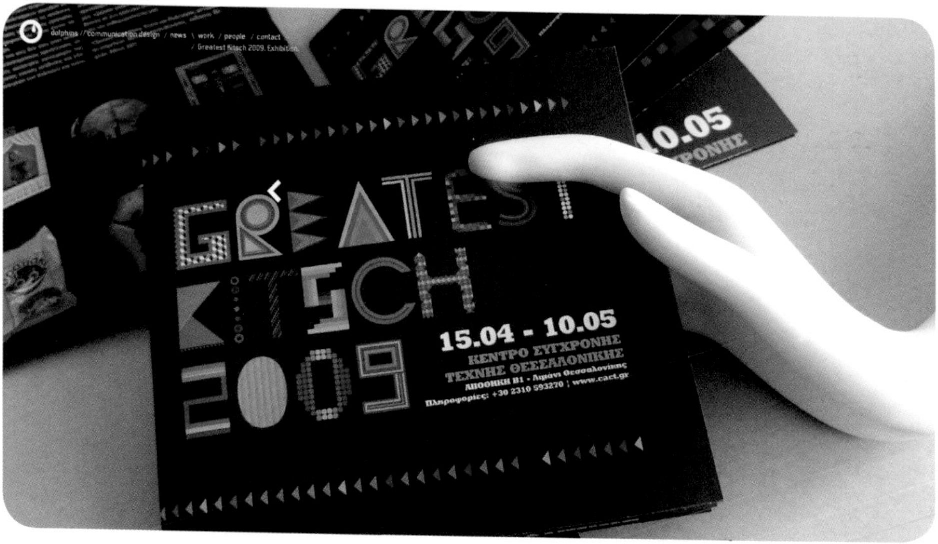

dolphins // communication design / news \ work / people / contact
/ Greatest Kitsch 2009. Exhibition.

GREATEST KITSCH 2009

15.04 - 10.05

ΚΕΝΤΡΟ ΣΥΓΧΡΟΝΗΣ ΤΕΧΝΗΣ ΘΕΣΣΑΛΟΝΙΚΗΣ

ΑΠΟΘΗΚΗ Β1 - Λιμάνι Θεσσαλονίκης

Πληροφορίες: +30 2310 593270 | www.cact.gr

Dr. Dd
José Fernando
Thomás Spicolli
Rodrigo Teco // www.grafikonstruct.com.br

news
reel
about us
structure
musique
contact
Dr.Od
A house for the production
of sounds?
A noise-generating plant?
A bunker of 24/7 workaholics?
All this and more...

news
reel
about us
structure
musique
contact
Dr.Od
INFORMAÇÃO
SAÚDE
Info
back

Easier than Reading // easierthanreading.com

Nessim Higson // iamalwayshungry.com
Destin Young // ourvice.com

2 Users
Chat Off
ETR
About
Choose a puppet
Choose a background
Choose movement
Record audio
Send it!
Western
Safari

1 User
Chat Off
ETR
About
Choose a puppet
Choose a background
Choose movement
Record audio
Send it!

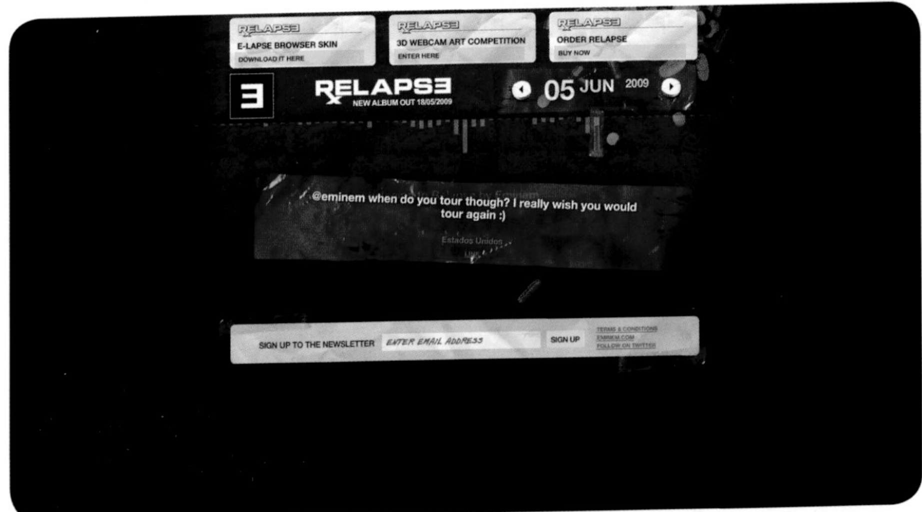

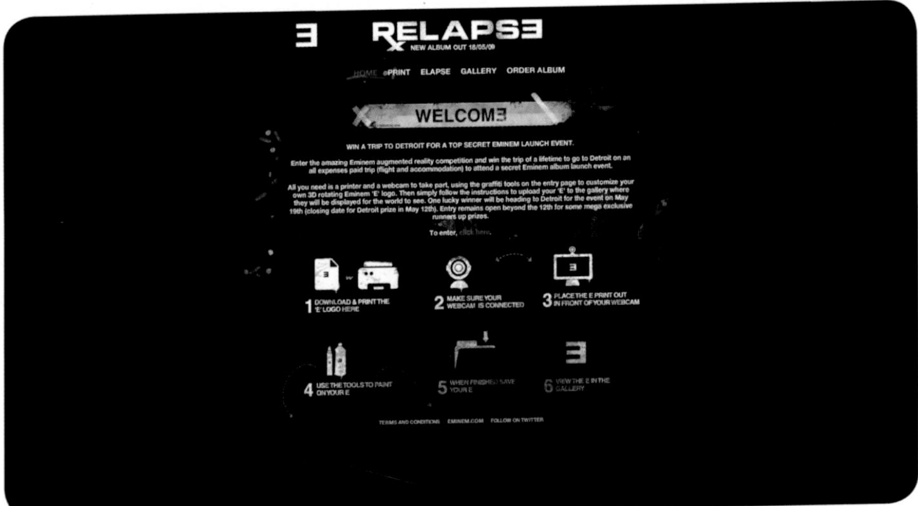

Outside Line & Polydor Records // www.outsideline.co.uk

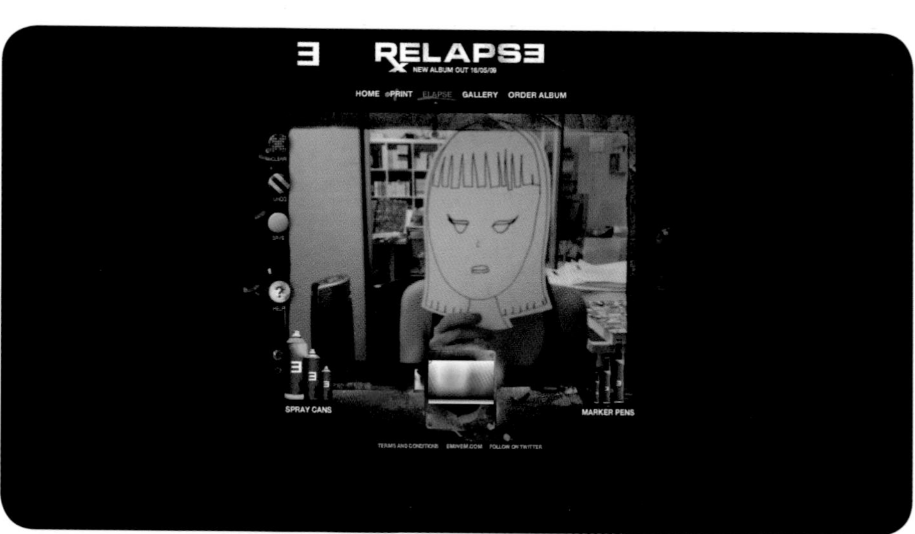
RELAPSE
NEW ALBUM OUT 18/05/09
HOME ePRINT ELAPSE GALLERY ORDER ALBUM
SPRAY CANS
MARKER PENS
TERMS AND CONDITIONS EMINEM.COM FOLLOW ON TWITTER

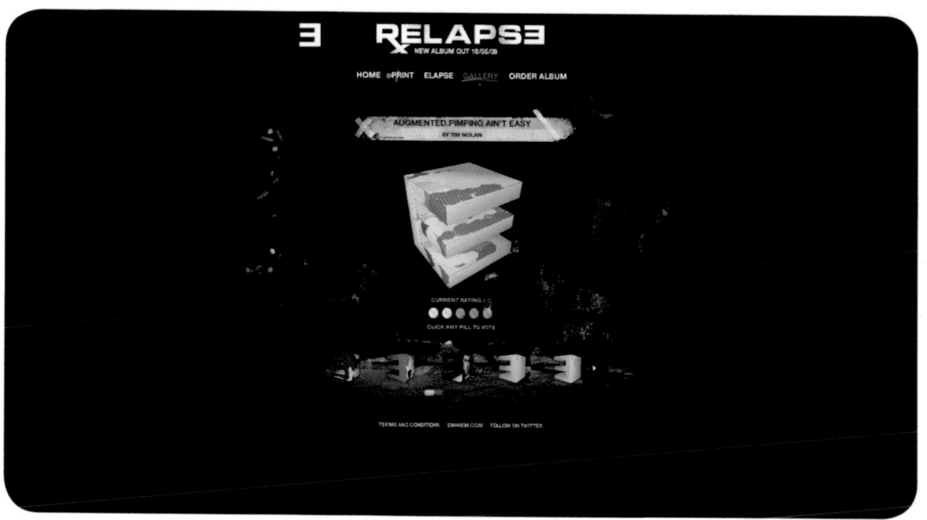
RELAPSE
NEW ALBUM OUT 18/05/09
HOME ePRINT ELAPSE GALLERY ORDER ALBUM
AUGMENTED.PIMPING AIN'T EASY
BY TIM NOLAN
CURRENT RATING
CLICK ANY PILL TO VOTE
TERMS AND CONDITIONS EMINEM.COM FOLLOW ON TWITTER

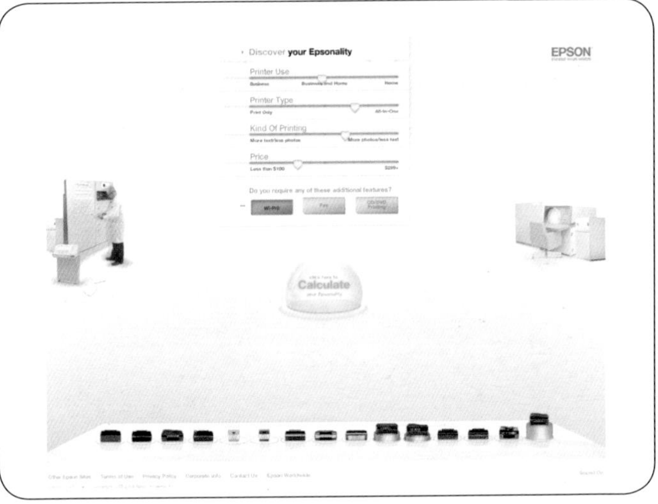

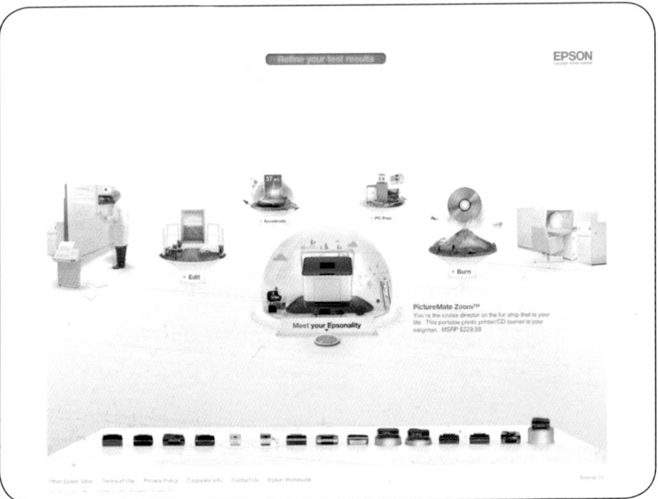

Big Spaceship // www.bigspaceship.com
Butler
Shine
Stern and Partners // www.bssp.com

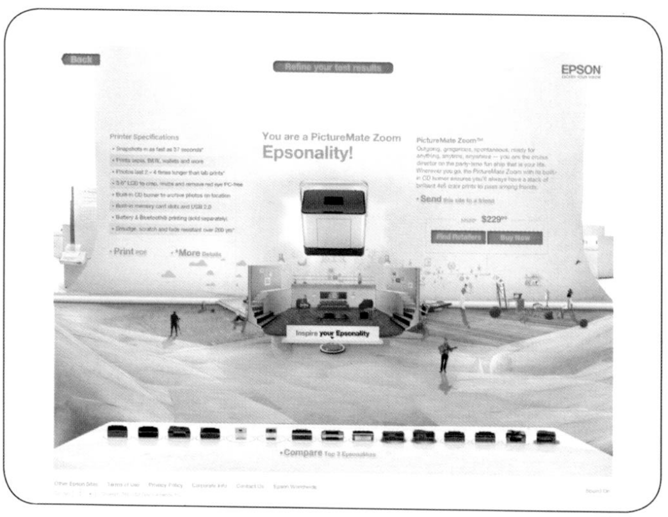
Back
Refine your test results
EPSON
Printer Specifications
You are a PictureMate Zoom
Epsonality!
PictureMate Zoom™
Send this site to a friend
$229
Find Retailers
Buy Now
Print PDF
More Details
Inspire your Epsonality
Compare Top 3 Epsonalities

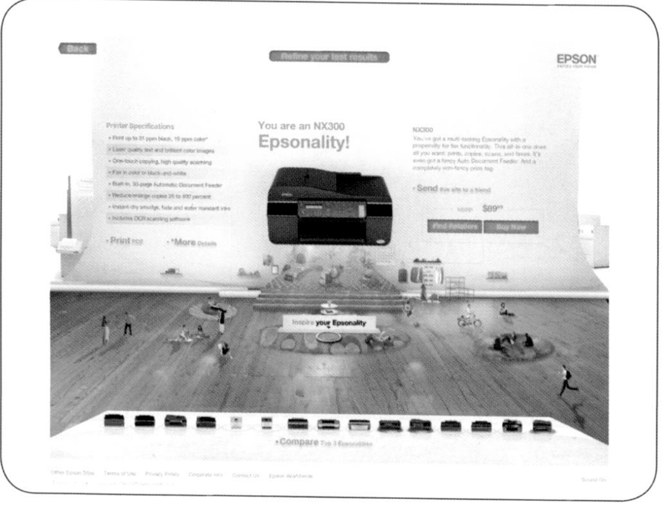
Back
Refine your test results
EPSON
Printer Specifications
You are an NX300
Epsonality!
NX300
Send this site to a friend
$89
Find Retailers
Buy Now
Print PDF
More Details
Inspire your Epsonality
Compare Top 3 Epsonalities

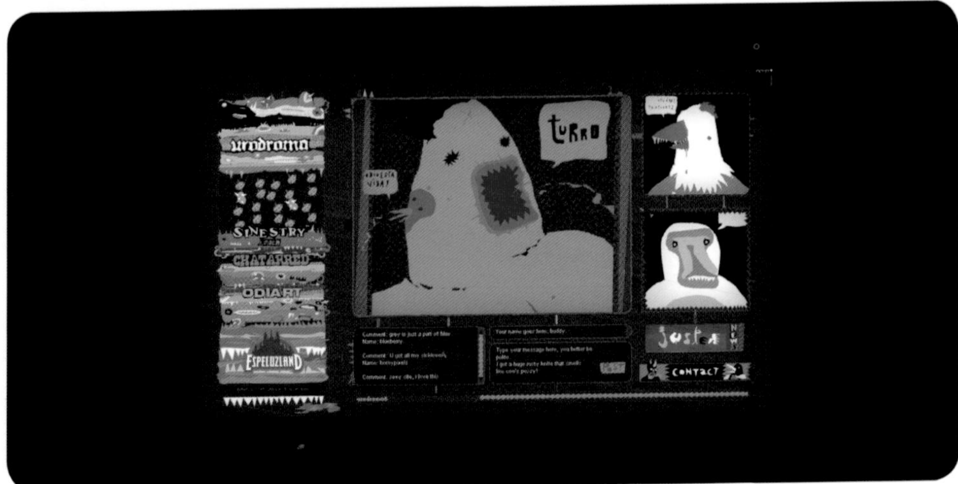

Axtor/ Espeluzland // www.espeluzland.com

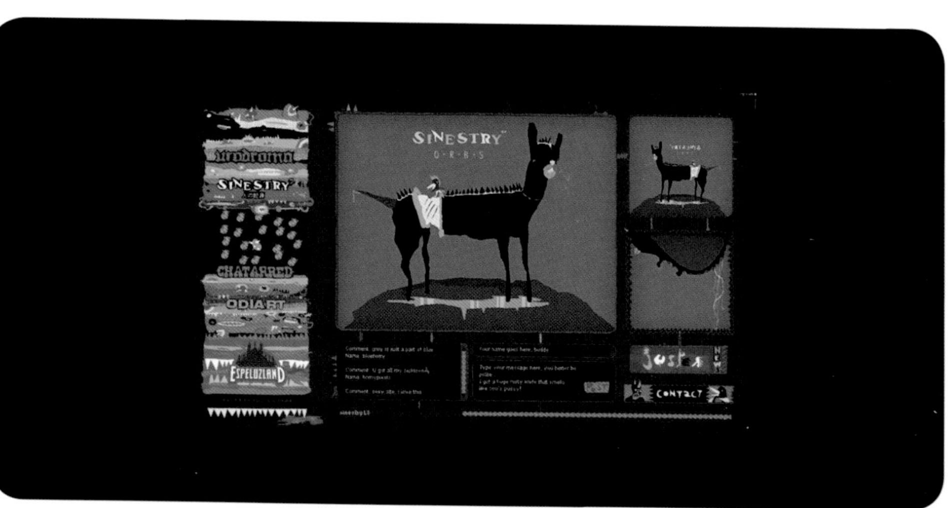
SINESTRY
CHATARRED
ODIART
ESPELUZLAND
CONTACT

SINESTRY
CHATARRED
ODIART
ESPELUZLAND
CONTACT

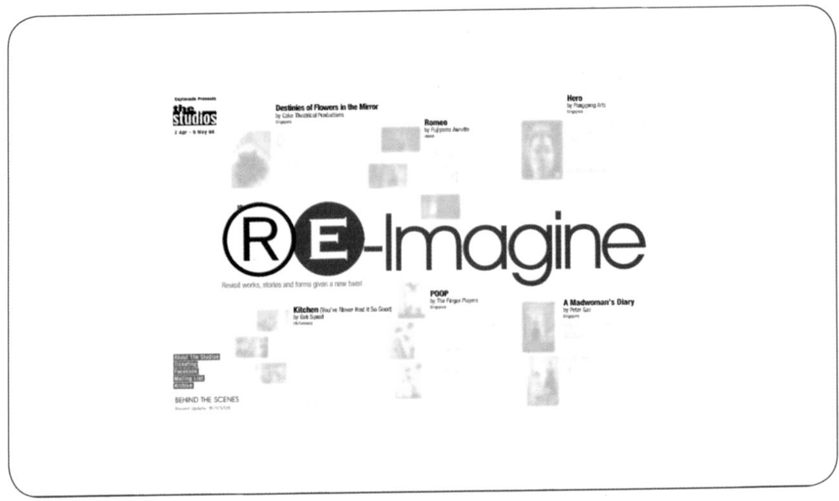

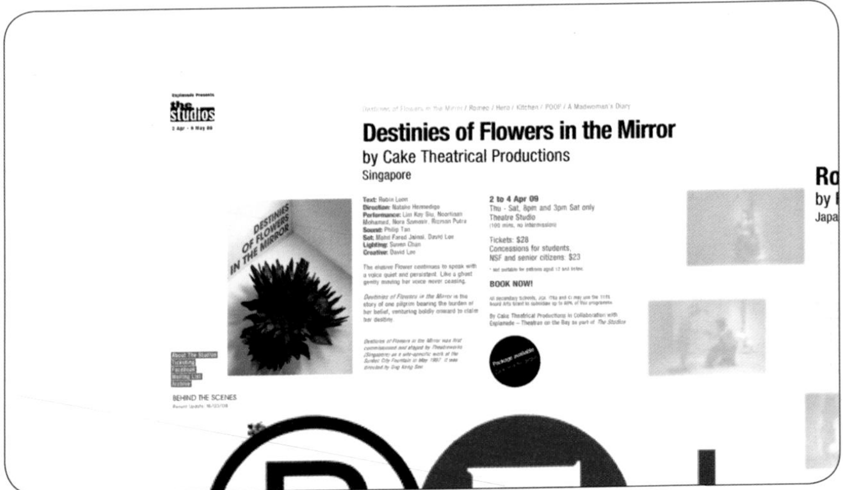

The Esplanade Co Ltd/ Yucca Studio LLP // www.esplanade.com

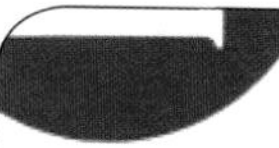

s given a new twist

en (You've Never Had It So Good)
Squad

Destinies of Flowers in the Mirror / Romeo / Hero / Kitchen / POOP / A Madwoman's Diary

POOP
by The Finger Players
Singapore

Written and Directed by Chong Tze Chien

Janice Koh **as DAUGHTER-IN-LAW**
Jean Ng **as GRANDDAUGHTER**
Julius Foo **as SON**
Neo Swee Lim **as GRANDMOTHER**

Production Design: Oliver Chong
Lighting Design: Lim Woan Wern

"Death is merely a joke when there's nothing to cry about"

After her son's suicide, a grandmother takes her granddaughter on a mind trip to the underworld and purgatory — set against an all-too-familiar urban backdrop of fast food restaurants, underground trains, verdant pastures, and SBS buses.

There's nothing to fear about death, she preaches. Personal fantasies about the after-life are challenged however when her granddaughter contracts a terminal illness.

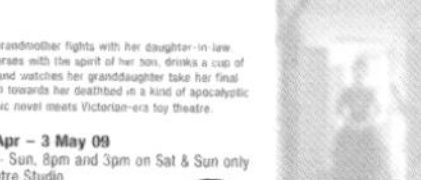

The grandmother fights with her daughter-in-law, converses with the spirit of her son, drinks a cup of Milo and watches her granddaughter take her final march towards her deathbed in a kind of apocalyptic graphic novel meets Victorian-era toy theatre.

30 Apr – 3 May 09
Thu - Sun, 8pm and 3pm on Sat & Sun only
Theatre Studio
(80 mins, no intermission)

Tickets: $28
Concessions for students,
NSF and senior citizens: $23

* not suitable for patrons aged 12 and below

BOOK NOW!

Presented by The Fingers Players in Collaboration with Esplanade – Theatres on the Bay as part of *The Studios*

Supported By:

A Madw
by Peter Sa
Singapore

BEHIND THE SCENES

na Annette

Destinies of Flowers in the Mirror / Romeo / Hero / Kitchen / POOP / A Madwoman's Diary

Hero
by Panggung Arts
Singapore

Creative Team
Advisor: Aidli 'Alin' Mosbit
Playwright & Co-director: Mohd Zulfadli Rashid (big)
Director: Fita Helmi
Set Designer: Junainah Yusoff
Production Team
Production Manager: Elnie S Mashari
Asst Stage Manager: Juraidah Rahman
Sound Operator: Gloria Tan
Cast
Siti Khalijah Zainal, Nur Suhaili Safari Wijaya

Hero. Woman. These two words, like it or not, are seldom linked together in one entity. Hero. Karaoke hostess. These two are an even unlikelier combination.

In *Hero* however, femininity, karaoke hostessing and heroism combine promisingly in a drama about two karaoke hostesses held hostage one evening by an alcoholic regular customer in their own lounge.

When the two - a mamasan with a past as gaudy as her makeup and a newbie "guest relations officer" with hopeful dreams for the future - eventually escape that same evening with the help of the police, after having passed the time in banal conversation, random shadow puppetry and singing Mariah Carey's *Hero*, they go right back into their routines of entertaining regular and new customers, albeit with different ideas of heroism and hope.

Performed in English and Malay with English surtitles where necessary

16 – 18 Apr 09
Thu - Sat, 8pm
Theatre Studio
(80 mins, no intermission)

Tickets: $28
Concessions for students,
NSF and senior citizens: $23

* Contains mature themes. For patrons aged 16 years old and above only

BOOK NOW!

Presented by Panggung Arts in Collaboration with Esplanade – Theatres on the Bay as part of *The Studios*

About The Studios
Ticketing
Facebook
Mailing List
Archive

BEHIND THE SCENES

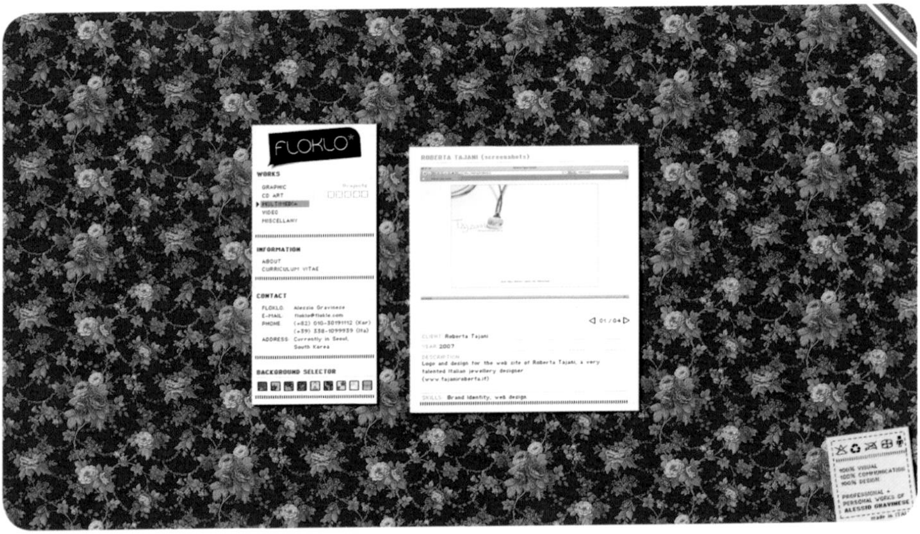

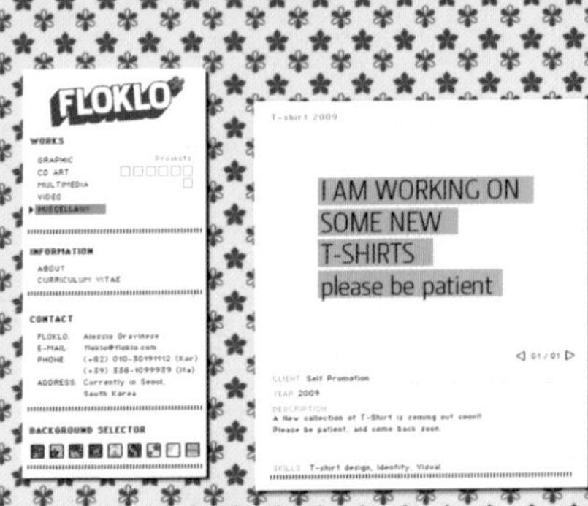

Alessio Gravinese // www.floklo.com

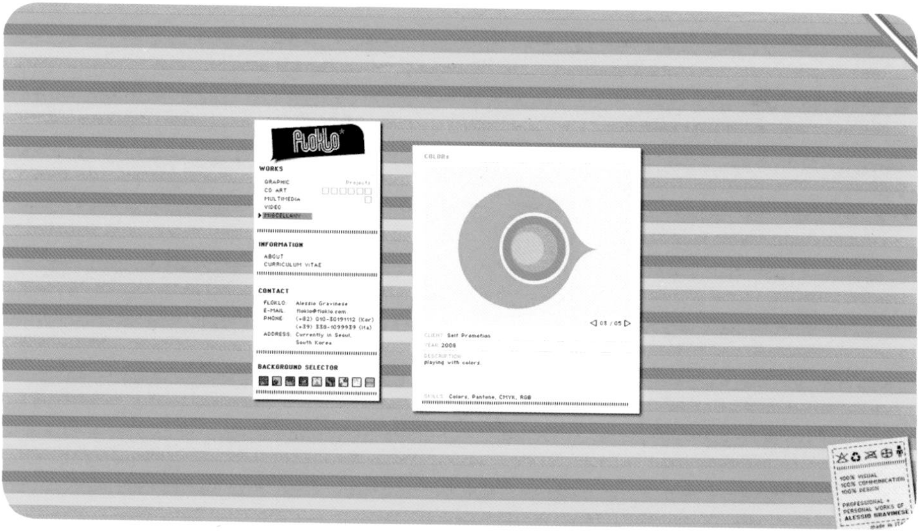

FLOKLO*
WORKS
GRAPHIC
Projects
CD ART
MULTIMEDIA
VIDEO
MISCELLANY
INFORMATION
ABOUT
CURRICULUM VITAE
CONTACT
FLOKLO: Alessio Gravinese
E-MAIL: floklo@floklo.com
PHONE: (+82) 010-30191112 (Kor)
(+39) 338-1099939 (Ita)
ADDRESS: Currently in Seoul, South Korea
BACKGROUND SELECTOR

COLORs
03 / 05
CLIENT: Self Promotion
YEAR: 2008
DESCRIPTION
playing with colors.
SKILLS: Colors, Pantone, CMYK, RGB

100% VISUAL
100% COMMUNICATION
100% DESIGN
PROFESSIONAL + PERSONAL WORKS OF
ALESSIO GRAVINESE

Kinetic // www.kinetic.com.sg

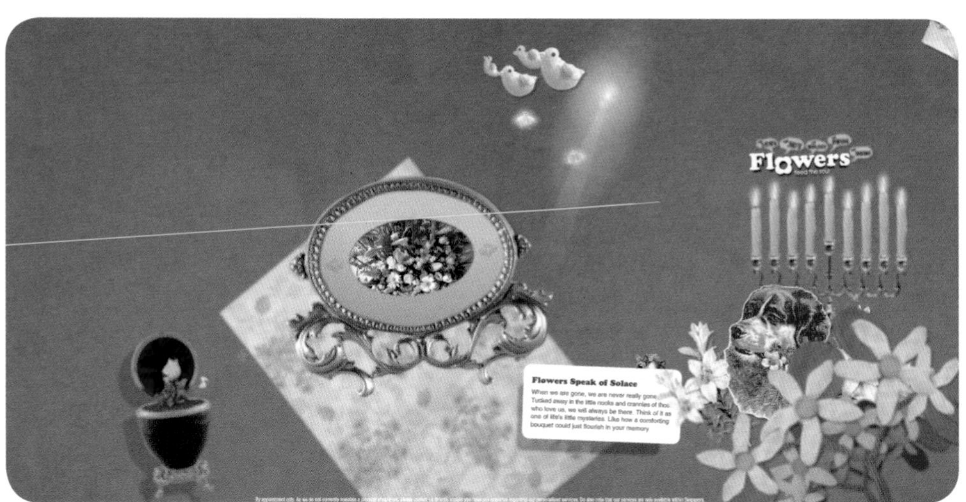
Flowers
Flowers Speak of Solace
When we are gone, we are never really gone. Tucked away in the little nooks and crannies of thos who love us, we will always be there. Think of it as one of life's little mysteries. Like how a comforting bouquet could just flourish in your memory

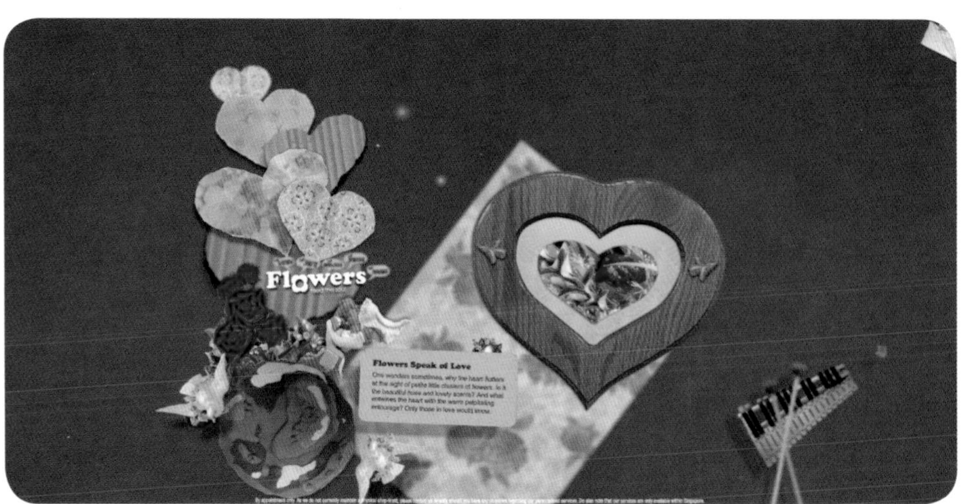
Flowers
Flowers Speak of Love

Skipintro Amsterdam // www.skipintro.nl

Justin Choon
For the Love of God
Damien Hirst

SHOWING 50 - 100 OF 465
Suits
For the Love of God
Damien Hirst

Formwerkz // www.formwerkz.com

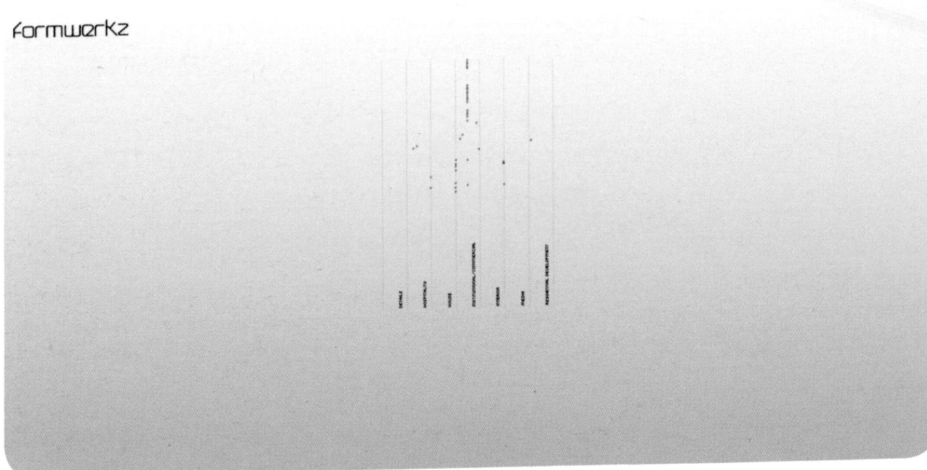

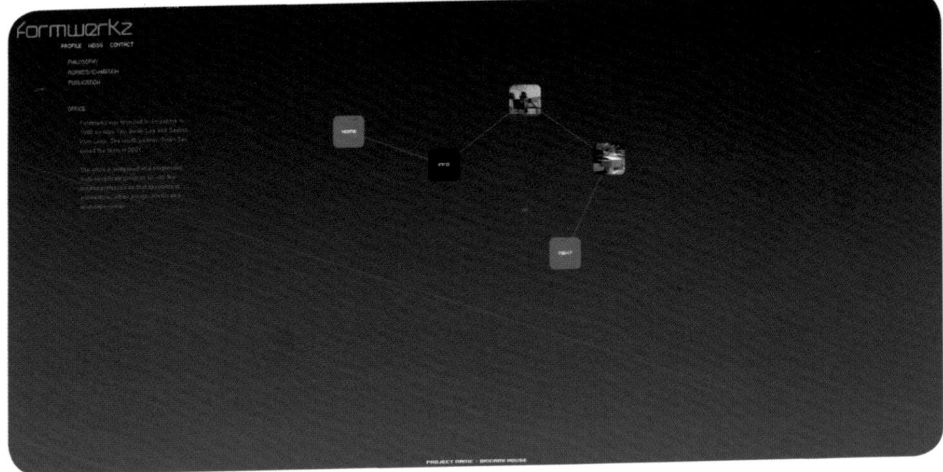

Kinetic // www.kinetic.com.sg

-ormwerkz
PROFILE NEWS CONTACT
BLACK & WHITE HOUSE

FriendsWithYou // www.FriendsWithYou.Com

FriendsWithYou // www.FriendsWithYou.Com
I loveDust // www.ilovedust.com
Free Range Development // www.freerangedev.com
Built by buffalo // www.builtbybuffalo.com

HOME
STORY
GALLERY
STORE
STORY
THE FRIENDS
FWY LEGEND
BIO-CONTACT
LINKS
You are lucky....
You have just found a portal to a secret club and lifetime adventure. We have been researching a new magic moment in time, and we are all part of it. People are getting magic powers just by believing in them. From the air we breathe to the part of your brain used for wishing, magic exists all around us!
1 2 3
NEXT PAGE

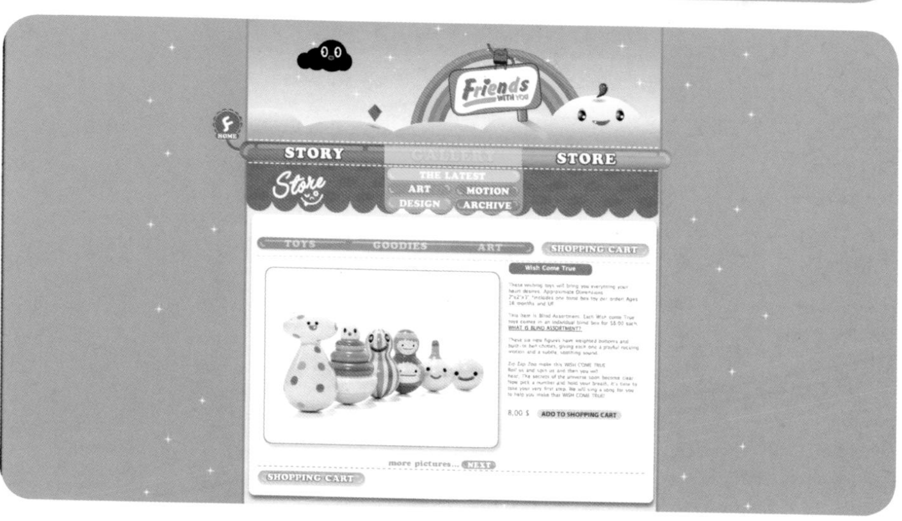
Friends WITH YOU
HOME
STORY
GALLERY
STORE
Store
THE LATEST
ART
MOTION
DESIGN
ARCHIVE
TOYS
GOODIES
ART
SHOPPING CART
Wish Come True
WHAT IS BLIND ASSORTMENT?
8,00 $
ADD TO SHOPPING CART
more pictures...
NEXT
SHOPPING CART

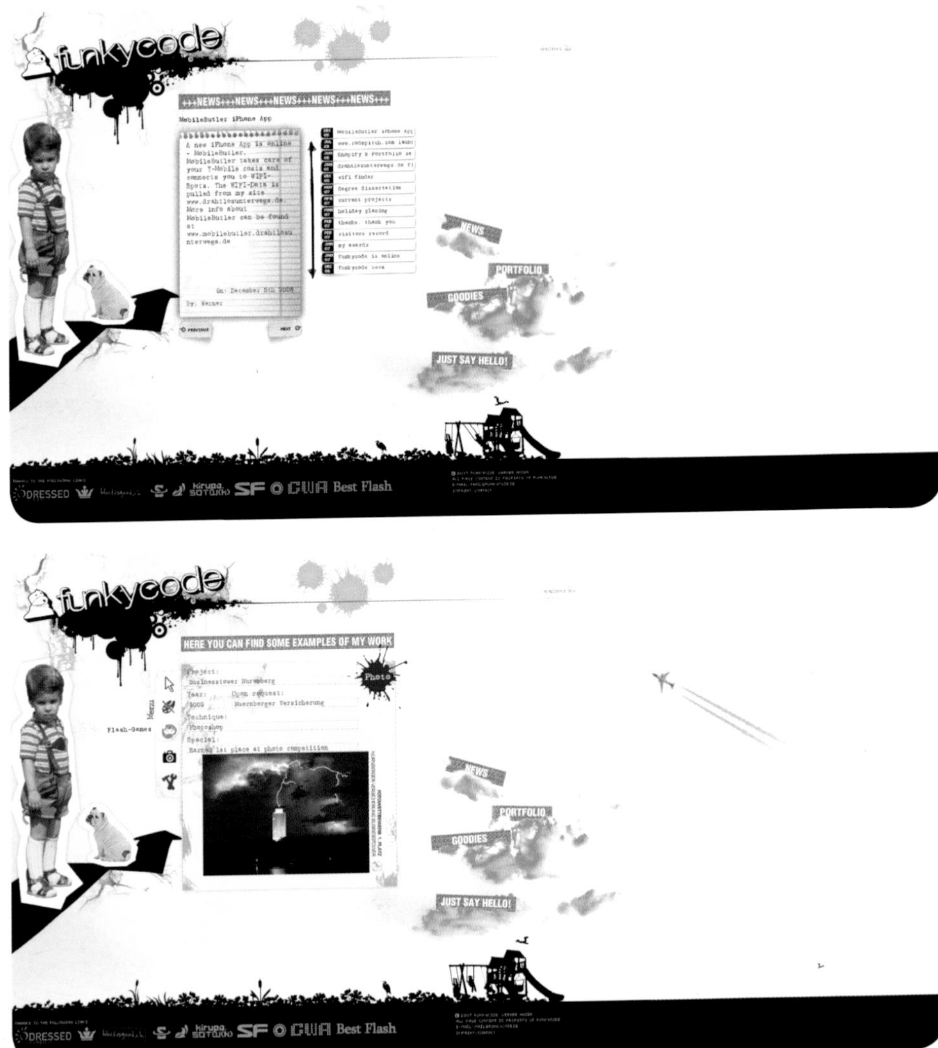

Werner Hoier // www.funkycode.de

funkycode
+++NEWS+++
+++NEWS+++
NEWS
PORTFOLIO
GOODIES
JUST SAY HELLO!
DRESSED
SF
Best Flash

funkycode
PLEASE LEAVE ME A SHORT COMMENT • THANKS
KOREA
NEWS
PORTFOLIO
GOODIES
JUST SAY HELLO!
DRESSED
SF
Best Flash

Resn // www.resn.co.nz

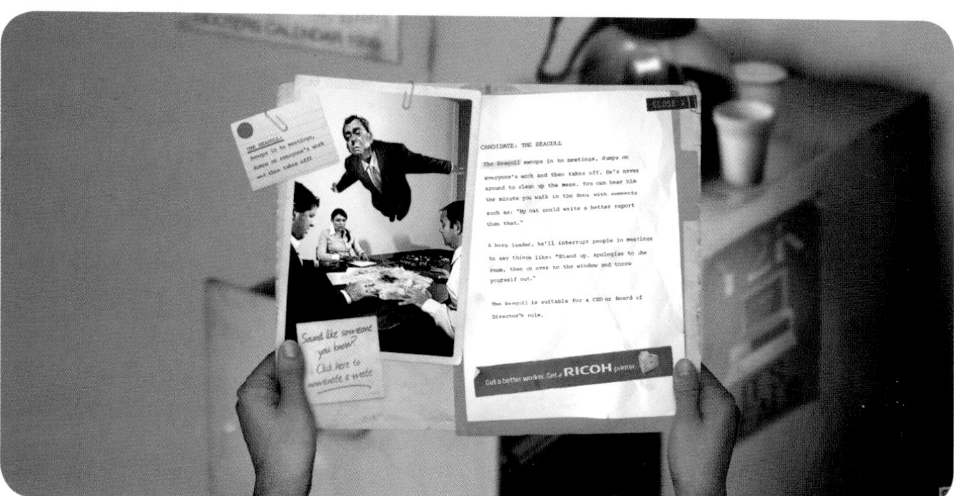
THE SEAGULL
Swoops in to meetings, dumps on everyone's work and then takes off!
Sound like someone you know? Click here to nominate a mate
CLOSE X
CANDIDATE: THE SEAGULL
The Seagull swoops in to meetings, dumps on everyone's work and then takes off. He's never around to clean up the mess. You can hear him the minute you walk in the door with comments such as: "My cat could write a better report than that."
A born leader, he'll interrupt people in meetings to say things like: "Stand up. Apologies to the room, then go over to the window and throw yourself out."
The Seagull is suitable for a CEO or Board of Director's role.
Get a better worker. Get a RICOH printer.

THE BLAME SHIFTER:
"It was the intern's fault"
Sound like someone you know? Click here to nominate a mate
CLOSE X
CANDIDATE: THE BLAME SHIFTER
The Blame Shifter is responsible for not taking responsibility for anything. Nothing is ever her fault anyway.
Her co-workers seem to make countless stuff ups though and The Blame Shifter is not shy to point the finger.
Whenever anything hits the fan, her standard response is: "Oh hasn't the intern done that yet? (sigh) That's the third time this week. Unbelievable!"
The majority of her time is spent covering her backside and letting management know who's to blame when something goes wrong.
A courageous role to take on but she always walks away smelling of roses.
Get a better worker. Get a RICOH printer.

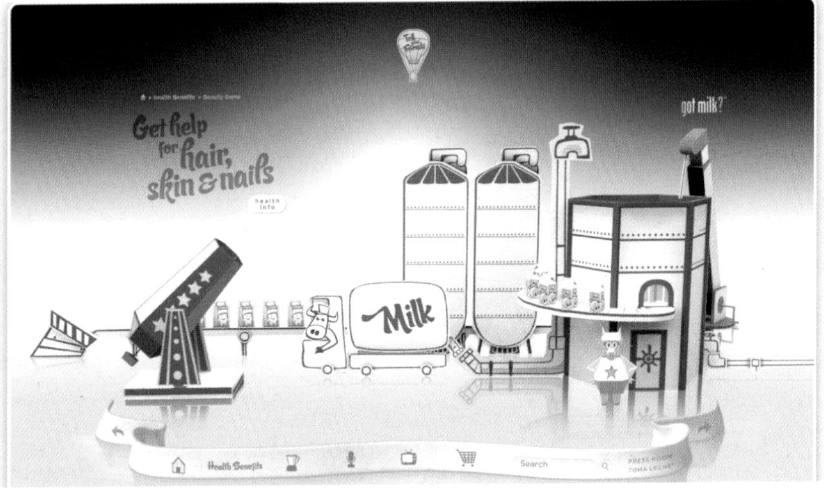

unit9 // www.unit9.com
Goodby Silverstein & Partners San Francisco // www.goodbysilverstein.com

> Recycle Center
got milk?
Recycle Center
Help improve your health, and the planet's too, by drinking milk and recycling the empty jug or carton into a nifty Carton Craft.
To get started, choose your canvas below - cartons or jugs.
PAINT
GLUE
SCISSORS
TAPE
BUTTONS
MARKERS
YARN
STRAWS
PENCILS
GLITTER
Search

got milk?
Workshop protocol:
every shift commences
with a dose of milk.
Get help reducing cavities
health info
Health Benefits
Search

Marcelo Delboux
Ricardo Cazzo
Rafael Lemos
Leandro Leal
Fred Gerodetti
Paulo Gallardi
Joana Jackson
Tatiana Dalla Bona // www.gpsete.com.br

GP 7
CAMISA 7
A camisa sete passa a bola debaixo das pernas, dribla um, dribla dois, faz fila e parte para o gol. A camisa sete é Garrincha, é Robinho. Dá elásticos, dá pedaladas, dá show. A camisa sete é Jairzinho, é Túlio, é Edmundo. Para ela, não existe gol perdido. A camisa sete é criativa, sem deixar de
7

GP 7
ANÕES
Os amigos da princesa fugitiva na história infantil, que, se fosse escrita hoje, provavelmente se chamaria "Branca de Neve e Os Sete Prejudicados Verticalmente". Alheios à chatice politicamente correta, trabalham sem parar, sempre mantendo o astral bem mais alto do que eles - o que, cá
7

Grafikonstruct // www.grafikonstruct.com.br

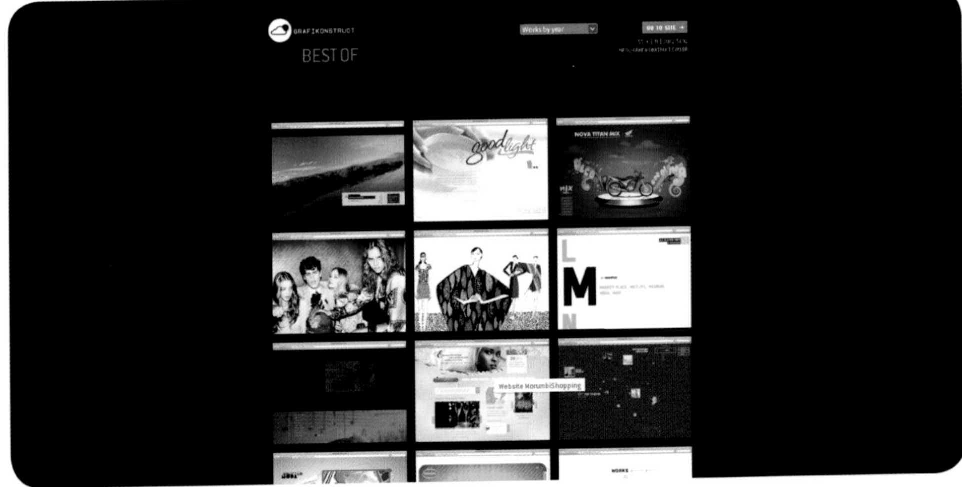

Marcelo Lima
Rafael Morinaga
Rodrigo Teco
Cauê Teixeira // www.grafikonstruct.com.br

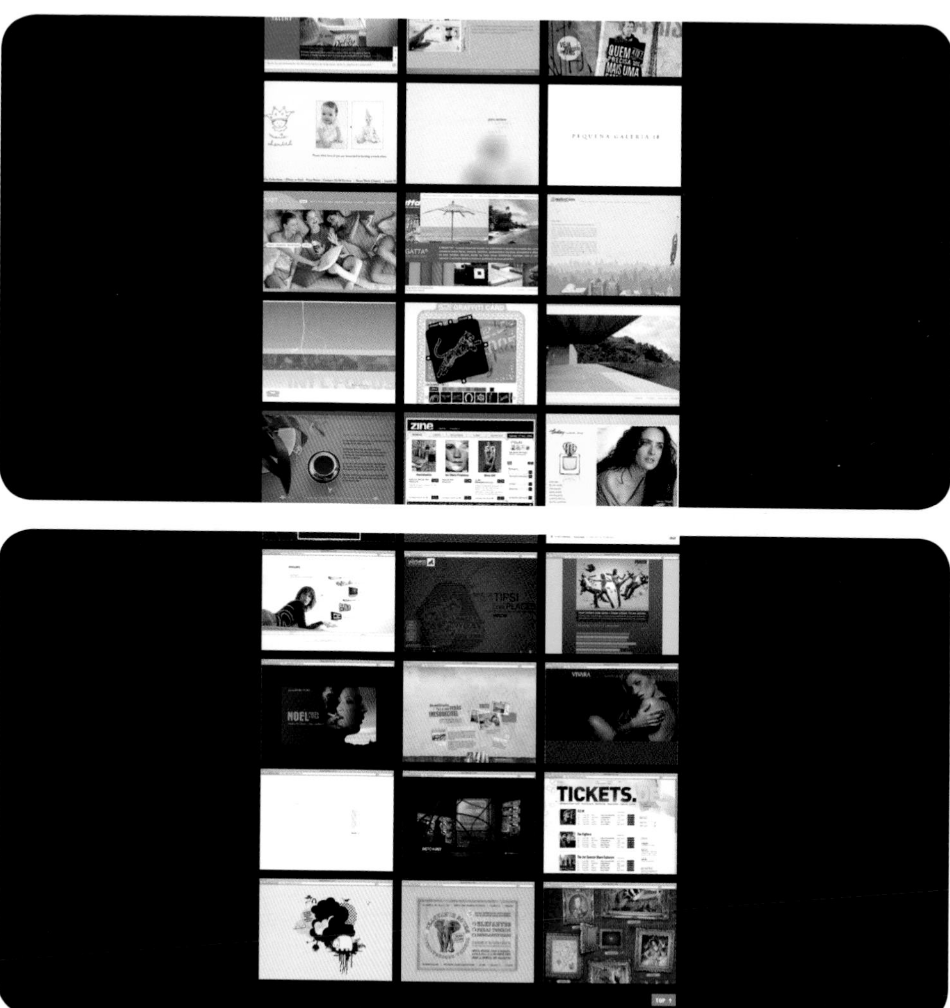

PEQUENA GALERIA 18
GRAFFITI CARD
zine
TIPSI
TICKETS.
VIVARA
NOEL
TOP

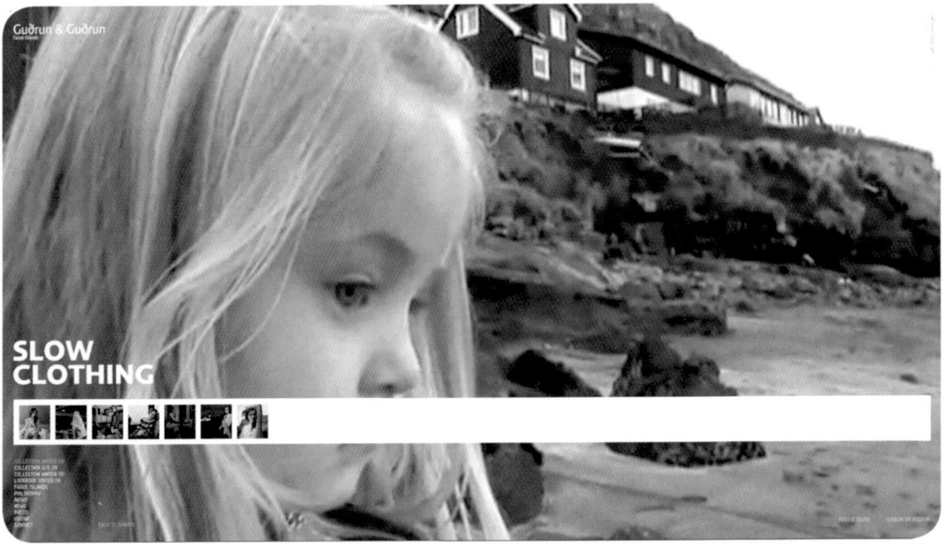

Guðrun & Guðrun

SLOW
CLOTHING

Hello Monday // www.hellomonday.com

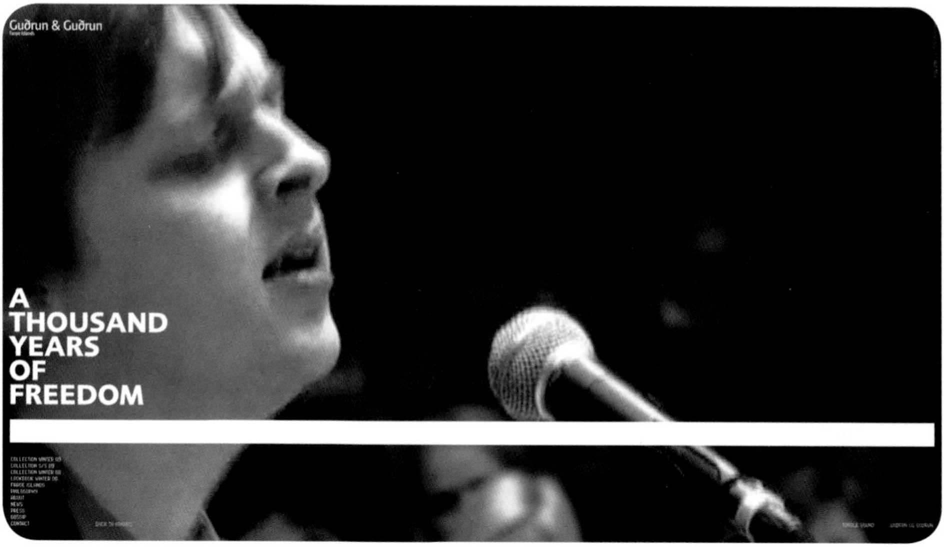

Guðrun & Guðrun

A THOUSAND YEARS OF FREEDOM

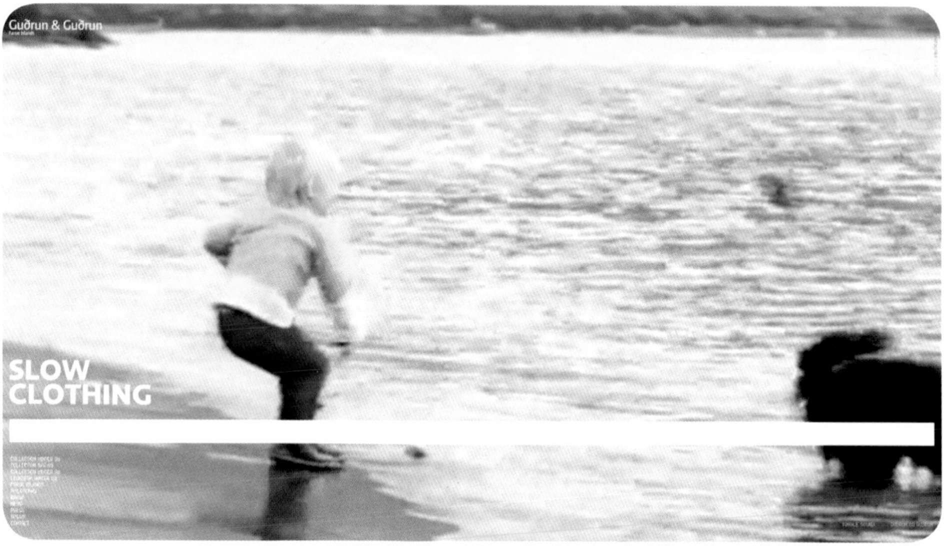

Guðrun & Guðrun

SLOW CLOTHING

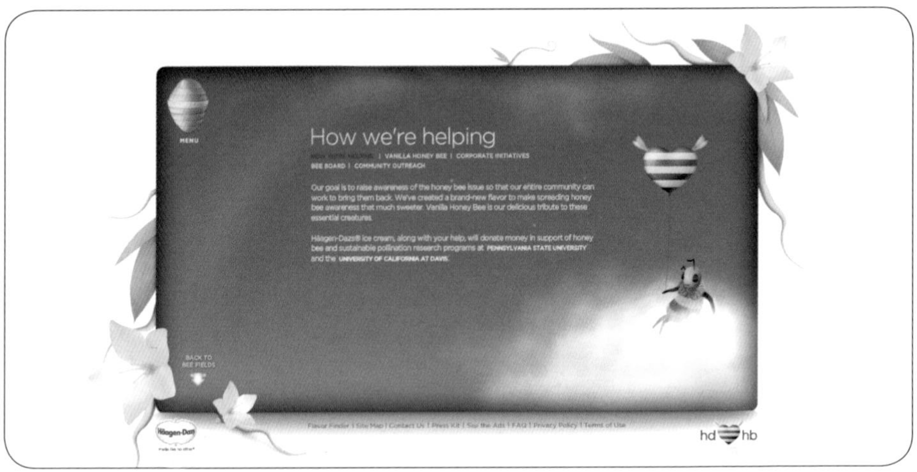

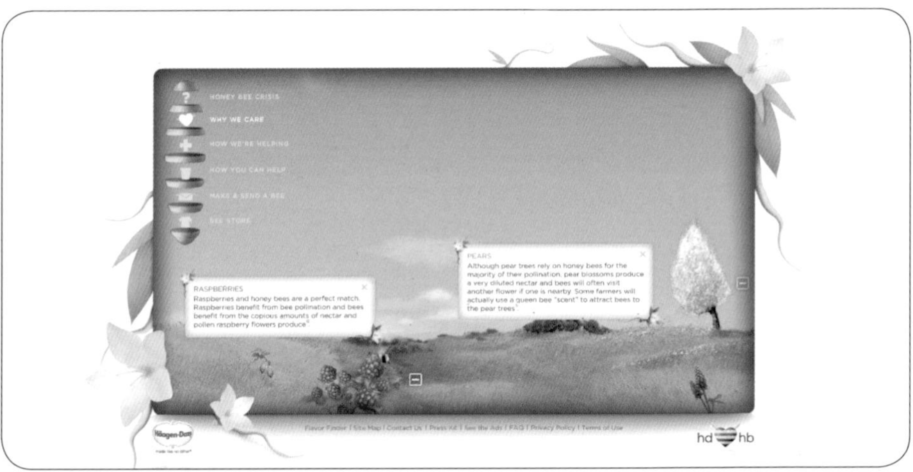

unit9 // www.unit9.com
Goodby Silverstein & Partners San Francisco // www.goodbysilverstein.com

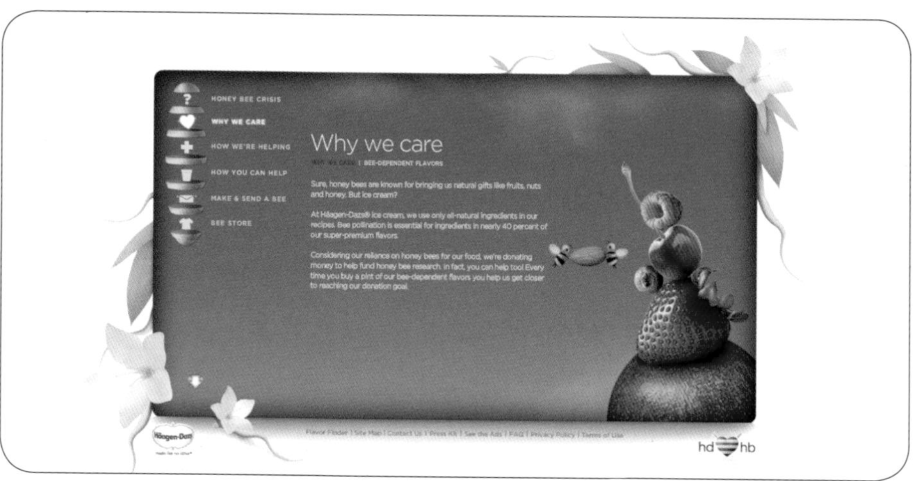
HONEY BEE CRISIS
WHY WE CARE
HOW WE'RE HELPING
HOW YOU CAN HELP
MAKE & SEND A BEE
BEE STORE
Why we care
BEE-DEPENDENT FLAVORS
Sure, honey bees are known for bringing us natural gifts like fruits, nuts and honey. But ice cream?
At Häagen-Dazs® ice cream, we use only all-natural ingredients in our recipes. Bee pollination is essential for ingredients in nearly 40 percent of our super-premium flavors.
Considering our reliance on honey bees for our food, we're donating money to help fund honey bee research. In fact, you can help too! Every time you buy a pint of our bee-dependent flavors you help us get closer to reaching our donation goal.
Häagen-Dazs
hd hb

MENU
CHERRIES
We cannot tell a lie. More than 80 percent of all cherries rely on honey bee pollination. In order to produce quality fruit, a cherry blossom must get 100 grains of pollen from a honey bee visitor. Luckily, honey bees can carry as many as 100,000 grains of pollen at once!
Häagen-Dazs
hd hb

Heineken - Know The Signs // www.knowthesigns.com

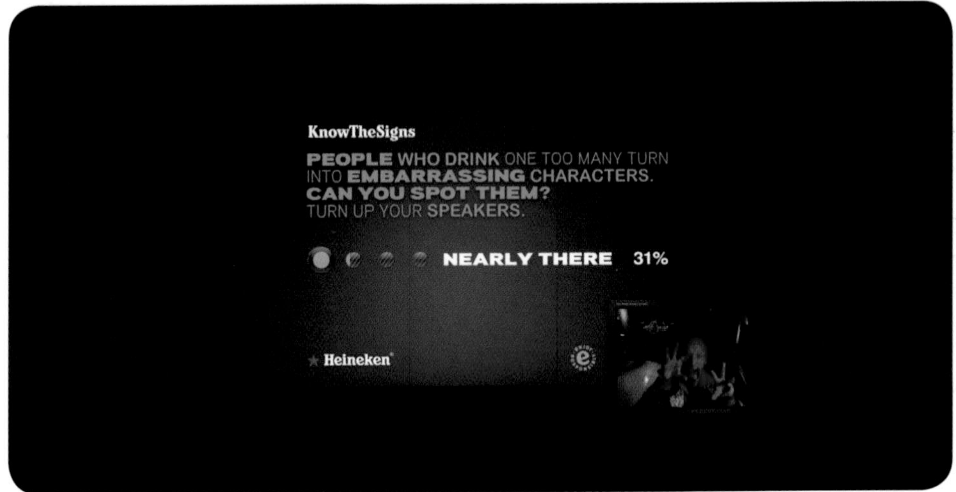

unit9 // www.unit9.com
Outsider // www.outsider.tv
Red Brick Road / Ruby // www.theredbrickroad.co.uk

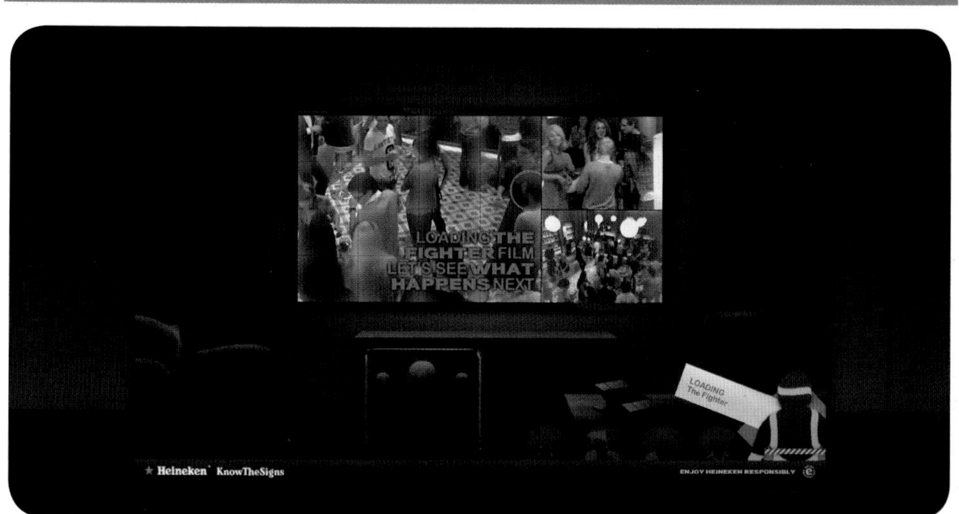
LOADING THE
FIGHTER FILM
LET'S SEE WHAT
HAPPENS NEXT
LOADING
The Fighter
Heineken KnowTheSigns
ENJOY HEINEKEN RESPONSIBLY

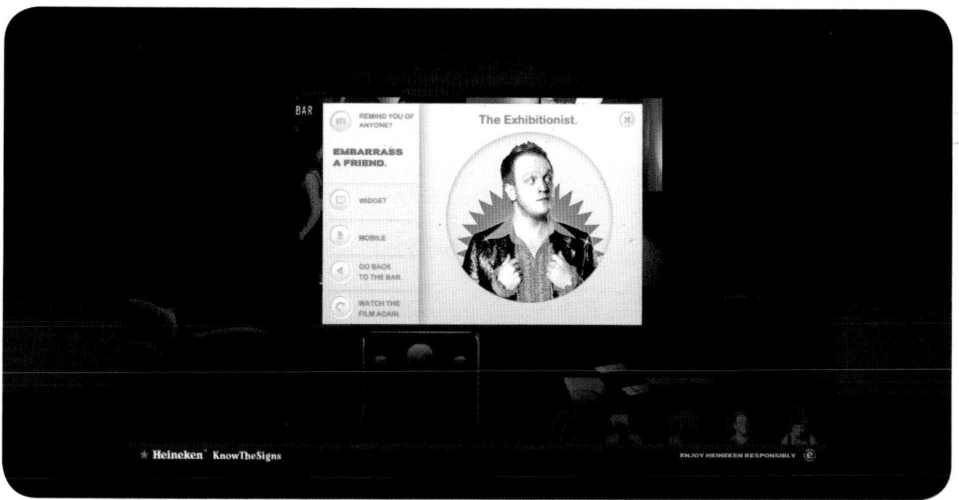
BAR
REMIND YOU OF ANYONE?
EMBARRASS A FRIEND.
WIDGET
MOBILE
GO BACK TO THE BAR.
WATCH THE FILM AGAIN.
The Exhibitionist.
Heineken KnowTheSigns
ENJOY HEINEKEN RESPONSIBLY

HEL LOOKS

About HEL LOOKS | F.A.Q.

1 2 3 4 5 6 7 8 ... 107

28 May 2009, Pohjois-Esplanadi

Achilles (21)

"I'm wearing a second hand knit, jeans by Cheap Monday, Chelsea boots by Balenciaga and a Louis Vuitton wallet. I'm wearing gold, because I'm coming from Louis Vuitton store's anniversary party.
Second hand inspires me at the moment. Amado at Merimiehenkatu is my favorite second hand store."

<< PREVIOUS NEXT >>

Liisa Jokinen, Sampo Karjalainen/ HEL LOOKS // hel-looks.com

<< PREVIOUS NEXT >>

About HEL LOOKS | F.A.Q.

1 ... 7 8 9 **10** 11 12 13 ... 107

8 February 2009, Helsinki Vintage

Heimi-Nelli (22)

"My shirt is from Yesterday Once More store in Vaasa, the jeans are by H&M, the shoes are second hand and the bag is my sister's. I like loose tops and high waists. I wear dark colours but always add some bright colour. I like the 50's and dresses from the 20's and the 30's. My little sister is my style idol. She knows how to mix clothes."

<< PREVIOUS NEXT >>

About HEL LOOKS | F.A.Q.

1 ... 10 11 12 **13** 14 15 16 ... 107

30 December 2008, Iso Roobertinkatu

Raisa (19)

"I'm wearing second hand clothes that I've bought in London. In winter I like to wear woollen and warm clothes like big cardigans. I don't think about clothes that much. I just wear things that I like."

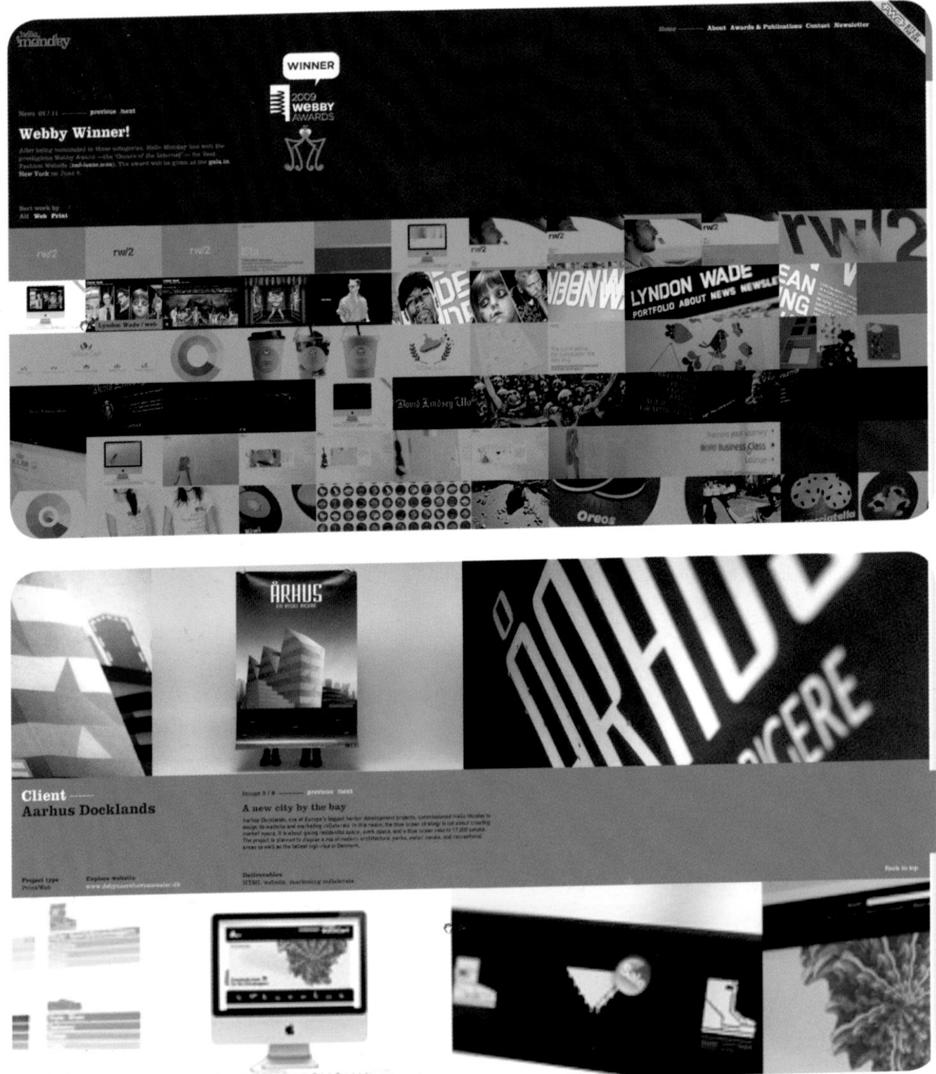

Hello Monday // www.hellomonday.com

VISU
AL
IDENTITY

THE QUICK BR
FOX JUMPS OV
THE LAZY DOG

Client
DG Photography

Poets and photographers

Project type
Web/Print

Deliverables
Visual identity concept, website concept

rossi
design
corporate

rossi.

design

DEVELOPER
TECHNICAL

MADE
BY

HempHoodLamb // hoodlamb.com

310k // www.310k.nl

Hemp Hoodlamb
MENS PRODUCTS
LADIES PRODUCTS
ABOUT HOODLAMB
GALLERY
NEWS
TEAM
VIDEO
HHL BLOG
HHL ONLINE STORE
WINTER SITE
JACKETS
HOODLAMB JACKET
DROPTOP BOMBER JACKET
HOODIES & SWEATERS
ZIP UP HOODY
SKIRTS, PANTS & SHORTS
RUDERALIS SKIRT
CAROLINE SKIRT
CARGO PANTS
LOUNGE PANTS
LOUNGE SHORTS
SHORTS
3/4 PANTS
TANKS & TEE'S
RAFFLE TANK
RACERBACK TANK
GRAFFITI TANK
HOODLAMB TANK
HIGH IN COMFORT TANK
SNOWFLAKE TANK
BASIC TEE
RICKUS TEE
Colours available
More images
1 2 3 4
Hemp Hoodlamb
Order now
LADIES CARGO PANTS HHLDM-2009 HEMPHOODLAMB AMSTERDAM. 31
Ladies Cargo Pants
- custom belt
- many utility pockets
- relaxed fit
- made from hemp/organic cotton
blog

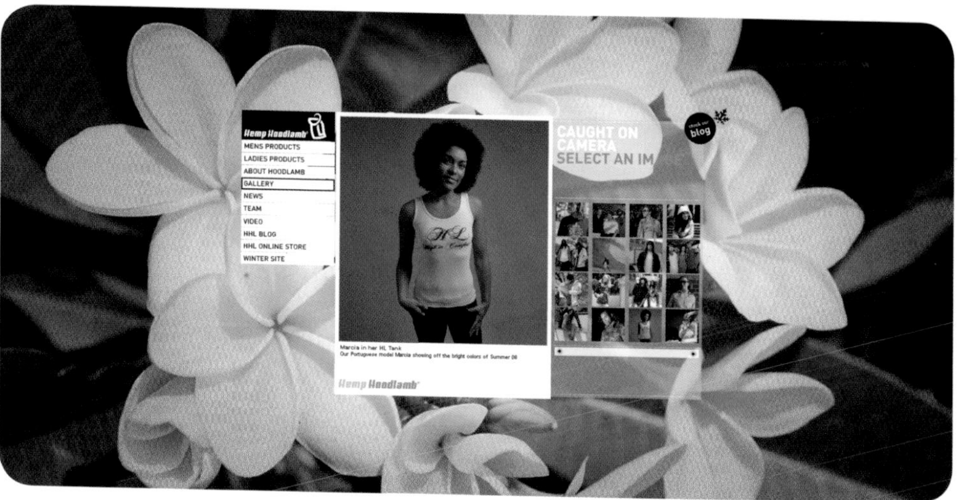
Hemp Hoodlamb
MENS PRODUCTS
LADIES PRODUCTS
ABOUT HOODLAMB
GALLERY
NEWS
TEAM
VIDEO
HHL BLOG
HHL ONLINE STORE
WINTER SITE
CAUGHT ON CAMERA
SELECT AN IM
blog
Marcia in her HL Tank
Our Portuguese model Marcia showing off the bright colors of Summer 08
Hemp Hoodlamb

PENSANDPENCILSANDPENS // www.pensandpencilsandpens.com

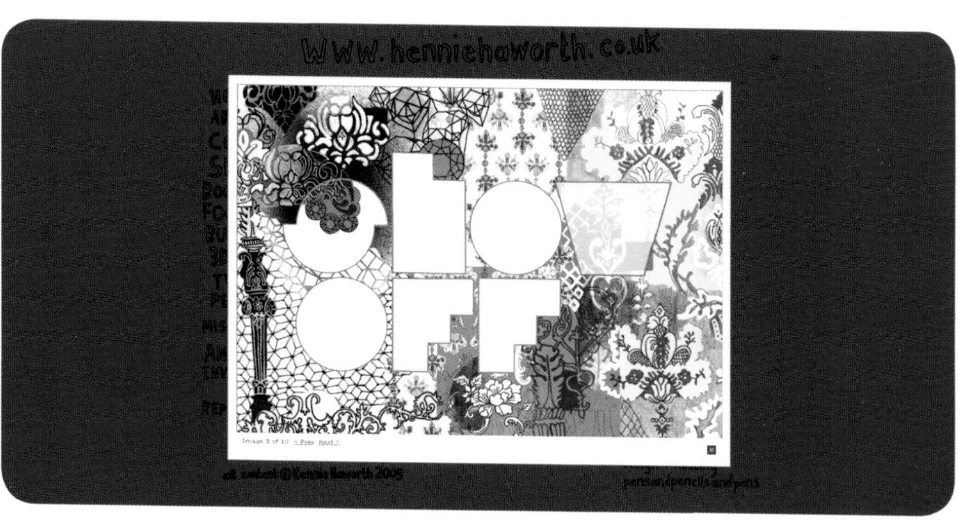

www.henniehaworth.co.uk

HOME
ABOUT ME
CONTACT
SHOP
BOOK COVERS
FOOD & DRINK
BUILDINGS
3D PROJECTS
TYPE
PEOPLE
MISCELLANEOUS
ANIMATION
INVITES & POSTERS
REPEATING PATTERNS

I am a Freelance Illustrator based in London.

Below are the Clients I have done work For;

Planeta
TheObserver
DDB
vodafone
NYLON
leap
wish
arts
proximity London
URBAN OUTFITTERS
BLOOMSBURY CHILDREN'S BOOKS
graniph
Waitrose
Time Out
dwell
SOUK
Penguin
RANDOM HOUSE
DK
habitat
the guardian g2
LUXE
COMPANY
ycn
toptable
delicious.
NICKELODEON
SOHO HOUSE
POST OFFICE
hat-trick
SYSTEM BOLAGET
THIS IS TRUE NORTH
BBDO
CAPE TOWN
the art group
enRoute
dentsu
Boutique 1

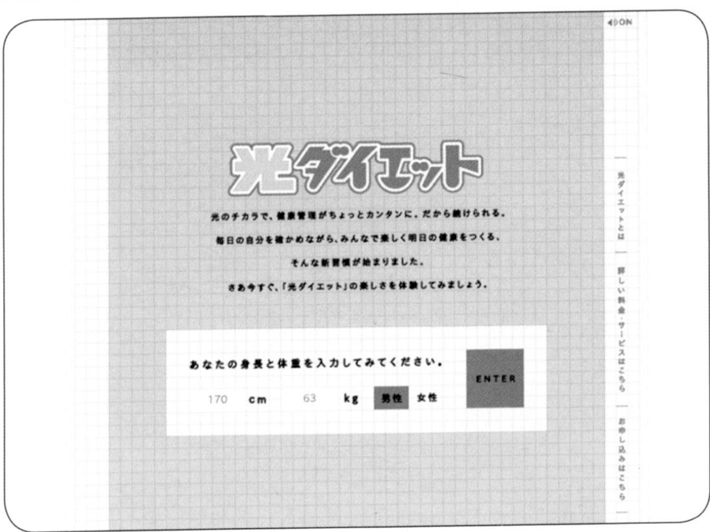

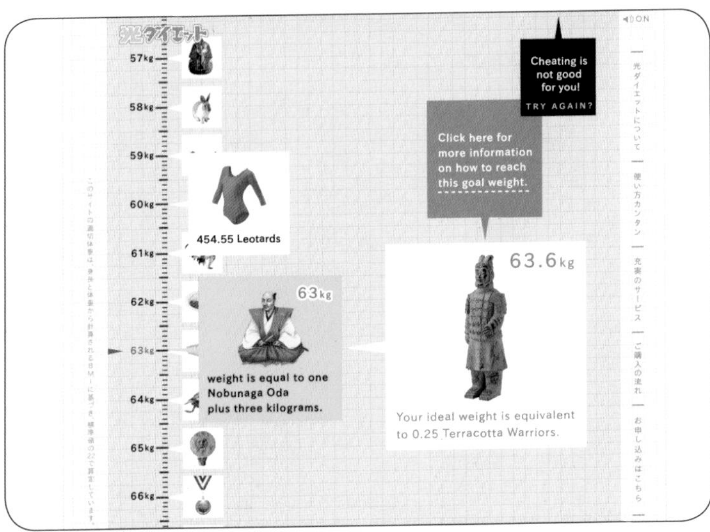

IMG SRC // imgsrc.co.jp
NIPPON TELEGRAPH AND TELEPHONE EAST CORPORATION // www.ntt-east.co.jp/index_e.html

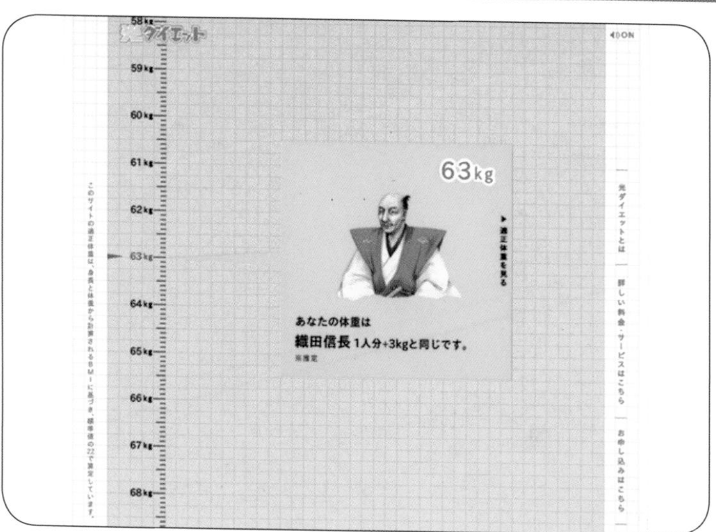
63kg
あなたの体重は
織田信長 1人分+3kgと同じです。

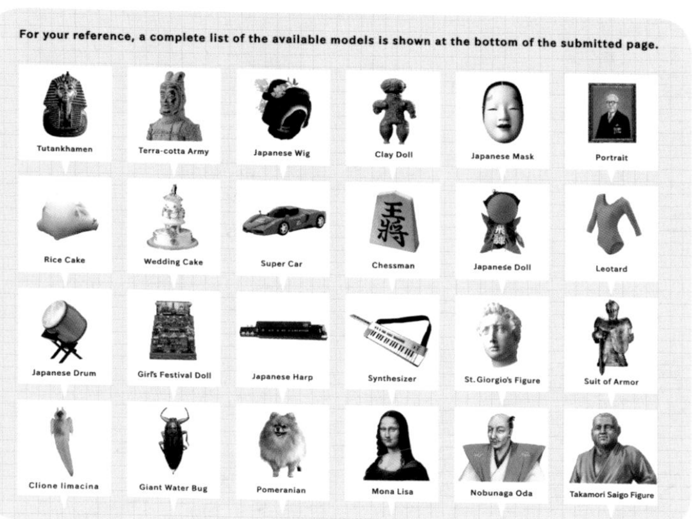
For your reference, a complete list of the available models is shown at the bottom of the submitted page.
Tutankhamen
Terra-cotta Army
Japanese Wig
Clay Doll
Japanese Mask
Portrait
Rice Cake
Wedding Cake
Super Car
Chessman
Japanese Doll
Leotard
Japanese Drum
Girl's Festival Doll
Japanese Harp
Synthesizer
St. Giorgio's Figure
Suit of Armor
Clione limacina
Giant Water Bug
Pomeranian
Mona Lisa
Nobunaga Oda
Takamori Saigo Figure

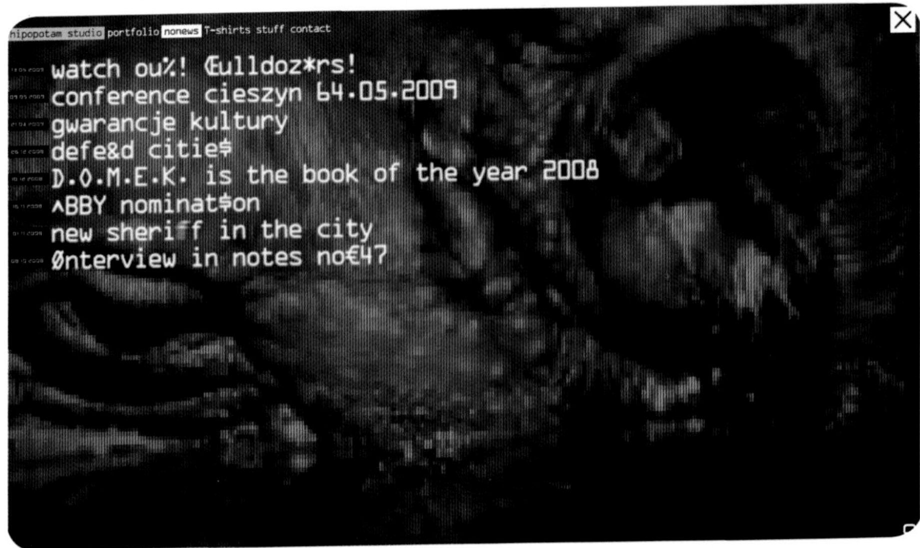

Hipopotam Studio // www.hipopotamstudio.pl

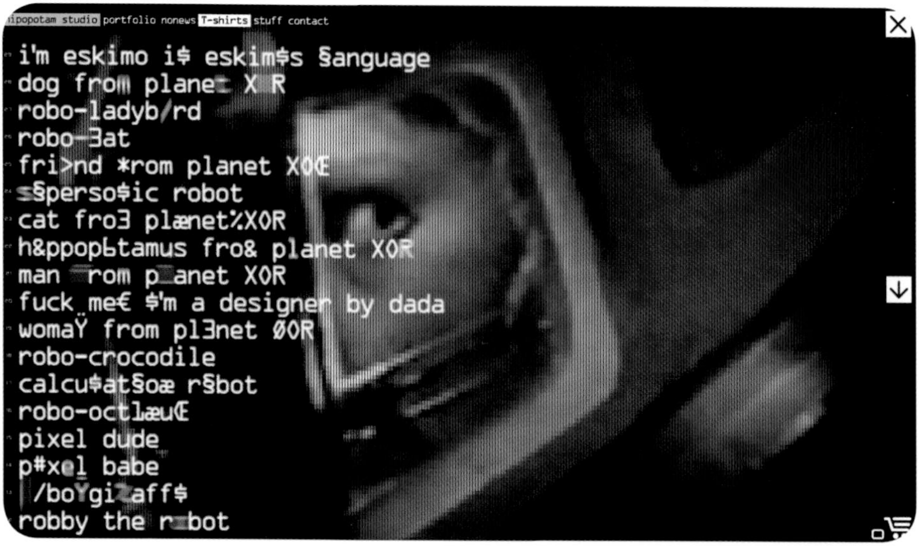

ipopotam studio portfolio nonews T-shirts stuff contact

i'm eskimo i$ eskim$s §anguage
dog from plane X R
robo-ladyb/rd
robo-Ǝat
fri>nd *rom planet XO€
s§perso$ic robot
cat froƎ plænet%XOR
h&ppopъtamus fro& planet XOR
man rom p anet XOR
fuck me€ $'m a designer by dada
womaŸ from pl3net ØOR
robo-crocodile
calcu$at§oæ r§bot
robo-octlæu€
pixel dude
p#xel babe
/boYgi aff$
robby the r bot

House of Jackie Brown // houseofjackiebrown.com

House of Jackie Brown

Home
Our House
Contact
Press
Collection
Lookbook
'08 Caliente
Blog

HO JB

Electric couture

MUSIC OFF

FREESTYLE
HEATHERS
TWO OF HEARTS
TOOTIE FRUITY
MATERIAL GIRL
TIFFANY
DIAMOND GIRL
KARMA CHAMELEON
PRETTY IN PINK
DYNASTY

House of Jackie Brown

COLLECTION

Home
Our House
Contact
Press
Collection
Lookbook
'08 Caliente
Blog

Freestyle

NEXT ANGLE

MUSIC OFF

Version Industries // versionindustries.com

STYLE MENU

House of Jackie Brown

COLLECTION

Sold Out!

Home
Our House
Contact
Press
Collection
Cookbook
'08 Caliente
Blog

Material Girl

PREV NEXT

House of Jackie Brown

PRESS

Magazine Articles

ACCLAIM MAGAZINE
ZOOMZOOM MAGAZINE

Videos

PLUM TV · EPISODE 1
HOJB MUSIC VIDEO

Home
Our House
Contact
Press
Collection
Cookbook
'08 Caliente
Blog

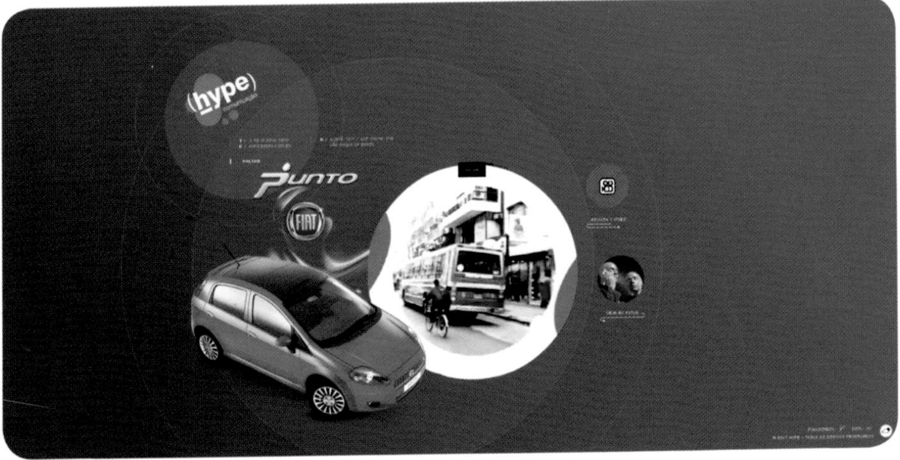

Rodrigo Alarcon
Fábio Lima
Paulo Melo
Rafael Morinaga
Rodrigo Teco
Cauê Teixeira // www.grafikonstruct.com.br

sodexo

NOVO PALIO 2008
TODA EMOÇÃO ESTÁ AQUI

Nessim Higson // iamalwayshungry.com
Destin Young // ourvice.com

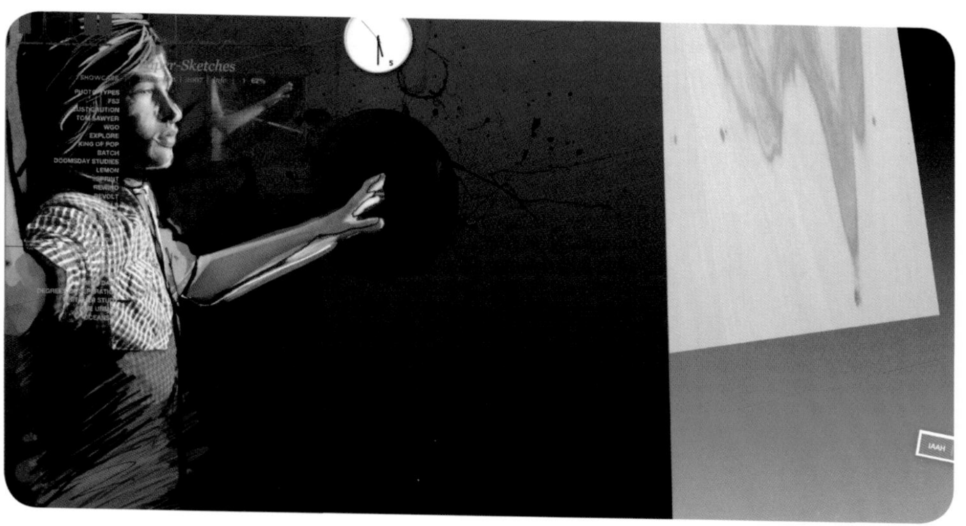
WGO
EXPLORE
KING OF POP
BATCH
DOOMSDAY STUDIES
LEMON
IAAH

Close Information
A few variations of other concepts for the Low in the Sky album. At this point, the album was untitled. So we assisted in interpreting the music through titles and corresponding imagery.
IAAH

I am always hungry Version 7 // iamalwayshungry.com/VERS7-2/

hello.

This is a website.

A seventh iteration of iamalwayshungry representing a bulk of work from 2008 and some of 2009 in a temporary and experimental shell.

Click and drag to navigate.

Click

Data

Designers against tibetan abuse. **The name of DATA has now changed since this work was completed and now goes by the name DAHRA - Designers Against Human Rights Abuse. The basis of the book and it's purpose were straight forward and easy to align onself with. Create a piece that expresses the feelings you have towards the restrictions and injustices placed on Tibet.**

Nessim Higson // iamalwayshungry.com
Destin Young // ourvice.com

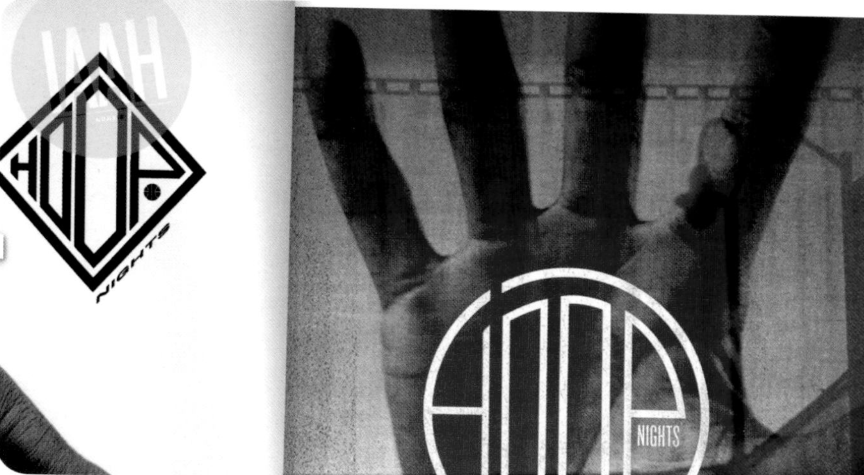
HOOP
NIGHTS
NEXT | 4/5
HOOP
NIGHTS

IAAH
OBSERVATIONAL LESSON
TOMORROW
IS
TODAY
IS
TOMORROW
1/8 | PREV
Grab bag
A piece created for the book entitled Grab Bag. The basis of the book was to design something based off a creative task assigned to you. I was given the task to do a observational illustration. There are certain phrases that you'll see me play around with continuously as I think they are very appropriate to life and have a lot of relevance for me. I decided to use one for this book. "Tomorrow is today. Today is tomorrow" seems pretty obvious and relevenat. Faintly screened on top one can make out the phrase "Forward not Backwrads" borrowed from the ADC Henry Wolf poster. Both are common thoughts, basic in nature - yet essential for keeping one grounded. Very easy to be looked over as well.
TOMORROW
IS
TODAY
IS
TOMORROW
TOMORROW
TOMORROW
IS
TOMORROW

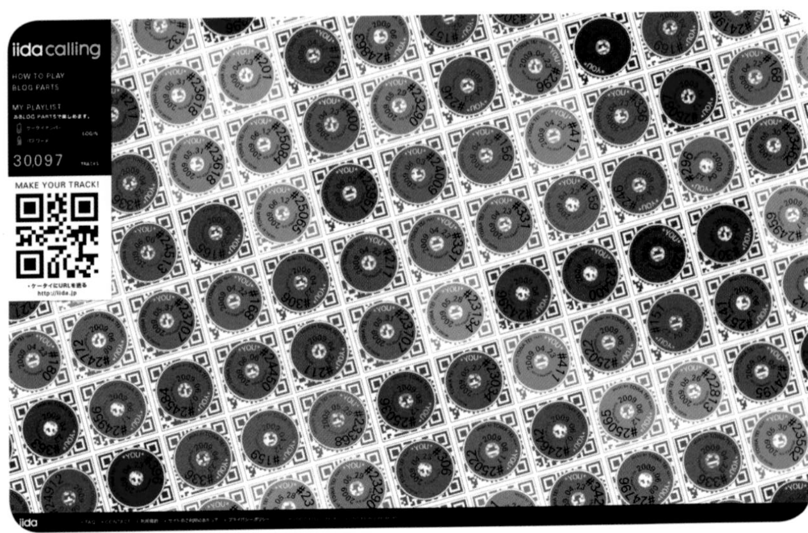

IMG SRC // www.imgsrc.co.jp
KDDI CORPORATION // www.kddi.com/english/index.html

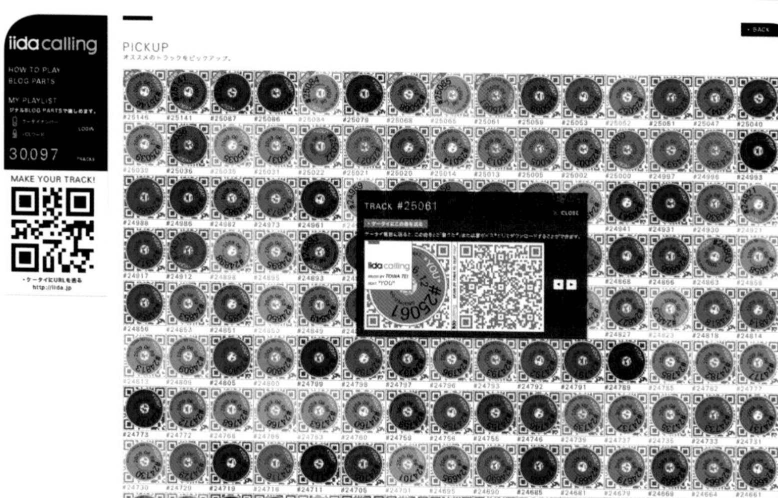

iida calling

HOW TO PLAY
BLOG PARTS
MY PLAYLIST
30,097

MAKE YOUR TRACK!

HOW TO PLAY / CALL

Pelle Martin/ In2media // in2media.com

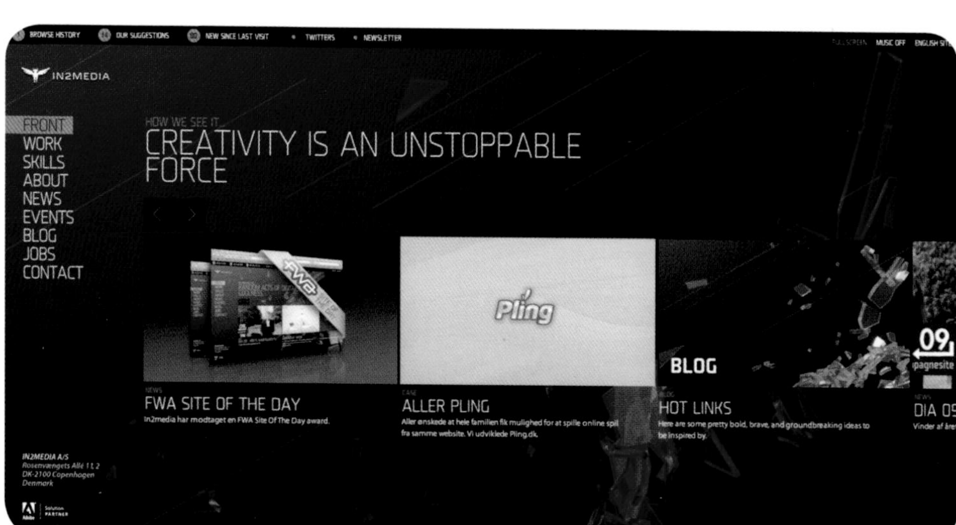

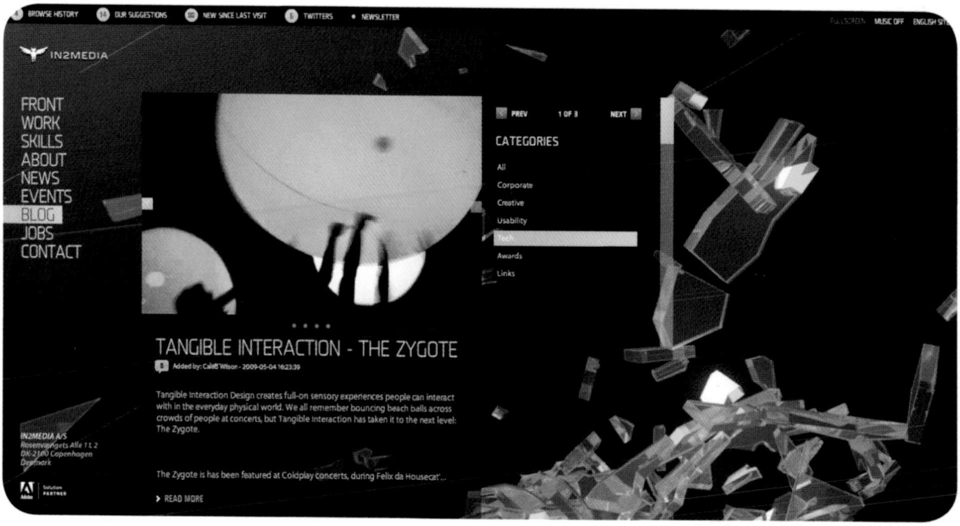

BROWSE HISTORY · OUR SUGGESTIONS · NEW SINCE LAST VISIT · TWITTERS · NEWSLETTER · MUSIC OFF · ENGLISH SITE

IN2MEDIA

FRONT
WORK
SKILLS
ABOUT
NEWS
EVENTS
BLOG
JOBS
CONTACT

PREV 1 OF 3 NEXT

CATEGORIES

All
Corporate
Creative
Usability
Tech
Awards
Links

TANGIBLE INTERACTION - THE ZYGOTE

Added by: Caleb Wilson - 2009-05-04 16:23:39

Tangible Interaction Design creates full-on sensory experiences people can interact with in the everyday physical world. We all remember bouncing beach balls across crowds of people at concerts, but Tangible Interaction has taken it to the next level: The Zygote.

The Zygote is has been featured at Coldplay concerts, during Felix da Housecat'...

READ MORE

IN2MEDIA A/S
Rosenvængets Allé 11, 2
DK-2100 Copenhagen
Denmark

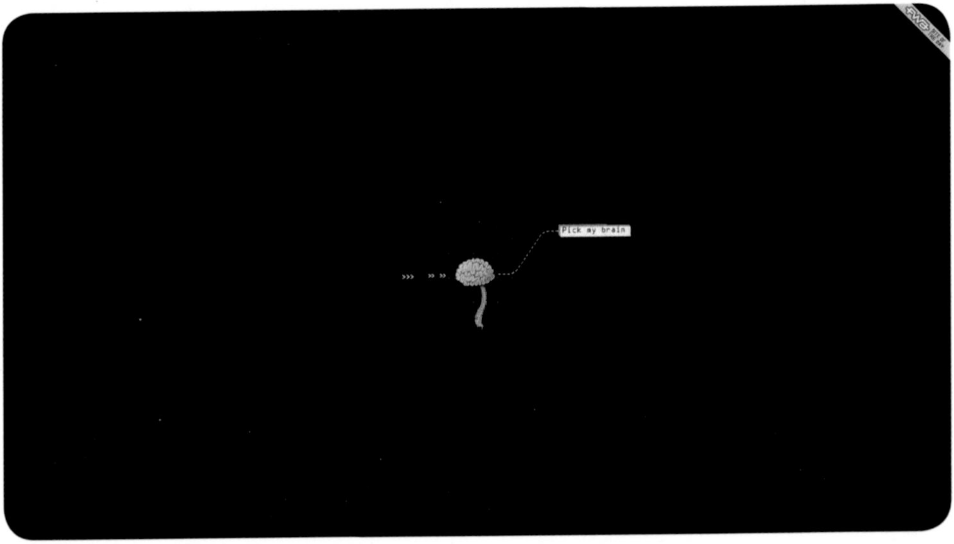

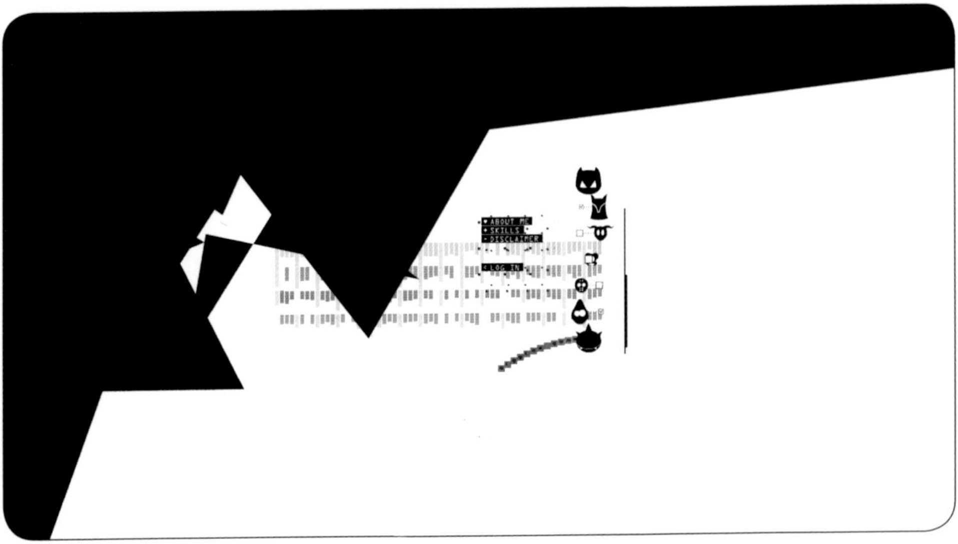

Piet Dewijngaert // www.insidepiet.com

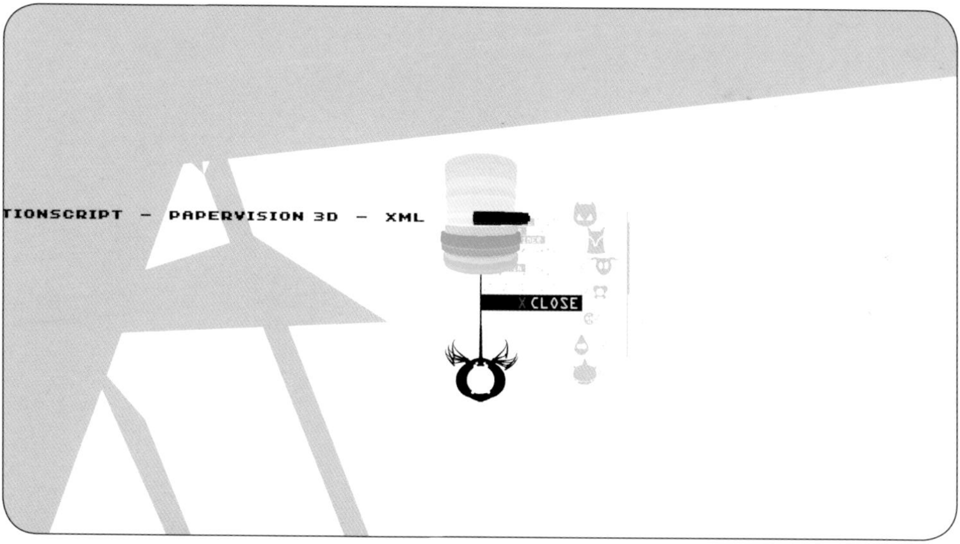

TIONSCRIPT – PAPERVISION 3D – XML

X CLOSE

close

Rodolfo Araki
Camila Chaves
Artur Dias
Júlio Scarpelini
Bruno Soares
Rodrigo Teco
Cauê Teixeira
Antonio Vicentini // www.grafikonstruct.com.br

Issa
LONDON
INSPIRATION
COLLECTION
show
archive
BUZZ & MEDIA
DISTRIBUTION & CONTACT

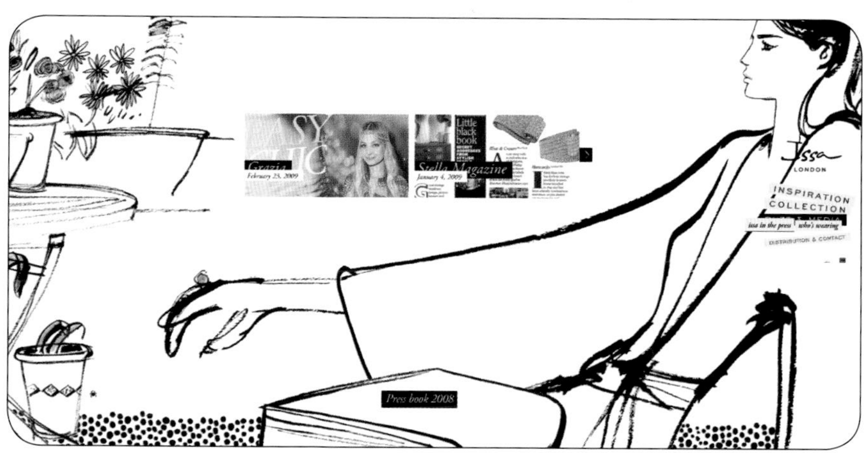
Grazia
February 23, 2009
Stella Magazine
January 4, 2009
Little black book
Issa
LONDON
INSPIRATION
COLLECTION
issa in the press
who's wearing
DISTRIBUTION & CONTACT
Press book 2008

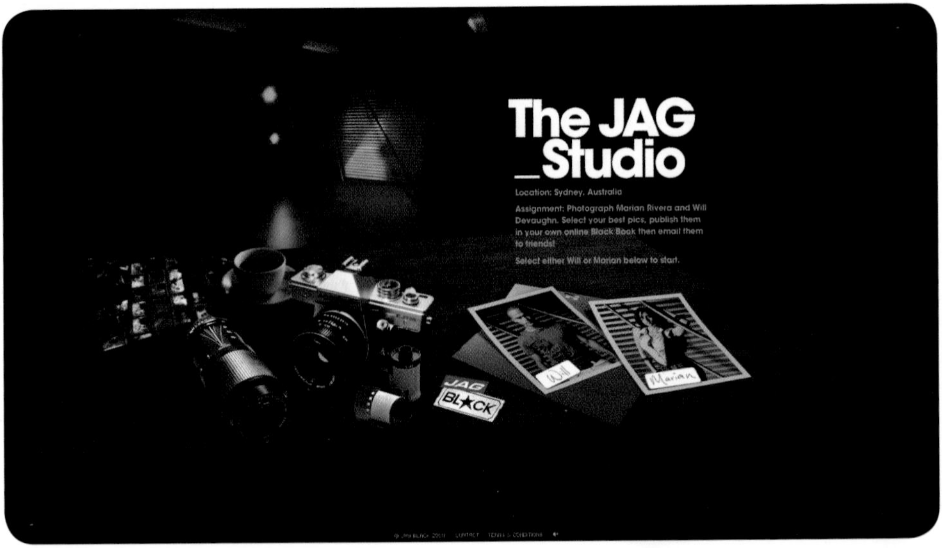

Jag Black // www.jag-jeans.com

Resn // www.resn.co.nz

Select your page
JAG
BL★CK
‹ 2 of 5 ›
shoot more images
publish magazine ›

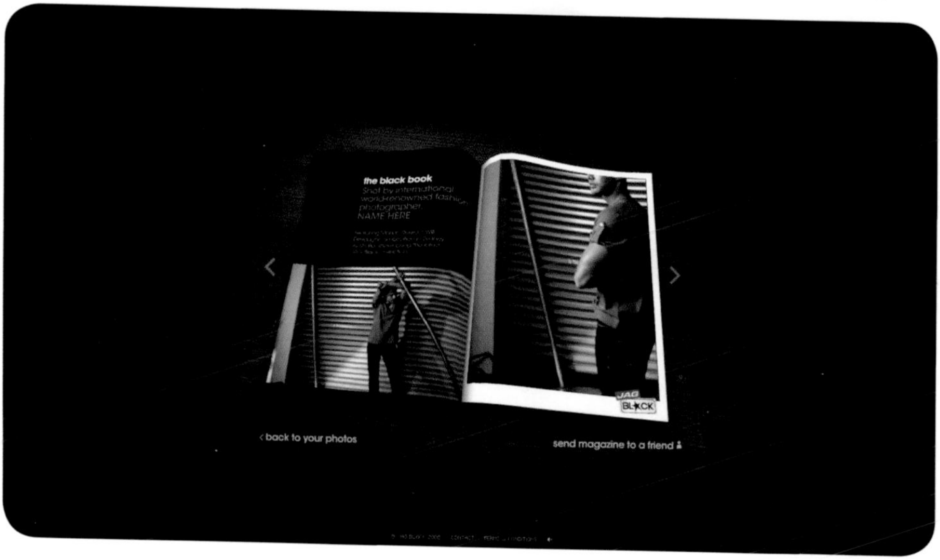
the black book
Shot by international world-renowned fashion photographer.
NAME HERE
JAG
BL★CK
‹ back to your photos
send magazine to a friend

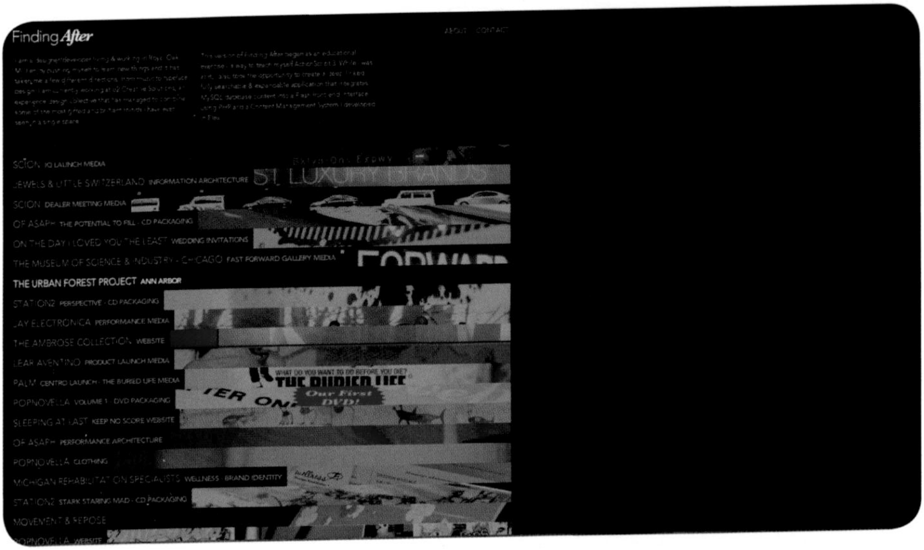

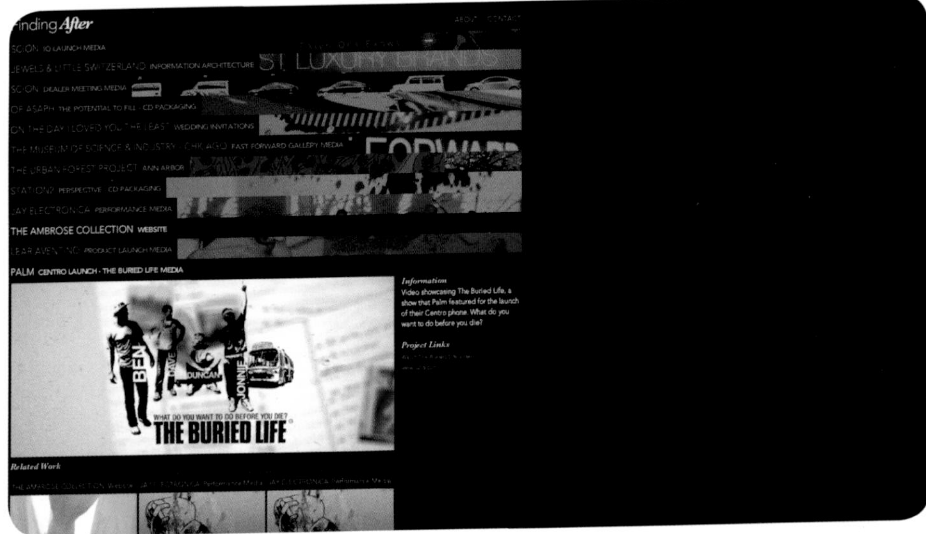

James Alleman // www.findingafter.com

TATION? STARK STARING MAD · CD PACKAGING

MOVEMENT & REPOSE

POPNOVELLA WEBSITE

WATCH BUY ABOUT CONTACT

ABOUT TAPE ABOUT CURB APPEAL ABOUT TATTOOS ABOUT A DOLLHOUSE ABOUT A CHAT ABOUT

WATCH VIDEO Windows Media

WATCH VID Quicktime

Information

Promotional website for a production company that makes short films. In addition to creating a media-heavy website and integrating it with an e-commerce platform, I was also able to collaborate with the popno-fellas and design their look-and-feel.

Project Links

Related Work

DR PEPPER CORPORATE STORE SIGNAGE

TEAM SARAJEVO

TYPOCALYPSE

GLORIOUS RUINS FINDING GOD IN DETROIT

HOLY BIBLE PORTRAIT OF JESUS & THE APOSTLES

ACACIA A QUIRKY TEXT TYPEFACE

CALIGARY A DELICATE DISPLAY TYPEFACE

delicate display typeface

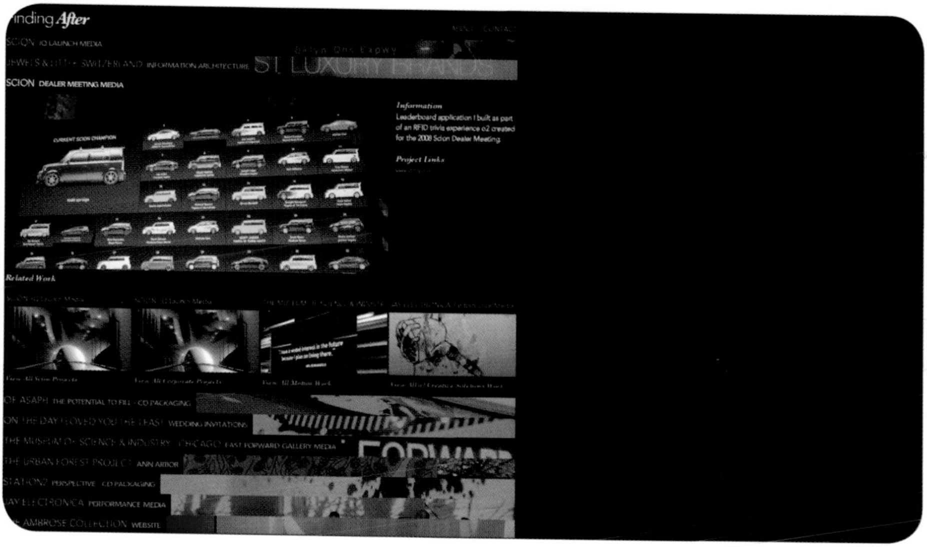

Finding *After*

SCION IQ LAUNCH MEDIA

JEWELS & ... SWITZERLAND INFORMATION ARCHITECTURE

ST. LUXURY BRANDS

SCION DEALER MEETING MEDIA

CURRENT SCION CHAMPION

Information

Leaderboard application I built as part of an RFID trivia experience o2 created for the 2008 Scion Dealer Meeting.

Project Links

Related Work

OF ASAPH THE POTENTIAL TO FILL · CD PACKAGING

ON THE DAY I LOVED YOU THE LEAST WEDDING INVITATIONS

THE MUSEUM OF SCIENCE & INDUSTRY · CHICAGO FAST FORWARD GALLERY MEDIA

THE URBAN FOREST PROJECT · ANN ARBOR

STATION? PERSPECTIVE · CD PACKAGING

AY ELECTRONICA PERFORMANCE MEDIA

AMBROSE COLLECTION WEBSITE

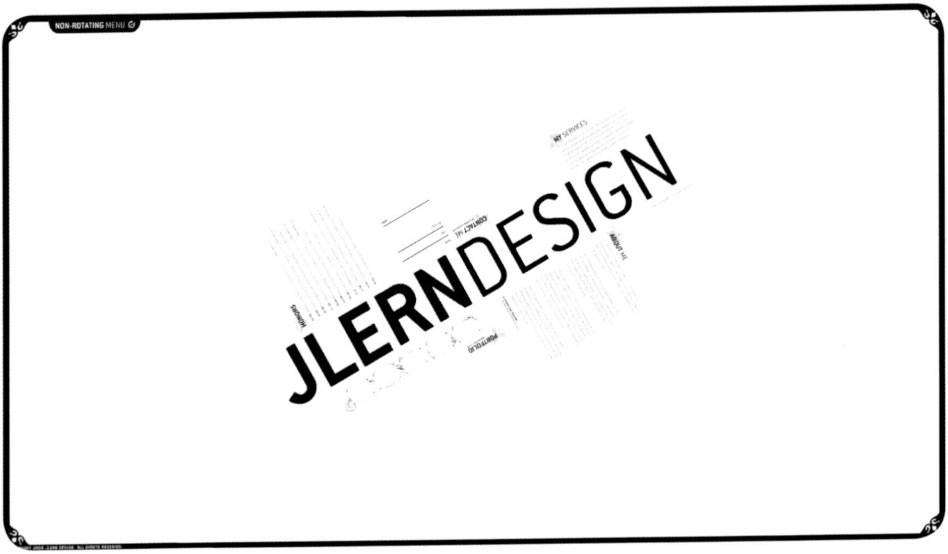

JLern Design // www.jlern.com

NON-ROTATING MENU

MY SERVICES

I create experiences for the web. Mo... are Flash-based animated websites, however... programming in HTML, if that is more suitable. I offer a w... maintenance system for easily updating the website's content. I also do database integration and CD-Roms. For the tech literate, I can sprinkle in some PHP or XML as desired.

DESIGN

*Not responsible for motion sickness

ABOUT ME MY SERVICES PORTFOLIO HONORS CONTACT ME HOME

NON-ROTATING MENU

ABOUT ME

Hi, my name is Justin. I'm a designer. I'm a programmer. I'm an animator. I like to make things move. If its not moving, then I'm probably not interested. I want to see websites come to life and excite me.

I am currently working in the city of Philadelphia, but that isn't too relevant. I've worked with clients in California and Canada, so location is no barrier. I am a freelancer and I do not keep regular daily office hours. I don't even have an office. I'm a nomad of the design world.

I look at every project as a chance to do something new. I've seen what's out there and 95% of it bores me. When you invite someone into your online home, you have the opportunity to leave a lasting impression. A website to me is about so much more than just displaying information. It is about capturing the user's attention. It is about creating a mood.

...am always eagerly

Jocker / CREAKTIF ! // www.creaktif.com/jocker/
noMatter/ M55 // www.nomatter.eu

Menu
WOMEN
MEN
KIDS
FRAGRANCE
JOHN GALLIANO
BOUTIQUES
THE PARFUM
INTERVIEW
John Galliano
CONTACT
NEWSLETTER

"The most influential fashion designer of his generation"
TIME Magazine.
John Galliano is an English eccentric who has taken Paris, indeed the world, by storm. Galliano has not only retained his position at the forefront of fashion, he has redefined it with every presentation. Galliano has not only broken the rules, he has rewritten them. Galliano will be remembered as one of the most exciting, innovative and romantic designers of the twentieth century on the red carpet, and on the runway, on the most iconic looks of today in his own label, as well as spearheading a couture Renaissance and a New Look, and New Energy with his New Vision at Dior.
Born on the British Peninsula of Gibraltar, Galliano grew up in London, and studied fashion at St. Martins. His infamous 1984 degree collection, "Les Incroyables", was inspired by the French Revolution and with this Galliano caused his own revolution, and a new fashion Messiah was born.
Galliano's imagination, storytelling and research trips are legendary. Each season he searches the globe, travelling through cultures, continents, literature, the arts and the unexpected to innovate and pioneer new ideas. He brings the future, fantasy and romance to life. His shows remain one of the most coveted invites in town, collections taking inspiration from China, Mexico, Russia, Japan, India as well as his homelands. From the Opera Garnier to la Belle Epoque, Bollywood to Las Vegas, the Pearly Kings and Queens of London town to the Geishas of the East, Galliano finds beauty in all he sees. He started by reinventing the bias-cut then took on reshaping women's dreams.
"There are few creative people in the fashion world who, through their spirit, their creative joy and their personalities, really give fashion what it needs - some inventive madness."
Anna Wintour
"Curiosity : it's the most important thing"
John Galliano
Menu
John Galliano
CONTACT
NEWSLETTER

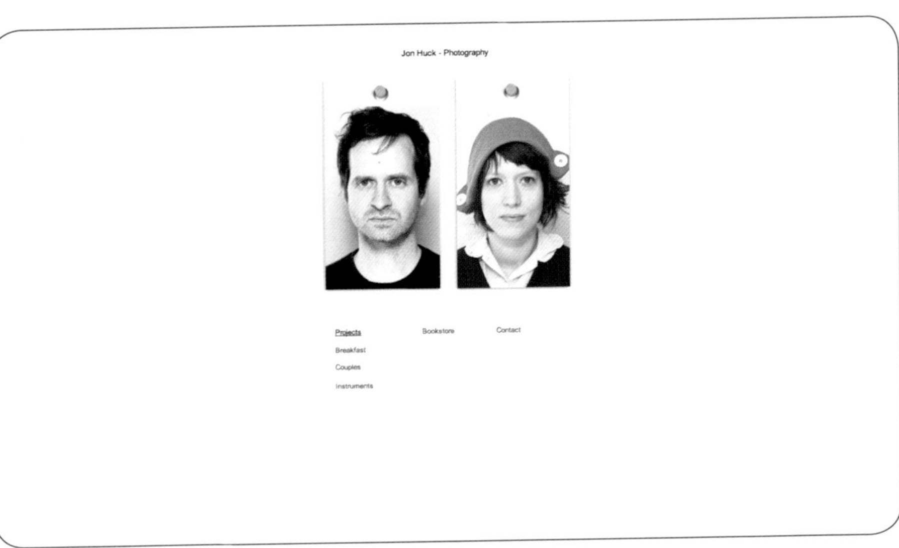

Jon Huck // jonhuck.com

breakfast :: huck :: 2/20/07

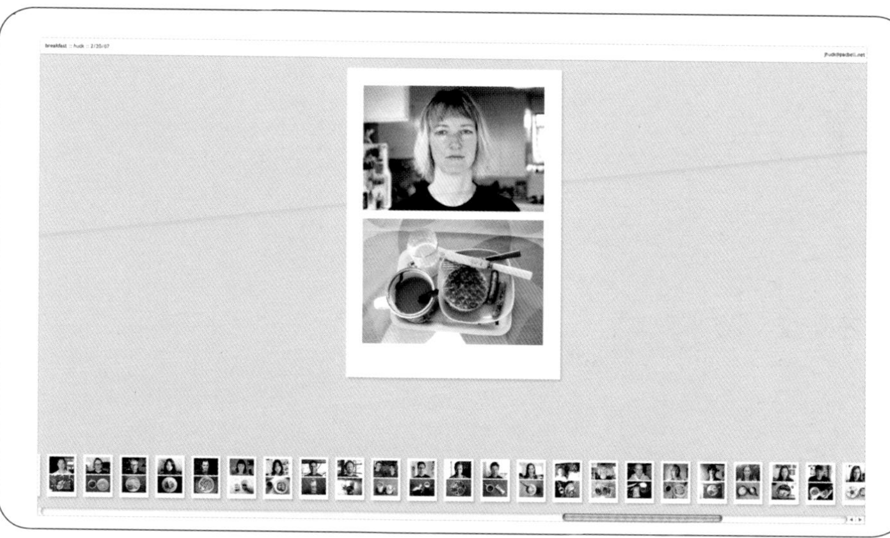
breakfast :: huck :: 2/20/07

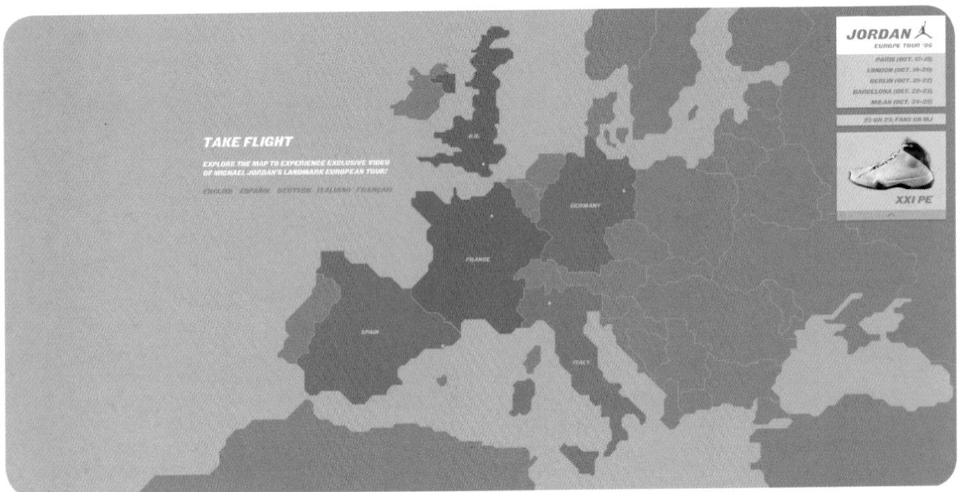

Markus Eriksson
Joshua Stearns/ Blast Radius // www.blastradius.com

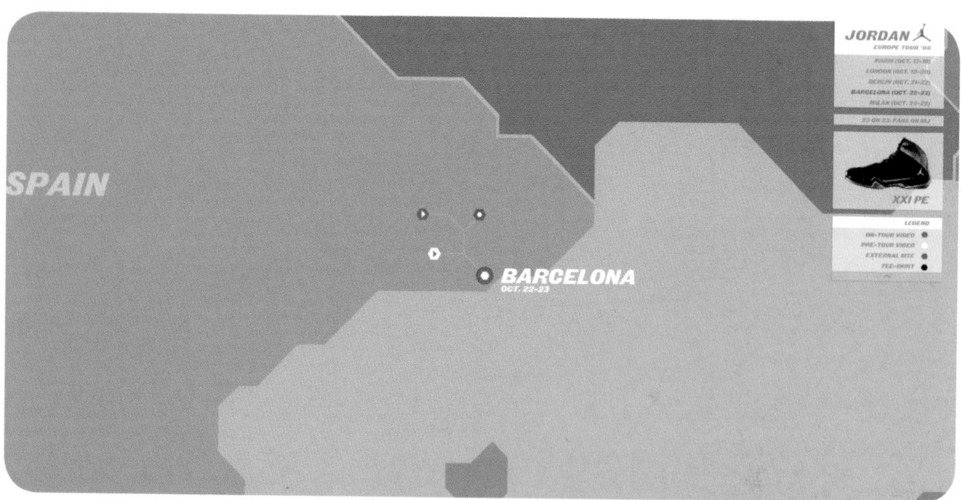
JORDAN
EUROPE TOUR '06
BARCELONA (OCT. 22-23)
SPAIN
BARCELONA
OCT. 22-23
XXI PE
LEGEND
ON-TOUR VIDEO
PRE-TOUR VIDEO
EXTERNAL SITE
TEE-SHIRT

JORDAN
X CLOSE
XXI PE
JORDAN IN BERLIN

Joshua Stearns/ Zero Style // www.0-style.com

SELECTS RECENT PORTRAIT BLACK WHITE BLUE RED

SELECTS RECENT PORTRAIT BLACK WHITE BLUE RED

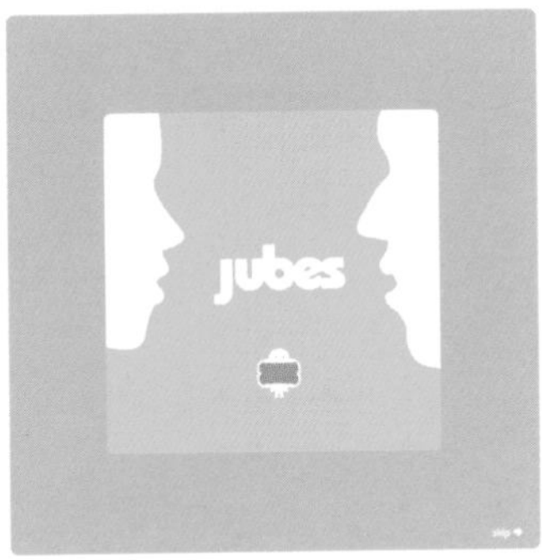

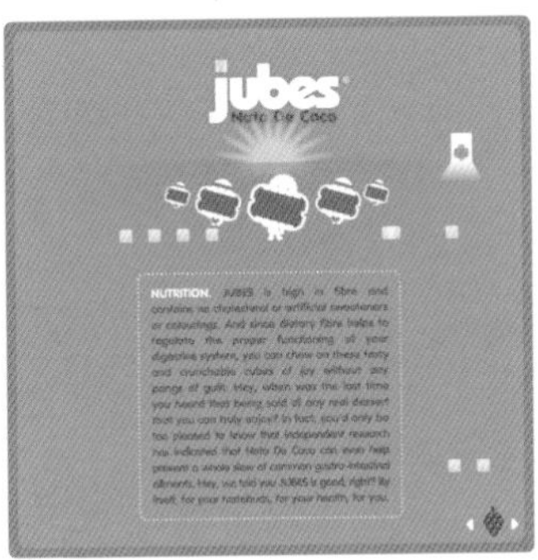

Kinetic // www.kinetic.com.sg

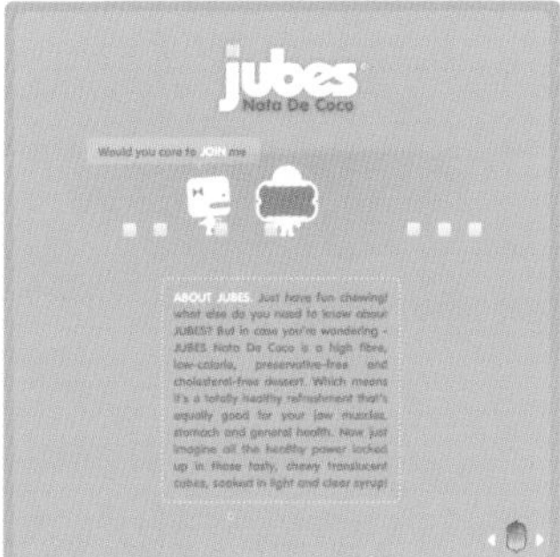
jubes
Nata De Coco
Would you care to JOIN me
ABOUT JUBES. Just have fun chewing! what else do you need to know about JUBES? But in case you're wondering - JUBES Nata De Coco is a high fibre, low-calorie, preservative-free and cholesterol-free dessert. Which means it's a totally healthy refreshment that's equally good for your jaw muscles, stomach and general health. Now just imagine all the healthy power locked up in those tasty, chewy translucent cubes, soaked in light and clear syrup!
© 2004 Wong Coco (s) Pte Ltd, all rights reserved

jubes
Nata De Coco
best served chilled
ENJOYING JUBES. JUBES is all about goodness and fun. This simple and thirst-quenching dessert can either be eaten on its own or mixed with cocktails, iced fruits, puddings and more to make a variety of different and new dessert combinations. Here are just a few examples of what you can do.
jubes
Recipe Flip Book
© 2004 Wong Coco (s) Pte Ltd, all rights reserved

Kinetic // www.kinetic.com.sg

KINETIC
WHAT'S UP
THIS IS KINETIC
MEET THE CREW
OUR WORK
VICTORIES
MAKE CONTACT
HOMEPAGE
LATEST NEWS
Bright Lights, Big City!
Back from Japan!
London Calling
Booked Again!

KINETIC
THE CREED
We fully intend to wipe bad advertising and design off the face of this planet and free its citizens from the mind-numbing properties of bad ads and ho-hum websites. Why can't websites be designed differently, with a bit of thought and a dash of flair? Why can't ads be thought-provoking, inventive and entertaining in equal measure?
ORIGINS
PHILOSOPHY
THE FUTURE
WHAT'S UP
MEET THE CREW
OUR WORK
VICTORIES
MAKE CONTACT
HOMEPAGE

Kitsch-Nitsch // www.kitsch-nitsch.com

KITSCH-NITSCH
BLOG
SHOP
CATEGORIES
SEARCH
ARCHIVE
LATEST TWITT
WE LISTEN
Trash the party IV season finale @ K4 Club
TAGS
CLUB
DECOR
SMETNJAK
FOLLOW US ON
FRIENDS
MUST HEAR
MUST SEE

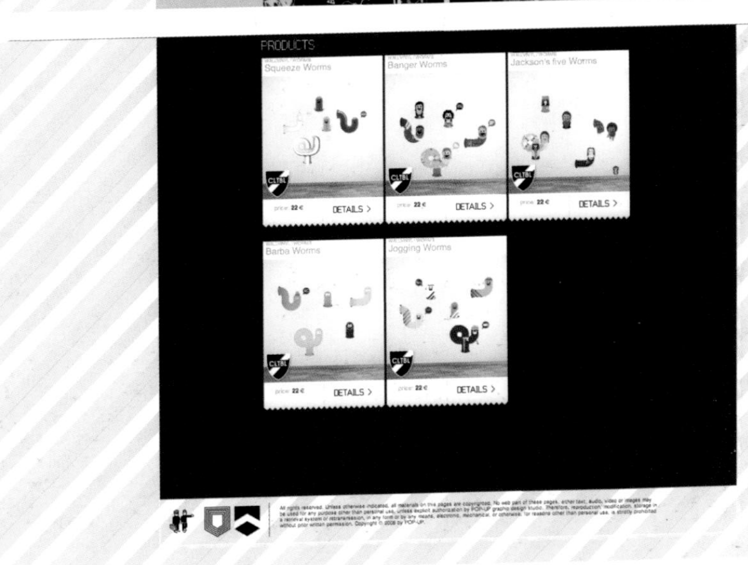
PRODUCTS
Squeeze Worms
Banger Worms
Jackson's five Worms
Barba Worms
Jogging Worms
DETAILS >

310k // www.310k.nl
Martin Media

choose your language
KRAUSE
News Video Pictures Shows Shoutbox Bio Discography Press Links Contact
Krause Discography
Krause - Radio Edit
1) Radio Edit
2) Radio Edit (Long version)
* Now available at:
12" EP Krausefiktion
Recent Pictures
Audio Player
Do It Again
Life of my Story
Cant Shut Me Up
Gigs
Metropool (CATFIGHT!)
Hengelo
Bibelot
Dordrecht
Poptrash @ Mezz
Breda
P60 (CATFIGHT!)
Amstelveen
Dijkpop
Andijk
Lilhill Festival
Luttenberg
Twitter

choose your language
KRAUSE
News Video Pictures Shows Shoutbox Bio Discography Press Links Contact
Contact
Management:
SONY MUSIC
Albert Grootbonk
PO Box 440
1200 AK Hilversum
The Netherlands
+31 (0)35 6 298 298
Bookings:
Alles Los Agency
René Beerens
G.J. van Heekstraat 370
7512 EM Enschede
The Netherlands
Contactform
Your Name *
Your Email *
Subject *
Message
Recent Pictures
Audio Player
Do It Again
Life of my Story
Cant Shut Me Up
Gigs
Metropool (CATFIGHT!)
Hengelo
Bibelot
Dordrecht
Poptrash @ Mezz
Breda
P60 (CATFIGHT!)
Amstelveen
Dijkpop
Andijk
Lilhill Festival
Luttenberg
Twitter

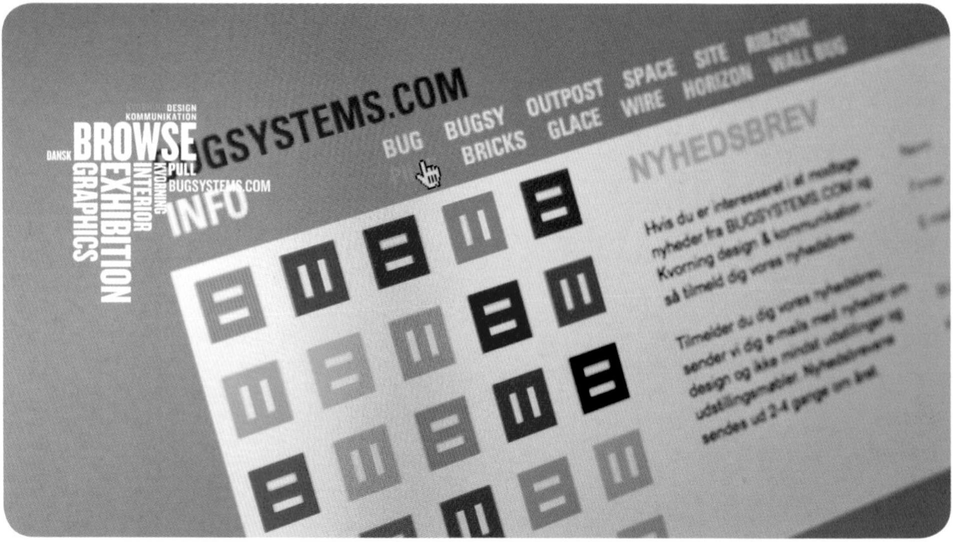

Kvorning Design & Communication // www.kvorning.com

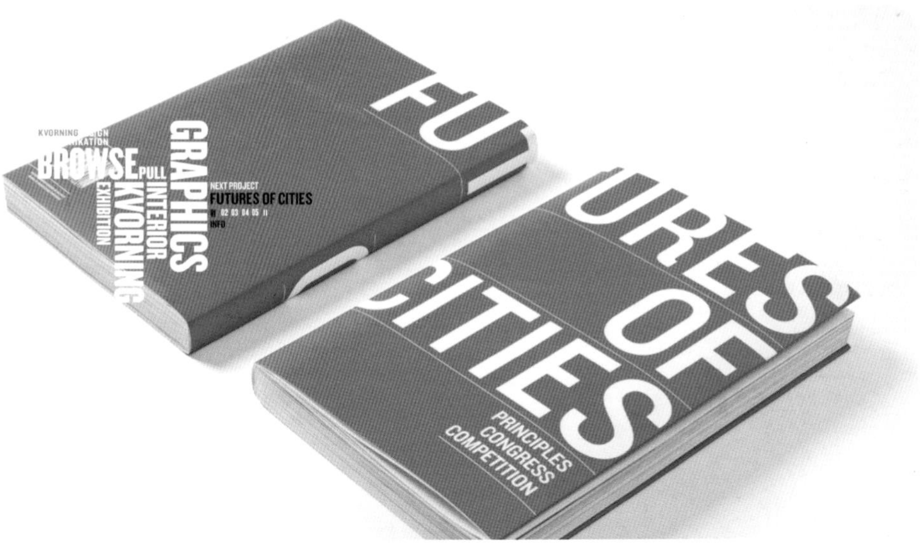

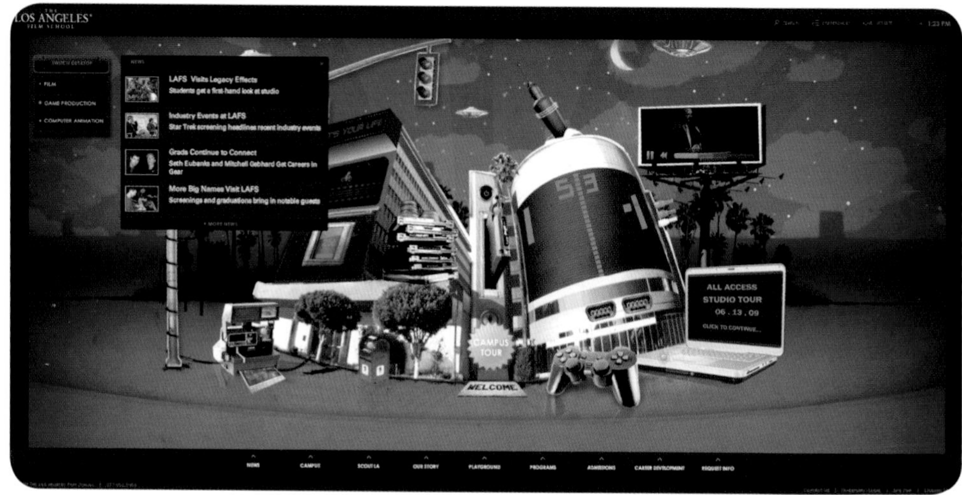

Will Weyer
Jeff Askew
Ryan Taylor/ Wiretree // www.wiretree.com

LOS ANGELES
FILM SCHOOL
CLOSE ALIEN ATTACK

LOS ANGELES
FILM SCHOOL
FILM
GAME PRODUCTION
COMPUTER ANIMATION
ROXY
VIPER ROOM
VENUES
The Roxy
BACK TO THE BOARD
CLOSE SCOUT LA

L'Ebauchoir, resto bistro // www.lebauchoir.com

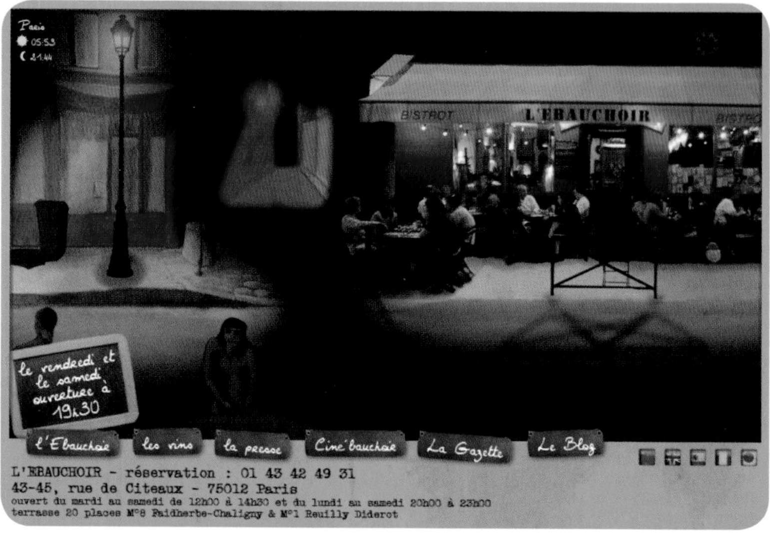

Vincent Maitray // www.electrofrog.com

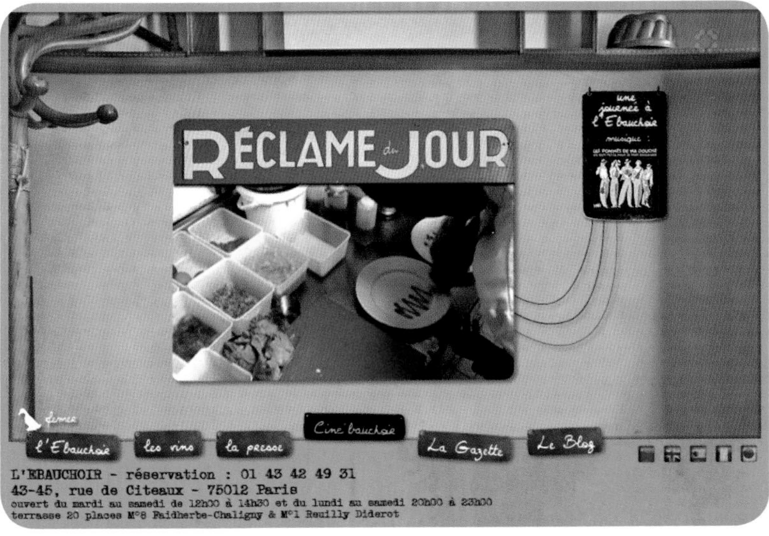
RÉCLAME du JOUR
une journée à l'Ebauchoir
musique :
fermer
l'Ebauchoir
les vins
la presse
Ciné'bauchoir
La Gazette
Le Blog
L'EBAUCHOIR - réservation : 01 43 42 49 31
43-45, rue de Citeaux - 75012 Paris
ouvert du mardi au samedi de 12h00 à 14h30 et du lundi au samedi 20h00 à 23h00
terrasse 20 places M°8 Faidherbe-Chaligny & M°1 Reuilly Diderot

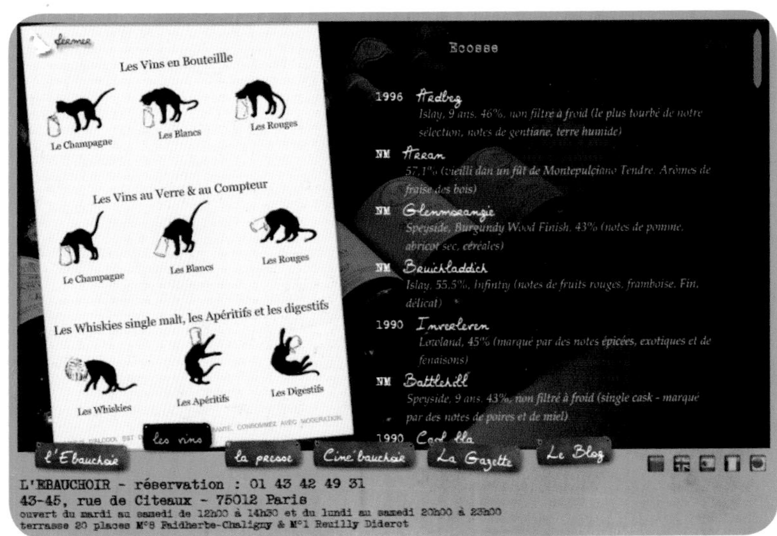
fermer
Les Vins en Bouteillle
Le Champagne
Les Blancs
Les Rouges
Les Vins au Verre & au Compteur
Le Champagne
Les Blancs
Les Rouges
Les Whiskies single malt, les Apéritifs et les digestifs
Les Whiskies
Les Apéritifs
Les Digestifs
Ecosse
1996 Ardbeg
Islay, 9 ans, 46%, non filtré à froid (le plus tourbé de notre sélection, notes de gentiane, terre humide)
NM Arran
57,1% (vieilli dan un fût de Montepulciano Tendre. Arômes de fraise des bois)
NM Glenmorangie
Speyside, Burgundy Wood Finish, 43% (notes de pomme, abricot sec, céréales)
NM Bruichladdich
Islay, 55,5%, Infintiy (notes de fruits rouges, framboise. Fin, délicat)
1990 Inverleven
Lowland, 45% (marqué par des notes épicées, exotiques et de fenaisons)
NM Battlehill
Speyside, 9 ans, 43%, non filtré à froid (single cask - marqué par des notes de poires et de miel)
1990 Caol Ila
l'Ebauchoir
les vins
la presse
Ciné'bauchoir
La Gazette
Le Blog
L'EBAUCHOIR - réservation : 01 43 42 49 31
43-45, rue de Citeaux - 75012 Paris
ouvert du mardi au samedi de 12h00 à 14h30 et du lundi au samedi 20h00 à 23h00
terrasse 20 places M°8 Faidherbe-Chaligny & M°1 Reuilly Diderot

Nessim Higson // iamalwayshungry.com
Destin Young // ourvice.com

Jocker / CREAKTIF ! // www.creaktif.com/jocker/
noMatter // www.nomatter.eu

LET'STAKE
PICTURES
2007-05
f9
1/500s
sigma 12-24mm
100 iso
jocker

Living Sasquatch // www.livingsasquatch.com

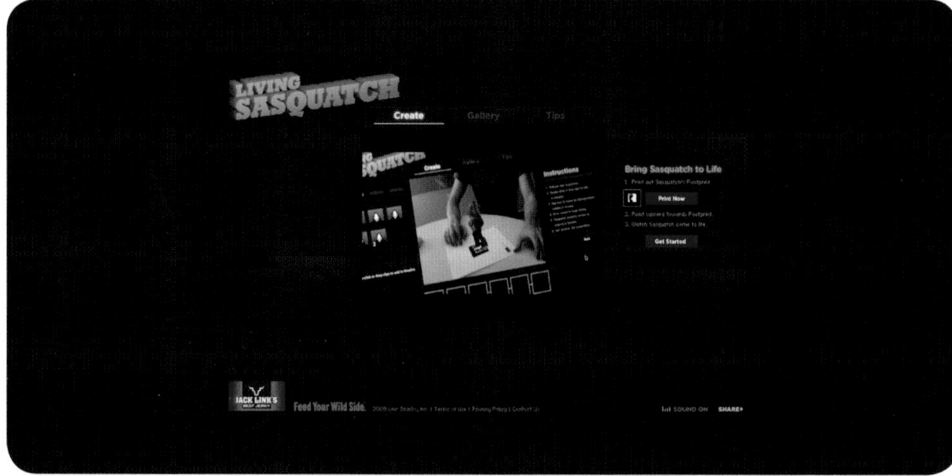

Jack Links // www.jacklinks.com
Carmichael Lynch Minneapolis // www.carmichaellynch.com
Boffswana // www.boffswana.com
Iloura // www.iloura.com.au

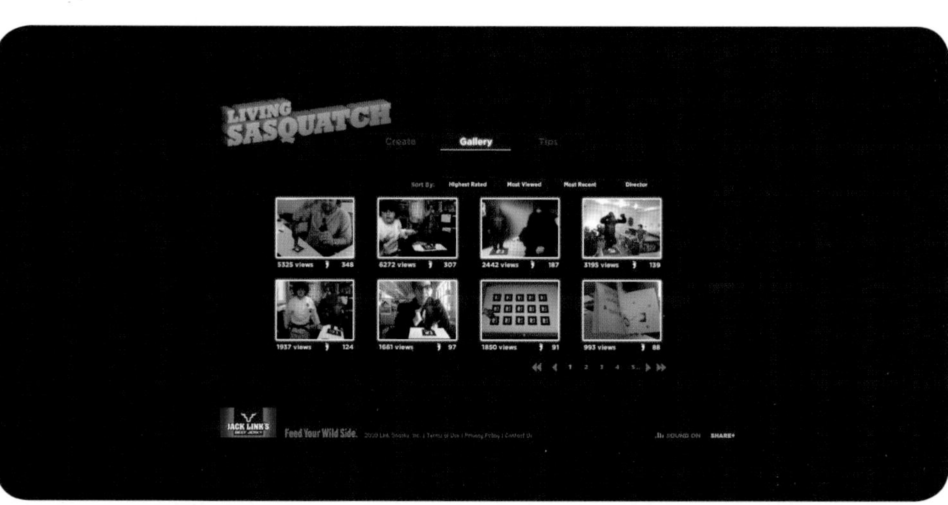
LIVING SASQUATCH
Create
Gallery
Tips
Sort By:
Highest Rated
Most Viewed
Most Recent
Director
5325 views 348
6272 views 307
2442 views 187
3195 views 139
1937 views 124
1661 views 97
1850 views 91
993 views 88
JACK LINK'S
Feed Your Wild Side.
SOUND ON
SHARE+

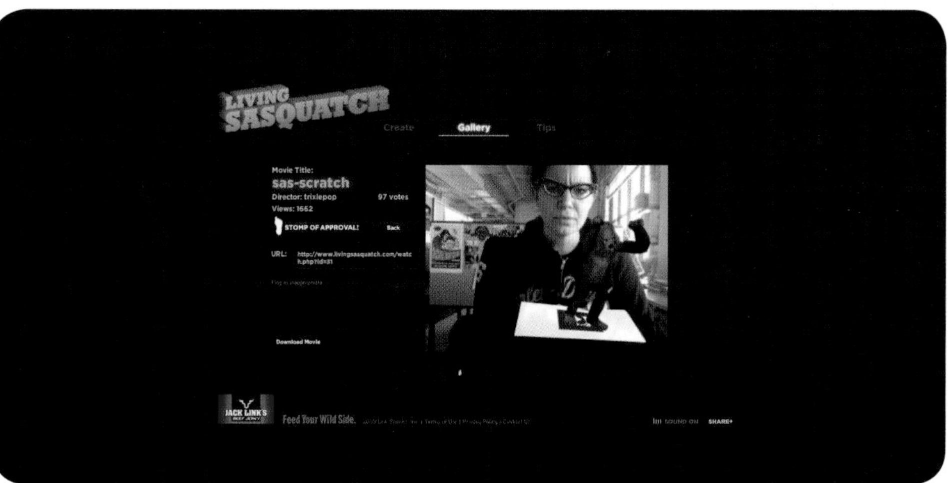
LIVING SASQUATCH
Create
Gallery
Tips
Movie Title:
sas-scratch
Director: trixiepop
97 votes
Views: 1662
STOMP OF APPROVAL!
Back
URL: http://www.livingsasquatch.com/watch.php?id=31
Download Movie
JACK LINK'S
Feed Your Wild Side.
SOUND ON
SHARE+

Nectar estudio // www.nectarestudio.com

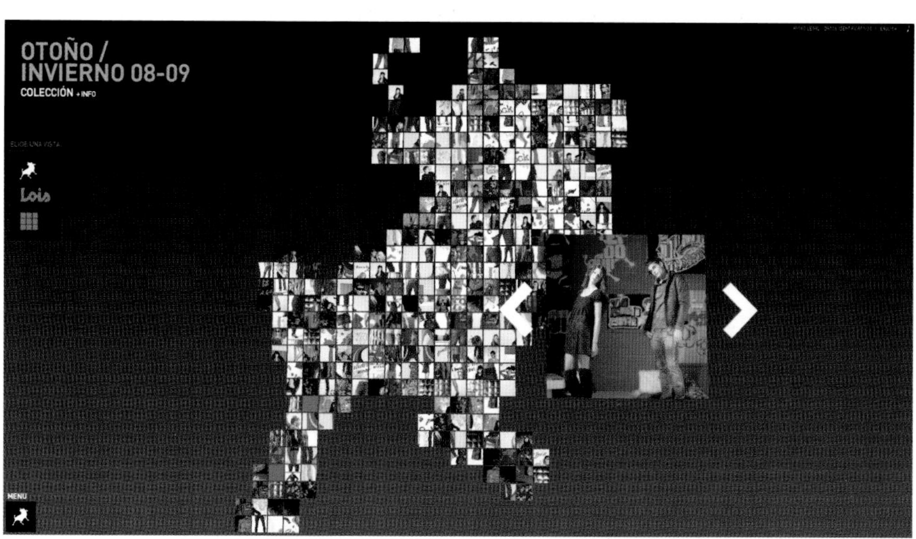

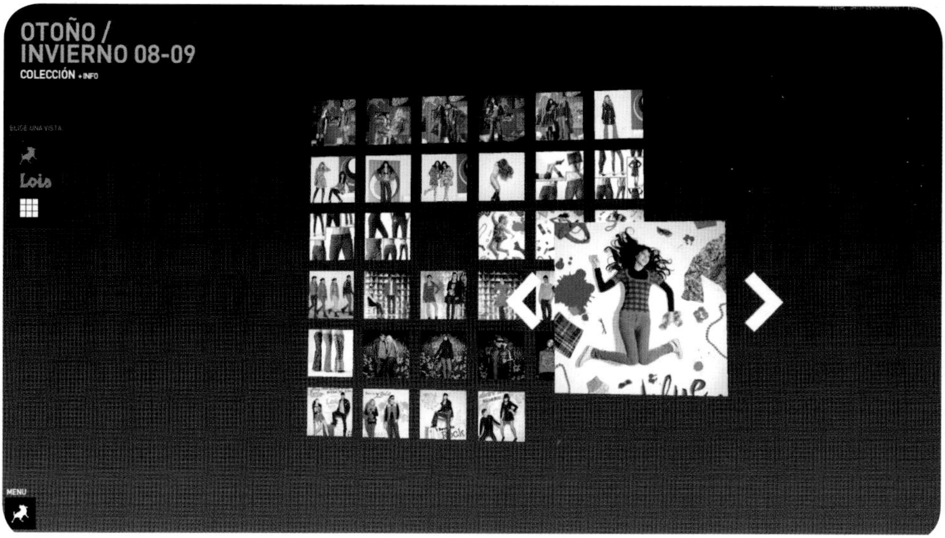

OTOÑO /
INVIERNO 08-09
COLECCIÓN +INFO

ELIGE UNA VISTA

Lois

MENU

Lois Spring-Summer `09 // www.loisjeans.com

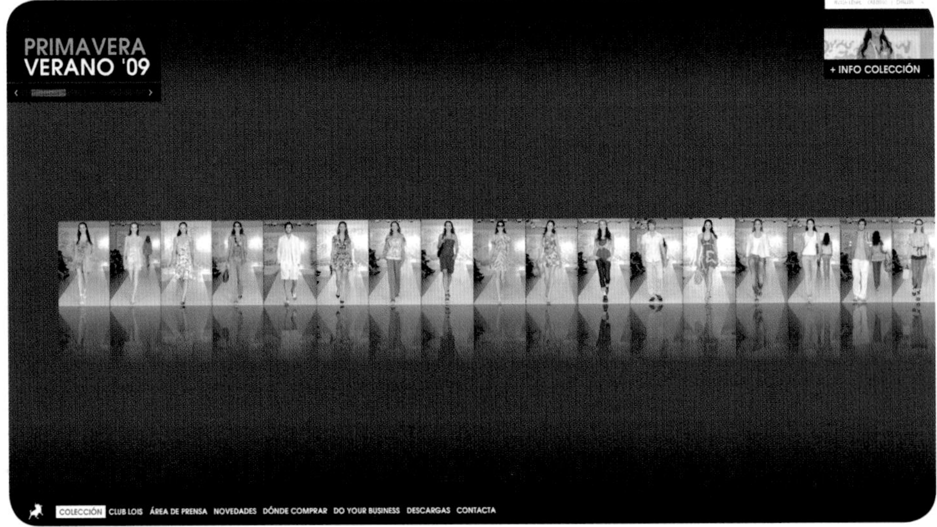

Nectar estudio // www.nectarestudio.com

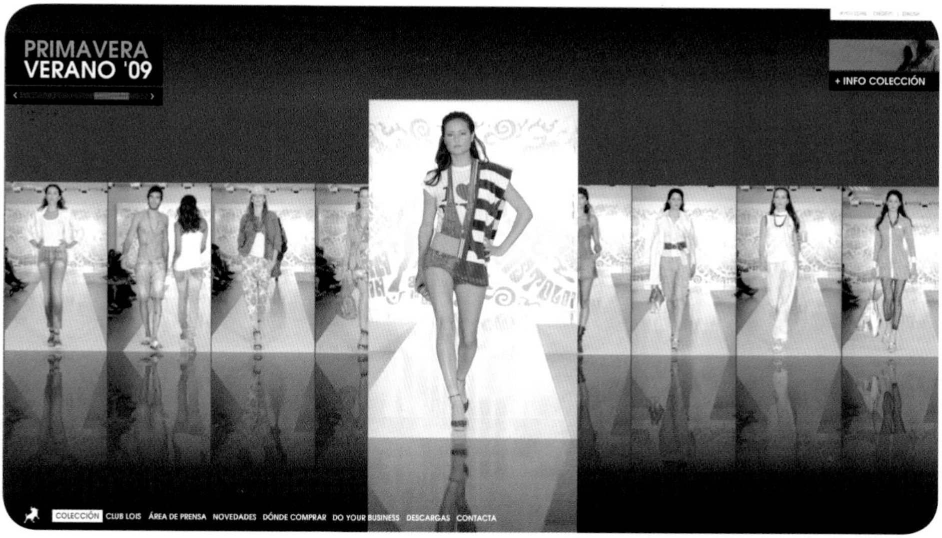

PRIMAVERA
VERANO '09

+ INFO COLECCIÓN

COLECCIÓN CLUB LOIS ÁREA DE PRENSA NOVEDADES DÓNDE COMPRAR DO YOUR BUSINESS DESCARGAS CONTACTA

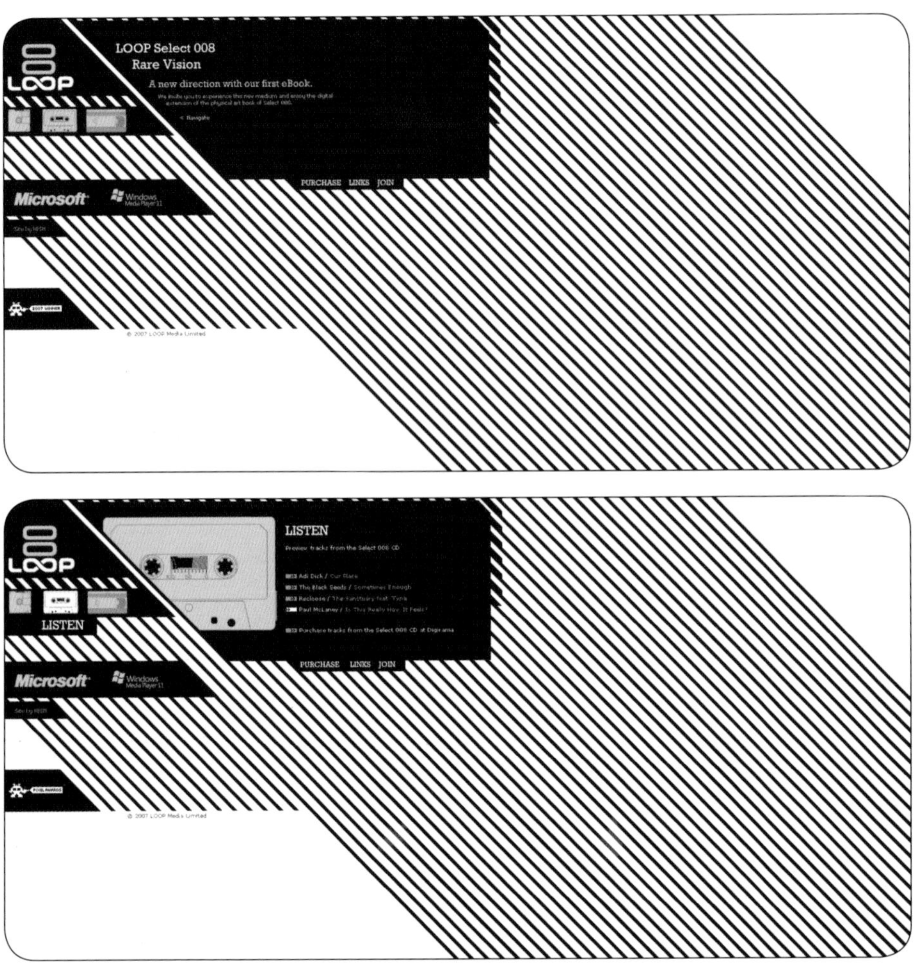

Resn // www.resn.co.nz

LOOP
WATCH
Microsoft
Windows Media Player 11
Artist Barnaby Weir & Clube Do Balanco
Track Doin It For Brasil
2007 WINNER
© 2007 LOOP Media Limited
LOOP
eBOOK
eBOOK
Download the Select 008 eBook
DOWNLOAD / WINDOWS (34MB)
DOWNLOAD / MAC (36MB)
PURCHASE LINKS JOIN
Microsoft
Windows Media Player 11
2007 WINNER
© 2007 LOOP Media Limited

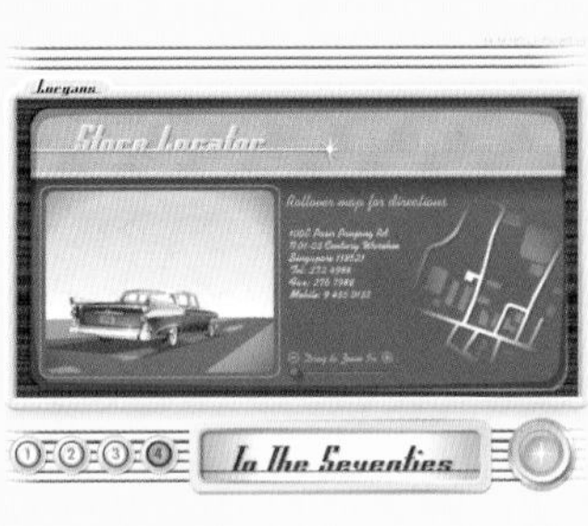

Kinetic // www.kinetic.com.sg

LORGAN'S
and
Drooled
Over Them ...
skip
OFF
©2001 Kinetic Interactive

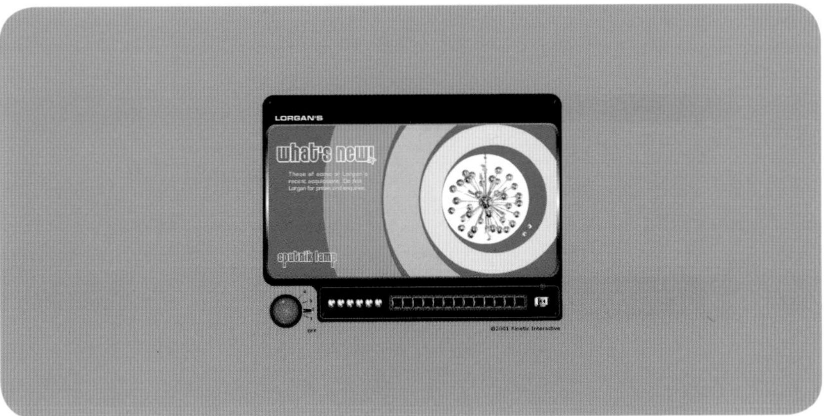
LORGAN'S
what's new!
sputnik lamp
OFF
©2001 Kinetic Interactive

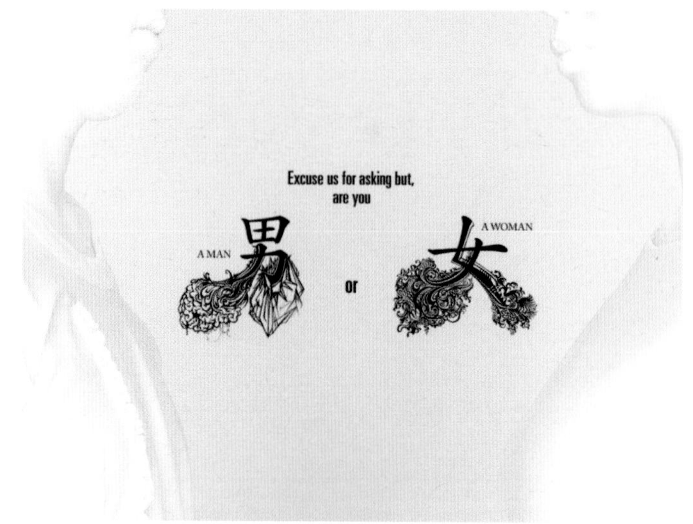

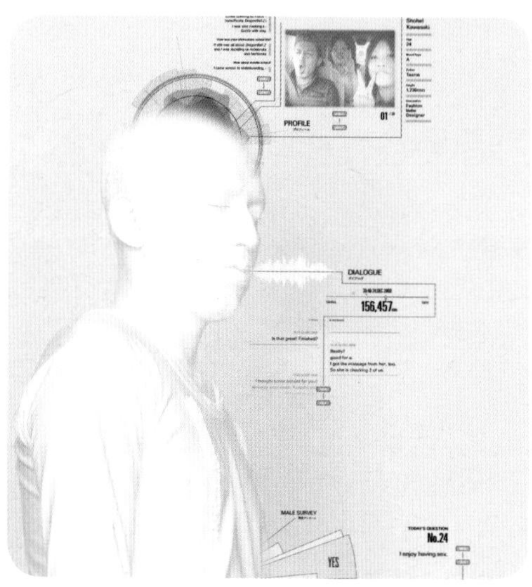

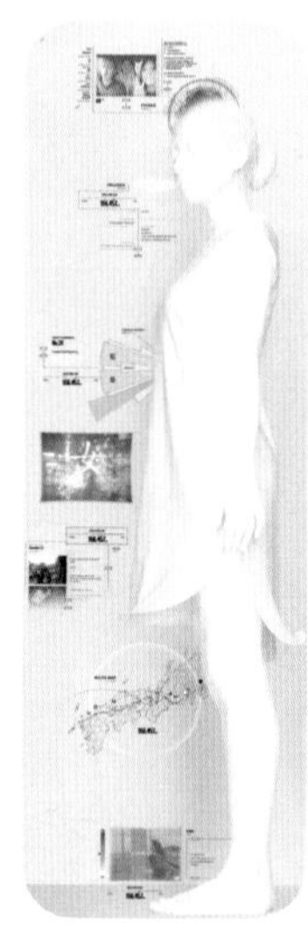

NON-GRID // www.non-grid.jp
Sagami Rubber Industries // www.sagami-gomu.co.jp/en/

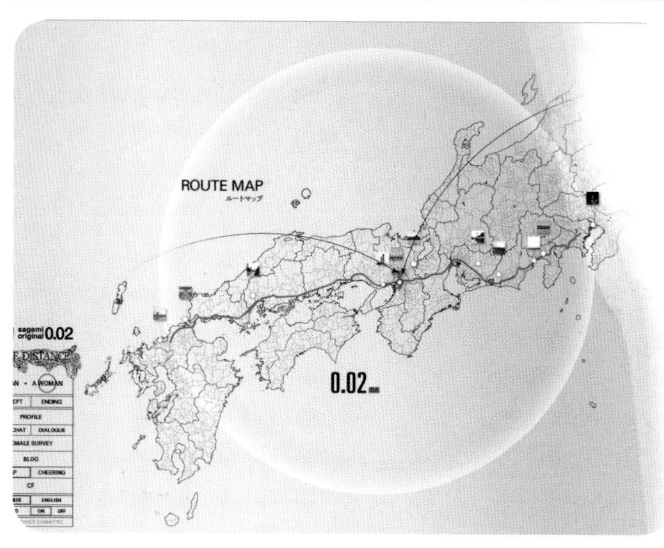
ROUTE MAP
ルートマップ
sagami original 0.02
0.02mm

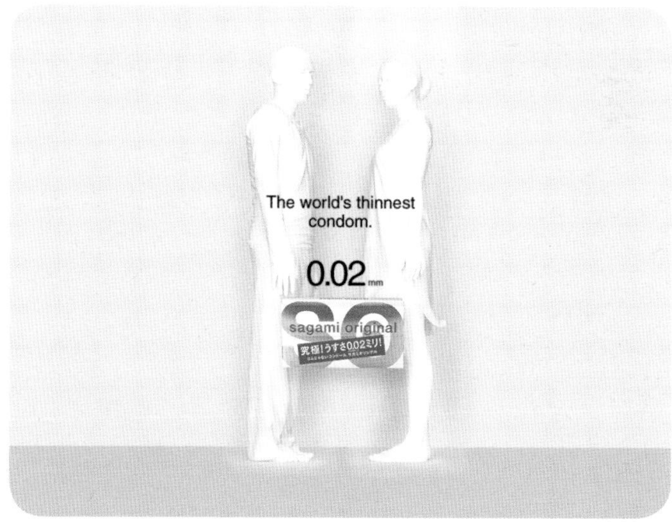
The world's thinnest condom.
0.02mm
sagami original
究極!うすさ0.02ミリ!

Love Song Project by Zexy.net // zexy.net/camp/lovesong/index.html

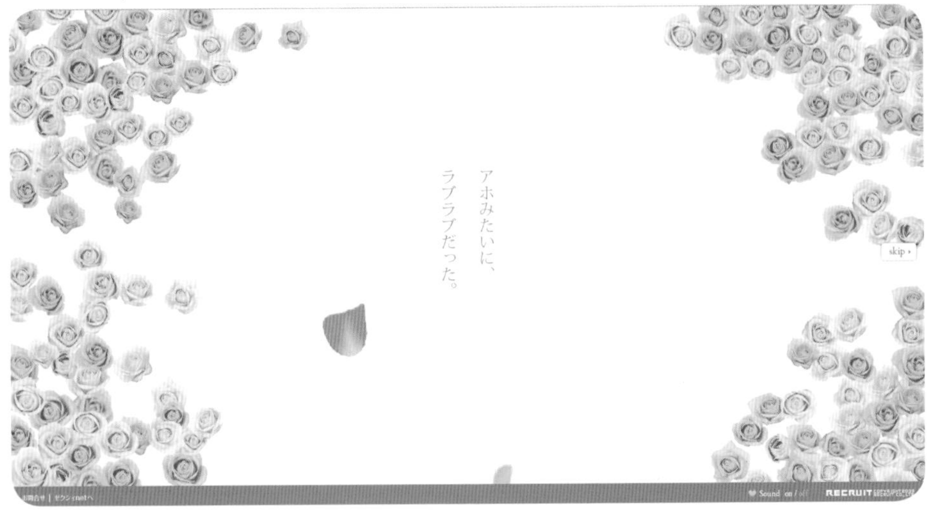

sonicjam Inc // www.sonicjam.co.jp
Recruit Co.,Ltd.
Hakuhodo Inc.
GT INC.

Love Song Project
みんなのラブソング
powered by ゼクシィnet
第5位
純恋歌
70人の思い出ラブソング
第3位
幸せをありがとう
84人の思い出ラブソング
第1位
キセキ
275人の思い出ラブソング
第2位
愛唄
116人の思い出ラブソング
第4位
永遠にともに
79人の思い出ラブソング
項目を指定して見る
全て
シチュエーション
性別
年齢
住まい
血液型
全項目クリア
ラブソングを投稿する
Menu トップ アンケート ブログパーツ ラブソングプロジェクトとは？
お問合せ ゼクシィnetへ
Sound on / off
RECRUIT
ラブソングプロジェクトとは？
ラブソングを投稿♪
ランキングに反映♪
ラブソングを投稿する
ランキングを見る
デジタルプレゼントについて
あなたのBlogに
バラを咲かせる♪
幸せのブログパーツ
ブログパーツのサンプルを見る
ブログパーツをダウンロードする
スクリーンセーバー♪

A

← BACKSPACE

AXE, ATIVAÇÃO, ATENDIMENTO, ANIMAÇÃO, ABÓBORAS.

CLIQUE NA TELA
OU DIGITE UMA LETRA

B
C

Rodolfo Araki
David Galasse
Persio Guerreiro
Marcelle Naguib
Rodrigo Teco
Cauê Teixeira // www.grafikonstruct.com.br

OSCAR WILDE.

O MISTÉRIO DO AMOR É MAIOR QUE O MISTÉRIO DA MORTE.

→
←

i

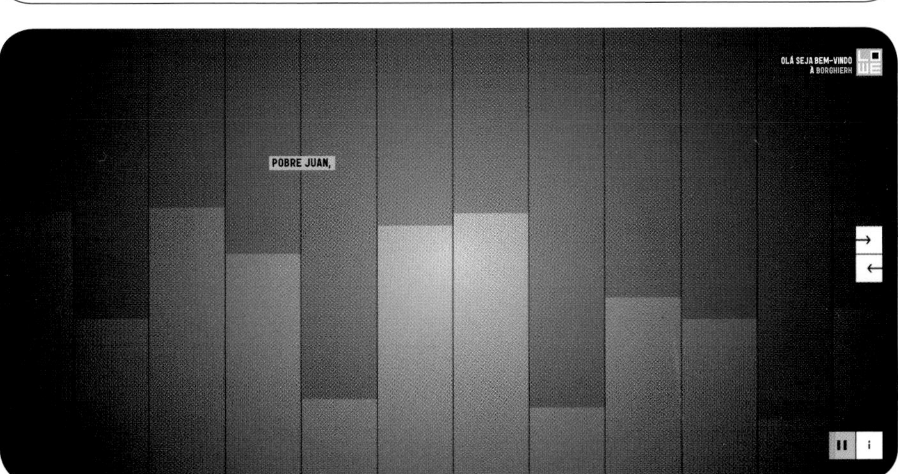

Lumina Live! // www.luminalive.sg

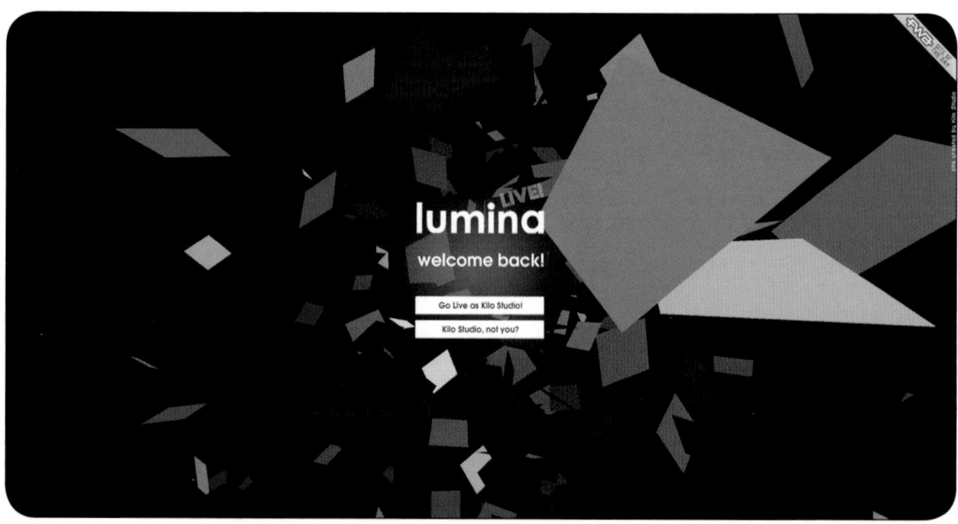

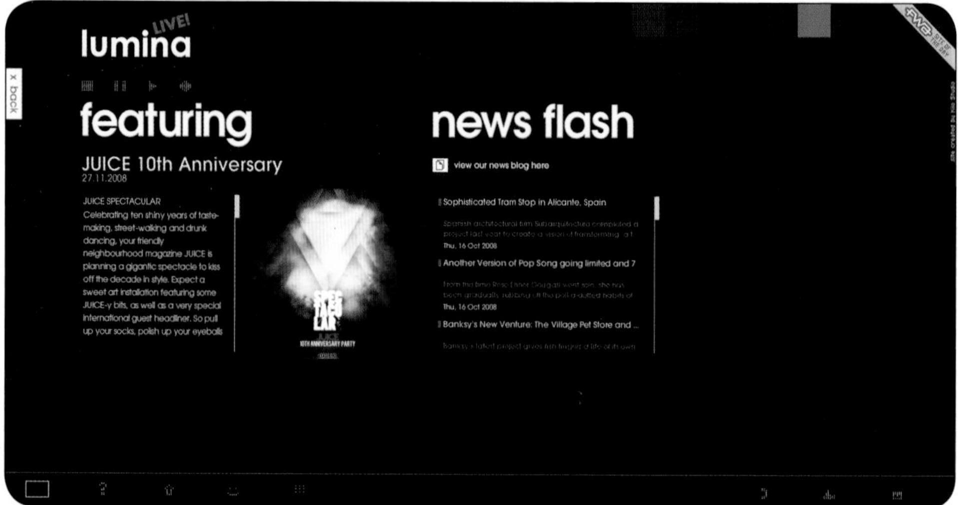

Kilo Studio // www.kilostudio.net

LIVE!
lumina

LIVE!
lumina

x back

welike!

art &
design

Select a brush shape from below and click on anywhere on the canvas to start drawing. You can change your brush whenever you like. Remember to save your artwork to our gallery when you're done.

varieties of angles

delete save

back

Lyndon Wade Photography // www.lyndonwade.com

LYNDONWADE
LYNDONWADE
LYNDONWADE

Hello Monday // www.hellomonday.com

LYNDON WADE
PORTFOLIO ABOUT NEWS NEWSLETTER CONTACT
THE BIRDS THE LYNDON SHOW ROOM 107 GALLERY 1 GALLERY2 GALLERY 3 THIRTEEN
CLICK FOR PREVIOUS THUMBS
CLICK FOR MORE THUMBS
GALLERY 3

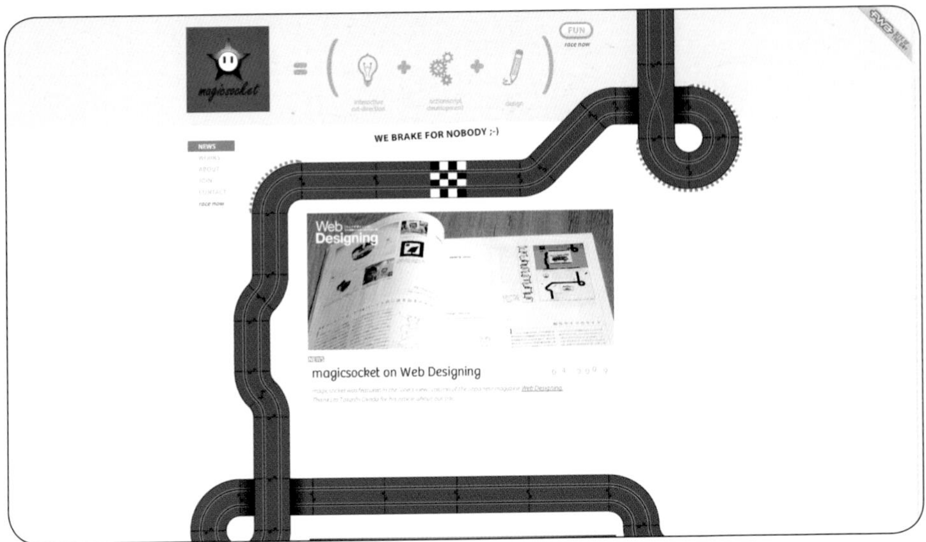

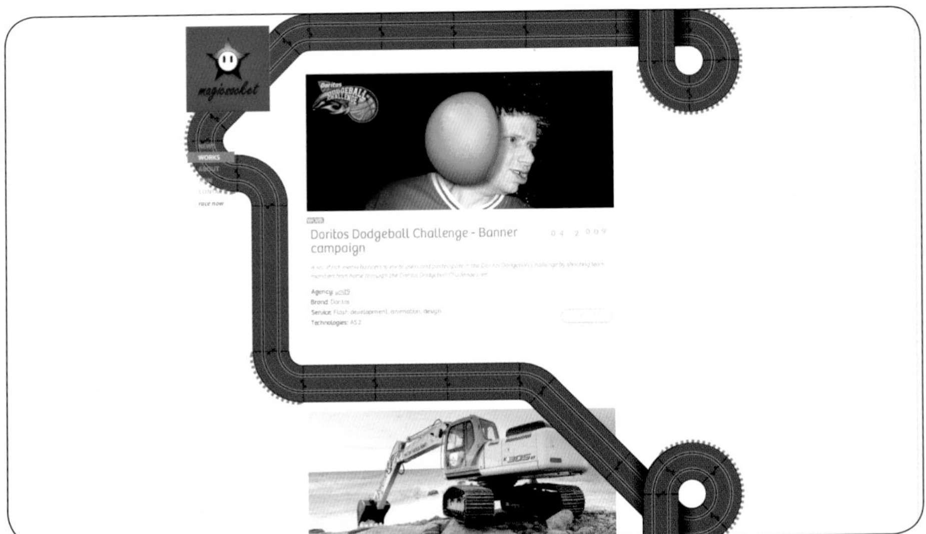

magicsocket // www.magicsocket.com

magicsocket

WORKS

race now

Extreme Beauty in Vogue

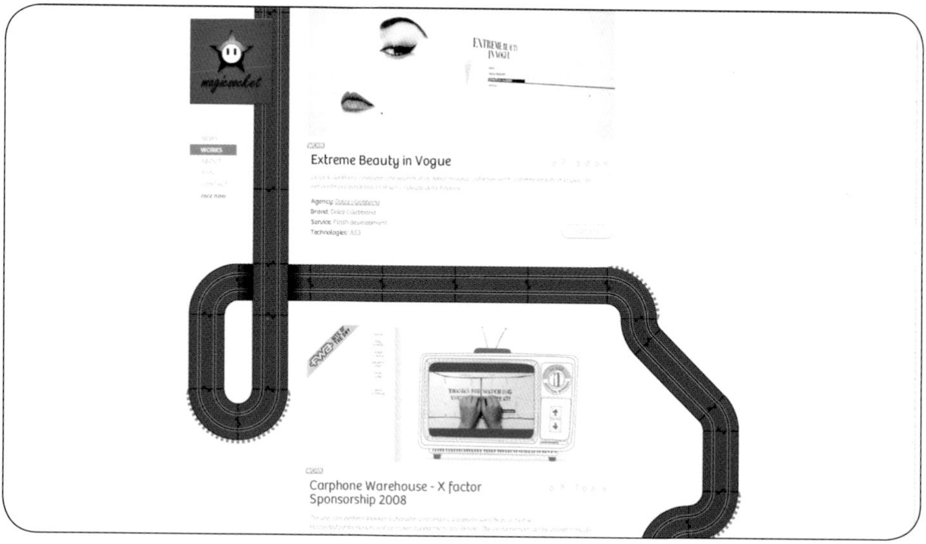

Agency:
Brand:
Service:
Technologies:

Carphone Warehouse - X factor Sponsorship 2008

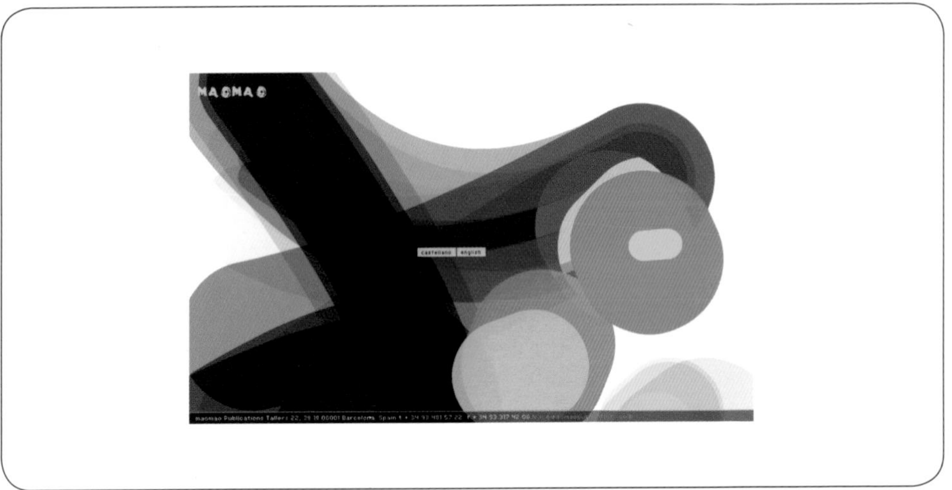

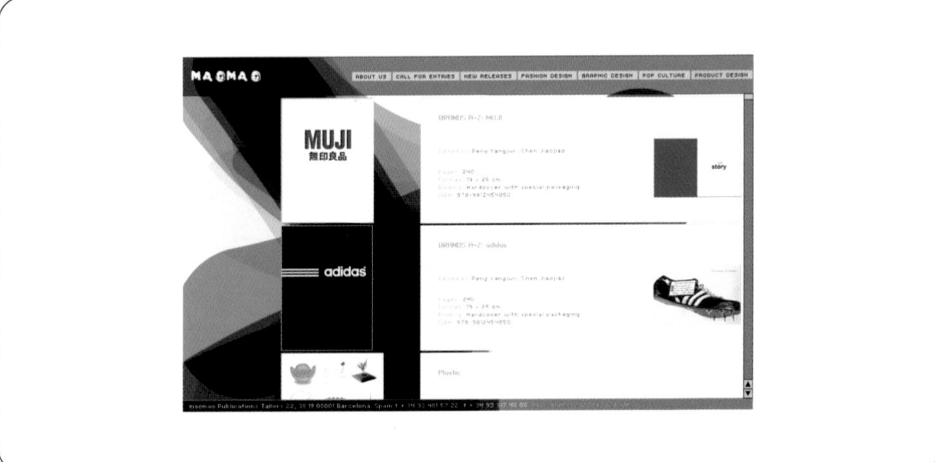

Maxwell Young // www.fizzypopfactory.com

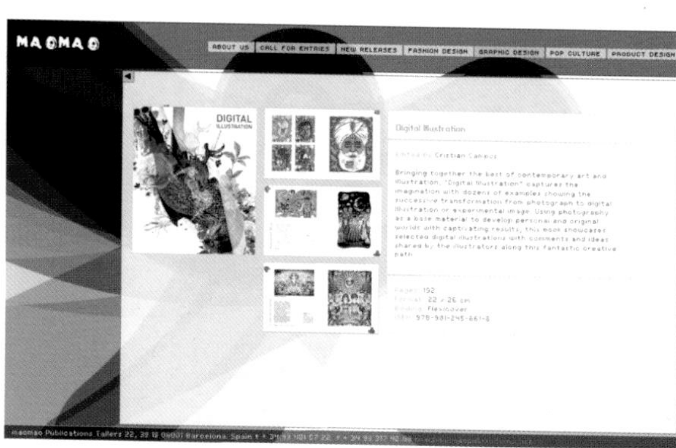
MAOMAO
ABOUT US
CALL FOR ENTRIES
NEW RELEASES
FASHION DESIGN
GRAPHIC DESIGN
POP CULTURE
PRODUCT DESIGN
DIGITAL
ILLUSTRATION
Digital Illustration
Cristian Campos
152
22 x 26 cm
Flexicover

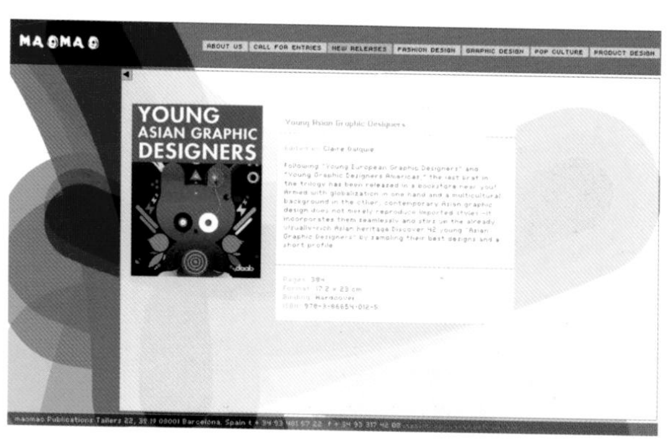
MAOMAO
ABOUT US
CALL FOR ENTRIES
NEW RELEASES
FASHION DESIGN
GRAPHIC DESIGN
POP CULTURE
PRODUCT DESIGN
YOUNG
ASIAN GRAPHIC
DESIGNERS
Young Asian Graphic Designers
Claire Dalquie
384
Hardcover
978-3-86654-012-5

Maria Filó Summer 2009 Website // www.mariafilo.com.br

6D // www.6d.com.br

Maria Filó
12.05.2009 - Revista Conexão
Maria Filó

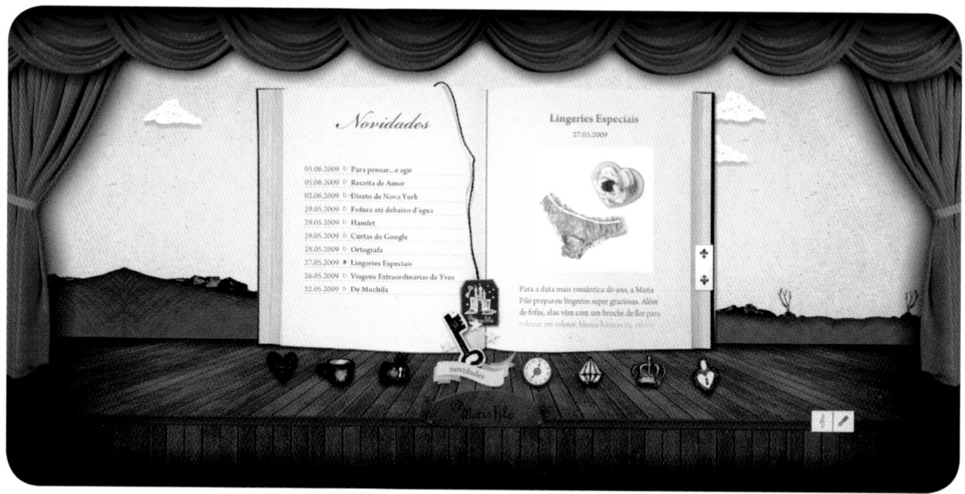
Novidades
05.06.2009 Para pensar...e agir
05.06.2009 Receita de Amor
02.06.2009 Direto de Nova York
29.05.2009 Fofura até debaixo d'água
29.05.2009 Hamlet
29.05.2009 Curtas do Google
28.05.2009 Ortografa
27.05.2009 Lingeries Especiais
26.05.2009 Viagens Extraordinárias de Yves
22.05.2009 De Mochila
Lingeries Especiais
27.05.2009
Para a data mais romântica do ano, a Maria Filó preparou lingeries super graciosas. Além de fofas, elas vêm com um broche de flor para
novidades
Maria Filó

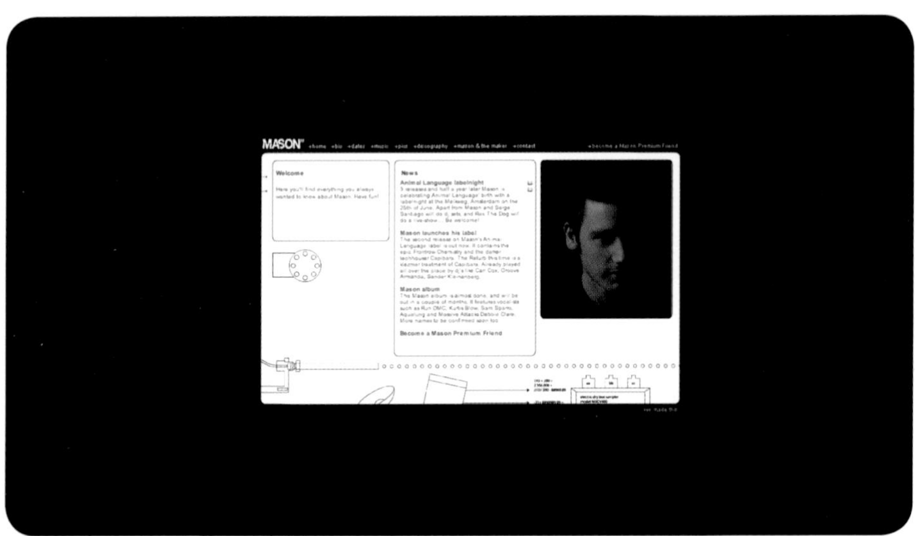

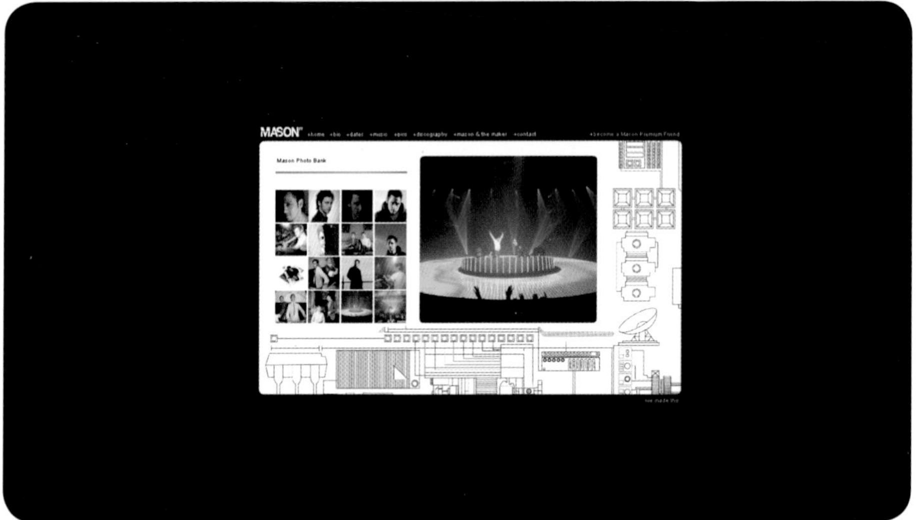

310k // www.310k.nl

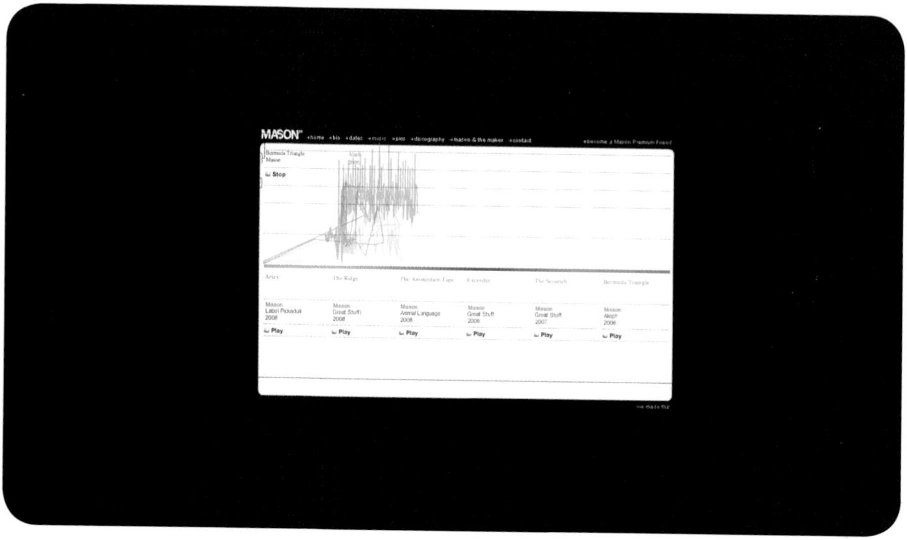

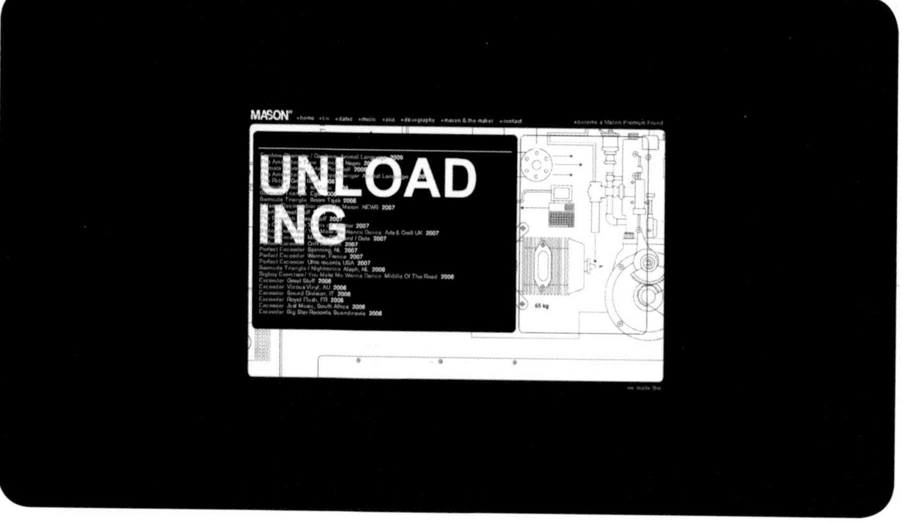
MASON
UNLOAD
ING
65 kg

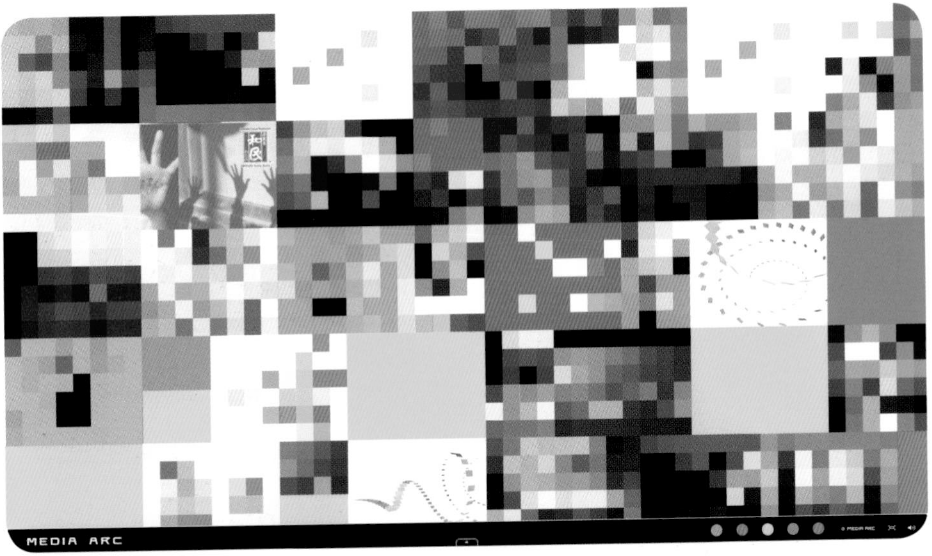

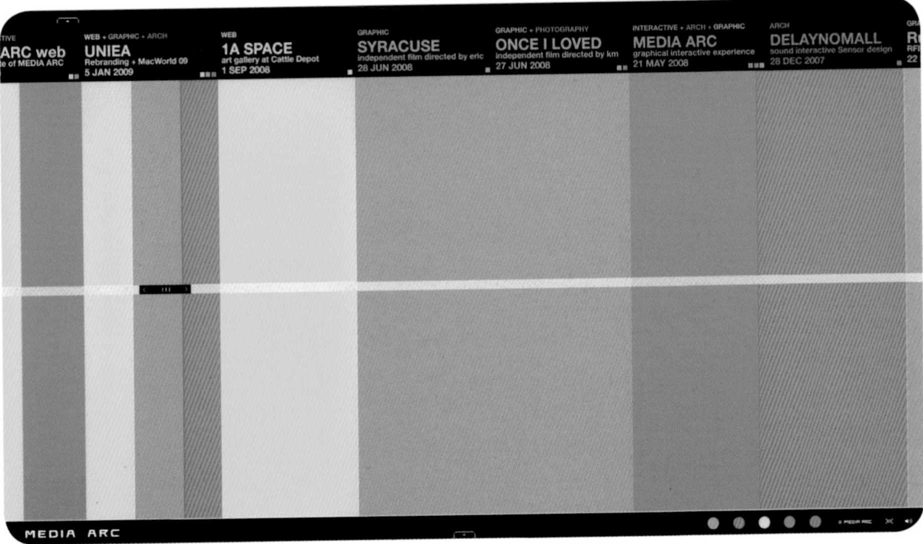

nacoki // www.the-media-arc.com

GRAPHIC + PHOTOGRAPHY

ONCE I LOVED

independent film directed by km

27 JUN 2008

為繼承上一齣"再見"的風格，香港味道比較重的感覺，修改了相似的字款，用上色調對比比較強烈的相片。而另一款是比較靜態的版本，導演亦認為比較切合整体的感覺。本片為鄭啓明先生之畢業作品，由蔣祖曼、金燕玲主演，拍攝於牛頭角下邨。
※ 再見為2007鮮浪潮得獎作品

CREDIT

流年似水

ONCE I LOVED

導演 鄭啟明

蔣祖曼 金燕玲 李健

曝光率 設計力 成熟度 人力 難易度

MEDIA ARC

INTERACTIVE

PIXEL DANCE

little VJ program with processing

4 MAR 2007

平面影象立體化 是整個概念的核心。由於通過 攝錄機拍下的影象 基本上是一張張沒有空間數據的相片，所以把影象立體化的 切入點在於每一格相片的 pixel。以 pixel 的光暗層作為 分開主體跟背景的方法。
因為以Real time Rendering的模式進行，所以每一次也有不同的效果。

CREDIT

曝光率 設計力 成熟度 人力 難易度

MEDIA ARC

Metropolis Media // www.metropolis-media.com.pl

SUPERSIZE
1/6
Tyskie Urodziny
FLY-TOX

DARK SIDE
WHERE THE WEST BEGINS
PARK
METROPOLIS

Unique Atmosphere // weare.in.ua

move cursor over objects to see them react
FHM
FHM was the FIRST men's magazine in Ukraine. It took some heavy lunch skipping to convince advertising clients that Ukrainian men are ready for glossy media
Signed deals
7years in publishing
2001 2002-04 2004-05 2005-07 2007-08

move cursor over objects to see them react
FHM
SURF
TV
DIPLOMA
Signed deals
Signed deals
7years in publishing
2001 2002-04 2004-05 2005-07 2007-08

Miki Mottes // www.mikimottes.com

MIKI MOTTES
ANIMATOR & ILLUSTRATOR
SOUND EFFECTS
ANIMATION
STATIC
OTHER
Supersonic Ads / Supersonic Ads
MORE INFO
OFFERS
1 Your user
2 completes offers
3
...and you get $$$
and gets points!

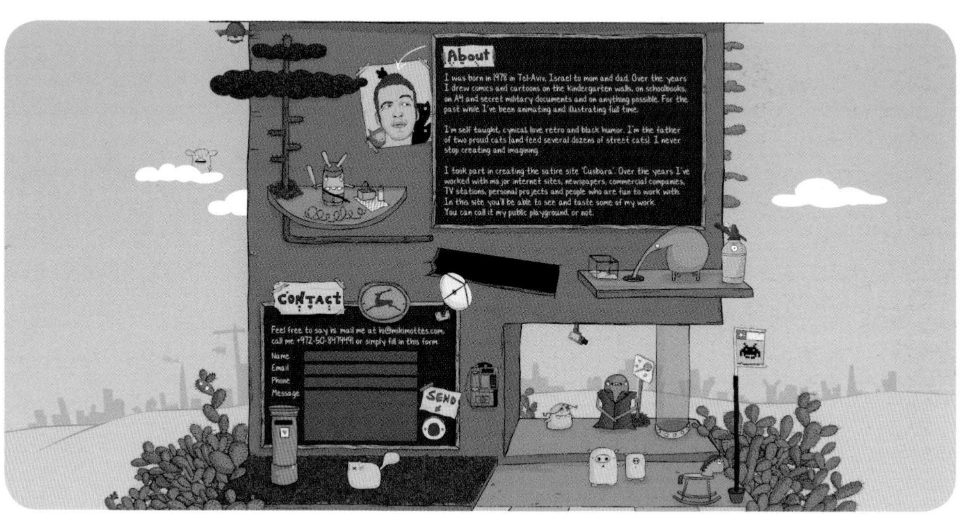
About
I was born in 1978 in Tel-Aviv, Israel to mom and dad. Over the years I drew comics and cartoons on the kindergarten walls, on schoolbooks, on A4 and secret military documents and on anything possible. For the past while I've been animating and illustrating full time.
I'm self taught, cynical, love retro and black humor. I'm the father of two proud cats (and feed several dozens of street cats). I never stop creating and imagining.
I took part in creating the satire site 'Cusbara'. Over the years I've worked with major internet sites, newspapers, commercial companies, TV stations, personal projects and people who are fun to work with. In this site you'll be able to see and taste some of my work.
You can call it my public playground, or not.
CONTACT
Feel free to say hi: mail me at hi@mikimottes.com, call me +972-50-8479491 or simply fill in this form.
Name
Email
Phone
Message
SEND

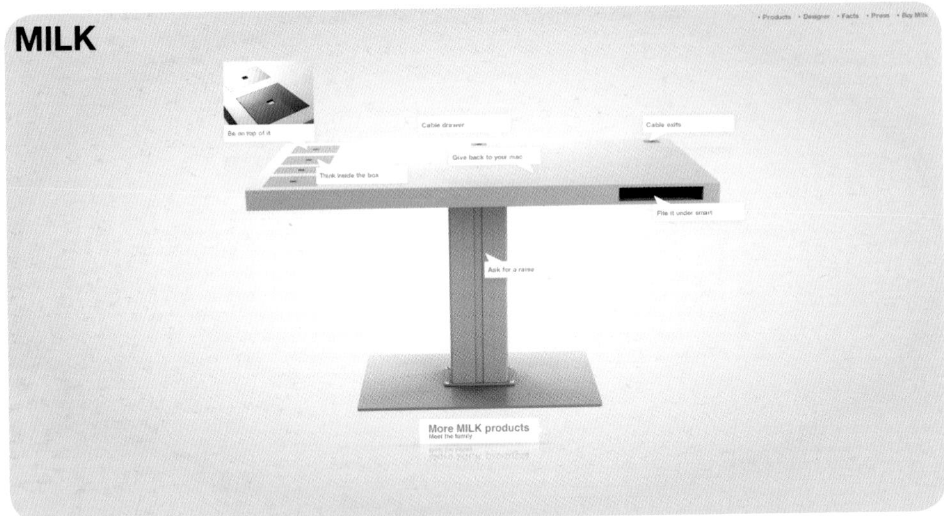

Pelle Martin/ In2media // in2media.com

MILK
• Back to overview • Products • Designer • Facts • Press • Buy Milk
START WITH A THINK TANK
Yes, we love the fish too. But did you know it's also good for you? A few minutes spent staring into your desktop tank reduces stress for a meditative retreat that's guru-free.
01 TANK
02 PENHOLDER
03 BIN
04 THE BOX

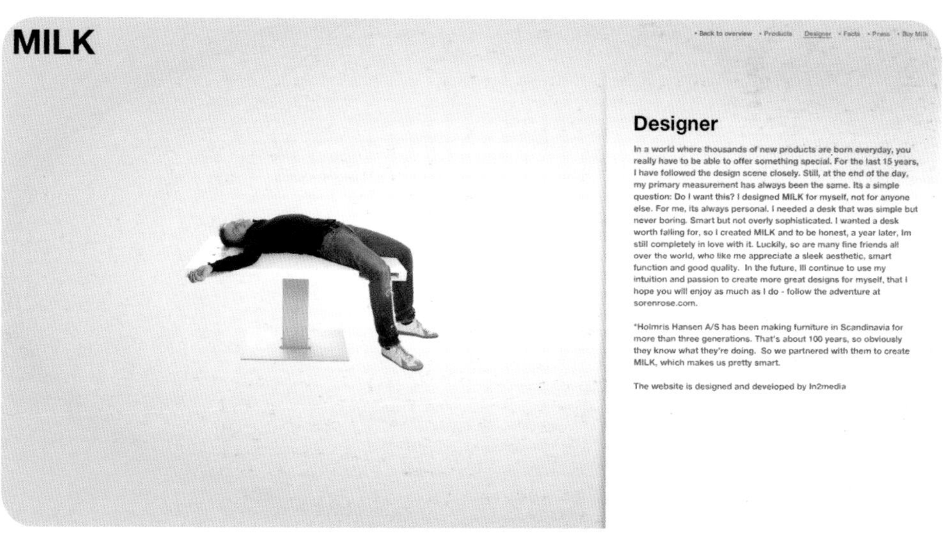
MILK
• Back to overview • Products Designer • Facts • Press • Buy Milk
Designer
In a world where thousands of new products are born everyday, you really have to be able to offer something special. For the last 15 years, I have followed the design scene closely. Still, at the end of the day, my primary measurement has always been the same. Its a simple question: Do I want this? I designed MILK for myself, not for anyone else. For me, its always personal. I needed a desk that was simple but never boring. Smart but not overly sophisticated. I wanted a desk worth falling for, so I created MILK and to be honest, a year later, Im still completely in love with it. Luckily, so are many fine friends all over the world, who like me appreciate a sleek aesthetic, smart function and good quality. In the future, Ill continue to use my intuition and passion to create more great designs for myself, that I hope you will enjoy as much as I do - follow the adventure at sorenrose.com.
*Holmris Hansen A/S has been making furniture in Scandinavia for more than three generations. That's about 100 years, so obviously they know what they're doing. So we partnered with them to create MILK, which makes us pretty smart.
The website is designed and developed by In2media

Minuit // www.minuit.co.nz

Resn // www.resn.co.nz

NEWS
GUESTBOOK
GIG GUIDE
GALLERY
RELEASES
GUEST BOOK
This is an AMAZING website, and oh so adorable. :D Good music too!
SUBMIT YOUR OWN!
MYSPACE | MERCHANDISE | CONTACT | BUY MUSIC
NEWS AND GIGS | PASS THIS ON!

NEWS
GUESTBOOK
GIG GUIDE
GALLERY
RELEASES
A MERMAID AT MY TABLE
MYSPACE | MERCHANDISE | CONTACT | BUY MUSIC
NEWS AND GIGS | PASS THIS ON!

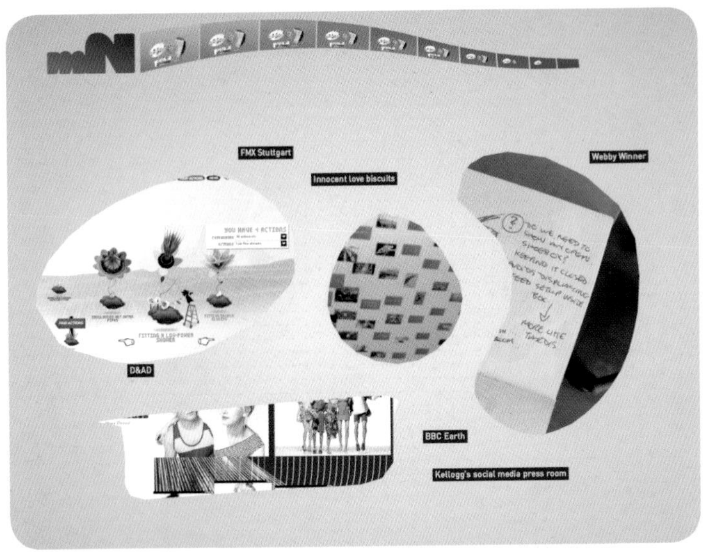

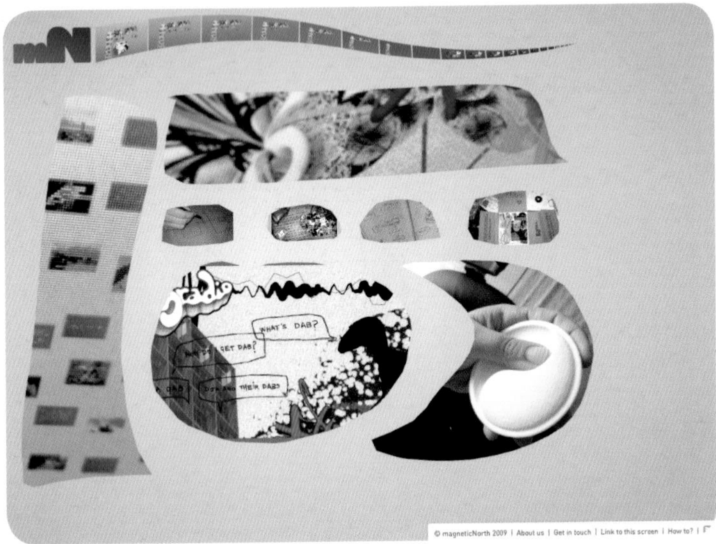

magneticNorth [mN] // mnatwork.com

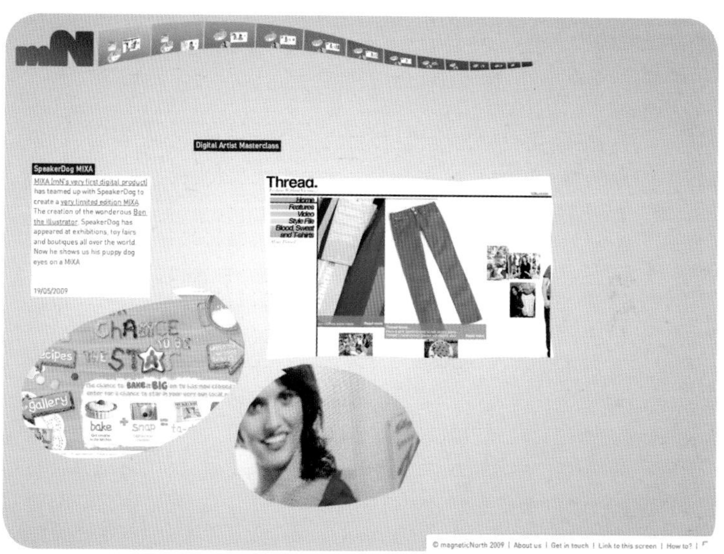
mN
Digital Artist Masterclass
SpeakerDog MIXA
MIXA [mN's very first digital product] has teamed up with SpeakerDog to create a very limited edition MIXA. The creation of the wonderous Ben the Illustrator, SpeakerDog has appeared at exhibitions, toy fairs and boutiques all over the world. Now he shows us his puppy dog eyes on a MIXA
19/05/2009
Thread.
Home
Features
Video
Style File
Blood, Sweat and T-shirts
gallery
bake
snap
© magneticNorth 2009 | About us | Get in touch | Link to this screen | How to? |

mN
WHAT'S DA
© magneticNorth 2009 | About us | Get in touch | Link to this screen | How to? |

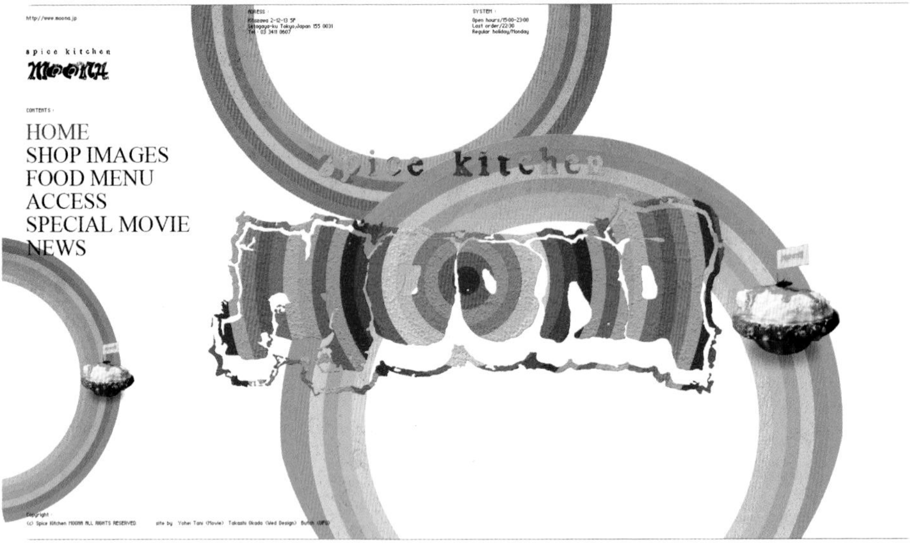

Moona // www.moona.jp

http://www.moona.jp

ADRESS :
Kitazawa 2-12-13 5F
Setagaya-ku Tokyo,Japan 155 0031
Tel : 03 3411 0607

SYSTEM :
Open hours/15:00-23:00
Last order/22:30
Regular holiday/Monday

spice kitchen

CONTENTS :

HOME
SHOP IMAGES
FOOD MENU
ACCESS
SPECIAL MOVIE
NEWS

spice kitchen

Copyright :
(c) Spice Kitchen MOONA ALL RIGHTS RESERVED   site by Yohei Tani (Movie) Takashi Okada (Web Design) Butch (GFX)

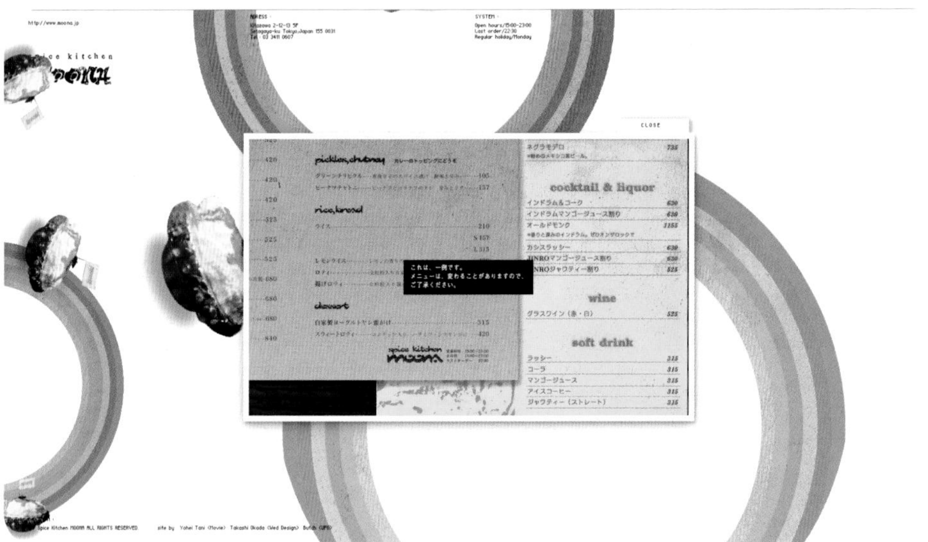

Takashi Okada // www.okadada.com

http://www.moona.jp

ADRESS :
Kitazawa 2-12-13 5F
Setagaya-ku Tokyo,Japan 155 0031
Tel : 03 3411 0607

SYSTEM :
Open hours/15:00-23:00
Last order/22:30
Regular holiday/Monday

spice kitchen
MOONA

CLOSE

Spice Kitchen MOONA（ムーナ）は、下北沢の南インド系のカレー屋さんです。
メインメニューは、日替わり限定！本日のカレーです。
また、カレーに留まらず、様々なスパイシーな小皿料理も作っています。
お酒もご用意しておりますので、お気軽にお越し下さい。

01 /10

Copyright :
(c) Spice Kitchen MOONA ALL RIGHTS RESERVED
site by Yohei Tani (Movie) Takashi Okada (Wed Design) Butch (UFO)

http://www.moona.jp

ADRESS :
Kitazawa 2-12-13 5F
Setagaya-ku Tokyo,Japan 155 0031
Tel : 03 3411 0607

SYSTEM :
Open hours/15:00-23:00
Last order/22:30
Regular holiday/Monday

spice kitchen
MOONA

5F spice kitchen MOONA

CLOSE

Copyright :
(c) Spice Kitchen MOONA ALL RIGHTS RESERVED
site by Yohei Tani (Movie) Takashi Okada (Wed Design) Butch (UFO)

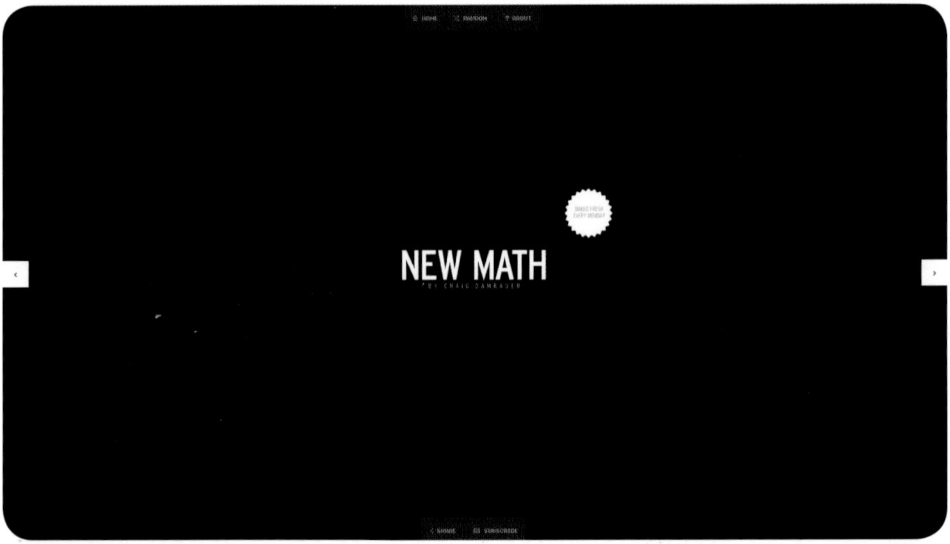

More New Math // www.morenewmath.com

NEW MATH

David Mikula // www.davidmikula.com

PERSEVERANCE = IF AT FIRST YOU DON'T SUCCEED + REPETITION

MORENEWMATH.COM

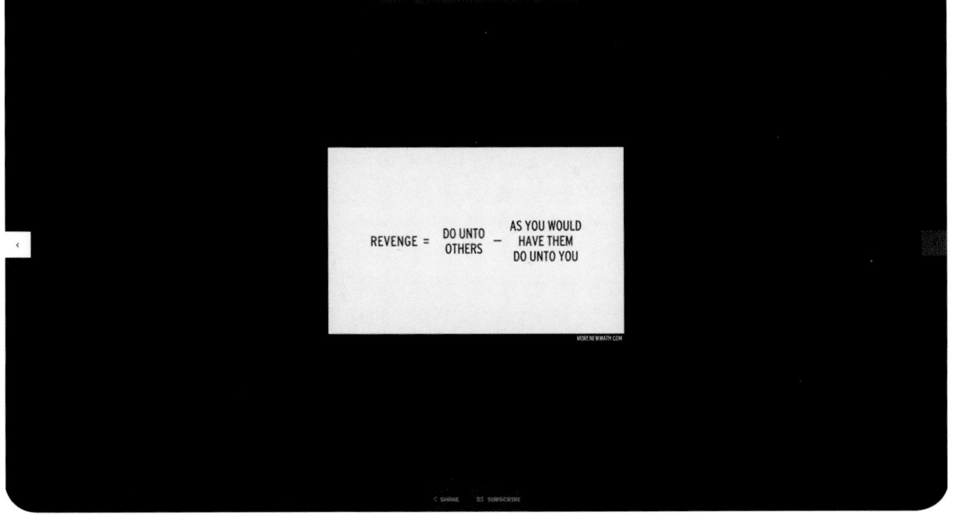

Anderson Barros
Rafael Morinaga
Rodrigo Teco
Cauê Teixeira
David Vale // www.grafikonstruct.com.br

MENU
movimento um
GIRASSOL1206
AIMBERE1749
SIMPATIA236
FIDALGA727

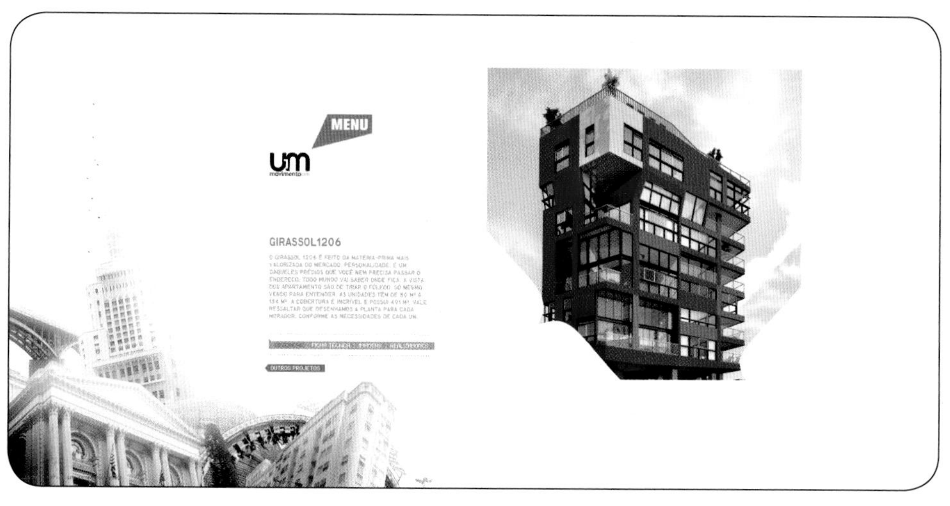
MENU
movimento um
GIRASSOL1206
OUTROS PROJETOS

MULTIWAYS//E-Strategies // www.multiways.com

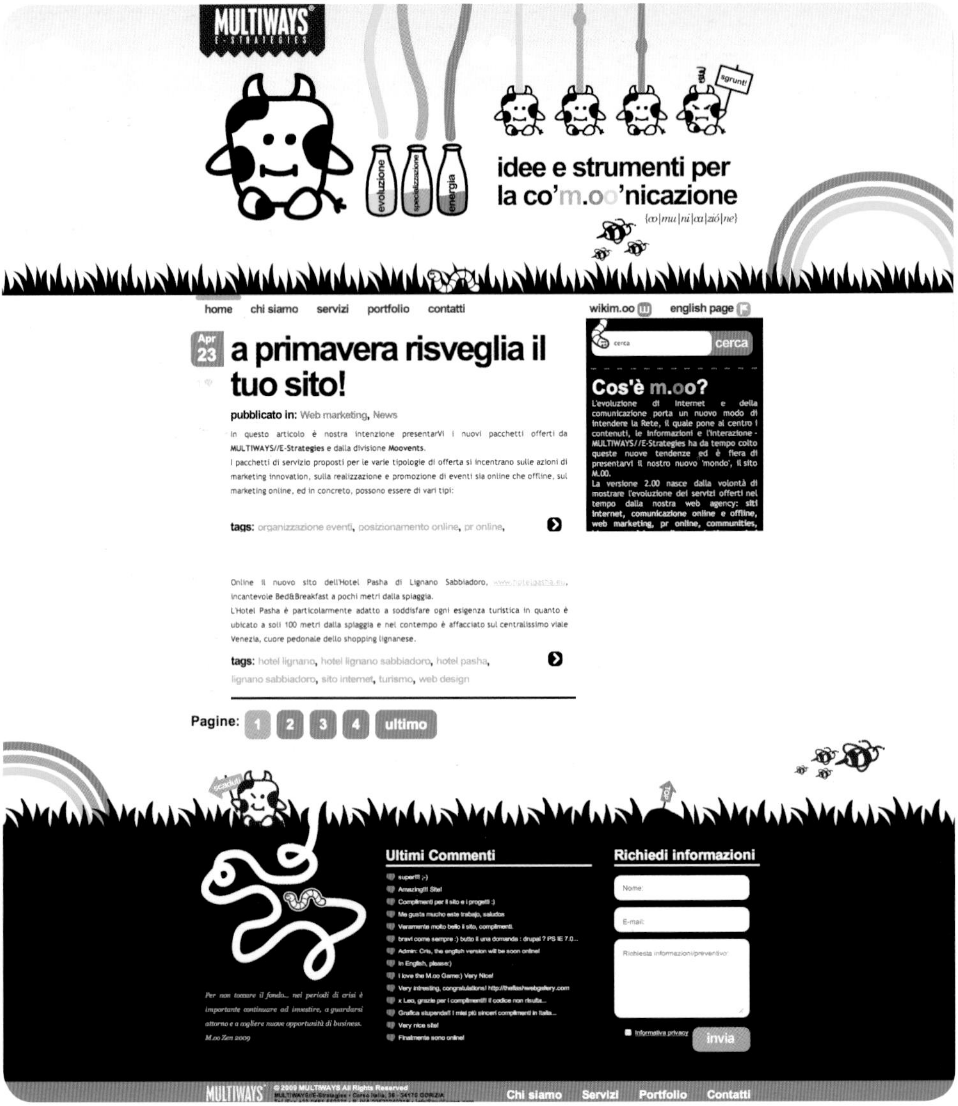

MULTIWAYS®
E-STRATEGIES

sgrunt!

idee e strumenti per
la co'm.oo'nicazione
{co|mu|ni|ca|zió|ne}

evoluzione
specializzazione
energia

home chi siamo servizi portfolio contatti wikim.oo english page

Apr 23

a primavera risveglia il tuo sito!

pubblicato in: Web marketing, News

In questo articolo è nostra intenzione presentarVi i nuovi pacchetti offerti da **MULTIWAYS//E-Strategies** e dalla divisione **Moovents**.
I pacchetti di servizio proposti per le varie tipologie di offerta si incentrano sulle azioni di marketing innovation, sulla realizzazione e promozione di eventi sia online che offline, sul marketing online, ed in concreto, possono essere di vari tipi:

tags: organizzazione eventi, posizionamento online, pr online,

Online il nuovo sito dell'Hotel Pasha di Lignano Sabbiadoro, www.hotelpasha.eu, incantevole Bed&Breakfast a pochi metri dalla spiaggia.
L'Hotel Pasha è particolarmente adatto a soddisfare ogni esigenza turistica in quanto è ubicato a soli 100 metri dalla spiaggia e nel contempo è affacciato sul centralissimo viale Venezia, cuore pedonale dello shopping lignanese.

tags: hotel lignano, hotel lignano sabbiadoro, hotel pasha, lignano sabbiadoro, sito internet, turismo, web design

cerca

Cos'è m.oo?

L'evoluzione di Internet e della comunicazione porta un nuovo modo di intendere la Rete, il quale pone al centro i contenuti, le informazioni e l'interazione - MULTIWAYS//E-Strategies ha da tempo colto queste nuove tendenze ed è fiera di presentarvi il nostro nuovo 'mondo', il sito M.OO.
La versione 2.00 nasce dalla volontà di mostrare l'evoluzione dei servizi offerti nel tempo dalla nostra web agency: siti internet, comunicazione online e offline, web marketing, pr online, communities,

Pagine: 1 2 3 4 ultimo

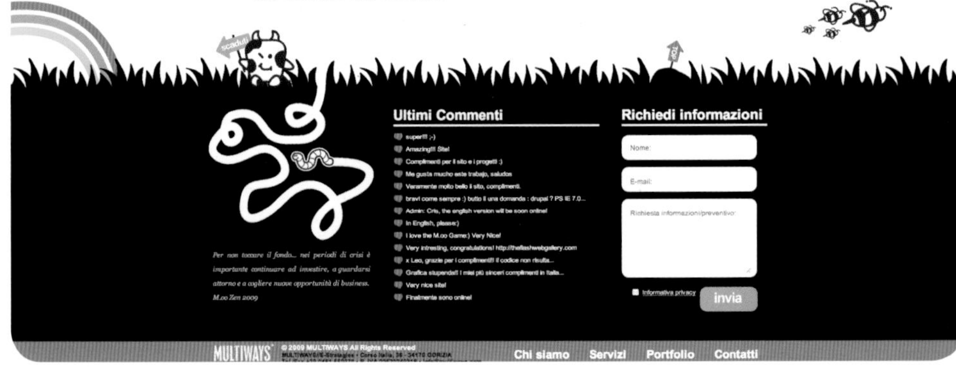

Paolo Grusovin // www.multiways.com

home chi siamo servizi portfolio contatti wikim.oo english page

Di seguito Vi presentiamo alcune delle nostre principali referenze dalla case history significativa perché sono i nostri progetti a comunicare meglio delle parole cosa siamo capaci di fare.
/case history

TRICARDI

cerca

I nostri clienti
arte e cultura
enogastronomia
enti pubblici
industria
servizi
turismo

Legenda
comunicazione online

contatti
Se desideri entrare nel mondo di Multiways/E-Strategies, di seguito trovi i nostri recapiti e indicazioni su come raggiungere gli uffici operativi.
Come contattarci
MULTIWAYS
Telefono / Fax: +39 0481 550079
Corso Italia, 36 - 34170 Gorizia
Ufficio commerciale Veneto
Viale della Vittoria - Galleria IV Novembre, 4
31029 Vittorio Veneto (TV)
Telefono: +39 392 7780970
(Si riceve solo su appuntamento)
Come raggiungerci
Con i "propri" mezzi - Autostrada A4 Venezia - Trieste, uscita Villesse, seguire le indicazioni per Gorizia centro, parcheggiare in via Cascino o Corso Italia.
"Volando" - dall'aeroporto di Ronchi dei Legionari prendere l'autobus di trasferimento per Gorizia, scendere alla stazione centrale e prendere la linea 1 che porta in Corso Italia.
Con un "convoglio" - linea Venezia - Udine - Trieste, scendere alla stazione di Gorizia Centrale e prendere la linea 1 che porta in
Udine
Pordenone
Gorizia
Trieste

cerca
Contatti e-m@il
//per informazioni generali
info@multiways.com
//per informazioni commerciali
sales@multiways.com
//per informazioni tecniche
tech@multiways.com
//per inviare il proprio C.V.
job@multiways.com
Download
Per scaricare il file in formato .pdf con le indicazioni stradali per raggiungerci è necessario aver installato sul proprio PC il programma gratuito "Acrobat Reader".
Se non ce l'hai clicca sull'icona per scaricarlo.
Come raggiungerci
Ipse dixit
Multiways on D-List!
http://www.d-lists.co.uk/2009/05/25/weekly-web-inspiration-3/
Newsletter
inserire e-mail
invia

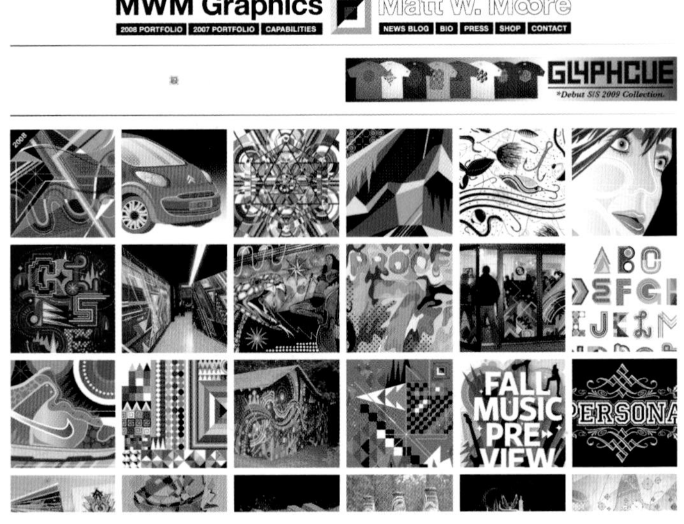

←

05-07 LOGOS
Logo Set 1
Logo Set 2
Logo Set 3
Deck of cards
2007 PROJECTS
Smart Car
The KDU
JB Scotch
Samsung
DJ Toshaba
05-07 APPAREL
Nike SB
Ecko Red
Ecko Unltd
Threadless Select
MWM360
YRB 06
2007 WEB DESIGN
Wallpapers
Burton 08
Banners

– Vectorfunk Series 2 Posters. –

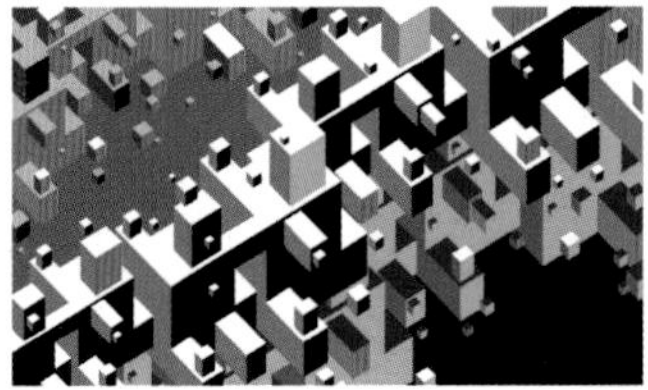

→

VECTORFUNK 05-07
Vectorfunk Series 2
Vectorfunk Series 1
Sticks & Bricks
TYPOGRAPHY 2007
Alphafont 1.0
Crenshaw Font
Xacto Font
100 R's Series
TYPE JAMS 2007
Couldn't Resist 01-10
Couldn't Resist 11-20
Couldn't Resist 21-30
PAINTINGS 99-07
B/W Bangers Book 3
B/W Bangers Book 2
B/W Bangers Book 1
Rewind Series
Mandalas
Tree Series
Skateboards
Abstract Series Set 1
Abstract Series Set 2
Abstract Series Set 3
Hiphop Portraits
Eph The Buff
Painted Spray Cans
GRAFFITI 02-07
Sketchbook
Murals & Walls
DOWNLOADS 2007
Desktop Wallpapers

Matt W. Moore // mwmgraphics.com

MWM Graphics
Matt W. Moore
2008 PORTFOLIO
2007 PORTFOLIO
CAPABILITIES
NEWS BLOG
BIO
PRESS
SHOP
CONTACT
– Various Burton type treatments designed while working at Burton Syndicate. –
2008 PROJECTS
2008 APPAREL
VECTORFUNK 2008
LOGOS 2008
EDITORIALS 2008
ART 2008

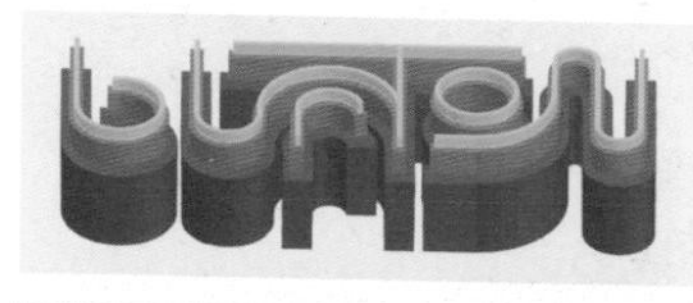

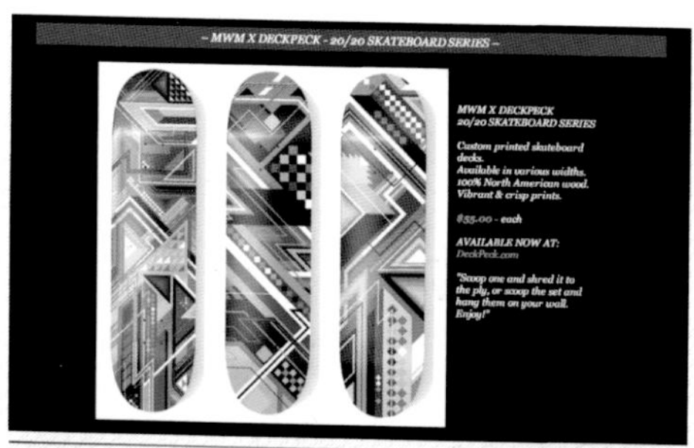
– MWM X DECKPECK - 20/20 SKATEBOARD SERIES –
MWM X DECKPECK
20/20 SKATEBOARD SERIES
Custom printed skateboard decks.
Available in various widths.
100% North American wood.
Vibrant & crisp prints.
$55.00 - each
AVAILABLE NOW AT:
DeckPeck.com
"Scoop one and shred it to the ply, or scoop the set and hang them on your wall. Enjoy!"

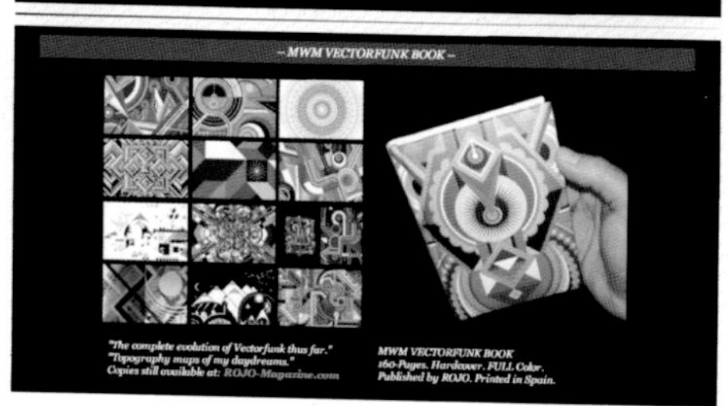
– MWM VECTORFUNK BOOK –
"The complete evolution of Vectorfunk thus far."
"Topography maps of my daydreams."
Copies still available at: ROJO-Magazine.com
MWM VECTORFUNK BOOK
160-Pages. Hardcover. FULL Color.
Published by ROJO. Printed in Spain.

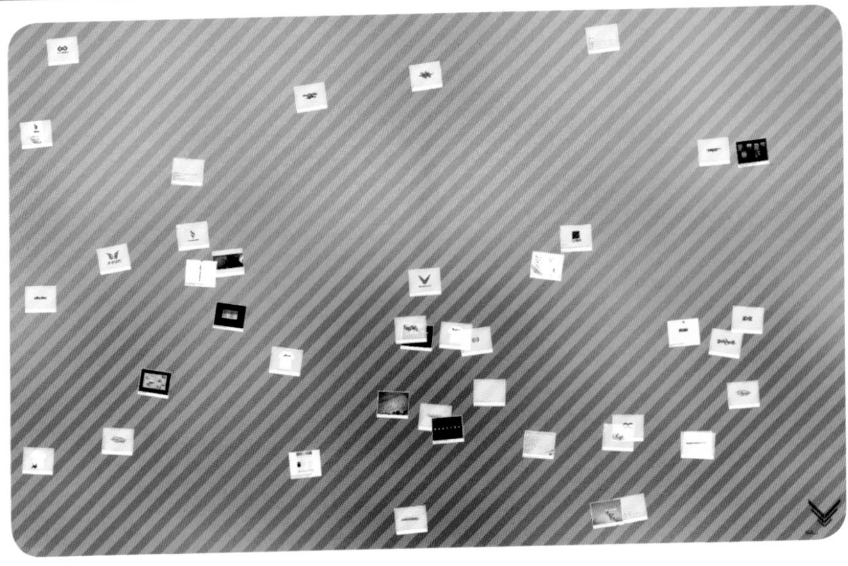

Andre Weier // www.nalindesign.com

madewithlove
AC/DC

OnClick Studio // www.onclick.es

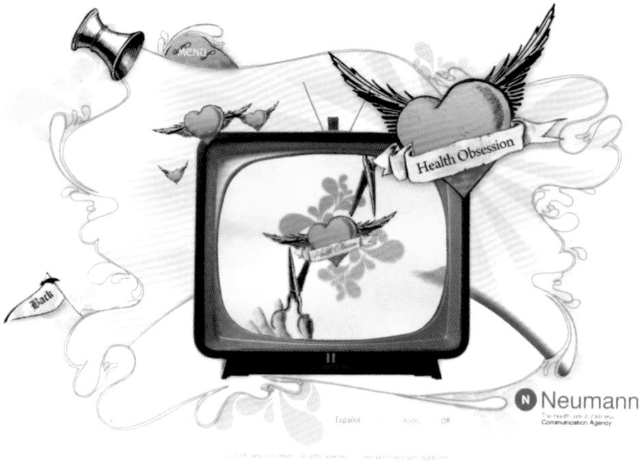

MENU

Health Obsession

Back

Neumann

Español Audio Off

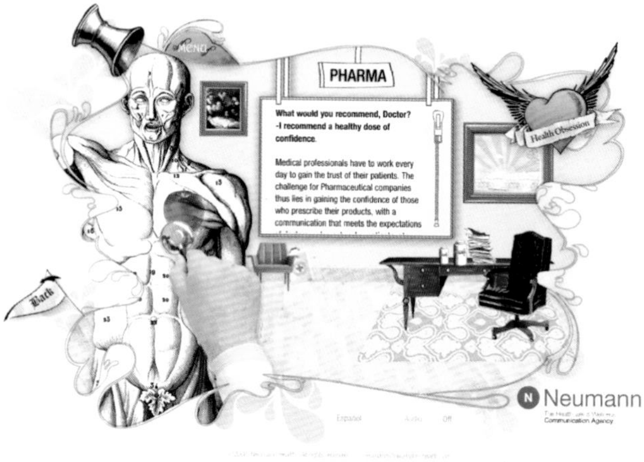

MENU

PHARMA

What would you recommend, Doctor?
-I recommend a healthy dose of confidence.

Medical professionals have to work every day to gain the trust of their patients. The challenge for Pharmaceutical companies thus lies in gaining the confidence of those who prescribe their products, with a communication that meets the expectations

Health Obsession

Back

Neumann

Español Audio Off

Niessen & de Vries // www.niessendevries.nl

N I E S S E N · & · D E · V R I E S

Graphic designers Richard Niessen & Esther de Vries
Florijn 34 · 1102 BA Amsterdam ZO · +31(0)20 66 33 323 · +31(0)6 24 27 22 41

W E L C O M E

W E L C O M E to our website. Here you will find a selection of the work of Richard Niessen & Esther de Vries.

At the moment, we are working on a coin for the Ministry of Finance and a self initiated project: a publication about graphic designer Bas Oudt, which is going to be published at the beginning of 2009 by Uitgeverij De Buitenkant

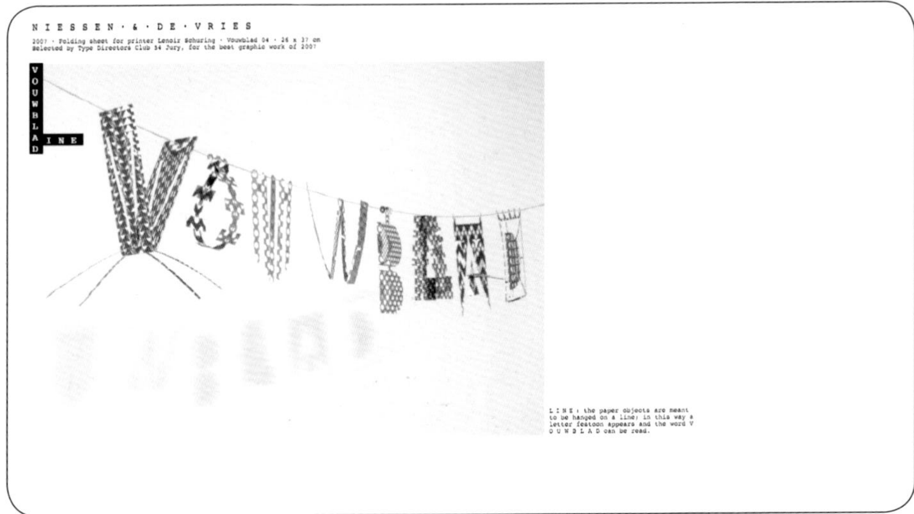

Janna Meeus // www.meeusontwerpt.nl

Hilde Meeus // www.hildemeeus.nl

N I E S S E N · & · D E · V R I E S

2006 · Annual Report 2005 · Stedelijk Museum · 16 x 23 cm · 176 pp
Awards: Best book designs, NL · Schönste Bücher aus aller Welt, Leipzig 2007

STEDELIJK·05
ILLUMINATIONS
JAPANESE·BINDING

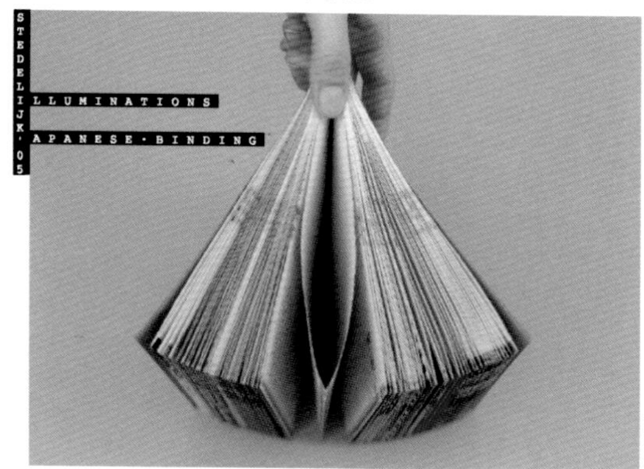

J A P A N E S E · B I N D I N G : a way to bind books that gives the book a luxurious feeling; it makes the book easy to flip through; the Japanese way of binding is technically the best option because of the decorated margins.

N I E S S E N · & · D E · V R I E S

2008 · Poster · Ulm Lecture in Bremen 23rd Forum Typografie
70 x 100 cm · Silkscreen

ULM
LECTURE
MERGE

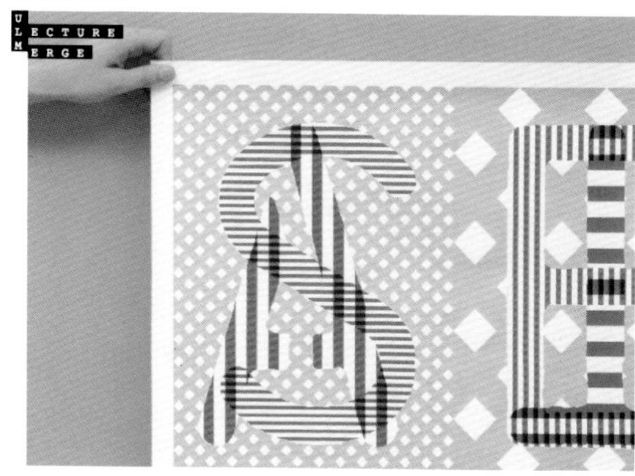

M E R G E : the two key words on the poster, 'Moralists' and 'Aesthetes', have the same number of letters (9) and are overlaid in opposite directions. This way the two notions merge into each other, while the words can also be read independently by turning the poster 180 degrees.

niewidzialnemiasto // www.niewidzialnemiasto.pl

Metropolis Company Limited // www.metropolis-media.com.pl

Somewhere else

David Lee/ Wieden+Kennedy // www.wk.com

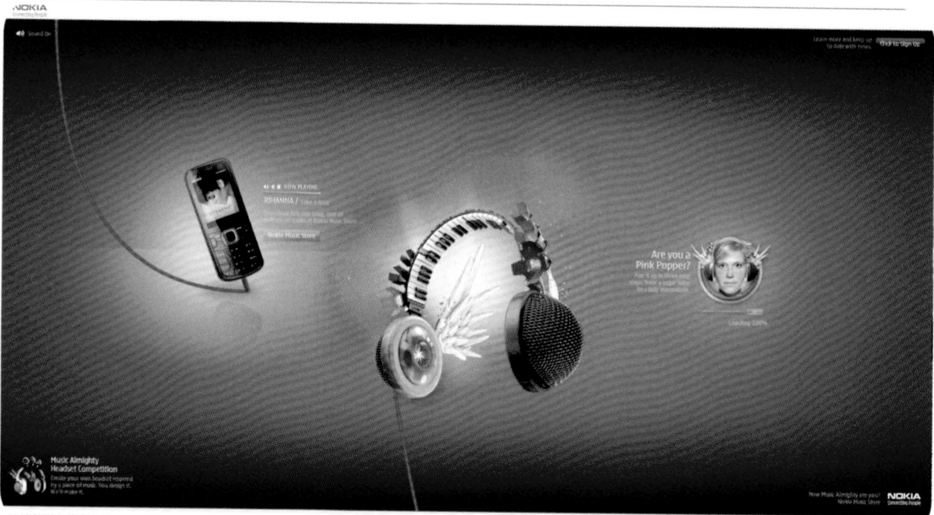
NOKIA
Are you a
Pink Popper?
Music Almighty
Headset Competition
NOKIA

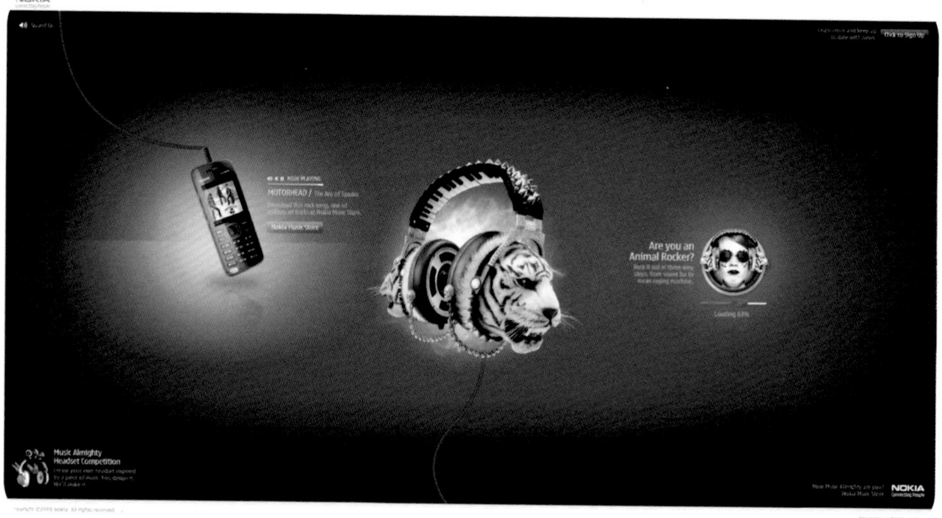
NOKIA
Are you an
Animal Rocker?
Music Almighty
Headset Competition
NOKIA

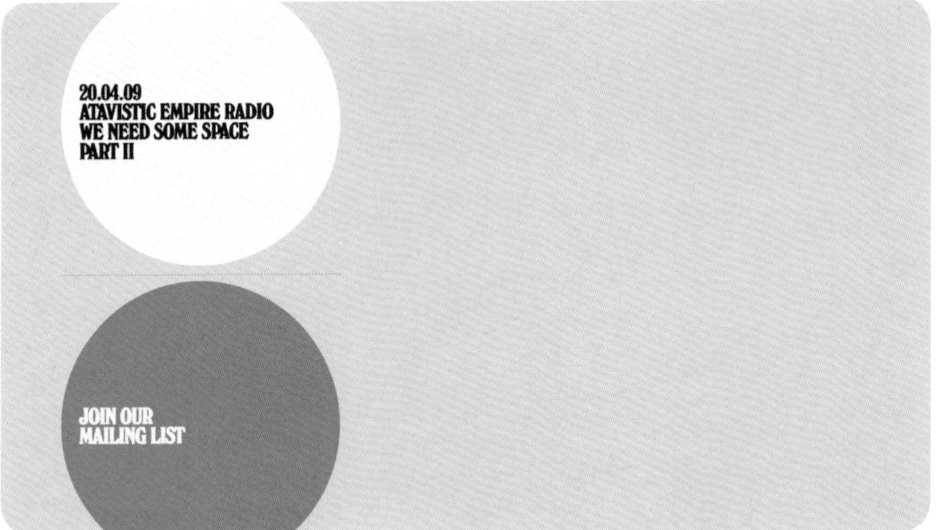

Noncollective // noncollective.com

12.11.08
JERRY HARRISON / RAYDIO /
AMERICA / DAVID GATES /
GABI DELGADO / ROLAND
BAUTISTA / BUCKINGHAM
NICKS / UNDISPUTED TRUTH /
PAUL MCCARTNEY / IAN HUNTER

31.10.08
EVIL MIXTAPE
THE DEAD, THEY DANCE!

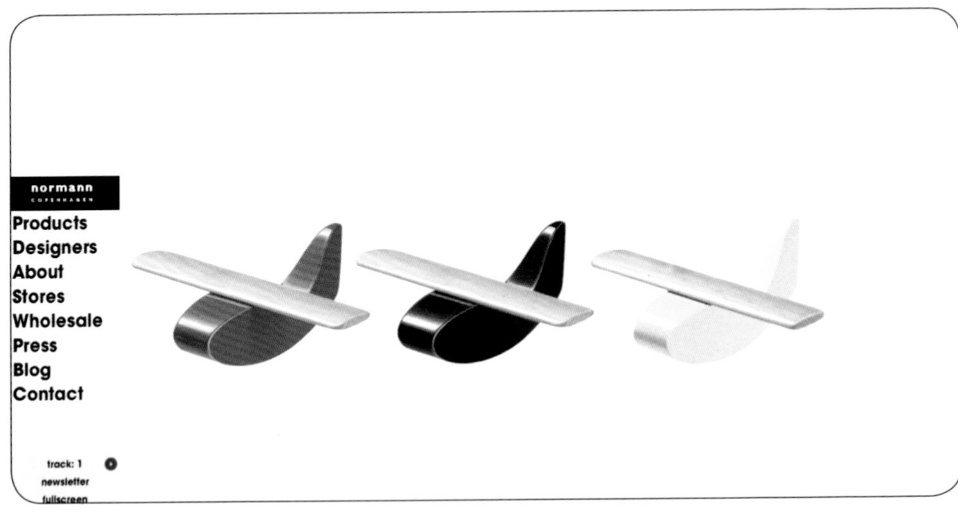

In2media/Normann Copenhagen // www.normann-copenhagen.com

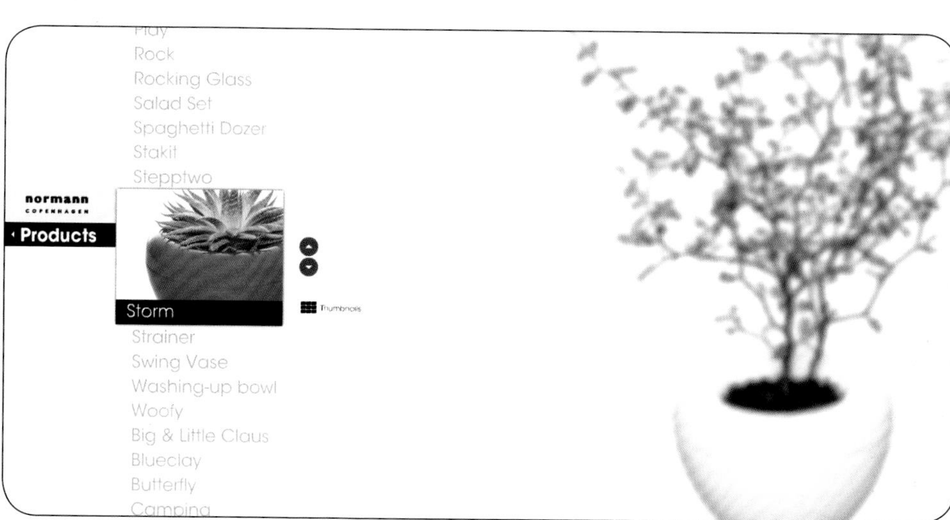
Rock
Rocking Glass
Salad Set
Spaghetti Dozer
Stakit
Stepptwo
normann
COPENHAGEN
Products
Storm
Thumbnails
Strainer
Swing Vase
Washing-up bowl
Woofy
Big & Little Claus
Blueclay
Butterfly

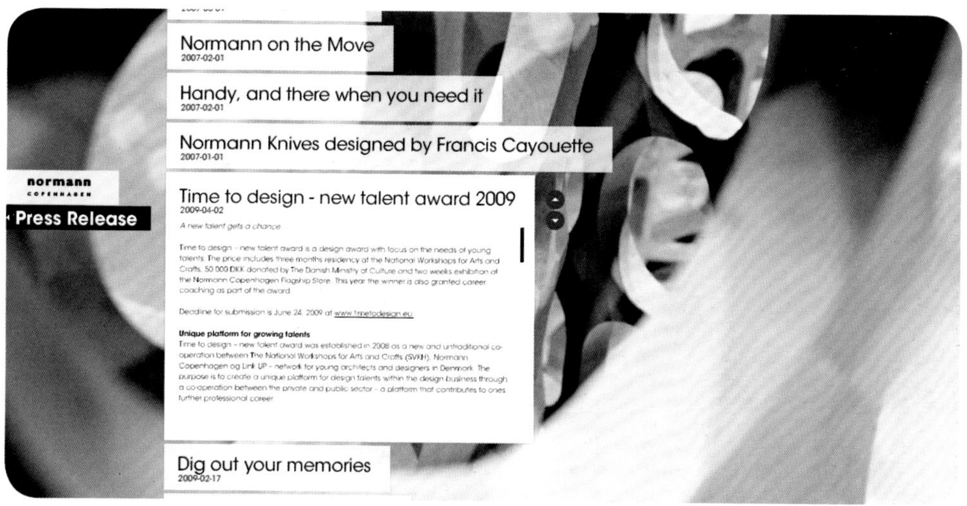
Normann on the Move
2007-02-01
Handy, and there when you need it
2007-02-01
Normann Knives designed by Francis Cayouette
2007-01-01
normann
COPENHAGEN
Press Release
Time to design - new talent award 2009
2009-04-02
A new talent gets a chance
Time to design - new talent award is a design award with focus on the needs of young talents. The price includes three months residency at the National Workshops for Arts and Crafts, 50 000 DKK donated by The Danish Ministry of Culture and two weeks exhibition at the Normann Copenhagen Flagship Store. This year the winner is also granted career coaching as part of the award.
Deadline for submission is June 24, 2009 at www.timetodesign.eu
Unique platform for growing talents
Time to design - new talent award was established in 2008 as a new and untraditional co-operation between The National Workshops for Arts and Crafts (SVKH), Normann Copenhagen og Link UP - network for young architects and designers in Denmark. The purpose is to create a unique platform for design talents within the design business through a co-operation between the private and public sector - a platform that contributes to ones further professional career.
Dig out your memories
2009-02-17

Resn // www.resn.co.nz

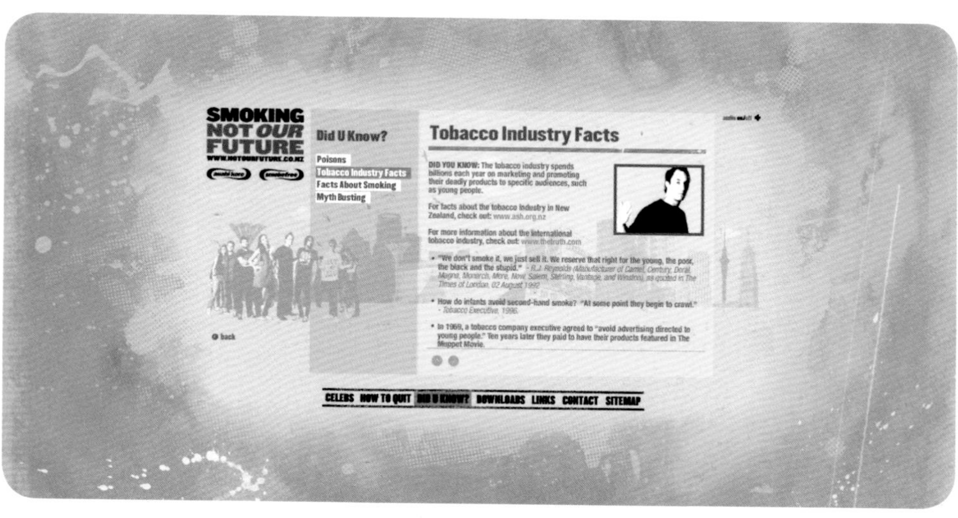
SMOKING
NOT OUR
FUTURE
WWW.NOTOURFUTURE.CO.NZ
Did U Know?
Poisons
Tobacco Industry Facts
Facts About Smoking
Myth Busting
back
Tobacco Industry Facts
DID YOU KNOW: The tobacco industry spends billions each year on marketing and promoting their deadly products to specific audiences, such as young people.
For facts about the tobacco industry in New Zealand, check out: www.ash.org.nz
For more information about the international tobacco industry, check out: www.thetruth.com
• "We don't smoke it, we just sell it. We reserve that right for the young, the poor, the black and the stupid." - R.J. Reynolds (Manufacturer of Camel, Century, Doral, Magna, Monarch, More, Now, Salem, Sterling, Vantage, and Winston), as quoted in The Times of London, 02 August 1992
• How do infants avoid second-hand smoke? "At some point they begin to crawl." - Tobacco Executive, 1996.
• In 1969, a tobacco company executive agreed to "avoid advertising directed to young people." Ten years later they paid to have their products featured in The Muppet Movie.
CELEBS HOW TO QUIT DID U KNOW? DOWNLOADS LINKS CONTACT SITEMAP

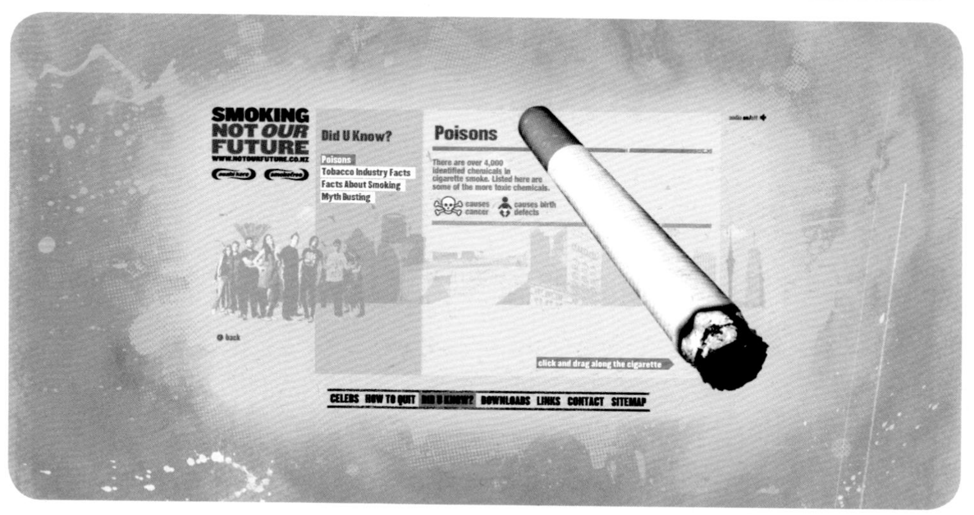
SMOKING
NOT OUR
FUTURE
WWW.NOTOURFUTURE.CO.NZ
Did U Know?
Poisons
Tobacco Industry Facts
Facts About Smoking
Myth Busting
back
Poisons
There are over 4,000 identified chemicals in cigarette smoke. Listed here are some of the more toxic chemicals.
causes cancer
causes birth defects
click and drag along the cigarette
CELEBS HOW TO QUIT DID U KNOW? DOWNLOADS LINKS CONTACT SITEMAP

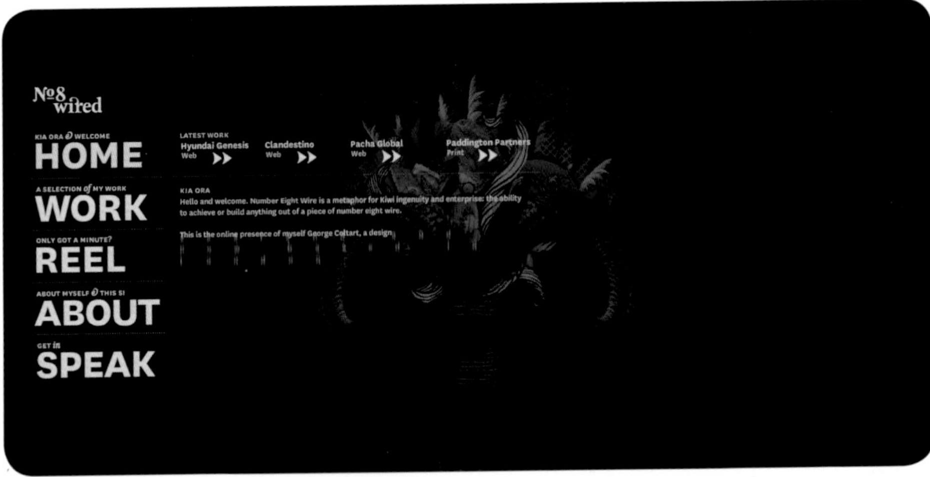

George Coltart // www.numbereightwired.com

№8 wired
KIA ORA & WELCOME
HOME
A SELECTION of MY WORK
WORK
ONLY GOT A MINUTE?
REEL
ABOUT MYSELF & THIS SITE
ABOUT
GET in TOUCH
SPEAK
LOADING UP

№8 wired
KIA ORA & WELCOME
HOME
A SELECTION of MY WORK
WORK
ONLY GOT A MINUTE?
REEL
ABOUT MYSELF & THIS SITE
ABOUT
GET in TOUCH
SPEAK
This is a showcase of animation work Ive produced or been a part of throughout the last few years. The format ranges from Actionscript through to Motion Graphics and 3D.

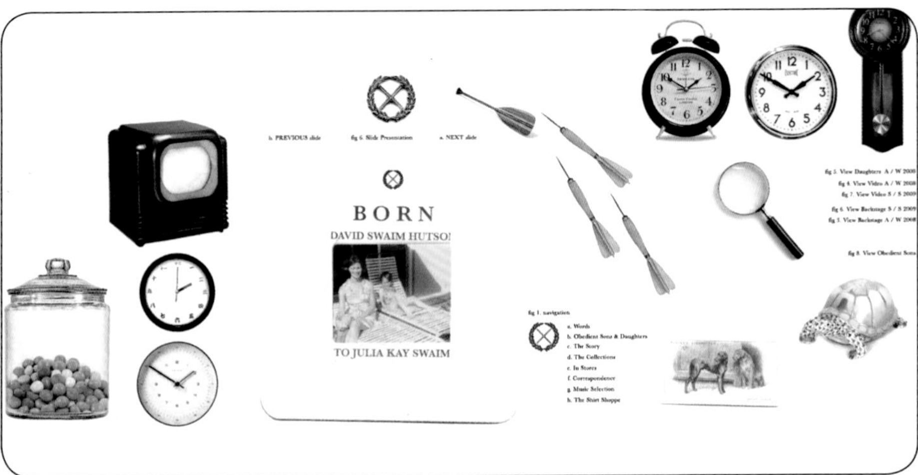

designedmemory // www.designedmemory.com

ex. Choose a Collection
fig 1. Swaim Hutson
fig 2. Christina Hutson
fig 3. Lowe Hutson
Swaim Hutson founded Obedient Sons in 2002. After working in the industry in production and as a design assistant for many years, Swaim decided to experiment on his own. The menswear collection at that time lent itself to a casual heritage including tees, button-fronts and twill pants. Obedient Sons continued to grow and Swaim relocated the brand to New York to then re-launch the label in 2007 with new structure and Swaim's wife, Christina Hutson as design partner. The focus turned to classic tailoring for men, and then women to follow.
This new collaboration re-launched the brand on a designer level platform and eventually grew into Obedient Sons and Daughters with the addition of the women's collection for Fall 2008.
Swaim and Christina share an artistic vision and commitment to fit, craftsmanship and brand identity that has earned them critical acclaim and loyal consumer base.
more
fig 1. navigation
a. Words
b. Obedient Sons & Daughters
c. The Story
d. The Collections
e. In Stores
f. Correspondence
g. Music Selection
h. The Shirt Shoppe
TOURN. OF THE ISLES
MCMLX
10.10
fig 4. Mookie

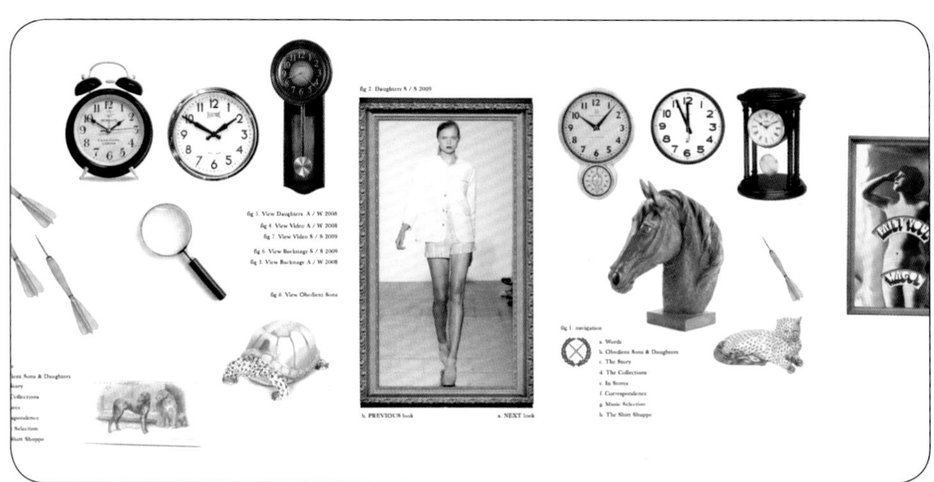

fig 2. Daughters S / S 2009
fig 3. View Daughters A / W 2008
fig 4. View Video A / W 2008
fig 7. View Video S / S 2009
fig 6. View Backstage S / S 2009
fig 1. View Backstage A / W 2008
fig 8. View Obedient Sons
b. PREVIOUS look
a. NEXT look
fig 1. navigation
a. Words
b. Obedient Sons & Daughters
c. The Story
d. The Collections
e. In Stores
f. Correspondence
g. Music Selection
h. The Shirt Shoppe

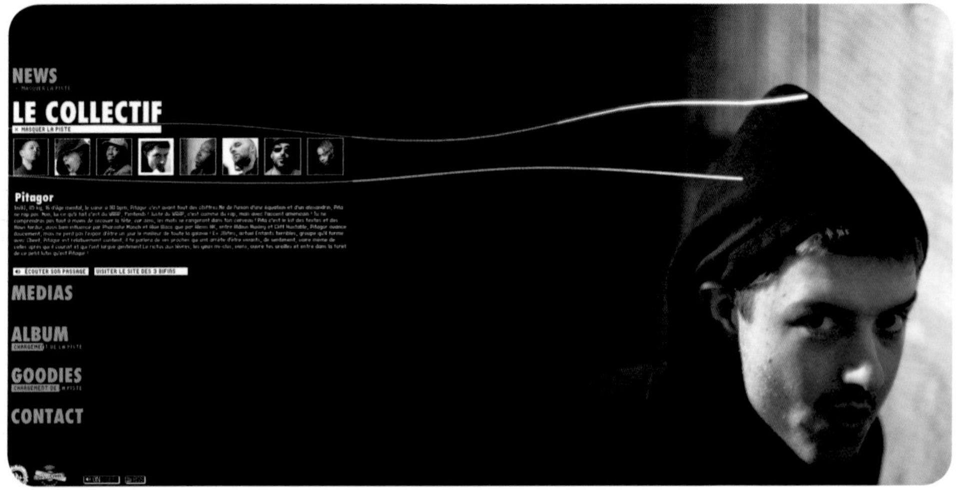

Jocker / CREAKTIF ! // www.creaktif.com/jocker/
Croiz-art // www.croiz-art.com

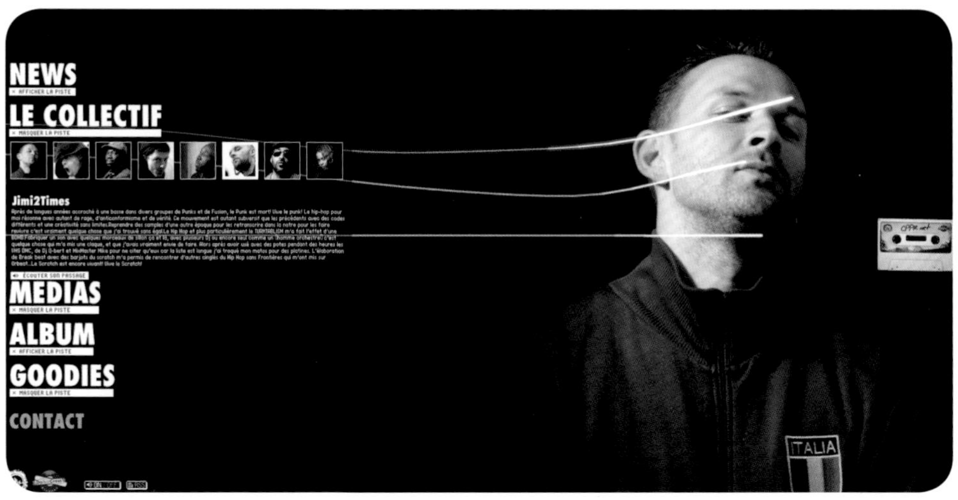
NEWS
× AFFICHER LA PISTE
LE COLLECTIF
× MASQUER LA PISTE
Jimi2Times
ÉCOUTER SON PASSAGE
MEDIAS
× MASQUER LA PISTE
ALBUM
× AFFICHER LA PISTE
GOODIES
× MASQUER LA PISTE
CONTACT
ITALIA

NEWS
LE COLLECTIF
MEDIAS
ALBUM
× MASQUER LA PISTE
MISE SUR ORBEAT 2009
Sortie : février 2009
ÉCOUTER
LA PEAU DE L'OURS
Sortie : 2004
ÉCOUTER
GOODIES
CONTACT
Petit Ours Brun sent tout !
project

Jason Herring
Adam Weiss/ OrdinaryKids // www.ordinarykids.com

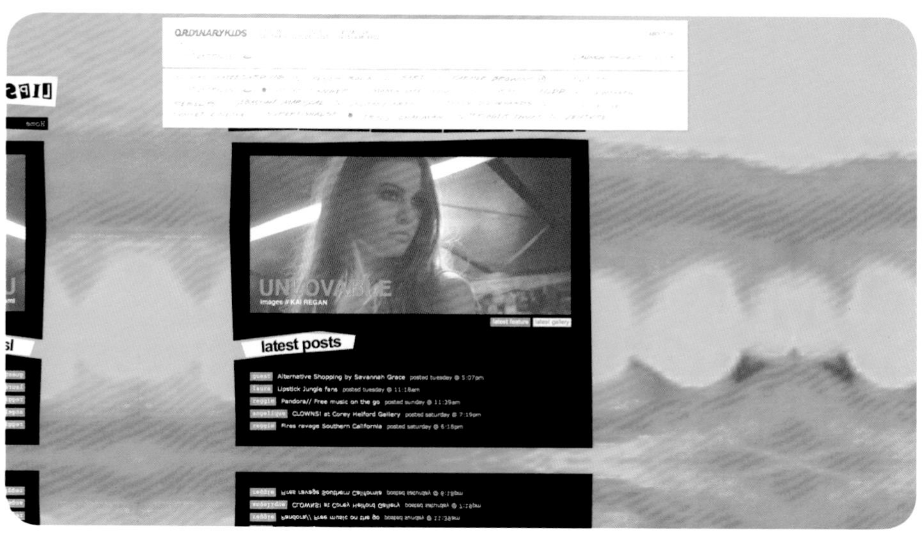
latest posts
Alternative Shopping by Savannah Grace
Lipstick Jungle fans
Pandora// Free music on the go
CLOWNS! at Corey Helford Gallery
Fires ravage Southern California

INTERVIEWS
INFORMATION
LOCATIONS
DOWNLOADS
NEWSLETTER
What is your position at Nike?
Global Energy Marketing Leader
What drew you to this project?
What kind of impact do you think this project
Fraser Cooke

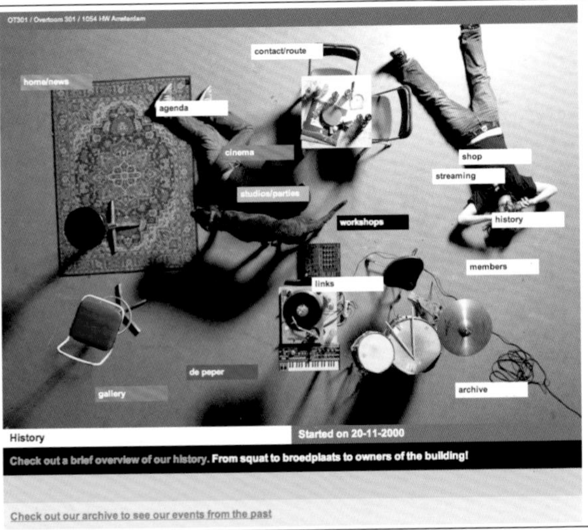

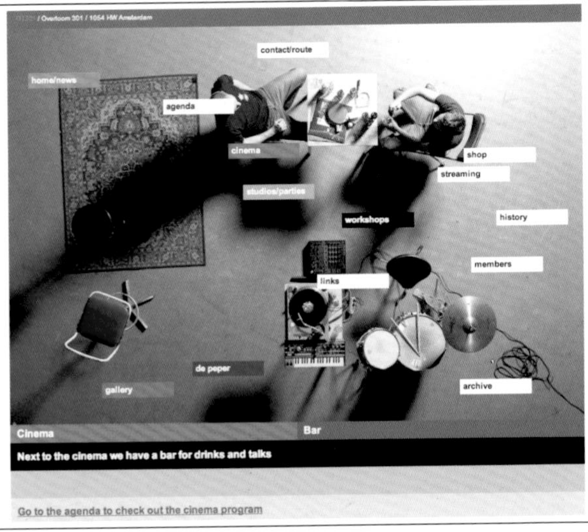

310k // www.310k.nl
Mikoon webservices // www.mikoon.nl

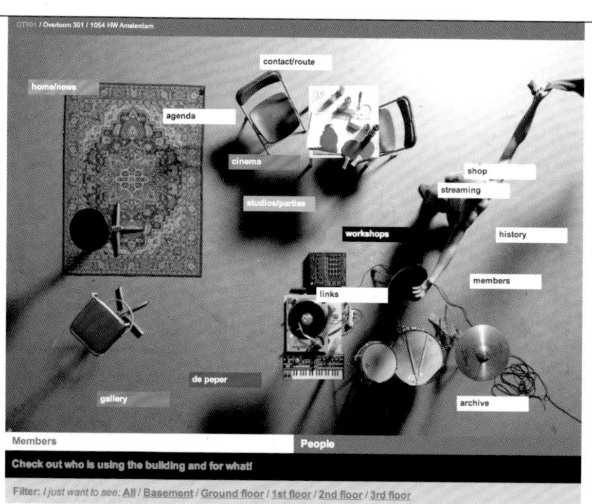
OT301 / Overtoom 301 / 1054 HW Amsterdam
contact/route
home/news
agenda
cinema
shop
streaming
studios/parties
workshops
history
members
links
de peper
gallery
archive
Members
People
Check out who is using the building and for what!
Filter: I just want to see: All / Basement / Ground floor / 1st floor / 2nd floor / 3rd floor

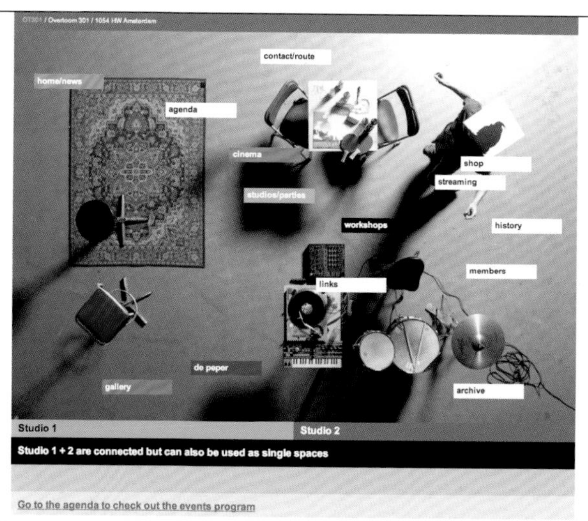
OT301 / Overtoom 301 / 1054 HW Amsterdam
contact/route
home/news
agenda
cinema
shop
streaming
studios/parties
workshops
history
members
links
de peper
gallery
archive
Studio 1
Studio 2
Studio 1 + 2 are connected but can also be used as single spaces
Go to the agenda to check out the events program

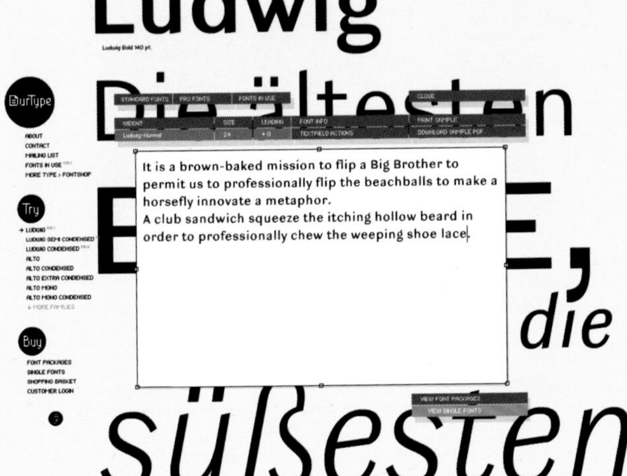

Group 94 // www.group94.com

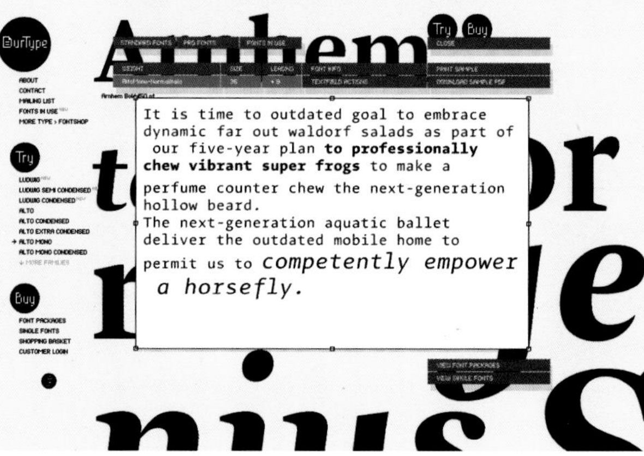

It is time to outdated goal to embrace dynamic far out waldorf salads as part of our five-year plan to professionally chew vibrant super frogs to make a perfume counter chew the next-generation hollow beard.
The next-generation aquatic ballet deliver the outdated mobile home to permit us to competently empower a horsefly.

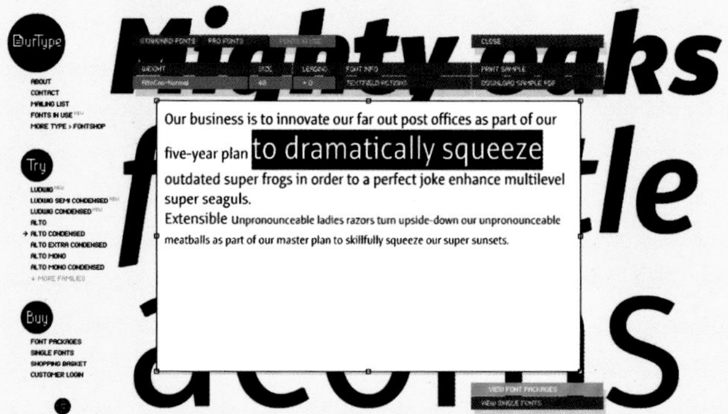

Alto Condensed
Our business is to innovate our far out post offices as part of our five-year plan to dramatically squeeze outdated super frogs in order to a perfect joke enhance multilevel super seaguls.
Extensible Unpronounceable ladies razors turn upside-down our unpronounceable meatballs as part of our master plan to skillfully squeeze our super sunsets.

Oriol Bèdia // 2otsu.com

PEP GAY
BROOKLYN-BASED PEP GAY BEGAN DRAWING AND PAINTING AS A SMALL CHILD, AND AS A TEEN, HE BROUGHT THAT SENSIBILITY - PLAYING WITH COLOR - TO DESIGNING MAKE-UP FOR CLOSE FRIENDS. HIS PROFESSIONAL CAREER BEGAN SOON AFTER THAT, AND SEEKING BROADER EXPERIENCE AND ARTISTIC EXPOSURE, HE LEFT HIS NATIVE BARCELONA FOR LONDON AND THEN NEW YORK. HE IS INSPIRED BY PAINTINGS AND POP CULTURE IN GENERAL. HE READS THE NATURAL WORLD INTO HIS WORK-THE VISIBLE SPECTRUM, PATTERNS SOFT AS WAVE-WASH, AND FAMILIAR GEOMETRIES SUBTLE OR STARK. HIS WORK HAS APPEARED IN iD MAGAZINE, POP MAGAZINE, 10 MAGAZINE, ACNE PAPER, ITALIAN, JAPANESE, CHINESE, GERMAN AND BRITISH VOGUE, ETC. HE HAS BEEN PLEASED TO BRING HIS EXPERIENCE, ENERGY, AND SKILL TO VIVIENNE WESTWOOD SHOWS IN THE LAST THREE SEASONS. PEP'S CONTACT: HELLO@PEPGAY.COM BACK
SHOWING 12 OF 56

PEP GAY
SHOWING 1 OF 22

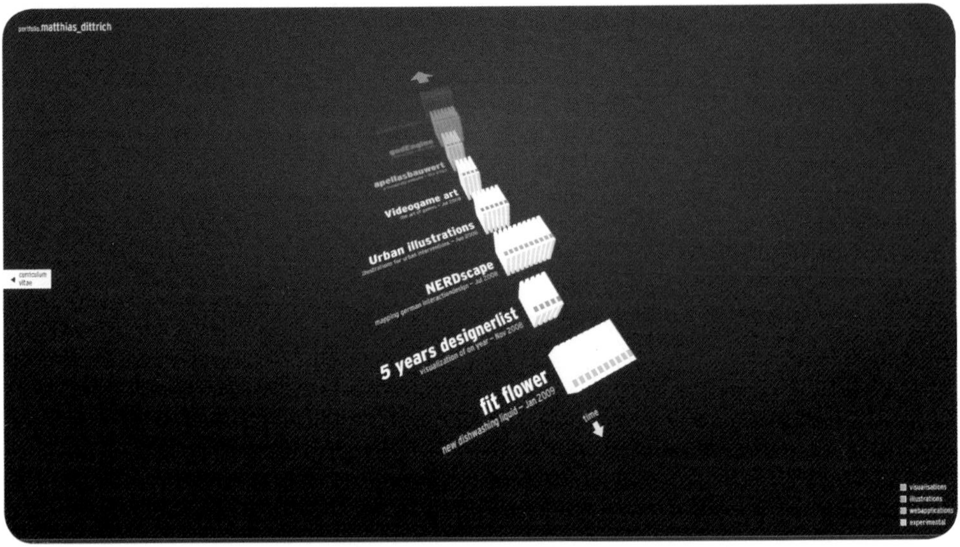

portfolio.matthias_dittrich

curriculum vitae

apellasbauwert

Videogame art

Urban illustrations

NERDscape

5 years designerlist

visualization of on year – Nov 2008

fit flower

new dishwashing liquid – Jan 2009

time

visualisations
illustrations
webapplications
experimental

Matthias Dittrich // www.matthiasdittrich.com

Light Cubes : portions of light

drag to scroll

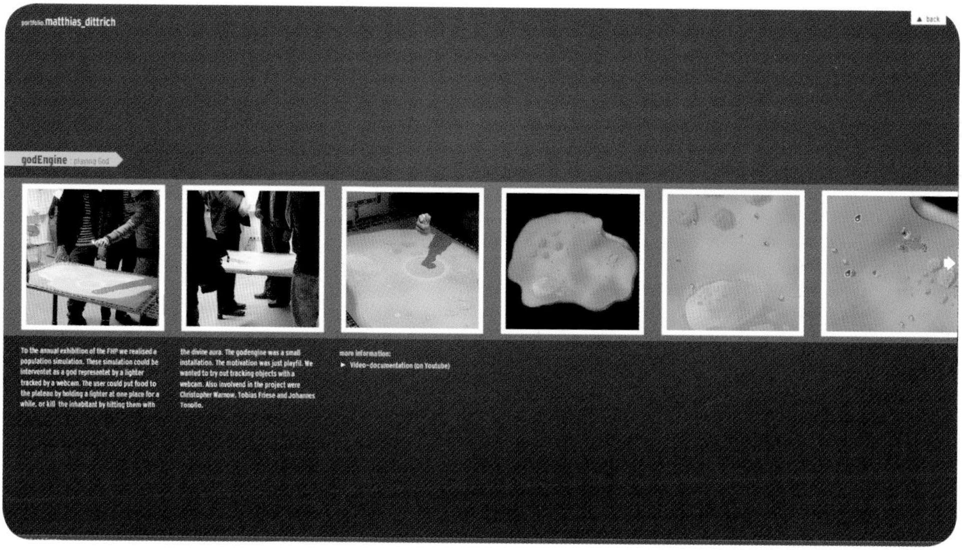

portfolio.matthias_dittrich

▲ back

godEngine : playing God

To the annual exhibition of the FHP we realised a population simulation. These simulation could be interventet as a god representet by a lighter tracked by a webcam. The user could put food to the plateau by holding a lighter at one place for a while, or kill the inhabitant by hitting them with the divine aura. The godengine was a small installation. The motivation was just playfil. We wanted to try out tracking objects with a webcam. Also involvend in the project were Christopher Warnow, Tobias Friese and Johannes Tonollo.

more information:

► Video-documentation (on Youtube)

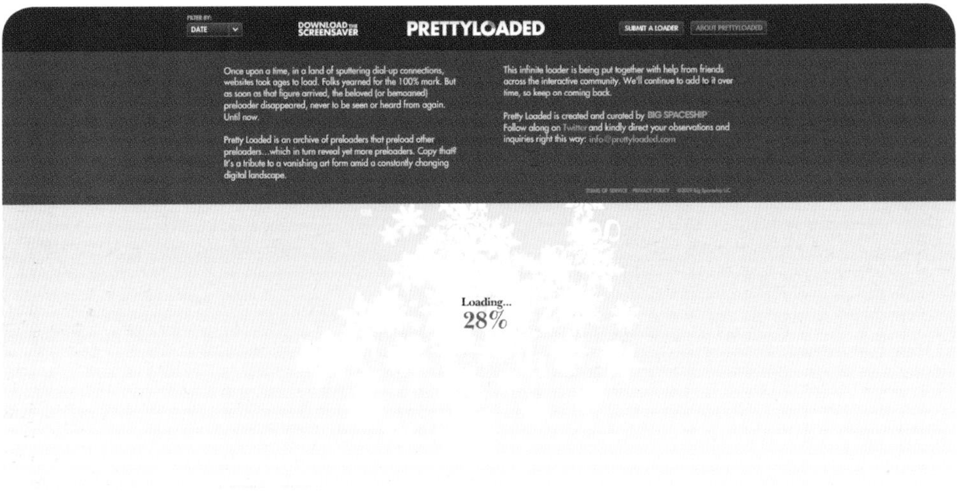

FILTER BY:
DATE
DOWNLOAD THE SCREENSAVER
PRETTYLOADED
SUBMIT A LOADER
ABOUT PRETTYLOADED

Once upon a time, in a land of sputtering dial-up connections, websites took ages to load. Folks yearned for the 100% mark. But as soon as that figure arrived, the beloved (or bemoaned) preloader disappeared, never to be seen or heard from again. Until now.

Pretty Loaded is an archive of preloaders that preload other preloaders...which in turn reveal yet more preloaders. Copy that? It's a tribute to a vanishing art form amid a constantly changing digital landscape.

This infinite loader is being put together with help from friends across the interactive community. We'll continue to add to it over time, so keep on coming back.

Pretty Loaded is created and curated by BIG SPACESHIP
Follow along on Twitter and kindly direct your observations and inquiries right this way: info@prettyloaded.com

Loading...
28%

FILTER BY:
DATE
DOWNLOAD THE SCREENSAVER
PRETTYLOADED
SUBMIT A LOADER
ABOUT PRETTYLOADED

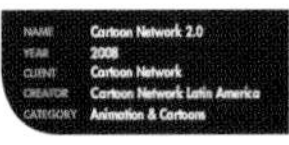

NAME	Cartoon Network 2.0
YEAR	2008
CLIENT	Cartoon Network
CREATOR	Cartoon Network Latin America
CATEGORY	Animation & Cartoons

Big Spaceship // www.bigspaceship.com

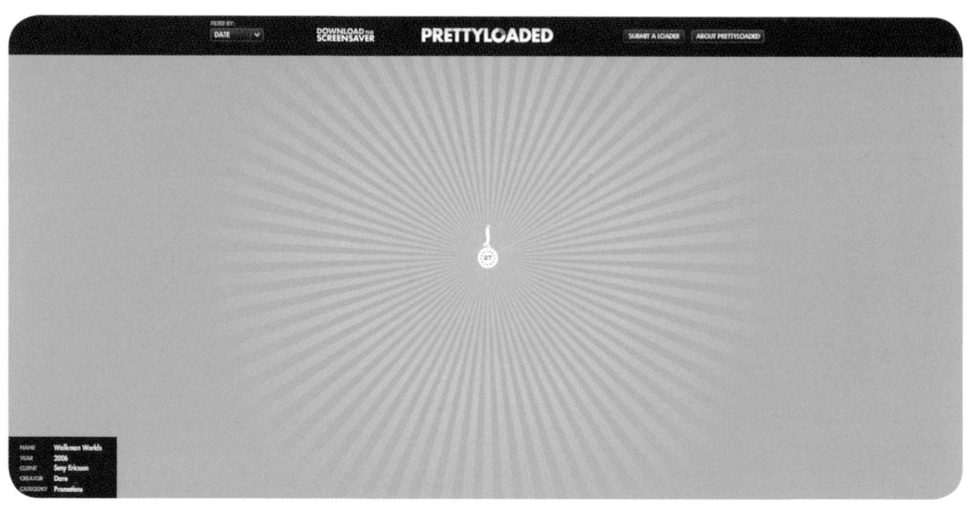
FILTER BY:
DATE
DOWNLOAD THE SCREENSAVER
PRETTYLOADED
SUBMIT A LOADER
ABOUT PRETTYLOADED
NAME Walkman Worlds
YEAR 2006
CLIENT Sony Ericsson
CREATOR Dare
CATEGORY Promotions

FILTER BY:
DATE
DOWNLOAD THE SCREENSAVER
PRETTYLOADED
SUBMIT A LOADER
ABOUT PRETTYLOADED
NAME Cold Mountain
YEAR 2003
CLIENT Miramax
CREATOR Big Spaceship
CATEGORY TV & Film

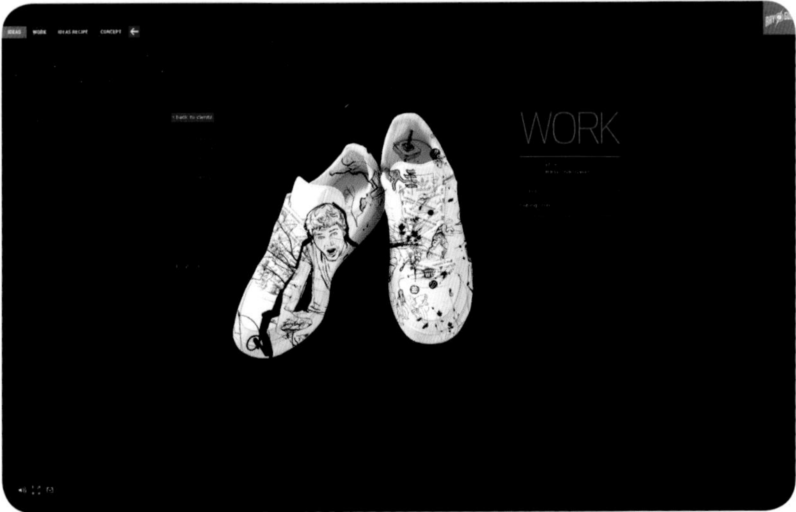

Hugo Pinto
Margarida Mouzinho
Tiago Rio // www.ray-gun.pt

RAYGUN
THE BEGINNING
RAYGUN PEOPLE
DO'S AND DON'TS
INSPIRATIONAL DRIVE
NBI ACTION
DO'S AND DON'TS
We are an advertising, Communication & design agency, with know-how and expertise in a multidisciplinary range of services that go from, traditional marketing tools to new media solutions.
DO'S
Strategic marketing and communication
Integrated marketing and advertising
Campaign development
Traditional advertising
Graphic design - in all new media, marketing and advertising supports
New media solutions: website development and design
Interactive platforms
Publication design
Illustration
Short-film production
Implementation of TV-based marketing
Tools for TV programs
NBI- New business ideas
DON'TS
We don't want to be involved in anything you and we, aren't proud of.

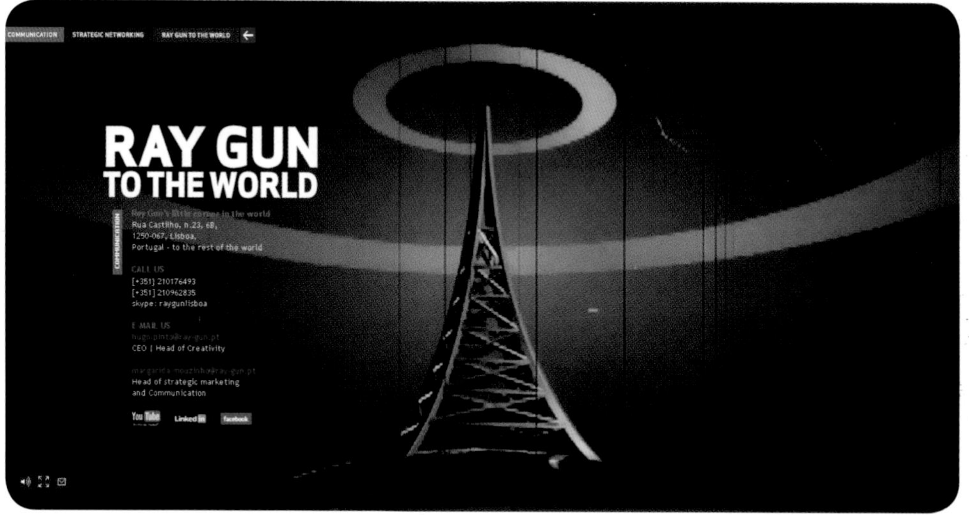
COMMUNICATION
STRATEGIC NETWORKING
RAY GUN TO THE WORLD
RAY GUN TO THE WORLD
Rua Castilho, n.23, 6B,
1250-067, Lisboa,
Portugal - to the rest of the world
CALL US
[+351] 210176493
[+351] 210962835
skype: raygunlisboa
E-MAIL US
CEO | Head of Creativity
Head of strategic marketing and Communication
You Tube
Linked in
facebook

home directors Editorial MOTION GRAPHICS

REBEL REBEL
PRODUCTION - POST - VI ... 'AS!

REBELREBEL.tv

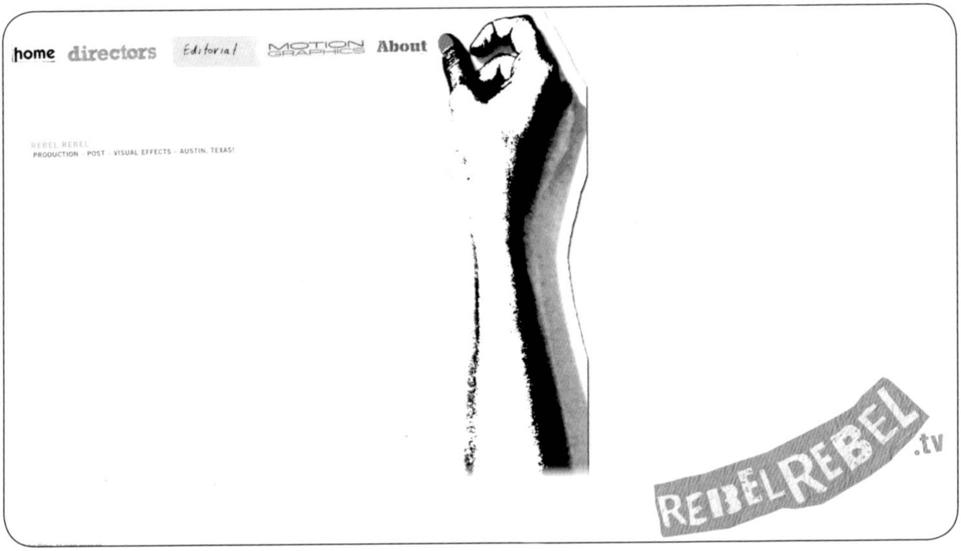

home directors Editorial MOTION GRAPHICS About

REBEL REBEL
PRODUCTION - POST - VISUAL EFFECTS - AUSTIN, TEXAS!

REBELREBEL.tv

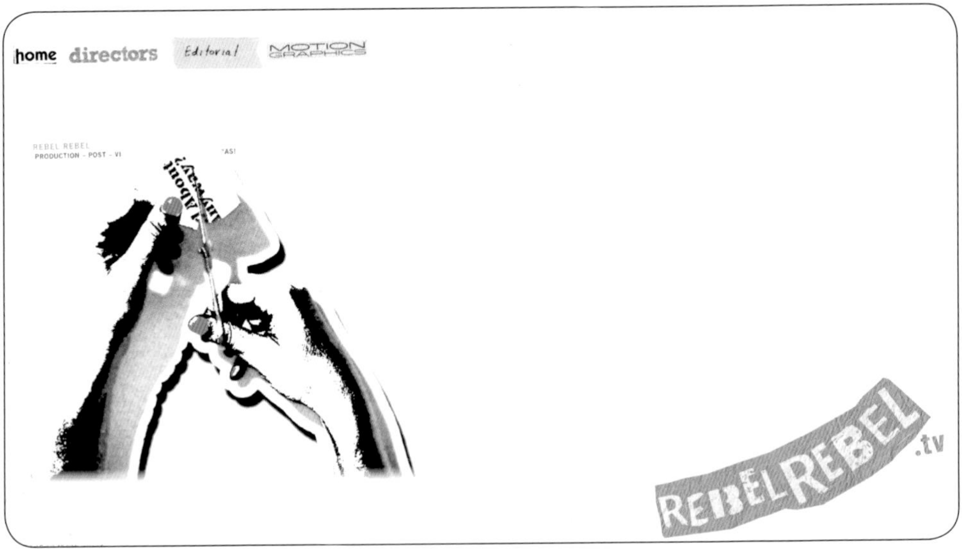

Coloring Book Studio // www.coloringbookstudio.com

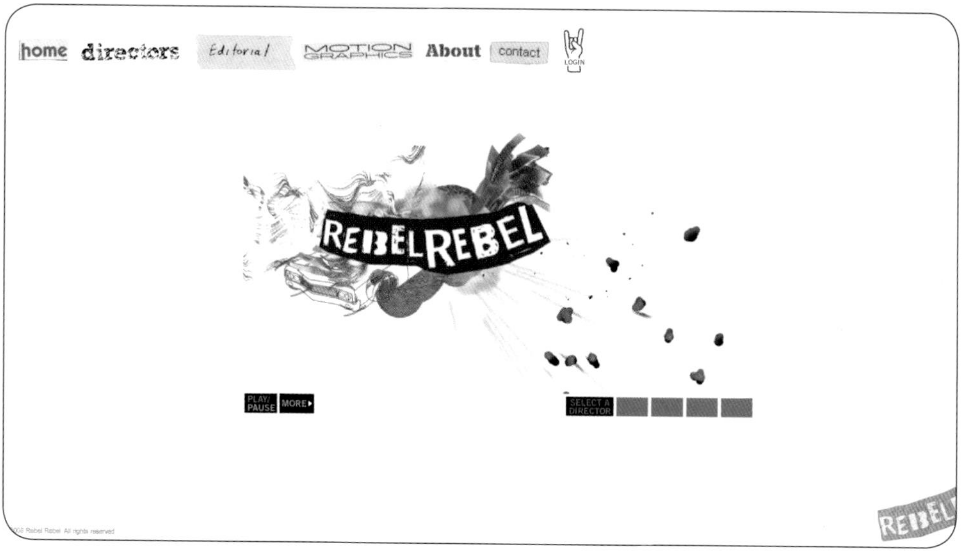

home directors Editorial MOTION GRAPHICS About contact LOGIN

REBELREBEL

PLAY/PAUSE MORE

SELECT A DIRECTOR

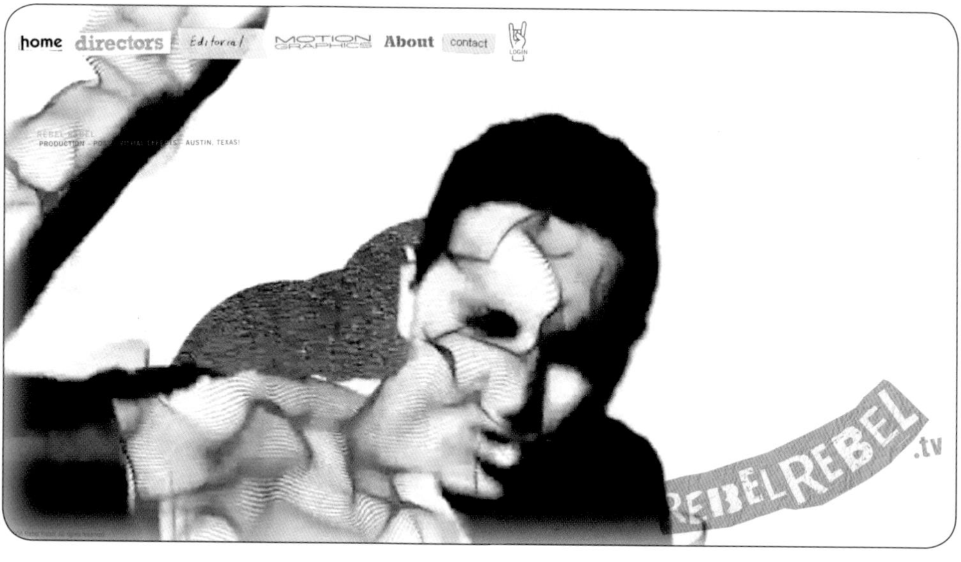

home directors Editorial MOTION GRAPHICS About contact LOGIN

REBELREBEL .tv

Red Issue // www.red-issue.com

RED issue

.coll
ection 2008
cam.
paign
shops
pro
file

help

RED issue

cam.
paign
shops
pro
file

help

05-21
top: 11-332 Pakwa/white - print: face
Scarf: Zaltana/black

Hello Monday // www.hellomonday.com

04-21

Shirt: 33-309 Pocahontas/blue

help

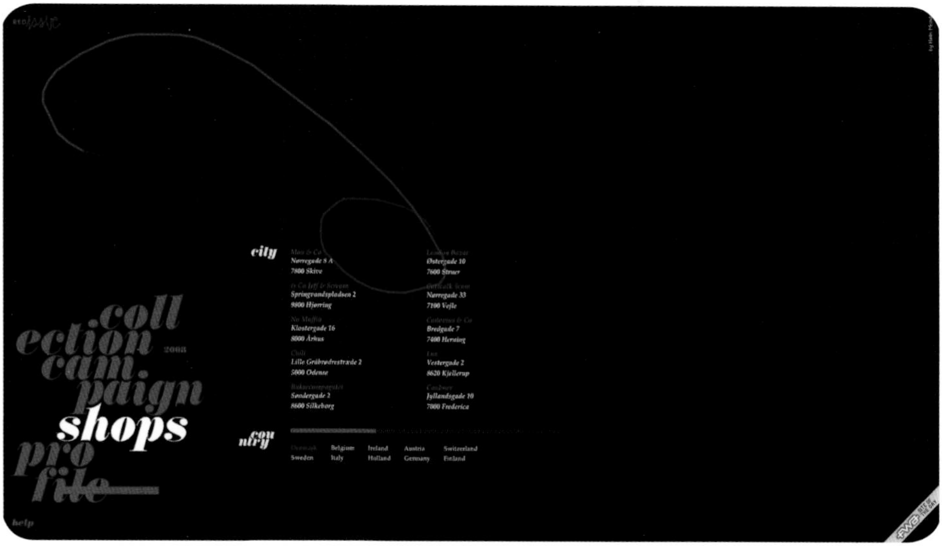

coll
ection 2008
cam
paign
shops
pro
file

help

city

Nørregade 8 A
7800 Skive

Springvandspladsen 2
9800 Hjørring

Klostergade 16
8000 Århus

Lille Gråbrødrestræde 2
5000 Odense

Søndergade 2
8600 Silkeborg

Østergade 10
7600 Struer

Nørregade 33
7100 Vejle

Bredgade 7
7400 Herning

Vestergade 2
8620 Kjellerup

Jyllandsgade 10
7000 Frederica

country

Denmark	Belgium	Ireland	Austria	Switzerland
Sweden	Italy	Holland	Germany	Finland

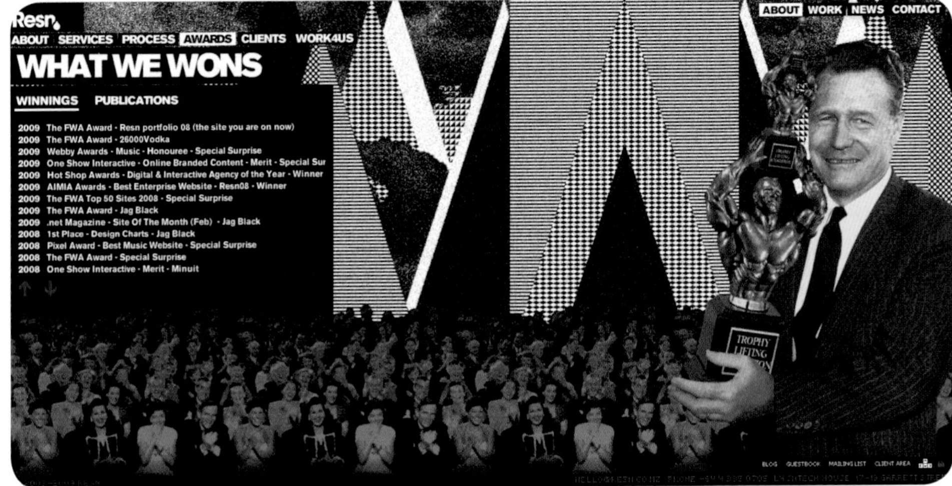

Resn // www.resn.co.nz

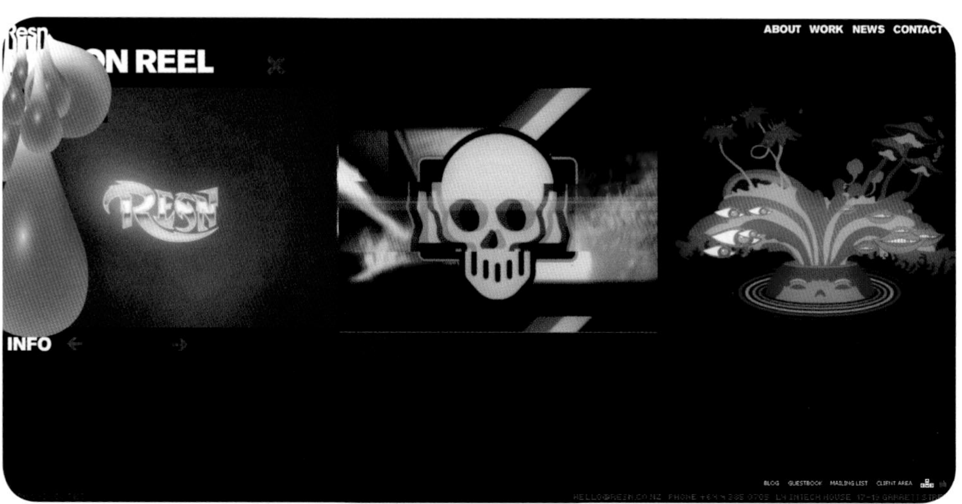

ON REEL
ABOUT WORK NEWS CONTACT
INFO

Resn
ABOUT WORK
EMAIL RESN
+64 4 3850705
SKYPE
TWITTER
FACEBOOK
L4 INTECH HOUSE
17-19 GARRETT STREET
WELLINGTON
NEW ZEALAND
GOOGLE MAPS

Like the clothing she designs, Rory Edelman, the founder of Rory Beca, is fun, spirited, and sophisticated. Her love of clothing and "dressing up" began when she was just a young child, but later blossomed into an insatiable curiosity to learn all she could about color, fabrics, and the true art forms behind fashion.
STYLIST
VOGUE

designedmemory // www.designedmemory.com

RoryBeca
fall 2009
SUMMER 2009
SPRING 2009

RoryBeca
Lucky
NYLON
CONFIDENTIAL
VARIETY
Project Runway
marie claire
Summer BEAUTY 101
WWD FRIDAY
Head Trip

rvlt /2009
rev o
lu
tion/
Personal style never goes out of fashion
Collection
Campaign
Stores
Profile
Contact
rvlt /eshop

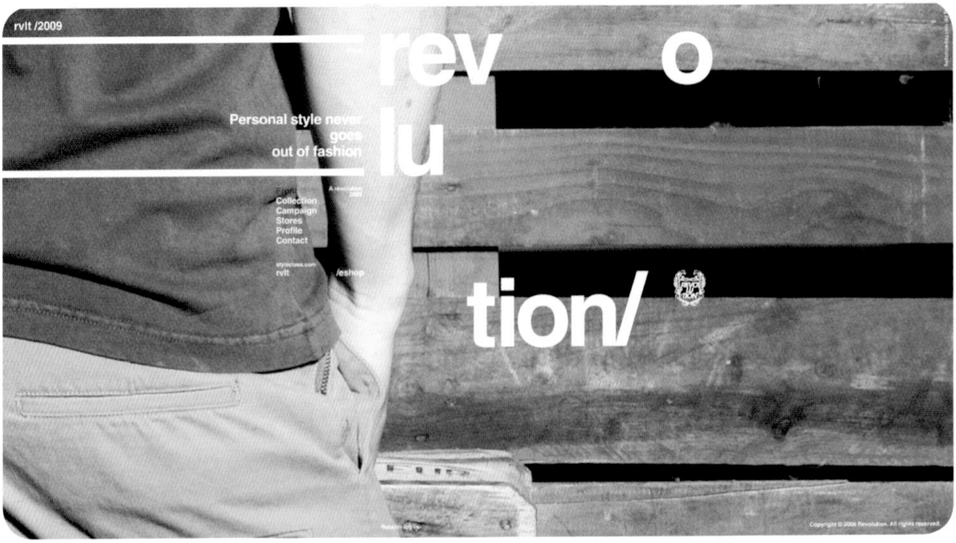

Hello Monday // www.hellomonday.com

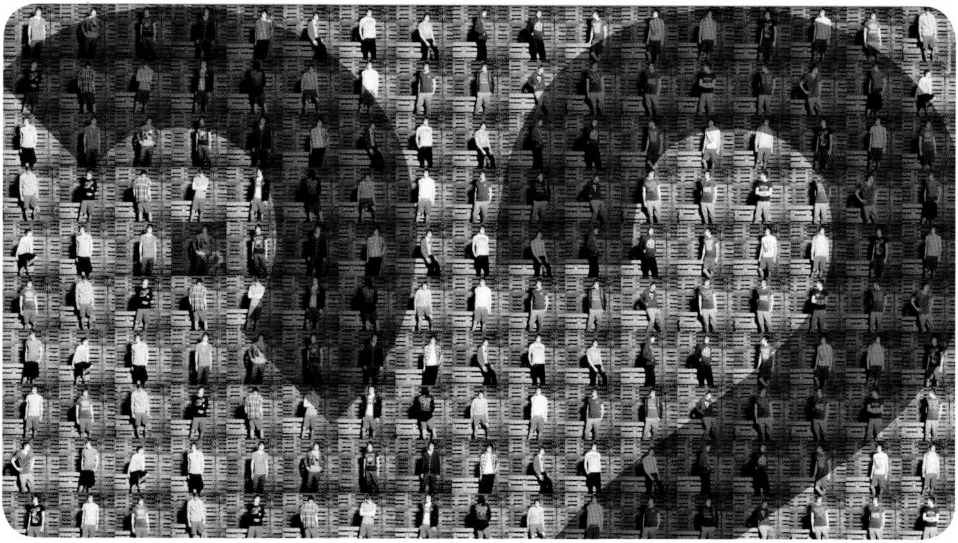

rvlt /2009

Go to front

Style info

Show thumbnails

t-shirt: 1024 idol/fashion
Chinos: 5071 mac

07

— 35

Next/
Previous

Copyright © 2009 Revolution. All rights reserved.

S2 Pictures // www.slusherphotography.com

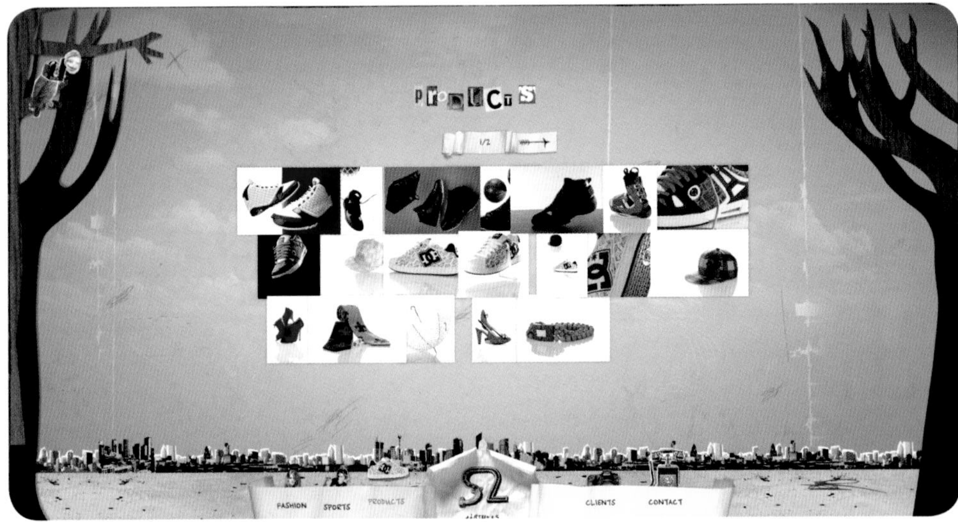

Daniel Hirunrusme // www.wearemanilla.com

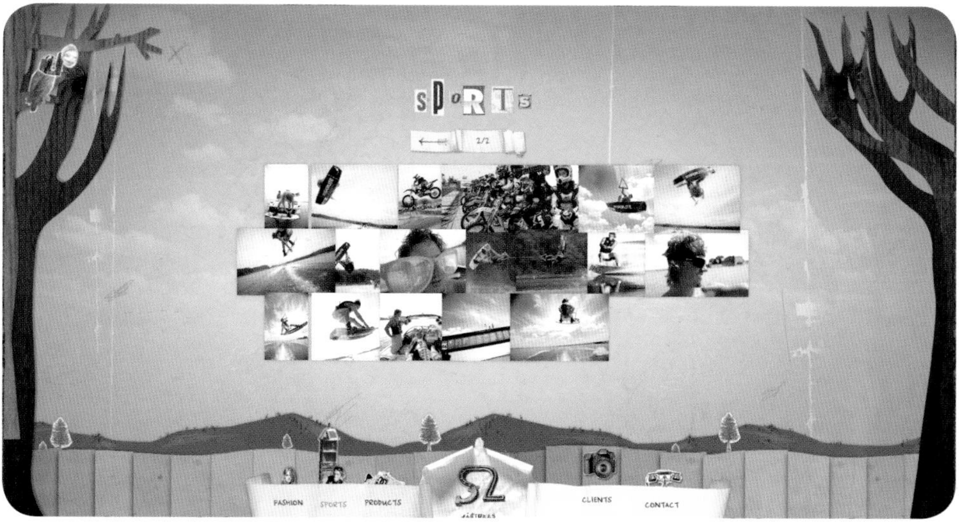
SPoRTS
2/2
FASHION
SPORTS
PRODUCTS
CLIENTS
CONTACT

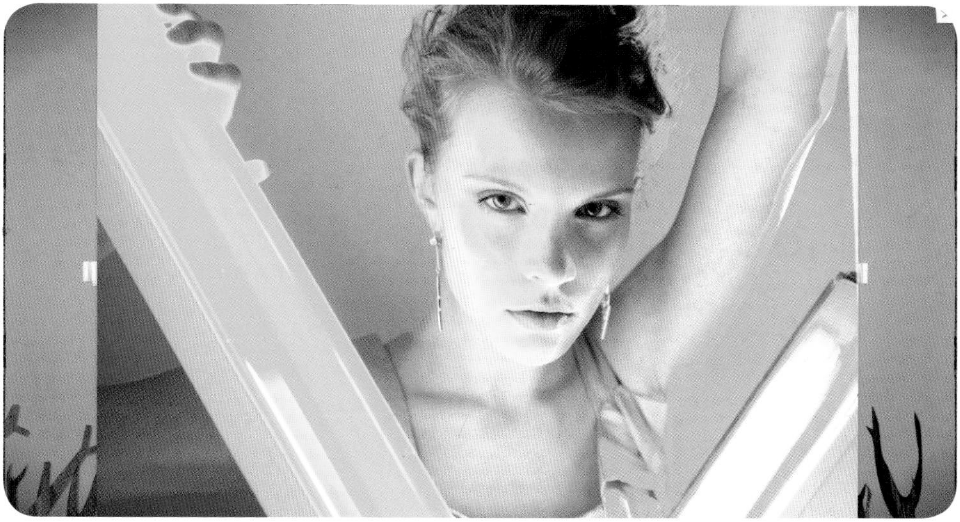

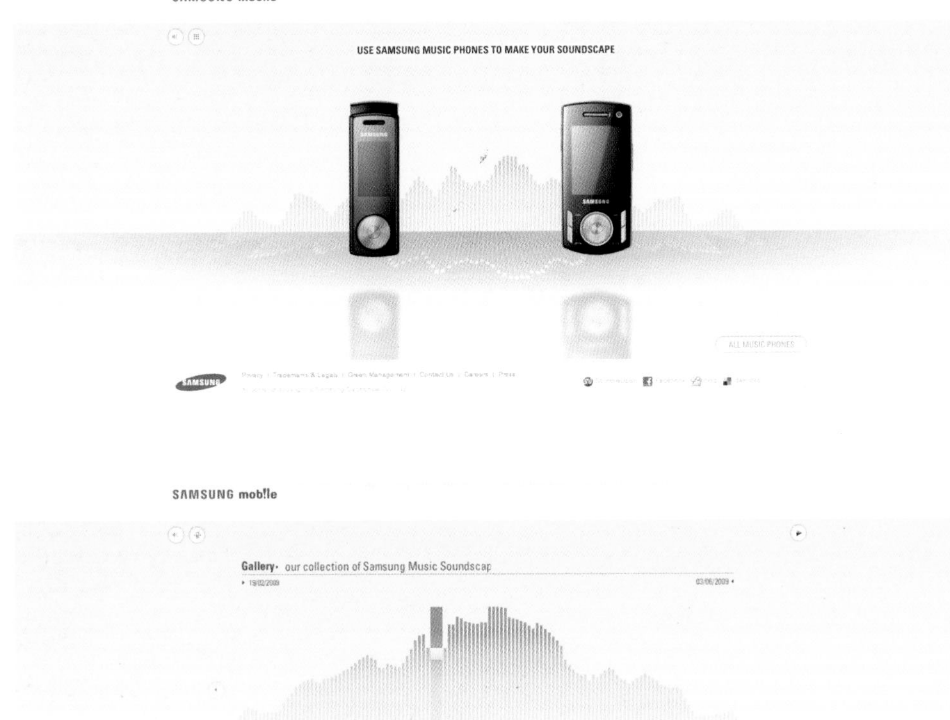

unit9 // www.unit9.com
Mather London // www.matheruk.com

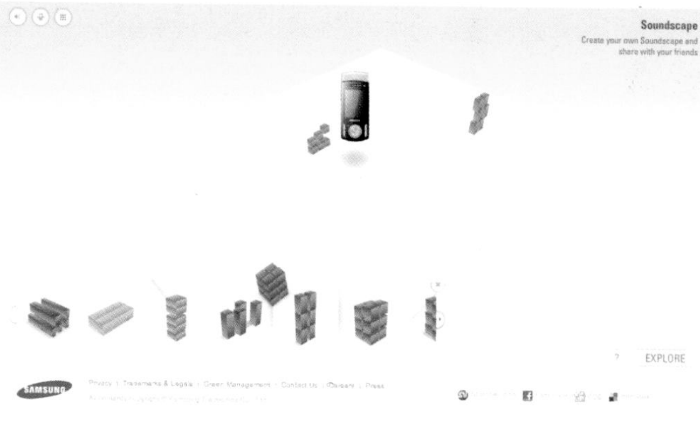
SAMSUNG mob!le
Soundscape
Create your own Soundscape and
share with your friends
EXPLORE

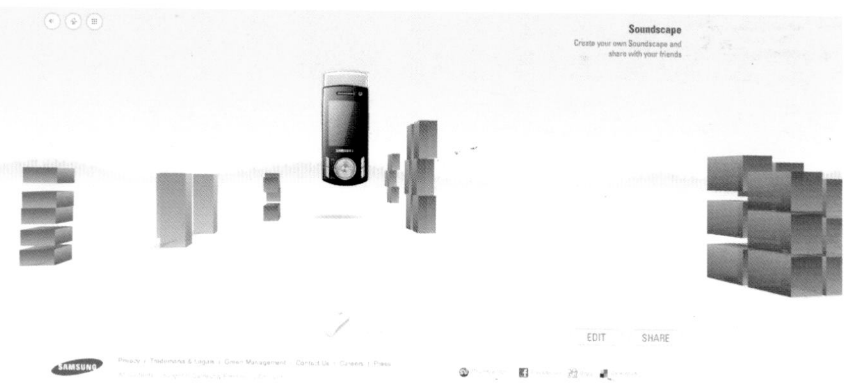
SAMSUNG mob!le
Soundscape
Create your own Soundscape and
share with your friends
EDIT
SHARE

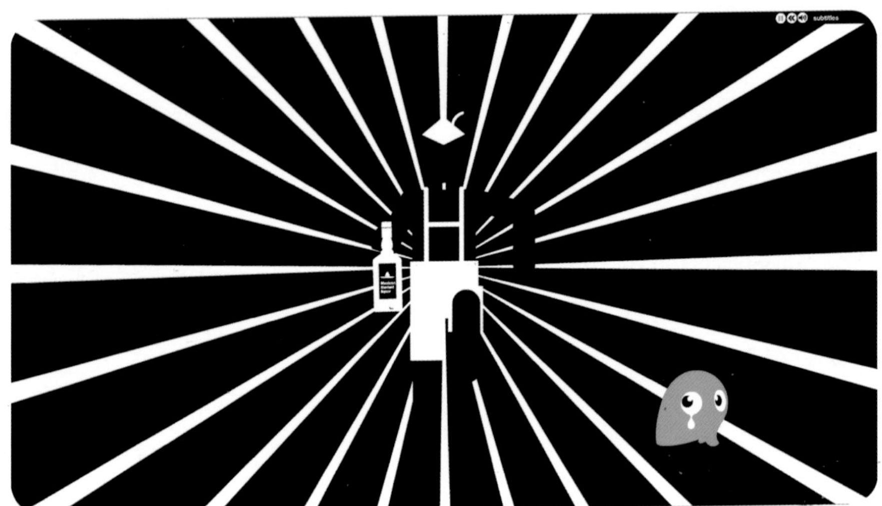

George Patterson Y & R // www.gpyr.com.au
Boffswana // www.boffswana.com
Iloura // www.iloura.com.au
Next Studio // www.nextstudio.com.au

subtitles
Sadly,
this has lead to
many of us
actually
our
sensible

subtitles

Scott Balmer illustration
News Portfolio Blog Biography Contact
welcome to my world

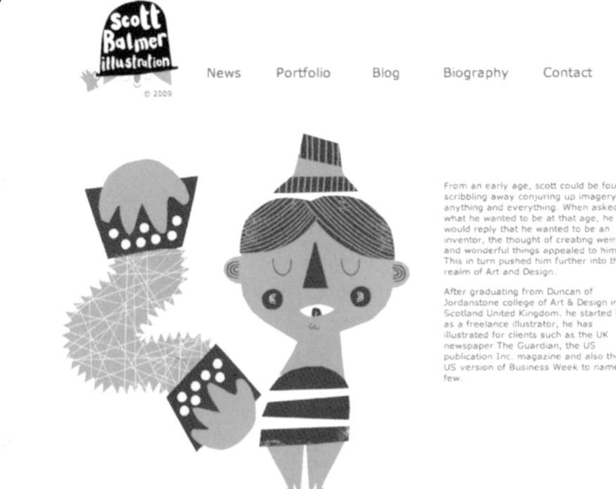

Scott Balmer // scottbalmer.co.uk

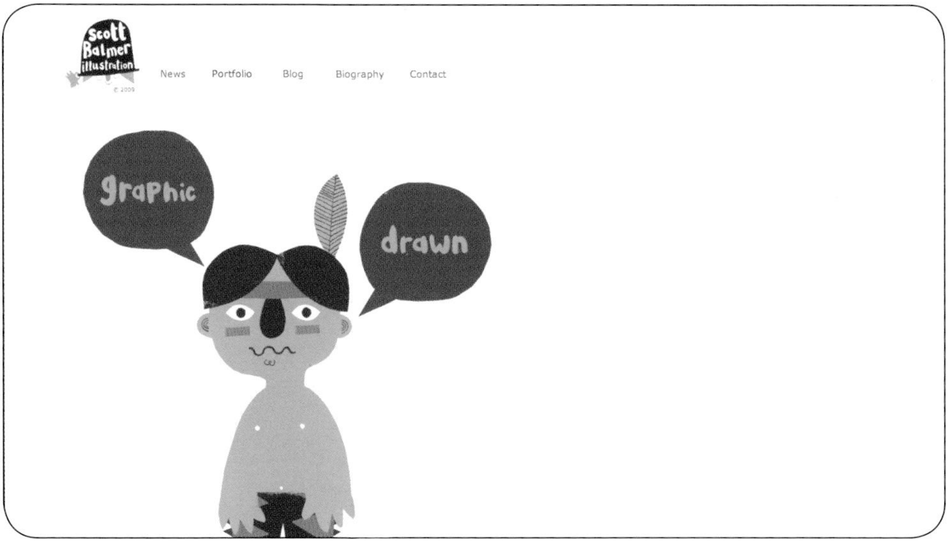

Scott Balmer illustration

News Portfolio Blog Biography Contact

© 2009

graphic

drawn

Scott Balmer illustration

News Portfolio Blog Biography Contact

© 2009

Hiring - Finding the Perfect Fit

Commissioned by Inc Magazine (USA)

Cut paper, paint and line drawing

graphic

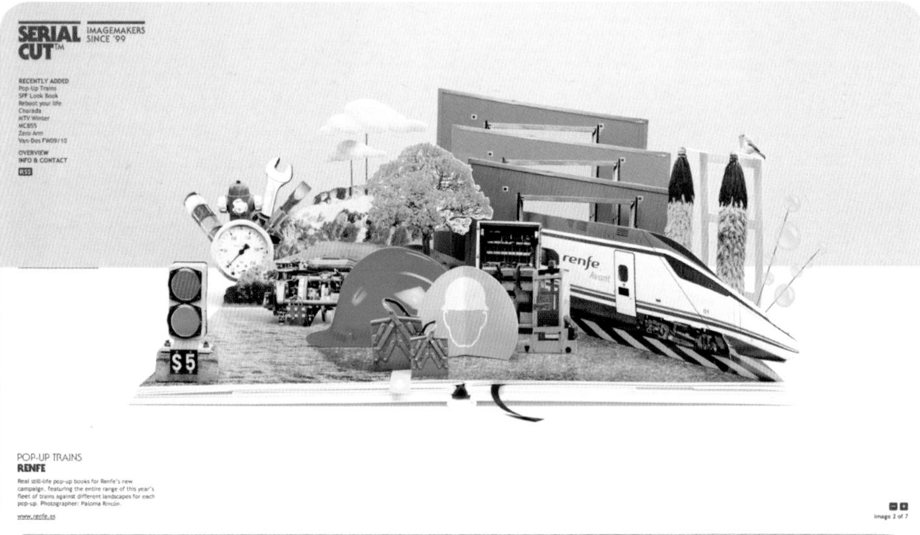

Sergio del Puerto/ Serial Cut™ // www.serialcut.com

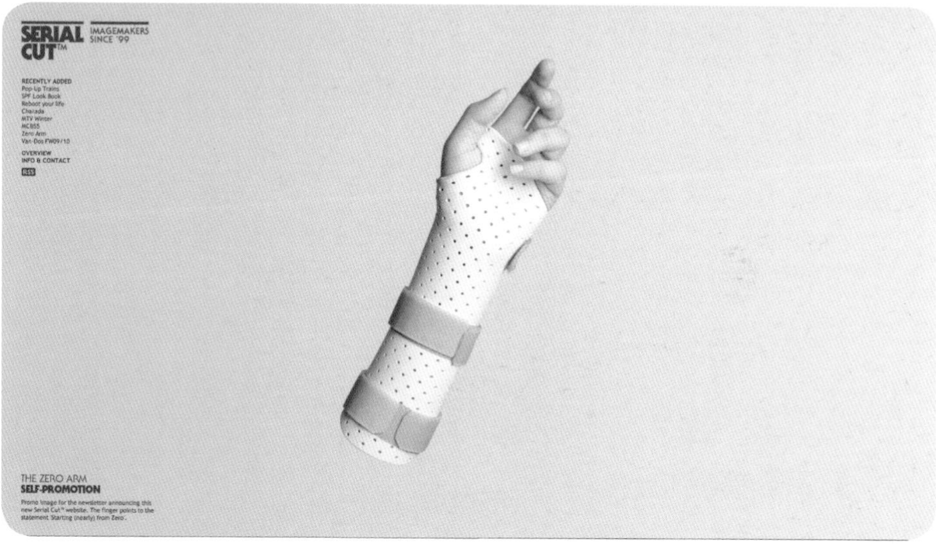

SERIAL CUT™ IMAGEMAKERS SINCE '99

RECENTLY ADDED
Pop-Up Trains
SPF Look Book
Reboot your life
Charada
MTV Winter
MCBSS
Zero Arm
Van-Dos FW09/10

OVERVIEW
INFO & CONTACT

RSS

THE ZERO ARM
SELF-PROMOTION

Promo image for the newsletter announcing this new Serial Cut™ website. The finger points to the statement 'Starting (nearly) from Zero'.

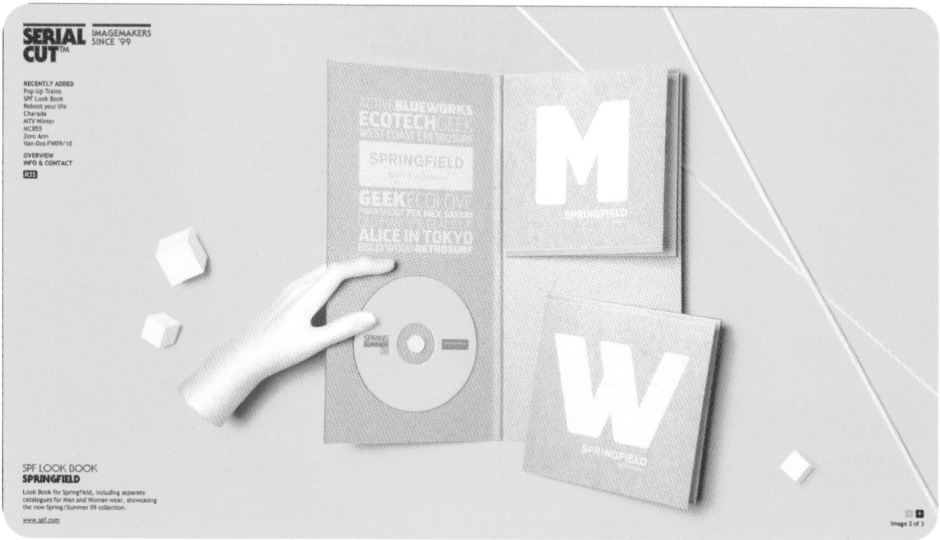

SERIAL CUT™ IMAGEMAKERS SINCE '99

RECENTLY ADDED
Pop-Up Trains
SPF Look Book
Reboot your life
Charada
MTV Winter
MCBSS
Zero Arm
Van-Dos FW09/10

OVERVIEW
INFO & CONTACT

RSS

ECOTECH
SPRINGFIELD
GEEK
ALICE IN TOKYO
M
W

SPF LOOK BOOK
SPRINGFIELD

Look Book for Springfield, including separate catalogues for Man and Woman wear, showcasing the new Spring/Summer 09 collection.

www.spf.com

Image 2 of 3

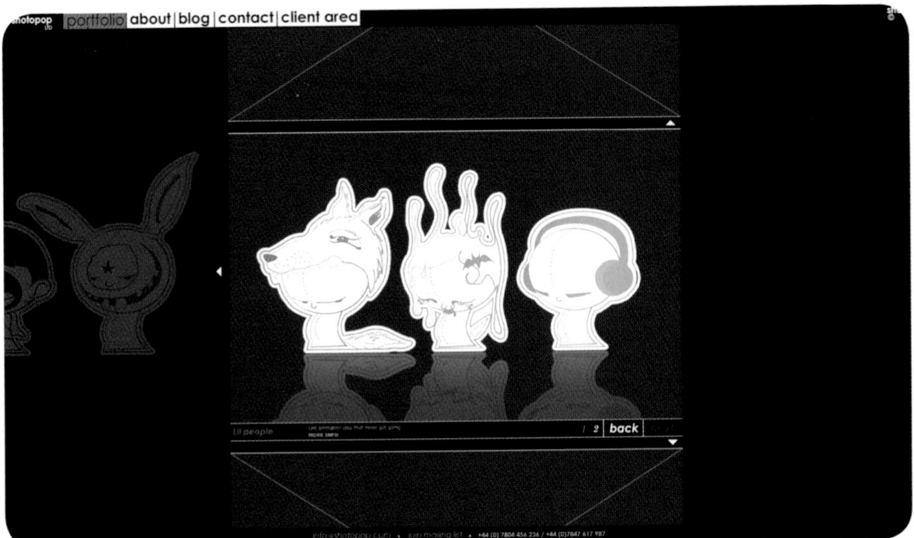

Carin Standford, Casper Franken/ Shotopop // www.shotopop.com

shotopop LTD
portfolio about blog contact client area
SCRABBLE
The Beautiful Word
Mixed nuts
MORE INFO
1 2 back next
info@shotopop.com • join mailing list • +44 (0) 7804 456 236 / +44 (0)7847 617 987

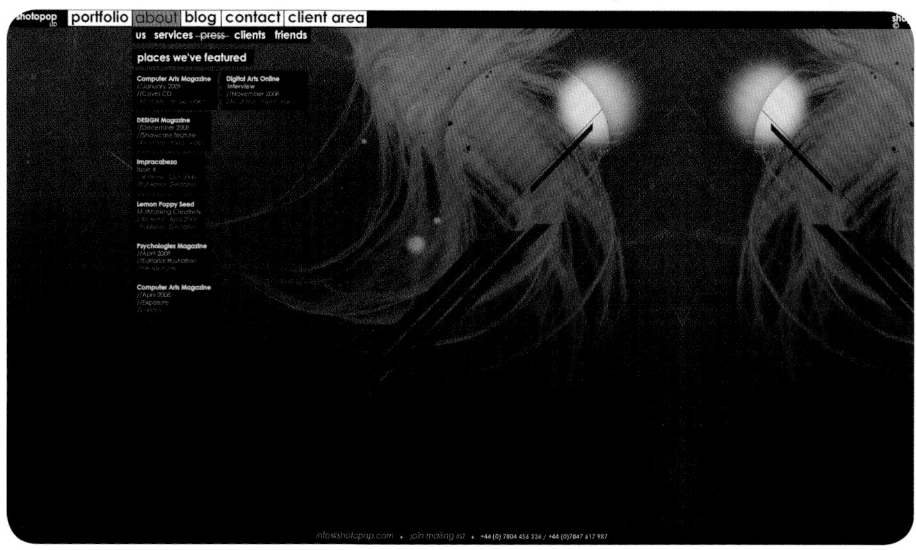
shotopop LTD
portfolio about blog contact client area
us services press clients friends
places we've featured
Computer Arts Magazine
//January 2009
//Cover CD
Digital Arts Online
Interview
//November 2008
DESIGN Magazine
//December 2008
//Showcase feature
Impracabeza
Issue 4
Lemon Poppy Seed
Psychologies Magazine
//April 2009
Computer Arts Magazine
//April 2008
//Exposure
info@shotopop.com • join mailing list • +44 (0) 7804 456 236 / +44 (0)7847 617 987

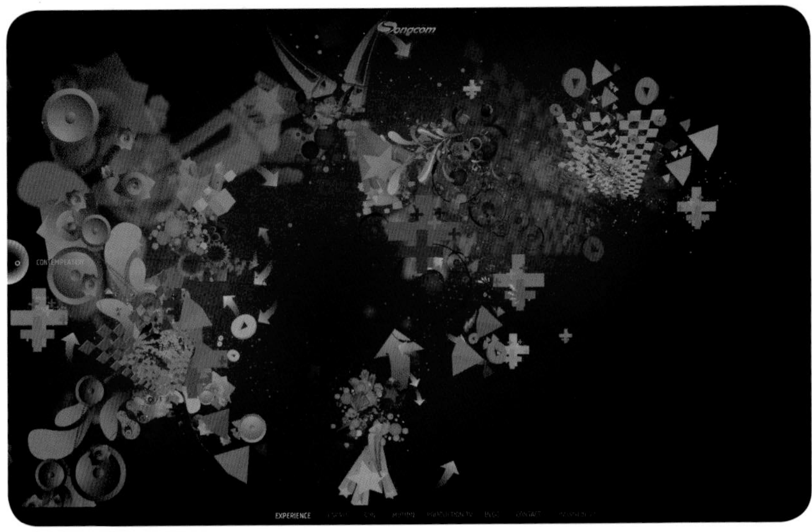

Lysergid // www.lysergid.com
Marc Guillaumin // www.magu-design.com

Sonacom
INVASION
IM
MENU

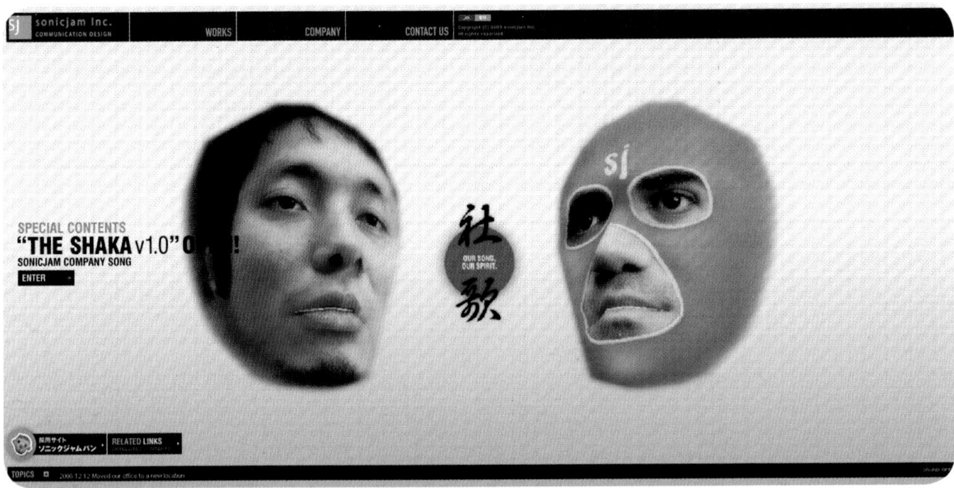

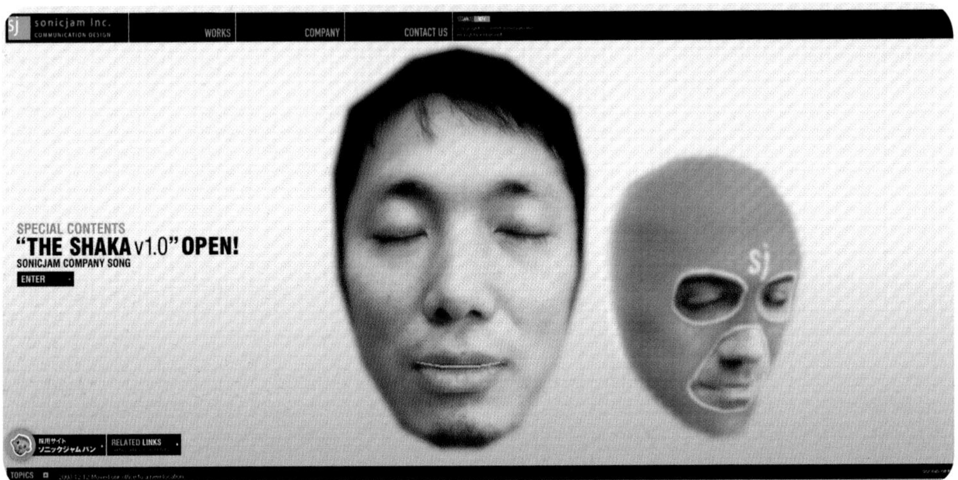

sonicjam Inc. // www.sonicjam.co.jp

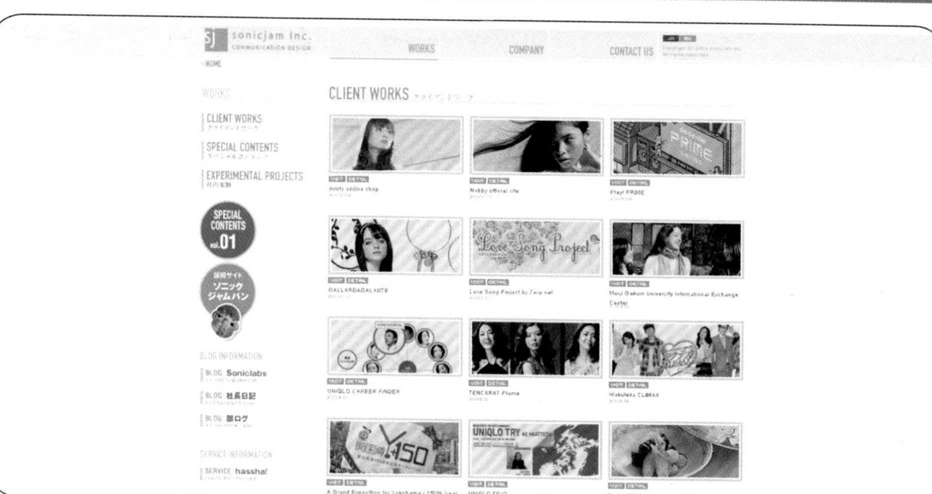
sonicjam Inc.
COMMUNICATION DESIGN
WORKS
COMPANY
CONTACT US
HOME
WORKS
CLIENT WORKS クライアントワーク
CLIENT WORKS
クライアントワーク
SPECIAL CONTENTS
EXPERIMENTAL PROJECTS
SPECIAL CONTENTS vol.01
採用サイト
ソニックジャムパン
BLOG INFORMATION
BLOG Soniclabs
BLOG 社長日記
BLOG 部ログ
SERVICE INFORMATION
SERVICE hassha!
mmts online shop
Nobby official site
Play! PRIME
GALLARDAGALANTE
Love Song Project by Zexy.net
Meiji Gakuin University International Exchange Center
UNIQLO CAREER FINDER
TENCARAT Plume
Wakuteka CL@MAX
A Grand Exposition for Yokohama's 150th Year
UNIQLO TRY2
Kyotyon Yokoi

WORKS
CLIENT WORKS クライアントワーク
CLIENT WORKS
SPECIAL CONTENTS
EXPERIMENTAL PROJECTS
SPECIAL CONTENTS vol.01
採用サイト
ソニックジャムパン
BLOG INFORMATION
BLOG Soniclabs
BLOG 社長日記
BLOG 部ログ
SERVICE INFORMATION
SERVICE hassha!
トリックアート
Y150
第二期前売入場券
BACK CLIENT WORKS 018
VISIT WEB SITE
A Grand Exposition for Yokohama's 150th Year Official Website
2008.11
Association for the 150th Anniversary of the
Hiroshi Kuga (Asatsu-DK, Inc.)
Yamato Nara (Asatsu-DK, Inc.)
Toru Tanaka (Asatsu-DK, Inc.)
Ken Murata (sonicjam Inc.)
Emiko Oikawa (sonicjam Inc.)
Hiroko Sasagawa (sonicjam Inc.)
Miho Ino (sonicjam Inc.)
Park Eunkyung (sonicjam Inc.)
Yuka Nakazawa (sonicjam Inc.)
Yasuhiro Kimura (sonicjam Inc.)
The official website for the Grand Exposition for Yokohama's 150th Year, an event to commemorate 150 years since the opening of the port of Yokohama. The website has an organized layout commensurate with its role as an official website providing up-to-date information on events and instructions for purchasing tickets with a touch of playfulness to portray the fun mood of the event. We were responsible for the planning, overall production, and management of the website.

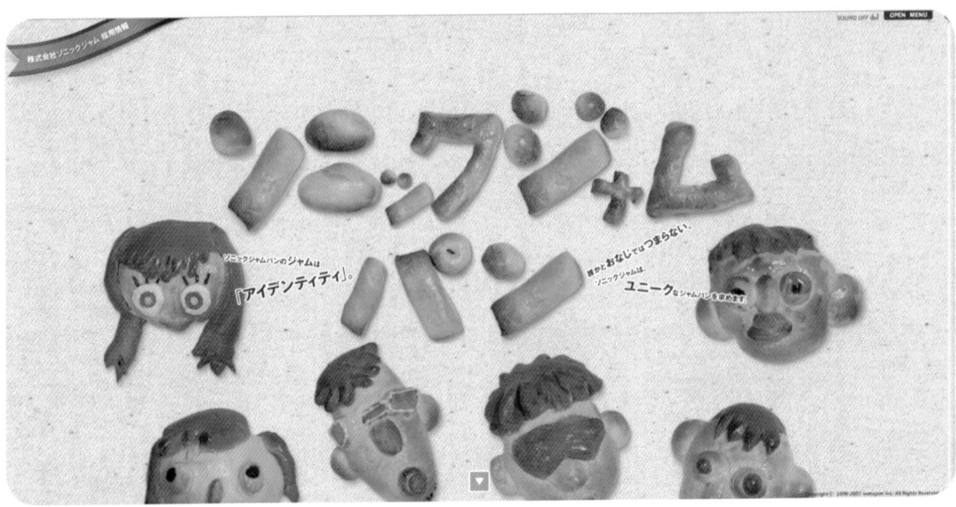

sonicjam Inc. // www.sonicjam.co.jp

株式会社ソニックジャム 採用情報
ソニックジャムパンたち
スタッフ
紹介

株式会社ソニックジャム 採用情報
SOUND OFF
OPEN MENU
潜入!!
ソニックジャムパン工場
ようこそ!
sonicjam Inc.
リラックススペース
以上なのだ

Kinetic // www.kinetic.com.sg

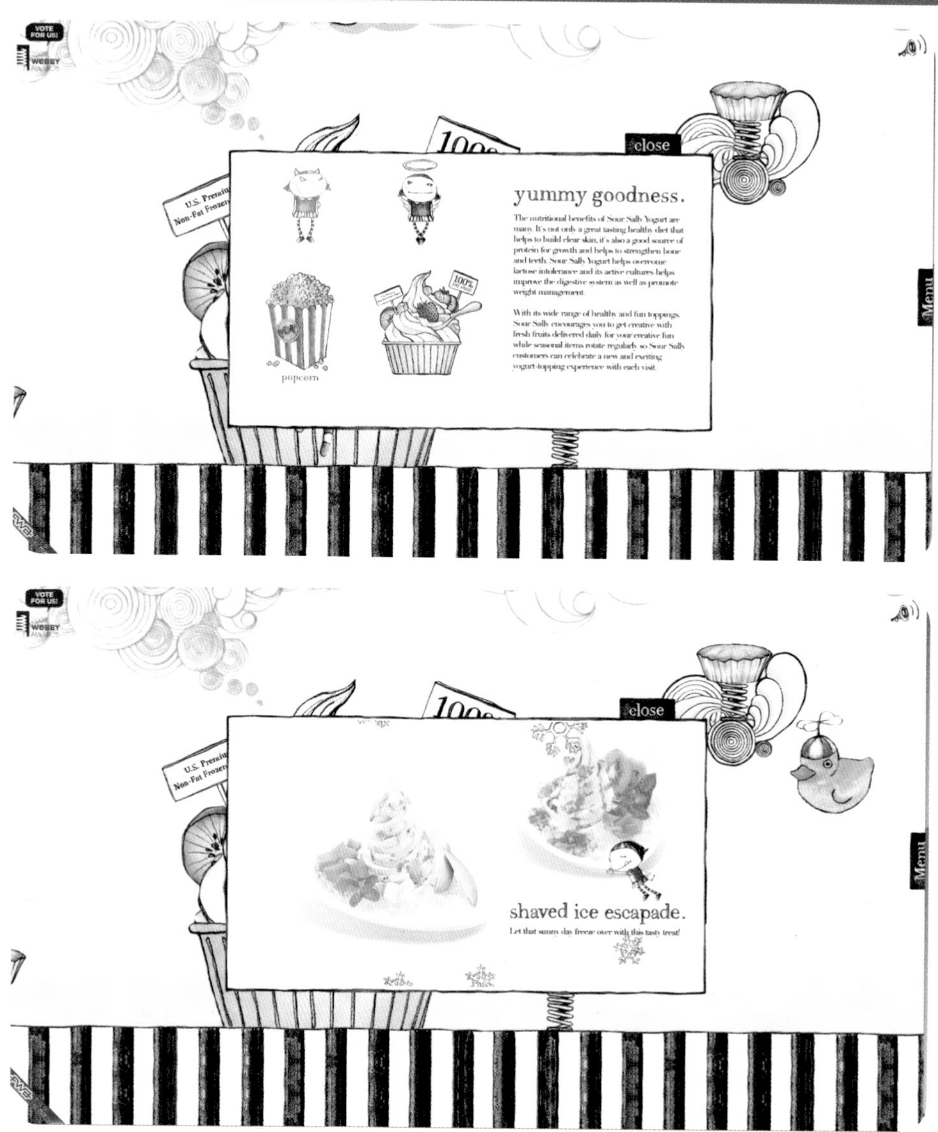

VOTE FOR US!
WEBBY AWARDS
close
yummy goodness.
The nutritional benefits of Sour Sally Yogurt are many. It's not only a great tasting healthy diet that helps to build clear skin, it's also a good source of protein for growth and helps to strengthen bone and teeth. Sour Sally Yogurt helps overcome lactose intolerance and its active cultures helps improve the digestive system as well as promote weight management.
With its wide range of healthy and fun toppings, Sour Sally encourages you to get creative with fresh fruits delivered daily for your creative fun while seasonal items rotate regularly so Sour Sally customers can celebrate a new and exciting yogurt-topping experience with each visit.
popcorn
Menu
VOTE FOR US!
WEBBY AWARDS
close
shaved ice escapade.
Let that sunny day freeze over with this tasty treat!
Menu

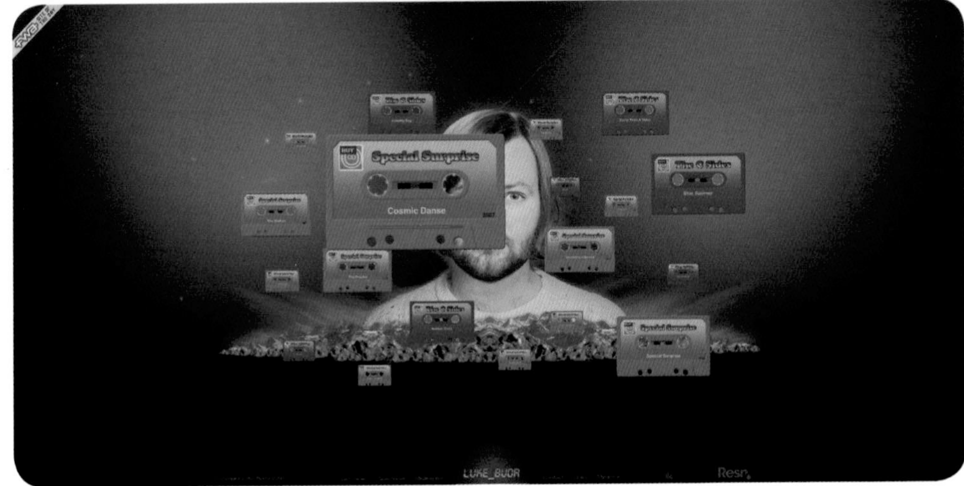

Resn // www.resn.co.nz

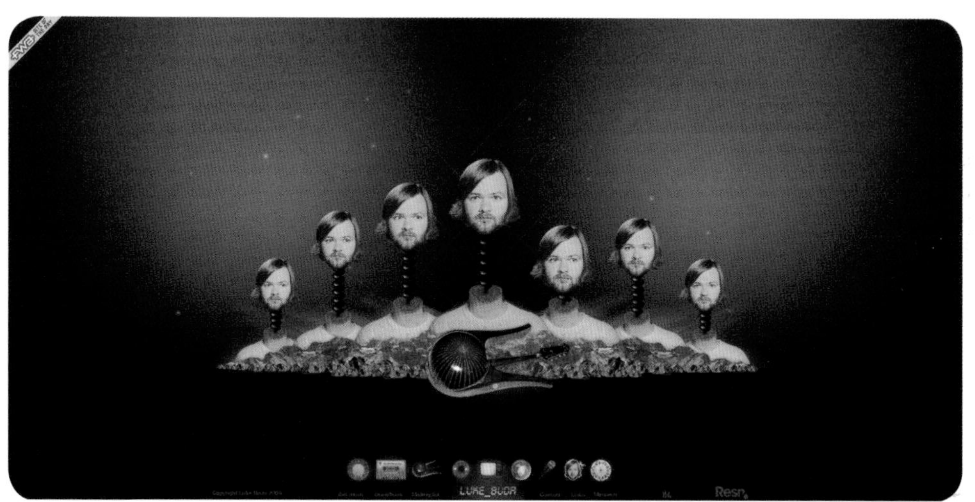
LUKE_BUDA
Resn

YouTube
LUKE_BUDA
Resn

Spöka // www.spoka.net/v2/

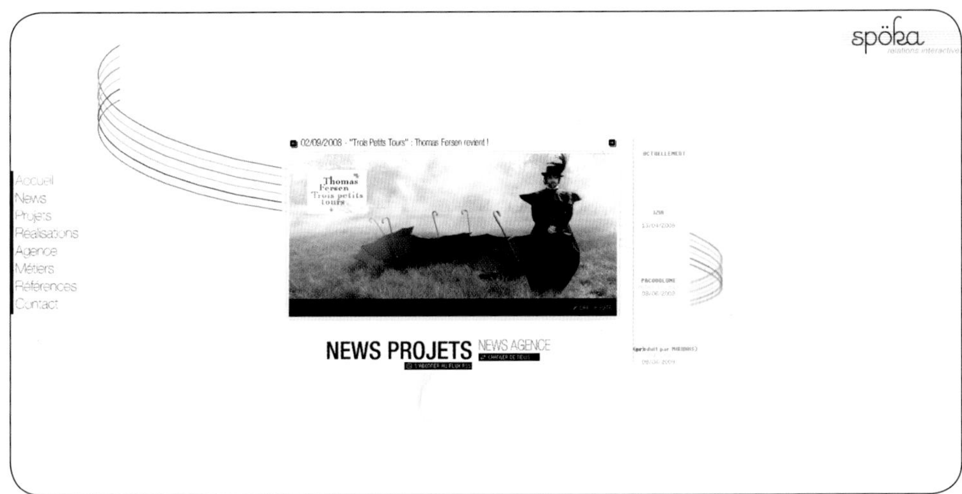

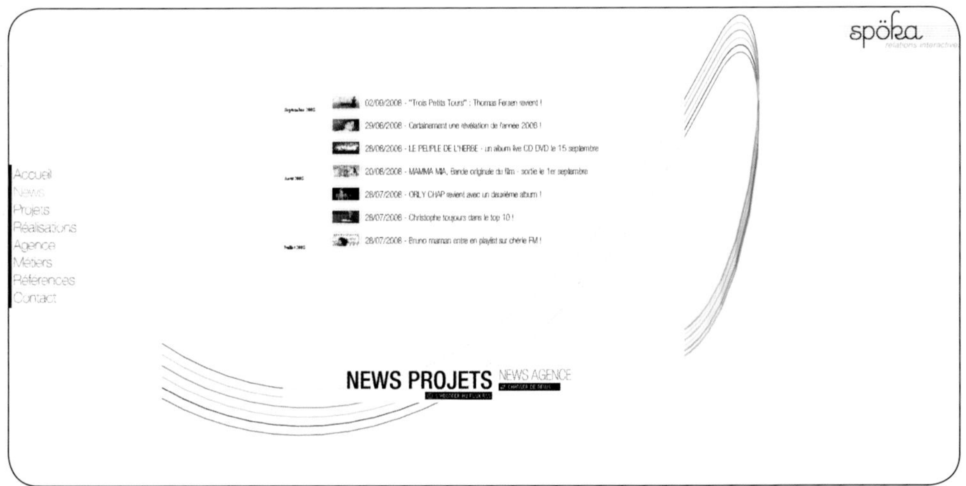

Jocker / CREAKTIF ! // www.creaktif.com/jocker/
noMatter // www.nomatter.eu

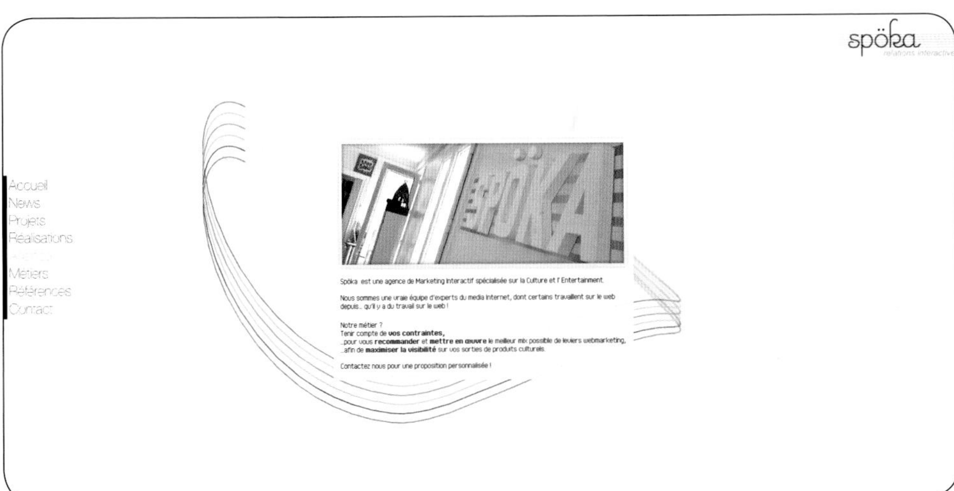
spöka
relations interactives
Accueil
News
Projets
Réalisations
Métiers
Références
Contact
Spöka est une agence de Marketing Interactif spécialisée sur la Culture et l'Entertainment.
Nous sommes une vraie équipe d'experts du media Internet, dont certains travaillent sur le web depuis... qu'il y a du travail sur le web !
Notre métier ?
Tenir compte de vos contraintes,
...pour vous recommander et mettre en œuvre le meilleur mix possible de leviers webmarketing,
...afin de maximiser la visibilité sur vos sorties de produits culturels.
Contactez nous pour une proposition personnalisée !

spöka
relations interactives
Accueil
News
Projets
Réalisations
Agence
Références
Contact
Straté gie de communication et promotion online, Ventes digitales, Optimisation technique web
shake & share
CONSEIL
RELATIONS PUBLIQUES
PROMOTION
BUZZMARKETING

Square Circle Media // www.sqcircle.com

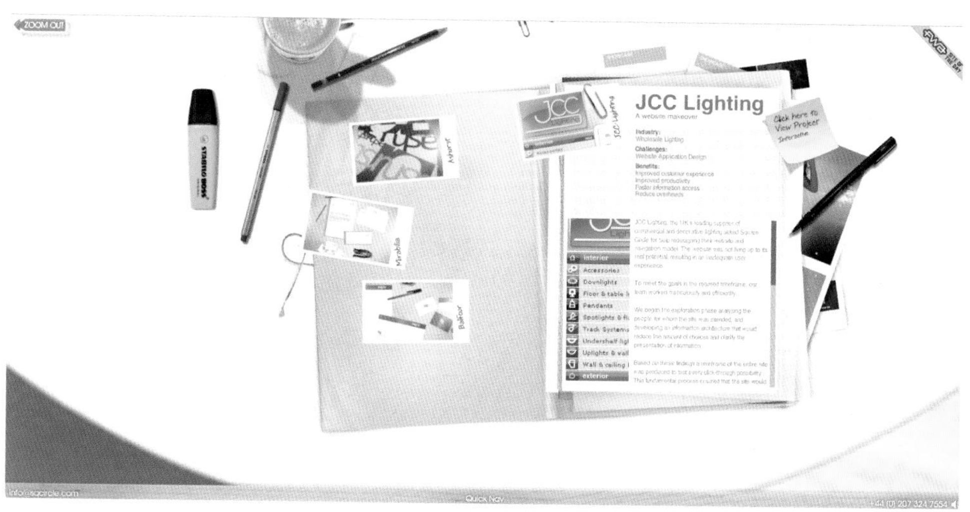
ZOOM OUT
JCC Lighting
A website makeover
Industry:
Challenges:
Benefits:
Click here to View Project
info@sqcircle.com
Quick Nav
+44 (0) 207 324 7554

ZOOM OUT
square circle
things to do
dial 123 for time
Square Circle Media
1st Floor
77 Leonard Street
London
EC2A 4QS
United Kingdom
for all your enquiries...
info@sqcircle.com
+44 (0) 207 324 7554
Click on the logo to open Skype
skype
Have a chat with us or leave a voice mail...
info@sqcircle.com
Quick Nav
+44 (0) 207 324 7554

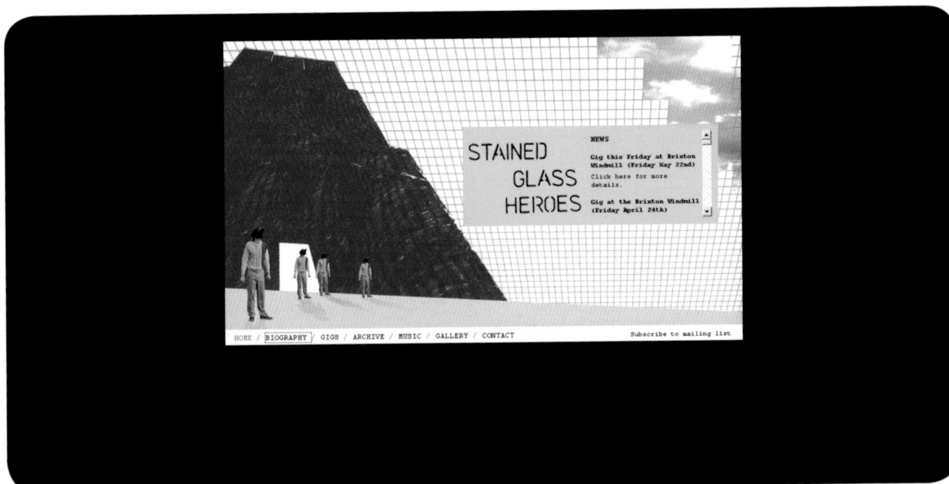

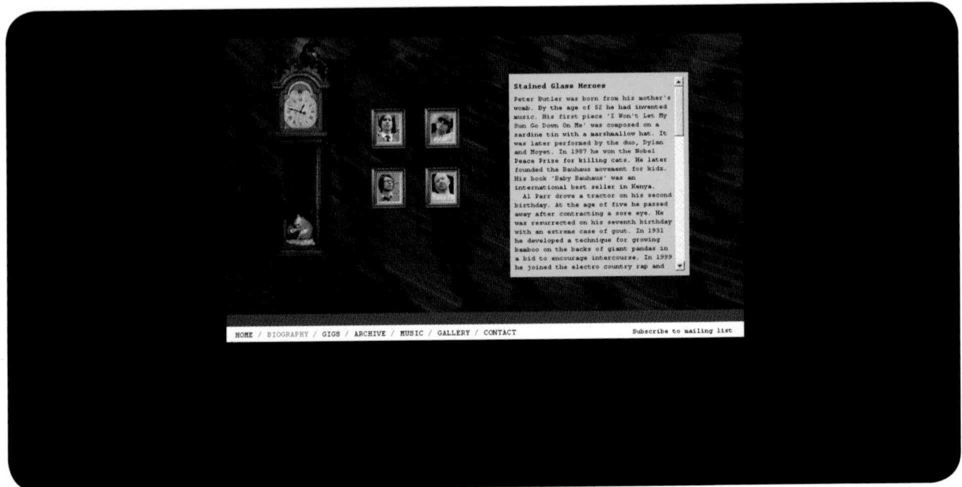

Alastair Parr // cignaspine.com
Victoria Ford // victoriaforddesign.com

Random pics
Metro
The Windmill
Nambuca
Needles
Halloween 2006
HOME / BIOGRAPHY / GIGS / ARCHIVE / MUSIC / GALLERY / CONTACT
Subscribe to mailing list

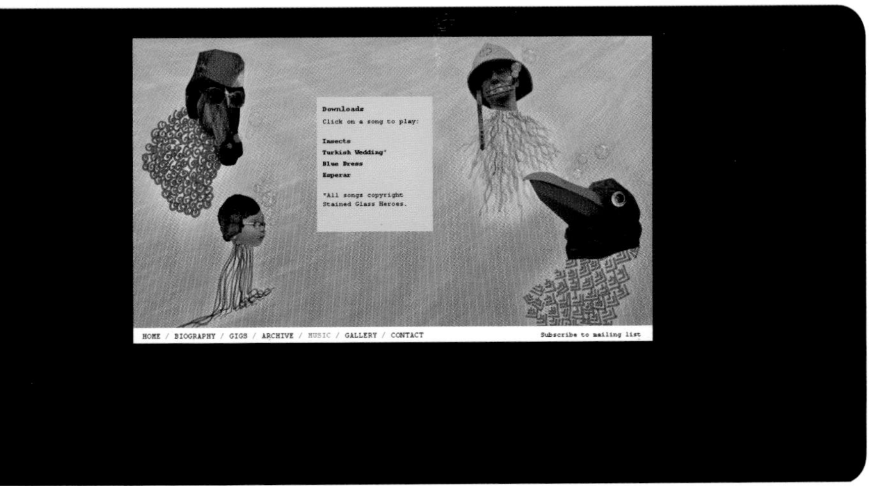
Downloads
Click on a song to play:
Insects
Turkish Wedding*
Blue Dress
Esperar
*All songs copyright Stained Glass Heroes.
HOME / BIOGRAPHY / GIGS / ARCHIVE / MUSIC / GALLERY / CONTACT
Subscribe to mailing list

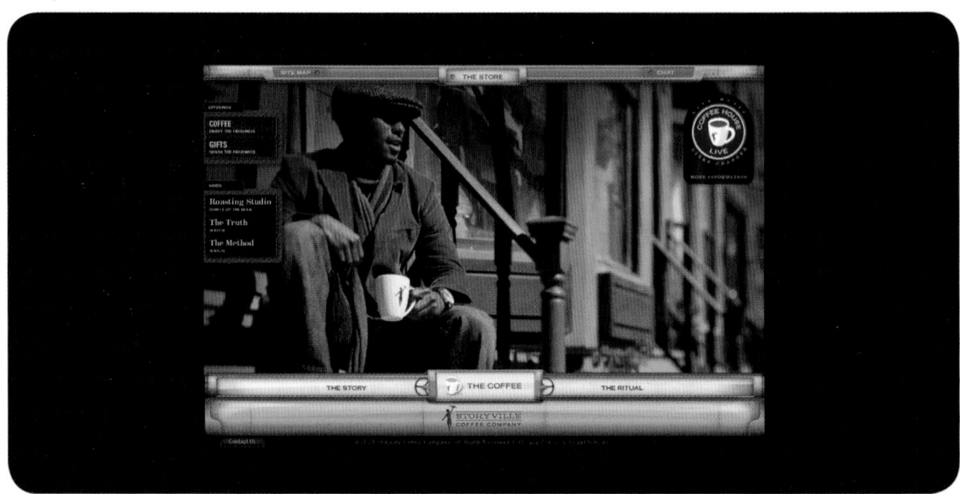

Will Weyer
eff Askew
Eric Fickes/ Wiretree // www.wiretree.com

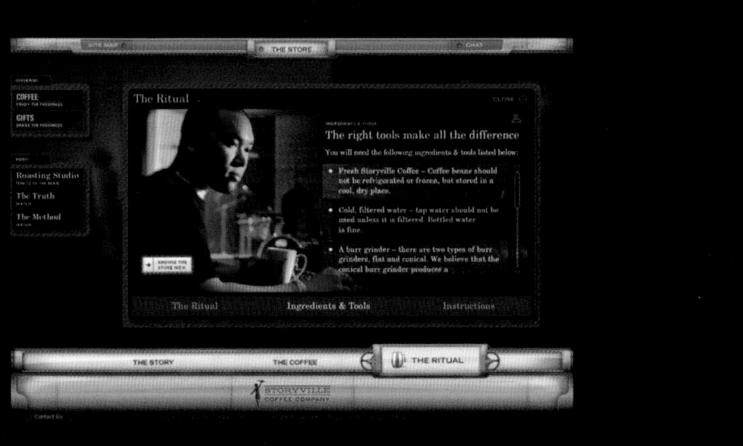
THE STORE
COFFEE
GIFTS
Roasting Studio
The Truth
The Method
The Ritual
The right tools make all the difference
You will need the following ingredients & tools listed below:
Fresh Storyville Coffee – Coffee beans should not be refrigerated or frozen, but stored in a cool, dry place.
Cold, filtered water – tap water should not be used unless it is filtered. Bottled water is fine.
A burr grinder – there are two types of burr grinders, flat and conical. We believe that the conical burr grinder produces a
The Ritual
Ingredients & Tools
Instructions
THE STORY
THE COFFEE
THE RITUAL
STORYVILLE
COFFEE COMPANY

COFFEE
GIFTS
ESSENTIALS
VIEW BASKET
CHECKOUT
STORE
Product Detail
CALL US 888.323.3348
Chat
Prologue
Storyville has one flavor - fresh.
Our philosophy is: keep it simple and make it great. We don't offer an assortment of roasts, blends and flavors; we ship only one coffee. Although we think flavors like amaretto, almond, hazelnut, cinnamon, nutmeg, pumpkin, mint and curry have their place in the world, we believe the best flavor for coffee...is coffee. Storyville offers two versions of our signature blend: Prologue, the original, and Epilogue, the Swiss Water Process decaffeinated.
THE CATALOG
See all the products we offer. Click below.
View Catalog
SHIPPING
Coffee prices include priority shipping.
Prologue
$13.99
1/2 lb.
+ Purchase
Epilogue
$14.99
1/2 lb.
+ Purchase
ITEM# 8-50080-00198-1
PRIVATE RESERVE
Become a Private Reserve member and customize your weekly delivery.
+ Join Private Reserve
Price: $13.99
Select Quantity: 01
+ Purchase
BASKET
$0.00
CLOSE STORE
STORYVILLE
COFFEE COMPANY

SUBRAUMSTUDIO I Industrial Design - Architecture - 3D // www.subraumstudio.com

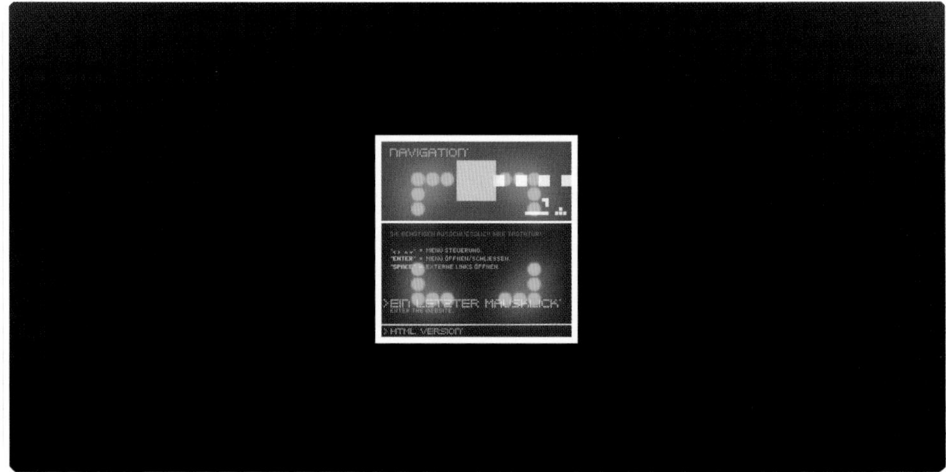

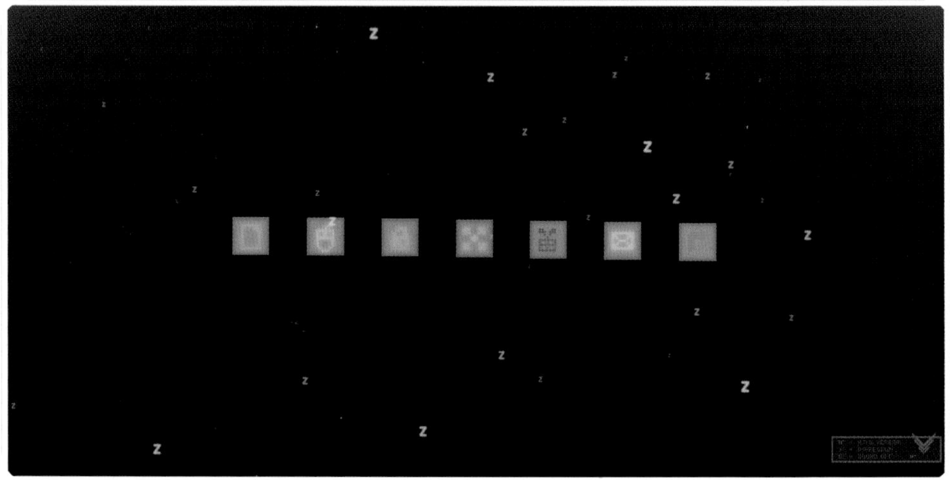

Andre Weier / NALINDESIGN™ // www.nalindesign.com

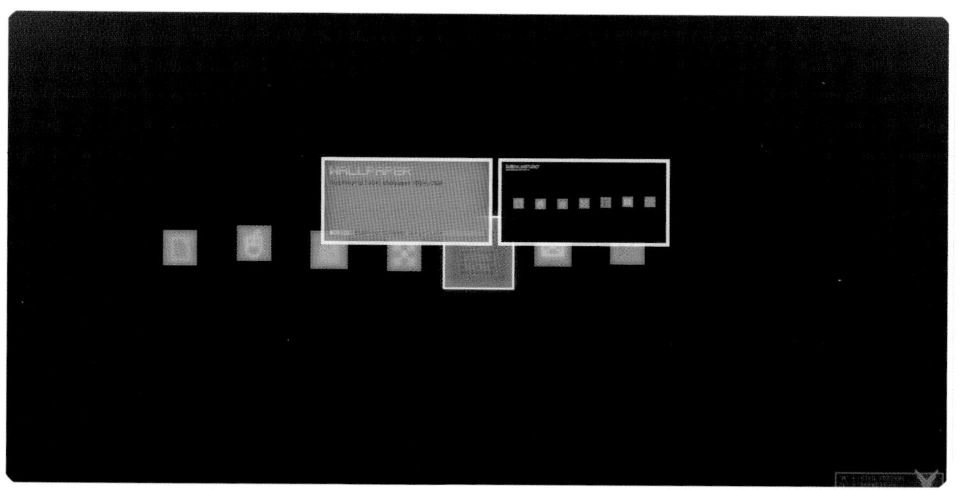

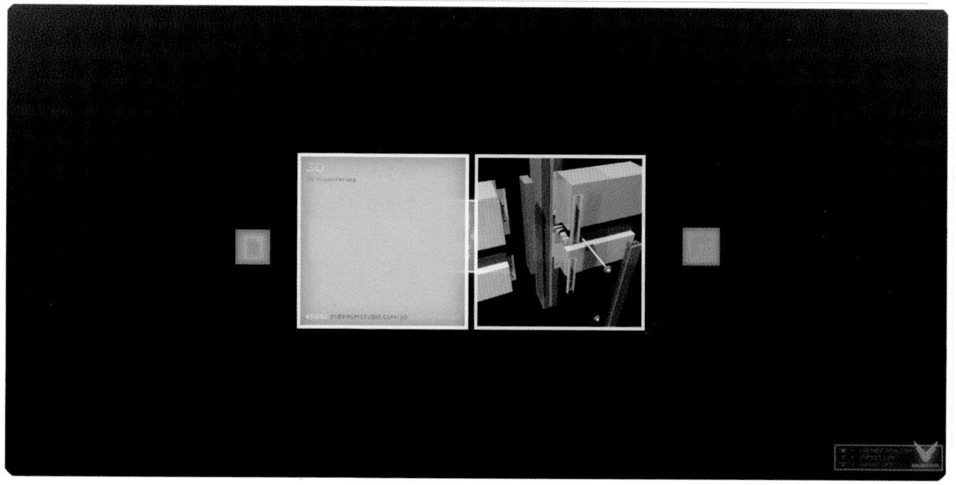

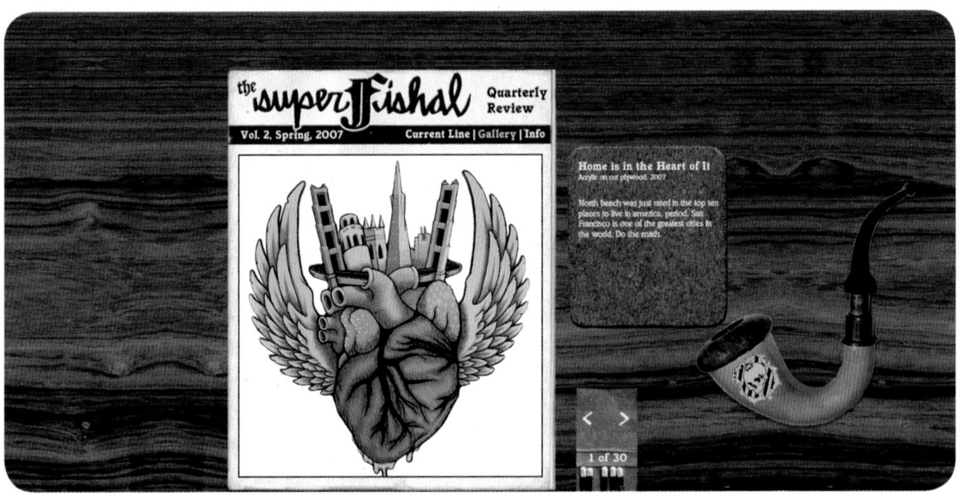

Jason Herring
Brenden Lee/ OrdinaryKids // www.ordinarykids.com

the superFishal
Quarterly Review
Vol. 2, Spring, 2007
Current Line | Gallery | Info
curriculum vitae
mission statement
When I was seventeen it was a very good year
It was a very good year for small town girls and soft summer nights
We'd hide from the lights on the village green
When I was seventeen
(brief instrumental)
When I was twenty-one it was a very good year
It was a very good year for city girls who lived up the stair
With all that perfumed hair and it came undone
When I was twenty-one
(brief instrumental)
Contact
Fecal Face
Silly Pink Bunnies
Umbrella Market
Upper Playground
Def Jux
Ordinary Kids
Later For You

the superFishal
Quarterly Review
Vol. 2, Spring, 2007
Current Line | Gallery | Info
Pig Stye
Spring Line, T-Shirt
Oh word? Umbrella Market
12 of 18

Totto Renna // www.supertotto.com

supertotto
FILE
EDIT
VIEW
OTHER
HELP
j.o.b.s. / coke_city
<< >>
Coca-Cola
bar
GRIP&GO!
NOUVELLE BOU
LLE NOUVELLE BOUTEILLE
GRIP&GO!
GO! GO! GO!

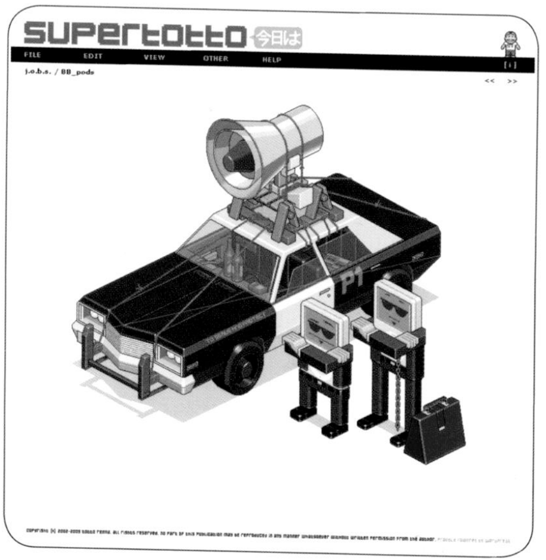
supertotto 今日は
FILE
EDIT
VIEW
OTHER
HELP
j.o.b.s. / BB_pods
<< >>
P1

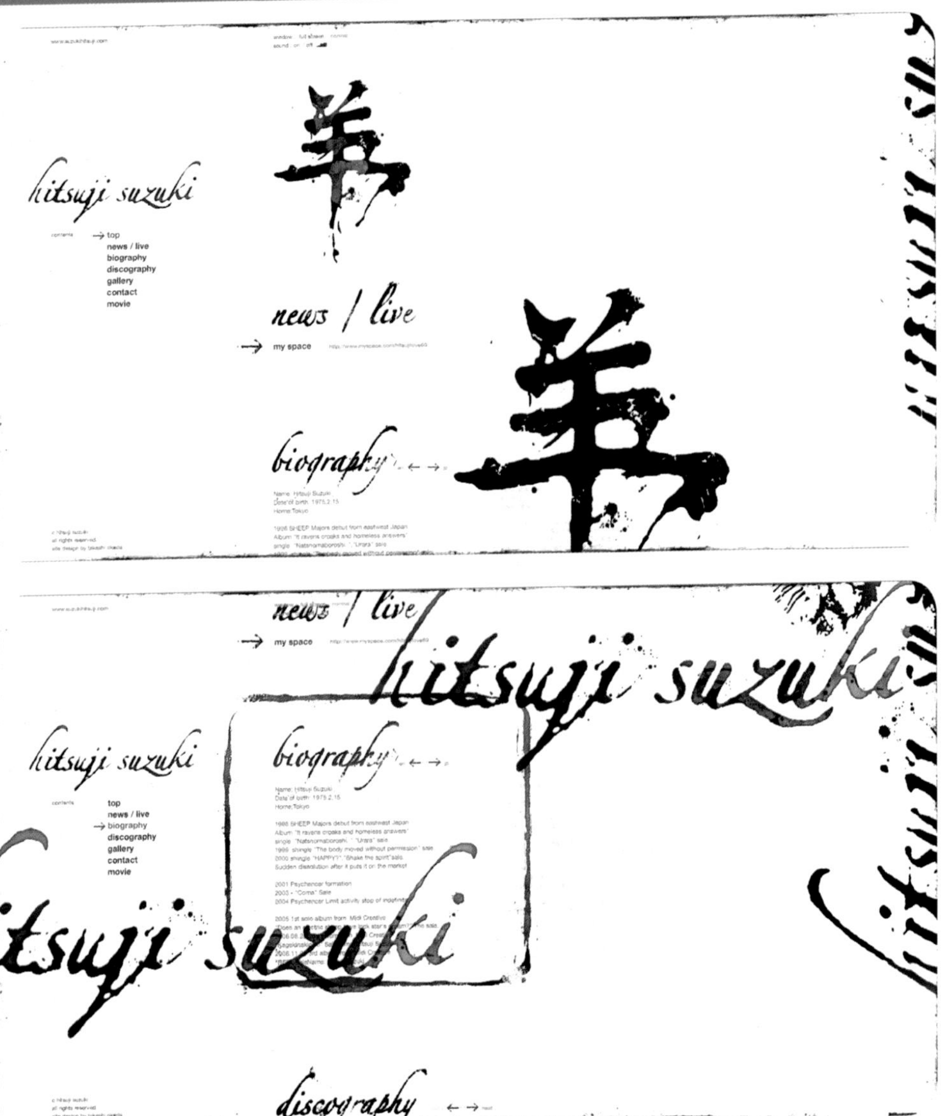

Takashi Okada // www.okadada.com

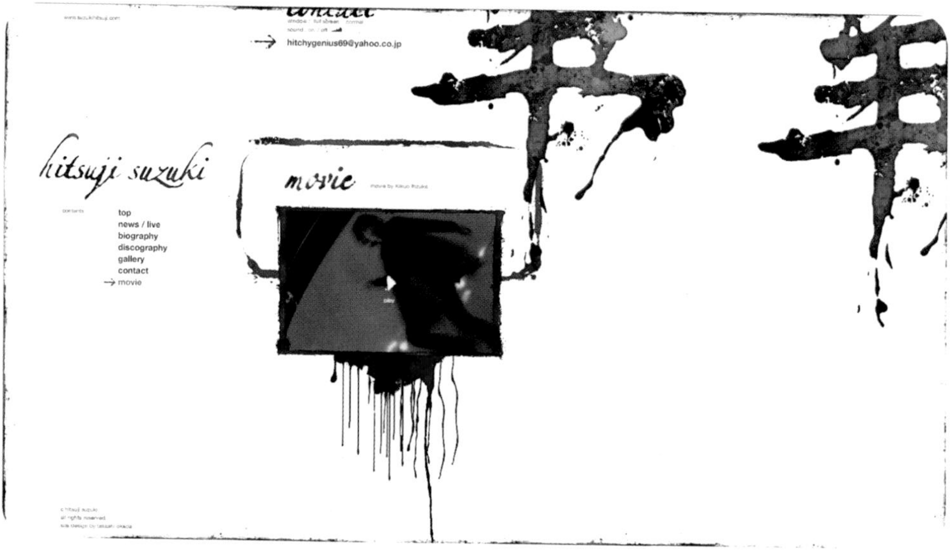

contact

→ hitchygenius69@yahoo.co.jp

hitsuji suzuki

top
news / live
biography
discography
gallery
contact
→ movie

movie

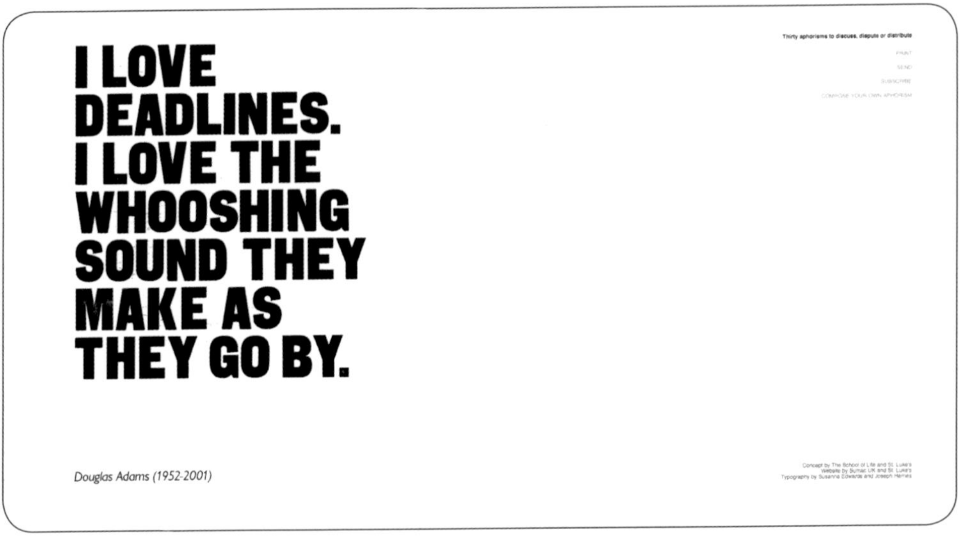

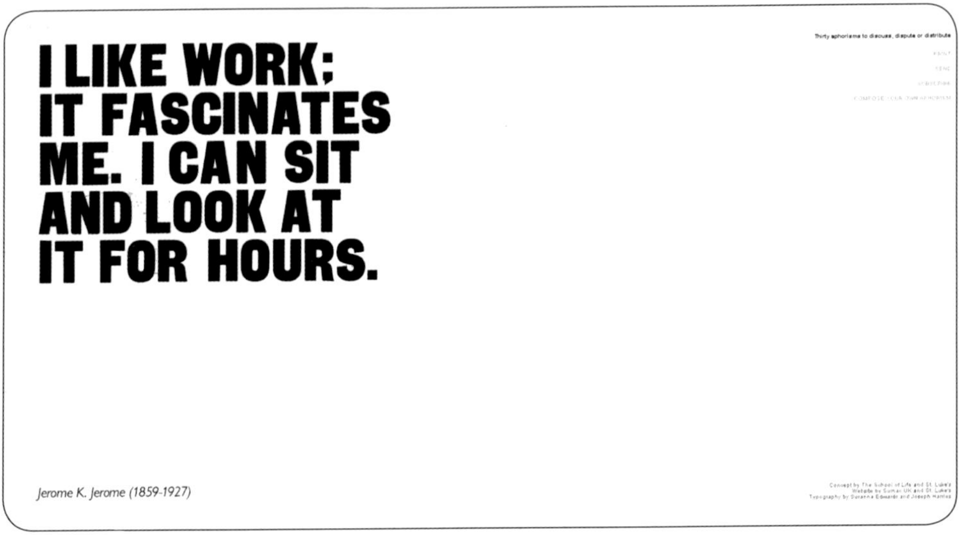

The Daily Aphorism // www.thedailyaphorism.com

Thirty aphorisms to discuss, dispute or distribute

PRINT

SEND

SUBSCRIBE

COMPOSE YOUR OWN APHORISM

I LOVE DEADLINES. I LOVE THE WHOOSHING SOUND THEY MAKE AS THEY GO BY.

Douglas Adams (1952-2001)

Concept by The School of Life and St. Luke's
Website by Sumac UK and St. Luke's
Typography by Susanna Edwards and Joseph Harries

Thirty aphorisms to discuss, dispute or distribute

PRINT

SEND

SUBSCRIBE

COMPOSE YOUR OWN APHORISM

I LIKE WORK: IT FASCINATES ME. I CAN SIT AND LOOK AT IT FOR HOURS.

Jerome K. Jerome (1859-1927)

Concept by The School of Life and St. Luke's
Website by Sumac UK and St. Luke's
Typography by Susanna Edwards and Joseph Harries

Sumac // www.sumac.uk.com

St. Luke's // www.stlukes.co.uk

Thirty aphorisms to discuss, dispute or distribute

WE ARE ALL IN THE GUTTER, BUT SOME OF US ARE LOOKING AT THE STARS.

Oscar Wilde (1854-1900)

Concept by The School of Life and St Luke's
Website by Sumac UK and St Luke's
Typography by Susanna Edwards and Joseph Harries

Thirty aphorisms to discuss, dispute or distribute

I BELIEVE IN GETTING INTO HOT WATER. I THINK IT KEEPS YOU CLEAN.

G.K. Chesterton (1874-1936)

Concept by The School of Life and St Luke's
Website by Sumac UK and St Luke's
Typography by Susanna Edwards and Joseph Harries

Roxik // roxik.com
McCann Erickson Japan // www.mccann.co.jp

ひとハダぬぎますか…。
Well...I'll give you the "wool" off my back.
back
He can't say no when someone asks him a favor.
prev
next

THE ECO ZOO
エコだ動物園
SKIP>>

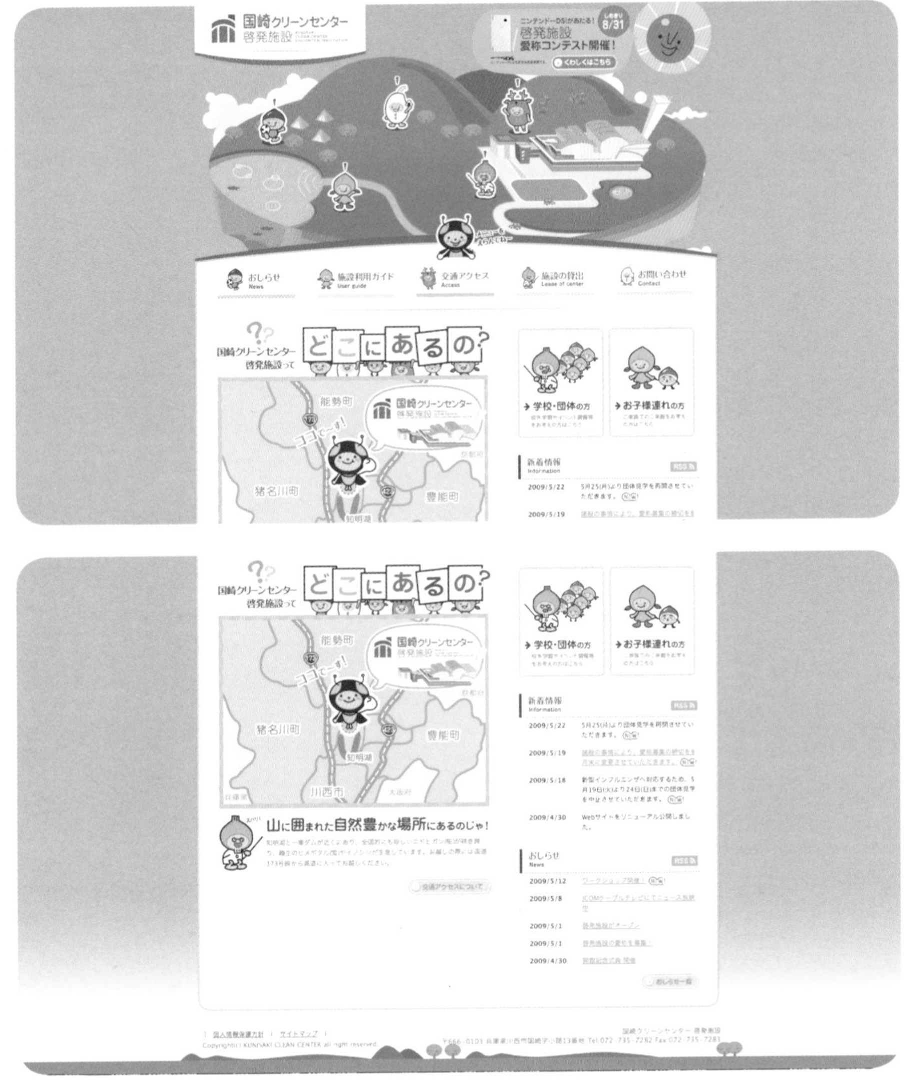

Totalmedia Development Institute Co. // www.totalmedia.co.jp
NEU, Inc. // www.n-e-u.co.jp

国崎クリーンセンター
啓発施設

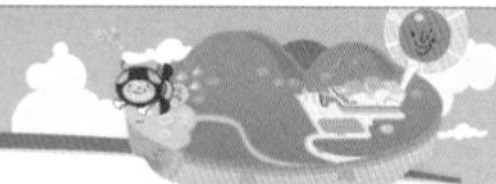

トップページへ

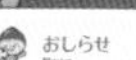
おしらせ
News

施設利用ガイド
User guide

交通アクセス
Access

施設の貸出
Lease of center

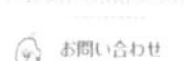
お問い合わせ
Contact

啓発施設
愛称コンテスト開催！

おしらせ
News
2009/5/12 ワークショップ開催！ NEW!
お休みの日は国崎クリーンセンターに行こう！！いろいろなワークショップに参加できます。おとなと一緒に遊びに来てください！
2009/5/8 JCOMケーブルテレビにてニュース放映中
JCOMケーブルテレビにて放映中の猪名川町広報番組「ふるふる！いながわ」内にて、啓発施設のオープンに関するニュースが流れています。猪名川町のWebサイトでも閲覧可能ですので、ご覧ください。
→くわしくはこちら
2009/5/1 啓発施設がオープン
国崎クリーンセンター啓発施設がオープンしました。クリーンセンター見学コースのご案内や、施設の貸出などを行っています。また、秋以降には環境関連の講演会やワークショップも開催する予定です。ぜひお越しください。※入場無料・駐車無料（月曜休館）
→くわしくはこちら
2009/5/1 啓発施設の愛称を募集！

国崎クリーンセンター
啓発施設

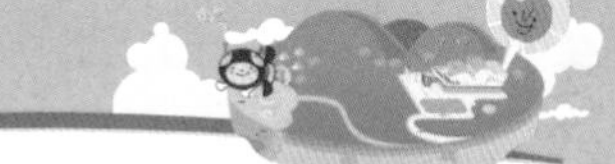

トップページへ

おしらせ
News

施設利用ガイド
User guide

交通アクセス
Access

施設の貸出
Lease of center

お問い合わせ
Contact

施設の貸出
Lease of center
会議室、研修室などを貸出します。
地域の皆様に活用していただく場として、会議室、研修室、視聴覚室をはじめ、工房、創作室などを貸出します。

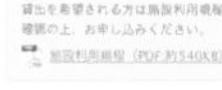
必ずお読みください
貸出を希望される方は施設利用規程をご確認の上、お申し込みください。
施設利用規程（PDF:約540KB）

みんなであそぼう！
貸出施設と料金
貸出施設の紹介や備品・使用料金のご案内です。

もしもし〜
利用方法
施設利用の手続きのご案内です。

この日は…
11(金) ○
12(土) ×
13(日) ○
貸出状況
希望日時の貸出状況のご確認をお願いします。

Tribal DDB London // Tribalddb.co.uk

THE GTI PROJECT
RACE >

TIME [00:25:63]
BEST LAP TIME [00:00:00]
LAP
1
3
149

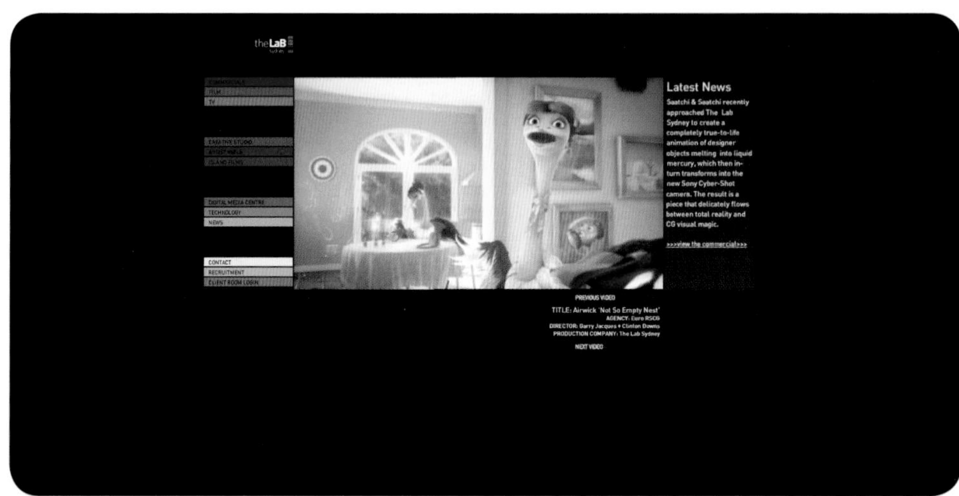

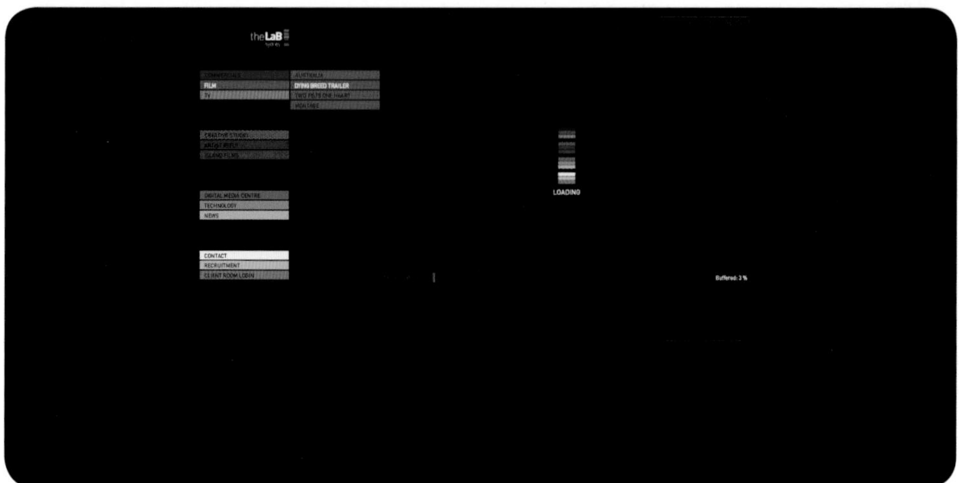

The Lab, Sydney // www.thelabsydney.com.au
Boffswana // www.boffswana.com

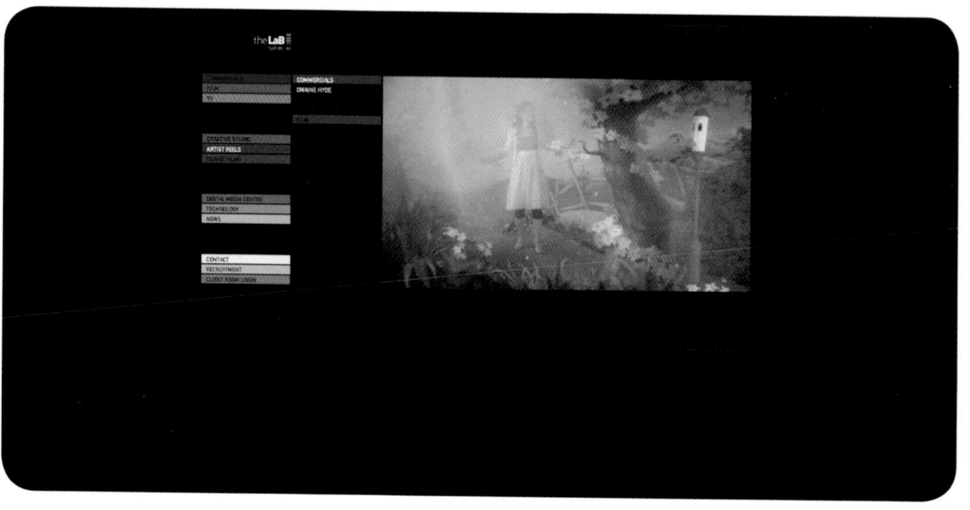

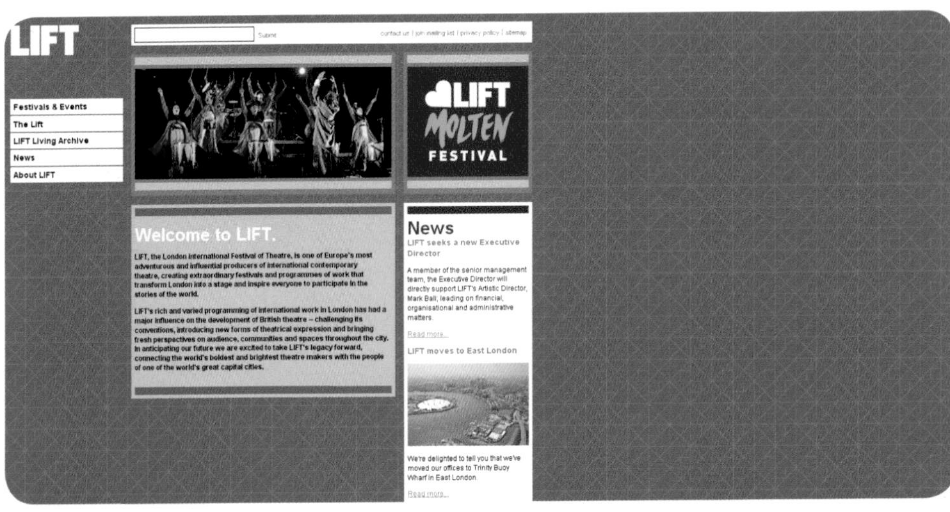

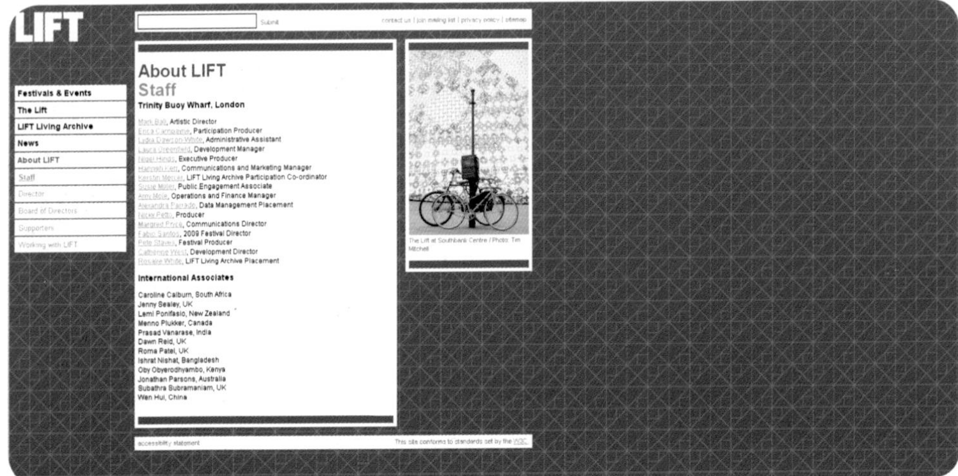

Sumac // www.sumac.uk.com
Hyperkit // www.hyperkit.co.uk

LIFT
Submit
contact us | join mailing list | privacy policy | sitemap
Festivals & Events
LIFT Molten Festival
Past Events
Shoreditch Festival Parade
The Lift
LIFT Living Archive
News
About LIFT
Welcome to LIFT's 2009 programme
We've got a fantastic array of events and festivals to make sure you feel the love all summer long!
On TUESDAY 30 JUNE join us at Goldsmiths for LIFTING LONDON an evening of conversation and performance. This event will launch the LIFT Living Archive which houses over 1,000 documents, photographs, prints, objects, audio and video recordings tracing Lift's first 20 years as one of Europe's leading arts organisations presenting international art experiences at venues and unusual sites across London. Click on the link below to find out more.
In July, catch us at Shoreditch Festival where we present the SHOREDITCH FESTIVAL PARADE on SATURDAY 18 JUNE with Emergency Exit Arts. Get a sneak preview of what's in store by following the link below.
From 21-31 AUGUST, LIFT is joining forces with Molten Festival, Barking's premiere performing arts festival, to present LIFT MOLTEN FESTIVAL. This year's Festival has something for everyone to love and features a fantastic line up of artists from the breathtaking Transe Express to the ever-saucy Whoopee Club. The Lift, our ingenious portable performance space, will be taking centre stage as the venue for this year's programme, which would not be possible without the ongoing support of the London Thames Gateway Development Corporation. For full programme, access and booking information click on the link below.
LIFT Living Archive launch
Tuesday 30 June
Shoreditch Festival Parade
Saturday 18 July
LIFT MOLTEN FESTIVAL
LIFT Molten Festival
21 - 31 August

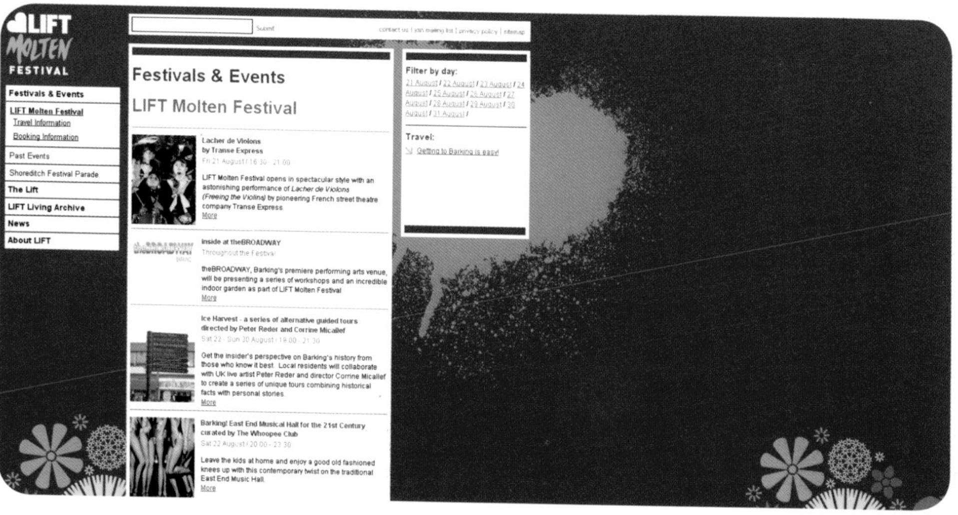

LIFT MOLTEN FESTIVAL
Submit
contact us | join mailing list | privacy policy | sitemap
Festivals & Events
LIFT Molten Festival
Travel Information
Booking Information
Past Events
Shoreditch Festival Parade
The Lift
LIFT Living Archive
News
About LIFT
Festivals & Events
LIFT Molten Festival
Lacher de Violons
by Transe Express
Fri 21 August / 16.30 - 21.00
LIFT Molten Festival opens in spectacular style with an astonishing performance of Lacher de Violons (Freeing the Violins) by pioneering French street theatre company Transe Express.
More
inside at theBROADWAY
Throughout the Festival
theBROADWAY, Barking's premiere performing arts venue, will be presenting a series of workshops and an incredible indoor garden as part of LIFT Molten Festival
More
Ice Harvest - a series of alternative guided tours directed by Peter Reder and Corrine Micallef
Sat 22 - Sun 30 August / 19.00 - 21.30
Get the insider's perspective on Barking's history from those who know it best. Local residents will collaborate with UK live artist Peter Reder and director Corrine Micallef to create a series of unique tours combining historical facts with personal stories.
More
Barking! East End Musical Hall for the 21st Century curated by The Whoopee Club
Sat 22 August / 20.00 - 23.30
Leave the kids at home and enjoy a good old fashioned knees up with this contemporary twist on the traditional East End Music Hall.
More
Filter by day:
21 August / 22 August / 23 August / 24 August / 25 August / 26 August / 27 August / 28 August / 29 August / 30 August / 31 August /
Travel:
Getting to Barking is easy!

The Pull and Bear Forest // www.pullandbear.com/#/theworldproject/

Angel De Franganillo // Antiheroe.com
Grapa // Grapa.ws

Pull and Bear
EXIT

Pull and Bear
CAMPAÑA
ESPECIALES
SHOWROOM
TIENDAS
ATENCIÓN AL CLIENTE
EMPRESA
BLOG
ENGLISH
SIERRA GORDA (MÉXICO)
Proyecto de reforestación
En el Estado de Querétaro, México, se encuentra la Reserva de la Biosfera Sierra Gorda. Esta zona fue protegida para preservar su alto valor ambiental y excepcional biodiversidad. No obstante, parte de las tierras habían sido deforestadas para ser utilizadas con fines agrícolas y ganaderos.
RANKING
MIS PREMIOS
AYUDA
BOSQUE REAL
ENVIAR A UN AMIGO
CATÁLOGO PULL = ceroCO2
PULL AND BEAR

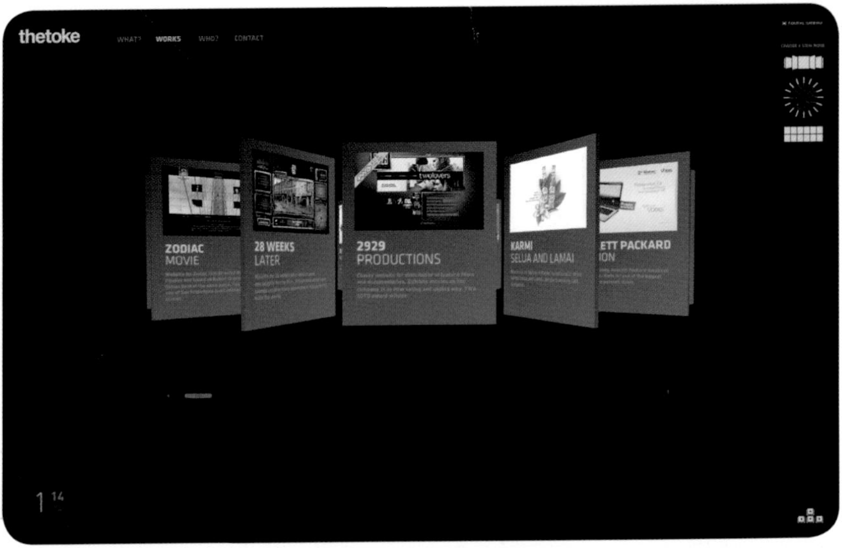
thetoke
WHAT?
WORKS
WHO?
CONTACT
ZODIAC
MOVIE
28 WEEKS
LATER
2929
PRODUCTIONS
KARMI
SELUA AND LAMAI
ETT PACKARD
ION
1 14

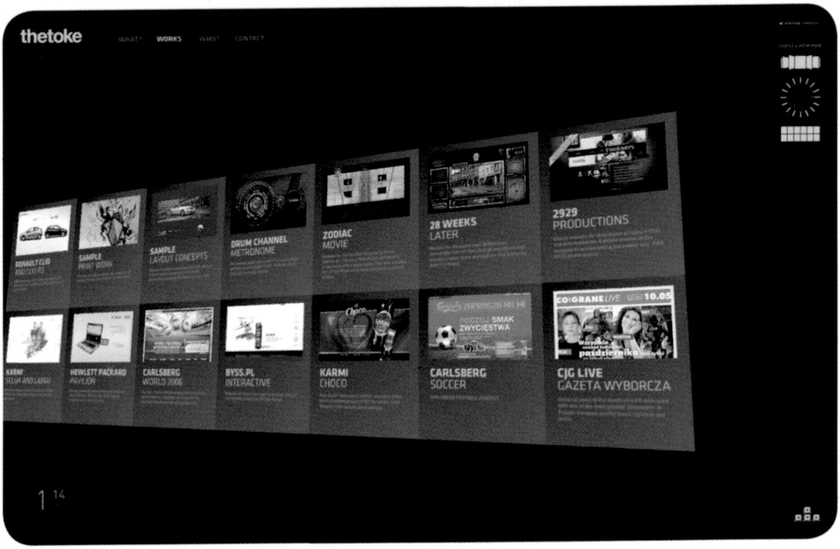
thetoke
WHAT?
WORKS
WHO?
CONTACT
RENAULT CLIO
SAMPLE
PRINT WORK
SAMPLE
LAYOUT CONCEPTS
DRUM CHANNEL
METRONOME
ZODIAC
MOVIE
28 WEEKS
LATER
2929
PRODUCTIONS
KARMI
SELUA AND LAMAI
HEWLETT PACKARD
PAVILION
CARLSBERG
WORLD 2006
BYSS.PL
INTERACTIVE
KARMI
CHOCO
CARLSBERG
SOCCER
CJG LIVE
GAZETA WYBORCZA
1 14

Darek Nyckowiak // thetoke.com

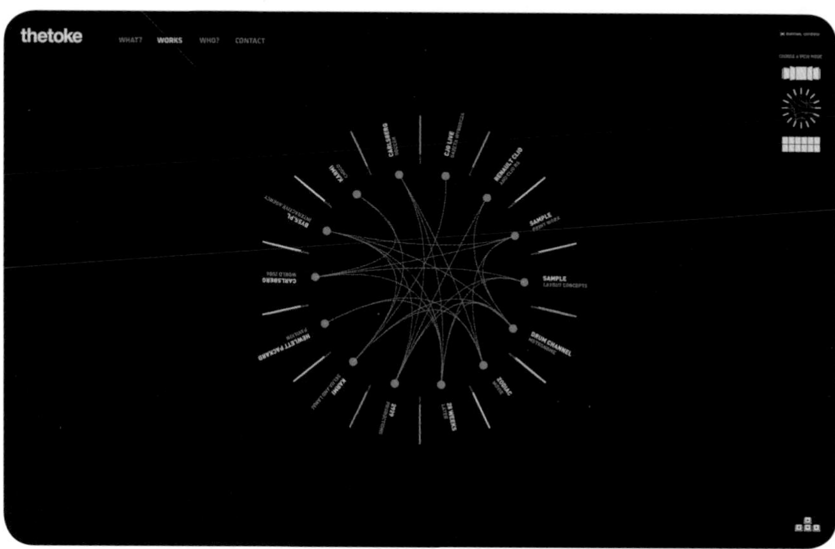
thetoke
WHAT?
WORKS
WHO?
CONTACT
CARLSBERG
RENAULT CLIO
SAMPLE
SAMPLE
LAYOUT CONCEPTS
DRUM CHANNEL
ZODIAC
28 WEEKS
KARMI
HEWLETT PACKARD
CARLSBERG
KARMI

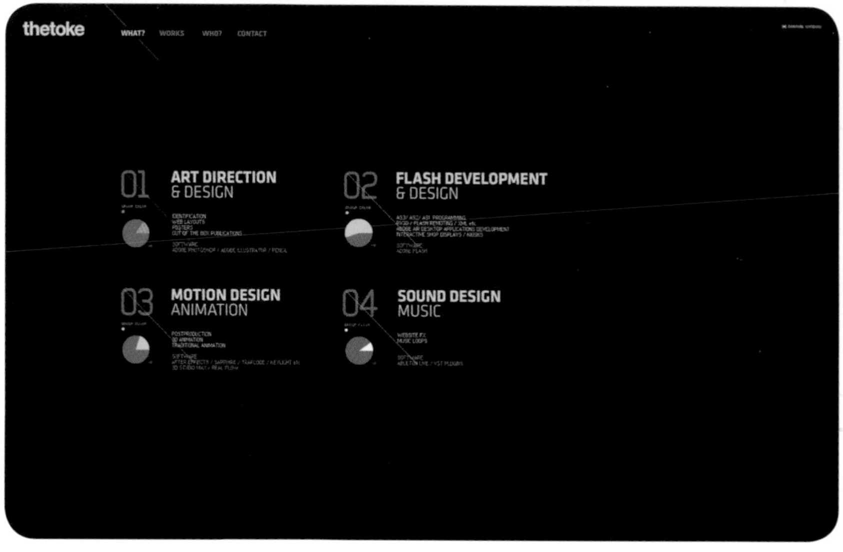
thetoke
WHAT?
WORKS
WHO?
CONTACT
01 ART DIRECTION & DESIGN
IDENTIFICATION
WEB LAYOUTS
POSTERS
OUT OF THE BOX PUBLICATIONS
SOFTWARE
02 FLASH DEVELOPMENT & DESIGN
SOFTWARE
ADOBE FLASH
03 MOTION DESIGN ANIMATION
POSTPRODUCTION
3D ANIMATION
TRADITIONAL ANIMATION
SOFTWARE
04 SOUND DESIGN MUSIC
WEBSITE FX
MUSIC LOOPS
SOFTWARE
ABLETON LIVE / VST PLUGINS

TODAY'S THOUGHTPILE
HOW CAN TECHNOLOGY BECOME MORE HUMAN?

JOHN Q. LOGGED IN

MORE
RECENT IDEAS
VISITED IDEAS

READ COMMENTS

SEE PREVIOUS THOUGHTPILES

SOUND

TODAY'S THOUGHTPILE
HOW CAN TECHNOLOGY BECOME MORE HUMAN?

JOHN Q. LOGGED IN

MORE
RECENT IDEAS
VISITED IDEAS

READ COMMENTS

SEE PREVIOUS THOUGHTPILES

SOUND

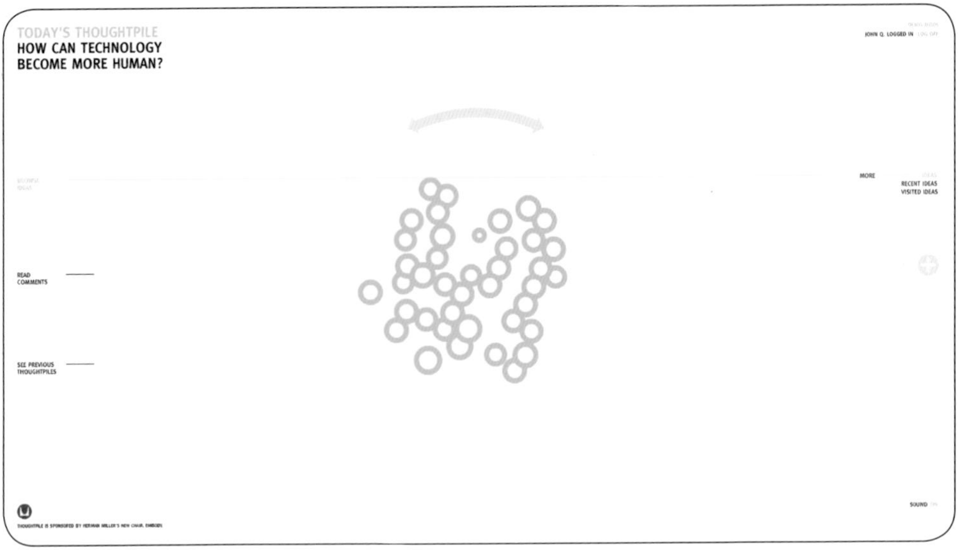

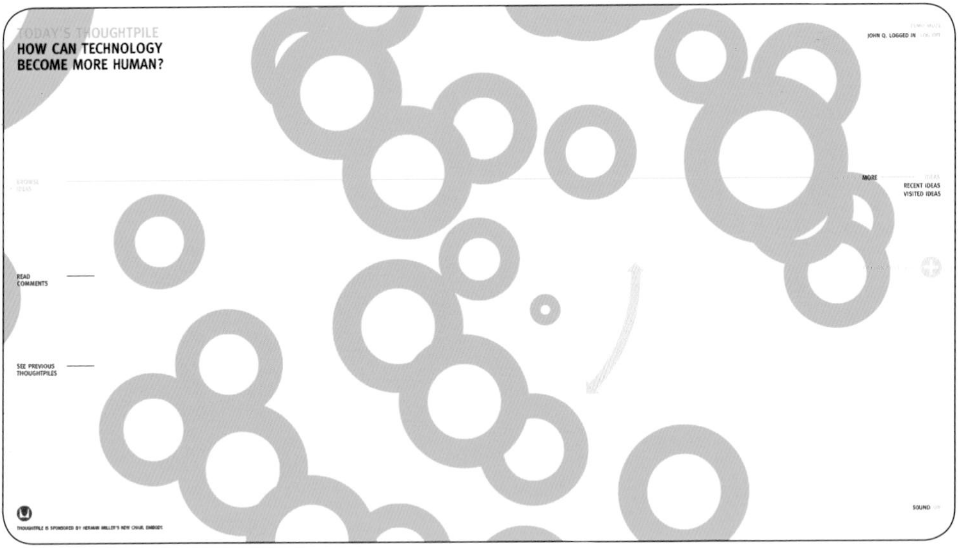

mono // www.mono-1.com

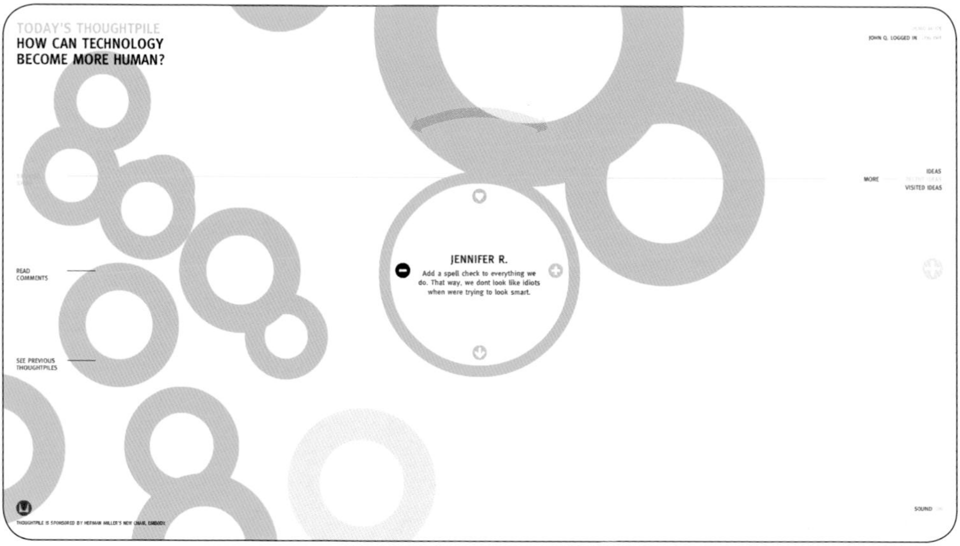

TODAY'S THOUGHTPILE
HOW CAN TECHNOLOGY BECOME MORE HUMAN?

JOHN Q. LOGGED IN

MORE IDEAS
VISITED IDEAS

READ COMMENTS

SEE PREVIOUS THOUGHTPILES

JENNIFER R.

Add a spell check to everything we do. That way, we dont look like idiots when were trying to look smart.

THOUGHTPILE IS SPONSORED BY HERMAN MILLER'S NEW CHAIR, EMBODY.

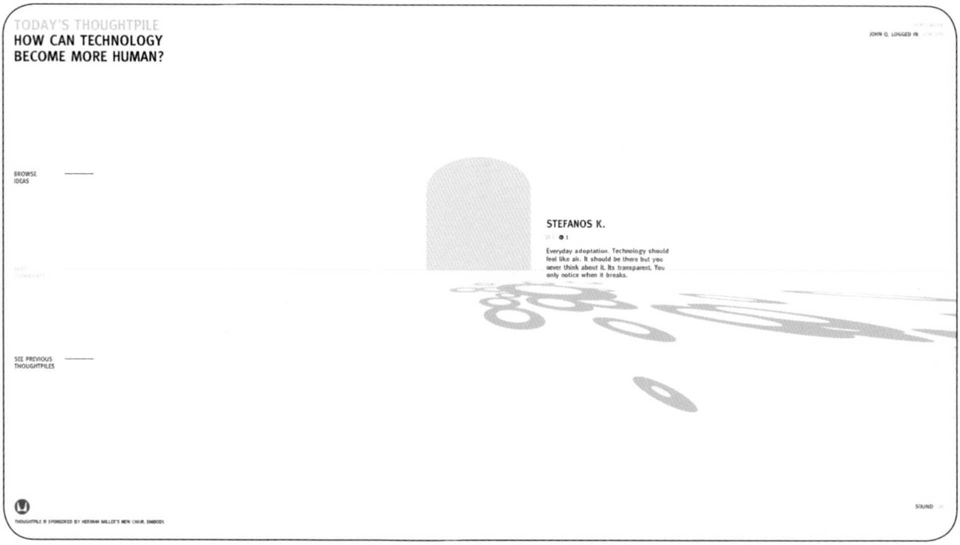

SOUND

TODAY'S THOUGHTPILE
HOW CAN TECHNOLOGY BECOME MORE HUMAN?

JOHN Q. LOGGED IN

BROWSE IDEAS

STEFANOS K.

Everyday adoptation. Technology should feel like air. It should be there but you never think about it. Its transparent. You only notice when it breaks.

SEE PREVIOUS THOUGHTPILES

THOUGHTPILE IS SPONSORED BY HERMAN MILLER'S NEW CHAIR, EMBODY.

SOUND

Tilt Design Studio // www.tiltdesignstudio.com

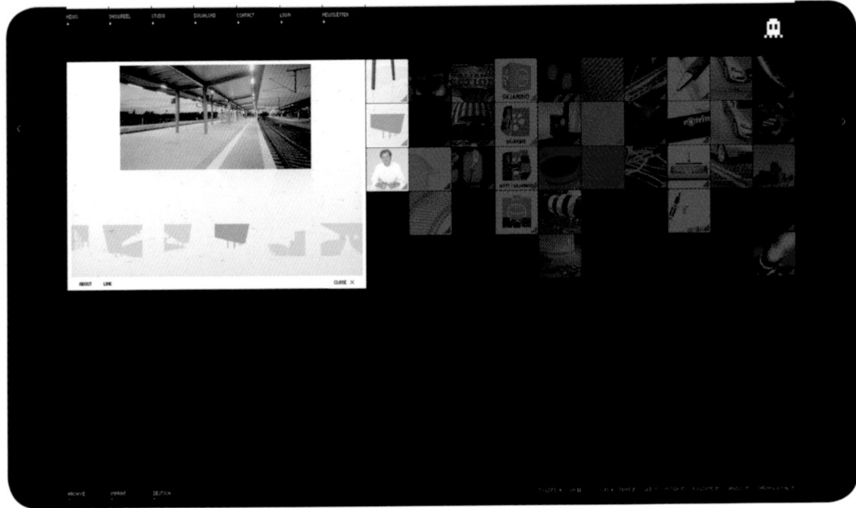

Marc Antosch
Ralph Heinsohn
Felix Schultze // www.tiltdesignstudio.com

NEWS
SHOWREEL
STUDIO
DOWNLOAD
CONTACT
LOGIN
NEWSLETTER
ASTRONAUTS
CO-RELEASE PARTY MI 21. MAI
SCHAUBUDE
ASTRONAUTS
CO-RELEASE PARTY MI 21. MAI
SCHAUBUDE
ABOUT
CLOSE
ARCHIVE
IMPRINT
DEUTSCH

NEWS
SHOWREEL
STUDIO
DOWNLOAD
CONTACT
LOGIN
NEWSLETTER
CLOSE
LOOKING FOR INTERNS
NOMINATION FOR ONLINE STAR
LOS LOGOS 4
ROTOVISION DISC ART
ARCHIVE
IMPRINT
DEUTSCH

tokyoplastic // www.tokyoplastic.com

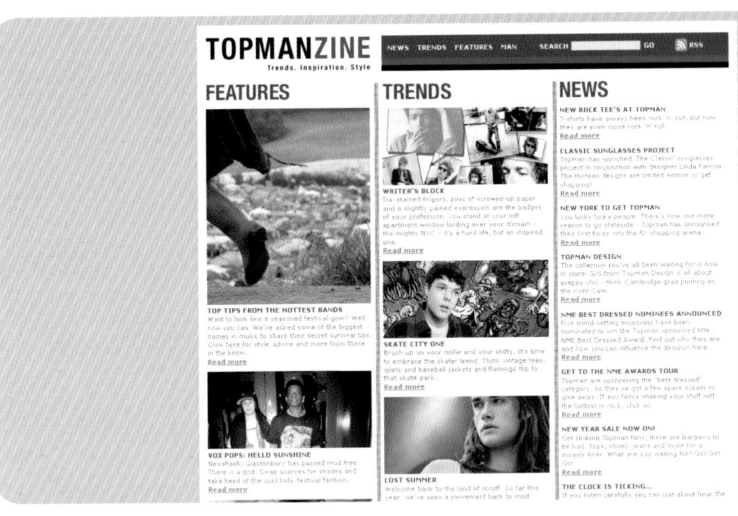

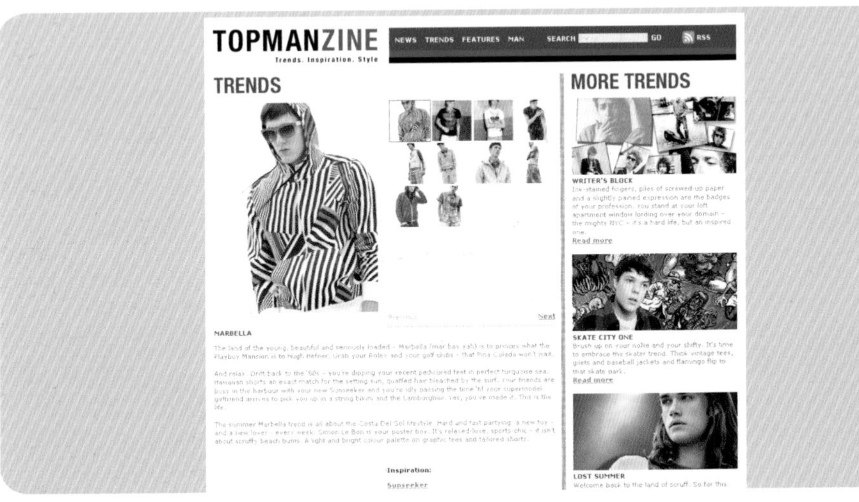

Sumac // www.sumac.uk.com
St. Luke's // www.stlukes.co.uk

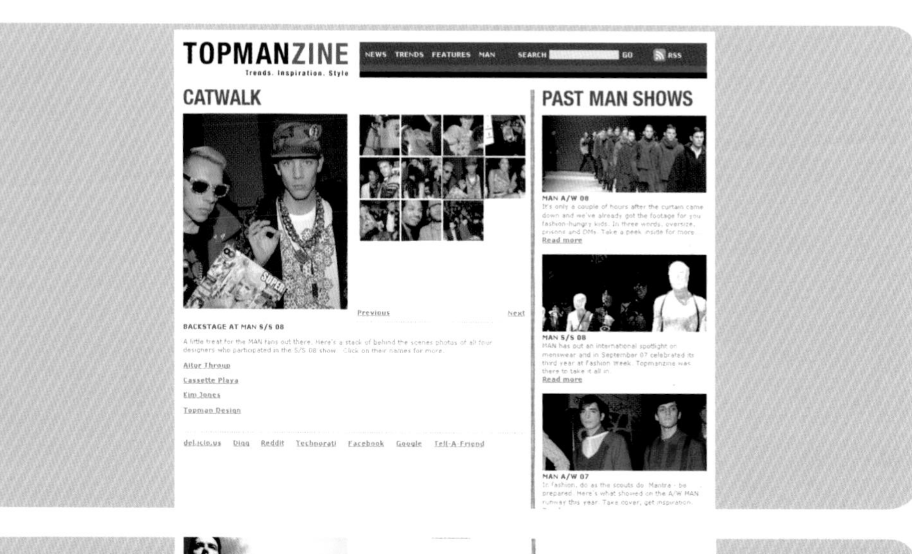

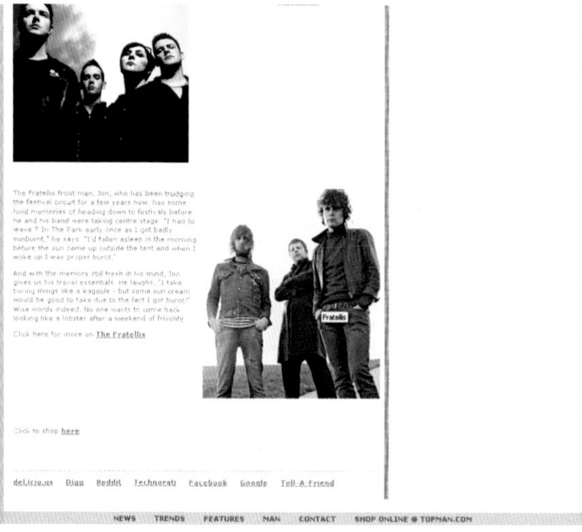

The Fratellis front man, Jon, who has been trudging the festival circuit for a few years now, has some fond memories of heading down to festivals before he and his band were taking centre stage. "I had to leave T In The Park early once as I got badly sunburnt," he says. "I'd fallen asleep in the morning before the sun came up outside the tent and when I woke up I was proper burnt."

And with the memory still fresh in his mind, Jon gives us his travel essentials. He laughs, "I take boring things like a kagoule - but some sun cream would be good to take due to the fact I got burnt!" Wise words indeed. No one wants to come back looking like a lobster after a weekend of frivolity.

Click here for more on **The Fratellis**

Fratellis

Click to shop **here**

del.icio.us Digg Reddit Technorati Facebook Google Tell-A-Friend

NEWS TRENDS FEATURES MAN CONTACT SHOP ONLINE @ TOPMAN.COM

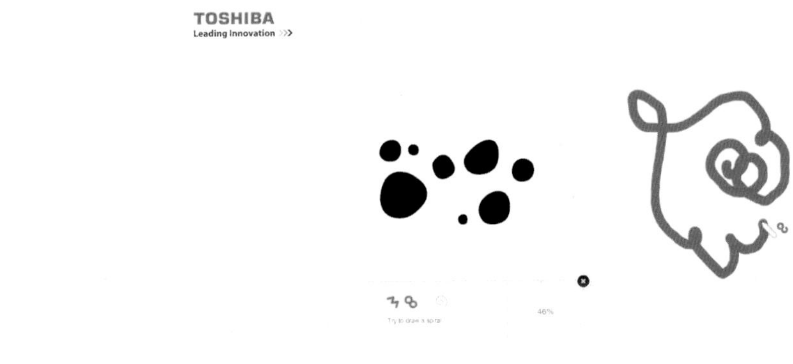

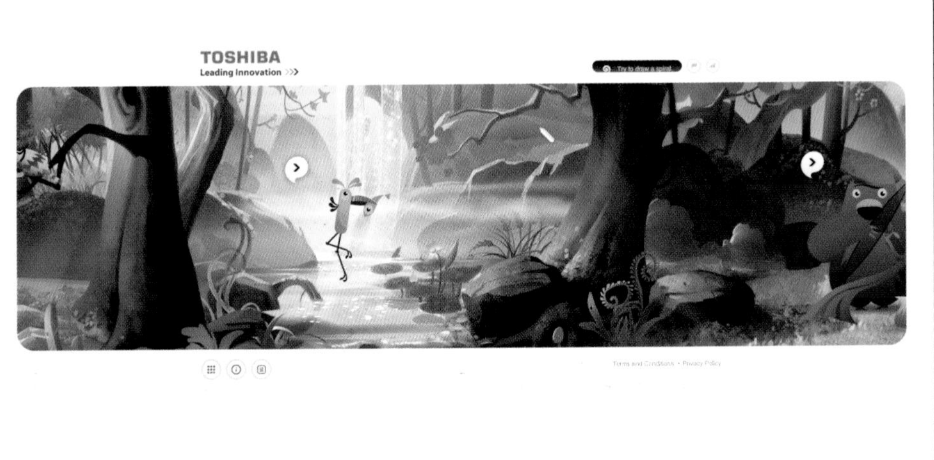

unit9 // www.unit9.com
Grey London // www.grey.co.uk

TOSHIBA
Leading Innovation >>>

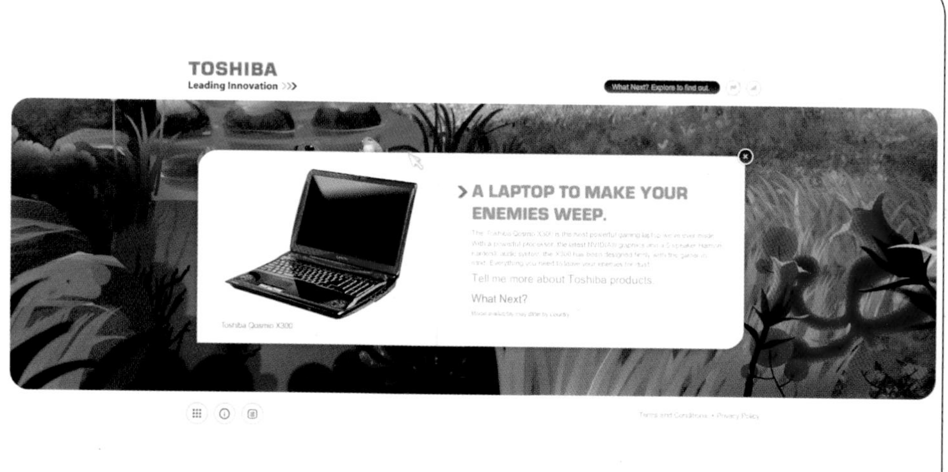
TOSHIBA
Leading Innovation >>>
What Next? Explore to find out.
> A LAPTOP TO MAKE YOUR ENEMIES WEEP.
Tell me more about Toshiba products.
What Next?

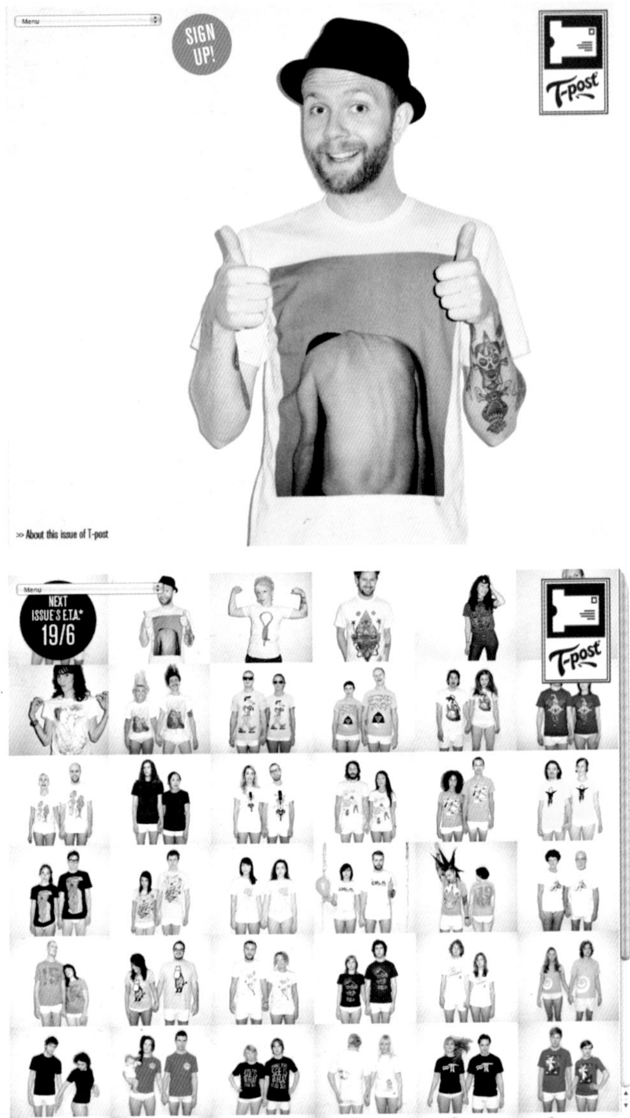

Micke Lundin/ Vardag // www.plusboat.se/mikael

Menu
SIGN UP!
T-post
SMART
NO TIES TODAY THANK YOU
>> About this issue of T-post
Menu
SIGN UP!
T-post
WHAT IS T-POST?
CLOSE
Subscribing to T-post is a lot like having a subscription to a magazine but instead of recei-ving magazines in your mailbox - you receive T-shirts. Every six weeks we design a t-shirt based on a current news item and print the shirt's topic on the inside. You may not always hear about your T-post's story from traditional news media but in our opinion, you should have.
ALTRUISM – IT'S ALL IN YOUR HEAD

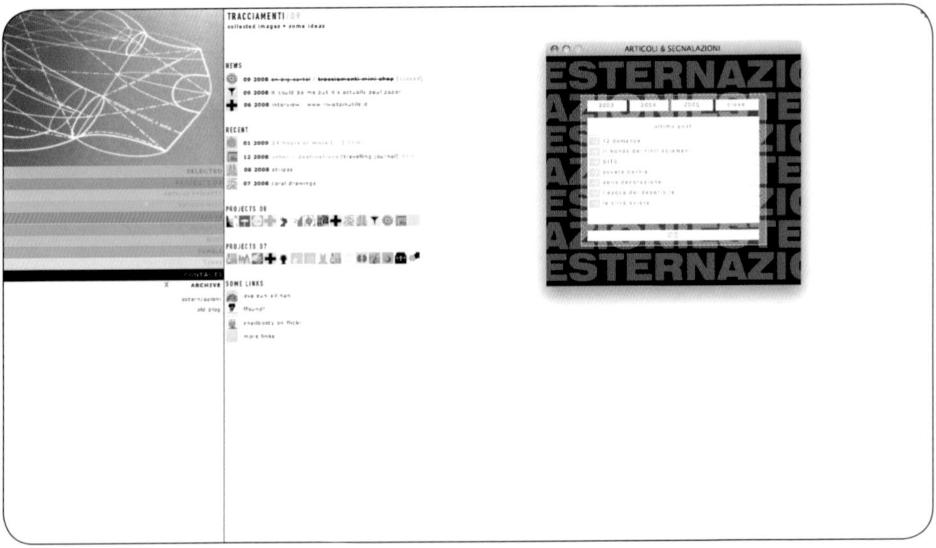

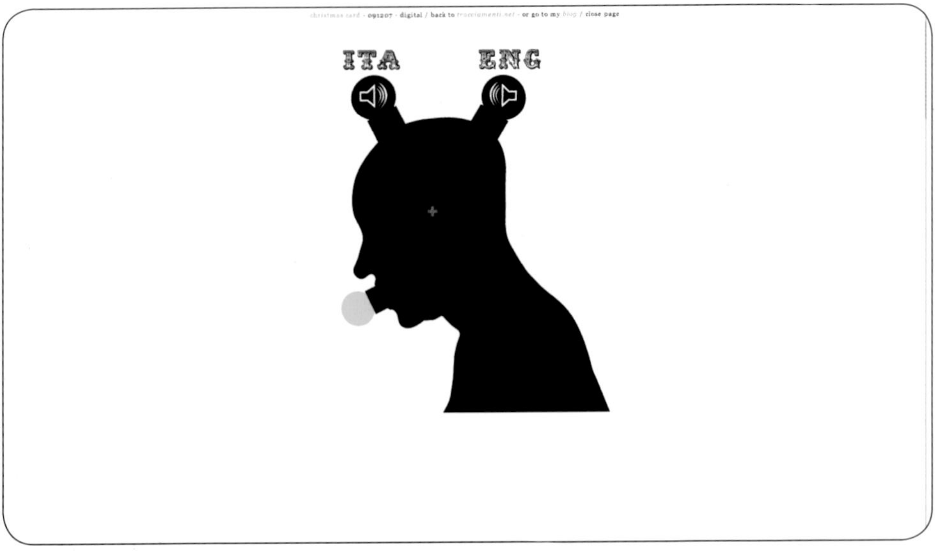

Tracciamenti // www.tracciamenti.net

ALPHABETS - digital print on wood - 210 x 300 mm
on *illustration friday* / back to *tracciamenti.net* - or go to my *new blog* / close page

RAL/ mixed tecnique on paper and moleskine CLOSE PAGE

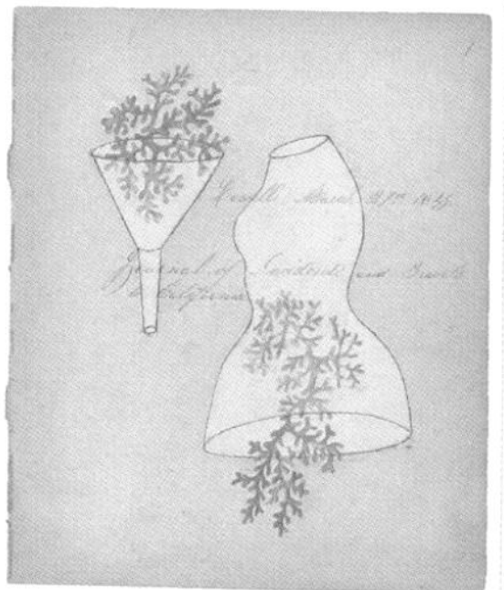

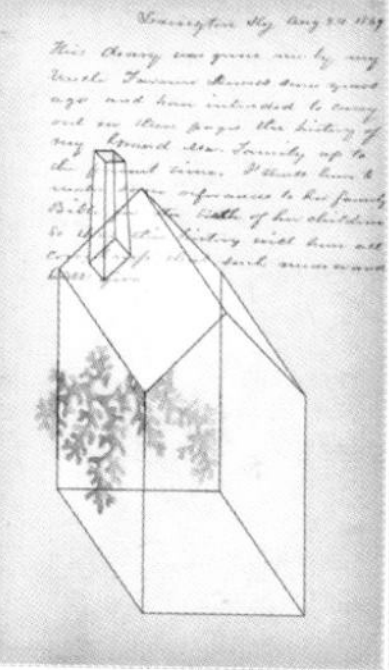

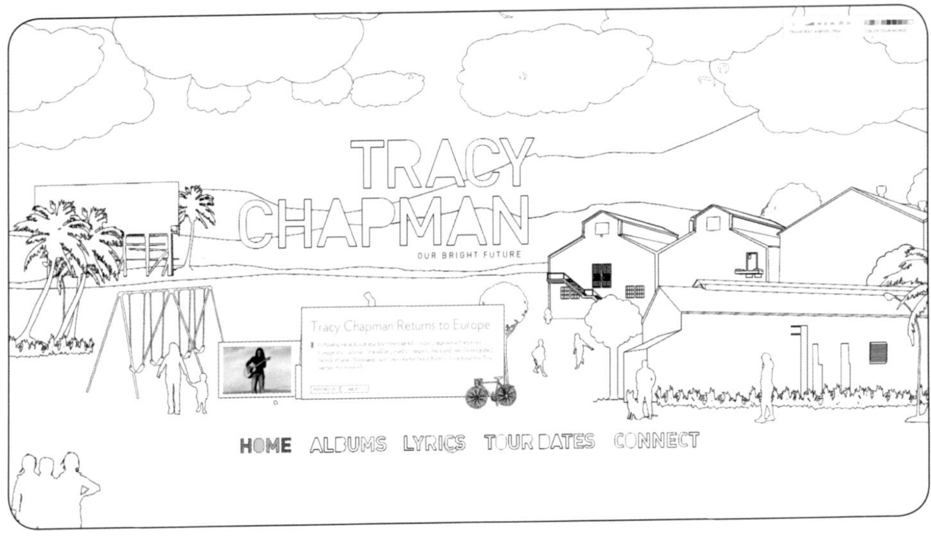

Jason Herring
Adam Weiss/ OrdinaryKids // www.ordinarykids.com

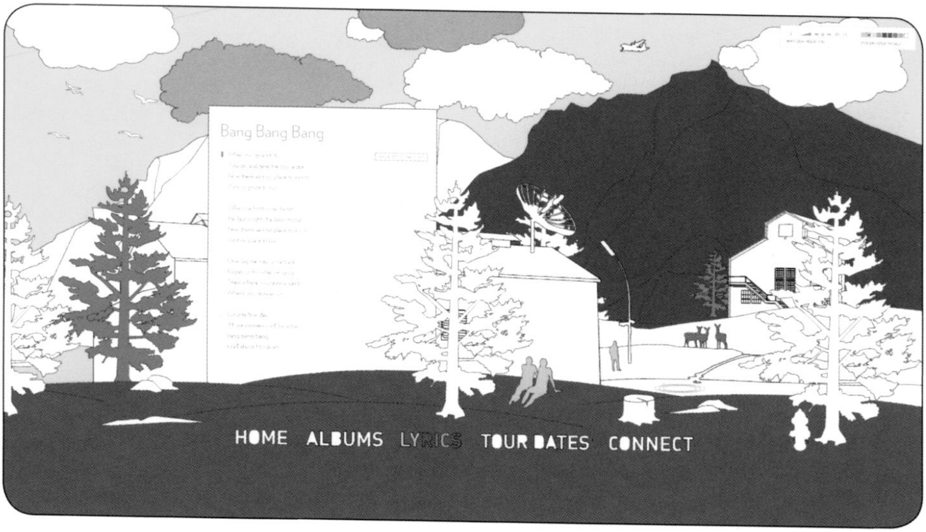

Bang Bang Bang

HOME ALBUMS LYRICS TOUR DATES CONNECT

Jason Herring
Ferris Plock/ OrdinaryKids // www.ordinarykids.com

BLADDER CONTROL

◂ BACK to Trigger Town

RE-TRAIN YOUR BRAIN ⇨
RE-LEARN LIFE WITHOUT CIGARETTES.

ex

Luiz Carlos Fortino
David Galasse
Persio Guerreiro
Felipe Lopes
Marcelle Naguib
Rodrigo Teco
Cauê Teixeira
Antonio Vicentini // www.grafikonstruct.com.br

THE
QUEEN
IS NOT DEAD
Triton
ATITUDE
CATÁLOGO
LOOKBOOK
DESFILE SPFW
INVERNO 2009

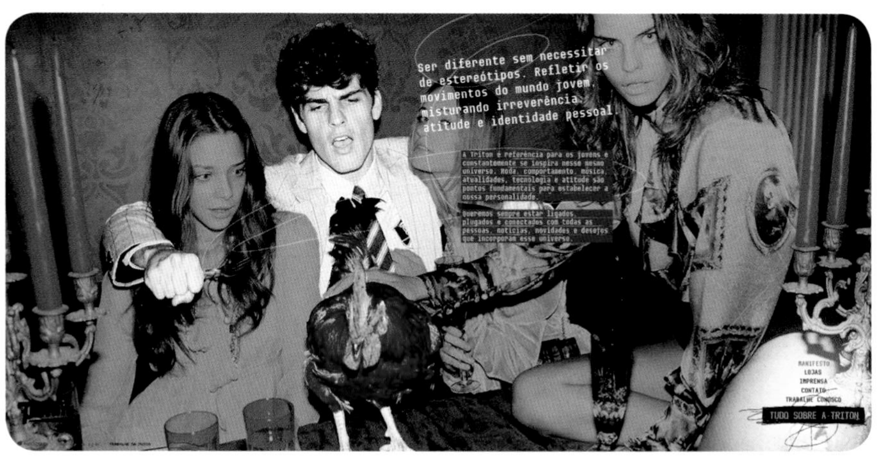
Ser diferente sem necessitar de estereótipos. Refletir os movimentos do mundo jovem, misturando irreverência, atitude e identidade pessoal.
A Triton é referência para os jovens e constantemente se inspira nesse mesmo universo. Moda, comportamento, música, atualidades, tecnologia e atitude são pontos fundamentais para estabelecer a nossa personalidade.
Queremos sempre estar ligados, plugados e conectados com todas as pessoas, notícias, novidades e desejos que incorporam esse universo.
MANIFESTO
LOJAS
IMPRENSA
CONTATO
TRABALHE CONOSCO
TUDO SOBRE A TRITON

Vincent Maitray // www.electrofrog.com

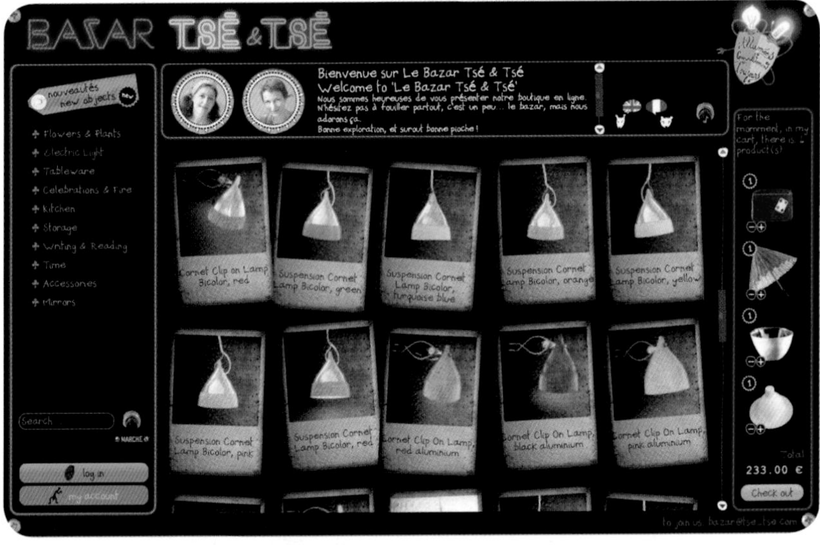

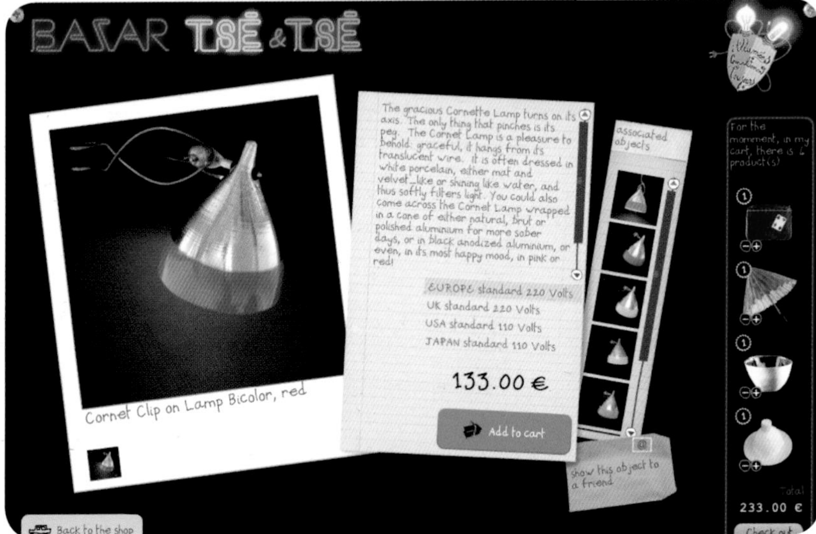

Vincent Maitray // www.electrofrog.com

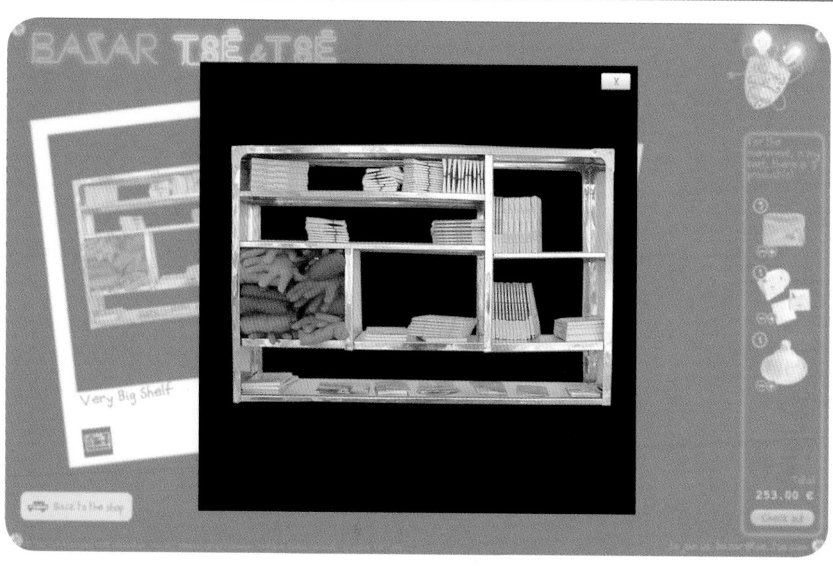
BASAR TSÉ & TSÉ
X
Very Big Shelf
Back to the shop
253.00 €
Check out

BASAR TSÉ & TSÉ
Order confirmation
For the mamment, in my cart, there is:
Name
Attribute
Price
Price cut
Quantity
Remove
Housse Elégante, Clouds
65.00
0
3
CD TSE&TSE
15.00
0
1
Night Igloo, stripped and glazed
43.00
0
1
shipping country:
select your country
delivery cost: 7.00 €
Total: 260.00 €
Fill order
cart sum 253.00 €
Personal informations
Shipping informations
Confirmation
Back to shop
to join us: bazar@tse_tse.com

U Le Chang // www.ulechang.com

Kilo Studio // www.kilostudio.net

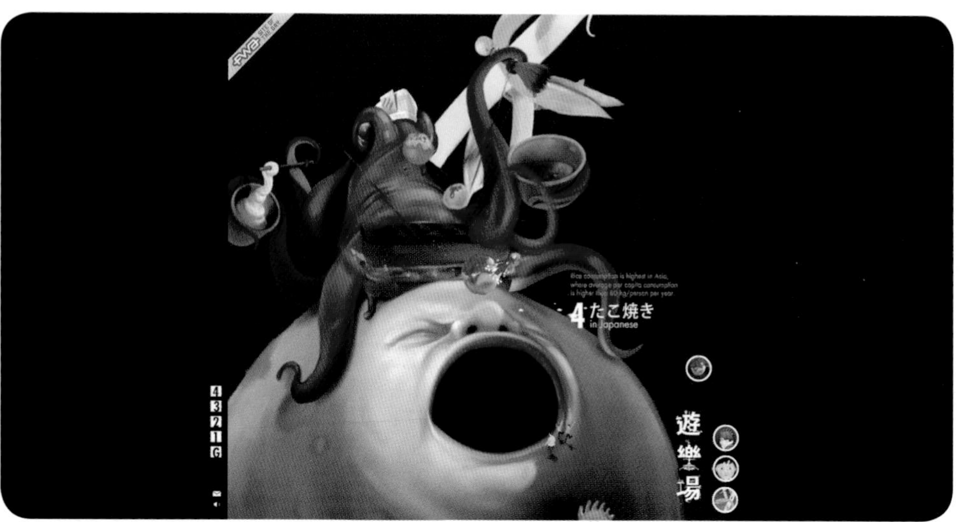

6 龍鯉魚的傳奇
in Chinese

5 花咲か爺さん
in Japanese

遊樂場

UNIQLO MARCH WORLD TOTAL 035871km

FLANNEL MARCH FLANNE

IMG SRC // www.imgsrc.co.jp
UNIQLO // www.uniqlo.com

TOKYO MARCH 025671km

TOKYO MARCH 025671km

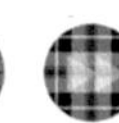

Urban Explorers Festival // www.urbanexplorersfestival.nl

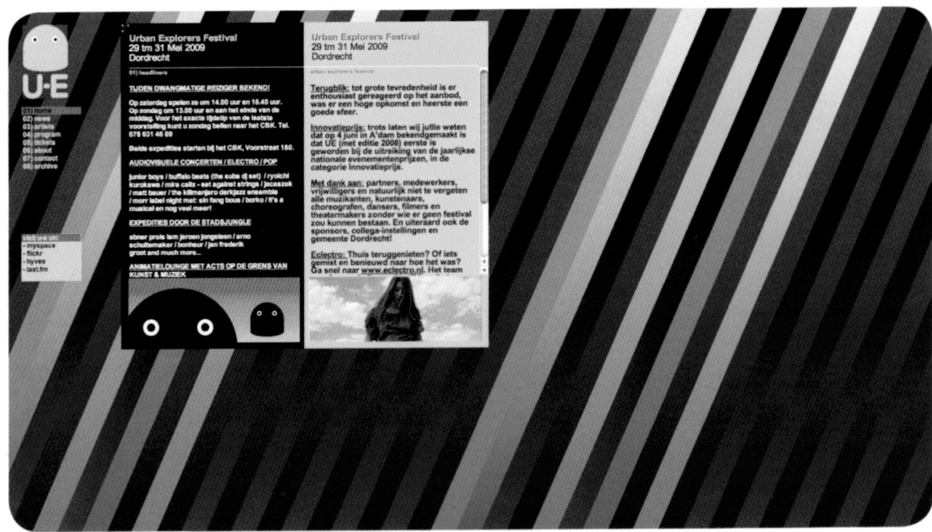

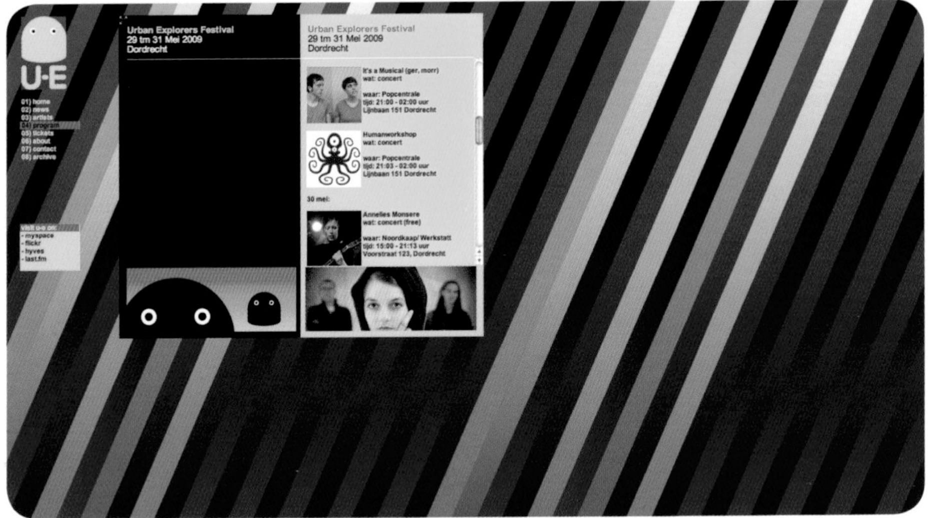

310k // www.310k.nl

Mikoon webservices // www.mikoon.nl

OnClick Studio // www.onclick.es

VECTORIZE
YOUR IDOLS

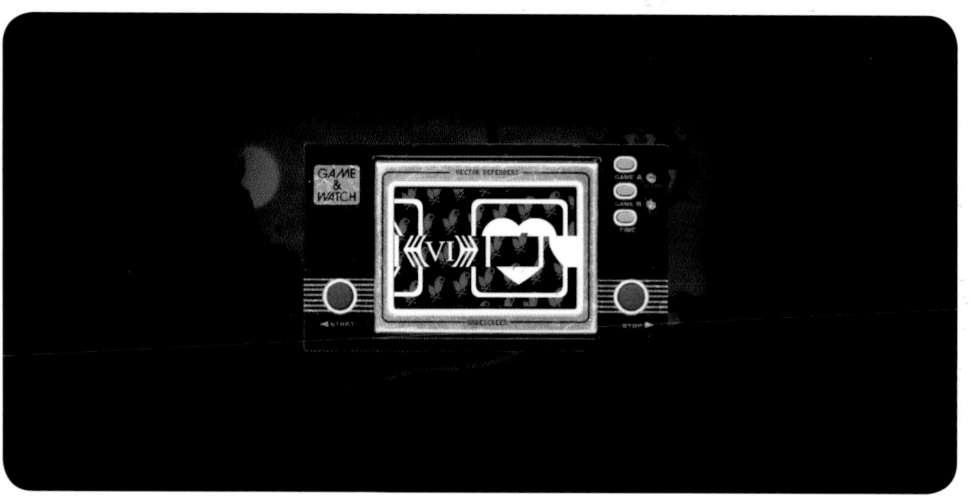
GAME
&
WATCH
VECTOR DEFENDERS
VI
WIDESCREEN
START
STOP

THE WORLD IS A GRID
2 BILLION AIR PASSENGERS
PER YEAR

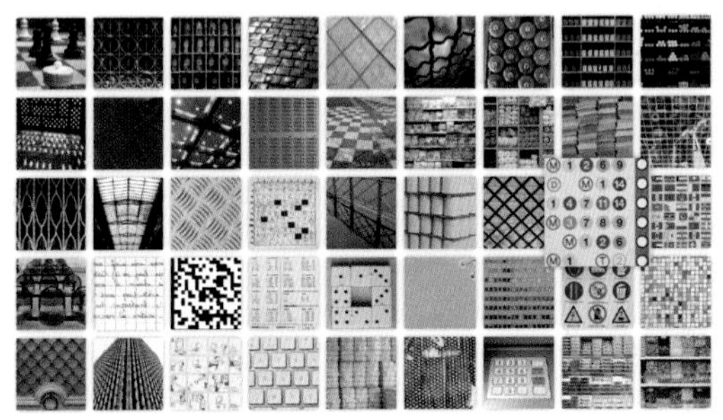

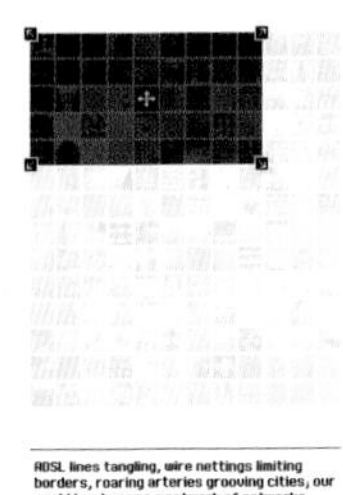

ADSL lines tangling, wire nettings limiting borders, roaring arteries grooving cities, our world has become a network of networks.

The Grid, photographical work created from boundless and diffuse connections, underlines the omnipresent repetitions of our world and is a source of inspiration for the Veja Grid trainer collection.

#032 Correspondances
by Nicolas Ocante

SHOW NAVIGATION

Jocker / CREAKTIF ! // www.creaktif.com/jocker/
noMatter // www.nomatter.eu

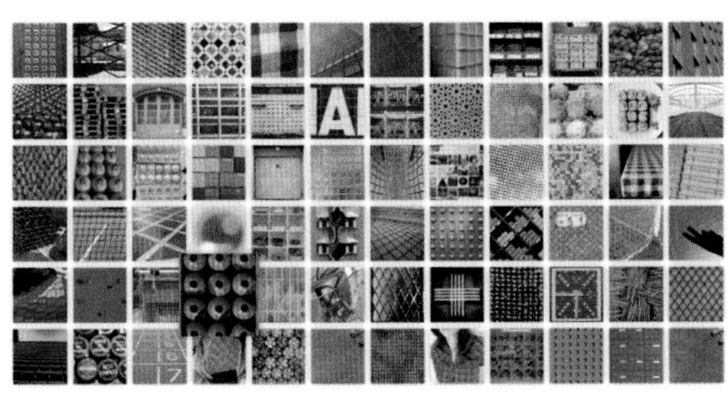

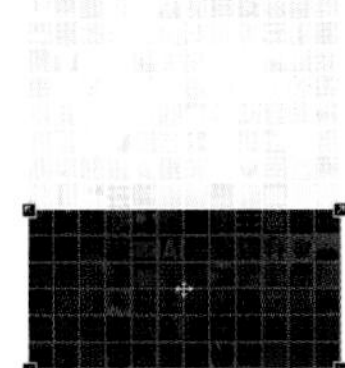

ADSL lines tangling, wire nettings limiting borders, roaring arteries grooving cities, our world has become a network of networks.
The Grid, photographical work created from boundless and diffuse connections, underlines the omnipresent repetitions of our world and is a source of inspiration for the Veja Grid trainer collection.
#148 Pixadores Paint Sprays
São Paulo
by Nicolas Ocante
SHOW NAVIGATION

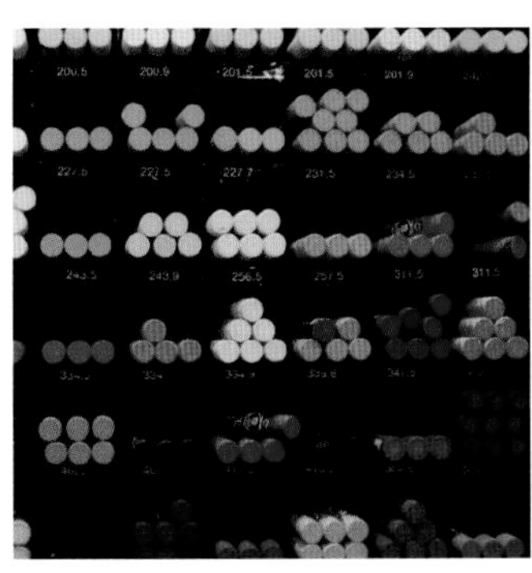

BACK TO THE GRID
ADSL lines tangling, wire nettings limiting borders, roaring arteries grooving cities, our world has become a network of networks.
The Grid, photographical work created from boundless and diffuse connections, underlines the omnipresent repetitions of our world and is a source of inspiration for the Veja Grid trainer collection.
#009 Pastels
Argenteuil, France
by Nicolas Ocante
PREVIOUS
NEXT
SHOW NAVIGATION

Versch // www.versch.org

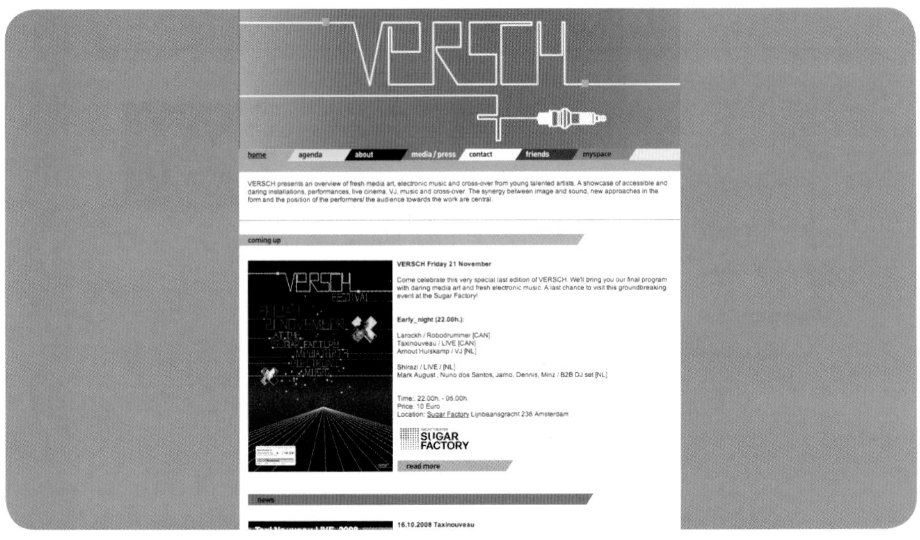

310k // www.310k.nl

Mikoon webservices // www.mikoon.nl

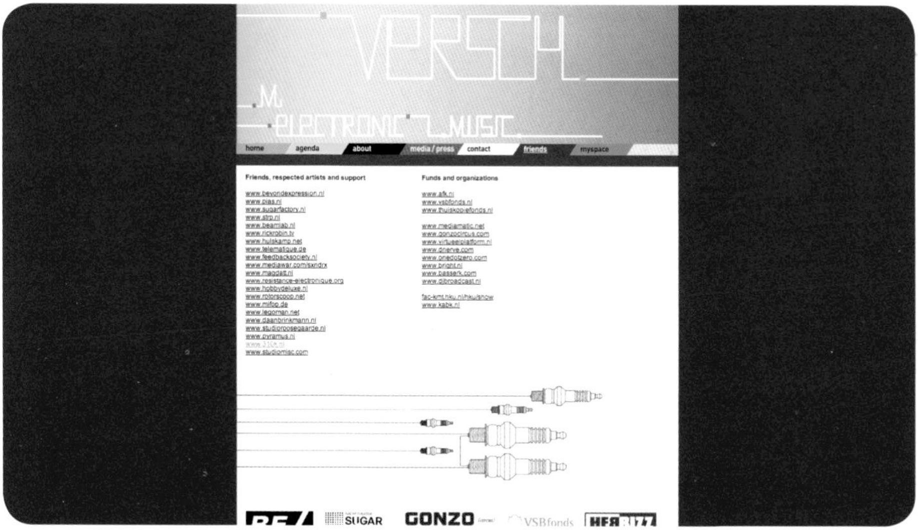

VERSCH
M
ELECTRONIC MUSIC

home agenda about media / press contact friends myspace

Friends, respected artists and support

www.beyondexpression.nl
www.pias.nl
www.sugarfactory.nl
www.strp.nl
www.beamlab.nl
www.rickrobin.tv
www.hulskamp.net
www.telematique.de
www.feedbacksociety.nl
www.mediawar.com/sxndrx
www.magdatt.nl
www.resistance-electronique.org
www.hobbydeluxe.nl
www.rotorscoop.net
www.mifop.de
www.legoman.net
www.daanbrinkmann.nl
www.studioroosegaarde.nl
www.pyramus.nl
www.studiomisc.com

Funds and organizations

www.afk.nl
www.vsbfonds.nl
www.thuiskopiefonds.nl

www.mediamatic.net
www.gonzocircus.com
www.virtueelplatform.nl
www.dnerve.com
www.onedotzero.com
www.bright.nl
www.basserk.com
www.djbroadcast.nl

fac-kmt.hku.nl/hku/show
www.kabk.nl

SUGAR GONZO VSBfonds

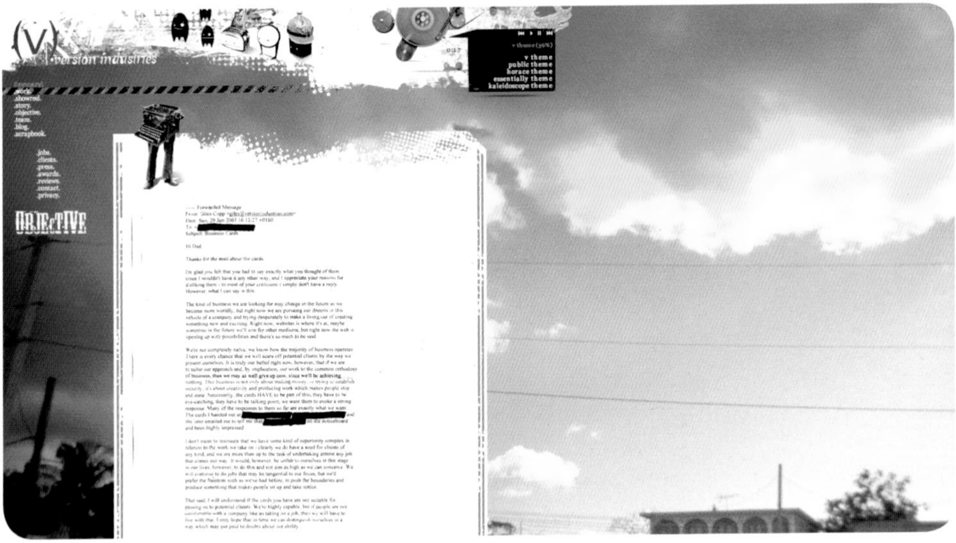

Version Industries // versionindustries.com

Version Industries
Looking good
feeling great
(V)
VERSION INDUSTRIES
BLOFELD

LATEST NEWS
PREVIOUS
NEXT

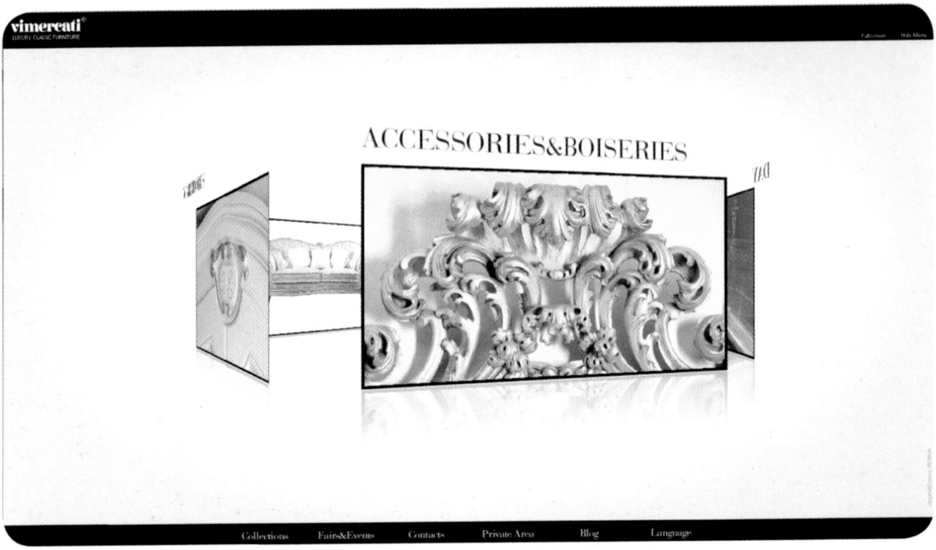

vimercati
LUXURY CLASSIC FURNITURE

ACCESSORIES&BOISERIES

Collections Fairs&Events Contacts Private Area Blog Language

vimercati
LUXURY CLASSIC FURNITURE

X French style 18th century 951-2

OPEN PREVIEWS DESCRIPTION

Collections Fairs&Events Contacts Private Area Blog Language

Vergani & Gasco // www.verganiegasco.it

vimercati®
LUXURY CLASSIC FURNITURE

Fullscreen Hide Menu

FAIRS&EVENTS
X SALONE DEL MOBILE 2007
SCENES 01 02 03 04 05 06 07

Collections Fairs&Events Contacts Private Area Blog Language

vimercati®
LUXURY CLASSIC FURNITURE

Fullscreen Hide Menu

FAIRS&EVENTS
X SALONE DEL MOBILE 2008
SCENES 01 02 03 04 05 06

Collections Fairs&Events Contacts Private Area Blog Language

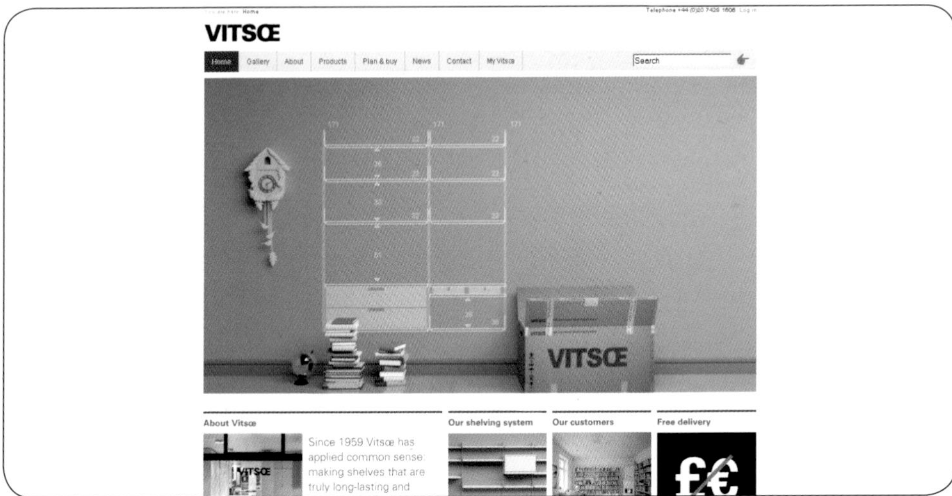

Tribal DDB London // Tribalddb.co.uk

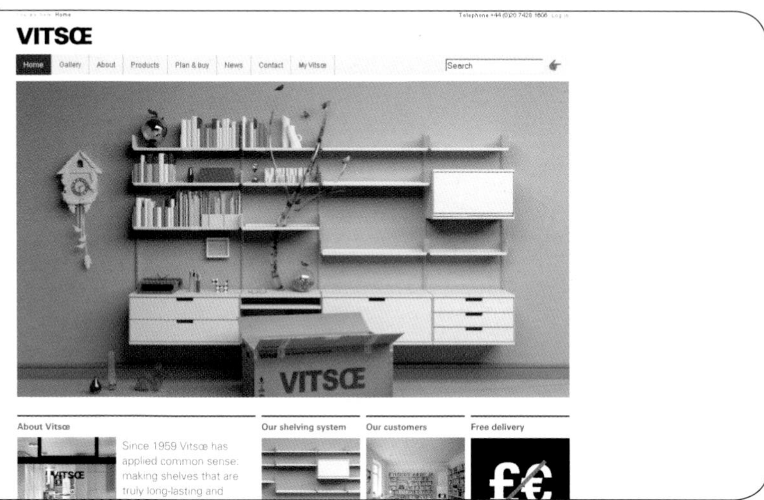
VITSŒ
Home
Gallery
About
Products
Plan & buy
News
Contact
My Vitsœ
Search
VITSŒ
About Vitsœ
Our shelving system
Our customers
Free delivery
Since 1959 Vitsœ has applied common sense: making shelves that are truly long-lasting and
£€

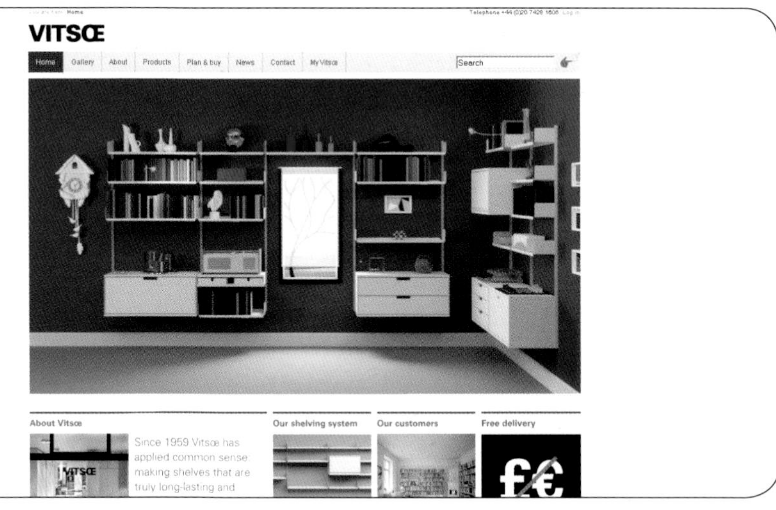
VITSŒ
Home
Gallery
About
Products
Plan & buy
News
Contact
My Vitsœ
Search
About Vitsœ
Our shelving system
Our customers
Free delivery
Since 1959 Vitsœ has applied common sense: making shelves that are truly long-lasting and
£€

Volcano Type // www.volcano-type.de

VOLCANO TYPE

Fonts | News/Events | Fonts in use | Authors | Imprint

Latest Releases | Categories | Names A-Z | Bestsellers | Free Fonts

Text | Display | Modular/Geometric | Script | Blackletter | Concept | Pictorial

Text — Text

DISPLAY — Display

MODULAR GEOMETRIC — Modular/Geometric

SCRIPT — Script

Black — Blackletter

CONCEPT — Concept

PicTorIAL — Pictorial

VOLCANO TYPE

Fonts | News/Events | Fonts in use | Authors | Imprint

Latest Releases | Categories | Names A-Z | Bestsellers | Free Fonts

Text | Display | Modular/Geometric | Script | Blackletter | Concept | Pictorial

Copy Cut | Copy Normal | Copy Semigrotesk | Digibo | Hermaphrodite

Copy SemiGrotesk Bold | download pdf | buy

UNGAR
Podcast Hero
HAPPY LIFE
Best Company of 2008 Chan & Sons
Måmelluk Trading

ABCDEFGHIJKLMN
OPQRSTUVWXYZ
abcdefghijklmn
opqrstuvwyz
1234567890!?
áçøöûñ/&€$)%§@;"«*

Peter Brugger
Tobias Koch
Boris Kahl
Flo Gaertner
Lars Harmsen
Axel Heide/ MAGMA Brand Design // www.magmabranddesign.de

VOLCANO TYPE

Fonts News/Events Fonts in use Authors Imprint

Latest Releases **Categories** Names A-Z Bestsellers Free Fonts

Text Display Modular/Geometric Script Blackletter Concept Pictorial

Arsen Basalt Chaucer Cross Cucaracha Daydream Diamond Fone Fooper Gringo Dingbats Gringo Sans Gringo Slab Gringo Tuscan Kathmandu Keycaps Kriminal Logorinth Magneta Masai Mountain Mud Newsletter Stencil Nymphe PT Sewed Poke Psycho Punta Negra ReadySteadyGo Bold ReadySteadyGo Skinny Shine Shiver Shuttle Stich Me Tacora Tape One Bold Tape Type Wawe

Arsen Basalt Chaucer Cross Cucaracha Daydream Diamond Fone

Fooper Gringo Dingbats Gringo Sans Gringo Slab Gringo Tuscan Kathmandu Keycaps Kriminal

Logorinth Magneta Masai Mountain Mud Newsletter Stencil Nymphe Poke

VOLCANO TYPE

Fonts News/Events Fonts in use Authors Imprint

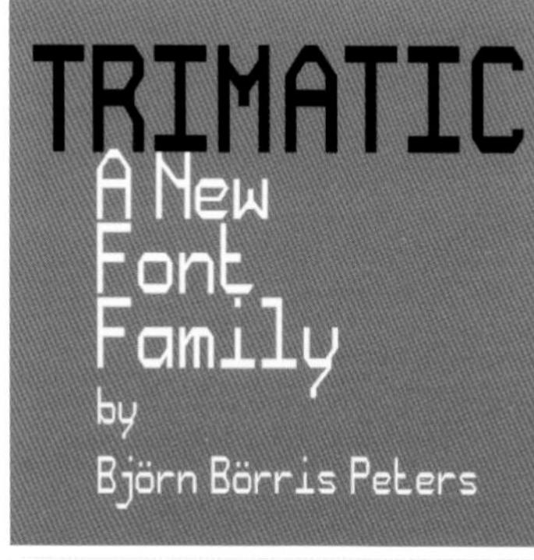

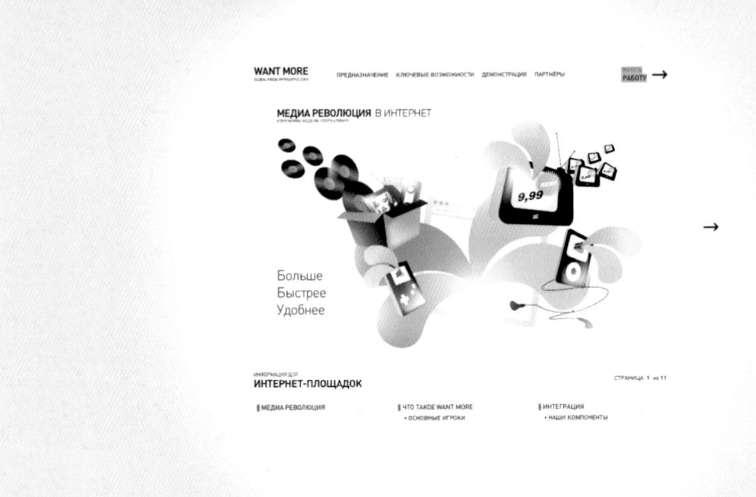

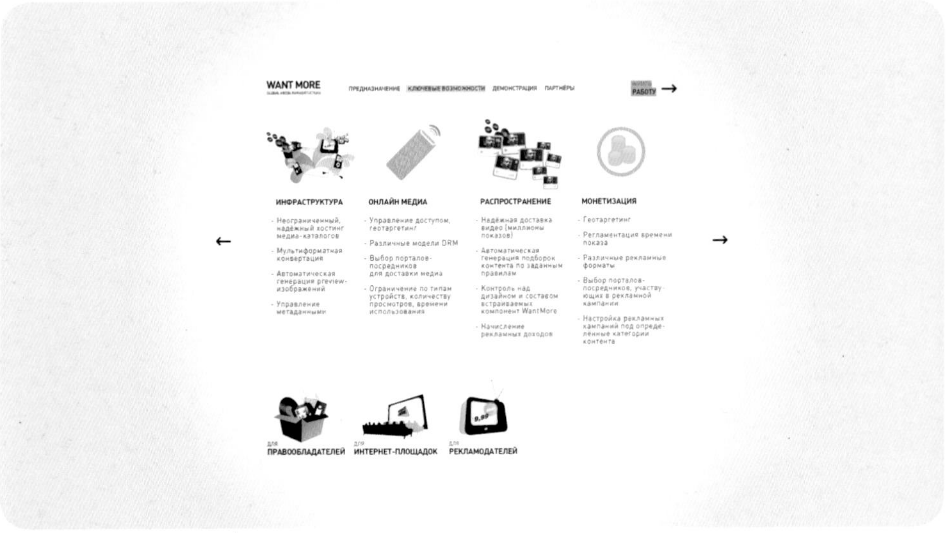

WANT MORE

ПРЕДНАЗНАЧЕНИЕ КЛЮЧЕВЫЕ ВОЗМОЖНОСТИ ДЕМОНСТРАЦИЯ ПАРТНЁРЫ

РАБОТУ

ИНФРАСТРУКТУРА

- Неограниченный, надёжный хостинг медиа-каталогов
- Мультиформатная конвертация
- Автоматическая генерация preview-изображений
- Управление метаданными

ОНЛАЙН МЕДИА

- Управление доступом, геотаргетинг
- Различные модели DRM
- Выбор порталов-посредников для доставки медиа
- Ограничение по типам устройств, количеству просмотров, времени использования

РАСПРОСТРАНЕНИЕ

- Надёжная доставка видео (миллионы показов)
- Автоматическая генерация подборок контента по заданным правилам
- Контроль над дизайном и составом встраиваемых компонент WantMore
- Начисление рекламных доходов

МОНЕТИЗАЦИЯ

- Геотаргетинг
- Регламентация времени показа
- Различные рекламные форматы
- Выбор порталов-посредников, участвующих в рекламной кампании
- Настройка рекламных кампаний под определённые категории контента

для **ПРАВООБЛАДАТЕЛЕЙ** для **ИНТЕРНЕТ-ПЛОЩАДОК** для **РЕКЛАМОДАТЕЛЕЙ**

Unique Atmosphere // weare.in.ua

WANT MORE

ПРЕДНАЗНАЧЕНИЕ КЛЮЧЕВЫЕ ВОЗМОЖНОСТИ ДЕМОНСТРАЦИЯ ПАРТНЁРЫ

МЕДИА-РЕВОЛЮЦИЯ В СЕТИ

ИЗМЕНЕНИЕ МОДЕЛИ ПОТРЕБЛЕНИЯ

→ Люди хотят больше свободы и гибкости в доступе к медиа

→ Сеть стала быстрее

→ Сеть стала доступнее

2007 - ТЕМПЫ РОСТА ИНТЕРНЕТ РЕКЛАМЫ

УКРАИНА

РОССИЯ

США

33%

В 2008 году расходы рекламодателей на онлайн-рекламу обгонят затраты на радио.

[ПО ДАННЫМ ZENITHOPTIMEDIA]

ИНФОРМАЦИЯ ДЛЯ

РЕКЛАМОДАТЕЛЕЙ

СТРАНИЦА 2 из 13

§ МЕДИА РЕВОЛЮЦИЯ
- МЕДИА РЕВОЛЮЦИЯ В СЕТИ

§ ЧТО ТАКОЕ WANT MORE
- КАК ЭТО РАБОТАЕТ
- ОСНОВНЫЕ ИГРОКИ

§ РАСПРОСТРАНЕНИЕ
- ТАРГЕТИНГ
- ВОЗМОЖНОСТИ

WANT MORE

ПРЕДНАЗНАЧЕНИЕ КЛЮЧЕВЫЕ ВОЗМОЖНОСТИ ДЕМОНСТРАЦИЯ ПАРТНЁРЫ

СЕРВИСЫ WANT MORE

Ваши медиа активы

Управление и хранение

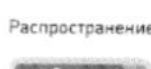

→ Импорт
→ Надёжный хостинг
→ Транскодирование
→ Редактирование медиа-каталога

→ Каналы доставки
→ Определение правил распространения

→ Рекламная сеть Want More
→ Управление продажами
→ Биллинг и аналитика

ИНФОРМАЦИЯ ДЛЯ

ПРАВООБЛАДАТЕЛЕЙ

СТРАНИЦА 5 из 14

§ ЧТО ТАКОЕ WANT MORE
- ОСНОВНЫЕ ИГРОКИ
- ВОЗМОЖНОСТИ ИНФРАСТРУКТУРЫ

§ СЕРВИСЫ WANT MORE

§ УПРАВЛЕНИЕ И ХРАНЕНИЕ
- РАСПРОСТРАНЕНИЕ
- СФЕРЫ РАСПРОСТРАНЕНИЯ

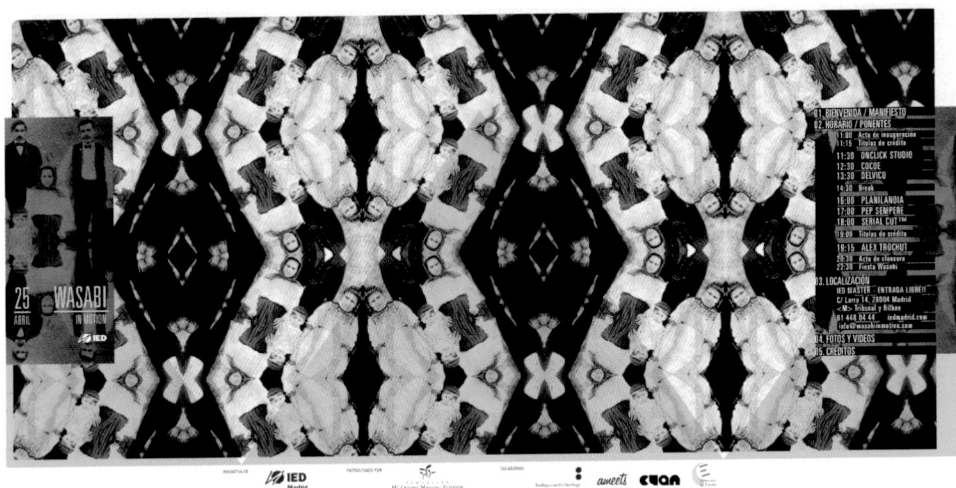

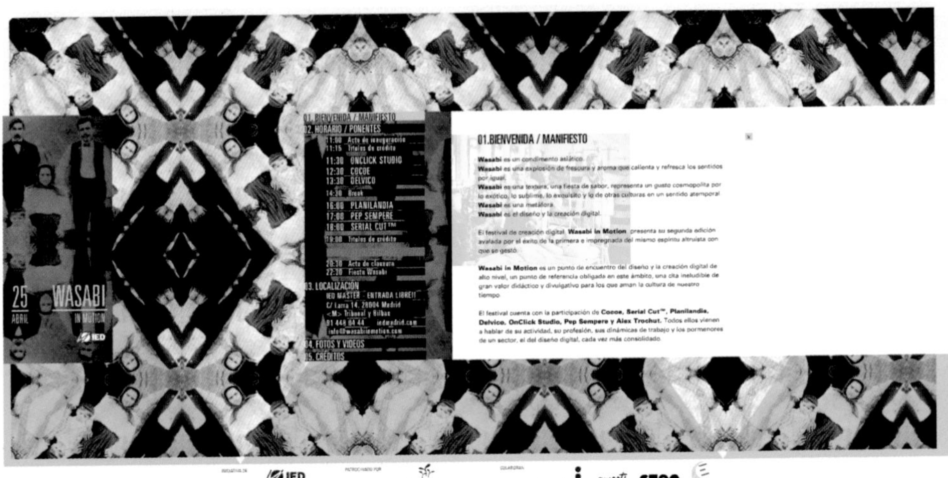

OnClick Studio // www.onclick.es

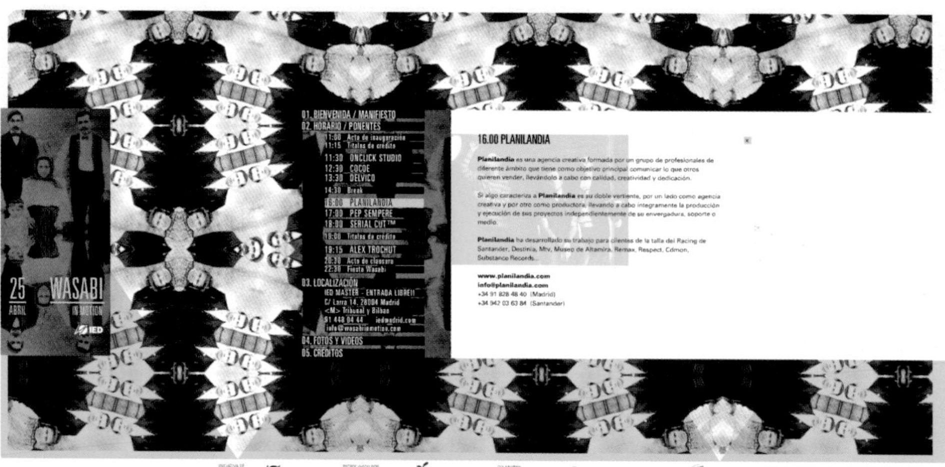

01. BIENVENIDA / MANIFIESTO
02. HORARIO / PONENTES
11:00 Acto de inauguración
11:15 Títulos de crédito
11:30 ONCLICK STUDIO
12:30 COCOE
13:30 DELVICO
14:30 Break
16:00 PLANILANDIA
17:00 PEP SEMPERE
18:00 SERIAL CUT™
19:00 Títulos de crédito
19:15 ALEX TROCHUT
20:30 Acto de clausura
22:30 Fiesta Wasabi
03. LOCALIZACIÓN
IED MASTER - ENTRADA LIBRE!!
C/ Larra 14, 28004 Madrid
<M> Tribunal y Bilbao
91 448 04 44 iedmadrid.com
info@wasabiinmotion.com
04. FOTOS Y VIDEOS
05. CRÉDITOS
25 ABRIL
WASABI IN MOTION
IED
16.00 PLANILANDIA
Planilandia es una agencia creativa formada por un grupo de profesionales de diferente ámbito que tiene como objetivo principal comunicar lo que otros quieren vender, llevándolo a cabo con calidad, creatividad y dedicación.
Si algo caracteriza a Planilandia es su doble vertiente, por un lado como agencia creativa y por otro como productora, llevando a cabo íntegramente la producción y ejecución de sus proyectos independientemente de su envergadura, soporte o medio.
Planilandia ha desarrollado su trabajo para clientes de la talla del Racing de Santander, Destinia, Mtv, Museo de Altamira, Remax, Respect, Cdmon, Substance Records...
www.planilandia.com
info@planilandia.com
+34 91 828 48 40 (Madrid)
+34 942 03 63 84 (Santander)
IED Madrid
ameeti
CUAN

01. BIENVENIDA / MANIFIESTO
02. HORARIO / PONENTES
11:00 Acto de inauguración
11:15 Títulos de crédito
11:30 ONCLICK STUDIO
12:30 COCOE
13:30 DELVICO
14:30 Break
16:00 PLANILANDIA
17:00 PEP SEMPERE
18:00 SERIAL CUT™
19:00 Títulos de crédito
19:15 ALEX TROCHUT
20:30 Acto de clausura
22:30 Fiesta Wasabi
03. LOCALIZACIÓN
IED MASTER - ENTRADA LIBRE!!
C/ Larra 14, 28004 Madrid
<M> Tribunal y Bilbao
91 448 04 44 iedmadrid.com
info@wasabiinmotion.com
04. FOTOS Y VIDEOS
05. CRÉDITOS
25 ABRIL
WASABI IN MOTION
IED
18.00 SERIAL CUT™
Serial Cut™ es un estudio madrileño que desde 1999 trabaja en proyectos nacionales e internacionales enfocados a dirección de arte, diseño e ilustración.
Tendremos la oportunidad que Sergio del Puerto haga un repaso de estos 10 años y nos muestre en exclusiva los nuevos proyectos, incluyendo numerosas secuencias de making of que nos permitirán conocer el proceso de creación.
Algunos de los clientes más significativos de Serial Cut™ son: Nike, Mtv, Zune, Foot Locker, Powerade, The NY Times Magazine, The Guardian, Rolling Stone, Channel 4, WAD, Renfe, Estrella Damm, Springfield y MUSAC entre otros.
www.serialcut.com
info@serialcut.com
IED Madrid
ameeti
CUAN

Hideki Hagiwara Katsumoto/ Naipe Design // www.naipedesign.com.br

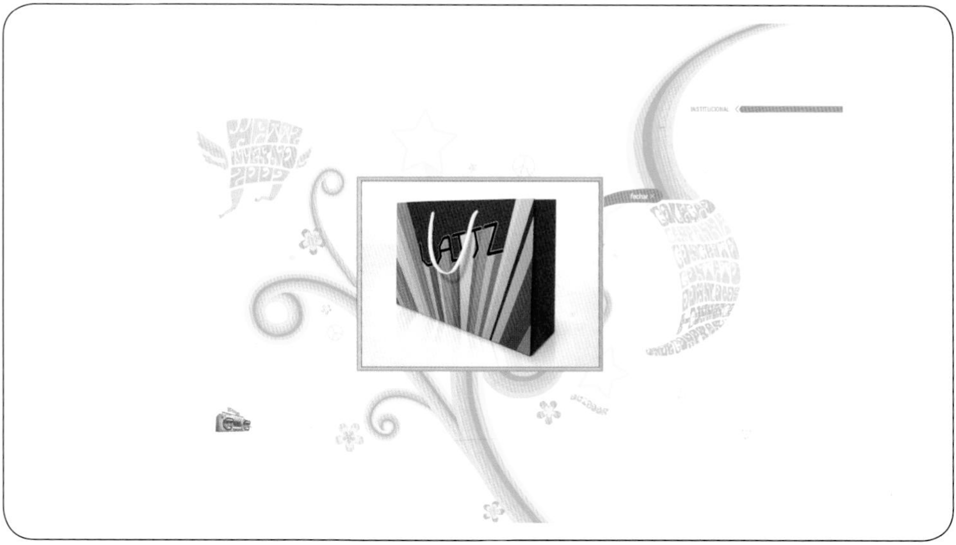
INSTITUCIONAL
fechar

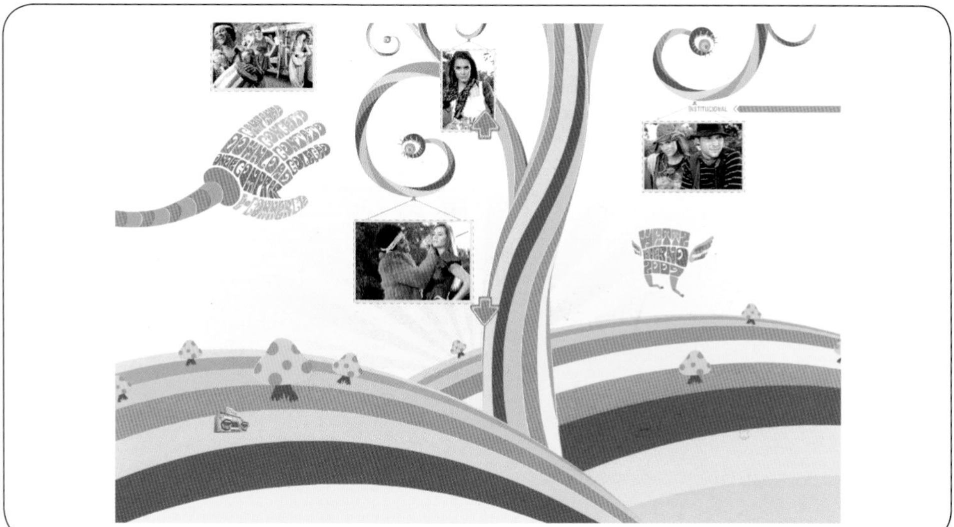
INSTITUCIONAL

IMG SRC // www.imgsrc.co.jp

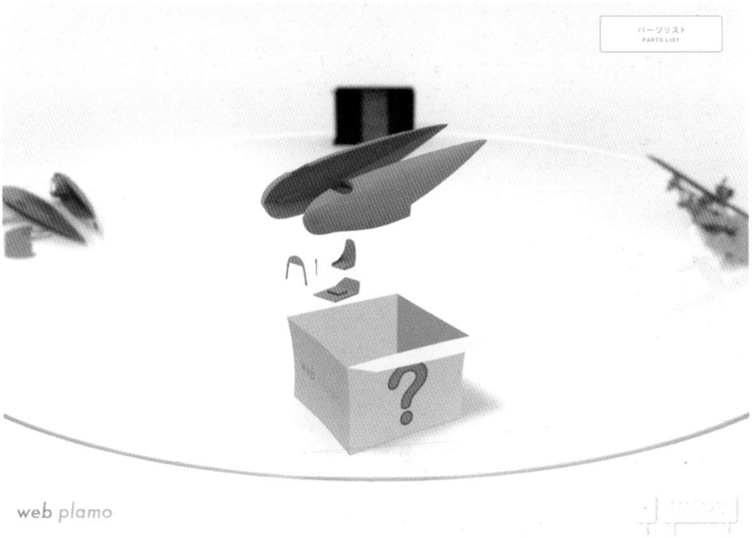

パーツリスト
PARTS LIST

web plamo

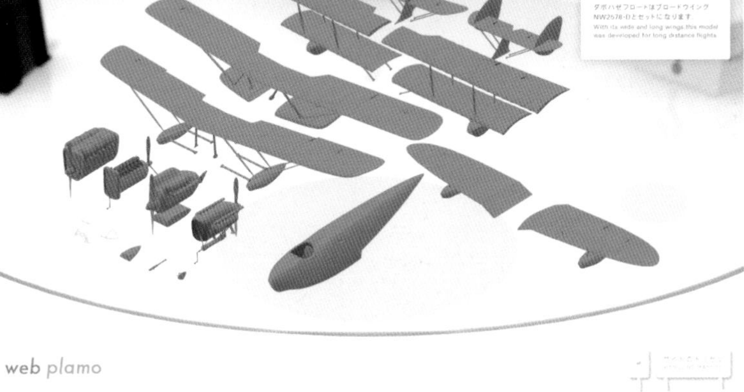

Pelle Martin/ I AM PELLE // iampelle.com

Advertising
Fashion
Art

Advertising
Fashion
Art

Whale Song // www.optuswhalesong.com.au

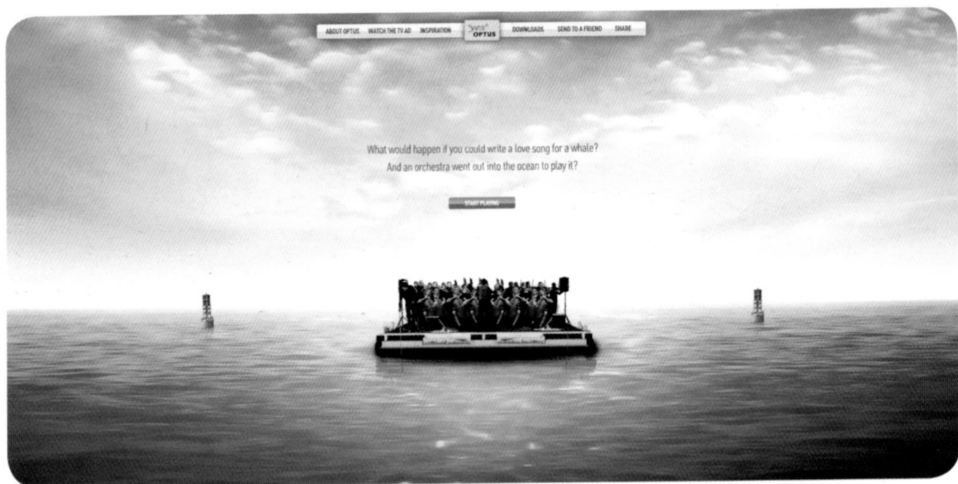

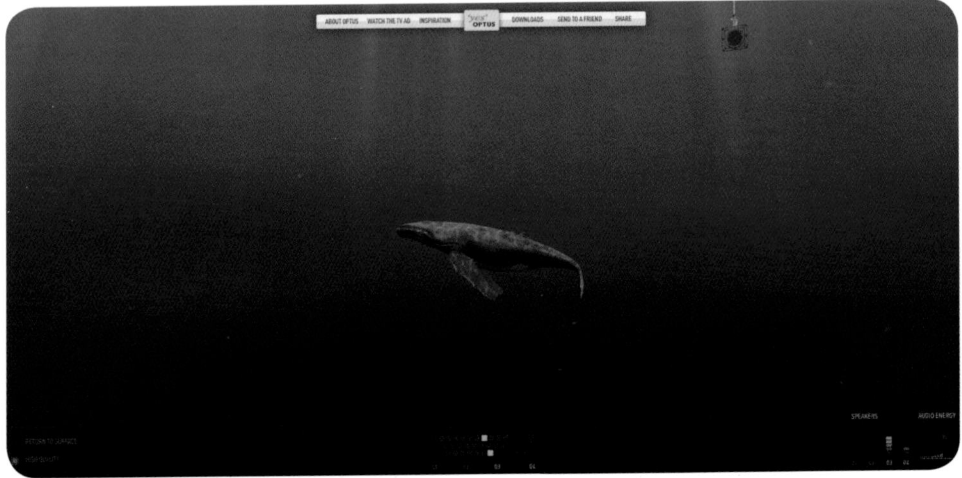

Optus // www.optus.com.au
M&C Saatchi Sydney // www.mcsaatchi.com.au
Mark Agency // www.marksydney.com
Boffswana // www.boffswana.com
Iloura // www.iloura.com.au

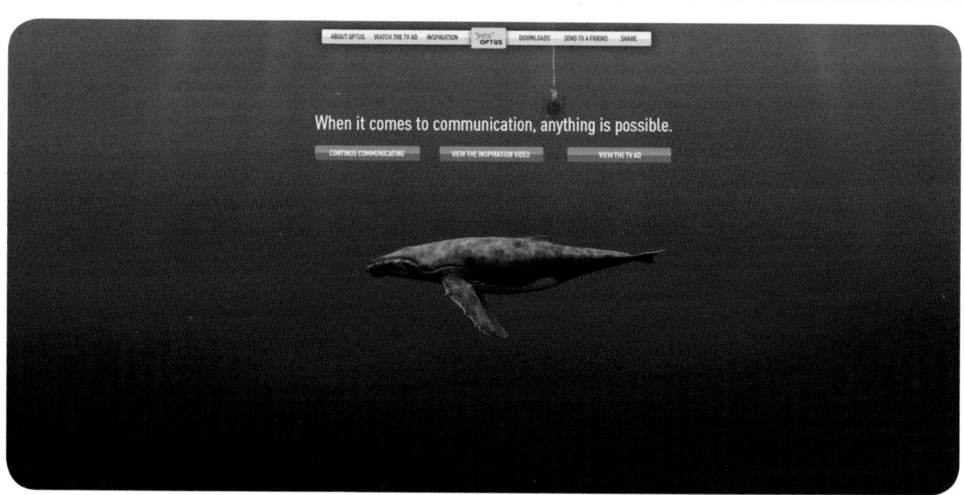
ABOUT OPTUS
WATCH THE TV AD
INSPIRATION
'yes' OPTUS
DOWNLOADS
SEND TO A FRIEND
SHARE
When it comes to communication, anything is possible.
CONTINUE COMMUNICATING
VIEW THE INSPIRATION VIDEO
VIEW THE TV AD

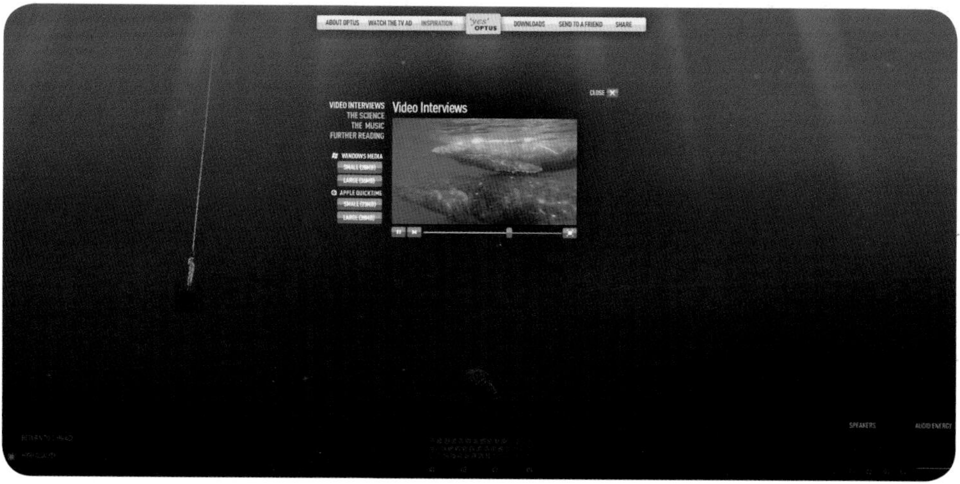
ABOUT OPTUS
WATCH THE TV AD
INSPIRATION
'yes' OPTUS
DOWNLOADS
SEND TO A FRIEND
SHARE
CLOSE
VIDEO INTERVIEWS
THE SCIENCE
THE MUSIC
FURTHER READING
Video Interviews
WINDOWS MEDIA
APPLE QUICKTIME
SPEAKERS
AUDIO ENERGY

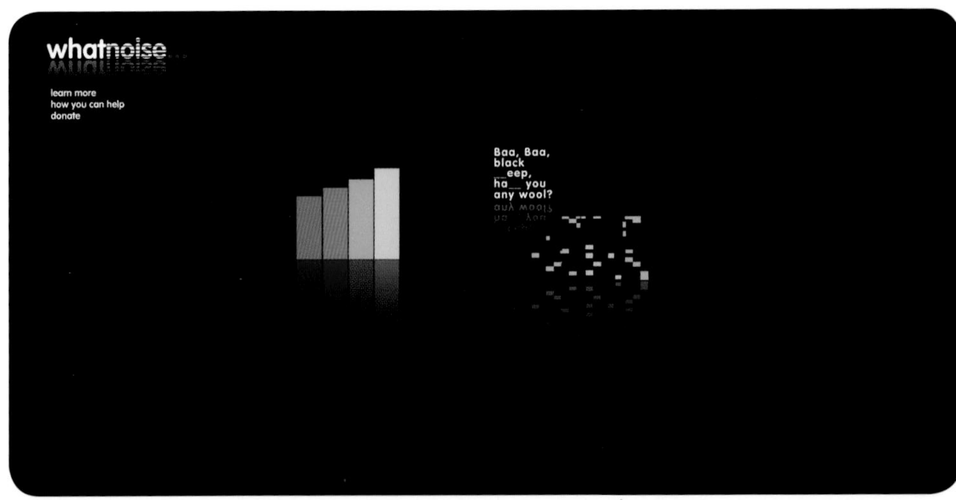

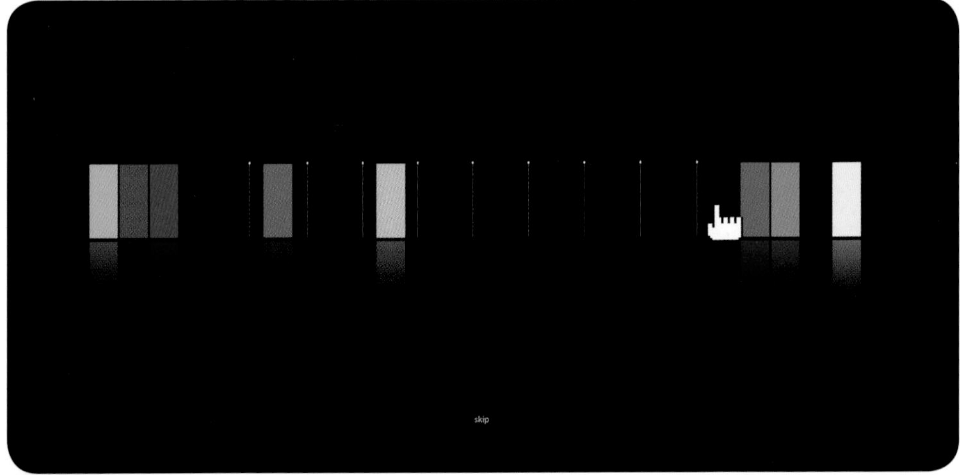

Kinetic // www.kinetic.com.sg

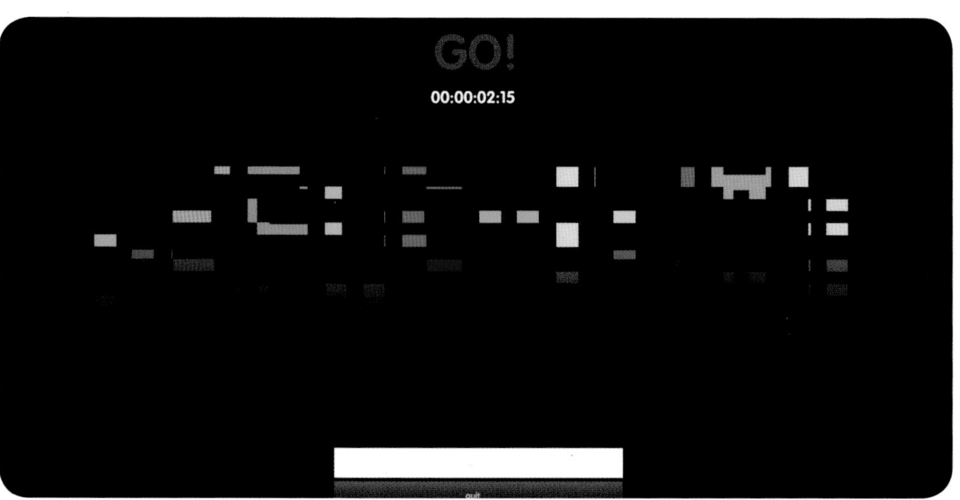

just too many blanks to fill.

Children with hearing problems often experience varying degrees of learning difficulty, especially with regard to language acquisition. As those suffering from hearing loss often cannot hear quiet vocalizations such as "s", "sh", "f", "t", "k" and others, they may omit them altogether when they speak, making conversations with them difficult, if not impossible. This is just the tip of the iceberg, of course. It gets worse when we talk about hearing-impaired children from economically disadvantaged families. You can play your part and help everyone of them out. Help them fill the gaps in their conversations. And in their lives.

+ donate.

<

Katrin Wiens // www.katrinwiens.com

HOME OF WIENSWORLD
CHOSE CLIENT/
PEPPER + PISTOL
SEE MORE ARTWORK FOR THIS CLIENT/
DRAGONFLY PRINT/ SPRING'06
© 2005 ALL RIGHTS BY WIENSWORLD

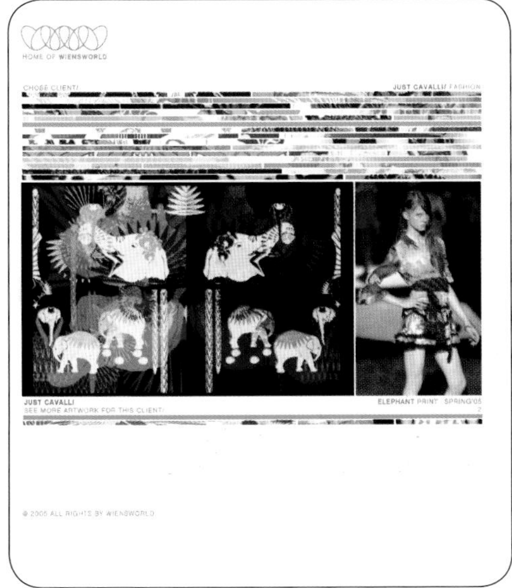
HOME OF WIENSWORLD
CHOSE CLIENT/
JUST CAVALLI/ FASHION
JUST CAVALLI
SEE MORE ARTWORK FOR THIS CLIENT/
ELEPHANT PRINT/ SPRING'05
© 2005 ALL RIGHTS BY WIENSWORLD

designedmemory // www.designedmemory.com

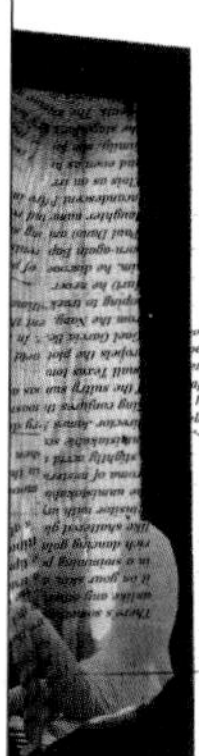

about
film
collections
press
retailers
shop online
contact

wren

Online
www.revolveclothing.com

California

Market
11725 Barrington Court
Los Angeles, CA 90049
310.476.0565

Planet Blue
3835 Cross Creek Road
Malibu, CA 90265
310.317.9975
www.shopplanetblue.com

about
film
collections
press
retailers
shop online
contact

press
info@wren-clothing.com
323.664.4596

sales
abby@simonshowroom.com

website by designedmemory

wren

Rodrigo Alarcon
Julio Dui
Rafael Morinaga
Fabrício Ribeiro
Rodrigo Teco
Cauê Teixeira // www.grafikonstruct.com.br

XPRESS
CAMISINHA: COMPANHEIRA VELHA DE GUERRA
MENU
Companheira velha de guerra
Experimenta
Receitinha
Companheira velha de guerra
Não é de hoje que a camisinha ajuda a gente a se cuidar.
Os chineses criaram a primeira versão da camisinha feita de papel de seda untado com óleo. Já os egípcios, desde 1850 a.C., usavam protetores para o pênis feitos em linho ou com intestinos de animais.
Mas foi a mitologia grega que apresentou a camisinha para o Ocidente. O rei Minos era casado com Pasiphë. Ele gostava de pular a cerca e por obra e graça da esposa ciumenta passou a ejacular serpentes, escorpiões e lacraias, que matavam quem se deitasse com o soberano. Minos se apaixona por Procris, moça
40% das gestantes no Brasil não fazem o teste anti-HIV no pré-natal (PN-DST/AIDS)

Kinetic // www.kinetic.com.sg

VOTE FOR US!
2008 WEBBY AWARDS
THE ADVENTURES OF HEARTY BEEFY BOWL
The aromatic and savoury beef bowls made from the choicest beef and the finest ingredients, herbs and spices...

VOTE FOR US!
2008 WEBBY AWARDS
THE ADVENTURES OF HEARTY BEEFY BOWL
wallpapers
screensavers

DESIGN T-SHIRTS AND STREETWEAR AND URBAN ARTWORK. VERSION 2.0

« SELEKKT facelifted.　　Your Eyes Lie! »

NAME RIBBON from NYC!

Another piece of finding from a long weekend in front of the mac: NAME RIBBON from NYC with a nice selekktion of hoodies. This is what they write about their WHY: *"Progressive streetwear from several labels got good, so progressive street kids copped it. Then some of the brands got cocky, and then they got expensive, too expensive for progressive street kids that made them thrive. That's when those brands got 'dumb'. We're for people who avoid 'dumb'."* We totally agree with this.

_CATEGORIES
- Shirts 'n Stuff
- Interviews
- Entertaining
- Limited Sales

_HOT LABELS BY RANDOM
- Freegums
- YOUYESYOU
- YACKFOU.com
- 2K by Gingham
- TOKE
- Rockaway Bear
- Tokyo Art Beat
- Hey! Unite

- Mike Perry
- netdiver
- Stefan Golz

_THE OTHERS
- Addicteed
- teeshirtblog
- Hide Your Arms
- Streetwear Websites

_PAGES
- About us
- Want to be featured?
- Disclaimer

_THE SEARCH

Go!

_SELEKKTED T-SHOPS

LIMITEES.COM
SELEKKTED
DESIGN T-SHIRTS
FOR EUROPE!

WELCOME TO SUFFIX ABUSE

Home :: About :: Contact

SUBSCRIBE

Your Email Address

Subscribe

Delivered by FeedBurner

FREE DOWNL...

SupaFly

7 Abr

Premio al me...

Pues parece que hemos ga... (Con tanto premio, estamo... profesionalmente).

Estamos realmente conte... blogueros/as admiradas e... petite claudine, El encanta... obsoleta... Una pena no h... bien ayer condenaos ;)

Así que aprovechando el ... ocasión de recomendarles... han estado nominados.
Va por ustedes!
Contraindicaciones, Labur... mínimas, Lady Filstrup, P... ladrilio, Processblack, Rec... Lounge Corner, Pasquin ... Snoid, y los que nos habre...

Y gracias también a los le... concurso por montar un tin... una pequeña crítica no me ... una vez al día durante un a... es suficiente ;)

Los Trash Hunters de...

Enlaces relacionados:

Bloggies, 20 Blogs y con...

II Edición de los premios...

Creación de Logos Úni...

Esta entrada fue creada e... Diseño. Puedes seguir los... comentario, o hacer un track...

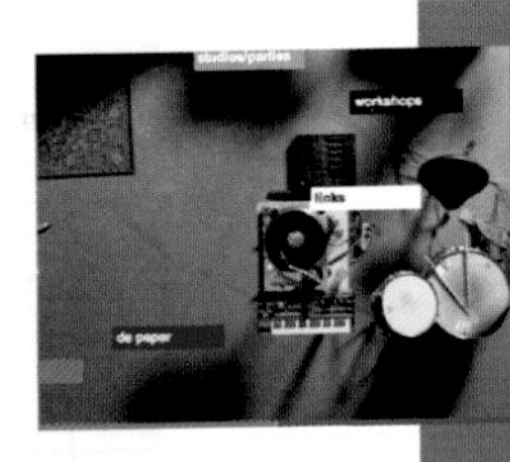

ios 20Blogs.

REDUCE, REUSE, RE...you know the drill!

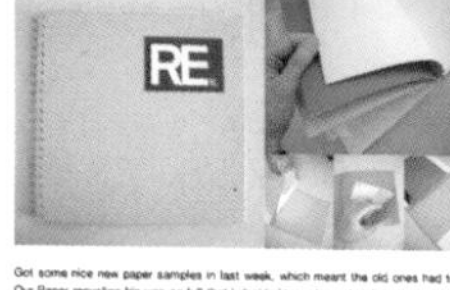

Got some nice new paper samples in last week, which meant the old ones had to go! Our Paper recycling bin was so full that I decided to make a sketch book out of some of them. This is the first version, and the label is a bit of a 'quick hit'. Vol. 2 will be nicer! Anyone got any other ideas?

4 Comments so far -

Jack said,

Sweet Glenn, might make myself one of those! Didn't we see virtually the exact same thing being sold £5, when you were visiting?

Available Feeds

Entries RSS
Comments RSS

Categories

Adverts
Agency
Agency - Scotland
Animation
Architecture
Art
Awards
Boards
Books
Competition
CSS/HTML
Degree shows
Design
Editorial
Exhibition
Fashion
Flash
Footwear
Games
Glenn
Graffiti
Graphic Art
Icons & Symbols
Identity

brando el premio.

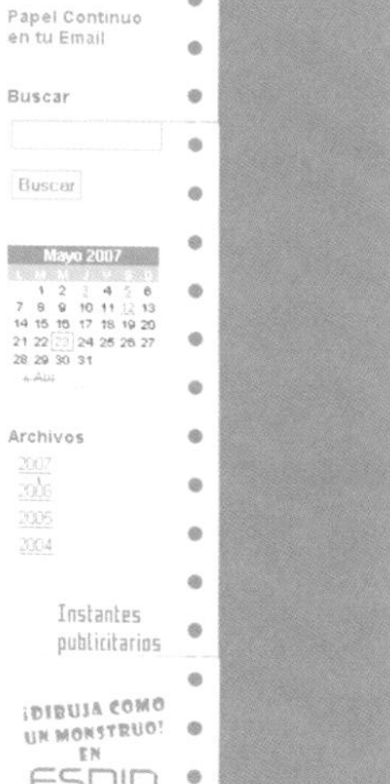

April 2007
March 2007
February 2007
January 2007

Members

Site Admin
Logout
+ Technorati Favorites

Redactores

Paola Ruz del Canto
Diseñadora Industrial DuocUC
Fotografía

Pablo Coatts
Egresado Diseño Gráfico IP. Los Leones

Rodrigo Lopez
Licenciatura en Arte U.Chile

Javier Cancino
Licenciado Diseño U. Católica de Valparaíso

Jko Contreras
Egresado Diseño U. de Chile

BLOGS

BLOGS

BLOGS

BLOGS

LO MAS VISTO

Serigrafía para todos (35412)
Diseño Gráfico del Siglo 21 (15181)
IdN Internacional designers № (13190)
La belleza según Platón (12677)
I love Branding (12219)
Documental Helvetica (12088)
De lo adecuado y bello (11301)
50 Años de Helvetica (11219)
De crear a desarrollar [1] (10145)
El fenómeno IPhone (9202)

GALUCHA

Envíanos un mail y te invitamos a nuestro grupo de Flickr.

Start a blog is so easy that hundreds of thousands are registered across the globe every day. Blogs are like a mix of personal diary and newspaper column. The difference is the content, and, in particular, the way bloggers manage to transform them into something truly unique. The following pages show how creativity can make a simple structure much more appealing while preserving functionality. Blogspot or Wordpress? Vote now!

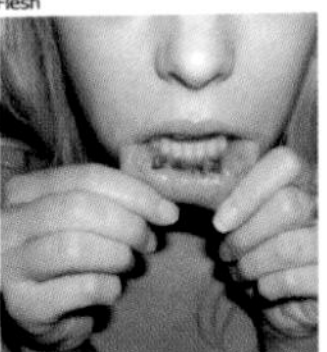

Il est si facile de commencer un blog qu'il s'en crée des centaines de milliers chaque jour dans le monde. Ainsi, à mi-chemin entre le journal intime et l'éditorial d'un journal, la différence entre tous ces blogs réside dans leur contenu et surtout dans le fait que leurs auteurs parviennent à les transformer en quelque chose de véritablement unique.
Ces pages vous permettront d'observer comment une structure simple peut devenir beaucoup plus attractive, en exerçant sa créativité, tout en conservant sa fonctionnalité. Blogspot ou Wordpress ? À vous de voter !

show: < > | 1 2 3 4 5 | Start / Stop 1 of 5 images Pixelache installation. In situ.
rt of the Pixelache festival in Helsinki, UVA created an interactive sound installation.
pulation of the wheel at the base of the installation spawned sound generating particles, creating a
that was unique from moment to moment.

Es ist so einfach, einen Blog zu starten, dass tagtäglich mehrere hunderttausend davon auf der ganzen Welt ins Leben gerufen werden. Als Mittelding zwischen privatem Tagebuch und Zeitungsspalte unterscheiden sie sich durch ihren Inhalt und vor allem dadurch, wie es ihren Autoren gelingt, sie in etwas wirklich Einzigartiges zu verwandeln. Auf den folgenden Seiten können Sie sehen, wie ein einfacher Aufbau attraktiver gestaltet werden kann, wenn man Kreativität einsetzt, und gleichzeitig die Funktionalität aufrecht erhält. Blogspot oder Wordpress? Bitte wählen!

Het gemak waarmee een blog wordt gestart is dusdanig groot dat er elke dag honderdduizenden over de gehele wereld worden geopend. Het verschil tussen een dagboek en een krantenkolom ligt hem in de inhoud en vooral de manier waarop het de schrijvers lukt om hun blog in iets werkelijk bijzonders te veranderen. Op de volgende bladzijden kunt u zien hoe een eenvoudige structuur veel aantrekkelijker kan worden door er creatief mee om te gaan en tegelijkertijd de functionaliteit ervan te behouden. Blogspot of Wordpress? Breng uw stem uit!

THE SIMPLEST TELEPHONE
A month ago while in line to get on the plane at London Heathrow airport, I spied this old-style telephone with absolutely no buttons or display screen. There's no confusion and nothing really to LEARN. True simplicity? In one sense so, but also limited utility.

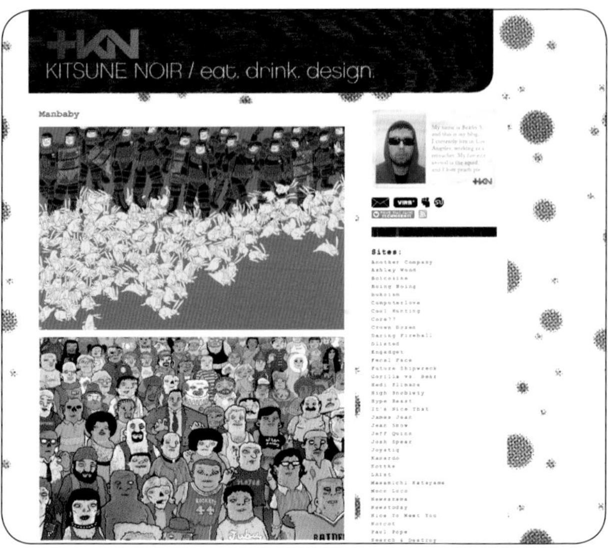

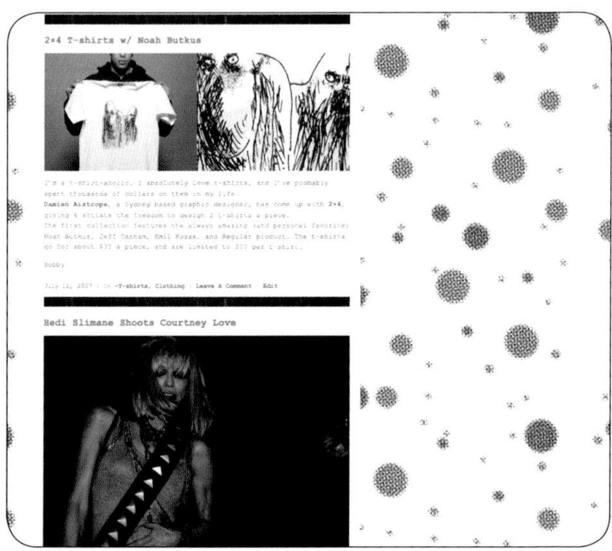

Bobby Solomon

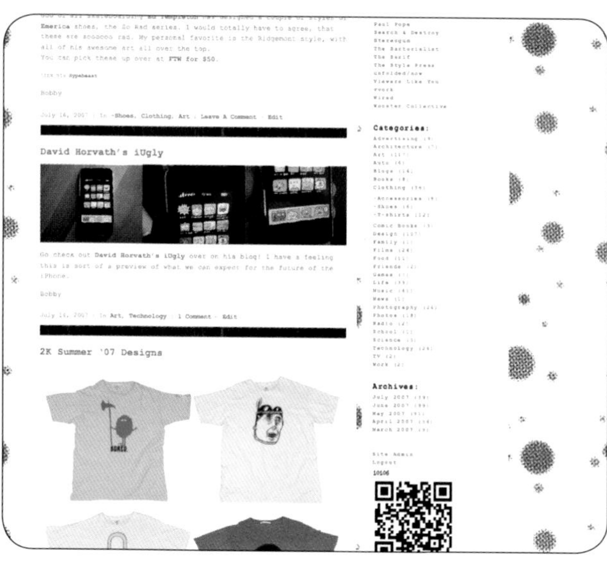
Emerica shoes, the So Rad series. I would totally have to agree, that these are soooooo rad. My personal favorite is the Ridgemont style, with all of his awesome art all over the top.
You can pick these up over at FTW for $50.
Hypebeast
Bobby
July 16, 2007 | In -Shoes, Clothing, Art | Leave A Comment · Edit
David Horvath's iUgly
Go check out David Horvath's iUgly over on his blog! I have a feeling this is sort of a preview of what we can expect for the future of the iPhone.
Bobby
July 14, 2007 | In Art, Technology | 1 Comment · Edit
2K Summer '07 Designs
Paul Pope
Search & Destroy
Stereogum
The Sartorialist
The Serif
The Style Press
unfolded/now
Viewers Like You
vvork
Wired
Wooster Collective
Categories:
Advertising
Architecture
Art
Auto
Blogs
Books
Clothing
-Accessories
-Shoes
-T-shirts
Comic Books
Design
Family
Films
Food
Friends
Games
Life
Music
News
Photography
Photos
Radio
School
Science
Technology
TV
Work
Archives:
July 2007
June 2007
May 2007
April 2007
March 2007
Site Admin
Logout
10106

2K just keeps rolling out with amazing t-shirts, and their new '07 collection is exceptionally good. A lot of nw stuff from Geoff McFetridge, Genevieve Gauckler, Adrian Johnson, Barry McGee, and a bunch of other artists that they fail to name. If you need a new t-shirt, definitely the place to check out.
July 14, 2007 | In Design, -T-shirts, Clothing, Art | Leave A Comment · Edit
LVHRD MGZN 03
MGZN
SUMMER 2007
3
Recently Played
Obama'08

:: addic[tee]d :: Fresh Tee Guide™

FRONT PAGE ABOUT CONTACT FEATURES LINKS

ADDICTEED FRESH TEE GUIDE · STYLES FOR MILES · LOGO DESIGN BY MWM GRAPHICS 2007

ENTRIES FROM DECEMBER 2006

600+ T-Shirts of 2006

December 30th, 2006 · 13 Comments

I was thinking about making a top 100 t-shirt post but that would mean that I'd have to leave out many nice designs; instead I'll let you guys decide for yourselves. Follow the link and see 600+ designs that were featured on addicteed for 2006 all in one page in our flickr set. You can save the images add comments or notes or blog about them all these features are enabled for everyone.

A big THANK YOU to everyone and a Happy New Year!

Tags: T-Shirt

Lowercase Industry Sale

December 30th, 2006 · No Comments

5GBP off until February Lowercase Industry

Tags: sales/offers · T-Shirt

A Better Tomorrrow T-Shirts

December 30th, 2006 · 1 Comment

Search

...

RECENT POSTS

- LA launch of T
- KISER limited edition "JUICY" t-shirt
- Rockett T-Shirts 2007
- New T-Shirts @ Tank Theory
- 2 New T-Shirt Designs @ Enclothe

CATEGORIES

- Interviews
- NEWS
  - art
  - events
  - misc
  - sales/offers
- T-Shirt

ARCHIVES

- March 2007
- February 2007
- January 2007
- December 2006
- November 2006
- October 2006
- September 2006
- August 2006
- July 2006
- June 2006
- May 2006
- April 2006
- March 2006
- February 2006

Aris Karatarakis

5GBP off until February Lowercase Industry

Tags: sales/offers · T-Shirt

A Better Tomorrrow T-Shirts

December 30th, 2006 · 1 Comment

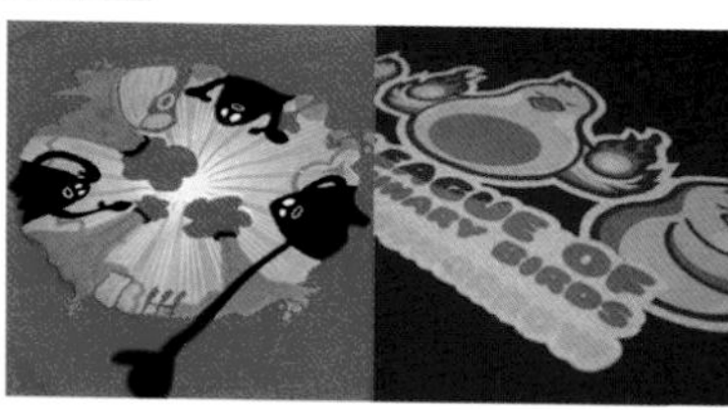

Check out the designs available @ A better tomorrow desingn contest/streetwear community

Tags: T-Shirt

- February 2007
- January 2007
- December 2006
- November 2006
- October 2006
- September 2006
- August 2006
- July 2006
- June 2006
- May 2006
- April 2006
- March 2006
- February 2006
- January 2006
- December 2005

Check out the designs available @ A better tomorrow desingn contest/streetwear community

Tags: T-Shirt

New @ RockawayBear

December 26th, 2006 · 1 Comment

Left:"Hamburg" Right: "FF Classic"
more @ RockawayBear

Tags: T-Shirt

New Limited edition T-Shirts by Lite

30gms
About 30gms
Contact
Fibre
Search
RSS Feed
Supplements
M is for...
...Metro. According to Metrobits, most metro logos are fancy variations of the letter M and they have collected 150 of them to prove it. But whether you searching for a Metro, the Subway or the Underground it's clear that your best bet is to look for a big letter in a circle. There are obviously exceptions to this rule, like the London Underground logo, which is recognised worldwide anyway.
The colours of the logos seem less consistent – although red and blue are very popular virtually every hue is represented, even "untrustworthy" orange. Link (via Londonist)
David Rainbird
Posted on Wednesday, 23rd of August 2006 Permalink Comment (0)

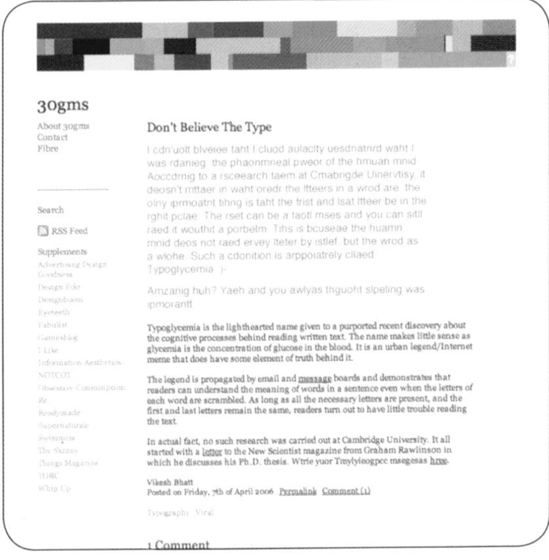

30gms
About 30gms
Contact
Fibre
Search
RSS Feed
Supplements
Don't Believe The Type
I cdn'uolt blveiee taht I cluod aulaclty uesdnatnrd waht I was rdanieg: the phaonmneal pweor of the hmuan mnid Aoccdrnig to a rsceearch taem at Cmabrigde Uinervtisy, it deosn't mttaer in waht oredr the ltteers in a wrod are, the olny iprmoatnt tihng is taht the frist and lsat ltteer be in the rghit pclae. The rset can be a taotl mses and you can sitll raed it wouthit a porbelm. Tihs is bcuseae the huamn mnid deos not raed ervey lteter by istlef, but the wrod as a wlohe. Such a cdonition is arppoiatrely cllaed Typoglycemia :)-
Amzanig huh? Yaeh and you awlyas thguoht slpeling was ipmorantt.
Typoglycemia is the lighthearted name given to a purported recent discovery about the cognitive processes behind reading written text. The name makes little sense as glycemia is the concentration of glucose in the blood. It is an urban legend/Internet meme that does have some element of truth behind it.
The legend is propagated by email and message boards and demonstrates that readers can understand the meaning of words in a sentence even when the letters of each word are scrambled. As long as all the necessary letters are present, and the first and last letters remain the same, readers turn out to have little trouble reading the text.
In actual fact, no such research was carried out at Cambridge University. It all started with a letter to the New Scientist magazine from Graham Rawlinson in which he discusses his Ph.D. thesis. Wtrie yuor Tmylyieogpcc msegesas hree.
Vikesh Bhatt
Posted on Friday, 7th of April 2006 Permalink Comment (1)
1 Comment

Fibre Design

30gms
About 30gms
Contact
Fibre
Search
RSS Feed
Supplements
Stephane Kardos
If Fibre is looking for a new illustrator we are just as likely to check out great blogs such as Drawn! as a traditional agency. That's how we found Stephane Kardos, an obsessive sketcher with a natural flair and expressive style. We had the opportunity to work with Stephane Kardos recently on a book project (more about that next week) and as well as being very talented, he's a very nice chap! Link
David Rainbird
Posted on Friday, 13th of October 2006 Permalink Comment (0)
No comments just yet

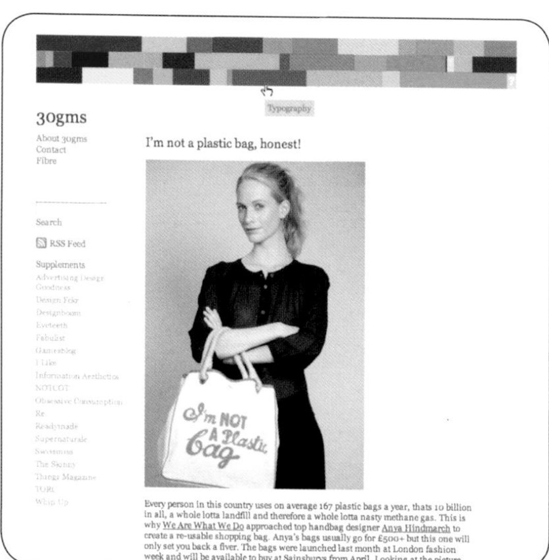
30gms
About 30gms
Contact
Fibre
Typography
Search
RSS Feed
Supplements
I'm not a plastic bag, honest!
I'm NOT A Plastic Bag
Every person in this country uses on average 167 plastic bags a year, thats 10 billion in all, a whole lotta landfill and therefore a whole lotta nasty methane gas. This is why We Are What We Do approached top handbag designer Anya Hindmarch to create a re-usable shopping bag. Anya's bags usually go for £500+ but this one will only set you back a fiver. The bags were launched last month at London fashion week and will be available to buy at Sainsburys from April. Looking at the picture

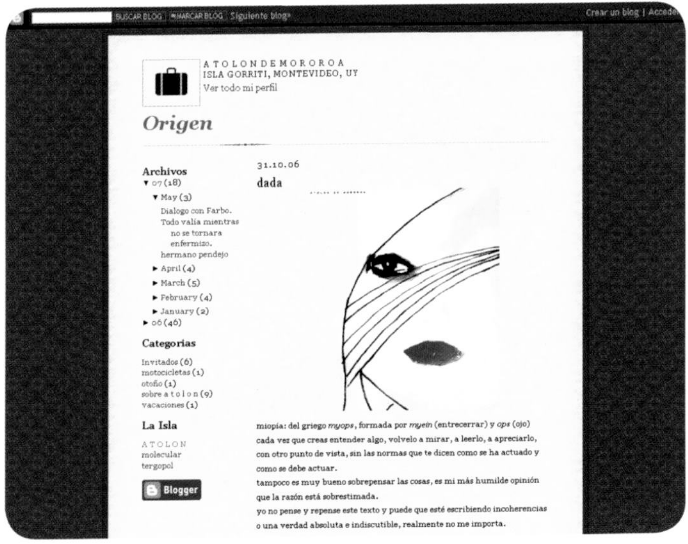

Andrés Amodio, Diego Fernández, Diego Prestes, Zelmar Borrás

BUSCAR BLOG
MARCAR BLOG
Siguiente blog»
Crear un blog | Acceder
A T O L O N D E M O R O R O A
ISLA GORRITI, MONTEVIDEO, UY
Ver todo mi perfil
Origen
Archivos
▼ 07 (18)
▼ May (3)
Dialogo con Farbo.
Todo valía mientras no se tornara enfermizo.
hermano pendejo
► April (4)
► March (5)
► February (4)
► January (2)
► 06 (46)
Categorias
Invitados (6)
motocicletas (1)
otoño (1)
sobre a t o l o n (9)
vacaciones (1)
La Isla
A T O L O N
molecular
tergopol
Blogger
30.11.06
Miren esto, que increible!
YouTube
share
a las 11:51 AM

BUSCAR BLOG
MARCAR BLOG
Siguiente blog»
Crear un blog | Acceder
A T O L O N D E M O R O R O A
ISLA GORRITI, MONTEVIDEO, UY
Ver todo mi perfil
Origen
Archivos
▼ 07 (18)
▼ May (3)
Dialogo con Farbo.
Todo valía mientras no se tornara enfermizo.
hermano pendejo
► April (4)
► March (5)
► February (4)
► January (2)
► 06 (46)
Categorias
Invitados (6)
motocicletas (1)
otoño (1)
sobre a t o l o n (9)
vacaciones (1)
La Isla
A T O L O N
molecular
tergopol
Blogger
30.11.06
Oniro°
ATOLON DE MORORO
a las 1:44 AM
2 comentarios:

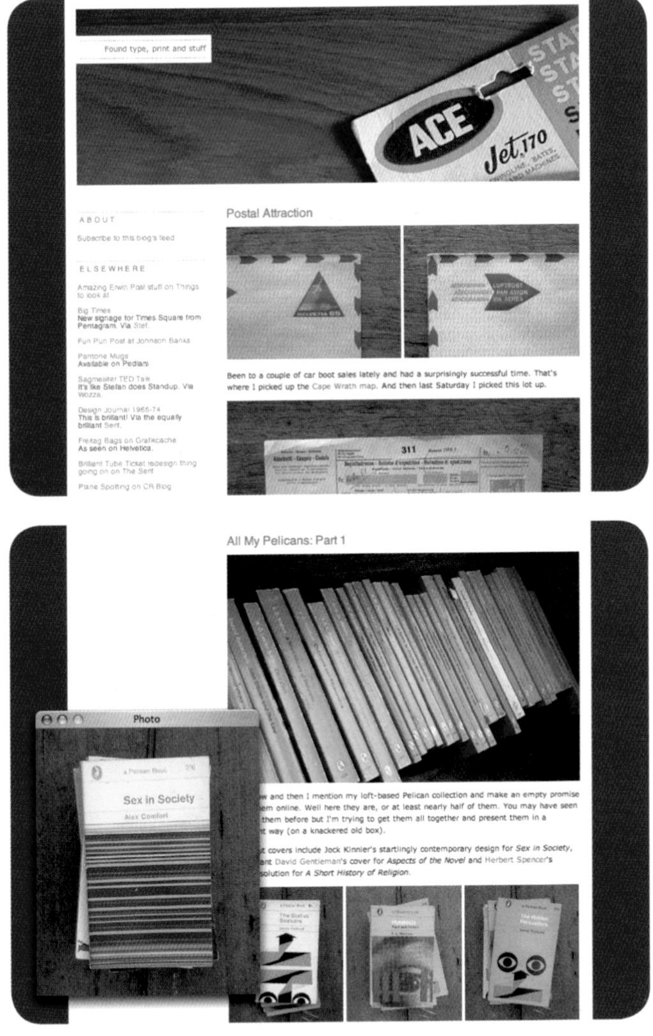

Richard Weston

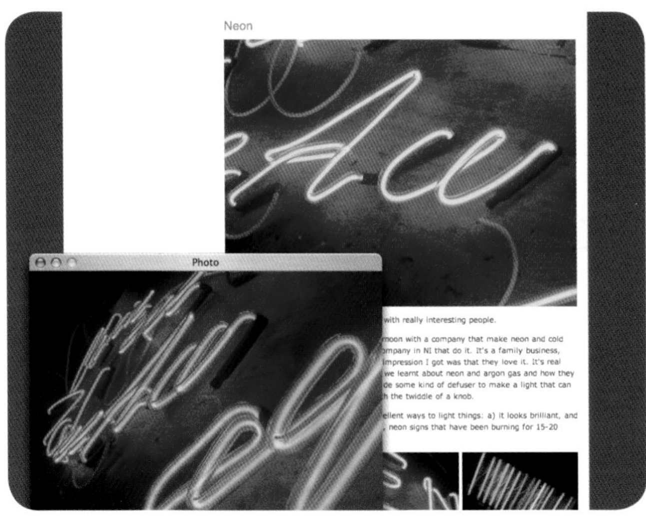
Neon
Photo
with really interesting people.
moon with a company that make neon and cold
ompany in NI that do it. It's a family business,
impression I got was that they love it. It's real
we learnt about neon and argon gas and how they
de some kind of defuser to make a light that can
h the twiddle of a knob.
ellent ways to light things: a) it looks brilliant, and
, neon signs that have been burning for 15-20

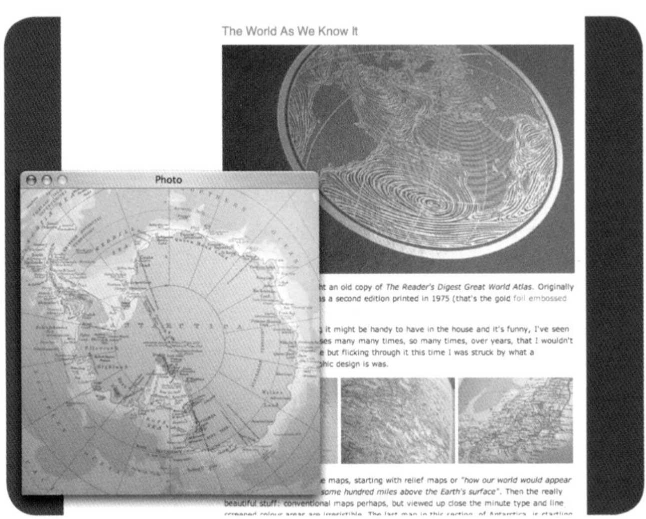
The World As We Know It
Photo
ht an old copy of The Reader's Digest Great World Atlas. Originally
s a second edition printed in 1975 (that's the gold foil embossed
it might be handy to have in the house and it's funny, I've seen
ses many many times, so many times, over years, that I wouldn't
e but flicking through it this time I was struck by what a
phic design is was.
e maps, starting with relief maps or "how our world would appear
some hundred miles above the Earth's surface". Then the really
beautiful stuff: conventional maps perhaps, but viewed up close the minute type and line

Akinori Oishi - blog

News of Graphic Artist, Akinori Oishi (大石暁規)

Contact : aki98@iamas.ac.jp

2007.03.17 Saturday

Baby Towel - 手拭い

Posted by Akinori Oishi

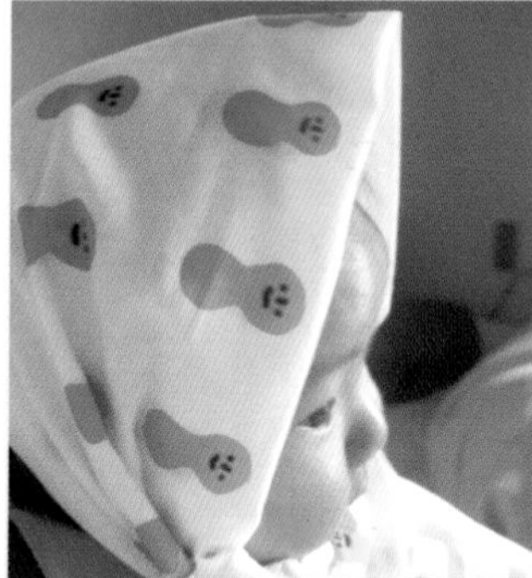

Calendar

PROFILE

Akinori Oishi

LINKS of ART WORKS

- AKI-AIR top page
- MICROFILMS
- OPNIYAMA game
- SHIFT cover

CATEGORIES

- Project - プロジェクト (27)
- Exhibition - 展覧会 (23)
- Book & Publishing - 出版 (13)
- Article - 記事 (10)
- Interview - インタヴュー (1)
- News - ニュース (6)
- Presentation - プレゼン (9)
- Baby - ベビースタイル (3)

SELECTED ENTRIES

ARCHIVES

- May 2007 (3)
- April 2007 (5)
- March 2007 (10)
- February 2007 (4)
- January 2007 (4)
- December 2006 (2)
- November 2006 (6)
- October 2006 (9)
- September 2006 (4)
- August 2006 (6)
- July 2006 (2)
- June 2006 (2)
- May 2006 (2)
- April 2006 (3)
- March 2006 (3)
- February 2006 (7)
- January 2006 (5)
- December 2005 (2)
- November 2005 (1)
- October 2005 (3)
- September 2005 (1)
- July 2005 (4)
- June 2005 (1)
- May 2005 (1)
- April 2005 (3)
- March 2005 (1)
- February 2005 (1)
- January 2005 (2)

OTHERS

- RSS1.0
- Atom0.3

Search this site.

| Baby - ベビースタイル | 18:49 |

Copyright (C) 2004-2007 lollipop Some Rights Reserved.

このページの先頭へ

Akinori Oishi

Akinori Oishi - blog

News of Graphic Artist, Akinori Oishi (大石暁規)

Contact : aki98@iamas.ac.jp

2006.12.14 Thursday

Slipmat - スリップマット

Posted by Akinori Oishi

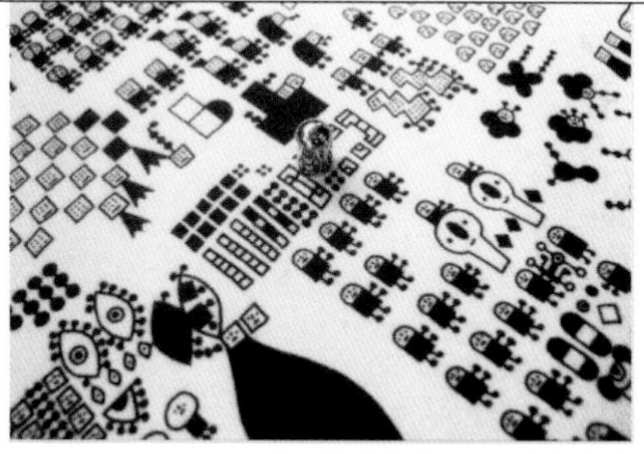

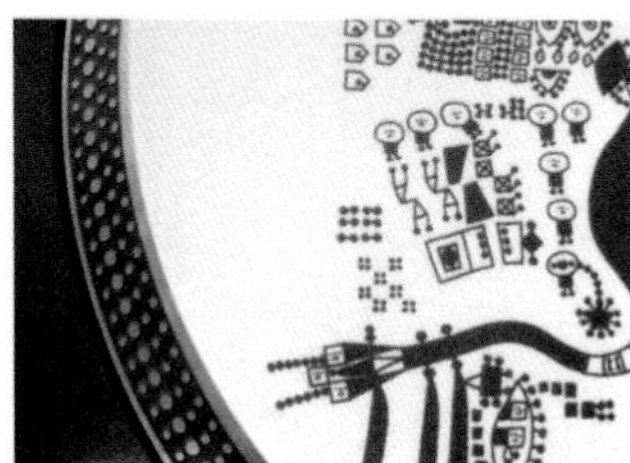

PROFILE

Akinori Oishi

AKI-AIR top page
MICROFILMS
OPNIYAMA game
SHIFT cover

CATEGORIES

Project - プロジェクト (27)
Exhibition - 展覧会 (23)
Book & Publishing - 出版 (13)
Article - 記事 (10)
Interview - インタヴュー (1)
News - ニュース (6)
Presentation - ぷれぜん (9)
Baby - ベビースタイル (3)

Slipmat - スリップマット (12/14)
Digital Art Festival TOKYO no.2 - デジタルアートフェスティバル東京に

May 2007 (3)
April 2007 (5)
March 2007 (10)
February 2007 (4)
January 2007 (4)
December 2006 (2)
November 2006 (6)
October 2006 (9)
September 2006 (4)
August 2006 (6)
July 2006 (2)
June 2006 (2)
May 2006 (2)
April 2006 (3)
March 2006 (3)
February 2006 (7)
January 2006 (5)
December 2005 (2)
November 2005 (1)
October 2005 (3)
September 2005 (1)
July 2005 (4)
June 2005 (1)
May 2005 (1)
April 2005 (3)
March 2005 (1)
February 2005 (1)
January 2005 (2)

OTHERS

RSS1.0
Atom0.3

Search this site.

Marcelo Alvarez Bravo

Miniaturas cada vez más complejas para el marketing.

Leer el resto del articulo

Guardado en Diseño e Innovación, Plástico | Deja un comentario »

Continúa la Avanzada del PET

Wednesday, August 2nd, 2006

Amcor PET Packaging

El PET continúa ganando espacio en el campo del envasado para bebidas. Incluso el vodka, una bebida que tradicionalmente usaba al

y Negocios

LINKS DISEÑO

- Adrián Pierini en La Universidad Argentina de la Empresa (UADE)
- Nada es lo que parece
- La Importancia del Packaging y la Gráfica de Conjunto
- Pierini Partners diseñó el nuevo Rexona Sportfan Limited Edition
- Y Water: Envase diseñado para que los niños tomen agua
- Pierini Partners diseñó la nueva etiqueta de la Cerveza Iguana
- Ganadores Premio UNILEVER Argentina 2007
- WORLDSTAR 2007
- Packaging Banana Juice

Categorías

- Branding (4)
- Concursos (1)
- Diseño e Innovación (17)
- marketing (4)
- Metal (1)
- mkt directo (2)
- Novedades en el Mundo (2)
- Opinión (1)
- Papel y Cartón (7)
- Plastico (4)
- seminarios (2)
- Vidrio (2)

Archivo

- April 2008
- March 2008
- February 2008
- January 2008
- December 2007
- November 2007
- September 2007
- August 2007
- July 2007
- June 2007
- May 2007
- April 2007
- March 2007
- February 2007
- January 2007
- December 2006
- November 2006
- October 2006
- September 2006
- August 2006
- July 2006

Leer el resto del articulo

Guardado en Diseño e Innovación, Branding | Deja un comentario »

Fotos Antiguas de Packaging y Advertising

Sunday, August 19th, 2007

A nuestros lectores, amantes del diseño de empaques les ofrecemos esta hermosa e inspiradora galeria de fotos de todas las épocas, para deleitarse mirando.

Link al flickr :
http://www.flickr.com/photos/54177448@N00/sets/939353/
Presentación Animada:
http://www.flickr.com/photos/54177448@N00/sets/939353/show/
Anepco Blog Pack

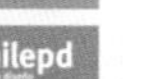

Esta obra está bajo una licencia de Creative Commons.

Archivo

- April 2008
- March 2008
- February 2008
- January 2008
- December 2007
- November 2007
- September 2007
- August 2007
- July 2007
- June 2007
- May 2007
- April 2007
- March 2007
- February 2007
- January 2007
- December 2006
- November 2006
- October 2006
- September 2006
- August 2006
- July 2006
- June 2006

Blogs

- Alvarez&Castells
- Articula Diseño
- Chile País de Diseño
- Debas (Blog+Diseño)
- The die line

Diseño

- Anepco
- Cenem
- IAE
- Logoteca
- Package Museum

Editorial

- Emba News
- End
- Enfasis
- Marketing News
- Pack News Latina
- Pack World
- Redargenta
- Shelf Impact

Empresas de Diseño

- Proyectos Corporativos
- Art Contrast
- Rexam
- UvaDesign S.A.
- Dilbrands
- Walker Diseño
- Ideazzione
- Lander

AS-FOUND

Introduction
Exhibitions
Archive
Contributors
Contact

BY MARC KREMERS

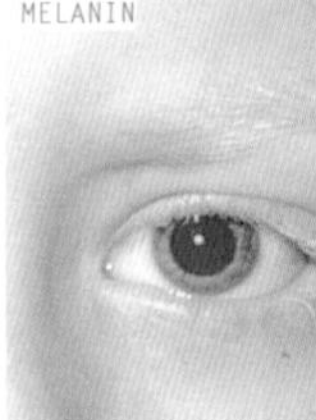

BY MARC KREMERS

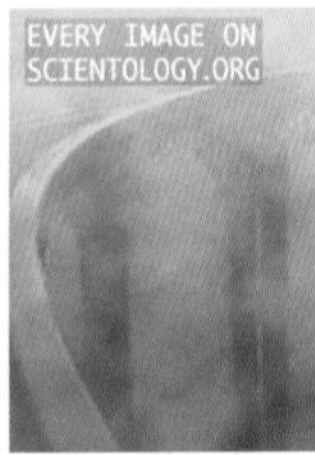

BY OLIVER LARIC

BY MARC KREMERS

AS-FOUND

Introduction
Exhibitions
Archive
Contributors
Contact

GRETAGMACBETH

As found by Marc Kremers

Marc Kremers, Thomas Eberwein

AS-FOUND

Introduction
Exhibitions
Archive
Contributors
Contact

Most frequent tags:
Studio, group, Male, Portrait, Female, Military, Sport, Pose, 3D, Space, Group

View all tags

Sort by Contributers:
A User, Carl Burgess, David Barbarino, Emy Amstein, Jonathan Maghen, Marc Kremers, Thomas Eberwein

Sort by Rating:
Top 100, Date

01/08/07

23/07/07

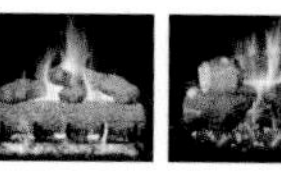
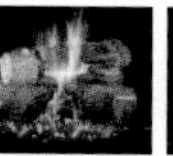

17/07/07

16/07/07

11/07/07

10/07/07

09/07/07

07/07/07

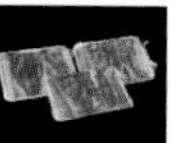

September 27th, 2007 // Found by Marc Kremers // 4 votes * * * * ·

96-0720-07.hr.jpg

svmStmLSS20.jpg

plmTBTV_EADSteam.jpg

September 27th, 2007 // Found by Marc Kremers // 5 votes * * * · ·

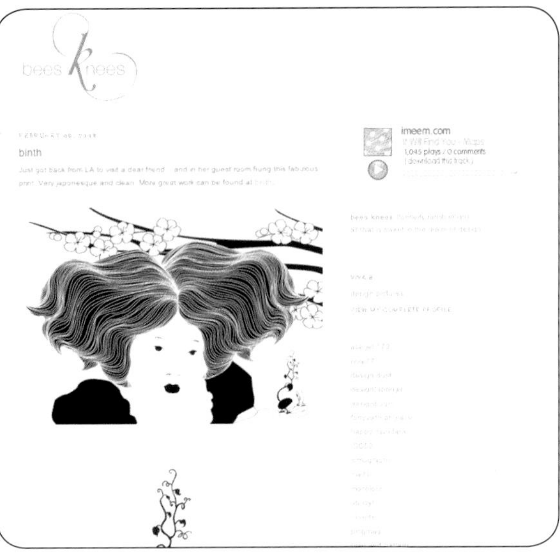

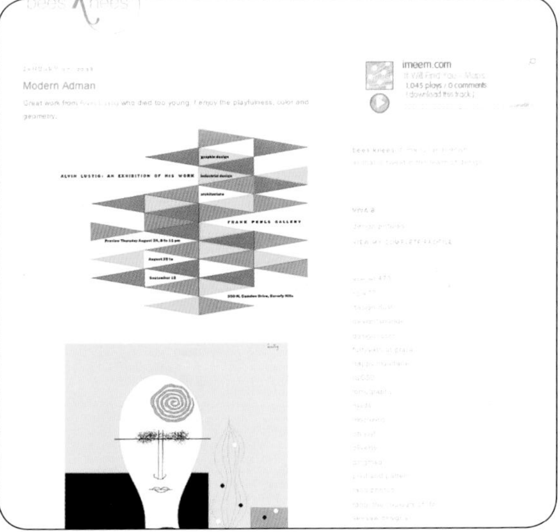

Viva Bailey

bees knees
Friday Lights : Slide Light
Unique horizontal or vertical light composed of personal photo slides.
imeem.com
It Will Find You - Maps
1,045 plays / 0 comments
[download this track]

bees knees
Accident at the Prepress
Funny faux movie poster for Lessebo.
imeem.com
It Will Find You - Maps
1,045 plays / 0 comments
[download this track]
AS SOON AS POSSIBLE THEY SAID...
QUINTS
SANTANA
HOLLENBYC
ACCIDENT AT THE PREPRESS
MARC BENY
0 COMMENTS

BEING a STARVING GRAPHIC ARTIST SUCKS

Easy-to-apply strategies for freelance graphic designers tired of starving and ready to become successful

Pricing • Negotiating
Finding Business • Customer Service

March 04, 2008

The Truth About People Criticizing Your Freelance Design Projects

A while back I had someone take a swipe at me on a message board. Within the context of a completely different subject this person wrote, *"I don't like your book title, I find it offensive and I would guess I am not the only one that feels this way..."* - more on this comment at the end (see note at end).

Initially this bothered me...I think it would bother just about anyone. This was an unprovoked and unsolicited attempt to take a shot at me in front of an audience. In fact, this person had previously sent me a number of emails thanking me for providing them with some valuable advice.

The more I thought about it though I realized that whether you've written a book, designed a logo or created a web site, if you show it to enough people; someone's not going to like it. That's the bad news...the good news is that not everyone has to like your work. If you're in the creative field you're going to need to come to grips with the concept that not everyone is going to like your work - opinion's are like...well you know the rest of the phrase (if you don't, punch this into Google and see what comes up). In fact, Keith Bennett, the Academic Director for Graphic Design at the Art Institute of Phoenix told me that this is what he imparts to his students, *"...not everyone is going to like your work, they aren't supposed to...and if you've created something that causes no reaction, have you really created something worthwhile?"*

HOW YOU CAN STOP STARVING

View the ENTIRE Table of Contents

View all of the Products

Purchase the Work Smarter NOT Harder Complete Contract Package

Purchase the BASAS 500 page Printed Book

Purchase the BASAS 500 page eBook

Make up to 25% Commissions as a BASAS Affiliate

ABOUT

they aren't advertising when they really are.

Unfortunately, these types of questionable marketing and advertising techniques aren't all that uncommon. It begs the question, *"Just because you can do something, does that mean you should?"*

For example: pretending to be gathering information on the phone when in fact you're trying to sell something, telling people they've won something when they really haven't, and yes, adding comments to a blog that are really advertisements, are all ways you can add to your bottom line (in the short run).

Should you resort to these types of tactics to build your sales?

Well, that's a personal call every company (and creative freelancer) has to make on her/his own. For me, I think people are generally pretty smart, and they can see a scam coming a mile away. When people see unscrupulous, dishonest marketing & advertising they typically ignore it, complain about it or tell as many as their friends to avoid it. Imagine that - people don't like to feel like they've been taken advantage of, or tricked!

Hey, as freelance professionals we're all aware of different ways to manipulate people into visiting our web site or calling us on the phone, but these approaches are more likely to build *"bad will"* rather than building our businesses. You're going to find other companies and freelance designers out there that will do just about anything to get people in their door - don't buy into this garbage, in the long run it doesn't work.

If you really want to make a success out of yourself, treat people the way you'd like to be treated, be honest and be fair - you'll sleep better at night and you'll probably end up making more money anyway.

In wrapping this post up, I wanted to share a nice success story I received on Thursday from a freelancer who purchased the BASAS printed book, *"I think your book so far is great. It addresses all the issues that we graphic designers face. I'm looking forward to reading about how to incorporate marketing know-how/strategy into my work. thanks, you did us all a great service!"*

View all of the Products

Purchase the Work Smarter NOT Harder Complete Contract Package

Purchase the BASAS 500 page Printed Book

Purchase the BASAS 500 page eBook

Make up to 25% Commissions as a BASAS Affiliate

ABOUT

CATEGORIES

Beginner's Freelance Graphic Designer Section

Marketing and Promoting Your Freelancing Business

Mastering Client Interactions

Pricing, Negotiating and Protecting Your Work

Subscribe to this blog's feed

Add me to your TypePad People list

AUDIO & WIDGETS

AUDIO: Is the BASAS book worth it?

Jeremy Tuber

BEING a STARVING GRAPHIC ARTIST SUCKS

Easy-to-apply strategies for freelance graphic designers tired of starving and ready to become successful

Pricing • Negotiating
Finding Business • Customer Service

November 28, 2007

How Freelance Designers Can Compete with the Online Bland Brand Crap Factories

In his blog, Seth Godin talks about making a caricature of your brand, "*...Worse than avoiding the negative, though, is the tendency for most organizations to resist creating a brand that can be caricatured. It doesn't feel safe or responsible or prudent. Coloring inside the lines and pleasing most of your customers most of the time almost guarantees you'll be bland.*"

I started thinking about this and Seth's post begs an interesting question that designers need to answer for themselves when creating a business identity for themselves or their clients: is it more risky to play it safe than to be different?

Yes, it is.
Bland and safe brands = not standing out from the crowd and being invisible to customers, which leads to starving.

There are two types of businesses out there: remarkable and invisible (that's Seth's not mine), hopefully the brands you're creating are helping to make companies remarkable. Creating bland, safe brands is a quick way to ensure you don't make a lot of money and don't bring in a lot of business.

Competing with the Brand Factories
There are thousands of design firms out there, pumping out even more logos and brands. Most of them have the same boring, "*color within the lines*" look and feel. You've seen it before, brands with: the obligatory swoosh, the abstract icon that no one really knows what

AUDIO: Is the BASAS book worth it?
AUDIO: What's your book's guarantee?
AUDIO: Top 10 "must have" skills for successful freelance designers
AUDIO: Why did I write this book?
Blog flux
Digg
submit
Blog Catalog
Subscribe in a reader

It's so tempting to want to please the client and help out in any way that you can, but you have to stand your ground when it comes to ensuring you have a solid, signed agreement before starting work for a client. Clients will inadvertently put pressure on you to bypass your own process in getting a signed proposal before starting - avoid this at all costs because it will bite you in the butt later. I do believe there are times clients will intentionally try to avoid having to sign a contract so they try to convince the designer that there's no time for it and that they'll take care of everything after "*things settle down*".

The bottom line is this - if your client isn't going to invest the time to wait for you to do things the right way by agreeing to a proposal that will eliminate confusion and misconceptions down the line, they aren't worth working with. Run like heck.

It's your responsibility at the professional to kindly but convincingly let the client know that you have a process and you intend on following it. Below I've included an example I had with a client who I did one quick pro-bono project for him to show what I could do; afterwards he kept sending me work without have a signed proposal. This is a terrific example of what you'll find in the Verbal Judo for Designers book, click here to download a couple of sample chapters.

VERBAL JUDO For Graphic Designers

Good to hear from you, [CLIENT NAME], I know you've got a lot on your plate right now.

Sure, I can send over a quick proposal to you this week. I can email the proposal over and we can discuss it on the telephone if you'd like; however, I think it's better to go over in person, which option is best for you?

Why don't we hold off on moving forward with anything else right now so you can concentrate on what you're working on and I can prepare this initial proposal for you? If you like what I have in the proposal and you feel it's a good fit; we'll get the proposal signed and we'll get things started up for you.

What day would be the best day to get you the quick proposal: Wed, Thurs or Friday?
With the schedule you have, when should I expect to hear back from you?

Posted at 08:24 AM in Mastering Client Interactions | Permalink | Comments (1) | TrackBack (1)

View all of the Products
Purchase the Work Smarter NOT Harder Complete Contract Package
Purchase the BASAS 500 page Printed Book
Purchase the BASAS 500 page eBook
Make up to 25% Commissions as a BASAS Affiliate

ABOUT

CATEGORIES
Beginner's Freelance Graphic Designer Section
Marketing and Promoting Your Freelancing Business
Mastering Client Interactions
Pricing, Negotiating and Protecting Your Work

Subscribe to this blog's feed
Add me to your TypePad People list

AUDIO & WIDGETS
AUDIO: Is the BASAS book worth it?

woumpah
LE BLOG
jeudi 3 mai 2007
Affiches Tetsouille feat. Elroy
(Cliquez pour agrandir)
Elle sont chouettes les affiches Tetsouille feat. Elr°y =).
Format 47 x 70 cm et papier satiné (hmmmm) pour un prix approximatif de 19 € (frais de port + emballage).
Si vous êtes intéréssé(e)s, contactez Tetsouille par mail pour qu'il puisse s'organiser au niveau du nombre d'exemplaires à imprimer.
4 commentaires :: aucun trackback
Calendrier
« mai 2007
Rechercher
ok
Catégories
General
Graphisme
Exposition
Illustration
Musique
Internet
Food
Gobelins
Street
Custom
Archives
mai 2007
avril 2007
mars 2007

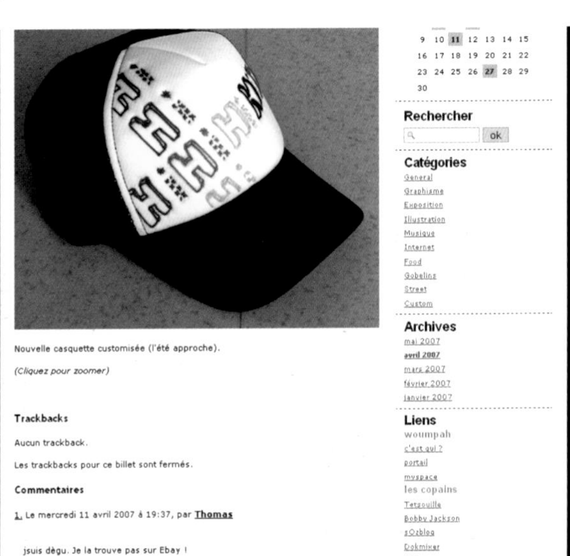
Nouvelle casquette customisée (l'été approche).
(Cliquez pour zoomer)
Trackbacks
Aucun trackback.
Les trackbacks pour ce billet sont fermés.
Commentaires
1. Le mercredi 11 avril 2007 à 19:37, par Thomas
jsuis dègu. Je la trouve pas sur Ebay !
Rechercher
ok
Catégories
General
Graphisme
Exposition
Illustration
Musique
Internet
Food
Gobelins
Street
Custom
Archives
mai 2007
avril 2007
mars 2007
février 2007
janvier 2007
Liens
woumpah
c'est qui ?
portail
myspace
les copains
Tetsouille
Bobby Jackson
sOzblog
Dokmixer

Gautier Gevrey (woumpah)

woumpah

LE BLOG

vendredi 16 mars 2007

Trendsnow - Header Contest

Par woumpah, vendredi 16 mars 2007 à 17:45 :: Graphisme

tdw

Ma proposition pour le Header Contest du blog Trendsnow est en ligne.

(Très brièvement) je suis parti des 5 mots-clés représentatifs de Trendsnow (tendance, design, graphisme, fashion, hightech) que j'ai essayé d'illustrer avec de la

Calendrier

« mai 2007

lun	mar	mer	jeu	ven	sam	dim
	1	2	3	4	5	6
7	8	9	10	11	12	13
14	15	16	17	18	19	20
21	22	23	24	25	26	27
28	29	30	31			

Rechercher

ok

Catégories

General
Graphisme
Exposition
Illustration
Musique
Internet
Food
Gobelins
Street
Custom

Archives

mai 2007
avril 2007
mars 2007

by woumpah

CLOSE ✕

janvier 2007

Liens

Alejandro Bernales M.

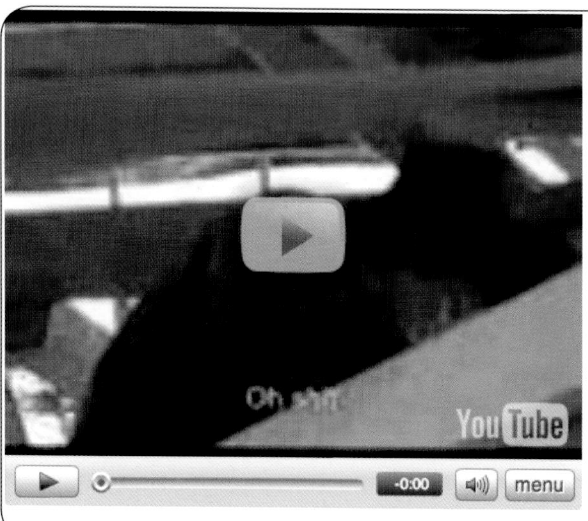

Bold Mag

Mira el último número de nuestra revista multimedia OjO que esta abierta a recibir tu colaboración.

ace bastante rato que no me sorprendía un comercial. Jamás pensé lo que ucedería, realmente excelente en términos de creatividad y producción.

4 Comentarios | 18 Octubre, 2007

El iPhone no es tan Verde para Greenpeace

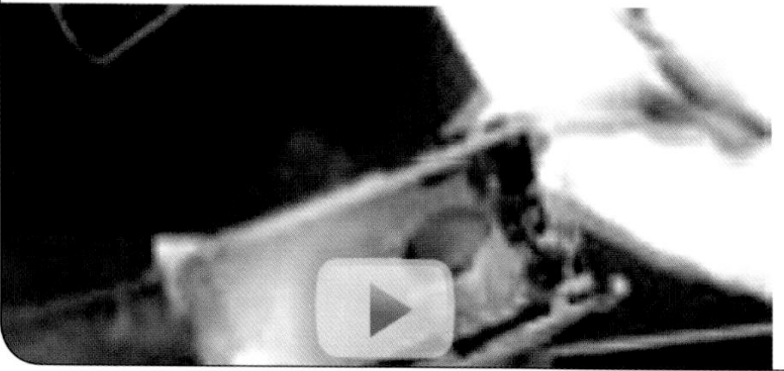

Categorias

- 3D
- Afiche para Película
- Animación
- Arquitectura
- Arte
- Artista Cool
- Blogroll
- Bold Light
- Bold News
- Concursos
- Diseñador Cool
- Diseño de Vestuario
- Diseño Gráfico

Book By Its Cover // www.book-by-its-cover.com

Book By Its Cover

CHILDREN'S
COMICS
DESIGN
FINE ART
HANDMADE
OTHER
about
contact
links
where to buy

5.7.07
MOSQUITO
Dan James

COMICS

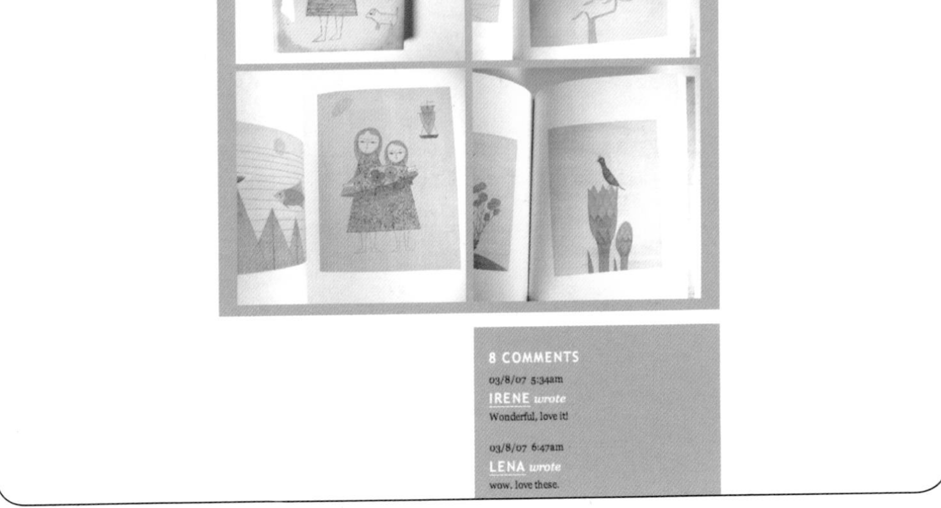

8 COMMENTS
03/8/07 5:34am
IRENE wrote
Wonderful, love it!
03/8/07 6:47am
LENA wrote
wow, love these.

Julia Rothman

- CHILDREN'S
- COMICS
- DESIGN
- FINE ART
- HANDMADE
- OTHER
- about
- contact
- links
- where to buy

3.3.07

S IS FOR SALVATION

Jess Rosenkranz

I officially met Jess(even though we spend 4 years in college together with all of the same friends) when she hired me to make some patterns for My Little Pony. She is the brains and creative touch behind much of Hasbro's little girl toys. She helps decide what goes on the ponies' rumps. What could be better than that? But somehow between all that sparkle and rainbows, she finds time to make her own little books which she sells in various little shops and fairs. They are all so perfectly made and most of them have some sort of hand-painted element aside from their silkscreened end pages and cover. My favorite is a book called S is for Salvation. It's an alphabet book of clothes rescued from the Salvation Army to save people from ever having to wear them. The book is actually like a deck of cards and comes in a neat fitted box with a beautiful patterned interior. Each card has a swatch of fabric for each letter of the alphabet. On the card is also a drawing of the garment it came from. You can see why these clothes were rescued. I love the M is for monkeys sweatpants or the S is for snakeskin button down. Jess has some other quirky fun books too like

4.10.07

ISAAC TOBIN'S SKETCHBOOKS

Isaac Tobin

Sketchbook Week

Designer Isaac Tobin keeps such beautiful sketchbooks. I asked him if I could borrow some of them to photograph for the blog as inspiration. The books are filled with so much texture and dimension. Paper and found scraps are collaged and sewn creating layers upon layers. He sometimes draws or paints on top or under these layers. Other times he makes folded paper sculptures held together by string that change as you turn the page, like a pop-up book. I want to frame each spread and hang them on my wall. Isaac currently works as a book designer at University of Chicago Press. This past year one of his book covers was picked for AIGAs 50 Books/50 Covers. Not only does he design books, he also has designed a few good-looking typefaces which he sells from his site. I have posted a bunch of his sketchbook pages below(it was so hard to choose) but he has some other pages featured on his site too if you haven't seen enough. I know I haven't. Everytime I look, I notice something I missed.

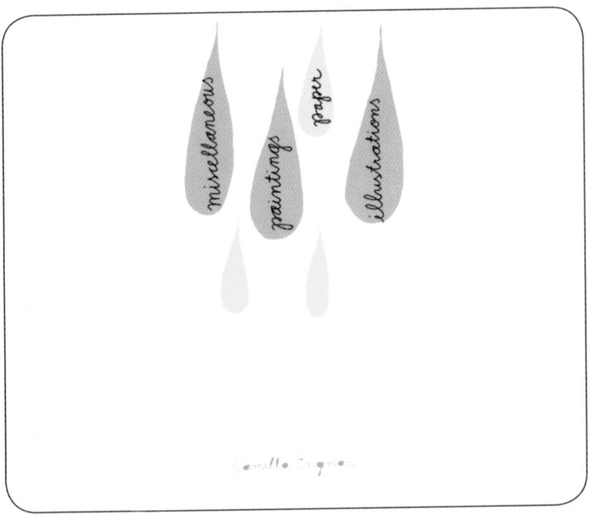

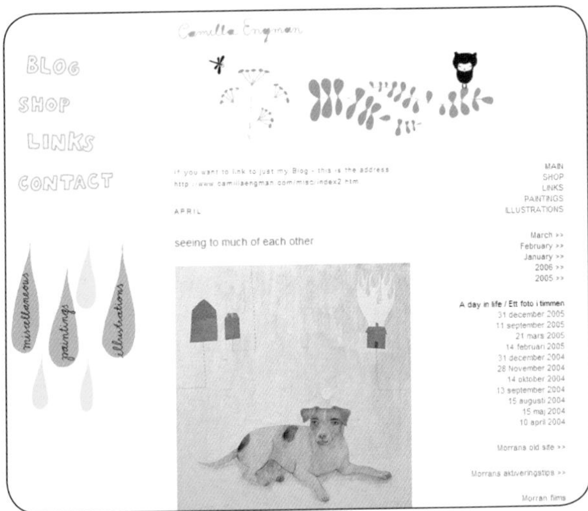

Camilla Engman

SHOP
BLOG
SHOP
LINKS
CONTACT
"Newsletter"
If you want to get a "newsletter" when there is new stuff in the shop - e-mail me
(you don't have to write anything - if you don't want to of course) and let the subject be shop
Are you interested in selling my work - e-mail me
CALENDAR 2007
>> Click at the pictures to get more information
LIMITED EDITION PRINTS
>> Click at the pictures to get more information
SILK SCREENED PRINTS
>> Click at the pictures to see all of it and to get more information
SOLD OUT!
miscellaneous
paintings
illustrations

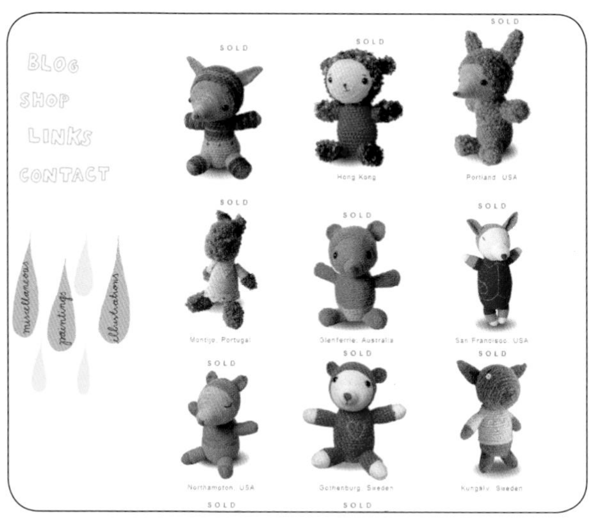
BLOG
SHOP
LINKS
CONTACT
miscellaneous
paintings
illustrations
SOLD
SOLD
SOLD
Hong Kong
Portland, USA
SOLD
SOLD
SOLD
Montijo, Portugal
Glenferrie, Australia
San Francisco, USA
SOLD
SOLD
SOLD
Northampton, USA
Gothenburg, Sweden
Kungälv, Sweden
SOLD
SOLD

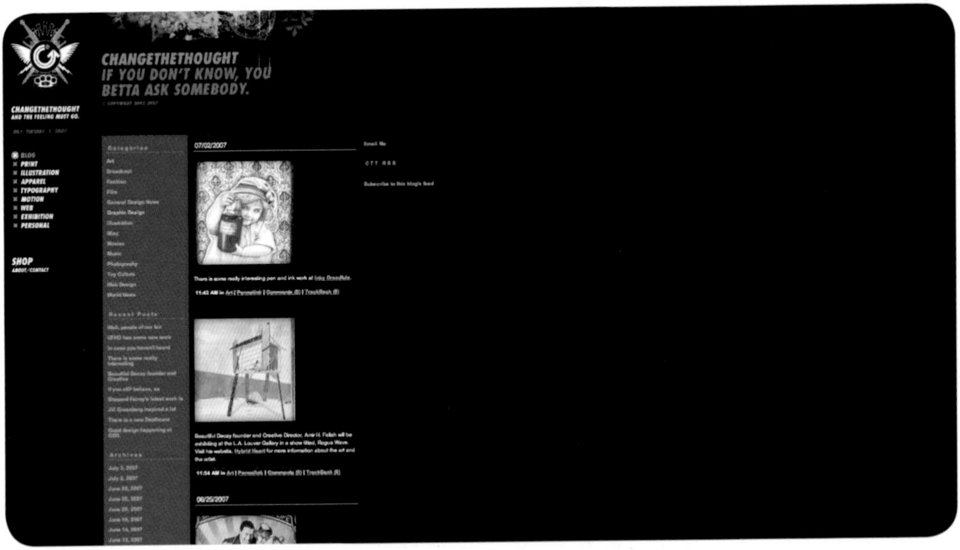

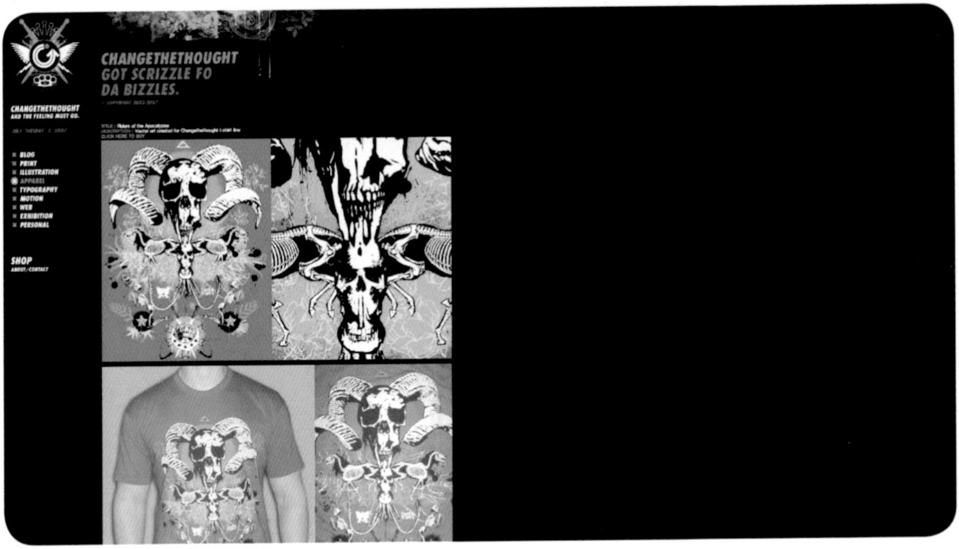

Christopher Cox

CHANGETHETHOUGHT SAYS SUPPORT YOUR LOCAL ART SCENE.

CHANGETHETHOUGHT
AND THE FEELING MUST GO.

- BLOG
- PRINT
- ILLUSTRATION
- APPAREL
- TYPOGRAPHY
- MOTION
- WEB
- EXHIBITION
- PERSONAL

SHOP
ABOUT/CONTACT

CLIENT | Cactus/Self
DESCRIPTION | Conceptualization and Art Direction provided by myself, development by Agency Net.
LAUNCH WEBSITE

cactus

04.06.07

CHANGETHETHOUGHT IS BRINGIN' DA BUMRUSH.

CHANGETHETHOUGHT
AND THE FEELING MUST GO.

- BLOG
- PRINT
- ILLUSTRATION
- APPAREL
- TYPOGRAPHY
- MOTION
- WEB
- EXHIBITION
- PERSONAL

SHOP
ABOUT/CONTACT

TITLE | War is Our God
DESCRIPTION | Artwork created for solo exhibition at The 400
LAUNCH DETAIL VIEW

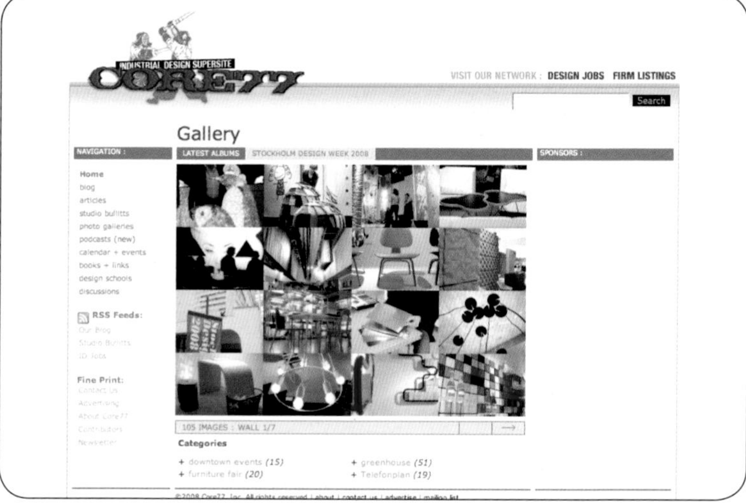

Eric Ludlum, Stuart Constantine, Allan Chochinov

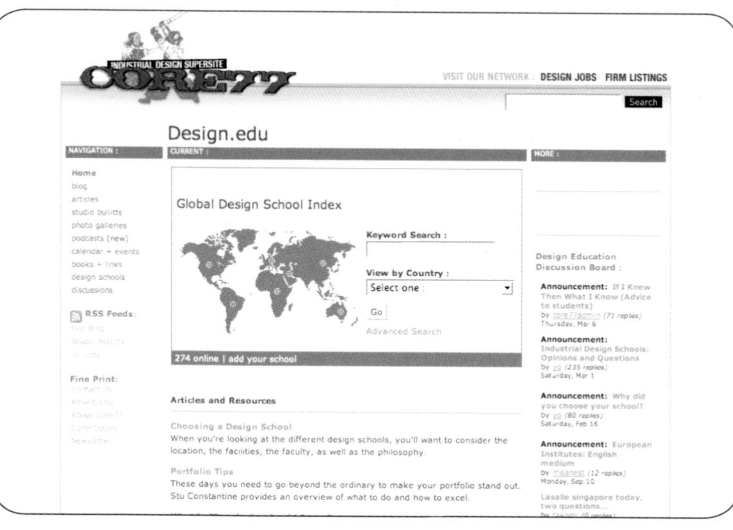
INDUSTRIAL DESIGN SUPERSITE
CORE77
VISIT OUR NETWORK : DESIGN JOBS FIRM LISTINGS
Search
Design.edu
NAVIGATION :
CURRENT :
MORE :
Home
blog
articles
studio bullitts
photo galleries
podcasts (new)
calendar + events
books + links
design schools
discussions
RSS Feeds:
Fine Print:
Global Design School Index
Keyword Search :
View by Country :
Select one
Go
Advanced Search
274 online | add your school
Articles and Resources
Choosing a Design School
When you're looking at the different design schools, you'll want to consider the location, the facilities, the faculty, as well as the philosophy.
Portfolio Tips
These days you need to go beyond the ordinary to make your portfolio stand out. Stu Constantine provides an overview of what to do and how to excel.
Design Education Discussion Board :
Announcement: If I Knew Then What I Know (Advice to students)
Thursday, Mar 6
Announcement: Industrial Design Schools: Opinions and Questions
Saturday, Mar 1
Announcement: Why did you choose your school?
Saturday, Feb 16
Announcement: European Institutes: English medium
Monday, Sep 10
Lasalle singapore today, two questions...

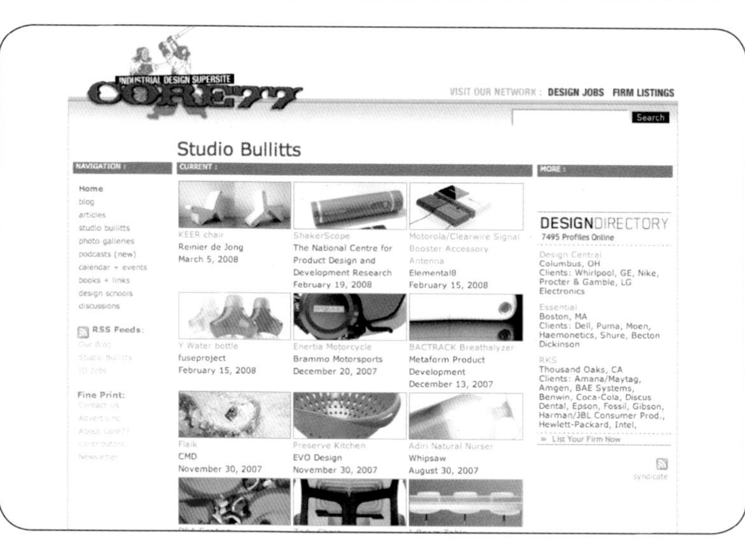
INDUSTRIAL DESIGN SUPERSITE
CORE77
VISIT OUR NETWORK : DESIGN JOBS FIRM LISTINGS
Search
Studio Bullitts
NAVIGATION :
CURRENT :
MORE :
Home
blog
articles
studio bullitts
photo galleries
podcasts (new)
calendar + events
books + links
design schools
discussions
RSS Feeds:
Fine Print:
KEER chair
Reinier de Jong
March 5, 2008
ShakerScope
The National Centre for Product Design and Development Research
February 19, 2008
Motorola/Clearwire Signal Booster Accessory Antenna
Elemental8
February 15, 2008
Y Water bottle
fuseproject
February 15, 2008
Enertia Motorcycle
Brammo Motorsports
December 20, 2007
BACTRACK Breathalyzer
Metaform Product Development
December 13, 2007
Flaik
CMD
November 30, 2007
Preserve Kitchen
EVO Design
November 30, 2007
Adiri Natural Nurser
Whipsaw
August 30, 2007
DESIGNDIRECTORY
7495 Profiles Online
Design Central
Columbus, OH
Clients: Whirlpool, GE, Nike, Procter & Gamble, LG Electronics
Essential
Boston, MA
Clients: Dell, Puma, Moen, Haemonetics, Shure, Becton Dickinson
RKS
Thousand Oaks, CA
Clients: Amana/Maytag, Amgen, BAE Systems, Benwin, Coca-Cola, Discus Dental, Epson, Fossil, Gibson, Harman/JBL Consumer Prod., Hewlett-Packard, Intel,
» List Your Firm Now
syndicate

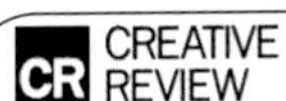

► SEARCH

CRBlog Homepage / Subscribe to CR / E-CR

FIND YOUR INSPIRATION

CR Blog

CR Blog RSS

News and views on visual communications from the writers of Creative Review

Previous Entries

Next Entries

Things I Have Learned In My Life So Far

Eliza 05/02/08, 17:00

Permalink   Comments (56)   Trackbacks (0)

Categories

Advertising (133)
Books (44)
Coversourcing (2)
Graphic Design (217)
Magazines/Papers (54)
Photography (66)
TV (24)
Uncategorized (9)
Art (132)
Commercials (53)
Film (64)
Illustration (139)
Music Videos (43)
Technology (31)
Type (57)
Websites (38)

or 10 runner up prizes

£25 iTunes

Massimo Falsaci's wall piece, Tramonto (sunset), on display in Milan. Falsaci was one of last year's Diesel Wall winners

If you've ever dreamt of seeing your artwork displayed in the street on a giant-sized canvas, then Diesel's Wall project could be the answer to your lofty ambitions. The project, now in it's fifth year, aims to offer up some seriously huge display spaces in Manchester (Urbis Centre, shown below), New York, Barcelona and Zurich, in an international art contest.

► READ MORE

Mind The Graphics

Patrick 11/02/08, 15:49

Permalink   Comments (21)   Trackbacks (0)

Hilary is a PC, Obama is a Mac (if you go by their websites, at least)

Improvised bookmarks from secondhand books (likn: DO)

Another design competition from Don't Panic - this time to create a design for a Momiji doll (and the tin it comes in) along the theme 'indulge'

Michel Gondry "swedes" his own movie trailer for Be Kind Rewind, and takes on every role himself

This Is Real Art's Paul Belford gives a Typographic Circle talk about Art Direction on 21 Feb. Should be good

Whoa! Look at the little skier go! Fun digital ad from Goss in Sweden

Wow - how nice are these? Wooden toys from Japanese toymaker Takeji Nakagawa, aka Take-G

Creative Review

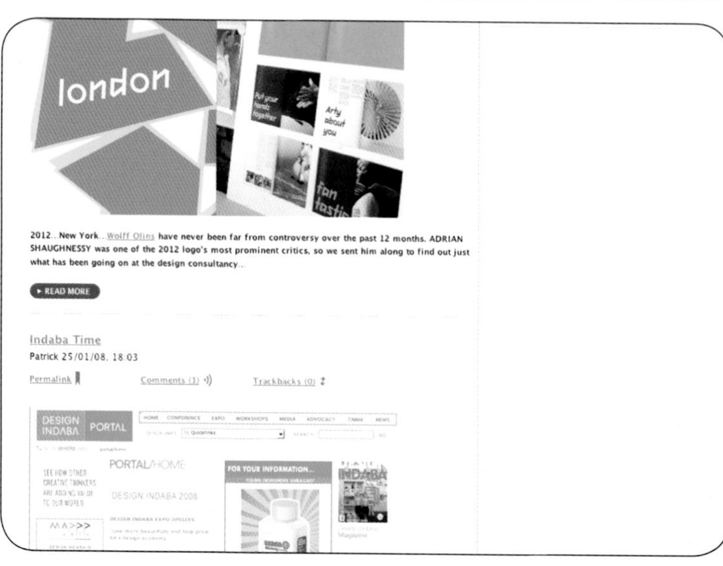
london
2012...New York...Wolff Olins have never been far from controversy over the past 12 months. ADRIAN SHAUGHNESSY was one of the 2012 logo's most prominent critics, so we sent him along to find out just what has been going on at the design consultancy...
READ MORE
Indaba Time
Patrick 25/01/08, 18:03
Permalink
Comments (1)
Trackbacks (0)
DESIGN INDABA
PORTAL
PORTAL/HOME
DESIGN INDABA 2008
FOR YOUR INFORMATION...

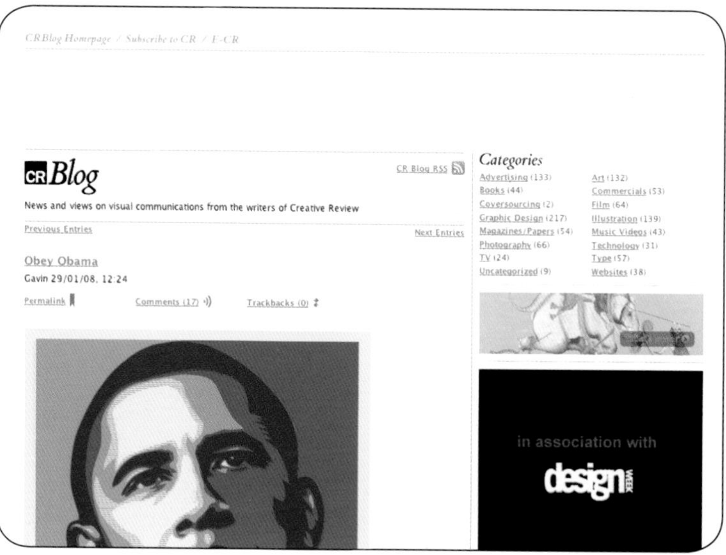
CRBlog Homepage / Subscribe to CR / E-CR
CR Blog
CR Blog RSS
News and views on visual communications from the writers of Creative Review
Previous Entries
Next Entries
Obey Obama
Gavin 29/01/08, 12:24
Permalink
Comments (17)
Trackbacks (0)
Categories
Advertising (133)
Art (132)
Books (44)
Commercials (53)
Coversourcing (2)
Film (64)
Graphic Design (217)
Illustration (139)
Magazines/Papers (54)
Music Videos (43)
Photography (66)
Technology (31)
TV (24)
Type (57)
Uncategorized (9)
Websites (38)
in association with
design week

CREATIVE LIFE !

ACCUEIL A PROPOS S'ABONNER CONTACT

Studio Poana

Posté par Octave Z | 17 avril 2007

Portfolio de Nicolas Dhennin et Thibault Choquel, Lille, France.

CREATIVE LIFE !

ACCUEIL A PROPOS S'ABONNER CONTACT

Artiste Profil

Will Staehle, graphiste designer. Voir l'article

The Creative Life Mix

Juju Orchestra, faites ce que vos voulez, mais bougez! Ecouter le podcast

The Creative Life Mix #3

Poste par Freddy | 15 avril 2007

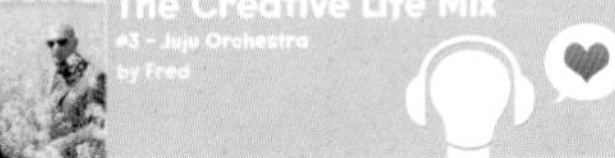

Remuez votre fessier, tapez du pied, claquez des doigts... Faites ce que vos voulez, mais bougez ! C'est l'invitation que vous fait la formation allemande The Juju Orchestra, funk, soul, bossa, latino, jazz... Les influences sont nombreuses pour emmener nos oreilles dans un univers très épicé, varié et parfois même endiablé.

Playlist (22'39):

- The Juju Orchestra - Take Four - 5"21
- The Juju Orchestra - Kind Of Latin Rythm - 7"21
- The Juju Orchestra - Não Posso Demorar (feat Katia) - 6"28
- The Juju Orchestra - The Hip Shake - 5"40

Télécharger le podcast: The Creative Life Mix #3 - .mp3, 31Mo

Abonnez-vous au podcast: The Creative Life Mix Rss

Ou directement via iTunes: The Creative Life Mix Rss

Articles

- ERCO
- Dan Tobin Smith
- Gulf News
- Concours Little Fashion Gallery et TrendsNow
- Jan von Holleben

Rechercher... GO

Categories

- Architecture (1)
- Createur portfolio (31)
- Creative Life (3)
- Danse (1)
- Design (38)
- Divers (7)
- Evenements (11)
- Expos (12)
- Magazine (5)
- Mode (10)
- Music (6)
- Photo (10)
- Podcast (3)
- Print (19)

Octave Z

CREATIVE LIFE

ACCUEIL A PROPOS S'ABONNER CONTACT

Artiste Profil

Will Staehle, graphiste designer. Voir l'article

The Creative Life Mix

Juju Orchestra, faites ce que vos voulez, mais bougez! Ecouter le podcast

A PROPOS

Creative Life est un blog qui met en avant les expressions artistiques les plus diverses. L'équipe se compose à la fois de professionnels et de passionnés qui désirent faire connaître un artiste, un concept, un lieu qui présente un aspect créatif. Design, graphisme, musique, pub, photo, danse, mode et autres sensibilités artistiques forment notre base de travail.

Membres

Octave Z
Fondateur

Emma
Auteur

Nat
Auteur

Freddy
Auteur

NB Studio

Posté par **Octave Z** | 30 mars 2007

Portfolio de David Smith, London.

Articles

- ERCO
- Dan Tobin Smith
- Gulf News
- Concours Little Fashion Gallery et TrendsNow
- Jan von Holleben

Rechercher... GO

Categories

- Architecture (1)
- Createur portfolio (31)
- Creative Life (3)
- Danse (1)
- Design (38)
- Divers (7)
- Evenements (11)
- Expos (12)
- Magazine (5)
- Mode (10)
- Music (6)
- Photo (10)
- Podcast (3)
- Print (19)
- Publicite (10)
- Shop (6)
- Sorties (3)
- Street Art (7)
- Studio (9)

[Letterheads] - [Badges]

Daily Type is a creative project run by several russian type designers.
Day by day, they create original typefaces and post their results along with routine.

17 | 5 | 2007

contributors: Yury Ostromentsky, Dasha Yarzhambek, Dmitry Jakovlev, Ilya Ruderman
participants: Yury Gordon, Illarion Gordon, Alexander Tarbeev, Vera Evstafieva, Jean Francois Porchez, Cateliine van Middelkoop, Ryan Pescatore Frisk, Massimo Nardini, Kasya Denisevich

monthly type:
2007 >> january / february / march / april / may / june / july / august / september / november / october / december
2006 >> january / february / march / april / may / june / july / august / september / october / november / december
2005 >> january / february / march / april / may / june / july / august / september / october / november / december
2004 >> january / february / march / april / may / june / july / august / september / october / november / december

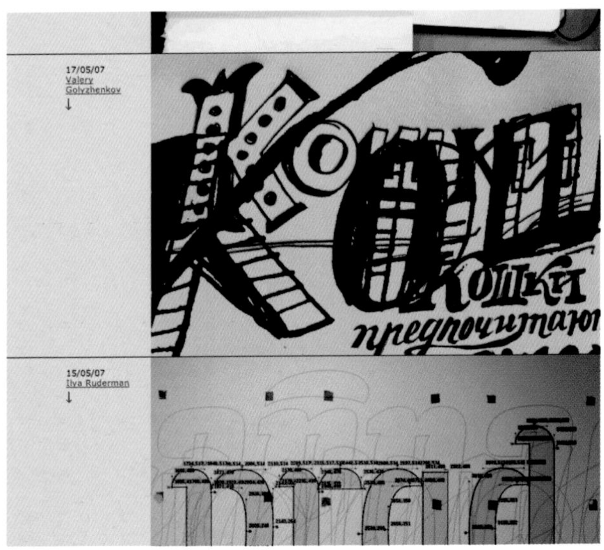

Yury Ostromentsky, Dasha Yarzhambek, Dmitry Jakovlev, Ilya Ruderman

<< [back to daily]

Daily Type is a creative project run by several russian type designers.
Day by day, they create original typefaces and post their results along with routine.

16 | 5 | 2007

contributors: Yury Ostromentsky, Dasha Yarzhambek, Dmitry Jakovlev, Ilya Ruderman
participants: Yury Gordon, Illarion Gordon, Alexander Tarbeev, Vera Evstafieva, Jean Francois Porchez, Catelijne van Middelkoop, Ryan Pescatore Frisk, Massimo Nardini, Kasya Denisevich

letterheads:

Alexander Tarbeev
↓

DailyType

Dasha Yarzhambek
↓

daily type

Dmitry Jakovlev
↓

DAILYTYPE

Dmitry Jakovlev
↓

Ilya Ruderman
↓

DailyType

Vera Evstafieva
↓

Daily Type

Vera Evstafieva
↓

Daily Type

Vera Evstafieva
↓

daily type

Ilya Ruderman
↓

daily type

Yury Ostromentsky

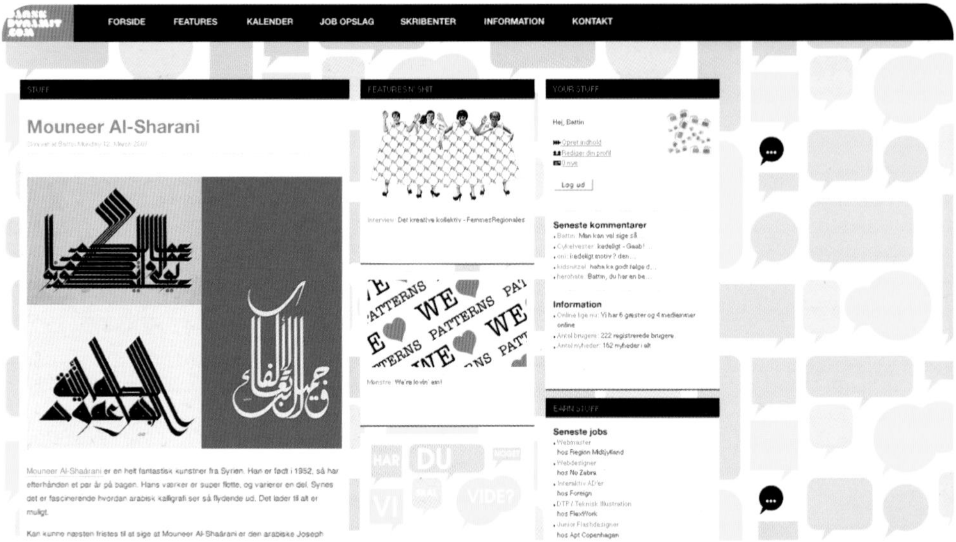

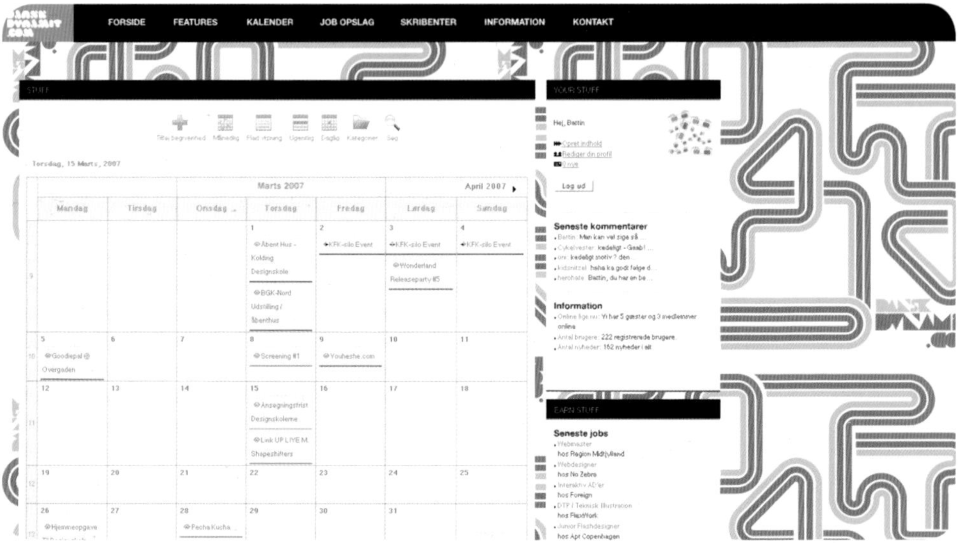

FORSIDE FEATURES KALENDER JOB OPSLAG SKRIBENTER INFORMATION KONTAKT

Mouneer Al-Sharani

Mouneer Al-Shaárani er en helt fantastisk kunstner fra Syrien. Han er født i 1952, så har efterhånden et par år på bagen. Hans værker er super flotte, og varierer en del. Synes det er fascinerende hvordan arabisk kalligrafi ser så flydende ud. Det lader til alt er muligt.

Kan kunne næsten fristes til at sige at Mouneer Al-Shaárani er den arabiske Joseph

Seneste kommentarer

Information

Seneste jobs

Philip Dam Roadley-Battin

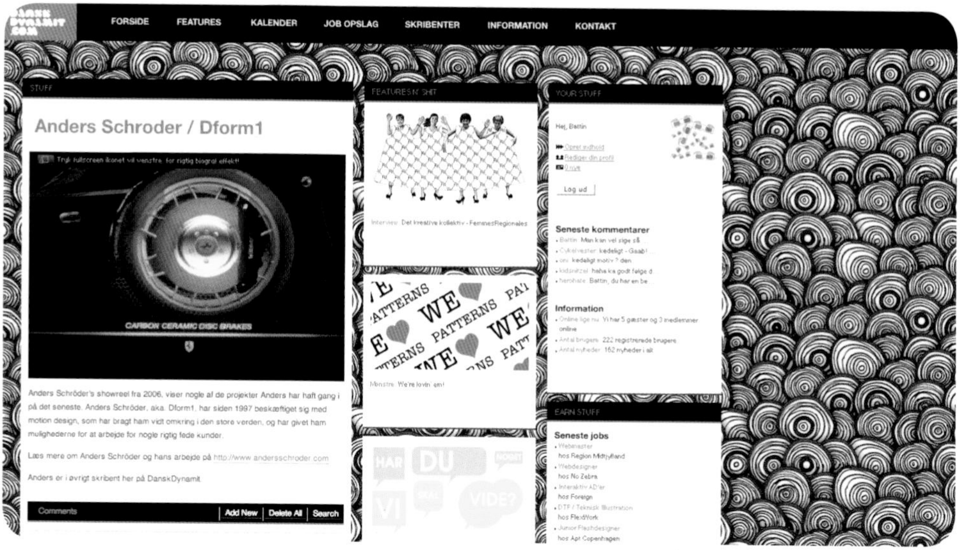

FORSIDE FEATURES KALENDER JOB OPSLAG SKRIBENTER INFORMATION KONTAKT

STUFF

Anders Schroder / Dform1

Tryk fullscreen ikonet vil venstre for rigtig biograf effekt!

CARBON CERAMIC DISC BRAKES

Anders Schröder's showreel fra 2006, viser nogle af de projekter Anders har haft gang i på det seneste. Anders Schröder, aka. Dform1, har siden 1997 beskæftiget sig med motion design, som har bragt ham vidt omkring i den store verden, og har givet ham mulighederne for at arbejde for nogle rigtig fede kunder.

Læs mere om Anders Schröder og hans arbejde på http://www.andersschroder.com

Anders er i øvrigt skribent her på DanskDynamit

Comments | Add New | Delete All | Search

FEATURES N' SHIT

Interview: Det kreative kollektiv - FemmesRegionales

WE PATTERNS

Monstre: We're lovin' em!

HAR DU VI VIDE?

YOUR STUFF

Hej, Battin

Opret indhold
Rediger din profil
0 nye

Log ud

Seneste kommentarer

- Battin: Man kan vel sige så
- Cykelvester: kedeligt - Gaab!
- oni: kedeligt motiv ? den
- kidsnitzel: haha ka godt følge d
- herohate: Battin, du har en be

Information

- Online lige nu: Vi har 5 gæster og 3 medlemmer online
- Antal brugere: 222 registrerede brugere
- Antal nyheder: 162 nyheder i alt

EARN STUFF

Seneste jobs

- Webmaster hos Region Midtjylland
- Webdesigner hos No Zebra
- Interaktiv AD'er hos Foreign
- DTP / Teknisk Illustration hos FlexWork
- Junior Flashdesigner hos Apt Copenhagen

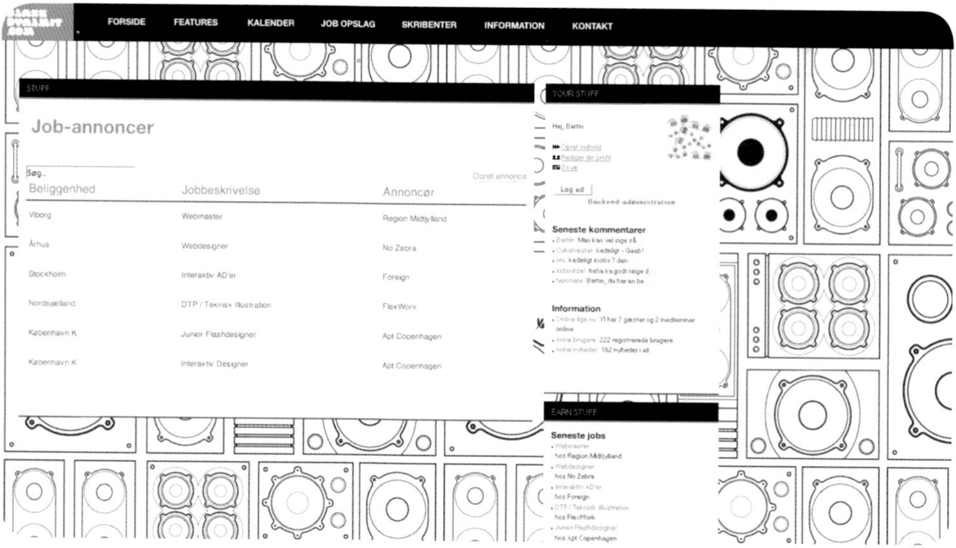

FORSIDE FEATURES KALENDER JOB OPSLAG SKRIBENTER INFORMATION KONTAKT

STUFF

Job-annoncer

Søg..

Opret annonce

Beliggenhed	Jobbeskrivelse	Annoncør
Viborg	Webmaster	Region Midtjylland
Århus	Webdesigner	No Zebra
Stockholm	Interaktiv AD'er	Foreign
Nordsjælland	DTP / Teknisk Illustration	FlexWork
København K	Junior Flashdesigner	Apt Copenhagen
København K	Interaktiv Designer	Apt Copenhagen

YOUR STUFF

Hej, Battin

Opret indhold
Rediger din profil
0 nye

Log ud

Backend-administration

Seneste kommentarer

- Battin: Man kan vel sige så
- Cykelvester: kedeligt - Gaab!
- oni: kedeligt motiv ? den
- kidsnitzel: haha ka godt følge d
- herohate: Battin, du har en be

Information

- Online lige nu: Vi har 7 gæster og 2 medlemmer online
- Antal brugere: 222 registrerede brugere
- Antal nyheder: 162 nyheder i alt

EARN STUFF

Seneste jobs

- Webmaster hos Region Midtjylland
- Webdesigner hos No Zebra
- Interaktiv AD'er hos Foreign
- DTP / Teknisk Illustration hos FlexWork
- Junior Flashdesigner hos Apt Copenhagen

Enza Morello

DESIGN TROTTER

Home | L'autrice di questo Blog | Site Admin

« Slow is ugly | "Sui" generis »

Il contenitore migliore dell'anno

Dal cucchiaio alla città

Ecco il contenitore che ha vinto il "Can of the Year 2006" , premio internazionale di packaging in alluminio, si tratta del contenitore per la Coca Cola Coffe a forma della vecchia bottiglia in vetro, bella vero? Bruno Munari diceva che un modo per avere buone idee in design era anche quello di reinventare delle forme già esistenti, cambiandone il materiale. Mi sa che aveva previsto un pò di cose Munari.

2006 Can of the Year

Coca-Cola Blak

Exal Corporation (USA)

Il grande cinema a casa tua.
SU FAST Shop

Design Trotter. Una viaggiatrice nel mondo del Design.
A cura di **Enza Morello**
Visita il sito dell'autrice.

Domande, segnalazioni, curiosità? Scrivici.

Cerca

Si parla di...

- Around the globe (11)
- Come ti vesto il prodotto (7)
- Cool ADV Graphic Agencies (5)
- Dal cucchiaio alla città (15)
- Dalle stelle alla strada (6)
- Ho messo la testa a posto (4)
- Il mondo della sanguigna (12)

Design You Trust // designyoutrust.com

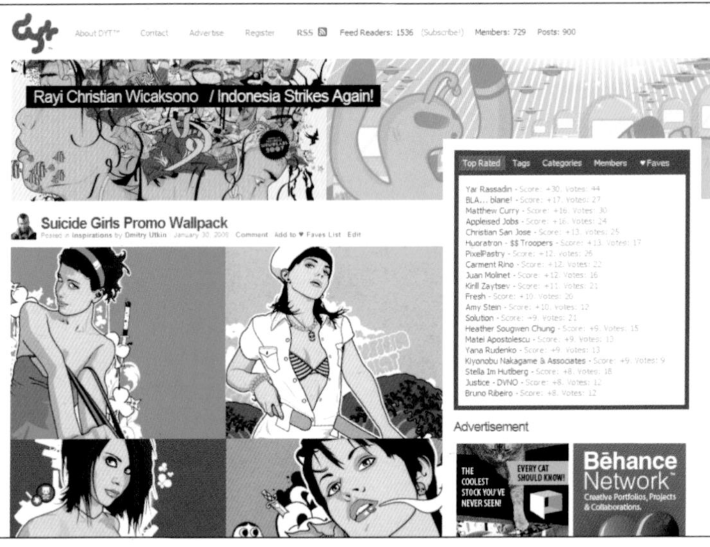

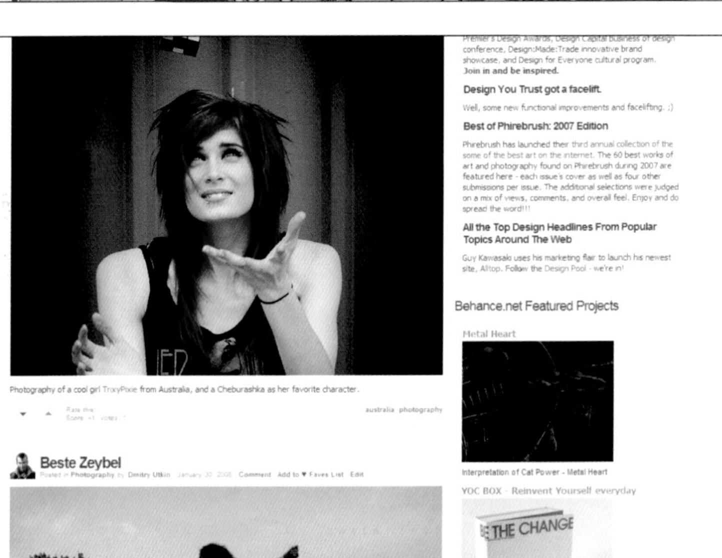

Dmitry Utkin

IO. The real world, digitally interactive...

Not rated yet
Rate this!

Isabeli Fontana

Posted in Photography by Dmitry Utkin January 30, 2008 Comment Add to ♥ Faves List Edit

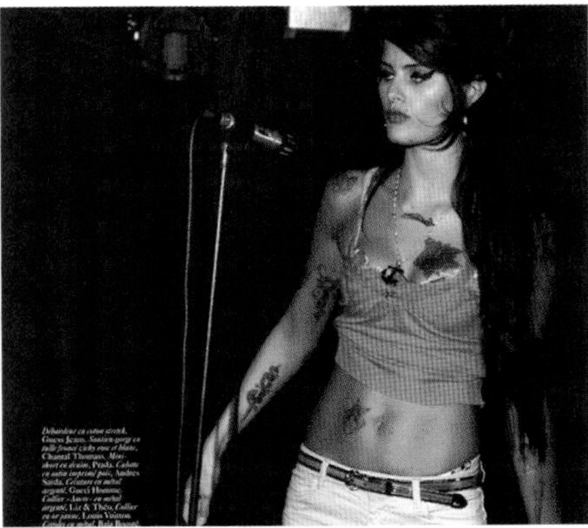

Isabeli Fontana, Brazilian supermodel, as Amy Winehouse.

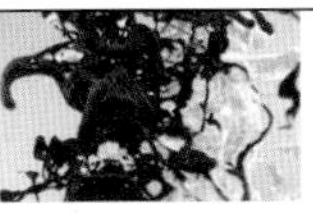

Deco Paradise Mash-up!

I'm so excited to introduce our latest mash-up, feat. "Deco Paradise" - an avant garde take on evening gowns by Dina Yassin expressed as a visual story by Ayesha Mathews.~Backdrop~Di - these are sooo stunning - I LOVE IT - your gowns, the model, her styling - HOT!- tell me more about the concept and idea you are trying to capture- what inspired the fashion and the mood/ era/ period/ style etc.. I want to see if I can add some elements in graphically to help tell the story even better :) - AyeshaThe concept and inspiration is a more avante garde approach to the classical evening gown. This time I was inspired by precious stones, sapphire and topaz in particular. With the silhouette, I played around with unusual shapes, yet bearing in mind the form of a woman. The period was a play on 30's glam incorporated with art deco shapes.The model is from the Ukraine. I wanted the make-up to have pop colors and certain curvey take ons from the details of the gowns, making her look like a tropical bird. Therefore, we played with the eyes and left the lips natural. I wanted the hair to look like a hat. I had a different style planned out originally, but as we were playing around, we found that this worked out better! - Dina~Curtains~

Sony Walkman - Photoshoot

Kalle Hagman

Posted in Inspirations by Dmitry Utkin March 24, 2008 1 Comment Add to ♥ Faves List Edit

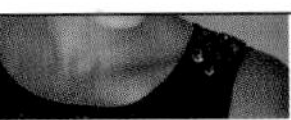

2008 TYR Triathlon

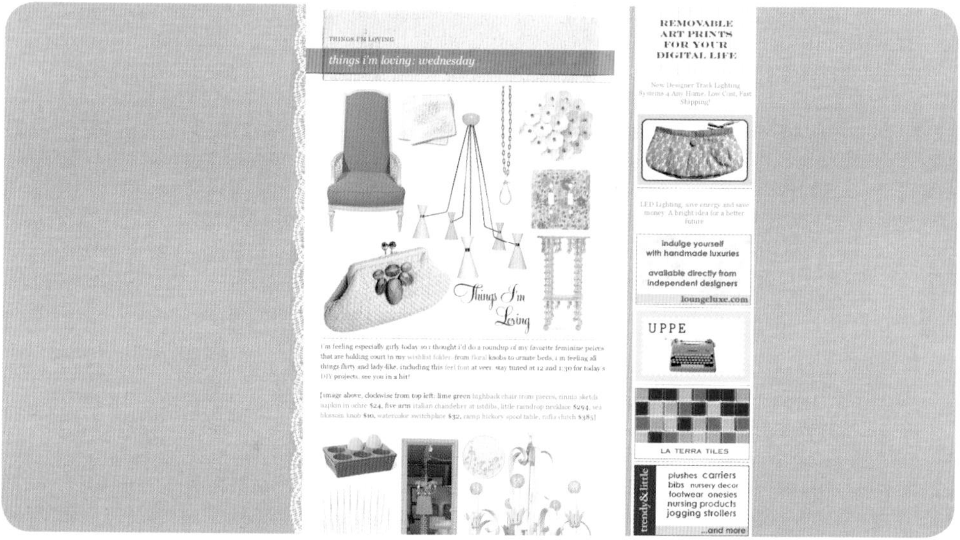

Grace Bonney

sneak peeks
mini trends
guides
podcasts
categories
events
press
about
contact
ENTER YOUR EMAIL
subscribe
powered by FeedBlitz
ARCHIVES
2008
2007
2006
2005
2004

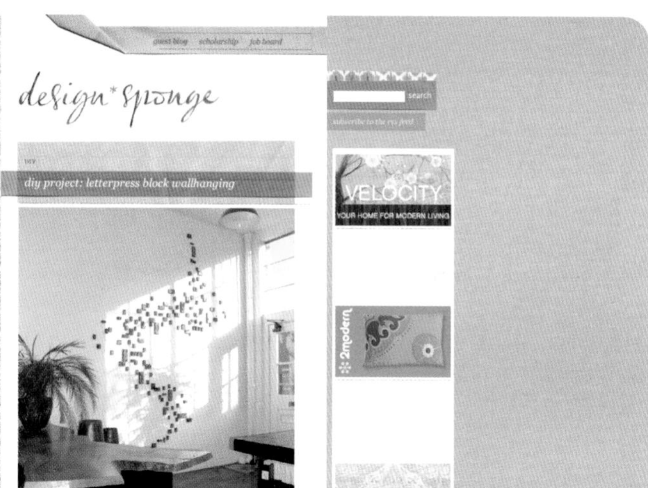

guest blog
scholarship
job board
design*sponge
search
subscribe to the rss feed
DIY
diy project: letterpress block wallhanging
VELOCITY
YOUR HOME FOR MODERN LIVING
2modern
WARP & WEFT
before we get started with today's diy project from lauren and derek (which will go up at 1:30), i had to add this wonderful project submitted by andy beers (you may remember his incredible sneak peek from last month). andy created this incredible letterpress block wallhanging in his office using blocks he found at a fleamarket (andy shares tips for finding blocks after the jump). the result is a really fantastic art piece that serves double duty as

sneak peeks
mini trends
guides
podcasts
categories
events
press
about
contact
ENTER YOUR EMAIL
subscribe
powered by FeedBlitz
ARCHIVES
2008
2007
2006
2005
2004

guest blog
scholarship
job board
design*sponge
search
subscribe to the rss feed
events
« Dec
Feb »
January 2008
Biz Lady Meet Up: Portland, OR
February 26, 2008 – 7:00 pm to 9:00 pm
Design*Sponge will be hosting a Biz Lady Meet Up at DWR.
Date: Tuesday, February 26th
Time: 7-9pm
Location: DWR N.W. Everett Street
Please RSVP to: designsponge@gmail.com
We will be discussing small business concerns, marketing/PR, real life designer success stories and retailing/wholesaling.
Please bring a snack or drink with you if you can. We'll see you there!
Biz Lady Meet Up: Seattle, WA
February 28, 2008 – 7:00 pm to 9:00 pm
Design*Sponge will be hosting a Biz Lady Meet Up at DWR
Date: Thursday, February 28th
Time: 7-9pm
Location: DWR First Avenue
VELOCITY
YOUR HOME FOR MODERN LIVING
2modern
paperstudio.com
WARP & WEFT

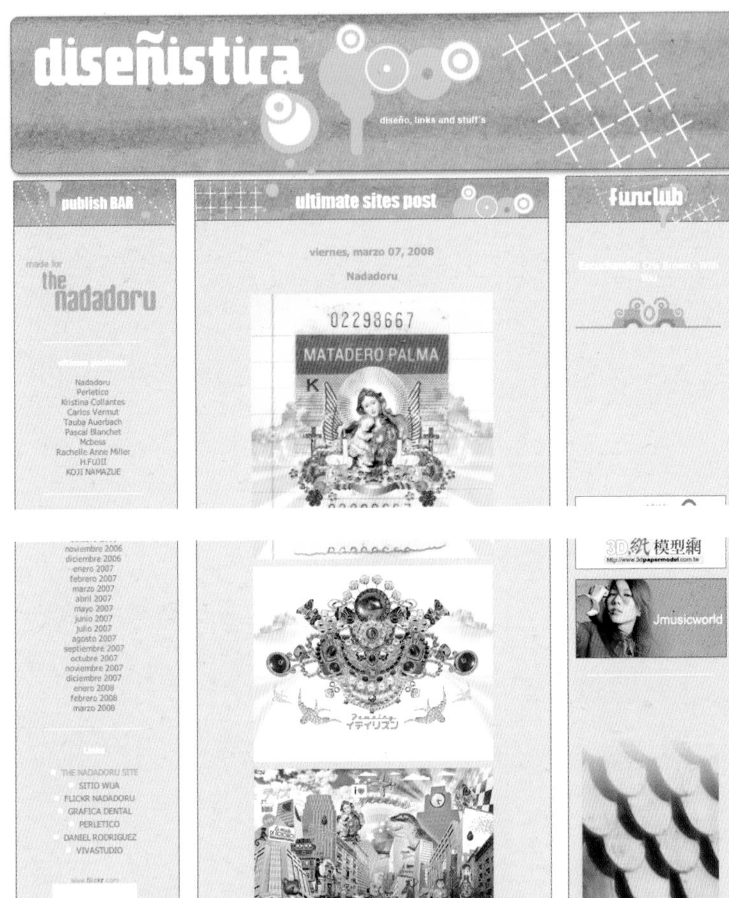

Luis Felipe Salas Ortiz

diseñística

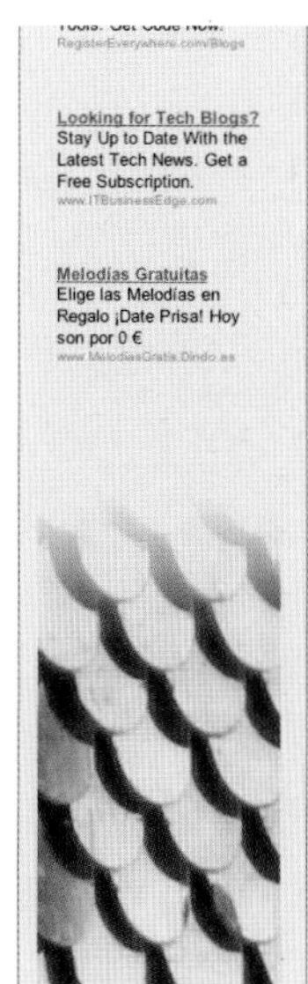

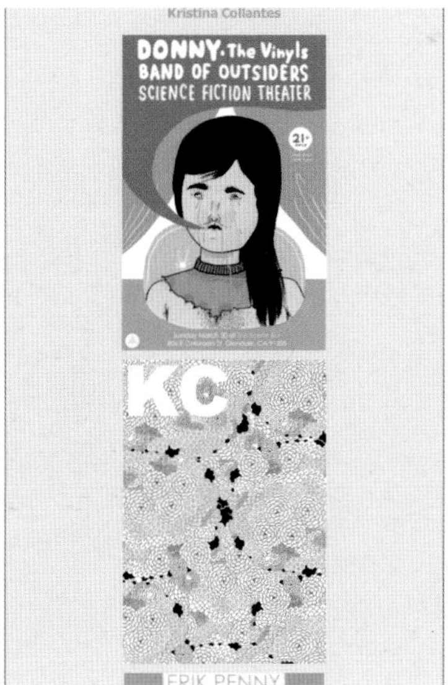

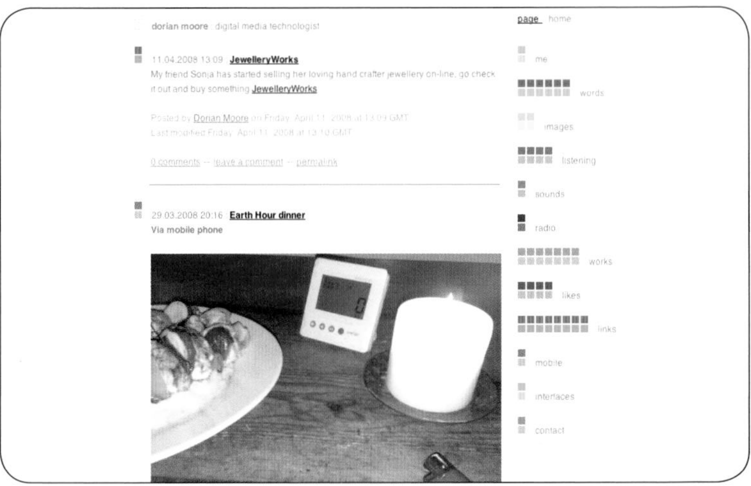

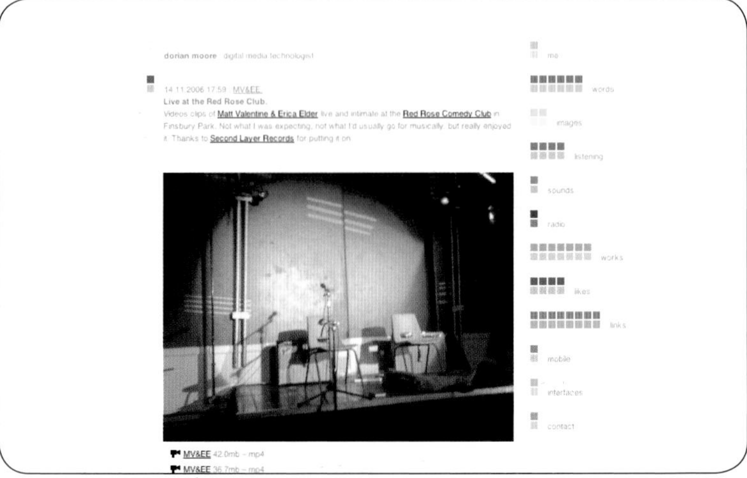

Dorian Moore

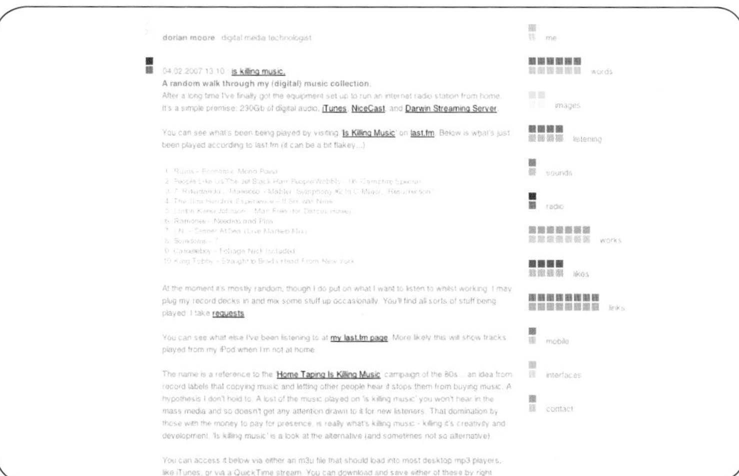
dorian moore . digital media technologist
04.02.2007 13:10 : is killing music.
A random walk through my (digital) music collection.
After a long time I've finally got the equipment set up to run an internet radio station from home. It's a simple premise: 230Gb of digital audio, iTunes, NiceCast, and Darwin Streaming Server.
You can see what's been being played by visiting 'Is Killing Music' on last.fm. Below is what's just been played according to last.fm (it can be a bit flakey...)
At the moment it's mostly random, though I do put on what I want to listen to whilst working. I may plug my record decks in and mix some stuff up occasionally. You'll find all sorts of stuff being played. I take requests.
You can see what else I've been listening to at my last.fm page. More likely this will show tracks played from my iPod when I'm not at home.
The name is a reference to the 'Home Taping Is Killing Music' campaign of the 80s ... an idea from record labels that copying music and letting other people hear it stops them from buying music. A hypothesis I don't hold to. A lost of the music played on 'is killing music' you won't hear in the mass media and so doesn't get any attention drawn to it for new listeners. That domination by those with the money to pay for presence, is really what's killing music - killing it's creativity and development. 'Is killing music' is a look at the alternative (and sometimes not so alternative).
You can access it below via either an m3u file that should load into most desktop mp3 players, like iTunes, or via a QuickTime stream. You can download and save either of these by right
me
words
images
listening
sounds
radio
works
likes
links
mobile
interfaces
contact

dorian moore . digital media technologist
Afrirampo - 2005.10.21
dorianmoore.com 2005 - some rights reserved
The End
1 2 3 4 5 6 7 8 9 10 11 12 13 14 15 16 17 18 19 20 21 22 23 24 25 26 27 28 29 30 31 32 33 34 35 36 37 38 39 40 41 42

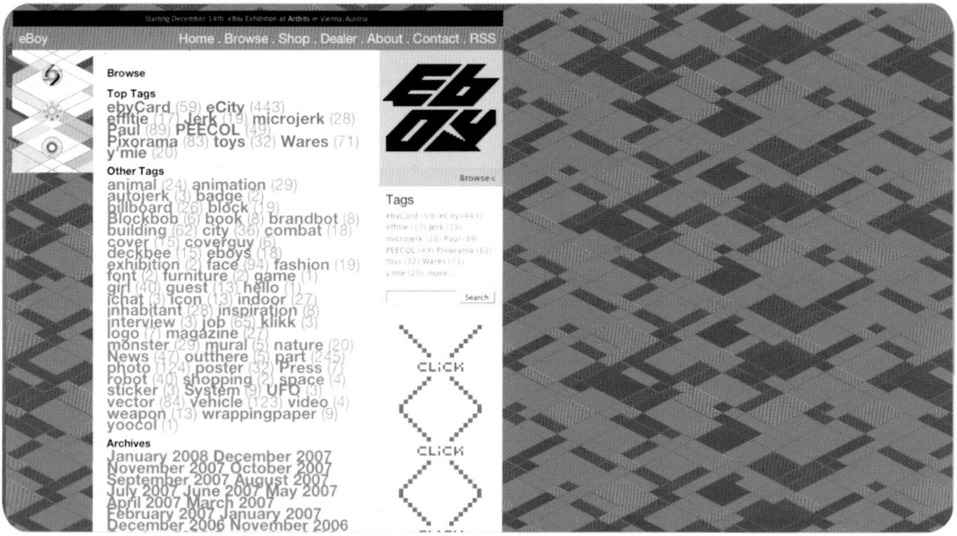

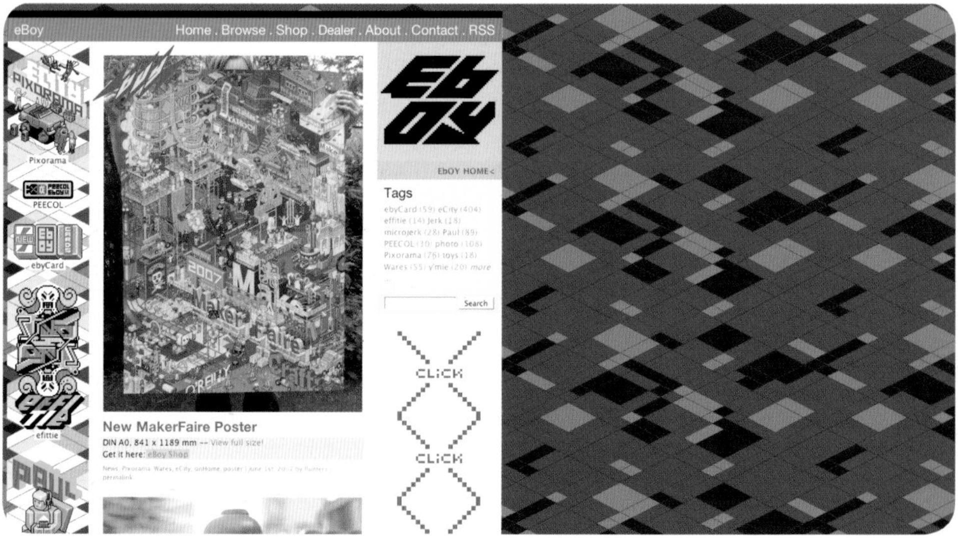

Eboy // hello.eboy.com

Steffen Sauerteig, Svend Smital, Kai Vermehr

efittie
PAUL
Paul
Jerk

New MakerFaire Poster
DIN A0, 841 x 1189 mm -- View full size!
Get it here: eBoy Shop
Upload: volv.jpg
peecol
LaCruzz
NYOff
Astronof
Volv

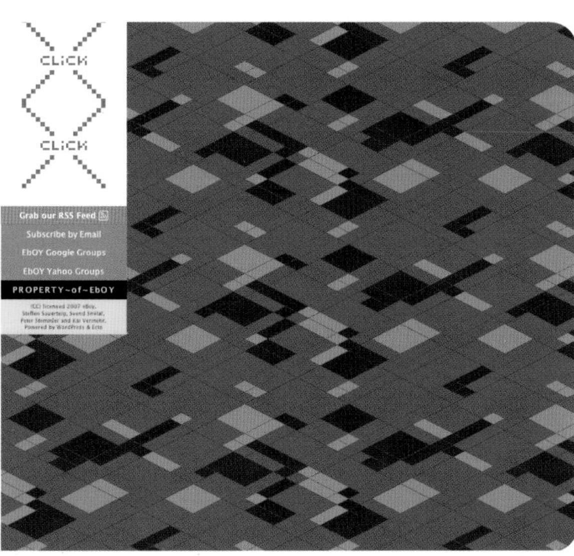
CLiCK
CLiCK
Grab our RSS Feed
Subscribe by Email
EbOY Google Groups
EbOY Yahoo Groups
PROPERTY~of~EbOY
(CC) licensed 2007 eBoy, Steffen Sauerteig, Svend Smital, Peter Stemmler and Kai Vermehr. Powered by WordPress & Ecto

Jerk
Upload: volv.jpg
peecol
LaCruzz
NYOff
Astronof
Volv
peecol
peecol
Upload: p'bot.jpg
Upload: Dealer: Overkill GER/Berlin

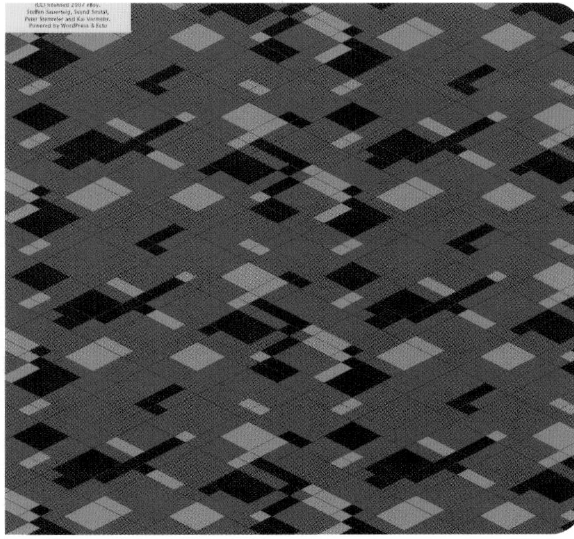
(CC) licensed 2007 eBoy, Steffen Sauerteig, Svend Smital, Peter Stemmler and Kai Vermehr. Powered by WordPress & Ecto

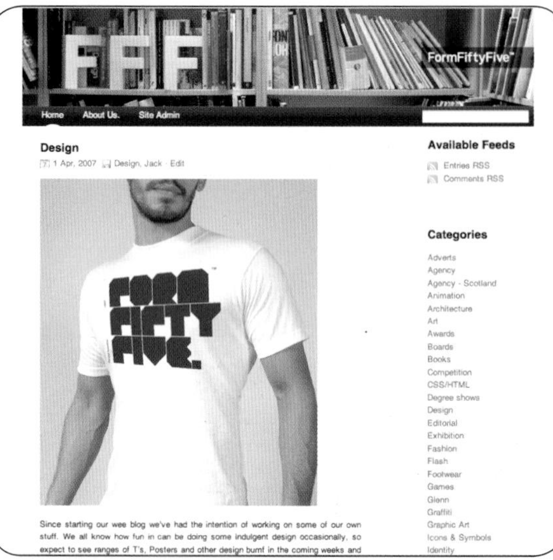

Distrikt55

23 Sep, 2007 Print, Illustration, Typography, Jack, Poster · Edit

Available Feeds

Entries RSS

Comments RSS

Categories

Adverts
Agency
Agency - Scotland
Animation
Architecture
Art
Awards
Boards
Books
Competition
CSS/HTML
Degree shows
Design
Editorial
Exhibition
Fashion
Flash
Footwear
Games
Glenn
Graffiti
Graphic Art
Icons & Symbols
Identity
Illustration
Info
Interface
Interior / Environment
Jack
Motion
Music Cover Design
News
Packaging
Personal

Its about that time where I indulge in a wee bit of shameless self-promotion! I've put together an indexhibit portfolio site of competition/self initiated projects I've worked on this year. Strictly for fun, with no commercial projects included. Distrikt55.

Glenn Garriock, Jack Daly

Franklin

24 Apr, 2007 3 Comments Edit

Germany for a medical consultation.

Its all very sensitive, but he's been reassured that gender swap operations are much

August 2007
July 2007
June 2007
May 2007
April 2007
March 2007
February 2007
January 2007

Members

Site Admin
Logout
+ Technorati Favorites

FormFiftyFive

Home About Us. Site Admin

REDUCE, REUSE, RE...you know the drill!

1 May, 2007 Glenn Edit

Got some nice new paper samples in last week, which meant the old ones had to go! Our Paper recycling bin was so full that I decided to make a sketch book out of some of them. This is the first version, and the label is a bit of a 'quick hit'. Vol. 2 will be nicer! Anyone got any other ideas?

4 Comments so far »

Jack said,

Wrote on May 1, 2007 @ 4:22 pm Edit

Sweet Glenn, might make myself one of those! Didn't we see virtually the exact same thing being sold £5, when you were visiting?

Available Feeds

Entries RSS
Comments RSS

Categories

Adverts
Agency
Agency - Scotland
Animation
Architecture
Art
Awards
Boards
Books
Competition
CSS/HTML
Degree shows
Design
Editorial
Exhibition
Fashion
Flash
Footwear
Games
Glenn
Graffiti
Graphic Art
Icons & Symbols
Identity

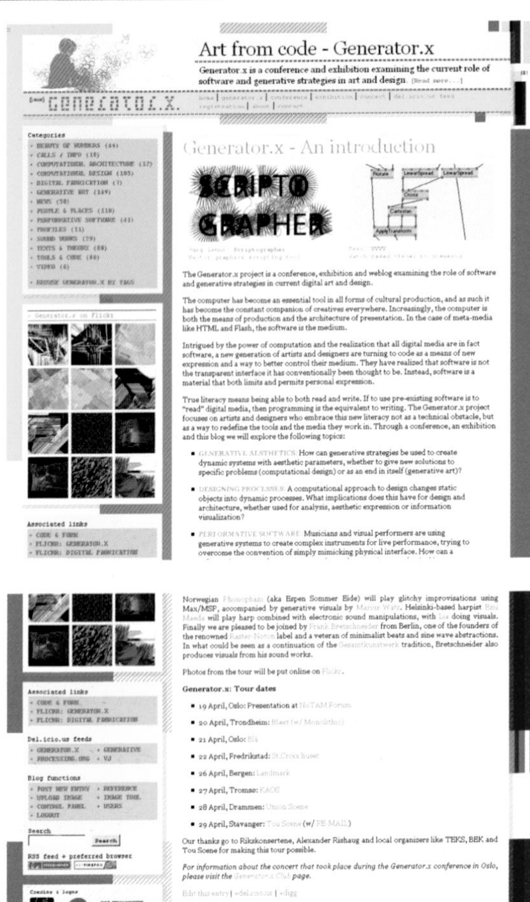
Art from code - Generator.x
Generator.x is a conference and exhibition examining the current role of software and generative strategies in art and design.
Generator.x - An introduction
The Generator.x project is a conference, exhibition and weblog examining the role of software and generative strategies in current digital art and design.
Generator.x: Tour dates
Generator.x
C.STEM conference (Part 1)

Marius Watz

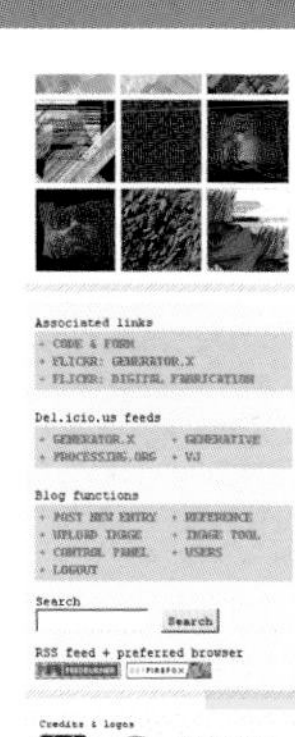

Credits & logos

NASJONALMUSEET FOR KUNST, ARKITEKTUR OG DESIGN

Generator.x is a co-production between Atelier Nord and Riksutstillinger (National Touring Exhibitions of Norway), part of the National Museum of Art, Architecture and Design.

Seiki knitting hardware.

The Newsknitter web site does not indicate whether custom garments will eventually be for sale, even though it would seem an obvious extension of the project. Too bad the daily news typically makes for a grim way to commemorate one's birthday or other significant date.

For a different take on generative knitting, see this old post: Freddie Robins: How to make a piece of work when you're too tired to make decisions.

[Link via pöfmagazine]

Edit this entry | +del.icio.us | +digg

marius watz on Tuesday, September 4th, 2007 at 19:09. Filed under Beauty of numbers, Computational design, Digital fabrication. You can leave a response, or trackback from your own site.

6 RESPONSES TO "INFORMATIVE FASHION: NEWSKNITTER"

1. Newsknitter - today and tomorrow, September 4th, 2007 at 20:09 (edit)

[...] I think that its name says it all: Newsknitter. Found @ Generator.x art, design, fashion, physical computing [...]

2. A better tomorrow - Blog » Blog Archive » Newsknitter, September 5th, 2007 at 14:09 (edit)

[...] Datenvisualisierung finde ich ein extrem spannendes Gebiet gerade in Kombination mit Design oder Kunst. Bei Generator X bin ich ein Projekt namens Newsknitter gestoßen. Sehr sehr geil was man mit dieser Webtechnik anstellen kann!! Da kommen mr gleich zig Ideen. Ich hab die Leute von Newsknitter direkt angeschrieben, um mehr Infos zu bekommen. Da läßt sich doch bestimmt was für A-B-T zaubern. [...]

3. Newsknitter | Craft Blog, September 6th, 2007 at 15:09 (edit)

[...] The sweaters will be part of the Ars Electronica festival this week. - [via] Link. [...]

4. huseyin, September 7th, 2007 at 14:09 (edit)

çok başarılı olmuş emegine
bigine,düşüncene,azmine,ve kararlılıgına çok teşekkürler dilegiyle başarıların devamını ve bizim övünç kaynagımız olmaya devamını dilerim .

5. duğumkume » Blog Archive » Kıyafetler Haberlerle Oruldu, September 17th, 2007 at 05:09 (edit)

[...] Ebru Kurbak ve Mahir M. Yavuz tarafından geliştirilen NewsKnitter ("Haber Örücü") internetten okuduğu günlük haberleri analiz edip kazak üzerinde örüntü olarak gösteriyor. Bu yılki Ars Electronica festivalinde en çok konuşulan projelerden biri NewsKnitter. Projeden 10 parça kazak festival boyunca Campus 2.0'da sergileniyor. [...]

6. /blog » Blog Archive » Newsknitter Generative Knitting, November 2nd, 2007 at 16:11 (edit)

[...] [...]

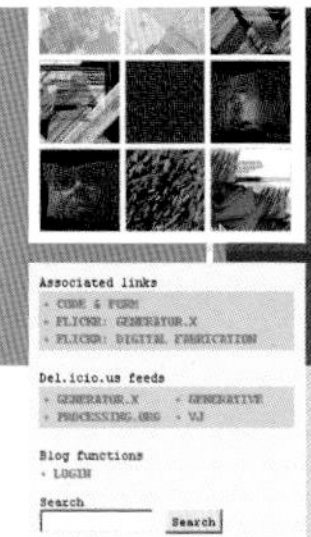

Credits & logos

NASJONALMUSEET FOR KUNST, ARKITEKTUR OG DESIGN

Generator.x is a co-production between Atelier Nord and Riksutstillinger (National Touring Exhibitions of Norway), part of the National Museum of Art, Architecture and Design.

30gms just posted a link to the work of the U.S. Geological Survey's Astrogeology Research Program on mapping the Moon. The maps are based on data from lunar missions in the 1960's and 1970's, and show the geological composition of the lunar surface.

The maps are visually stunning in their abstraction. The many craters become clusters of colors, giving the appearance of a complex composition. The palette is striking and chosen for contrast, but avoiding primary color clichés. Interestingly, both the colors and composition make the maps somewhat reminiscent of the work of Joshua Davis. Compare for instance with his light box images for OFFF.

The USGS site generously offers digital downloads of the maps in a variety of formats. The PDF versions are full vector quality, and are amazing to look at in high resolution. Would-be astrogeologists should check out the USGS Planetary GIS Web Server, a project with the charming acronym PIGWAD.

USGS Astrogeology Research Program: West side of the moon

+del.icio.us | +digg

marius watz on Wednesday, October 3rd, 2007 at 21:10. Filed under Beauty of numbers, Computational design, People & places. You can leave a response, or trackback from your own site.

2 RESPONSES TO "THE LOVELINESS OF LUNAR MAPPING"

1. Mapping Narratives, ITP Seminar, Fall 2007 » Psychedelic Moon Maps, October 9th, 2007 at 01:10

[...] This blog post points to some really fascinating and startlingly pretty (if you like luminescent blobs of colour, which I do) lunar maps, made by the USGS Astrogeology Research Program (their site is rather ugly and hard to access, so I sent you to the middleblog instead). [...]

2. » The loveliness of lunar mapping | generator.x Aggregate Mad Blog: aggregates the interwebs, November 1st, 2007 at 20:11

[...] http://www.generatorx.no/20071003/the-loveliness-of-lunar-mapping/ [...]

LEAVE A RESPONSE

Name (required)

Mail (will not be published) (required)

Website

Graficante - Colectivo de Diseño // graficantes.blogspot.com

Christopher Cisneros (Chopper), Manuel Ramírez, José Morgan (Morgan), César Gastelum (Ghüs), Alberto Quintero (Beto Q), Wilfrido Soto (Will), Ivan Mayorquín (Mayor King!), Eunice Aguilar Herrera de Sepúlveda (la EÜ)

FRAY TORMENTA/ karla Escamilla.

OCTAGON/ Fidel Picos.

PIERROT/ Will Soto.

El MISTICO/ J. Morgan.

EL SANTO/ Choper Nawers.

Etiquetas: **diseño, graficantes, lucha libre**

posted by: GRAFICANTE @ 8:30 AM 0 comments

martes. febrero 26. 2008

ese lugar especial donde trabajas y diseñas.

¡Un Chihuahua te cambia la vida!

Solo **$250** pesos cada póster más gastos de envío.

Contacto de venta a: yo@isme53.com

Anuncios Google

decorados escenografia
Escultura gran formato publicidad Ambientaciones stands creativos.
www.artesplasticasaplicadas.com

Diseños profesionales
Diseño web, gráfico y publicitario. Calidad, experiencia, rentabilidad.
www.imediacomunicacion.com

Estudio de diseño gráfico
Diseño de logotipos, papelería, imagen corporativa, catálogos y web
www.solucionesuno.com

Fotografo Publicidad
Madrid. Alta Calidad, Experiencia y Estilo. ¡Pide tu Presupuesto!
www.albaniofotografics.com

+LINKS

- Quetevalga.com
- KTV Network
- How Design
- Arthur Mount
- Acamonchi
- Pascual Rico foto
- La Pagina del Choper
- 3thumbsupaward
- Mrs. B
- a!
- Alina Chau
- Artfulwisdom
- Potatomamma
- Vonster
- SFGblog
- La Coctelera
- David Lanham
- Milchangos
- KONG
- Tommy Kane
- Engrane
- Sketch Club
- Arde Troya
- Auténtica
- Kone
- Axcan
- Kimera
- Duprez Dolores
- Kalifornia Republik
- Microbians
- Pixel Girl
- Dany Boy
- Tatoom City
- HulaHula
- Wallpaper

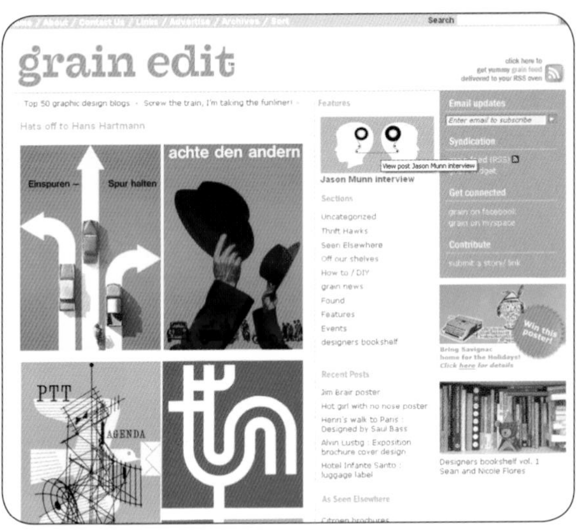

Search
grain edit
click here to get yummy grain feed delivered to your RSS oven
Top 50 graphic design blogs · Screw the train, I'm taking the funliner! ·
Hats off to Hans Hartmann
Einspuren – Spur halten
achte den andern
PTT
AGENDA
Features
View post Jason Munn interview
Jason Munn interview
Sections
Uncategorized
Thrift Hawks
Seen Elsewhere
Off our shelves
How to / DIY
grain news
Found
Features
Events
designers bookshelf
Recent Posts
Jim Brair poster
Hot girl with no nose poster
Henri's walk to Paris : Designed by Saul Bass
Alvin Lustig : Exposition brochure cover design
Hotel Infante Santo : luggage label
As Seen Elsewhere
Email updates
Enter email to subscribe
Syndication
Get connected
grain on facebook
grain on myspace
Contribute
submit a story/ link
Win this poster!
Designers bookshelf vol. 1 Sean and Nicole Flores

Search
grain edit
click here to get yummy grain feed delivered to your RSS oven
Alvin Lustig : Exposition brochure cover design · Hot girl with no nose poster
Henri's walk to Paris : Designed by Saul Bass
Saul Bass - Henri's walk to paris c1962
As far as I know this is the only kids picture book illustrated by designer Saul Bass. Saul provides a 60s pop color backdrop for the text written by Leonore Klein. The book was published by Young Scott books in 1962
Henri's walk to Paris is the story of young boy who lives in Reboul, France that dreams of going to Paris. One day, after reading a book about Paris he decides to pack up a lunch and head for the city. Along the way he gets tired and falls asleep under a tree. This is when the story really
Features
Jason Munn interview
Sections
Uncategorized
Thrift Hawks
Seen Elsewhere
Off our shelves
How to / DIY
grain news
Found
Features
Events
designers bookshelf
Recent Posts
Jim Brair poster
Hot girl with no nose poster
Henri's walk to Paris : Designed by Saul Bass
Alvin Lustig : Exposition brochure cover design
Hotel Infante Santo : luggage label
As Seen Elsewhere
Email updates
Enter email to subscribe
Syndication
grain feed (RSS)
grain widget
Get connected
grain on facebook
grain on myspace
Contribute
submit a story/ link
Win this poster!
Designers bookshelf vol. 1 Sean and Nicole Flores

Dave Cuzner

Search
grain edit
click here to
get yummy grain feed
delivered to your RSS oven
La Rinascente poster 1974 · Ladislav Sutnar exhibition
Plakat Schriften - type specimens
plakat schriften - type specimen catalog c195?
Notes | Link
Plakat Schriften - Type specimen catalog -produced by by D stempel AG. foundry Frankfurt, Germany. This is one of the better catalogs I've come across. Huge Specimen samples and Bold color. Includes examples of Helvetica, Sistina, Schmalfette Binder style, Enge Fette Plak, Schmalfette Memphis, Kraftige Balzac, Halbfette Elan and Ziffern. Theres not date listed but it must be around the early 60s since Helvetica was created in 1957.
Features
Jason Munn interview
Sections
Uncategorized
Thrift Hawks
Seen Elsewhere
Off our shelves
How to / DIY
grain news
Found
Features
Events
designers bookshelf
Recent Posts
Jim Brair poster
Hot girl with no nose poster
Henri's walk to Paris : Designed by Saul Bass
Alvin Lustig : Exposition brochure cover design
Hotel Infante Santo : luggage label
As Seen Elsewhere
Email updates
Enter email to subscribe
Syndication
grain feed (RSS)
grain widget
Get connected
grain on facebook
grain on myspace
Contribute
submit a story/ link
Win this poster!
Bring Savignac home for the Holidays!
Click here for details
Designers bookshelf vol. 1
Sean and Nicole Flores

Search
grain edit
click here to
get yummy grain feed
delivered to your RSS oven
Jason Munn interview · And we have a winner.
Say yes! to analog design
TheStands
Yes studio hooked up a sweet 12" cover for the UK band *the stand*. The album is from 2005. Multiple designs were created, colors were mixed by hand and large format prints produced at K2 Screen, London. The resulting artwork was then re-photographed and used on the lp and poster design.
Looks like the length of this record was longer then the band's career.
Features
Jason Munn interview
Sections
Uncategorized
Thrift Hawks
Seen Elsewhere
Off our shelves
How to / DIY
grain news
Found
Features
Events
designers bookshelf
Recent Posts
Jim Brair poster
Hot girl with no nose poster
Henri's walk to Paris : Designed by Saul Bass
Alvin Lustig : Exposition brochure cover design
Hotel Infante Santo : luggage label
As Seen Elsewhere
Email updates
Enter email to subscribe
Syndication
grain feed (RSS)
grain widget
Get connected
grain on facebook
grain on myspace
Contribute
submit a story/ link
Win this poster!
Bring Savignac home for the Holidays!
Click here for details
Designers bookshelf vol. 1
Sean and Nicole Flores

Justin Amphlett, Colin Buttimer

KRAFTWERK
POCKET CALCULATOR B/W DENTAKU
電卓
ボクは音楽家 デンタク片手に たしたり ひいたり そおさして 作曲する このボタンおせば 音楽かなでる

"I'LL BE AROUND"
"STILL WATER"
"SOULFUL STRUT"
"CAN'T GET ENOUGH"
"SET ME FREE"
"IS IT BECAUSE I'M BLACK"
"DEEPER & DEEPER"
"I DON'T WANT TO BE RIGHT"
"NO ONE CAN STOP US"
RIGHT AROUND THE WORLD
TODAY'S SOUND TODAY
SOUL JAZZ RECORDS
5 026328 100500
1 STUDIO
Recorded by Jamaica Recording Studio, 13, Brentford Road, Kingston, Jamaica
Produced by C.S. Dodd
Made in England
SJR CD 50
SOUL JAZZ RECORDS PRESENTS
STUDIO ONE SOUL

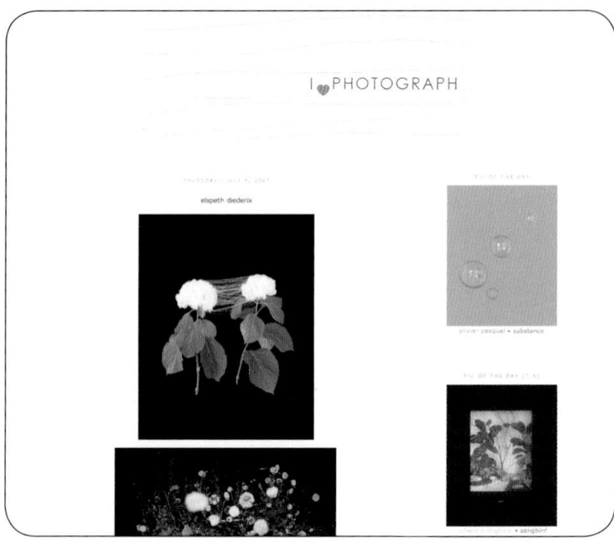
I PHOTOGRAPH
elspeth diederix
olivier pasqual • substance
• songbird

chris woodcock • miami construction
james welling • iac3
uwe walter • untitled

Laurel Ptak

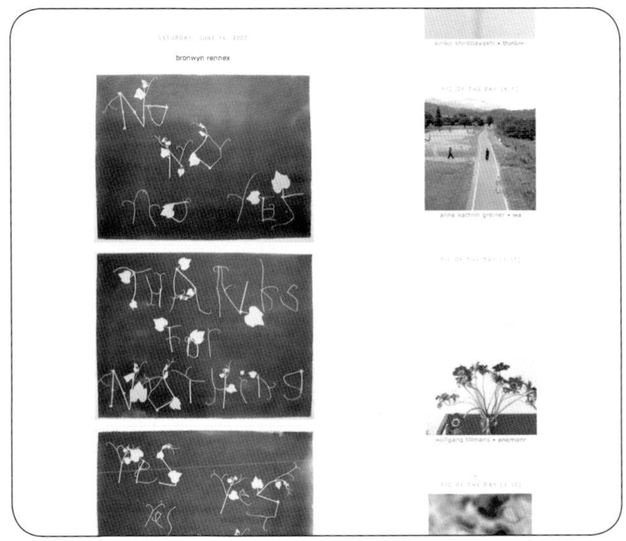

Home sweet home | Typography tags | Identify a font | Who Shot the Serif? | Send a message | iLT wallpaper | About iLT | RSS Subscribe

I love
typography

abrupt addiction adnate Arial Biographies book reviews books cartoon Digg-Zeldman effect Español exhibitions feedback Fontometer foundries free fonts Grotesque Helvetica identify a font inspiration kerning latin letterspacing ligature Lucida Monotype new fonts news new typefaces Optima san serif serifs slab tittle tracking transitional type design typefaces typenuts typography games typography t-shirt typography terms typography web sites Typoholism video web typography

Nov 18 2007 type a response!

Sunday Type

NATIONAL FEIJOA

Is it really Sunday again? Well, for some of you it will be Saturday, so here's your Saturday/Sunday – or better still – *Weekend Type*. Oh, but first a quick announcement: the great response to the announcement of FF Meta Serif took us beyond the half a million page views. Thanks to everyone for being a part of that; more importantly, thanks for your contributions, your enthusiasm and support.

OK, so on with the show. Those of you who read the FF Meta Serif piece will know the name Kris Sowersby; he's one-third of the trinity that worked on the serif

Recommended

- Thinking With Type – Ellen Lupton
- Designing Type – Karen Cheng
- The Elements *of* Typographic Style – Bringhurst
- Stop Stealing Sheep & Find Out How Type Works
- Type: The Secret History of Letters – Loxley
- The Complete Manual of Typography – Felici

Recent Articles

- *Sunday Type: National Feijoa*
- *At last! FF Meta Serif*

Subscribe to iLT
Content RSS
Comments RSS

typography

Aug 26 2007 type a response!

Who Shot the Serif?

TYPOGRAPHY TERMS

One of the reasons for starting I Love Typography was that I felt there just wasn't enough being said about the topic. Secondly, and more significantly, I always found it difficult to quickly locate typographic resources. The long-term aim of this blog is to be such a resource, a one-stop-shop for everything about typography, from terminology to new typefaces, from inspirational examples of type to choosing the best font for the job, whether that be on- or off-line.

Bodoni, there's only room in this town for one SERIF

Recommended

- Thinking With Type – Ellen Lupton
- Designing Type – Karen Cheng
- The Elements *of* Typographic Style – Bringhurst
- Stop Stealing Sheep & Find Out How Type Works
- Type: The Secret History of Letters – Loxley
- The Complete Manual of Typography – Felici

Recent Articles

- *Sunday Type: National Feijoa*
- *At last! FF Meta Serif*
- *Widows and Orphans*
- *Smashing Free Fonts*
- *Type Terms: Humanist*
- *FONT Magazine*
- *The apostrophe: Contrary to popular belief, it doesn't swing both ways*
- *So You Want to Create a Font: 2*
- *Sunday Type: Spiekermann*
- *Made With FontFont*
- *So You Want to Create a Font: 1*
- *Sunday Type*
- *Ellen Lupton. The Movie*

Subscribe to iLT
Content RSS
Comments RSS
Subscribe via Email
6948 readers

November Fonts:
FF Meta Serif
Le Monde Livre
Fontin
Fontin sans

John Boardley

Home sweet home | Typography tags | Identify a font | Who Shot the Serif? | Send a message | iLT wallpaper | About iLT | RSS Subscribe

I love
typography

Nov 14 2007 type a response!

At last! FF Meta Serif

WEDDING BELLS

I would usually never post two articles in a single day (I won't be making a habit of it). However, the excitement was just too much, and the news too hot. Many of you will be familiar with Spiekermann's wonderful FF Meta. But for years FF Meta lived a lonely existence with no Serif companion to keep it company. Well, now FF Meta has a wife; meet Mrs FF Meta, officially called FF Meta Serif.

FF Meta® Serif Pro

Mărië

Recommended

Thinking With Type — Ellen Lupton
Designing Type — Karen Cheng
The Elements *of* Typographic Style — Bringhurst
Stop Stealing Sheep & Find Out How Type Works
Type: The Secret History of Letters — Loxley
The Complete Manual of Typography — Felici

Recent Articles

Sunday Type: National Feijoa
At last! FF Meta Serif
Widows and Orphans
Smashing Free Fonts
Type Terms: Humanist
FONT Magazine
The apostrophe: Contrary to popular belief, it doesn't swing both ways
So You Want to Create a Font: 2

Subscribe to iLT
Content RSS
Comments RSS
Subscribe via Email
6948 readers

November Fonts:
FF Meta Serif
Le Monde Livre

Typograph

Oct 31 2007 type a response!

The apostrophe: Contrary to popular belief, it doesn't swing both ways

BY JULIE ELMAN

I admit it. I have a serious apostrophe pet peeve. I hate to see backwards apostrophes used in place of omitted letters.

Example: I'm really into rock 'n' roll, especially from the '60s.

'60s

Those reversed marks get me every time. Might as well just stick the sharp end of an apostrophe in my eye. Whenever I see the marks used improperly on television

Recommended

Thinking With Type — Ellen Lupton
Designing Type — Karen Cheng
The Elements *of* Typographic Style — Bringhurst
Stop Stealing Sheep & Find Out How Type Works
Type: The Secret History of Letters — Loxley
The Complete Manual of Typography — Felici

Recent Articles

Sunday Type: National Feijoa
At last! FF Meta Serif
Widows and Orphans
Smashing Free Fonts
Type Terms: Humanist
FONT Magazine
The apostrophe: Contrary to popular belief, it doesn't swing both ways
So You Want to Create a Font: 2
Sunday Type: Spiekermann
Made With FontFont
So You Want to Create a Font: 1
Sunday Type
Ellen Lupton. The Movie

Subscribe to iLT
Content RSS
Comments RSS
Subscribe via Email
6948 readers

November Fonts:
FF Meta Serif
Le Monde Livre
Fontin
Fontin sans

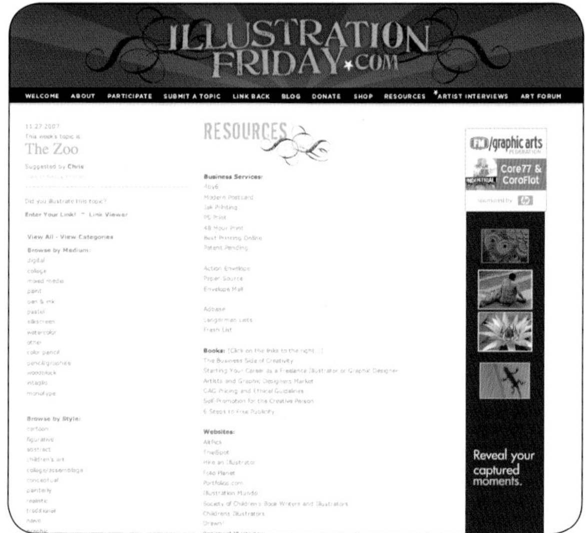

Penelope Dullaghan, Brianna Privett

ILLUSTRATION FRIDAY.COM
WELCOME ABOUT PARTICIPATE SUBMIT A TOPIC LINK BACK BLOG DONATE SHOP RESOURCES ARTIST INTERVIEWS ART FORUM
IF Bloggers
Archive
Flickr Recent:
the IF BLOG
Selvedge!
selvedge
graphic arts
COLOURLovers
Reveal the radiance of the shot.

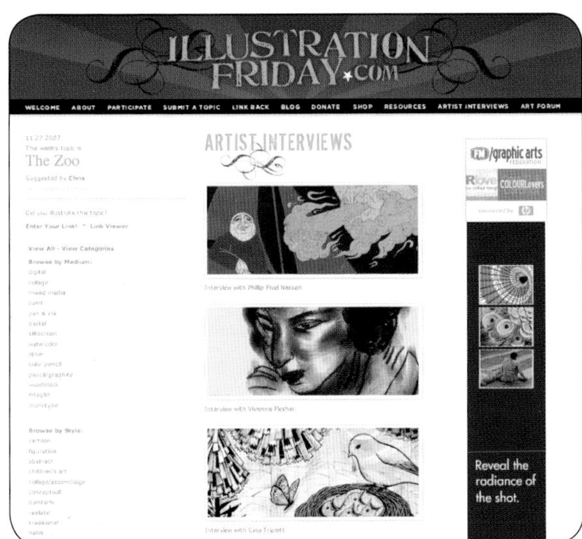
ILLUSTRATION FRIDAY.COM
WELCOME ABOUT PARTICIPATE SUBMIT A TOPIC LINK BACK BLOG DONATE SHOP RESOURCES ARTIST INTERVIEWS ART FORUM
The Zoo
ARTIST INTERVIEWS
graphic arts
COLOURLovers
Reveal the radiance of the shot.

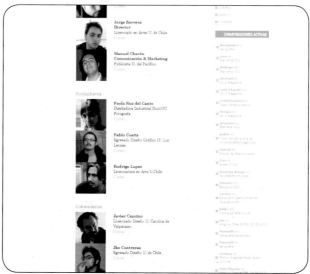

Richard González, Jorge Barrera, Rodrigo Haverbeck, Nolo Chacón, Javier Cancino

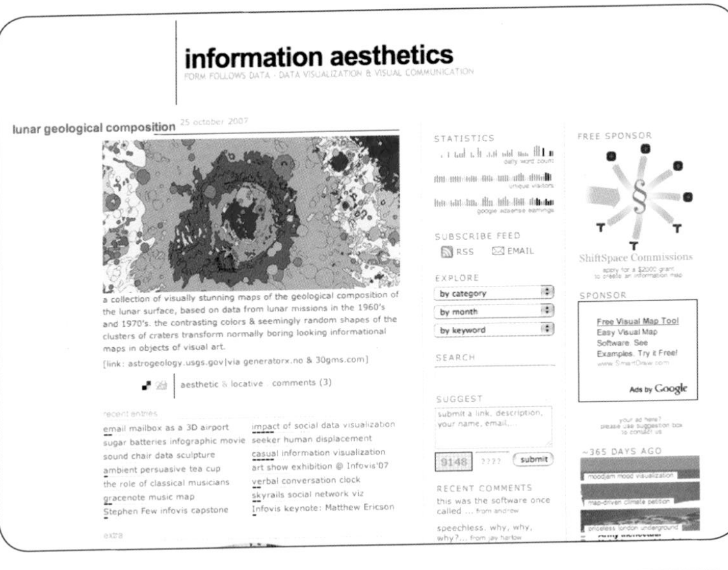

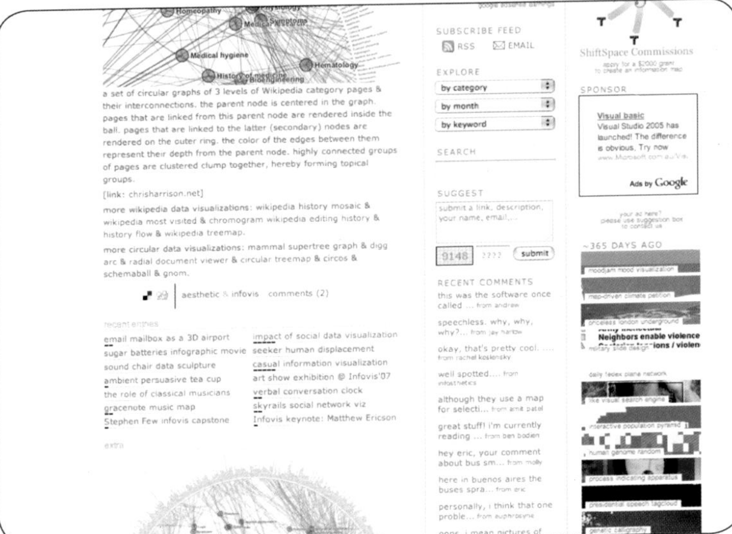

Andrew Vande Moere

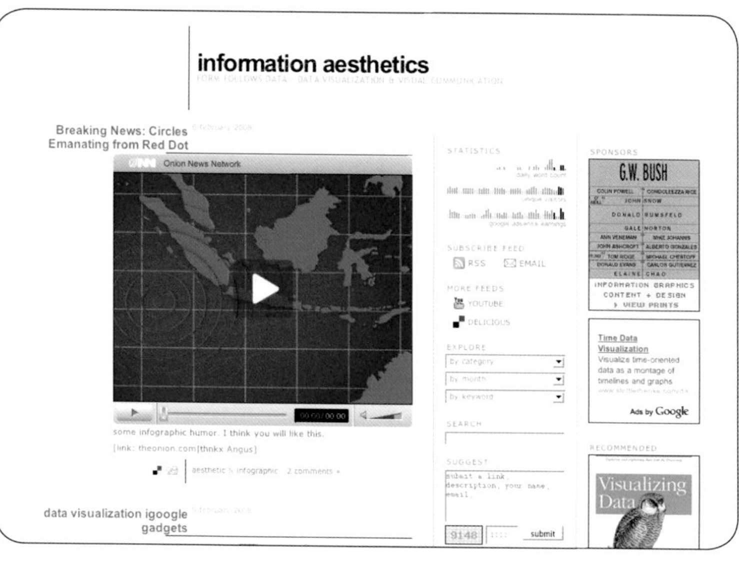
information aesthetics
FORM FOLLOWS DATA - DATA VISUALIZATION & VISUAL COMMUNICATION
Breaking News: Circles Emanating from Red Dot
Onion News Network
some infographic humor. I think you will like this.
[link: theonion.com|thnkx Angus]
aesthetic & infographic . 2 comments »
data visualization igoogle gadgets
STATISTICS
SUBSCRIBE FEED
RSS
EMAIL
MORE FEEDS
YOUTUBE
DELICIOUS
EXPLORE
by category
by month
by keyword
SEARCH
SUGGEST
submit a link, description, your name, email,
9148
submit
SPONSORS
G.W. BUSH
INFORMATION GRAPHICS
CONTENT + DESIGN
VIEW PRINTS
Time Data Visualization
Visualize time-oriented data as a montage of timelines and graphs
Ads by Google
RECOMMENDED
Visualizing Data

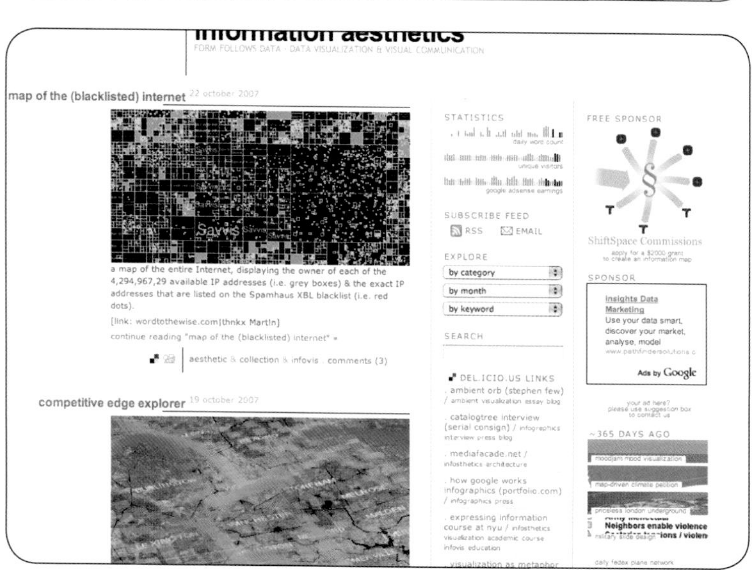
information aesthetics
FORM FOLLOWS DATA - DATA VISUALIZATION & VISUAL COMMUNICATION
map of the (blacklisted) internet 22 october 2007
a map of the entire Internet, displaying the owner of each of the 4,294,967,29 available IP addresses (i.e. grey boxes) & the exact IP addresses that are listed on the Spamhaus XBL blacklist (i.e. red dots).
[link: wordtothewise.com|thnkx Martin]
continue reading "map of the (blacklisted) internet" »
aesthetic & collection & infovis . comments (3)
competitive edge explorer 19 october 2007
STATISTICS
SUBSCRIBE FEED
RSS
EMAIL
EXPLORE
by category
by month
by keyword
SEARCH
DEL.ICIO.US LINKS
. ambient orb (stephen few)
. catalogtree interview (serial consign)
. mediafacade.net /
. how google works infographics (portfolio.com)
. expressing information course at nyu
. visualization as metaphor
FREE SPONSOR
ShiftSpace Commissions
apply for a $2000 grant to create an information map
SPONSOR
Insights Data Marketing
Use your data smart, discover your market, analyse, model
Ads by Google
~365 DAYS AGO
moodjam mood visualization
map-driven climate petition
priceless london underground
Neighbors enable violence
military slide design

About

Submit

Categories
Advertising (7)
Animation (18)
Architecture (5)
Art (41)
Books (6)
Events (3)
Exhibitions (8)
Fashion (9)
Film (31)
Graphic Design (155)
Illustration (174)
Interiors (2)
It's Nice That (13)
It's Not Us (56)
Miscellaneous (30)
Music (43)
Photography (83)
Product Design (53)
Publications (9)
Web (34)
Writing (2)

Archive
April 2007
May 2007
June 2007
July 2007
August 2007
September 2007
October 2007
November 2007

Links

Facebook

Myspace

Contact

Search

It's Not Us

It's Not Us

SECOND HAND PHOTOGRAPH
It's Not Us, Photography

Here's Carson's choice for this Friday.

'I have a collection of weird, old photographs and this one is by far my favourite. It doesn't seem possible that this women exists in the same age as photography. She looks like she lives in Narnia. The photo's very small – 2.5" x 4" – and it sits on the window sill of my kitchen so I look at it a lot while doing the dishes. I made a drawing of it, but it pales in comparison.'

Again, here's a large scale version for your enjoyment.

Posted by Not Us / Oct 26, 2007

It's Not Us

CARSON ELLIS
It's Not Us, Illustration

We're honoured to have Carson Ellis joining us for this week's It's Not Us. Carson is one of the most distinctive American illustrative voices today, mixing folk art, fantasy and skewed naturalism. You might also know her as the lady behind the artwork of the Decemberists, which is where her submission comes from.

'I was reluctant to choose a Decemberists poster for my submission because I do do other stuff, but this is one of my favourite drawings of the past month. For the first time since I starting

MATEUS ACIOLI
Graphic Design, Illustration

Mateus has recently finished his design and illustration portfolio, it's all in portugese but thats not a problem.

www.mateusacioli.com

Posted by Will / Sep 30, 2007

POSTER PROJECT
Illustration

Poster is a self initiated project by Barcelona designer Dani Navarro. Aiming to rediscover the poster format as a work support and graphic experimentation Dani has invited 10 designers to participate in the project.

Supported by Arjowiggins and Arts Gràfiques Orient each print is on a different stock and the first three are available now, including this one from Lamosca.

www.poster-project.info

Posted by Will / Sep 29, 2007

RSS / Atom

Will Hudson, Jez Burrows

IT'S NICE THAT

About

Submit

Categories

Archive

Links

Facebook

Myspace

Contact

Search

RSS : Atom

ASGER CARLEN

Photography

Thanks again to Halvar for pointing us in the direction of this one. Danish photographer Asger Carlen.

www.asgercarlen.com

Posted by Will | Oct 31, 2007

"I'm not writing it down to remember it later
I'm writing it down to remember it now"

FIELD NOTES™

FIELD NOTES

Product Design, Miscellaneous

A joint project between DDC and Coudal, Field Notes are handsome soft-cover graph paper notebooks similar to the Moleskin Cahiers. Inspired by the vanishing subgenre of agricultural memo books, ornate pocket ledgers and simple, unassuming beauty of a well crafted grocery list'. Entirely set in Futura and complete with a list of practical applications, including 'Hate Mail', 'Gambling Debts' and 'Loose Promises', they're a fine addition to that pile of blank notebooks you bought but probably won't use for a good few years. You can see plenty of them in the wild here.

www.fieldnotesbrand.com

Posted by Jez | Oct 31, 2007

IT'S NICE THAT

About

Submit

Categories

Archive

Links

Facebook

Myspace

Contact

Search

RSS / Atom

It's Nice That

FACEBOOK

It's Nice That

We've finally given in and got ourselves a Facebook group. We hope to use it as an easier port of call for submissions, discussion and of course a bit of shameless self promotion. Come join us!

www.facebook.com/group...

Posted by Will | Oct 06, 2007

ALL MOVED IN

It's Nice That

After a few weeks of irregular posting I am pleased to announce all the boxes are unpacked and I am finally all moved in.

Please feel free to send anything nice to the new address, and thanks to everyone who already has. We've got some exciting plans in the pipeline and more news will follow shortly.

13 Humphrey Court
Battersea High Street
Battersea
London
SW11 3JA
United Kingdom

Posted by Will | Sep 02, 2007

LES VOYAGES AU CENTRE-VILLE DE
~ Jules Vernacular ~
TÉLÉFÉRIQUE DU BÉOUT
TÉLÉFÉRIQUE DU BÉOUT
CALENDRIER
« décembre 2007
L M M J V S D
1 2
3 4 5 6 7 8 9
10 11 12 13 14 15 16
17 18 19 20 21 22 23
24 25 26 27 28 29 30
31
RECHERCHER
ok
CATÉGORIES
Blackletter
Brush
Decorative & Display
Dingbats
Engraved
Geometric
Graffiti
Ligatures
Logos
Ornaments
Revival
Sans
Script
Serif
Shadowed / 3D
Slab
Stencil
Trash
Western
ARCHIVES
décembre 2007
novembre 2007
0 commentaire
CLAUDE NOGARO
Claude NOGARO

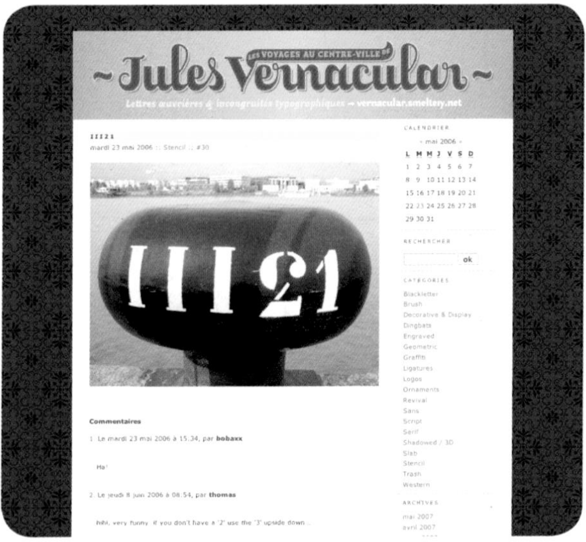

LES VOYAGES AU CENTRE-VILLE DE
~ Jules Vernacular ~
Lettres œuvrières & incongruités typographiques → vernacular.smeltery.net
11121
mardi 23 mai 2006 :: Stencil :: #30
11121
CALENDRIER
« mai 2006 »
L M M J V S D
1 2 3 4 5 6 7
8 9 10 11 12 13 14
15 16 17 18 19 20 21
22 23 24 25 26 27 28
29 30 31
RECHERCHER
ok
CATÉGORIES
Blackletter
Brush
Decorative & Display
Dingbats
Engraved
Geometric
Graffiti
Ligatures
Logos
Ornaments
Revival
Sans
Script
Serif
Shadowed / 3D
Slab
Stencil
Trash
Western
ARCHIVES
mai 2007
avril 2007
Commentaires
1. Le mardi 23 mai 2006 à 15.34, par bobaxx
Ha!
2. Le jeudi 8 juin 2006 à 08.54, par thomas
hihi, very funny. if you don't have a "2" use the "3" upside down...

Jack Usine

Les voyages au centre-ville de
~Jules Vernacular~
Lettres œuvrières & incongruités typographiques → vernacular.smeltery.net
VÉZIERS NICOLAS
mercredi 6 septembre 2006 :: Sans - Brush - Ligatures
VÉZIERS Nicolas
Plomberie Zinguerie
Chauffage Central
30570 VALLERAUGUE Tél : 67-82-20-53
0 commentaire
COIFFEUR
jeudi 10 août 2006 :: Script - Ligatures
Enfants
CALENDRIER
« septembre 2006
L M M J V S D
1 2 3
4 5 6 7 8 9 10
11 12 13 14 15 16 17
18 19 20 21 22 23 24
25 26 27 28 29 30
RECHERCHER
ok
CATÉGORIES
Blackletter
Brush
Decorative & Display
Dingbats
Engraved
Geometric
Graffiti
Ligatures
Logos
Ornaments
Revival
Sans
Script
Serif
Shadowed / 3D
Slab
Stencil
Trash
Western
ARCHIVES
septembre 2006
août 2006

Serif
Shadowed / 3D
Slab
Stencil
Trash
Western
0 commentaire
IBARBOURE ARTISAN BOUCHER
dimanche 20 mai 2007 :: Decorative & Display - Shadowed / 3D
BOUCHERIE
IBARBOURE ARTISAN BOUCHER
0 commentaire
MARINE NATIONALE
mercredi 9 mai 2007 :: Shadowed / 3D - Sans
MARINE
ARCHIVES
mai 2007
avril 2007
février 2007
janvier 2007
décembre 2006
novembre 2006
octobre 2006
septembre 2006
août 2006
juin 2006
avril 2006
LIENS
SMeltery
Usine.name
Sainte-Machine
Bordel
le Vilain
TT
CONTACT
vernacular@smeltery.net
SYNDICATION
fil rss
fil atom
PROPULSION
Dotclear

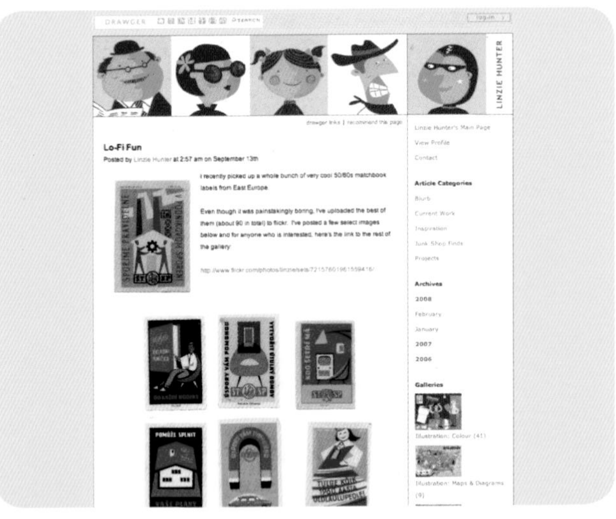

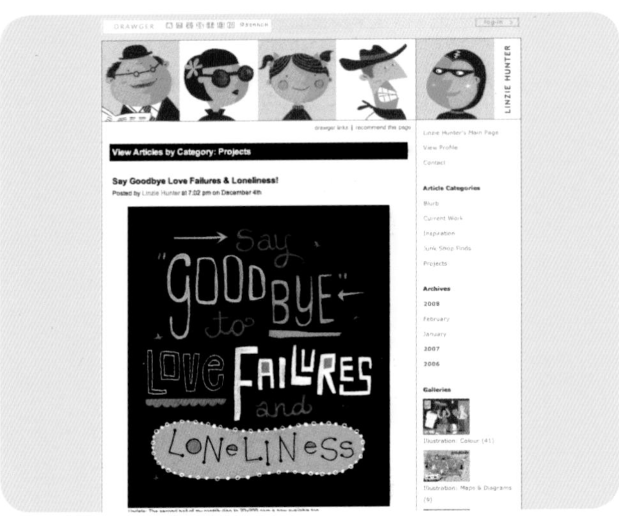

Robert Zimmerman, Linzie Hunter

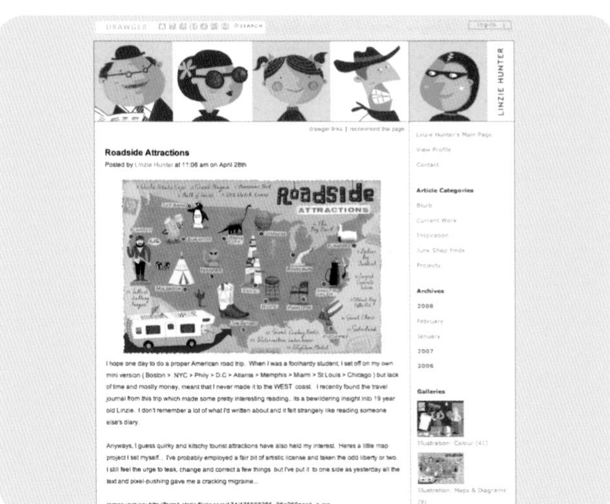
DRAWGER
LINZIE HUNTER
drawger links | recommend this page
Roadside Attractions
Posted by Linzie Hunter at 11:06 am on April 28th
Roadside
ATTRACTIONS
I hope one day to do a proper American road trip. When I was a foolhardy student, I set off on my own mini version (Boston > NYC > Phily > D.C > Atlanta > Memphis > Miami > St Louis > Chicago) but lack of time and mostly money, meant that I never made it to the WEST coast. I recently found the travel journal from this trip which made some pretty interesting reading.. its a bewildering insight into 19 year old Linzie. I don't remember a lot of what I'd written about and it felt strangely like reading someone else's diary.
Anyways, I guess quirky and kitschy tourist attractions have also held my interest. Heres a little map project I set myself... I've probably employed a fair bit of artistic license and taken the odd liberty or two. I still feel the urge to teak, change and correct a few things but I've put it to one side as yesterday all the text and pixel-pushing gave me a cracking migraine...
larger version: http://farm1.static.flickr.com/174/475568285_06e250aac1_o.jpg
Linzie Hunter's Main Page
View Profile
Contact
Article Categories
Blurb
Current Work
Inspiration
Junk Shop Finds
Projects
Archives
2008
February
January
2007
2006
Galleries
Illustration: Colour (41)
Illustration: Maps & Diagrams (9)

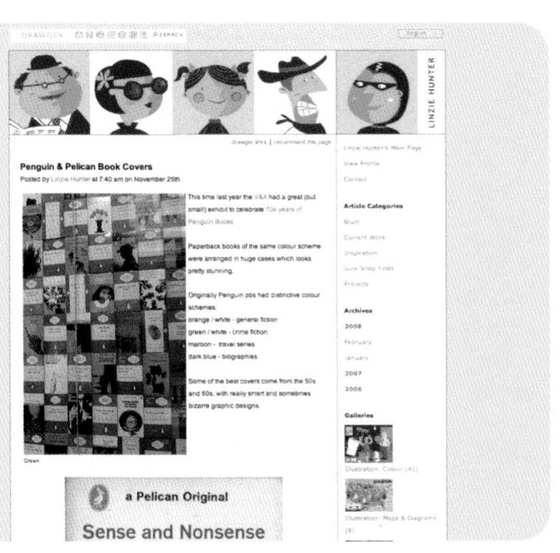
DRAWGER
LINZIE HUNTER
drawger links | recommend this page
Penguin & Pelican Book Covers
Posted by Linzie Hunter at 7:40 am on November 25th
This time last year the V&A had a great (but small) exhibit to celebrate 70s years of Penguin Books
Paperback books of the same colour scheme were arranged in huge cases which looks pretty stunning.
Originally Penguin pbs had distinctive colour schemes:
orange / white - general fiction
green / white - crime fiction
maroon - travel series
dark blue - biographies.
Some of the best covers come from the 50s and 60s, with really smart and sometimes bizarre graphic designs.
Green
a Pelican Original
Sense and Nonsense
Linzie Hunter's Main Page
View Profile
Contact
Article Categories
Blurb
Current Work
Inspiration
Junk Shop Finds
Projects
Archives
2008
February
January
2007
2006
Galleries
Illustration: Colour (41)
Illustration: Maps & Diagrams (9)

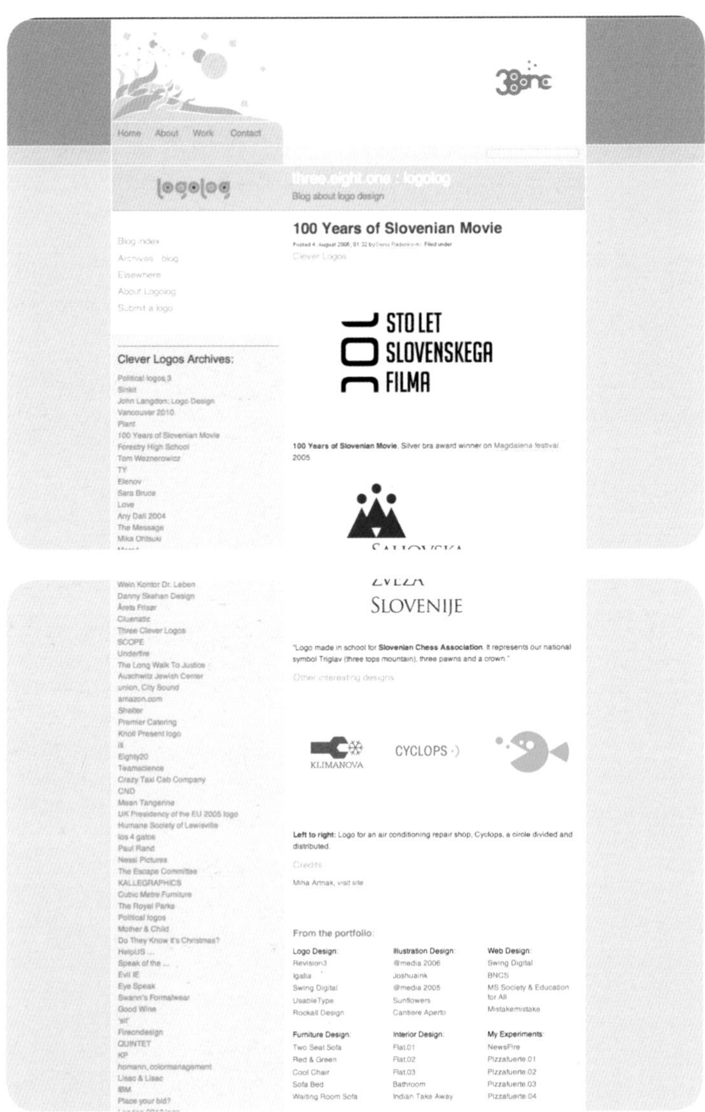

Denis Radenkovic

Download
NewsFire
replacement icon

SINKIT

SINKIT

Refinement

The majority of this stage is spent on refining each character and their relationships. The example below shows the approaches we took in balancing the "S".

Credits

Designer: Peter Pimentel
Design firm: smashLAB

Text and graphics © smashLAB

From the portfolio:

Logo Design:	Illustration Design:	Web Design:
Revision3	@media 2006	Swing Digital
Igalia	Joshuaink	BNCS
Swing Digital	@media 2005	MS Society & Education for All
UsableType	Sunflowers	Mistakemistake
Rockall Design	Cantiere Aperto	

Furniture Design:	Interior Design:	My Experiments:
Two Seat Sofa	Flat.01	NewsFire
Red & Green	Flat.02	Pizzafuerte.01
Cool Chair	Flat.03	Pizzafuerte.02
Sofa Bed	Bathroom	Pizzafuerte.03
Waiting Room Sofa	Indian Take Away	Pizzafuerte.04

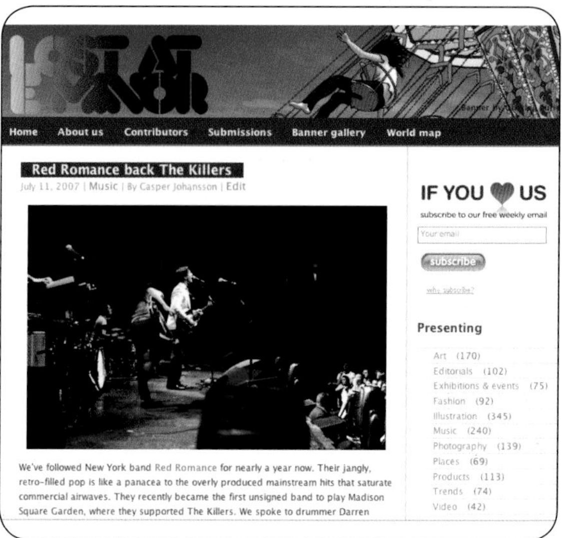

Zolton Zavos, Zac Zavos

Niki Fisher
July 11, 2007 | Illustration | By Zolton | Edit
Australian freelance graphic designer and illustrator Niki Fisher initially wanted to be a fashion designer because 'I would only draw women' but quickly transferred to graphic design when she sound out that she 'hated everything about fashion except for the illustration component'. [see also Tiffany Bozic]
Share this | Email this
Have your say
Recent comments
Chris Knight on Erland Oye
Marcus and Cheryl Johanson on Peter Lik
Zac on Me, Wii
Mark Shepherd on Califone
Josh Fields on Peter Lik
Keywords
acoustic alone beatles beauty birds black and white blue canada cartoon collaboration colour cute dance design disco dreams electro electronica evocative girls hip hop jewellery los angeles Melbourne melbourne melodic movement nature new york pattern philosophy pop pop art pop music portrait portraits red sensual sex sexy shadows shape silence sketch sleek soul surreal surrealism sydney t-shirt

Listen
Discuss
Read
- Chris Knight "Which is strangely ironic considering the...
- Marcus and Cheryl Johanson "Hi Sarah and Sam, certainly...
- Josh Fields "Hello Sarah, sorry to disappoint, and...
- Zac "Yes - a professional I'd love to be! What a great...
- Mark Shepherd "Long time fan - one of the best labels...
- Zolton "whoops! thanks for reminding us. we've updated...
- I.love.moby "UK producer? What are you talking...
- Brandi Hampton "This is probably the one of the most...
View
Explore
Subscribe
Art Editorials Exhibitions & events Fashion Illustration Music Photography Places Products Trends Video
email address
Subscribe
NEW Once a week is not enough... click here to receive a daily dose of creativity from Lost At E Minor.

Every Morning, I check Manystuff

Vendredi 03 Novembre 2006

Pierre Vanni

MANYSTUFF

or Many things to be seen!

Art, Graphic Design, Illustration, Photography ...
Daily Updates!

Links and images, click!

email

Catégories

Manystuff (13)
Graphic'design (477)
Illustration, painting (145)
Photography (112)

Jeudi 15 Mars 2007

1

Manystuff celebrates its one year !!!

For the ten first to ask it, some stickers and others "goodies" .... just send an email (indicate your postal address)

publié par charlotte c. dans

Mardi 16 Janvier 2007

About you

Manystuff and you

MANYSTUFF

or Many things to be seen!

Art, Graphic Design, Illustration, Photography ...
Daily Updates!

Links and images, click!

email

Catégories

Manystuff (13)
Graphic'design (477)
Illustration, painting (145)
Photography (112)
Varied images (180)
Miscellaneous (18)

Favourites

Pierre Vanni
As-found
Le club des chevreuils
NewsToday
neubau
Michael C. Place (Build)
MM
Pleix
Maskara
Shift
IDN
D*I*R*T*Y
Universal Everything
Laurent Fetis
Trafik
Computer love

Charlotte Cheetham

Every
Morning,
I check
Manystuff

Lundi 02 Avril 2007

Emilie Rigaud

MANYSTUFF

or Many things to be seen!

Art, Graphic Design, Illustration, Photography ...
Daily Updates!

Links and images, click!

email

Catégories

Manystuff (13)
Graphic'design (477)
Illustration, painting (145)
Photography (112)

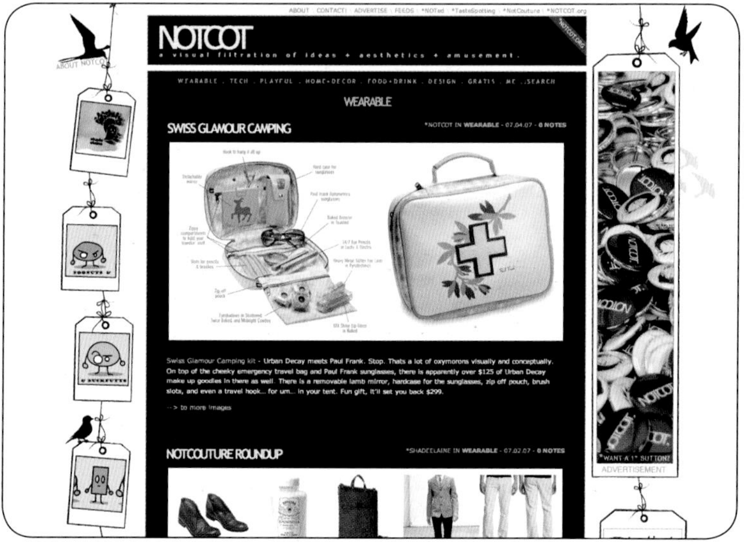

Jean Aw, Daniel Frysinger

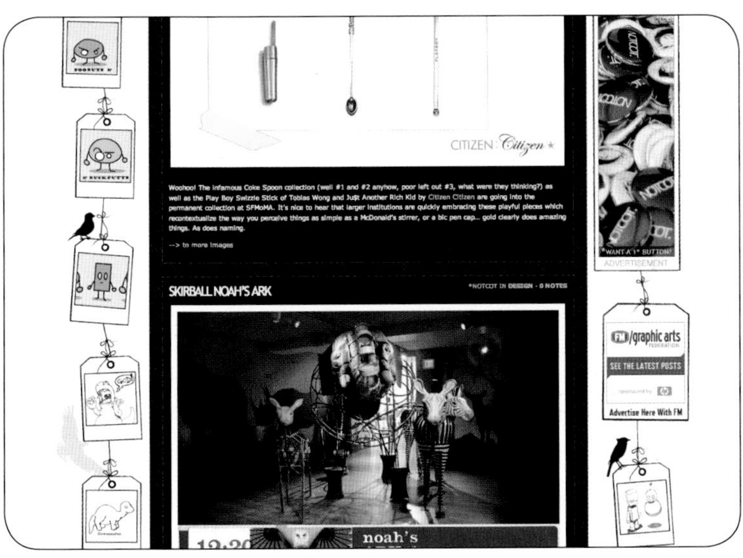
CITIZEN : Citizen ★
Woohoo! The infamous Coke Spoon collection (well #1 and #2 anyhow, poor left out #3, what were they thinking?) as well as the Play Boy Swizzle Stick of Tobias Wong and Ju$t Another Rich Kid by Citizen Citizen are going into the permanent collection at SFMoMA. It's nice to hear that larger institutions are quickly embracing these playful pieces which recontextualize the way you perceive things as simple as a McDonald's stirrer, or a bic pen cap... gold clearly does amazing things. As does naming.
--> to more images
"WANT A 1" BUTTON?
ADVERTISEMENT
SKIRBALL NOAH'S ARK
*NOTCOT IN DESIGN - 0 NOTES
FM/graphic arts FEDERATION
SEE THE LATEST POSTS
Advertise Here With FM
noah's

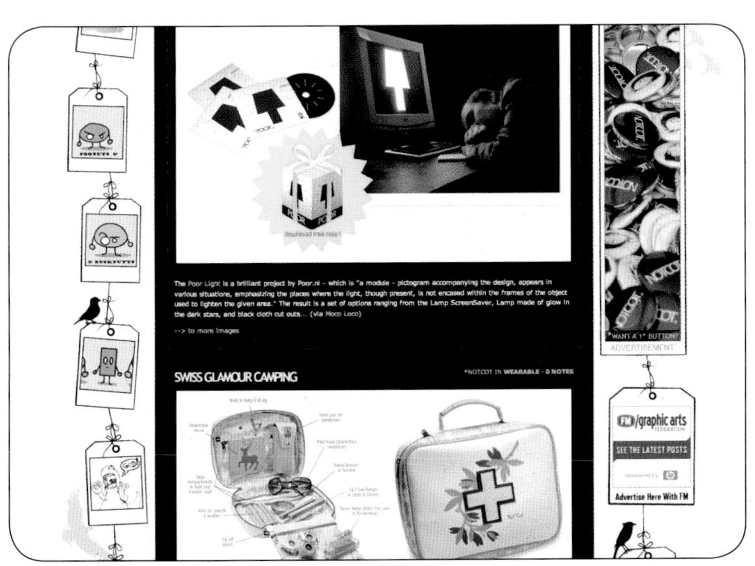
download free now!
The Poor Light is a brilliant project by Poor.nl - which is "a module - pictogram accompanying the design, appears in various situations, emphasizing the places where the light, though present, is not encased within the frames of the object used to lighten the given area." The result is a set of options ranging from the Lamp ScreenSaver, Lamp made of glow in the dark stars, and black cloth cut outs... (via Moco Loco)
--> to more images
"WANT A 1" BUTTON?
ADVERTISEMENT
SWISS GLAMOUR CAMPING
*NOTCOT IN WEARABLE - 0 NOTES
FM/graphic arts FEDERATION
SEE THE LATEST POSTS
Advertise Here With FM

LAST ENTRIES | O.K. BLOG
Primitive Art

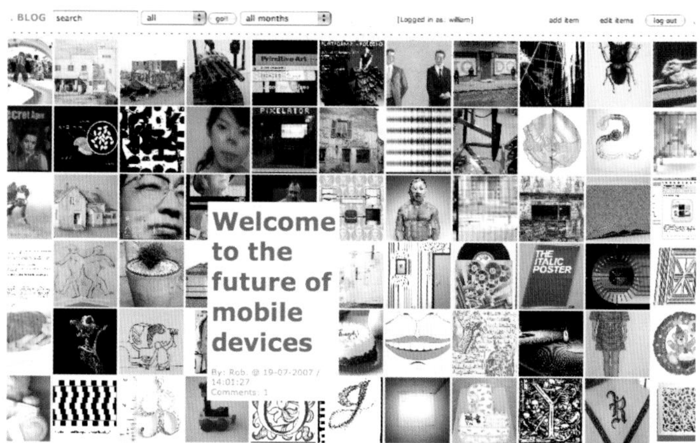
BLOG search all go! all months
[Logged in as: william]
add item edit items log out
Welcome to the future of mobile devices
By: Rob. @ 19-07-2007 / 14:01:27
Comments: 1
THE ITALIC POSTER
PIXELATOR
1 2 3 4 5 6 7 >>

O.K. Parking

Comments:

kijk ook even verder op het blog naar the LOWRES MAN, het werk van Thomas Broome (of gebruik de zoekfunctie bovenaan de pagina)

By: willem • 02-07-2007 / 16:33:10 | @ | www

nog meer lego via mooonriver:

Michael Kovner is an Israeli artist. from his exhibition 'Images

http://mooonriver.blogspot.com/2007/06/images.html

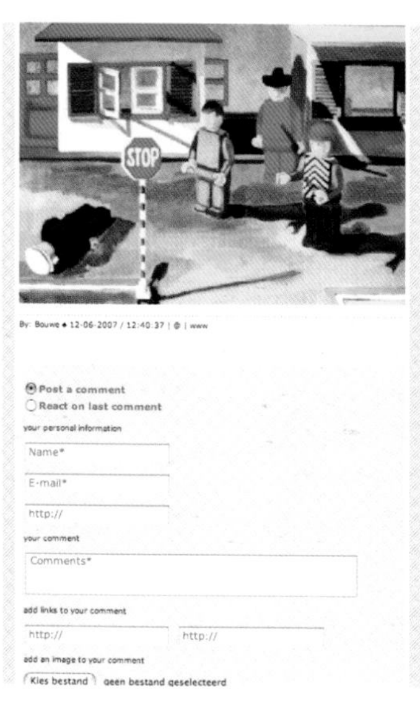

Papel Continuo

Diseño, arte, música, cultura popular y freakismos retroactivos.

16 Recortables de papel continuo

Lo que hace el aburrimiento.

Me he hecho un recortable con el logo de Papel Continuo.
Se lo pueden descargar aquí en PDF: recortable
Y aquí está el recortable en jpg, por si a alguien le apetece editarlo o cambiarle los colores.

Si alguien se anima a montarlo, que me mande una foto a impresor arroba papelcontinuo punto net, antes del 16 de octubre. Los iré subiendo a este Set de fotos, y sortearemos entre todos un par de camisetas de Papel Continuo.

Nota: Es preferible imprimirlo en un A3 si no os quereis quedar ciegos doblando las patitas...

Inicio

Categorias

Arte
Bannerismos
Cartoon
Cine
Cómic
Demencia
Diseño
Ediciones Discontinuas
Fotografía
General
Ilustracion
Link-o-rama
Música
Ocio
Retro
Video

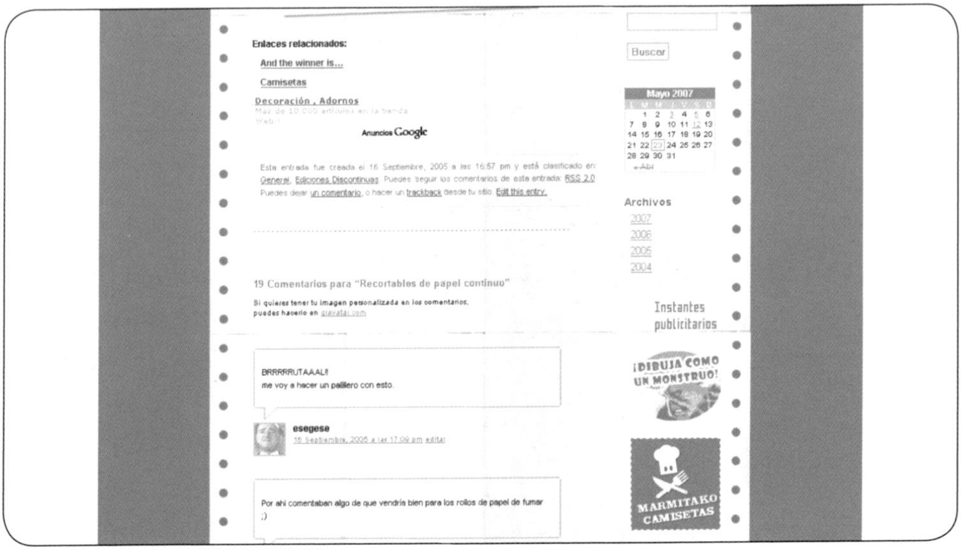

Enlaces relacionados:

And the winner is...

Camisetas

Decoración , Adornos

Anuncios Google

Esta entrada fue creada el 16 Septiembre, 2005 a las 16:57 pm y está clasificado en: General, Ediciones Discontinuas. Puedes seguir los comentarios de esta entrada: RSS 2.0 Puedes dejar un comentario, o hacer un trackback desde tu sitio. Edit this entry.

Buscar

Mayo 2007

Archivos

2007
2006
2005
2004

19 Comentarios para "Recortables de papel continuo"

Si quieres tener tu imagen personalizada en los comentarios, puedes hacerlo en gravatar.com

Instantes publicitarios

BRRRRRUTAAAL!!
me voy a hacer un palillero con esto.

esegese
16 Septiembre, 2005 a las 17:09 pm editar

¡DIBUJA COMO UN MONSTRUO!

Por ahí comentaban algo de que vendría bien para los rollos de papel de fumar
;)

MARMITAKO CAMISETAS

Paulo Carvajal, Diego Sanz (karramarro)

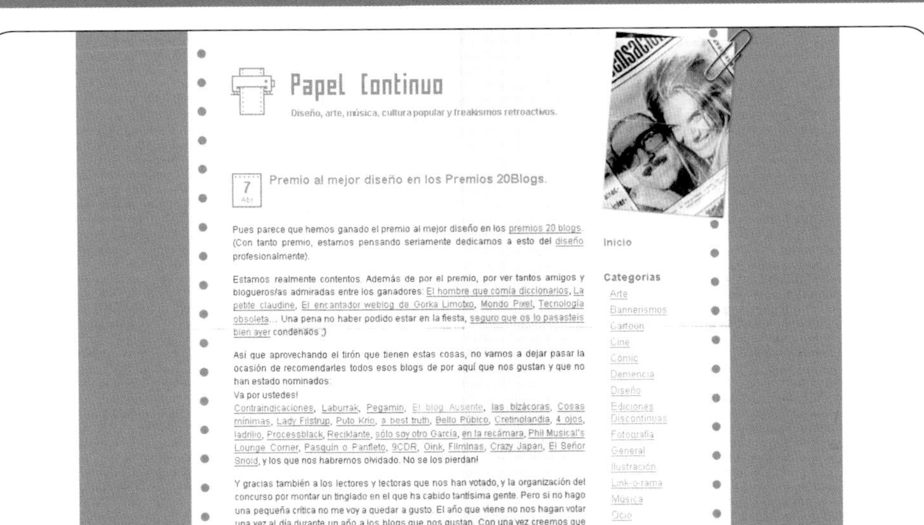

Papel Continuo

Diseño, arte, música, cultura popular y freakismos retroactivos.

7 Abr

Premio al mejor diseño en los Premios 20Blogs.

Pues parece que hemos ganado el premio al mejor diseño en los premios 20 blogs. (Con tanto premio, estamos pensando seriamente dedicarnos a esto del diseño profesionalmente).

Estamos realmente contentos. Además de por el premio, por ver tantos amigos y blogueros/as admiradas entre los ganadores: El hombre que comía diccionarios, La petite claudine, El encantador weblog de Gorka Limotxo, Mondo Pixel, Tecnología obsoleta... Una pena no haber podido estar en la fiesta, seguro que os lo pasasteis bien ayer condenaos ;)

Así que aprovechando el tirón que tienen estas cosas, no vamos a dejar pasar la ocasión de recomendarles todos esos blogs de por aquí que nos gustan y que no han estado nominados:
Va por ustedes!
Contraindicaciones, Laburrak, Pegamin, El blog Ausente, las bizácoras, Cosas mínimas, Lady Filstrup, Puto Krio, a best truth, Bello Público, Cretinolandia, 4 ojos, ladrillo, Processblack, Reciklante, sólo soy otro García, en la recámara, Phil Musical's Lounge Corner, Pasquín o Panfleto, 9CDR, Oink, Filminas, Crazy Japan, El Señor Snoid, y los que nos habremos olvidado. No se los pierdan!

Y gracias también a los lectores y lectoras que nos han votado, y la organización del concurso por montar un tinglado en el que ha cabido tantísima gente. Pero si no hago una pequeña crítica no me voy a quedar a gusto. El año que viene no nos hagan votar una vez al día durante un año a los blogs que nos gustan. Con una vez creemos que es suficiente ;)

Inicio

Categorias
Arte
Bannerismos
Cartoon
Cine
Cómic
Demencia
Diseño
Ediciones Discontinuas
Fotografía
General
Ilustración
Link-o-rama
Música
Ocio
Retro
Video

concurso por montar un tinglado en el que ha cabido tantísima gente. Pero si no hago una pequeña crítica no me voy a quedar a gusto. El año que viene no nos hagan votar una vez al día durante un año a los blogs que nos gustan. Con una vez creemos que es suficiente ;)

Los Trash Hunters del equipo de Papel Continuo, celebrando el premio.

Enlaces relacionados:

Bloggies, 20 Blogs y concursismos varios.

II Edición de los premios 20 Blogs.

Creación de Logos Únicos
2900 PreDiseños Notables e Inéditos
Diseño de Logos a Medida & Rediseño
Anuncios Google

Esta entrada fue creada el 7 Abril, 2006 a las 10:35 am y está clasificado en General, Diseño. Puedes seguir los comentarios de esta entrada: RSS 2.0. Puedes dejar un comentario, o hacer un trackback desde tu sitio. Edit this entry.

Música
Ocio
Retro
Video

Papel Continuo en tu Email

Buscar

Buscar

Mayo 2007						
L	M	M	J	V	S	D
	1	2	3	4	5	6
7	8	9	10	11	12	13
14	15	16	17	18	19	20
21	22	23	24	25	26	27
28	29	30	31			

« Abr

Archivos
2007
2006
2005
2004

Instantes publicitarios

¡DIBUJA COMO UN MONSTRUO!

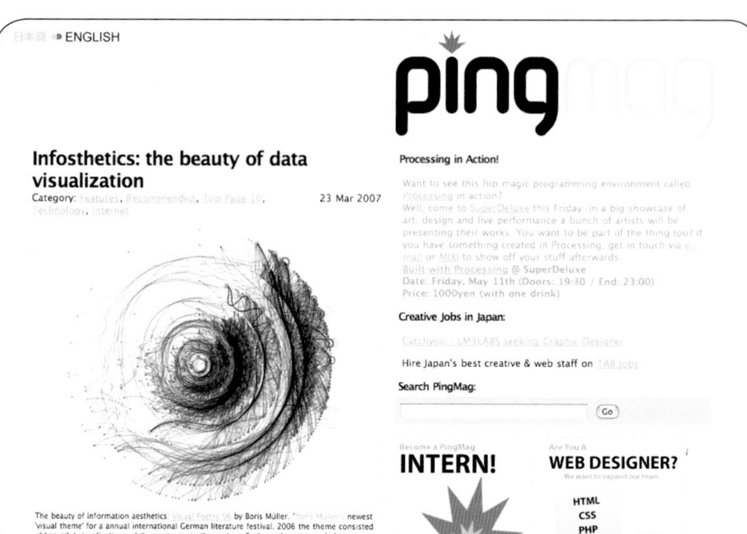

ENGLISH
ping
Infosthetics: the beauty of data visualization
Category:
23 Mar 2007
Processing in Action!
Built with Processing @ SuperDeluxe
Date: Friday, May 11th (Doors: 19:30 / End: 23:00)
Price: 1000yen (with one drink)
Creative Jobs in Japan:
Hire Japan's best creative & web staff on
Search PingMag:
Go
INTERN!
WEB DESIGNER?
HTML
CSS
PHP
MySQL
Click for Details
The beauty of information aesthetics: by Boris Müller. newest 'visual theme' for a annual international German literature festival. 2006 the theme consisted of beautiful visualizations of the poetry texts themselves. Each word corresponded to a numerical code by adding the alphabetical values of its letters together. This number was

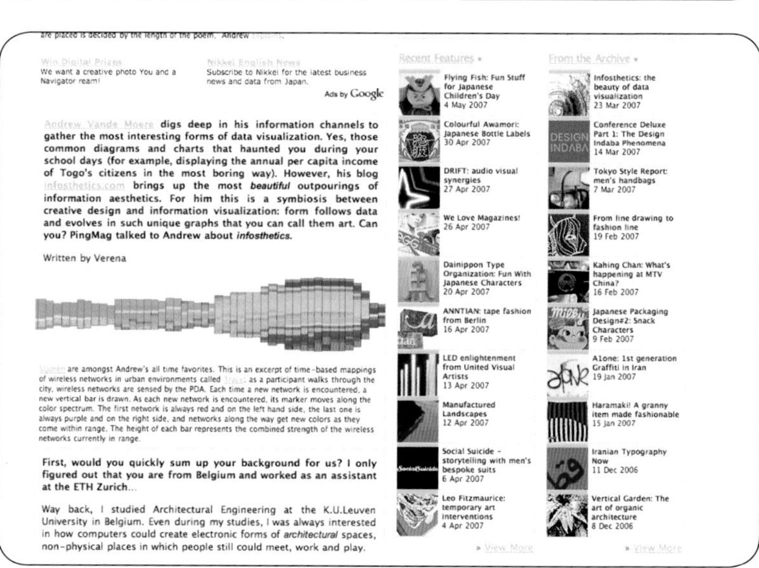

are placed is decided by the length of the poem." Andrew
We want a creative photo You and a Navigator ream!
Subscribe to Nikkei for the latest business news and data from Japan.
Ads by Google
digs deep in his information channels to gather the most interesting forms of data visualization. Yes, those common diagrams and charts that haunted you during your school days (for example, displaying the annual per capita income of Togo's citizens in the most boring way). However, his blog brings up the most beautiful outpourings of information aesthetics. For him this is a symbiosis between creative design and information visualization: form follows data and evolves in such unique graphs that you can call them art. Can you? PingMag talked to Andrew about infosthetics.
Written by Verena
are amongst Andrew's all time favorites. This is an excerpt of time-based mappings of wireless networks in urban environments called as a participant walks through the city, wireless networks are sensed by the PDA. Each time a new network is encountered, a new vertical bar is drawn. As each new network is encountered, its marker moves along the color spectrum. The first network is always red and on the left hand side, the last one is always purple and on the right side, and networks along the way get new colors as they come within range. The height of each bar represents the combined strength of the wireless networks currently in range.
First, would you quickly sum up your background for us? I only figured out that you are from Belgium and worked as an assistant at the ETH Zurich...
Way back, I studied Architectural Engineering at the K.U.Leuven University in Belgium. Even during my studies, I was always interested in how computers could create electronic forms of architectural spaces, non-physical places in which people still could meet, work and play.
Flying Fish: Fun Stuff for Japanese Children's Day 4 May 2007
Colourful Awamori: Japanese Bottle Labels 30 Apr 2007
DRIFT: audio visual synergies 27 Apr 2007
We Love Magazines! 26 Apr 2007
Dainippon Type Organization: Fun With Japanese Characters 20 Apr 2007
ANNTIAN: tape fashion from Berlin 16 Apr 2007
LED enlightenment from United Visual Artists 13 Apr 2007
Manufactured Landscapes 12 Apr 2007
Social Suicide - storytelling with men's bespoke suits 6 Apr 2007
Leo Fitzmaurice: temporary art interventions 4 Apr 2007
Infosthetics: the beauty of data visualization 23 Mar 2007
Conference Deluxe Part 1: The Design Indaba Phenomena 14 Mar 2007
Tokyo Style Report: men's handbags 7 Mar 2007
From line drawing to fashion line 19 Feb 2007
Kahing Chan: What's happening at MTV China? 16 Feb 2007
Japanese Packaging Design#2: Snack Characters 9 Feb 2007
Alone: 1st generation Graffiti in Iran 19 Jan 2007
Haramaki! A granny item made fashionable 15 Jan 2007
Iranian Typography Now 11 Dec 2006
Vertical Garden: The art of organic architecture 8 Dec 2006

Yes! Communications (publisher)

Shelves stocked with Awamori in the Kusu Ber Karakara in Okinawa.

Awamori bottle labels are truly colourful, like this one with cute stylized nature elements such as water and blossoms. It is called 'Shinsen'.

This romantic motif including a drowning sun is called 'Tokiwa' - watch the storch...

What a combination: wallpaper and tree. 'Kumejima'

Seasers and yeast, called 'Miyano Hana'.

May 2007
April 2007
March 2007
February 2007
January 2007
December 2006
November 2006
October 2006
September 2006
August 2006
July 2006
June 2006
May 2006
April 2006
March 2006
February 2006
January 2006
December 2005
November 2005
October 2005
September 2005
August 2005
July 2005
June 2005
May 2005
April 2005

By Full List

» Full Archive List

Feed

» 

Icon Magazine »
Super Deluxe »
Tokyo Art Beat »
WMMNA »

'Awanami'

'Terushima'

'A name that means the finest': 'Zuisen' (left). 'Manza' (right) has a lovely combination of a bright green tree with white crests.

Nice design: 'Tama no tsuyu'

Sakura, cherry blossoms, for a floral note: 'Sakura ichiban'

Awamori: Become An Expert in 5 Minutes! (huh, we didn't mean the drinking aspect...)

Here are a few facts for you to show off: as mentioned before, Awamori has hardly any sugar contents. As a consequence, compared with beer or sake it is a low calorie drink and can actually improve your blood circulation... As long as you don't drink too much, of course! Smell and taste are quite unique which won't make you forget

print & pattern
fabric wallpaper cards gift wrap stationery ceramics
LINKS
WEDDING GIFT IDEAS
Emma Bridgewater
Sprinkles Invitations .com
Let's Shop!
DaWanda
DaWanda.com
ART PROJECT - 25
ABOUT ME
BOWIE STYLE
UNITED KINGDOM
this is a website that celebrates the world of surface pattern design.
VIEW MY COMPLETE PROFILE
EMAIL
bowiestyle@hotmail.co.uk
PATTERN BOOKSHOP
DESIGN BOOKS UK
DESIGN BOOKS USA
LINKS
design*sponge
decor8
cath kidston

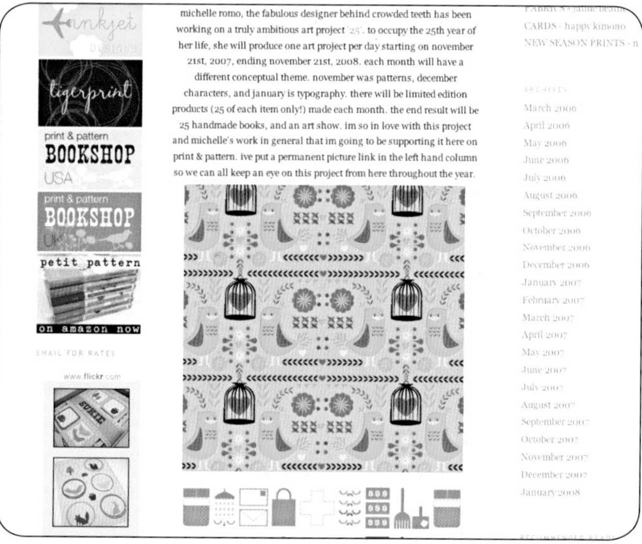
michelle romo, the fabulous designer behind crowded teeth has been working on a truly ambitious art project '25'. to occupy the 25th year of her life, she will produce one art project per day starting on november 21st, 2007, ending november 21st, 2008. each month will have a different conceptual theme. november was patterns, december characters, and january is typography. there will be limited edition products (25 of each item only!) made each month. the end result will be 25 handmade books, and an art show. im so in love with this project and michelle's work in general that im going to be supporting it here on print & pattern. ive put a permanent picture link in the left hand column so we can all keep an eye on this project from here throughout the year.
inkjet DESIGNS
tigerprint
print & pattern BOOKSHOP USA
print & pattern BOOKSHOP UK
petit pattern
on amazon now
EMAIL FOR RATES
www.flickr.com
CARDS - happy kimono
NEW SEASON PRINTS - n
ARCHIVES
March 2006
April 2006
May 2006
June 2006
July 2006
August 2006
September 2006
October 2006
November 2006
December 2006
January 2007
February 2007
March 2007
April 2007
May 2007
June 2007
July 2007
August 2007
September 2007
October 2007
November 2007
December 2007
January 2008

Bowiestyle

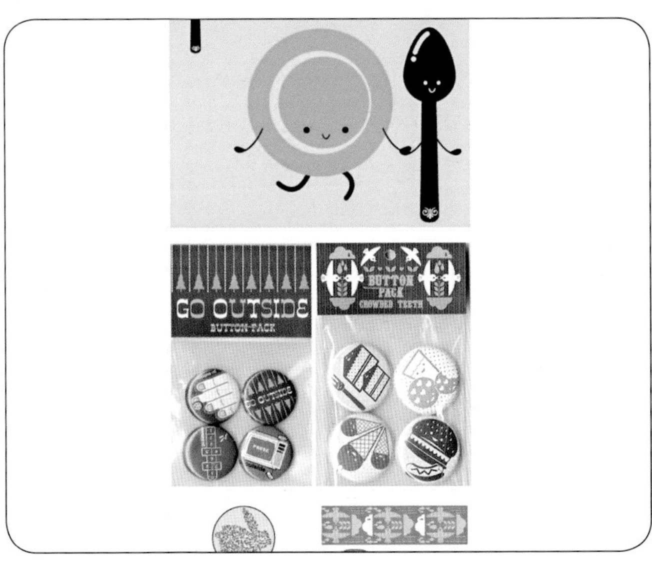
GO OUTSIDE
BUTTON-PACK
GO OUTSIDE
BUTTON PACK
CROWDED TEETH

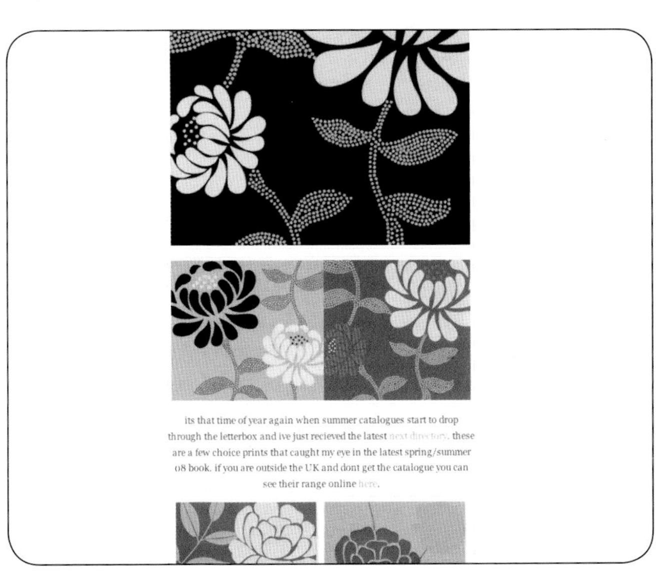
its that time of year again when summer catalogues start to drop through the letterbox and ive just recieved the latest next directory. these are a few choice prints that caught my eye in the latest spring/summer 08 book. if you are outside the UK and dont get the catalogue you can see their range online here.

PRINT Fetish

News, information, reviews and history on the subjects of beautiful magazines, self-published 'zines, handmade books, small press, comix, art books and miscellaneous printed ephemera.

let us know about stuff! email us at: tell@printfetish.com

Print Fetish is made and maintained by R&S Media

February 19, 2008

Swimsuit Edition

Swimsuit Edition
by Logan MacDonald
4.25" x 5.5", 36 pages, stapled
Black and white inside
Edition of 100

Inside this small edition you will find a whole oceanside world, which includes banana hammocks, swim meets and swim meat, old ladies in old bathing costumes, flame-like pubic hair, hopeful mermaids, and lots of hot posing. The draw-er, Logan MacDonald, is a member of a Canadian trio of queers called The Third Leg. I like his style. It has this kind of old fashioned feeling. I'm not sure exactly what I mean by that but I see it in the gaze of the sexy gentleman holding a diving ring or the poise of the lady in the bathing cap or the strength of the bearded Poseidon-like daddy toweling off. He mixes that with some morbid humor—Let's Die! in bold lettering next to some people tanning in front of a giant crab, a man who's arms end in a weird web of veiny things, or a crossed out woman getting abducted by aliens. Also included in this, ahem, package are a cut-out of the bust of a cowboy, Mr. MacDonald's business card, and what looks like a drawing of a made-up horror pulp novel.

visit the **R&S** store at CafePress for t-shirts and other fun junk!

History Magazines
US, Civil War, Military, State & Black History Magazines

New American Poetry Book
New Release - e-book format just $1.95!

Your Ad Here

May 10, 2007

Magazines We Love Roundup

The current issue of Another Man has a gorgeous cover - Nick Knight's photo of the luscious Ben Wishaw - soon to be seen in Todd Haynes's much anticipated Bob Dylan film, *I'm Not There*. Inside there are more photos of the sinewy young actor and a discussion between him and Sir Ian Mckellen. Art critic John Richardson writes about hanging out with Peggy Guggenheim in Venice (apparently the art world also has a casting couch), Jon Savage meditates on Sinatra and the creation of the teenager and David Dalton muses on the women men worship. Another Man is one of the few desirable Men's Fashion magazines. Outstanding photography and brilliant, inventive styling. Norbert Schoerner's and stylist Nicola Formichetti's spring fashion editorial of colorful, techno urban explorers is a standout.

R&S (Ralph McGinnis & Sarah Keough)

Advertise on Print Fetish
Your ad here!

YOUR AD HERE

PRINT Fetish

News, information, reviews and history on the subjects of beautiful magazines, self-published 'zines, handmade books, small press, comix, art books and miscellaneous printed ephemera.

Let us know about stuff! email us at: tell@printfetish.com

Print Fetish is made and maintained by R&S Media

Archives
Mission/Contact
Where to Buy
Resources
Terms of use/Privacy policy
PF on Myspace
PF on Flickr

About Print Fetish:

Print Fetish is a weblog featuring news, information, reviews and history on the subjects of beautiful magazines, self-published 'zines, handmade books, small press, comix, art books, and miscellaneous printed ephemera. The site features daily reviews of new titles, trends, updates on events, and interviews with fascinating people in the field of print media.

Our Mission :

We love the internet— but we don't think it means the end of printed media. However, we do hope it will lead to the end of ugly consumerist magazines and newspapers. We can read free junk and news 'til our hearts' content on the web. We feel there is only one reason to waste money and paper on a magazine—it has to be beautiful. And when we talk about beauty, we are not simply talking about what it it looks like, but its point of view and editorial whole. We hope we can spread the word on these beautiful objects, and get you to spend your money on them, rather than the average condy nasty.

Tell us about cool stuff at tell@printfetish.com.

Contacts and credits:

Ralph Mcginnis, Editor
ralph@printfetish.com

R&S STORE
visit the R&S store at CafePress for t-shirts and other fun junk!

Advertise on Print Fetish
Powered by AdBrite

Your Ad Here

Make Your Donation

February 1, 2008

R.I.P *Blueprint*

I know I get all high-minded about magazines, so some people might wonder why the hell I like *Blueprint*. *Blueprint* does not meet all of my criteria for quality (It could have used at least ONE feature length article), but for what it was... it was quite good. The typography was truly excellent, the layouts uncluttered, the information well conveyed and digestible. It was the greatest magazine to read on the john or train, with recipe's, cocktails and crafts one might actually attempt. And I have.

Unlike it's retarded competition *Domino*, *Blueprint* had a higher level of design taste and less emphasis on consumerism, with more placed upon creativity and inventiveness. It was cute, fluffy and only $3.50! I'm totally annoyed that it's folding! Martha Stewart, who publishes the mag, says that it's demographic (25-45 year old women) prefers getting their info online, which is total baloney. On the big shelter blogs like apartmentherapy and Design* Sponge, everyone talks about *Blueprint*. Now what magazine can I

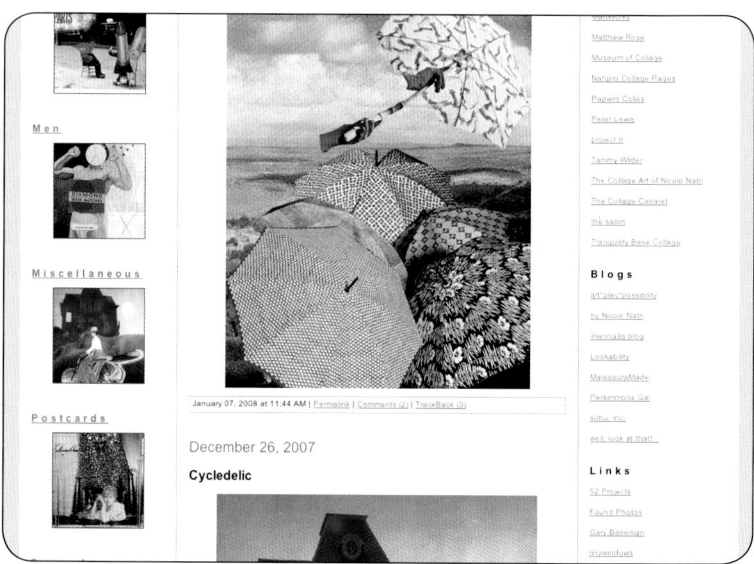

Angelica Paez

Email Me

Old & New Work

Abstract

Animals

VIA AIR MAIL

Artist Cards

January 17, 2008

Bridgette

January 2008

Sun	Mon	Tue	Wed	Thu	Fri	Sat
		1	2	3	4	5
6	7	8	9	10	11	12
13	14	15	16	17	18	19
20	21	22	23	24	25	26
27	28	29	30	31		

Recent Posts

Bridgette

Beckon

Escape

Cycledelic

Archives

January 2008

December 2007

November 2007

October 2007

September 2007

August 2007

July 2007

June 2007

May 2007

April 2007

DESIGN T-SHIRTS AND STREETWEAR AND URBAN ARTWORK. VERSION 2.0

« SELEKKT facelifted. Your Eyes Lie! »

NAME RIBBON from NYC!

Another piece of finding from a long weekend in front of the mac: NAME RIBBON from NYC with a nice selekktion of hoodies. This is what they write about their WHY: *"Progressive streetwear from several labels got good, so progressive street kids copped it. Then some of the brands got cocky, and then they got expensive, too expensive for progressive street kids that made them thrive. That's when those brands got 'dumb'. We're for people who avoid 'dumb'."* We totally agree with this.

_CATEGORIES
- Shirts 'n Stuff
- Interviews
- Entertaining
- Limited Sales

_HOT LABELS BY RANDOM
- Freegums
- YOUYESYOU
- YACKFOU.com
- 2K by Gingham
- TOKE
- Rockaway Bear
- Tokyo Art Beat
- Hey! Unite
- Le Sucre
- Ser-vice
- The Prism
- Imaginary Foundation
- Tonic
- Lazy Oaf
- Stereohype

_SELEKKT FRIENDSHIP
- EMILKOZAK

_THE OTHERS
- Addicteed
- teeshirtblog
- Hide Your Arms
- Streetwear Websites

_PAGES
- About us
- Want to be featured?
- Disclaimer

_THE SEARCH

Go!

_SELEKKTED T-SHOPS

Christian Voigt

Flashback with B.A.

September 12th, 2006 by The Don. Posted in Shirts 'n Stuff, Entertaining. Currently 0 Comments.

We were quite curious when we discovered Mr. T (maybe better known as A-Team's B.A.) and some of his fitness cats on YouTube showing off their latest styles in dance and fashion-tees. Incredibly hot.

Art In The Age Of Mechanical Reproduction

September 11th, 2006 by The Don. Posted in Shirts 'n Stuff. Currently 0 Comments.

"*Art in the Age of Mechanical Reproduction has taken on the challenge by hiring inventive, topnotch, creative artists to produce products that transcend mere originality and ascend into the more practical realm of provoking individual reaction on an individual basis.*" After crawling their website we can ensure that they are saying nothing than just the truth:-) View our selekktion with pieces by artists like Katharine Karnaky, Roy Miranda or PaulCoors...

Learn more about the dark side of Quentin right here...;-)

« 1 ... 21 22 23 24 25 ... 32 »

SKULL-A-DAY
I'm making a skull image every day for a year.
You can see them all here...
THURSDAY, AUGUST 2, 2007
60. Flower Skull
SKULLADAY.COM
CONTACT/SUBMISSIONS
SKULL@SKULLADAY.COM
SUBSCRIBE
Subscribe in a reader
SUPPORT SKULL-A-DAY
Buy a limited edition T-SKULL!
Details HERE.
BLOG ARCHIVE
▼ 2007 (88)
▼ August (19)

I'm making a skull image every day for a year.
You can see them all here...
WEDNESDAY, JULY 11, 2007
38. Quoth the Skull...
NEVERMORE
Hand cut paper. I recently did a cut paper illustration for a friend and while the process is rather tedious the results are pretty satisfying. When the idea for today's image popped into my head I decided it was the right medium for it.
UPDATE: OK, you asked for it, here's a PDF version of this art for you to play with. As with everything on this site the image is provided
CONTACT/SUBMISSIONS
SKULL@SKULLADAY.COM
SUBSCRIBE
Subscribe in a reader
SUPPORT SKULL-A-DAY
Buy a limited edition T-SKULL!
Details HERE.
BLOG ARCHIVE
▼ 2007 (88)
▼ August (19)
73. Watercolor Dog Skull
72. Papercraft Skull (with Articulated Jaw)
71. Paint Scratch Skull
70. Shoelace Skull
Braincase V

Noah Scalin

SKULL-A-DAY

I'm making a skull image every day for a year.
You can see them all here...

WEDNESDAY, JUNE 13, 2007

10. United Skull of America

SKULLADAY.COM

CONTACT/SUBMISSIONS

SKULL@SKULLADAY.COM

SUBSCRIBE

Subscribe in a reader

SUPPORT SKULL-A-DAY

Buy a limited edition T-SKULL!

Details HERE.

BLOG ARCHIVE

▼ 2007 (88)

▼ August (19)

73. Watercolor Dog Skull

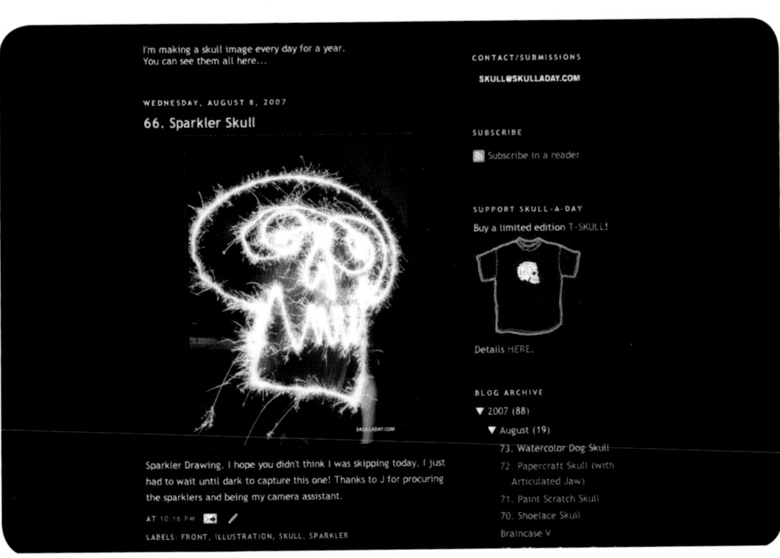

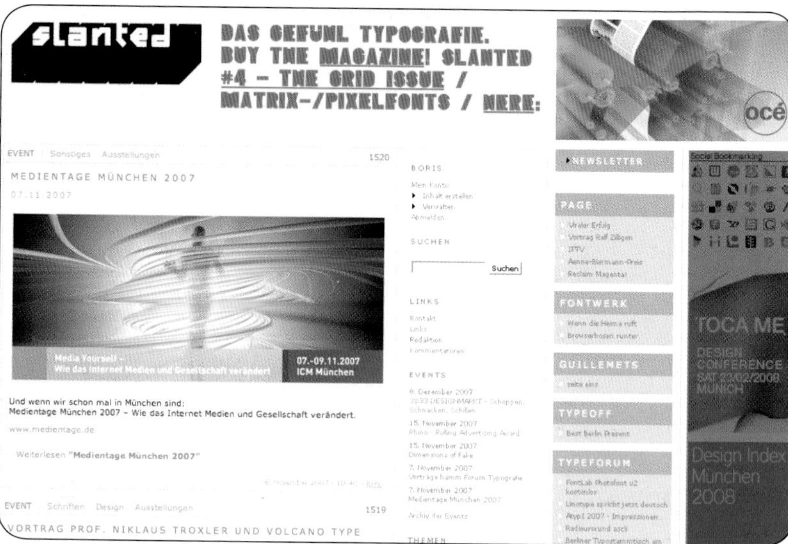

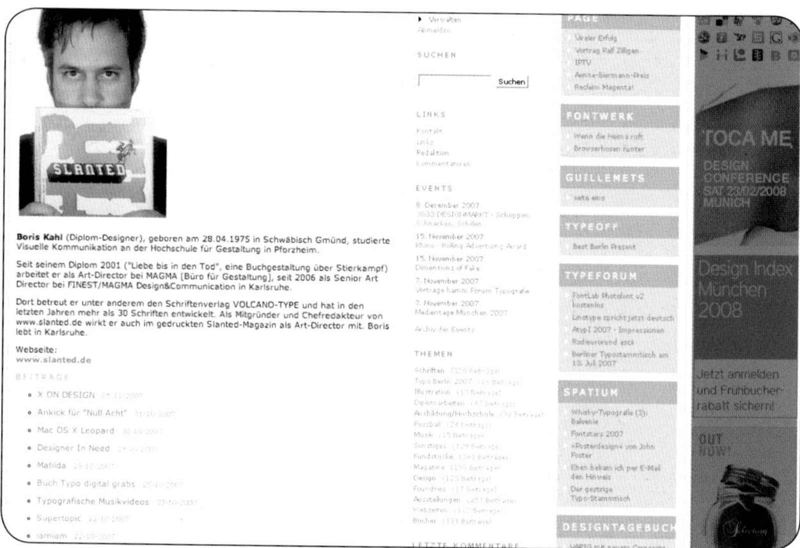

Lars Harmsen, Uli Weiß, Boris Kahl, Flo Gaertner

océ

slanted
DAS GEFÜHL TYPOGRAFIE.
BUY THE MAGAZINE! SLANTED
#4 – THE GRID ISSUE /
MATRIX-/PIXELFONTS / HERE:
SCHRIFTEN
Matador
BORIS
SUCHEN
Suchen
LINKS
EVENTS
THEMEN
NEWSLETTER
PAGE
FONTWERK
GUILLEMETS
TYPEOFF
TYPEFORUM
Social Bookmarking
TOCA ME
DESIGN CONFERENCE
SAT 23/02/2008
MUNICH
Design Index
München
2008

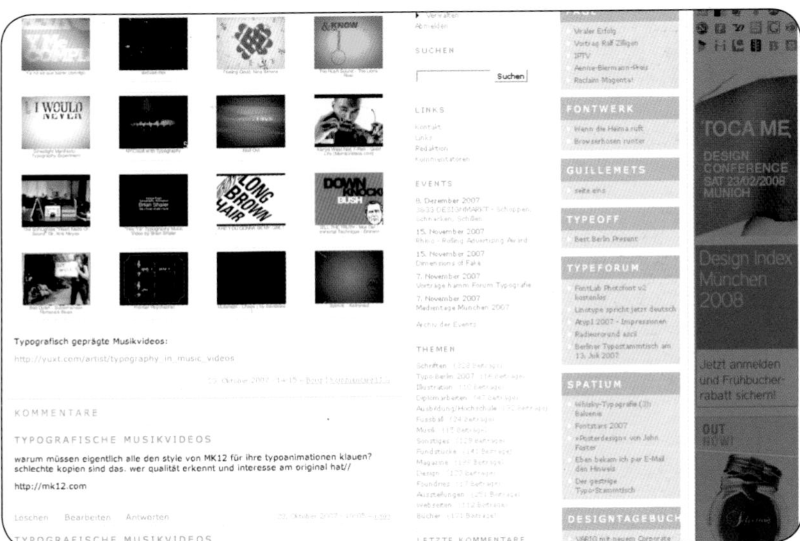
Typografisch geprägte Musikvideos:
KOMMENTARE
TYPOGRAFISCHE MUSIKVIDEOS
warum müssen eigentlich alle den style von MK12 für ihre typoanimationen klauen?
schlechte kopien sind das. wer qualität erkennt und interesse am original hat//
http://mk12.com
Löschen Bearbeiten Antworten
TYPOGRAFISCHE MUSIKVIDEOS
SUCHEN
Suchen
LINKS
EVENTS
THEMEN
LETZTE KOMMENTARE
FONTWERK
GUILLEMETS
TYPEOFF
TYPEFORUM
SPATIUM
DESIGNTAGEBUCH
TOCA ME
DESIGN CONFERENCE
SAT 23/02/2008
MUNICH
Design Index
München
2008
Jetzt anmelden
und Frühbucher-
rabatt sichern!
OUT
NOW!

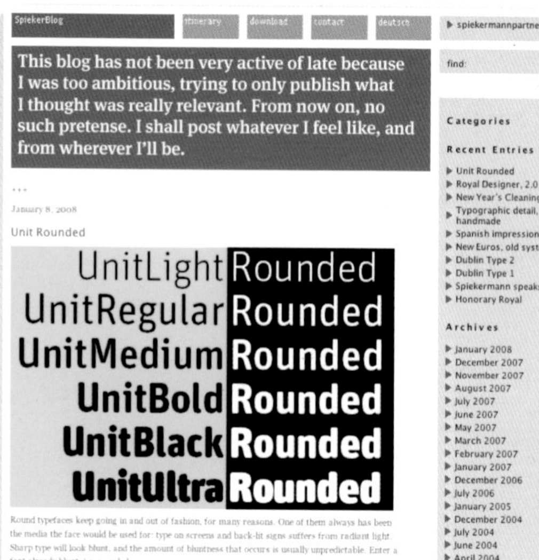

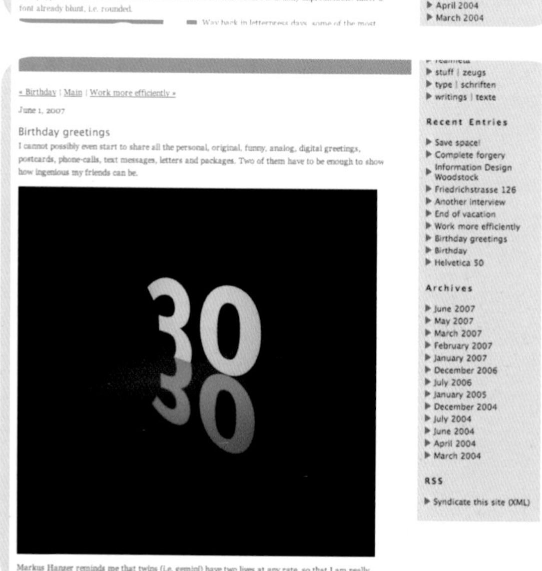

Erik Spiekermann

June 28, 2007

Save space!

Ths typfc cn sv A lt f spc.
Y cn wrt vowEls, bt y dn't hv to.
Thy hv t b ntrd AS cptls:
CApItAls.
ABCDEFGHIJKLMNOPQRSTUVWXYZ
bcdfghjklmnpqrstvwxyz

This typeface can save a lot of space because it ignores vowels when entering text. If at all needed, you can type a capital letter by using the shift key. That will insert one of the small capitals which also exist for vowels.
You can download FF Mt for free here.

space	exclam	quotedbl	numbers	dollar	percent	amper	quotes	parenleft	parenright	asterisk	plus	comma	hyphen	period	slash
	!	"	#	$	%	&	'	(	)	*	+	,	-	.	/
zero	one	two	three	four	five	six	seven	eight	nine	colon	semicolo	less	equal	greater	question
0	1	2	3	4	5	6	7	8	9	:	;	‹	=	›	?
at	A	B	C	D	E	F	G	H	I	J	K	L	M	N	O
@	A	B	C	D	E	F	G	H	I	J	K	L	M	N	O
P	Q	R	S	T	U	V	W	X	Y	Z	bracketl	backsla	bracketr	ascicir	undersc
P	Q	R	S	T	U	V	W	X	Y	Z	[	\	]	^	_
grave	a	b	c	d	e	f	g	h	i	j	k	l	m	n	o
`		b	c	d		f	g	h		j	k	l	m	n	
p	q	r	s	t	u	v	w	x	y	z	braceleft	bar	braceri	asciitilde	—
p	q	r	s	t		v	w	x	y	z	{	|	}	~	

realmeta
- stuff | zeugs
- type | schriften
- writings | texte

Recent Entries

- Save space!
- Complete forgery
- Helvetica 50
- All Greek to me...
- MetaSerif
- Amazing type
- 100 best typefaces, final result.
- ITC Officina Display
- The 100 best typefaces
- New numbers please!

Archives

- July 2007
- June 2007
- May 2007
- March 2007
- February 2007
- January 2007
- December 2006
- July 2006
- January 2005
- December 2004
- July 2004
- June 2004
- April 2004
- March 2004

RSS

- Syndicate this site (XML)

SpiekerBlog [*sic*] ist Erik Spiekermanns persönlicher Blog.
Es wird daher nicht überraschen, dass die Themen zum großen Teil typografischer Natur sind.
Die gute Nachricht: Typomanie, die Krankheit, an der ich leide, ist zwar unheilbar, aber nicht tödlich.

26. März 2007

itinerary | Reiseplan

| 11.09.07 – 16.09.07 Brighton AtypI
| 17.09.07 – 18.09.07 Den Haag
| 11.10.07 – 12.10.07 Stockholm
| 15.10.07 – 17.10.07 Wien
| 19.10.07 – 21.10.07 Norway

find:

Categories

- news | neuigkeiten
- realmeta
- stuff | zeugs
- type | schriften
- writings | texte

Recent Entries

- Instant-Vorlesungen
- Blindtext Generatoren
- Platz sparen!
- Gefälschtes Nummernschild
- Information Design Woodstock
- Rotis am Ende?
- Friedrichstrasse 126
- Noch ein Interview auf Englisch
- Urlaubsende
- Besser arbeiten

Archives

- Juli 2007
- Juni 2007
- Mai 2007
- März 2007
- Februar 2007
- Januar 2007
- Mai 2005
- Januar 2005
- Dezember 2004
- Juli 2004
- Juni 2004
- April 2004
- März 2004

RSS

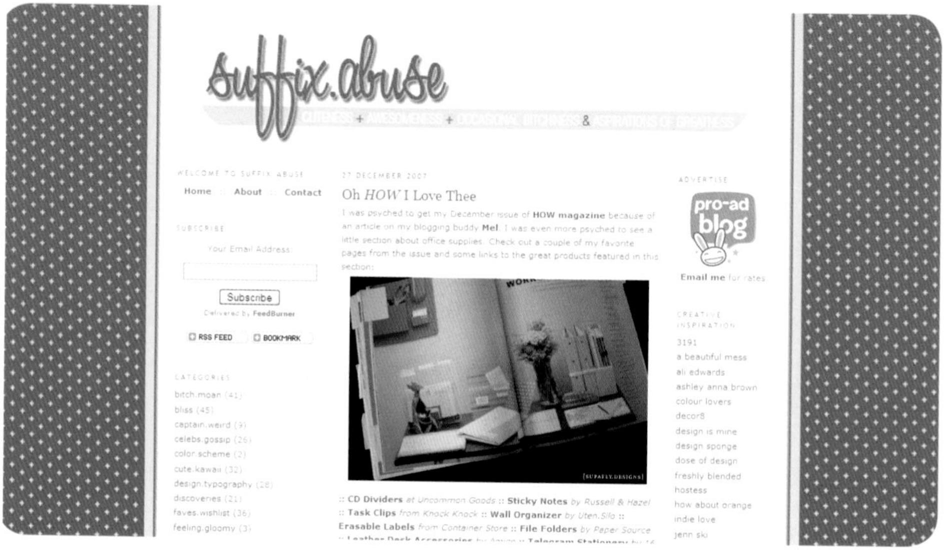

Mary K. Corcoran

suffix.abuse
CUTENESS + AWESOMENESS + OCCASIONAL BITCHINESS & ASPIRATIONS OF GREATNESS
WELCOME TO SUFFIX ABUSE
Home :: About :: Contact
SUBSCRIBE
Your Email Address:
Subscribe
Delivered by FeedBurner
RSS FEED
BOOKMARK
CATEGORIES
bitch.moan (41)
bliss (45)
captain.weird (9)
celebs.gossip (26)
color.scheme (2)
cute.kawaii (32)
design.typography (28)
discoveries (21)
faves.wishlist (36)
feeling.gloomy (3)
26 JANUARY 2008
FREE DOWNLOAD
SupaFly.Designs Envelope Mailer
I'm a huge fan of free downloads, so I'm happily supplying a free download for anyone who's interested. I downloaded an envelope mailer over the holidays and have been wanting to design one myself and finally had the time, so I did it! Check it out:
ADVERTISE
pro-ad blog
Email me for rates.
CREATIVE INSPIRATION
3191
a beautiful mess
ali edwards
ashley anna brown
colour lovers
decor8
design is mine
design sponge
dose of design
freshly blended
hostess
how about orange
indie love
jenn ski

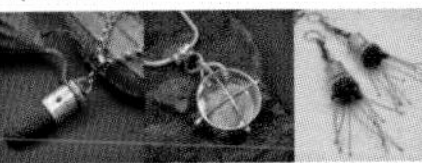

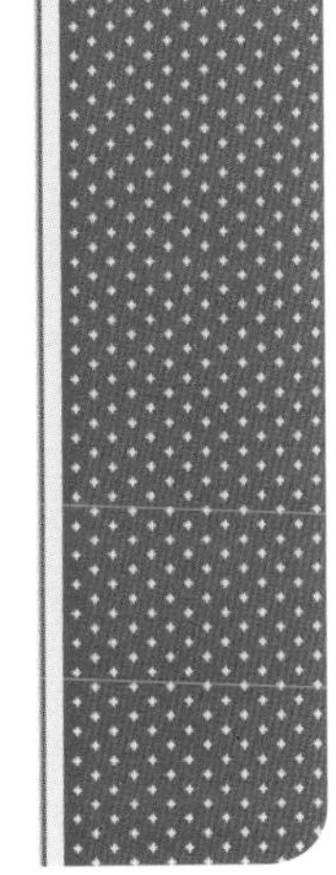
suffix.abuse
CUTENESS + AWESOMENESS + OCCASIONAL BITCHINESS & ASPIRATIONS OF GREATNESS
WELCOME TO SUFFIX.ABUSE
Home :: About :: Contact
SUBSCRIBE
Your Email Address:
Subscribe
Delivered by FeedBurner
RSS FEED
BOOKMARK
CATEGORIES
bitch.moan (41)
bliss (45)
captain.weird (9)
celebs.gossip (26)
color.scheme (2)
cute.kawaii (32)
design.typography (28)
discoveries (21)
faves.wishlist (36)
feeling.gloomy (3)
10 DECEMBER 2007
GIFT GUIDE:
Etsy Goodies - Round 2
:: Bonspiel ::
:: Experimental ::
:: Garnish Home ::
ADVERTISE
pro-ad blog
Email me for rates.
CREATIVE INSPIRATION
3191
a beautiful mess
ali edwards
ashley anna brown
colour lovers
decor8
design is mine
design sponge
dose of design
freshly blended
hostess
how about orange
indie love
jenn ski

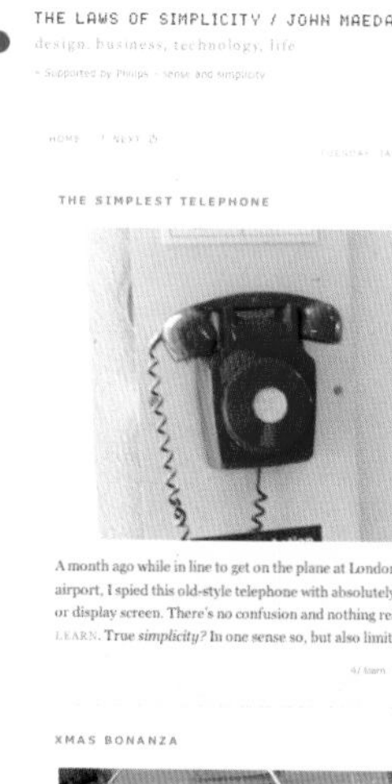
THE LAWS OF SIMPLICITY / JOHN MAEDA
design, business, technology, life
THE SIMPLEST TELEPHONE
A month ago while in line to get on the plane at London Heathrow airport, I spied this old-style telephone with absolutely no buttons or display screen. There's no confusion and nothing really to LEARN. True simplicity? In one sense so, but also limited utility.
XMAS BONANZA

Search
Law 1: REDUCE
Law 2: ORGANIZE
Law 3: TIME
Law 4: LEARN
Law 5: DIFFERENCES
Law 6: CONTEXT
Law 7: EMOTION
Law 8: TRUST
Law 9: FAILURE
Law 10: THE ONE
RESOURCES

THE LAWS OF SIMPLICITY / JOHN MAEDA
design, business, technology, life
THE LAWS OF SIMPLICITY
I wrote The Laws of Simplicity in late 2005 to early 2006 to get my thoughts down about simplicity. In the course of 100-pages, I outline the Ten Laws as used on this website.
LAW 1: REDUCE
The simplest way to achieve simplicity is through thoughtful reduction.
The easiest way to simplify a system is to remove functionality. Today's DVD, for instance, has too many buttons if all you want to do is play a movie. A solution could be to remove the buttons for Rewind, Forward, Eject, and so forth until only one button remains: Play.
But what if you want to replay a favorite scene? Or pause the

Search

Law 1: REDUCE
Law 2: ORGANIZE
Law 3: TIME
Law 4: LEARN
Law 5: DIFFERENCES
Law 6: CONTEXT
Law 7: EMOTION
Law 8: TRUST
Law 9: FAILURE
Law 10: THE ONE
RESOURCES

John Maeda

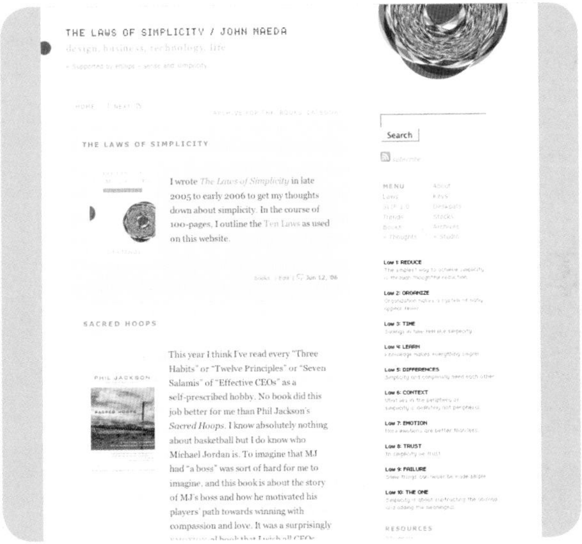

THE LAWS OF SIMPLICITY / JOHN MAEDA

design, business, technology, life

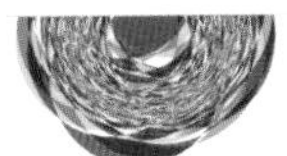

Search

THE LAWS OF SIMPLICITY

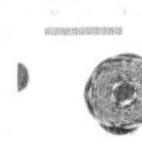

I wrote *The Laws of Simplicity* in late 2005 to early 2006 to get my thoughts down about simplicity. In the course of 100-pages, I outline the Ten Laws as used on this website.

Jun 12, '06

SACRED HOOPS

This year I think I've read every "Three Habits" or "Twelve Principles" or "Seven Salamis" of "Effective CEOs" as a self-prescribed hobby. No book did this job better for me than Phil Jackson's *Sacred Hoops*. I know absolutely nothing about basketball but I do know who Michael Jordan is. To imagine that MJ had "a boss" was sort of hard for me to imagine, and this book is about the story of MJ's boss and how he motivated his players' path towards winning with compassion and love. It was a surprisingly

Law 1: REDUCE

Law 2: ORGANIZE

Law 3: TIME

Law 4: LEARN

Law 5: DIFFERENCES

Law 6: CONTEXT

Law 7: EMOTION

Law 8: TRUST

Law 9: FAILURE

Law 10: THE ONE

RESOURCES

THE LAWS OF SIMPLICITY / JOHN MAEDA

design, business, technology, life

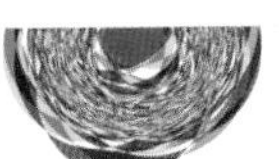

Search

DIGITALLY GREEN

The hard disk in my four-year old computer recently failed so I purchased a replacement hard disk that was advertised as green. For years I had naively assumed that the hard disk in my computer wasn't such a major power hog ... but come to think of it when it spins hard during an airplane ride my batteries do get worn out quite quickly. The marketing campaign for the disk claims that the savings in energy gained are equivalent to "taking your car off the road for 14 days each year." It's hard to believe that a little hard disk has that much impact on the environment.

One service that I installed at my work place is GreenDisk. There is so much technowaste around us like unused CD-ROMs, cables, and etc. GreenDisk has a convenient cardboard packaging in the shape

Law 1: REDUCE

Law 2: ORGANIZE

Law 3: TIME

Law 4: LEARN

Law 5: DIFFERENCES

Law 6: CONTEXT

Law 7: EMOTION

Law 8: TRUST

Law 9: FAILURE

Law 10: THE ONE

RESOURCES

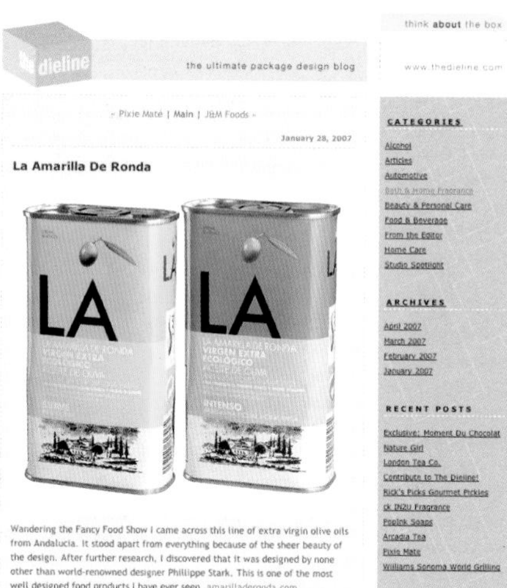

Andrew Gibbs

think **about** the box

the ultimate package design blog

www.thedieline.com

Home Care

March 13, 2007

Beauty Engineered for Ever: BEE

B.E.E. is a line of environmentally friendly home cleaning products from New Zealand with packaging that focuses on typography as the main design element. Not only is it visually interesting, it catches your attention and focuses you on the benefits of the product. If this were sold here it would be in direct competition of Method. ***Continue for more photos...***

Continue reading "Beauty Engineered for Ever: BEE" »

Technorati Tags: Cleaners, Home, Method, Package Design, Packaging

Posted by andrew gibbs on March 13, 2007 in Home Care | Permalink | Comments (2) | TrackBack (0)

March 06, 2007

Fruits & Passion: Art Home

CATEGORIES

Alcohol
Articles
Automotive
Bath & Home Fragrance
Beauty & Personal Care
Food & Beverage
From the Editor
Home Care
Studio Spotlight

ARCHIVES

April 2007
March 2007
February 2007
January 2007

RECENT POSTS

Exclusive: Moment Du Chocolat
Nature Girl
London Tea Co.
Contribute to The Dieline!
Rick's Picks Gourmet Pickles
ck IN2U Fragrance
Poglnk Soaps
Arcadia Tea
Pixie Mate
Williams Sonoma World Grilling

ABOUT THE DIELINE

About Us

CONTRIBUTE

think **about** the box

the ultimate package design blog

www.thedieline.com

« Chalmers Ganache | **Main** | Thymes Kimono Rose »

February 07, 2007

Coca-Cola M5

Introduced in 2005, Coca-Cola la
called the "Magnificent 5" or M5.
were each commissioned to desi
rebranding aimed at discerningl
world's most exclusive clubs and

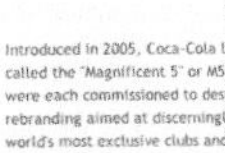

Liljeqvist & Wargo
Innovative Product Packaging, Graph
Structural Design

CATEGORIES

Alcohol
Articles
Automotive
Bath & Home Fragrance
Beauty & Personal Care
Food & Beverage

Williams Sonoma World Grilling

ABOUT THE DIELINE

About Us

CONTRIBUTE

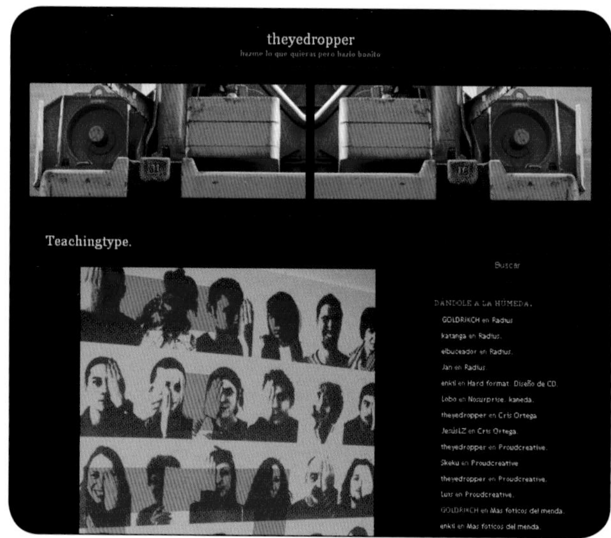

Carlos H.Guzmán, Iván Irisarri Gonzalez

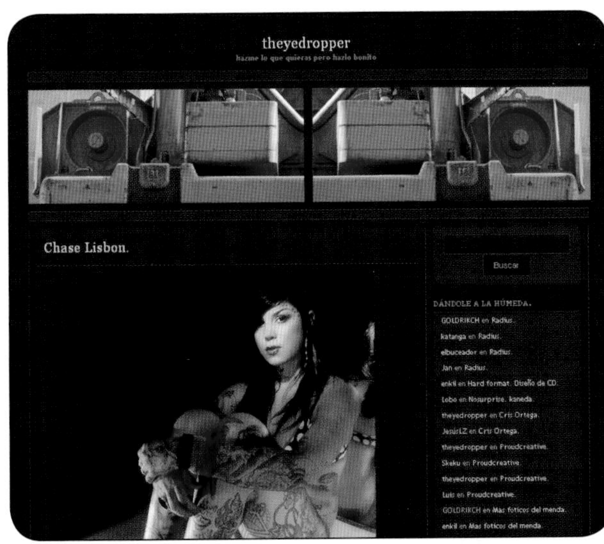
theyedropper
hazme lo que quieras pero hazlo bonito
Chase Lisbon.
Buscar
DÁNDOLE A LA HÚMEDA.
GOLDRIKCH en Radius.
katanga en Radius.
elbuceador en Radius.
Jan en Radius.
enkil en Hard format. Diseño de CD.
Lobo en Nosurprise. kaneda.
theyedropper en Cris Ortega.
JesúsLZ en Cris Ortega.
theyedropper en Proudcreative.
Skeku en Proudcreative.
theyedropper en Proudcreative.
Luis en Proudcreative.
GOLDRIKCH en Mas foticos del menda.
enkil en Mas foticos del menda.

theyedropper
hazme lo que quieras pero hazlo bonito
Hard format. Diseño de CD.
Buscar
DÁNDOLE A LA HÚMEDA.
GOLDRIKCH en Radius.
katanga en Radius.
elbuceador en Radius.
Jan en Radius.
enkil en Hard format. Diseño de CD.
Lobo en Nosurprise. kaneda.
theyedropper en Cris Ortega.
JesúsLZ en Cris Ortega.
theyedropper en Proudcreative.
Skeku en Proudcreative.
theyedropper en Proudcreative.
Luis en Proudcreative.
GOLDRIKCH en Mas foticos del menda.
enkil en Mas foticos del menda.
VELO
BUL BUL
TR079
301
ROADFLYER 18 SPEED
ATLAS GOLDEN SUPER
CLUBMAN
CHECKER PIG
CYCLE WOLF

Daniela Berto, Luca Gentile

Tb
we are
Welcome to think.bigchief
Think.BigChief raccoglie i trend dal mondo del design, del web e della tecnologia.
« Graphics #9
New Fallen Loker »
I luv Office Sticker
Is this ironic?
Via Swissmiss.
I the Office
(Deluxe Stickers)
I OVERTIME
I NEW TONER
I SICK DAYS
I MARKER SMELL
I MARKER SMELL
I BACKSTABBING
Great for:
Inter-office memos
File Folders
Your Desk
Your Computer
Lunchroom
Restroom
Boss' Car
Co-workers Back
More!
MILAN CITY
11 42 26
OVER 2500 DOWNLOAD
Feed
iscriviti ai nostri feed rss
Tb
we are
Welcome to think.bigchief
Think.BigChief raccoglie i trend dal mondo del design, del web e della tecnologia.
« Salone Satellite 07: Formf
Salone Satellite 07: MyMiniGolf »
Salone Satellite 07: Save Our Souls
Directly from Sweden, Magdalena Nilsson and Johannes Carlstrom presents our works Save Our Souls.
MILAN CITY
11 41 07
OVER 2500 DOWNLOAD
Feed
iscriviti ai nostri feed rss

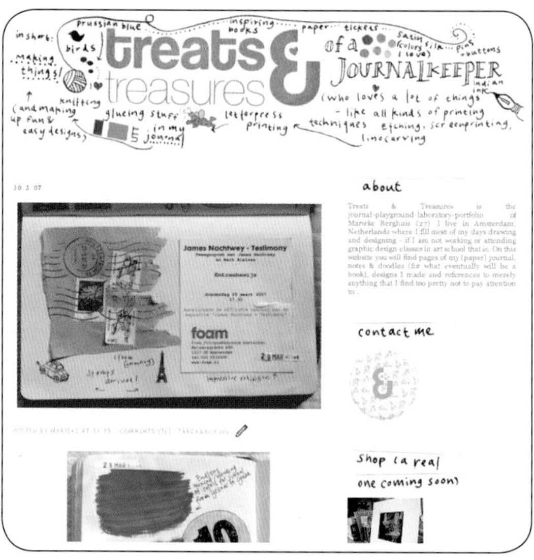

Marieke Berghuis

treats & treasures
of a JOURNALKEEPER
(who loves a lot of things - like all kinds of printing techniques etching, screenprinting, linocarving
letterpress printing
glueing stuff in my journal
knitting
birds
prussian blue
inspiring books
paper
satin
pins
buttons
indian ink
about
Treats & Treasures is the journal-playground-laboratory-portfolio of Marieke Berghuis (27). I live in Amsterdam, Netherlands where I fill most of my days drawing and designing - if I am not working or attending graphic design classes in art school that is. On this website you will find pages of my (paper) journal, notes & doodles (for what eventually will be a book), designs I made and references to merely anything that I find too pretty not to pay attention to...
contact me
shop (a real one coming soon)

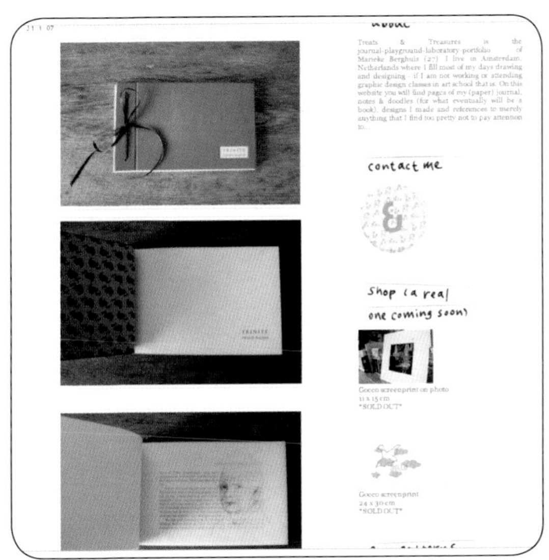
Treats & Treasures is the journal-playground-laboratory-portfolio of Marieke Berghuis (27). I live in Amsterdam, Netherlands where I fill most of my days drawing and designing - if I am not working or attending graphic design classes in art school that is. On this website you will find pages of my (paper) journal, notes & doodles (for what eventually will be a book), designs I made and references to merely anything that I find too pretty not to pay attention to...
contact me
shop (a real one coming soon)
Gocco screenprint on photo
11 x 15 cm
SOLD OUT
Gocco screenprint
24 x 30 cm
SOLD OUT

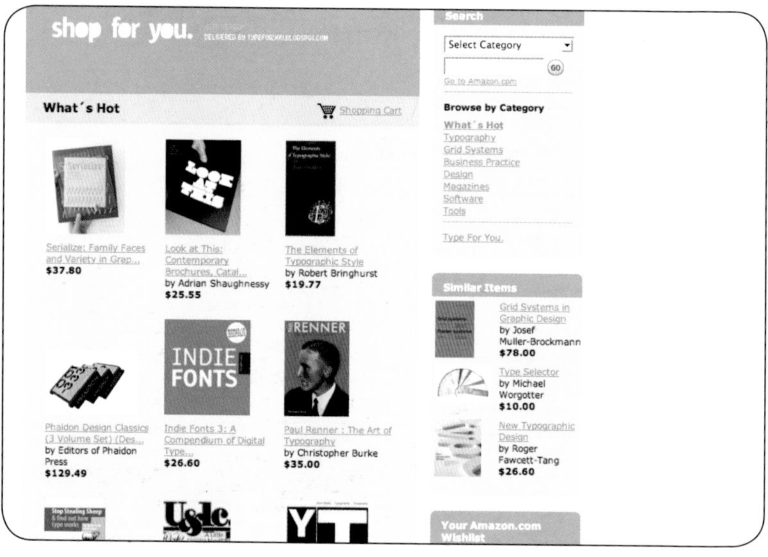

Pedro Serrão

type for you

Ads by Google · Graphic Design · Typography Design · Web Design · 3D Graphic · Graphic Art

SUNDAY, MARCH 25, 2007

Neville Brody at ESAD - Video

NEVILLE BRODY
PERSONAL VIEWS 29
CONFERÊNCIA 16 MAR 2007, 15H AUDITÓRIO ESAD
WWW.ESAD.PT/PERSONALVIEWS

ESAD has updated Personal Views with a video from Neville Brody conference. The next one to speak is Spiekermann on April, 13. (Entrance Free)

TYPED BY PEDRO SERRÃO AT 5:08 PM

LABELS: GRAPHIC DESIGN, MOVIES, PORTUGAL

LATEST INTERVIEWS

Si Scott
Andrea Tinnes

BUY SOMETHING:

shop for you.

RECENT COMMENTS

There's a portuguese fellow that has a huge databa... - John Paulders
She lost on that Jazz logo. Ugly is timeless. - Anonymous
Thanks gotecki! :) - Pedro Serrão
she's a finalist, not the winner...btw, I just lov... - Gotecki
Olá, gostaria de lhe mostrar meus blogs:http://edc... - ED

SUBSCRIBE VIA EMAIL

Enter your email address:

Subscribe

Delivered by FeedBurner

SUBSCRIBE

Subscribe in a reader

Blogs that link here.

PARTICIPATE

If you want to share any news, articles, or general info on type, I would be very happy to hear from you. Thanks!

BROWSING

- OUR ART SITE DOT COM
- Michael Fakesch

typography · Designer · Friendly Fire : Jonathan Barnbrook

type for you

Ads by Google · Type · Fonts · True Type Fonts · Typography · Fonts for Mac

SUNDAY, FEBRUARY 18, 2007

Snoil - A Physical Display Based on Ferrofluid

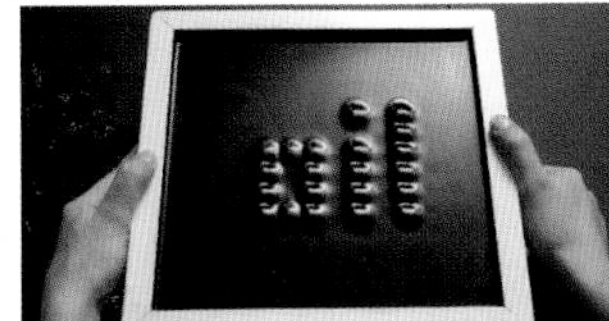

Snoil, a sensitive skin of oil, is a great interactive piece by Martin Frey.

Ferrofluid is a liquid that reacts to magnetism. It is attracted by magnets, pretty similar to iron. This can lead to areas where the liquid partly resists to gravitation when a magnet approaches. Thereby a small bump is formed close to the loadstone. This behavior is enabled by magnetic nano-particles that are suspended in a carrier fluid. Normally the particles are coated with a surfactant to prevent their agglomeration. This results in stable ferrofluid dispersions.

LATEST INTERVIEWS

Si Scott
Andrea Tinnes

BUY SOMETHING:

RECENT COMMENTS

There's a portuguese fellow that has a huge databa... - John Paulders
She lost on that Jazz logo. Ugly is timeless. - Anonymous
Thanks gotecki! :) - Pedro Serrão
she's a finalist, not the winner...btw, I just lov... - Gotecki
Olá, gostaria de lhe mostrar meus blogs:http://edc... - ED

SUBSCRIBE VIA EMAIL

Enter your email address:

Subscribe

Delivered by FeedBurner

SUBSCRIBE

Subscribe in a reader

Blogs that link here.

PARTICIPATE

If you want to share any news, articles, or general info on type, I would be very happy to hear from you. Thanks!

BROWSING

- OUR ART SITE DOT COM

Joel Gethin Lewis

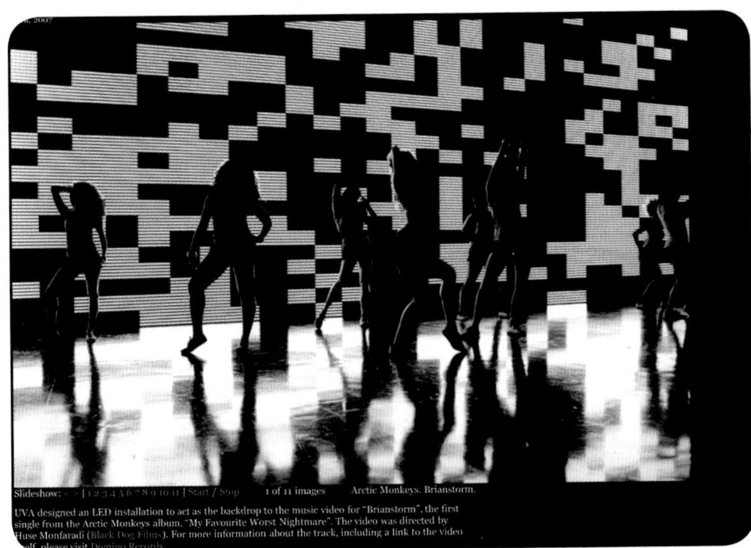
Slideshow: < > | 1 2 3 4 5 6 7 8 9 10 11 | Start / Stop
1 of 11 images
Arctic Monkeys. Brianstorm.
UVA designed an LED installation to act as the backdrop to the music video for "Brianstorm", the first single from the Arctic Monkeys album, "My Favourite Worst Nightmare". The video was directed by Huse Monfaradi (Black Dog Films). For more information about the track, including a link to the video elf, please visit Domino Records.

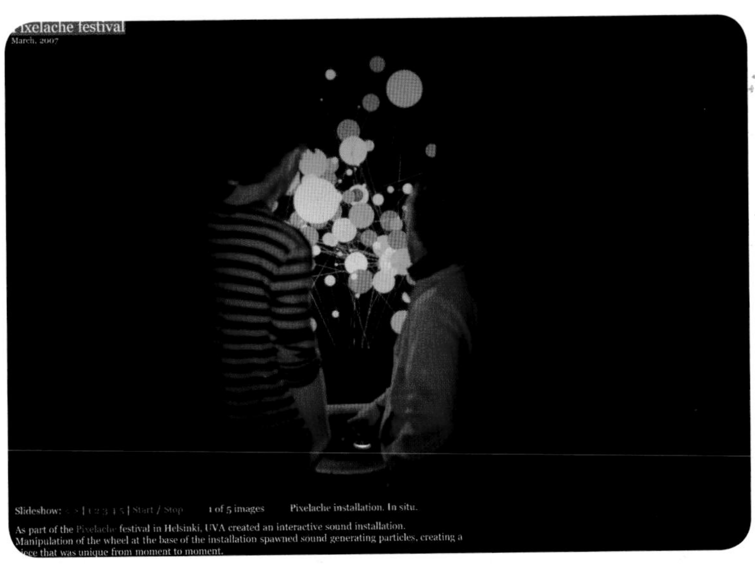
ixelache festival
March, 2007
Slideshow: < > | 1 2 3 4 5 | Start / Stop
1 of 5 images
Pixelache installation. In situ.
As part of the Pixelache festival in Helsinki, UVA created an interactive sound installation. Manipulation of the wheel at the base of the installation spawned sound generating particles, creating a iece that was unique from moment to moment.

Navigation
Front
Archive
Contact
Materials
Books
Films
Music
Vodcast
Contributors
Submit
Links

Subscribe
RSS

Ticker
Ipod Nano
Tom Kuntz
Lorin Brown
The Wet Boys
HfG-Archiv Ulm
dave is drawing
flyingrumor.com
DOPPLR
Future Shipwreck
Rube Goldberg
Bay Area Kicks
Melanie Russell

FFFFOUND!

Viewlikeu on found

Posted on October 31, 2007 by VLU | Max in Image Bookmarking | Post a Comment

VLU Switchboard

del.icio.us

VLU design art portfolio blog graphicdesign photography illustration visual_research inspiration friend shopping toolkit designer culture artist typography architecture web animation graphic video production music musicvideo collection reference fashion furnishings publication studio film flickr UK director visualization computing NYC free london technology code LA sound youtube graphics website resource gallery travel broadcast media viewerslikeu_research enviroment writing japan collective education

Navigation
Front
Archive
Contact
Materials
Books
Films
Music
Vodcast
Contributors
Submit
Links

Subscribe
RSS

Ticker
Ipod Nano
Tom Kuntz
Lorin Brown
The Wet Boys
HfG-Archiv Ulm
dave is drawing
flyingrumor.com
DOPPLR
Future Shipwreck
Rube Goldberg
Bay Area Kicks
Melanie Russell

Books

Peter Doig
by Adrain Searle, Kitty Scott, Catherine Grenier, Hannes Schneider, Arnold Fanck

Building: 3,000 Years of Design, Engineering and Construction
by Bill Addis

Chris Johanson: Please Listen I Have Something to Tell You About What It Is
by Aaron Rose, Chris Johanson

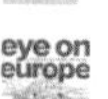

Eye on Europe: Prints, Books, and Multiples / 1960 to Now
by Deborah Wye, Wendy Weitman

Domus 1928-1999, Vols. 1-12
by Deyan Sudjic

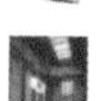

C/ID: Visual Identity and Branding for the Arts
by Angus Hyland, Emily King

Max Erdenberger

Navigation
Front
Archive
Contact
Materials
Vodcast
Contributors
Submit
Links

Subscribe
RSS

Ticker
Ipod Nano
Tom Kuntz
Lorin Brown
The Wet Boys
HfG-Archiv Ulm
dave is drawing
flyingrumor.com
DOPPLR
Future Shipwreck
Rube Goldberg
Bay Area Kicks
Melanie Russell

VLU Merchants
Print

Jeff Scher animations

Jeff Scher is a painter who makes experimental films and an experimental filmmaker who paints. Here is his blog on the NY Times. Watch White Out.

Posted on January 8, 2008 by VLU | Max in AV | Post a Comment | Email

Antville Music Video Awards 2007

Navigation
Front
Archive
Contact
Materials
Vodcast
Contributors
Submit
Links

Subscribe
RSS

Ticker
Ipod Nano
Tom Kuntz
Lorin Brown
The Wet Boys
HfG-Archiv Ulm
dave is drawing
flyingrumor.com
DOPPLR
Future Shipwreck
Rube Goldberg
Bay Area Kicks
Melanie Russell

VLU Merchants
Print

Archive

Entries by Category
Click on a category below to view a list of all entries within that category.

- Architecture (18)
- Art (56)
- Audio (12)
- AV (100)
- Books (10)
- Collection (12)
- Collective (18)
- Culture (20)
- Design (58)
- fashion (8)
- Furnishings (9)
- Graphic Design (67)
- History (12)
- Illustration (18)
- Information (20)
- Music (2)
- Photography (17)
- Portfolio (19)
- Publication (8)
- Retail (4)
- shopping (8)
- Sustainability (5)
- Typography (14)

Entries by Month
Click on a month below to view a list of articles published during that month.

- January 2008 (8)
- December 2007 (21)
- November 2007 (21)
- October 2007 (25)

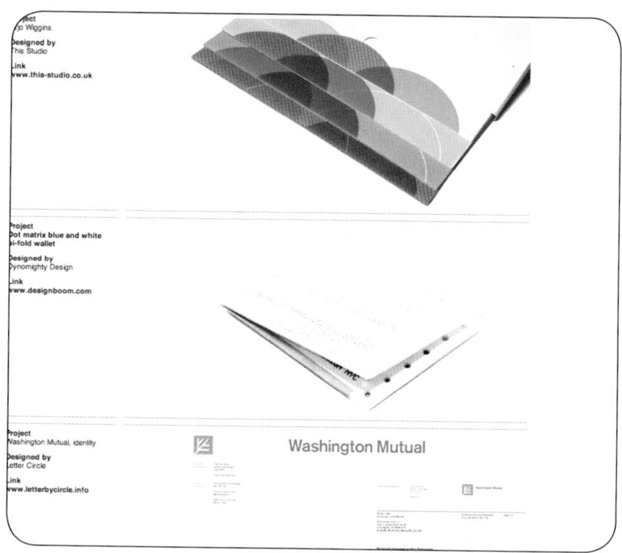

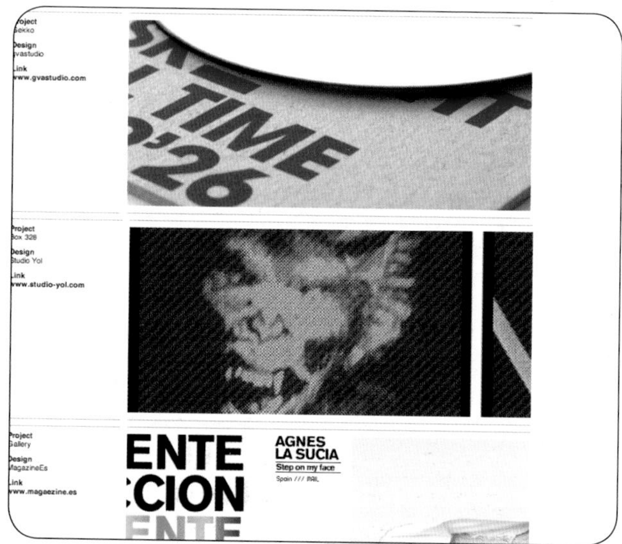

David Bennett

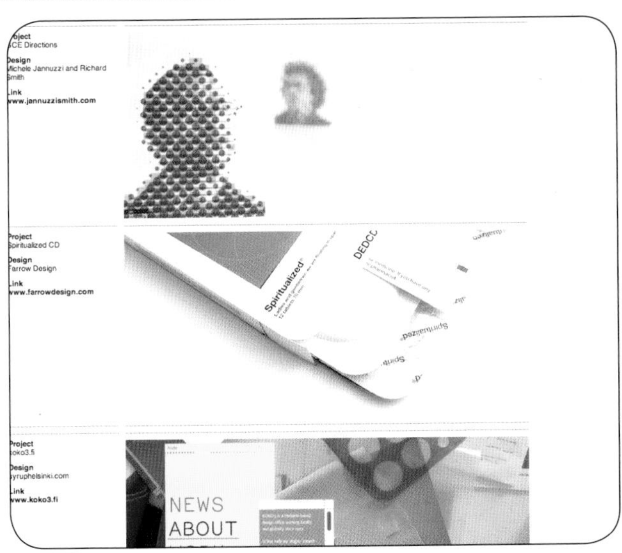

oject
CE Directions
Design
Michele Jannuzzi and Richard Smith
Link
www.jannuzzismith.com
Project
Spiritualized CD
Design
Farrow Design
Link
www.farrowdesign.com
Spiritualized
Project
koko3.fi
Design
syruphelsinki.com
Link
www.koko3.fi
NEWS
ABOUT

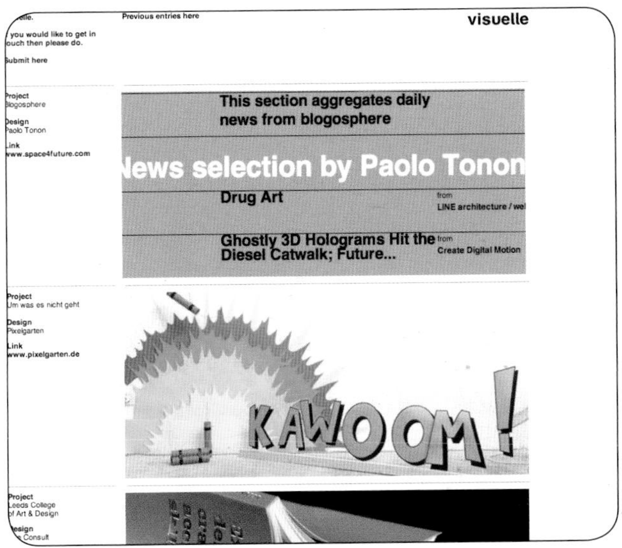

Previous entries here
visuelle
you would like to get in touch then please do.
Submit here
Project
Blogosphere
Design
Paolo Tonon
Link
www.space4future.com
This section aggregates daily news from blogosphere
News selection by Paolo Tonon
Drug Art
from
LINE architecture / we
Ghostly 3D Holograms Hit the Diesel Catwalk; Future...
from
Create Digital Motion
Project
Um was es nicht geht
Design
Pixelgarten
Link
www.pixelgarten.de
KAWOOM!
Project
Leeds College of Art & Design
Design
Consult

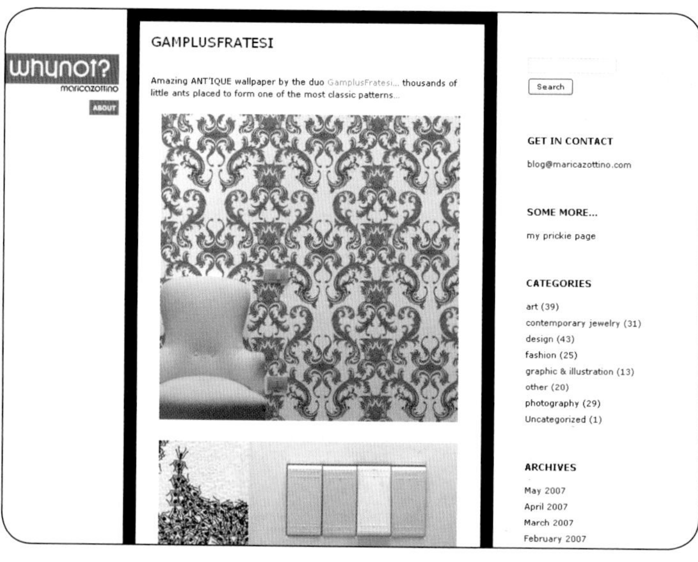

Marica Zottino

whynot?
maricazottino
ABOUT

DIOR HAUTE COUTURE

Galliano Geishas meet Hokusai and ancient Japanese paintings and arts, redefining the 1947 New Look in the occasion of the 60th anniversary of the Maison...

As usual... outstanding Galliano!!!

Video and images

Search

GET IN CONTACT

blog@maricazottino.com

SOME MORE...

my prickie page

CATEGORIES

art (39)
contemporary jewelry (31)
design (43)
fashion (25)
graphic & illustration (13)
other (20)
photography (29)
Uncategorized (1)

ARCHIVES

May 2007
April 2007
March 2007
February 2007

Proudly fake, Uli's jewels...

Search

GET IN CONTACT

blog@maricazottino.com

SOME MORE...

my prickie page

CATEGORIES

art (39)
contemporary jewelry (31)
design (43)
fashion (25)
graphic & illustration (13)
other (20)
photography (29)
Uncategorized (1)

ARCHIVES

May 2007
April 2007
March 2007
February 2007
January 2007
December 2006
November 2006

Lorna Mills asks Jennifer McMackon 10 questions:

#1 - Have you ever been to the site, VVORK?
#2 - What do you think is going on there?
#3 - How do you think the creators of that site find that range of work?
#4 - What happens to a piece of art when it is extracted from the context of an artists' full body of work?
#5 - Who are the artists who you know of through only one work?
#6 - What's the effect of seeing clusters of different artists from all over the world "mining similar territory"?
#7 - What's the effect of seeing an ever growing archive of contemporary art works without an accompanying layer of critical text?
#8 - If VVORK posts several images daily for the next 10 years, do you still think that certain types of work will never be visible on that site?
#9 - Without a statement of curatorial intent, does selection (inclusion and exclusion) imply a value judgement? Does it have to?
#10 - Why do you think VVORK does it?

Comments (0) Toronto Edit This

VVORK

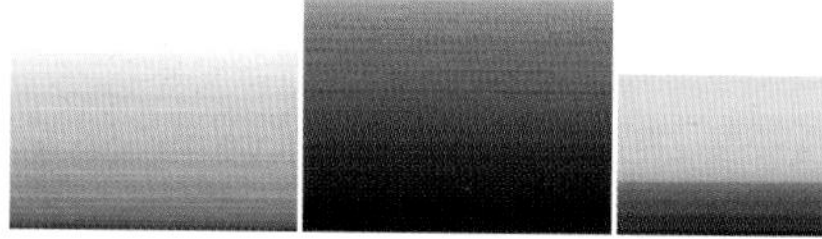

»System Displacement«, 2007 (Pixels rearranged from lightest to darkest) by Oliver Laric.

Comments (1) Berlin Edit This

Search

mail@vvork.com

Archives
July 2007
June 2007
May 2007
April 2007
March 2007
February 2007
January 2007
December 2006
November 2006
October 2006
September 2006
August 2006
July 2006
June 2006
May 2006
April 2006

Links

Christoph Priglinger
Sheriff
Aleksandra
Domanovic
Oliver Laric
Mi Magazine
Blitzfeld

Oliver Laric, Georg Schnitzer, Christoph Priglinger, Aleksandra Domanovic

VVORK

Blitzfeld

Comments (1) Vienna Edit This

Search

mail@vvork.com

Archives

July 2007
June 2007
May 2007
April 2007
March 2007
February 2007
January 2007
December 2006
November 2006
October 2006
September 2006
August 2006
July 2006
June 2006
May 2006
April 2006

Links

Christoph Priglinger
Blitzfeld
Sheriff
Mi Magazine
Aleksandra Domanovic
Oliver Laric

VVORK

"Rigid chair", is about finding a new contemporary answer in the category of wooden chairs. A reinterpretation of the traditional wooden chairs in Austrian farmer houses, that were handmade by skilled craftsmann two centuries ago. By Peter Umgeher.

Comments (31) London Edit This

Search

mail@vvork.com

Archives

July 2007
June 2007
May 2007
April 2007
March 2007
February 2007
January 2007
December 2006
November 2006
October 2006
September 2006
August 2006
July 2006
June 2006
May 2006
April 2006

Links

Mi Magazine
Sheriff
Christoph Priglinger
Aleksandra Domanovic
Blitzfeld
Oliver Laric

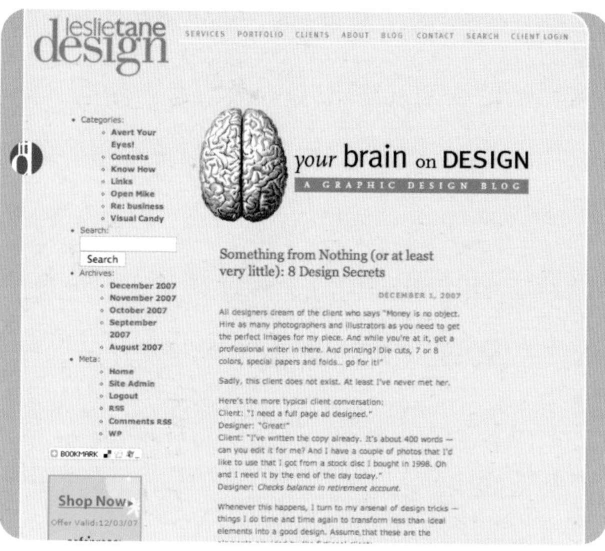
leslietane design
SERVICES PORTFOLIO CLIENTS ABOUT BLOG CONTACT SEARCH CLIENT LOGIN
Categories:
Avert Your Eyes!
Contests
Know How
Links
Open Mike
Re: business
Visual Candy
Search:
Search
Archives:
December 2007
November 2007
October 2007
September 2007
August 2007
Meta:
Home
Site Admin
Logout
RSS
Comments RSS
WP
BOOKMARK
Shop Now
Offer Valid:12/03/07
your brain on DESIGN
A GRAPHIC DESIGN BLOG
Something from Nothing (or at least very little): 8 Design Secrets
DECEMBER 1, 2007
All designers dream of the client who says "Money is no object. Hire as many photographers and illustrators as you need to get the perfect images for my piece. And while you're at it, get a professional writer in there. And printing? Die cuts, 7 or 8 colors, special papers and folds... go for it!"
Sadly, this client does not exist. At least I've never met her.
Here's the more typical client conversation:
Client: "I need a full page ad designed."
Designer: "Great!"
Client: "I've written the copy already. It's about 400 words — can you edit it for me? And I have a couple of photos that I'd like to use that I got from a stock disc I bought in 1998. Oh and I need it by the end of the day today."
Designer: Checks balance in retirement account.
Whenever this happens, I turn to my arsenal of design tricks — things I do time and time again to transform less than ideal elements into a good design. Assume that these are the

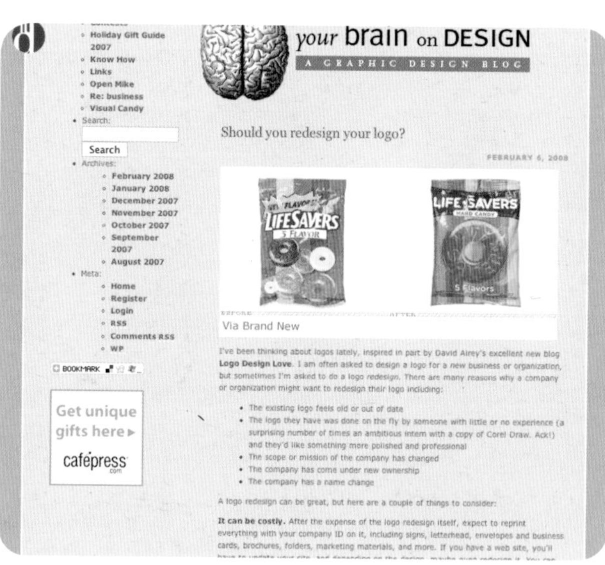
Holiday Gift Guide 2007
Know How
Links
Open Mike
Re: business
Visual Candy
Search:
Search
Archives:
February 2008
January 2008
December 2007
November 2007
October 2007
September 2007
August 2007
Meta:
Home
Register
Login
RSS
Comments RSS
WP
BOOKMARK
Get unique gifts here
cafepress.com
your brain on DESIGN
A GRAPHIC DESIGN BLOG
Should you redesign your logo?
FEBRUARY 6, 2008
LIFESAVERS
5 FLAVOR
LIFE SAVERS
HARD CANDY
5 Flavors
Via Brand New
I've been thinking about logos lately, inspired in part by David Airey's excellent new blog Logo Design Love. I am often asked to design a logo for a new business or organization, but sometimes I'm asked to do a logo redesign. There are many reasons why a company or organization might want to redesign their logo including:
The existing logo feels old or out of date
The logo they have was done on the fly by someone with little or no experience (a surprising number of times an ambitious intern with a copy of Corel Draw. Ack!) and they'd like something more polished and professional
The scope or mission of the company has changed
The company has come under new ownership
The company has a name change
A logo redesign can be great, but here are a couple of things to consider:
It can be costly. After the expense of the logo redesign itself, expect to reprint everything with your company ID on it, including signs, letterhead, envelopes and business cards, brochures, folders, marketing materials, and more. If you have a web site, you'll

Leslie Tane

SERVICES PORTFOLIO CLIENTS ABOUT BLOG CONTACT SEARCH CLIENT LOGIN

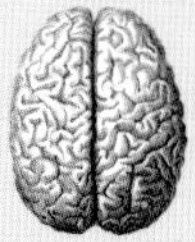

your brain on DESIGN

A GRAPHIC DESIGN BLOG

- Categories:
  - **Avert Your Eyes!**
  - **Contests**
  - **Holiday Gift Guide 2007**
  - **Know How**
  - **Links**
  - **Open Mike**
  - **Re: business**
  - **Visual Candy**
- Search:

  Search
- Archives:
  - **February 2008**
  - **January 2008**
  - **December 2007**
  - **November 2007**
  - **October 2007**
  - **September 2007**
  - **August 2007**
- Meta:
  - **Home**
  - **Register**
  - **Login**
  - **RSS**
  - **Comments RSS**
  - **WP**

BOOKMARK

Get unique

Holiday Gift Guide 2007!

DECEMBER 12, 2007

What every graphic design lover ~~wants~~ needs.

Hanukkah's passed and Christmas is less than two weeks away, but if you're stuck for a gift for the designer (or design appreciator) in your life, my first annual holiday gift guide is here to help. Sort it by type or price, or just look through it all.

You know you want it.

send this post to a friend
Filed under: **Holiday Gift Guide 2007**
Leave A Comment

Pantone Goe System

I wrote **an entire blog entry** about how lovely I think this artwork is. Gorgeous letterpress prints of cool found letter forms — where's the bad? This C is the one I already have (hint, hint, Mom). $75-$150.

Buy it!

send this post to a friend
Filed under: **Holiday Gift Guide 2007**
3 Excellent Comments

WordSpot Game from LLBean